Great Britain
&
Reza Shah

Great Britain

&

Reza Shah

The Plunder of Iran, 1921–1941

Mohammad Gholi Majd

University Press of Florida
Gainesville/Tallahassee/Tampa/Boca Raton
Pensacola/Orlando/Miami/Jacksonville/Ft. Myers

Library of Congress Cataloging-in-Publication Data
Majd, Mohammad Gholi, 1946–
    Great Britain and Reza Shah: the plunder of Iran, 1921–1941 / Mohammad Gholi Majd.
    p. cm.
    Includes bibliographical references and index.
    ISBN 0-8130-2111-1 (cloth : alk. paper)
        1. Iran—Relations—Great Britain. 2. Great Britain—Relations—Iran.   3. Iran—
        History—Pahlavi dynasty, 1925–1979.   4. Reza Shah Pahlavi, Shah of Iran,
        1878–1944. I. Title.
DS274.2.G7 M35 2001
955.05'2—dc21   2001023565

The University Press of Florida is the scholarly publishing agency for the State University
System of Florida, comprising Florida A&M University, Florida Atlantic University,
Florida Gulf Coast University, Florida International University, Florida State University,
University of Central Florida, University of Florida, University of North Florida, Univer-
sity of South Florida, and University of West Florida.

University Press of Florida
15 Northwest 15th Street
Gainesville, FL 32611–2079
http://www.upf.com

Dedicated to the memory
of all the victims of the reign of terror
and murder in Iran from 1921 to 1941

ILLUSTRATIONS

I thank the staff of the National Archives and Records Administration (NARA) in College Park, Maryland, for their help and courtesy during the many days I spent there in 1999 and 2000. Dr. Milton Gustafson, senior specialist at NARA, helped in navigating the records of the Department of State pertaining to Iran. I am deeply grateful to Professor Hafez Farmayan for his comments on the earlier version of the manuscript, his excitement at the discovery of the records, his keen interest in the project, and his helpful suggestions. I also thank Chris Hofgren and Amy Gorelick, acquisitions editors at the University Press of Florida, for their interest in the book and for their professional and helpful approach. The task of assembling the photos again fell to my brother Mohammad Hossein Majd, and I thank him greatly. I am grateful to the Bureau of Cultural Heritage for permission to photograph and reproduce a portrait of Reza Shah on a tapestry located in Niavaran Palace. I thank the Institute for Iranian Contemporary Historical Studies in Tehran for providing several of the photographs reproduced in this book.

Finally, I am vastly indebted to my family for help and understanding that made the completion of this book possible. The computer skills of my son, Ali, as usual rescued me at the appropriate time.

CHAPTER ONE

Introduction

THE RUSSIAN REVOLUTION IN OCTOBER 1917 and the defeat of the Ottoman forces in Mesopotamia and its conquest by the British in 1918 resulted in a de facto encirclement of Persia (as Iran was then known in the West) by Britain from the east, south, and west. Taking advantage of its predominance in the region, British forces invaded Iran from the east and the west. The main invasion took place in April 1918, and the entire country, with the exception of Azerbaijan province, was occupied by the British.

The British military invasion and occupation of 1918 is a cardinal event in the history of Iran. For the next sixty years, Iran effectively lost its independence. For nearly twenty-five years (1918–42), Iran was completely controlled by Britain, and thereafter, and until the Islamic revolution of 1979, Iran fell under the domination of the United States.

Despite its historical significance, the British invasion of 1918 has received relatively little attention in the literature. From the very beginning, the British maintained extraordinary secrecy about the invasion of Iran. The main British invasion force, the so-called Dunster Expeditionary Force, was nicknamed the hush-hush force because its very existence could not be openly discussed even in Baghdad, the location of British headquarters. Evidently, this hush-hush approach has continued to this day. Little information on the subject is to be found in several relatively recent books on this period.[1] In another study based on the British records, the British invasion force is portrayed as a relatively friendly force whose aim was to protect Persia from the "Bolshevik threat,"[2] but little credence or even mention of such a threat to Persia is to be found in the American legation's political and military reports from Tehran.

Having gained military control, the British set about deepening their political grip by engineering the downfall of the cabinet of Samsam-es-Saltaneh and the appointment of Hassan Vossough, Vossough-ed-Dowleh, as prime minister in August 1918. The Vossough government can best be described as a British-backed civilian dictatorship through which the British intended to bring about permanent control of Persia and its economic resources, especially its petroleum, and to direct Persia's economic development in ways favorable to Britain. Formal British control was to be achieved through the Anglo-Persian Convention of August 9, 1919. Faced with the bitter hostility of the people to the British and the proposed agreement, it was clear by early 1920 that the agreement could not be implemented and that the experiment in Vossough's civilian dictatorship had failed.

Effective and long-term British control of Persia and its resources was achieved through the establishment of a military dictatorship. This military dictatorship was brought about by the coup d'état of February 21, 1921, that made an obscure and nearly illiterate Cossack officer of peasant parentage the military dictator of Persia for the next twenty years. This man was Reza Khan. In 1925, with yet another British coup, the Qajar dynasty was abolished, and Reza Khan was made shah of Persia. He was forced to abdicate in September 1941, following the Allied invasion in August, and departed in a British ship and under British protection.

Reza Shah: The Myth and the Reality

The traditional view of Reza Shah Pahlavi and the period between 1921 and 1941 is that it was a heroic age during which, through the efforts and sacrifice of a brave and patriotic soldier, namely Reza Khan Pahlavi, a new national army was created that unified Iran and saved it from disintegration. The national army subdued the lawless tribes and marauding feudal elements and brought them under government control. After Reza Khan ascended the throne in 1925, the country became Westernized and the grip of the reactionary clergy weakened. The Islamic veil was abolished and women were emancipated. Great reforms and modernization were introduced. Factories, roads, and railroads were built. Tehran University was constructed. It was Iran's tragedy, so the view goes, that Iran was so treacherously attacked by Britain and Russia in August 1941 and its capable sovereign, Reza Shah Pahlavi, driven from his throne and country.[3]

A cursory examination of some of the salient facts concerning the history of this period makes it immediately clear that there are serious problems with this interpretation. Even writers who are great admirers of Reza Shah, such as Cyrus Ghani, cannot conceal the crucial role of the British in helping Reza Shah gain power. Iran's "great leader" was placed in power by a British coup d'état in 1921, and another coup d'état by the British effectively gave him the throne once occupied by Shah Abbas. Reza Khan was unquestionably a creation of the British. Furthermore, in August 1941, at the time of the Allied invasion of Iran, the so-called national army put up little resistance to the invaders. Army commanders and most government officials abandoned their posts and ran. Most ignominiously, Reza Shah himself, it was learned later, sought asylum in the British legation in Tehran, but he was discouraged from pursuing the matter. Subsequently, he meekly abdicated and was whisked away to safety in a British ship and under British protection, under which he lived out his remaining years. One reads in contemporary diaries and memoirs, as well as in the American diplomatic reports, that the departure of Reza Shah was greeted with a huge outpouring of joy by the population. One reads of severe food shortages and near famine conditions at the end of his reign.

In Ghani's book, as well as others dealing with this period, one reads the names and often sees the photos of notable individuals who were put to death on the orders of Reza Shah. It is also learned that these unfortunate individuals, who had often served as Reza Shah's ministers or had been prominent politicians, were put to death in prison, not because they had broken a law or had been condemned in a court of law, but because they were suspected of treachery by Reza Shah. The names include Teymourtache, Nosrat-ed-Dowleh, Modarres, and Sardar Assad. In civilized and law-abiding societies, in a country supposed to be a constitutional monarchy, individuals are not murdered in prison on the orders of the king simply because he suspected them of treachery. Such savage killings can only happen in the most brutal and lawless dictatorships (in Stalin's Russia death sentences were often handed out after show trials). In Iran of Reza Shah, the victims were simply murdered in prison, with no questions asked. In the diaries of Amir Asadollah Alam one reads of the bloody massacre of pilgrims and protesters in the Shrine of Imam Reza in Mashhad in July 1935, during which, according to Alam, 200 people were slaughtered by machine gun fire. From the American diplomatic reports it is learned that the toll from the machine guns was far more than the 200 claimed by Alam.[4]

In addition to this brutality, we have learned of massive financial corruption and embezzlement by Reza Shah. For instance, at the time of his abdication in 1941, he had on deposit at Bank Melli more than 760 million rials ($50 million). Vast amounts were deposited in foreign banks. Thanks to the records of the U.S. Departments of State and Treasury, we know that Reza Shah amassed as much as £20–30 million ($100–150 million) in London, and that this sum, an unbelievable amount in 1941, was inherited by his son and successor, Mohammad Reza Pahlavi. Thanks to the records of the Treasury Department and the Federal Reserve Bank of New York, we now also know that Reza Shah held vast sums in Swiss and New York banks, sums that were also inherited by his children. On the basis of the

Census of Foreign-Owned Assets in the United States, conducted in June 1941, we can infer that Reza Shah's holdings in America amounted to $18.5 million. From the documents and records that surfaced after the Islamic revolution, we learned that vast areas of Iran, including well over 6,000 villages and hamlets, were acquired by Reza Shah. From a map prepared by the American embassy in the 1950s, we can see the magnitude of the land he confiscated. Clearly, there are difficulties with the "golden age–great leader–reformer" interpretation of the period's history. What is amazing is that it should have persisted for so long. It was clearly a clever piece of myth and propaganda that was generated and has been maintained to this day with the help of the British.

State Department Records on Iran, 1921–1941

The history of Iran from 1921 to 1941 is a void. Despite numerous works of history, little is known about this period. This dearth of knowledge is demonstrated by the publication in Tehran in 1999 of a volume of documents pertaining to Reza Shah for this time. For several obvious reasons, it contains amazingly few concrete documents. The period was one of strict censorship during which events were not freely or accurately recorded. In addition, during the rule of the second Pahlavi (1941–79), most incriminating documents pertaining to Reza Shah were destroyed and any active scrutiny of the period by historians greatly discouraged. Another reason the period has been shrouded in mystery is that scholars have tended to rely almost exclusively on British diplomatic records on Iran. However, given the control of Persian affairs achieved through military occupation and the coup d'état, the complicity and pivotal British role in bringing the first and second Pahlavis to power, and their deep involvement with Reza Shah, British diplomatic papers cannot be expected to provide an accurate and objective account of events. As will be documented here, terrible things happened in Iran from 1921 and 1941. The British are fully cognizant that because Reza Shah was brought to power and kept in power for twenty years with their assistance and protection, the ultimate responsibility for the misdeeds that were perpetrated during this period must fall on them. For this reason, from the beginning, they set out to conceal their role. Outstanding examples of British mendacity and deception concerning their role in Persia can be found in their parliamentary records and statements, a sample of which is documented here.

A completely unexplored and surprisingly rich and complete source of primary historical records for Iranian history are the records of the State Department. They provide detailed political, social, economic, and military reports on Iran. Using these records, one can begin to rewrite a detailed history of the 1921–41 period. American interest in Iran greatly increased after the British invasion and occupation of Persia in 1918. Shortly thereafter, the American legation in Tehran began compiling and submitting detailed reports on political, military, and economic matters. The military and quarterly reports submitted by the American legation from October 1918 to April 1921 constitute a valuable set of historical documents, and some will be given in this study. American interest during the 1920s was maintained with the appointment of a team of financial advisers led by Arthur Chester Millspaugh of Washington, D.C., and the attempts by American oil companies to gain a foothold in Persian oil matters. A rich source of documentation was generated by his correspondence with the State Department and his reports to the American legation in Tehran that were duly conveyed to Washington and thus preserved in the archives of the State Department.

From the American diplomatic records one learns of the profound unhappiness and outright hostility of the American government to the policies of their British cousins in Persia. It is clear that American diplomats posted there were appalled by the policies of the British in Persia, the plunder of Persia's oil, and the imposition of a brutal and illiterate military dictator. They also greatly resented Britain's exclusion of American oil interests and the subsequent British domination of Iranian military aviation at the expense of American concerns, but they were not willing to take on the British directly.[5] They did not have to wait long. In 1942, taking advantage of Britain's difficulties during World War II, the Roosevelt administration quickly put an end to twenty-five years of exclusive British domination of Iran. The era of American domination had begun, and it was maintained during the Cold War until it became evident that the Soviet Union was collapsing. As State Department records clearly establish, the American government had a profound aversion to the Pahlavis even from 1921. Some of the comments on Reza Khan by the American ministers and chargés d'affaires are most undiplomatic. Nor was the American government enamored of Reza Shah's son and successor. American assistance and protection of the Pahlavi regime from 1942 to 1978 was due solely to strategic and geopolitical considerations. The approaching end of the Cold War doomed the regime. Thereafter, the United States distanced itself from the Pahlavis, and without the support of a foreign power the regime crumbled. In 1979, for the first time since 1918, Iran was able to reclaim its independence.

An indication of the keen American interest in Persia from 1918 to 1941 was the assignment of some able diplomats to this post, of whom Charles

Calmer Hart, the American minister from 1930 to 1933, was the most notable. His prolific, insightful, and often brilliant reports on conditions in Persia and on Reza Shah make extremely interesting reading, and some will be given here. Hart's reports on Reza Shah's "maniacal avarice," his acquisition of wealth, and his personal cruelties are remarkable pieces of diplomatic reporting. Hart's reports on the arrest and murder of his friend Abdol Hossein Teymourtache, Reza Shah's able minister of the court, are classics. Hart's reports on the 1933 oil concession to the British, and the personal role of Reza Shah in forcing the agreement on the reluctant Persian negotiators, is a valuable historical document. Historians of Iran owe Hart a profound debt of gratitude. From his successors, we have a detailed account of the renewed reign of terror that was unleashed on the people of Iran after 1933, the prison murders, the extra-judicial killings, and, most of all, the brutal massacre of protesters and pilgrims that took place in Mashhad from July 12 to July 14, 1935.

With the outbreak of World War II, there was increased American interest in Iran. The reports on economic conditions in Iran in 1940–41 reveal a country that had been traumatized for twenty years. We learned that in 1941, after twenty years of plunder and brutality, the people of Iran were faced with a severe shortage of food. There were bread riots in Tehran in 1940–41. Thus, we can begin to debunk the various myths, lies, and propaganda concerning Reza Shah and his golden age that have been constructed by the British and maintained to this day.

Reign of Terror, 1921–1941

In his 1946 book, Millspaugh provides an indication of the prevailing terror practiced by Reza Shah. Millspaugh states that Reza Shah "had imprisoned thousands and killed hundreds, some of the latter by his own hand." As the consequence of the terror, "Fear settled upon the people. No one knew whom to trust; and none dared to protest or criticize. . . . Evidence also appeared abundant and pitifully convincing, that the [shah's] terror operating on a timid and sensitive people had shaken nerves and unbalanced minds. Moreover, he let loose a spirit of violence that lent sinister implications to the mercurial temperament of the people, the disunity of the country, and the disorganization and weakness of the government."[6]

State Department records provide a vivid account of the reign of terror inflicted on the people of Iran between 1921 and 1941. For twenty years, the country was a complete and brutal military dictatorship. Parliament became a rubber stamp and complete censorship was imposed.[7] Iran's newspapers and their editors were early victims of the dictatorship. The suppression of newspapers, the physical violence (specially the savage beatings administered by Reza Khan himself), and even murder of recalcitrant editors are described in the records. There are many instances of arrest and subsequent disappearance of opponents, including numerous members of the ulema, the most notable that of Seyed Hassan Modarres. The arrests and extrajudicial killings of political personalities are described in detail in the American records, such as the murders of Teymourtache, Sardar Assad, Haim, Solated-Dowleh, Firouz, and others. From Hart's numerous reports on the arrest and murder of Teymourtache, we learn that just prior to his death he was visited in prison by Reza Shah, who administered a savage beating to the former minister of the court, leaving him unconscious. The subsequent administration of the "little white pill" to Teymourtache shortly before his death is also recorded by Hart. Invariably, the cause of death in such cases was given as heart failure or an attack of apoplexy.

To historians, an interesting aspect of these tragic affairs was the attempt by the British minister to attribute some of the prison deaths to natural causes. Most remarkable was the insistence of the British minister to his American colleague, William H. Hornibrook, that the prison death of Sardar Assad in 1934, former minister of war and a Bakhtiari tribal chief, was to be attributed to apoplexy. The prison official subsequently convicted of the murder of Sardar Assad was hanged in a Tehran square in 1944, near an equestrian statue of Reza Shah. This ironic scene prompted the American chargé d'affaires, Richard Ford, to comment in his report that while the prison official was hanged, the real murderer, Reza Shah, whose statue still stood there, had escaped justice.

The brutal suppression of the tribal populations by the army, the plunder of their valuables, and the forced relocation of these unfortunate people is also described in the records. One reads with deep horror of the forced marches of old men, women, and children across hundreds of miles of barren territory from their tribal homes in western Iran to remote regions in Khorasan. That such outrages have been suppressed for seventy years is remarkable. Even more disturbing are the detailed descriptions of the massacre in Mashhad in July 1935. As described by the American minister, the demonstrators were attacked by army troops on the orders of the shah himself, and machine guns were "brought into play, resulting in a frightful loss of life." A conservative estimate of killed and wounded was 500 persons. In addition, as many as 2,000 were arrested and were being "flogged daily in groups of thirty."[8] In the initial British reaction to this grave tragedy, just as they had insisted that some of the prison deaths in 1934 were from natural causes, they now attempted to play down the number of casualties, insisting that "only" sixty were killed and 120 arrested.

As recorded by the American minister, the main concern of the British minister after this tragic affair was to safeguard the life of Reza Shah and to protect him from assassination. In the words of Hart, "On him [Reza Shah] the British had always counted for the success of their policy." And they wanted to keep him alive, thus guaranteeing that the killings would continue. By 1938 the reign of terror had expanded to include Modarres, Ali Akbar Davar, Nosrat-ed-Dowleh Firouz, Hossein Dadgar, Ali Dashti, and Zein-ol-Abedine Rahnema, to name but a few. The first four were to meet a gruesome end. Others were permitted to go into exile or languished in a prison hospital. Admittedly, Modarres had been a bitter enemy of Reza Khan, but some of the others had been intimately associated with Reza Khan since his earlier days and had helped him to power.

Cultural Plunder and Violence, 1921–1941

In addition to brutality, the country was subjected at the same time to immense cultural degradation, destruction, and plunder. Irreparable damage was wreaked on Iran's architectural heritage. C. Van H. Engert, the American chargé d'affaires, reported the demolition of as many as 30,000 old houses in Tehran alone on the orders of Reza Shah, and their replacement with new buildings. This wanton and criminal destruction of Iran's cultural heritage was called modernization and progress. It was Engert's sad duty to also report the destruction of majestic, centuries-old trees ruthlessly sacrificed for the purpose of building wider, European-looking boulevards.

From State Department records and the reports by Millspaugh, a documentary account emerges of the manner in which Iran's crown jewels were systematically looted by Reza Shah. We learn that in 1937 a quantity of the crown jewels that were of "special interest" to Reza Shah were put aside. He took these when he left in 1941. Given Reza Shah's avarice, the looting of the crown jewels was not surprising. State Department records document vast amounts of antiques and archeological finds taken out of Iran between 1925 and 1941, a period when most of the Persian objects in European and American museums were acquired. Not only had Iran's oil resources been plundered, its very cultural heritage had been systematically looted or destroyed, and the Universities of Pennsylvania and Chicago were among the culprits.

How could such calamities befall Iran? It is easy to blame Reza Shah's lack of education (the American diplomats sometimes in their charitable moments called it cultural shortcomings), or his brutality and greed (in the words of Millspaugh, "brutality and greed came to him easily"). But the real responsibility lies with the British. When, as Hart says, "an illiterate son of an equally illiterate peasant" is "selected" and made the brutal military dictator of Persia, what else could be expected? In order to plunder Persia's oil, and to direct its "economic development in ways favorable to Britain," the British had no qualms about destroying Persia and its civilization. Evidently, the only thing that mattered was continued access to its cheap oil.

Petroleum and Financial Records: The Plunder of Iran's Oil

In addition to being brutalized for twenty years after the 1921 coup, Iran was plundered by the British and their chosen partner, Reza Khan, as illustrated by the systematic looting of its oil. U.S. Treasury and State Department records provide ample details of this plunder. One lengthy report details the manner in which the British took Iran's oil between 1911 and 1951, and the vast sums that Iran was "deprived of" by British malfeasance. What is specially important about this report is the wealth of statistics it contains and the vast sums that are mentioned. The report, discussed in detail in chapter 9, contains information and insight not found in other studies of the history of Iran's oil. The records show that while the bulk of Iran's oil wealth was stolen by the British, the few crumbs that were left for Iran were in turn stolen by Reza Shah.

After the downfall of Reza Shah in 1941, Mohammad Mossadeq and others claimed that much of Iran's oil revenues had been diverted to the shah's personal bank accounts in Europe and America on the pretext of buying armaments. One of the first acts by the Majlis after the downfall of Reza Shah in 1941 was to enact a law by which the oil revenues paid by the Anglo-Iranian Oil Company were to be brought under the control of the Ministry of Finance, to be counted as part of the regular budget. Thanks to the meticulous oil and financial reporting by American diplomats, we have exact figures for royalty payments by the Anglo-Persian Oil Company to Iran, and we know what subsequently became of this money. From the statistics on oil and the detailed reporting on Iran's arms purchases and military matters by American diplomats and by American military intelligence (the United States had maintained a military attaché as far back as 1922), a detailed account of arms purchases can be constructed for 1928–41. A small fraction of the oil income marked for arms purchases had actually been spent for that purpose. There is documentary evidence that out of $155 million in oil royalty payments, at least $100 million was stolen by Reza Shah. To appreciate the magnitude of this sum at the time, the total lending capacity of the U.S. Import-Export Bank in 1939 was $100 million.

That Iran's oil revenues were being diverted to Reza Shah's bank accounts was fully suspected by the American legation. When Hart, the American minister, reported in 1931 on Reza Shah's recent personal bank deposit of "more than a million" pounds in London, he knew that such sums could have only come from oil revenues. That at least $100 million of Iran's oil revenues had been diverted to Reza Shah's bank accounts was suspected by the American minister to Tehran during 1940–44, Louis G. Dreyfus, Jr. Dreyfus also ruefully remarks that nothing had yet been said about the former shah's stocks and bonds in America and Europe. Moreover, the facts were widely known in Iran. As noted, immediately after the downfall of Reza Shah, a law was enacted by the Majlis to take control of Iran's oil revenues. During 1927–41, the Iranian government had no control over or access to oil revenues, which were under the control of Reza Shah himself. This arrangement enabled Reza Shah to divert most of Iran's oil revenues to his private accounts in Europe and America.

Thanks to the intervention of the Federal Bureau of Investigation, we are able to provide a documented instance of the diversion of Iran's oil revenues to banks in Switzerland. The money had supposedly been allocated for arms purchases in the United States. Records of the U.S. Treasury and State Department show that the shah stashed vast sums in Swiss banks. This looting of Iran's oil revenues was accomplished with the full knowledge and connivance of the British government—much of the money was banked in London. The point is that while Britain itself was engaged in large-scale plunder of Iran's oil, it could hardly expect abstinence from its partner in plunder. Moreover, we can begin to understand why Reza Shah so quickly surrendered to the British in 1941 and left Iran on a British ship: to save his £20–30 million fortune in London.

To understand the origins of the Islamic revolution of 1979, knowledge and understanding of the tragic events of 1921–41 are imperative. I hope that this study, by examining State Department records, will make a small contribution to a serious analysis of this period. We are beginning to understand the dreadful events of 1921–41: all liberties were suppressed, the Constitution was effectively suspended, the population was terrorized, the tribes (one-fourth of the population) were brutalized, Parliament was turned into a rubber stamp, and the country was plundered. We can begin to understand why Iran did not develop despite its history and culture and its vast resources: It was because of the plunder, brutality, and lawlessness inflicted on the country between 1921 and 1941, from which it never recovered. Some of the long-term consequences of Reza Shah's misrule are described by Millspaugh in his 1946 book. Millspaugh's most damaging indictment of Reza Shah included the following:

However one may apprise the program, it is evident that Reza's most damaging failure lay in the means that he employed: dictatorship, corruption, and terror. . . . From the institutional point of view, Persia had the Church and the Throne; and the Revolution created a third institution, the Parliament, custodian of the constitution. The dictatorship not only weakened all three of these institutions from the standpoint of their place in the feelings of the people, but it also suspended and discredited that evolutionary course which might have consolidated popular affection and respect for the fundamental law. . . . The dictatorship destroyed both leaders and capacity for leadership. It was as if Reza had followed the advice given to the Greek dictator, to go through the grainfield and lop off all the heads that arose above the rest. No new men of capacity and courage, with possibly one or two exceptions, have appeared on the scene. For political leadership, Persia is now using the vestiges of what it had twenty years ago, and it did not have much then. No country could be closer to political bankruptcy.

By 1926 all of the preliminary essentials of progress—political, economic, and social—had appeared in Persia. Had it not been for the beginnings of large-scale looting by Reza Khan and his Army, popular confidence in the government, indispensable to national unity, might have been gradually created in the minds of the people. It seems clear that if Reza could have restricted himself to the function of keeping order, and if a continuing American mission had guarded the treasury and guided the country's development, Persia might gradually have achieved the requisites of self-government and permanent stability. But in that year, Reza Khan, who had used the Army to control parliamentary elections, made himself Shah, and the country returned to absolutism with hardly a sign of protest from the so-called good men whose timidity and confusion lost for their country its golden opportunity to win lasting freedom.[9]

Plan of Study

In chapter 2, I first provide a documentary account of the British invasion and subjugation of Persia in April and May 1918. It was very clear to American diplomats and officials on special assignment in Persia that the British intended to take permanent control of Persia. I then describe the establishment of a civilian dictatorship through the government of Vossough-ed-Dowleh. Beginning in October 1918, the American legation submitted quarterly reports on political and economic conditions in Persia. The practice continued until 1922, when a new American minister was appointed to Tehran. The first eleven of these reports, covering a period from October 1918, shortly after the appointment of Vossough-ed-Dowleh, to April 1921, or shortly after the coup d'état of February 1921, constitute an extremely valuable set of historical documents. Quarterly report 11, written by American Minister John L. Caldwell, provides a detailed and firsthand account of the coup and the British role therein. The first eight quarterly reports describe the government of Vossough-ed-Dowleh. It is clear from these reports that the Vossough-ed-Dowleh experiment by the British was an attempt to gain permanent control of Persia and its resources by establishing a civilian dictatorship.

Upon coming to power, the regime set about establishing law and order and suppressing the tribes. It closed down newspapers, jailed newspaper editors, and established rigid censorship. Opponents were imprisoned or exiled. The regime openly interfered with Majlis elections, and tried to pack the Majlis with its own supporters. In short, the Vossough experiment was a small and mild version of what was to transpire under Reza Khan. The Anglo-Persian Convention of August 9, 1919, was an attempt to formalize and institutionalize British control of political and economic affairs of Persia. The inability of the Vossough government to force the ratification of the Anglo-Persian Convention and the consequent fall of the government was a serious setback to British policy in Persia. It showed the failure of a British-sponsored civilian dictatorship. It showed that faced with a hostile population, political establishment, and shah, the British plans for formal control of Persia and the exploitation of its oil had failed. The successor of Vossough-ed-Dowleh was Moshir-ed-Dowleh. Caldwell expressed surprise that the British had even permitted the appointment of Moshir-ed-Dowleh, a popular and respected politician. It turned out that the British would get rid of him when it suited their purpose. What the British needed was to establish a military dictatorship. The desirability of succeeding and their satisfaction at the rapid rise of Reza Khan as military dictator of Persia is openly discussed in the British records.

Soon after the departure of Vossough, the British set about preparing for a coup d'état. To mount one, they needed to get direct control of the Cossacks, the country's only organized military force. To do that, the Russian officers of the Cossacks had to be dismissed. The Russian Commander of the Cossacks, Colonel Starosselski, was particularly close to Ahmad Shah and had often been accused of intriguing with the shah against the British. The manner in which the Cossack force was destroyed as a fighting unit and its Russian officers first discredited and then dismissed is described in chapter 2. The British took direct control of the Cossacks in November 1920, and the stage was set for the coup. In December the British announced that they were withdrawing from Persia, and leaving it to its fate.

With the deliberate destruction and decapitation of the Cossacks, it appeared that with this withdrawal, Tehran itself was likely to fall to the

Bolsheviks, causing a general panic in the capital. Even the American minister, Caldwell, was taken in by the announced withdrawal. Caldwell had reported to his government the desperate pleas of Ahmad Shah for American help to Persia in its hour of peril. In the State Department records, Ahmad Shah emerges as an educated and cultured young man (a contrast to the illiterate brute who was to succeed him), a true constitutional monarch, and a patriot who, unlike Reza Khan, was not willing to betray his country to the British in order to maintain his throne. Caldwell's lengthy telegram about the "historic" opportunity created in Persia for America by the departure of the British, and his conversations with Ahmad Shah about possible American assistance to Persia, is an interesting document. Ahmad Shah's previous intrigues against the British, his close relationship with the American minister and subsequent appeals for American help, must have rendered him persona non grata to the British. Before the Americans could do anything the British had struck.

Few events in Iran's modern history can equal the importance of the coup d'état of February 21, 1921. From State Department records we learn that the coup was entirely British, intended to take forceful control of Iran, its people, and its resources "through native tools" (see chapter 3). The coup launched the political career of Reza Khan. With British financial, political, and military assistance and protection, Reza Khan became the military dictator of Persia. In the words of Joseph S. Kornfeld, the American minister in Tehran in 1921–24, in Reza Khan the British had found "an admirable tool" to achieve their ends. For the next four years, the British repeatedly intervened to protect their protégé and maintain him in power. As documented in chapter 3, the British "drove the bandwagon" that put Reza Khan on the throne of Persia in 1925. When the dominant (de facto occupying) foreign power could so easily change Persia's monarchy, deposing its reigning house of 140 years and substituting a person who could barely read and write, it was assuredly one of the lowest points in Persia's recorded history. As described in the reports of the American chargé d'affaires in Tehran, the way in which this was brought about was deeply humiliating to the people of Iran. Establishing that Reza Shah was a British creation and tool demonstrates British responsibility for the events that took place under his rule.

The appointment of Millspaugh and an American team of financial experts in 1922 was a happy event for future historians of Iran (see chapter 4). The work of the Americans generated a large number of financial and political records for 1922–27. Millspaugh's reports provide a great deal of information on the early financial practices of Reza Khan, including the systematic looting of army funds by him and his army officers, and the looting of the tribes by him and his army. The matter of what became of the looted gold and valuables belonging to the tribes of Azerbaijan provoked an acrimonious exchange between Reza Khan and Millspaugh, who in 1924 had attempted to obtain an accounting of what had become of the loot. Millspaugh's report on the establishment and operation of Bank Pahlavi, whose principal stockholder was Reza Khan himself, is a valuable historical document. In addition to systematic and organized extortion, the bank obtained a monopoly of bus service in Tehran, and the "postal operation" between Tehran and the Iraqi border. It was all done with army funds. While soldiers and junior officers were not being paid for months at a time, over the strenuous protests of Millspaugh, army funds were being used to establish a bus service in Tehran. The hungry soldiers in the provinces had in turn resorted to looting and extortion from the hapless merchants. All this is recorded by Millspaugh and by the American consuls in such cities as Bushire and Tabriz. We also learn of large sums being extorted from the merchants and citizens of Mashhad by army commanders prior to the coronation of His Pahlavi Majesty.

Another valuable contribution by Millspaugh was his long memo on the proposed granting of the concession for Caspian fisheries to the Soviets. The proposed concession was described as a betrayal of Persia's fundamental interests. No sooner had Millspaugh been dismissed than the very concession that he had denounced was granted to the Soviets. If the British could plunder the oil in the south, the Soviets insisted on the exploitation of the Caspian fisheries in the north. It was learned that the Soviets had paid "large presents—very large presents" to His Pahlavi Majesty in connection with the Caspian fisheries (see chapter 4). Hart describes a conversation with Teymourtache in which the latter casually told of a payment of $850,000 by the Soviets in order to prevent American participation in the fisheries. Hart also remarks that Teymourtache was but a "channel to the Shah."

Chapter 4 also briefly describes the granting of an oil concession by Reza Khan in 1923 to Sinclair Oil, an American concern. It was claimed at the time in both American and Persian newspapers that a bribe of $300,000 had been paid by Sinclair, of which the share of Mohammad Ali Foroughi, Reza Khan's foreign minister, had been $100,000. The rest had gone to Reza Khan. The matter had been vehemently denied. That the bribery had in fact been received was confirmed by Millspaugh's report that shortly after the granting of the concession, a sum of $200,000 had been transferred by Reza Khan to his bank accounts in Europe. In 1931, Hart learned that Foroughi was a partner in a group attempting to obtain an oil concession by another American concern. Hart commented on Foroughi's reputed honesty. In the world of crooks and thieves, Hart declared, Foroughi was a "veritable collector's piece." The American financial team and Millspaugh in particular were greatly resented by the British and by

Reza Khan. That Millspaugh lasted for nearly five years (November 1922 to August 1927) was remarkable.

With the accession of Reza Khan to the throne, the fate of the American financial team was sealed. The British greatly resented the intrusion of the Americans onto their turf. Reza Shah himself was anxious to get complete control of financial and fiscal affairs, in particular, to lay his hands on the oil revenues. This could not be done with Millspaugh and his powers as Persia's general administrator of finance. He had to go. The occasion of Millspaugh's dismissal had provoked some angry comments by the American diplomats at their British cousins and at Reza Shah. With the departure of Millspaugh in 1927, the large-scale looting of Iran's oil revenues by Reza Shah commenced. Thereafter, until 1941, oil revenues were no longer treated as government revenue or part of the regular budget, but rather as the Reserve Fund of the Nation, to be banked in London. As documented here, nearly all of Iran's oil revenues between 1927 and 1941 were systematically diverted by Reza Shah to his bank accounts in London, Switzerland, and New York. It must be considered the most scandalous episode in the history of Iran.

Chapter 5 describes the character of Reza Khan. Specifically it documents what American diplomats recorded about his personal brutality and unbounded greed. Hart's report on his first meeting with Reza Shah in February 1930 is revealing. His first impression was that he had met a man "who was only a few jumps from savagery." By the end of his mission in December 1933, Hart had concluded that his first impression of Reza Shah had been overly charitable. He was far worse. Numerous instances of savage beatings administered by Reza Khan to those unable to defend themselves are described in detail. Newspaper editors, mullahs, policemen, and subsequently cabinet ministers had figured prominently in Reza Khan's displays of "animal instincts." The violence had become institutionalized throughout society. The merciless police beatings and deportation of the silk weavers of Yazd who had been reluctantly recruited for employment in Reza Shah's silk mill in Chalus, Mazandaran, is ably described by the American consul. Hart's description of the forced relocation of the hapless tribal populations, the long marches, and the Majlis discussion of the matter of nonpayment of camel drivers who had transported the belongings of the relocated tribes is priceless. Equally valuable and revealing are his reports on land acquisition by Reza Shah and his extortion of money out of such wealthy individuals as Haj Moin-ot-Tojjar Bushehri, who were forced to share nearly all their wealth with His Pahlavi Majesty. Immediately upon gaining power, Reza Khan had resorted to extortion of wealthy individuals, and systematic looting of the government. Another prominent personality who had been forced to share much his wealth, including the "donation" of villages in Kermanshah and his house and garden in Tehran to His Pahlavi Majesty, was Prince Abdol Hossein Farman Farma.

Chapters 6 through 8 provide a sampling of the reign of terror that was inflicted on the people of Iran during 1921–41. The prison murders described here are only those of the most prominent victims of Reza Shah. As I have documented elsewhere, many other lesser known individuals had shared a similar fate in the hands of the Pahlavi poison squad and in the prison that Hart had named the Persian Bastille. Also, from State Department records we can begin to understand the role of the British in assuring Reza Shah's personal security. In response to Hart's rhetorical question of why someone did not kill Reza Khan, the simple answer was that the British would not allow it. The ruthlessly efficient army intelligence service that had discovered and foiled numerous plots to assassinate Reza Khan was operated by the British. An assassination plan by Colonel Mahmoud Poulladin in 1926 had been foiled by the British, and its participants, including Poulladin and Major Ruhollah Khan, Major Ahmad Khan, and Sheik Al-Araqein, were executed. Another participant who paid with his life for plotting against His Pahlavi Majesty was Samuel Haim, a former Persian government employee and a former Jewish Majlis deputy.[10] The extreme care that the British took to safeguard the life of Reza Shah after the brutal massacre of 1935 in Mashhad is indicative of the protection they had provided him.

Chapter 9 provides the reason why the British were so anxious to safeguard the life of Reza Shah: it gives a documentary and quantitative account of the plunder of Iran's oil by the British during 1911–51. As described in the U.S. Treasury Department records, the much maligned and frequently denounced D'Arcy Concession of 1901 was extremely favorable to Persia. By 1908 the magnitude of the enormously rich reserves had been established, and thereafter the British had set about a systematic violation of the agreement and attempted to change the agreement itself. They succeeded in 1933. The entire crisis and subsequent cancellation of the D'Arcy Agreement by the Persian government in 1932, it is revealed, were all engineered by the British. The annulment of the D'Arcy Concession by the Iranian government and its replacement by the 1933 Agreement was the greatest act of betrayal and treason committed by any Persian government against Iran and its people. No other episode provides a better illustration of the role of Reza Shah as a British tool. The chapter concludes with the adjustment to the concession that was made in September 1940: Iran's oil revenues were to be converted into dollars for deposit in bank accounts in New York—the plunder of Iran's oil revenues by Reza Shah had entered its final stage. Chapter 10 describes the establishment and operation of the Reserve Fund of the Nation in London in 1927. During 1927–41, oil revenues were deposited into this fund and were no longer considered as part of the budget or treated as government revenue. For all practical purposes, Iran had become a non-oil-producing economy. Chapters 10–12 document the manner in which Iran's oil revenues were stolen by Reza Shah under the pretext of buying arms and various other measures and diverted to his bank accounts in Europe and America. It is shown that of the £31.3 million in oil royalty payments, £18,412,000 was allocated for the purchase of armaments in Europe and America, £6 million for railroads and port construction, and £3 million for the purchase of gold. A balance of £1.3 million remained when Reza Shah departed in 1941. In reality, the people of Iran had derived no benefit from the oil revenues—none.

Chapter 11 examines Iranian arms purchases during 1928–41. Thanks to American military intelligence and legation reports, we have a comprehensive list of army, naval, and air force purchases during 1928–41, and the prices actually paid for the arms. In July 1941, the American legation obtained access to a secret report, "The Battle Order of the Iranian Army." Produced by the British military attaché, it provided a comprehensive account of the state of the Iranian armed forces and their equipment. With this information at hand, and the prices paid for the arms, it becomes obvious that only a small fraction of the £18,412,000 ($92 million) allocated to arms purchases abroad had actually been spent on arms. In short, out of $155 million in oil royalties paid by the Anglo-Iranian Oil Company during 1928–41, there is documentary evidence that at least two-thirds was stolen by Reza Shah—one of the greatest robberies ever committed by an individual.

Chapter 12 documents the diversion of Iran's oil revenues to Reza Shah's bank accounts in Europe and America. Thanks to the intervention of the Federal Bureau of Investigation we have documentary evidence that in one instance $1.13 million of Iranian army funds that had been allocated for arms purchases in the United States were transferred to the Swiss National Bank in May 1941 and thereafter disappeared. Treasury Department records indicate that at the same time Iran was faced with an acute dollar shortage, vast sums were being transferred to Iranian accounts in New York, then transferred to Swiss banks. There can be absolutely no doubt that these transfers were for the benefit of Reza Shah. Thanks to the June 1941 Census of Foreign-Owned Assets in the United States, we can conclude that Reza Shah's assets in America amounted to $18.5 million.

Evidence that he had transferred vast sums to London and to Swiss banks is found in several reports. These London funds were to resurface and are discussed in a 1957 State Department report in reference to the shah's attempts to convert these "blocked" personal funds into dollars and Swiss francs. Another report described the extensive purchase of real estate in Geneva by Mohammad Reza Shah in the 1950s and his frequent consultation with Swiss bankers handling his financial affairs. Given the date of the report, there can be little doubt that the money consisted of sums transferred by Reza Shah and subsequently inherited by his son and successor. Finally, just like his father, as soon as he came to power, Mohammad Reza Shah began transferring large sums from Iran to American banks. Thanks to the State Department records we have detailed and completely documented proof of the transfer of $1 million by Mohammad Reza Shah in April 1943 to the Guaranty Trust Company of New York. We also have documentation that the Shah's transfers to Guaranty Trust continued at least up to the time of Mossadeq. We cannot imagine the vast sums that were transferred to foreign banks by the Pahlavis during the 1960s and 1970s, when the oil money began to flow in earnest.

Given that Reza Shah stole most of Iran's oil revenues and a great deal of prime rural and urban real estate, it would have been most uncharacteristic if he had not similarly helped himself to Iran's crown jewels. Chapter 13 documents the looting of Iran's crown jewels by Reza Shah and his subordinates during 1924–41. Finally, the records indicate that the transfer of the crown jewels to America was continued by his son and successor, at least during the 1950s.

Conditions in Iran in 1941 and the End of Reza Shah

Finally, chapters 14 and 15 describe the grim economic conditions in Iran during 1930–41. The reality is in sharp contrast to the propaganda and myth of economic progress under Reza Shah that has been spread for much of a century. State Department records contain detailed reports on economic and social conditions in Iran at the end of Reza Shah's rule. As amply documented by the quarterly reports for 1918–20 (see chapter 2), in 1920 Iran was a land of relative prosperity, despite the ravages of the war, Britain's failure to pay oil royalties, and its withholding of customs revenues. It took only four krans to buy one dollar. In 1941, Iran was a wasteland in which the people even lacked bread. Tehran itself had been shaken by bread riots in 1940. Fortunately for historians of Iran, the American consuls and legation members had undertaken extensive travels in Iran during 1940–41 and duly recorded their findings. Their reports are reproduced here. Most revealing are the observations on the plight of Iran's peasantry. The reports provide ample justification for Millspaugh's statement that "Reza Shah cruelly exploited the peasants who form the mass of the population."[11]

To foreign observers in Iran in 1941, it was no longer a question of if Reza Shah had to go, it was only a question of when. The country was faced with revolutionary conditions. In a conversation in 1941, a British diplomat told his American colleague that "it was imperative to get rid of the Shah," adding that Reza Shah had overplayed his hand in all things and had to go. In the early hours of August 25, 1941, British and Soviet forces invaded Iran from the west and north. Reza Khan's national army, on which each year at least 50 percent of the government budget had been spent for twenty years—the same army on which the bulk of Iran's oil revenues had supposedly been spent, the same army that had shown such valor against the unarmed demonstrators in Mashhad in 1935—offered hardly any resistance to the invaders. Ignominiously, Reza Shah sought asylum in the British legation.

Assuredly, the resistance to the British invasion in 1918 by such patriots as Mirza Kuchik Khan and Solat-ed-Dowleh Qashqai was far more determined and honorable than the pathetic performance of the Pahlavis' so-called national army. Quickly Reza Shah was sent off in a British ship under British protection to enjoy his ill-gotten wealth and thus was saved from the wrath of his own people. In a manner reminiscent of the events of 1925, when Reza Khan had been "chosen by the people" to be shah, in September 1941 his son was similarly chosen. By removing Reza Shah, the British had saved the Pahlavi regime. By installing his son, they wished to ensure that the dreadful events of 1921–41 would remain hidden and the incriminating evidence and documents destroyed. August 1941, however, was the beginning of the end of British domination of Iran. For the people of Iran it meant freedom from the nightmare of British rule through Reza Khan. In early 1942, taking advantage of the difficulties and weakness of the British, the United States had begun to take control of Iranian affairs. The presidential finding signed by Franklin D. Roosevelt on March 10, 1942, declared the defense of the government of Iran to be vital to the defense of the United States. It opened the way for assumption of Lend-Lease assistance to Iran and the appointment of various American advisory missions, including military, police, gendarmerie, and financial missions to Iran. Millspaugh was once again appointed administrator general of finance. The era of American domination had begun.

CHAPTER 2

The British Invasion and the Strangulation of Persia, 1918–1920

IN APRIL 1918 THE AMERICAN CONSUL IN ADEN, Addison E. Southard, received instruction to proceed to Persia for the specific purpose of reporting on the British conquest of Persia and assess British intentions toward Persia. In a series of reports between July and September 1918, Southard provided a detailed account of British military and political activity in Persia. In addition, as a clear sign of increased American interest in Persia, the American legation, at about the same time, also began submitting detailed quarterly reports on political and economic conditions. Before invading Iran in April 1918, the British legation sent a note, signed by Sir Charles M. Marling, the British minister in Tehran, to the Persian government informing them that British troops were about to invade, and gave the "justifications" for the act.[1] While announcing the temporary nature of the invasion, the British government undertook not to infringe on Persia's independence. But as Southard was soon to discover and report, the British, having first encircled and then conquered Persia, intended to take permanent control of the country and its economic resources, a euphemism for its petroleum resources. The justifications for the act of aggression against a weak nation are the usual ones given by an imperialist power. They included the supposed inability of the Persian government to maintain law and order, and the seizure of the British vice consul and the manager of the Imperial Bank of Persia by the Jangalis in Rasht.

In response to the British ultimatum, the Committee of Public Indignation held a public meeting in Tehran on March 19 and a translation of its declaration was sent to all foreign legations in Tehran, except the British. The Persians protested in vain against the act of aggression, and in vain they sought the support of the "civilized" world in deterring aggression. On April 16, 1918, the British consul in Kermanshah, Colonel Kennion, distributed a pamphlet, "For the Understanding and Tranquillity of Mind of the People of Persia," that informed the people that the British forces were about to invade Persia and sought to reassure them. It also warned that any resistance to the British forces would be crushed by the "all-powerful and victorious British Army." The pamphlet, enclosed with Southard's dispatch, was unlikely to provide reassurance to the unfortunate people of Persia. By early summer of 1918, the British military conquest of Persia was complete.

Resistance to British Aggression: Qashqai, Jangali, and Sanjabi

Formal military resistance to British aggression was negligible because Persia had no standing army in the true sense of the word. The resistance by the tribes, however, as the reports show, was formidable. In addition to opposition from the Qashqai tribes and Jangalis, the invading forces met resistance from the Sanjabi Kurdish tribes. Against the Jangalis and Sanjabis the British used armored cars and airplanes with devastating effect. A telegram from Southard states:

> Confidential. British have well established military line of communication from Bagdad across Persia via Kermanshah, Hamadan, Kasvin [Qazvin] to Enzeli [Bandar-e Anzali, or Bandar-e Pahlavi], headquarters Kasvin. Expedition called Dunsterville forces from the name of Major General Commanding and is supplied from Mesopotamia, but directly controlled by British War Office. Persian military opposition to British occupation is negligible. Occasional sniping at motor convoys has occurred in mountain stretch between Hamadan and Resht [Rasht]. Near Resht small fights have occurred with jungle tribes. Most serious one six days ago; when enemy casualties forty four and British three. Aeroplanes and armored vehicles used with success. . . . Motor convoys of troops and supplies continue uninterrupted. Indications are that British have Persian military situation well controlled.[2]

A follow-up telegram provides additional military information:

> Strictly confidential. In all parts of Persia south of Bagdad-Caspian line of communication, British have practically control of military and political affairs. From Hamadan small detachments have gone to Sultanabad and Teheran. Sultanabad-Kermanshah road is under British control. British and Indian troops are at all important points in provinces [of] Kermanshah, Luristan, and Arabistan. At Shiraz, Yezd [Yazd], Kerman, and Meshed [Mashhad]

there are reported increased detachments [of] Indian cavalry, nominally maintained as consular guards. British consuls or political officers are reported to be in all important points closely in touch with conditions. Inimical political agitators are kept under surveillance and I have ascertained from reasonably reliable sources that many arrests of tribal leaders have been made in Arabistan and that one or two have been executed for pernicious political offenses against Allied interests. Supplementing this organization there are about seven thousand native police known as [South] Persia Rifles with British officers and paid by British government. Some native tribes have attacked Persia Rifles at various places but discounting wilder reports and rumors, it is improbable that the tribes will be able to offer serious resistance to present British control of south Persia. Occurrence [of] important trouble in south Persia is considered improbable.[3]

The main resistance to the British as recorded by the American legation came from the Qashqai tribes in the south and from Mirza Kuchik Khan and the Jangalis in the north. John L. Caldwell, the American minister in Tehran, describes a bloody encounter between the Qashqais and the British army. A detachment of South Persia Rifles under a British officer and noncommissioned officer was sent to the town of Khan-i-Zinian in the province of Fars on May 11, 1918.

The Kashgai [Qashqai] tribesmen, who, under the instigation of the German agent Wassmus, have been very hostile to the British, surrounded this force and cut off their running water supply. A column of Indian troops was despatched from Shiraz for their relief, but before their arrival at Khan-i-Zinian the British officer and non-commissioned officer had been murdered by their Persian command, who then gave over their rifles and ammunitions to the Kashgai. An engagement took place on the 25th instant between the British-Indian troops and the Persian tribesmen, resulting in the route of the latter after losing about three hundred and fifty men. The British losses, which are reported to have been moderately heavy, included the loss of a British Major and Captain. After the encounter the British are reported to have fallen back on Shiraz. It is too early as yet to know what future action will be necessary on the part of the British authorities in regard to this matter, but as the Kashgais appear to be excellent fighters and determined in their resistance, further trouble is to be expected.[4]

Francis White, secretary of the American legation, reports on Mirza Kuchik Khan and his cause:

Resht and Enzeli are in the hands of the Bolsheviks and the Jungali [Jangali] tribe under their leader Kuchik Khan, who is opposed to the British occupation of Persian territory. Kuchik Khan, from all accounts, is a man of some education, who is very much opposed to what he conscientiously considers the high handed actions of the British in Persia. He is a member of the so-called Democratic party and appears to be honest and patriotic and a man of some force of character, but short sighted and perhaps a bit fanatical.[5]

By late May 1918, the British were preparing a push to the north against the Jangalis. Despite the rumored division among the Jangalis,[6] they attacked the British headquarters on July 20, 1918. This desperate attack by Mirza Kuchik Khan was repulsed with heavy casualties.

Twelve hundred jungle tribesmen attacked British headquarters in Resht on July 20, and were repulsed with about two hundred killed and wounded. They then attacked British bank and consulate, looting the latter. Fighting continued for four days and tribesmen were driven from Resht by aeroplanes and armored motors. To do this the British burned hotel, theater and six other buildings surrounding American missionary school, and school building had a large hole torn in the roof by a bomb from aeroplanes. No Americans injured or molested by tribesmen who expressed friendship for American missionaries. Two young Persians from the missionary school have joined the tribesmen. British losses not much and there is no interruption [of] line of communication to Caspian. Successful attacks by tribesmen very improbable as they cannot oppose British aeroplanes, armored motors, and increasing British forces now numbering about a thousand in Resht.[7]

A month after the above report, Caldwell described the collapse of the Turkish forces and their withdrawal from Persia.[8] With the revolution in Russia and the collapse of the Ottoman armies in Persia and Mesopotamia, the British had become the unchallenged military power. As outlined below, they quickly set about transforming their military supremacy into political domination and economic control.

Southard's Reports on British Invasions and the Occupation of Persia

Southard details the British military invasion of Persia:

Not considering the South Persia Rifles and the unusually large detachments of so-called Consular guards at British consulates and political agencies in Persia, there have been three distinct invasions of Persia by British troops. In 1915 Indian cavalry to the strength of about a battalion was sent into Arabistan to protect the wells and pipe lines of the Anglo-Persian Oil Company from possible attacks from Turkish troops and by Persian tribes in German pay. This invasion can be explained as necessary to protect a source of fuel oil supply of great importance to the British Admiralty and which, although in Persian territory, the Persian Government was unable to protect because it neither had soldiers nor police at its disposal. Judging from personal observation it seems that the general attitude of British military and political officers on the gulf and Mesopotamia suggests that they consider their government definitely and permanently responsible for the proper policing of Arabistan, although that territory may remain nominally Persian.

Probably the most important invasion of Persia by British troops has been the occupation of the Bagdad-Caspian line of communication, actively begun at the first of this year and following the Russian retirement. This invasion

seems to have been justified so far as military necessity was concerned, because
of the inability of the Persian government to protect its own neutrality. It had
the double objective of throwing a barrier across Persia in the way of a possible
enemy invasion from the north, and of gaining control of the Caspian sea
and cutting off the pan-Turanian movement or invasion into Turkestan and
beyond. Both objectives have been accomplished, and as the British have control of the Caspian it is my opinion that the present military and political situation in Persia and Turkestan is unlikely to change pending decisive results on the
Western front, as Turkey's possible military efforts can at best be but feeble ones
in either Persia or the Caucasus without definite and considerable German aid.
The control of the Caspian sea has, according to recent developments, been the
key to the entire situation in Persia and Turkestan, and as it is now apparently
firmly in the hands of the British further developments of importance during
the present year seem improbable so far as enemy progress is concerned.

The British had before this time established themselves in Bagdad and
shortly after the withdrawal of the Russians became probable [end of 1917]
British plans were underway for the occupation of the line from Bagdad across
Persia via Kermanshah and Hamadan to the Caspian at Enzeli. A small British
detachment with wireless equipment is understood to have been established in
Kermanshah as early as the middle of 1917, this place being 304 miles by caravan from Bagdad.

After the occupation of Bagdad a railroad was begun by the British running
towards the Persian frontier and early this year it had reached the small town of
Ruz, sixty miles north-east of Bagdad. Ruz is not shown on most maps, but may
be located as about half way between Shahroban [Shahraban] and Kizil-Robat,
which are shown on good maps. With Ruz as base preparations were made for
the occupation by British troops of the route across Persia to the Caspian. In
January of this year [1918] Major General Dunsterville went into Persia with a
small party of hand picked officers. He went as far as the Caspian and returned
to Mesopotamia to organize the expeditionary force. Great secrecy was maintained and this expedition into Persia, although officially known as the Dunster
force, was known among the military people as the "hush-hush" force, because
it was not permitted to be discussed even in Bagdad.

By the middle of June [1918] the British had approximately 2,500 troops in
Persia, the force being spread out over the line of communication from Ruz to
the Caspian. At this time the Dunster force consisted of parts of one mixed division from Mesopotamia, the thirteenth and the fourteenth divisions. Between
Kermanshah and Ruz some Indian battalions [a battalion consists of approximately 1,000 men] were observed, but beyond Kermanshah the troops seemed
to be all British with the exception of parts of two battalions of Ghurkas
[Indians belonging to the mixed division mentioned above], brought in for
special work, and who are considered equal to British troops in being able to
stand cold weather which they will experience in Persia and on the Caspian
during the coming winter. The Ghurkas are considered to be the best fighters in
the Indian army. The latter part of August there were possibly 10,000 troops
along the Bagdad-Caspian line, in addition to 5,000 at that time in Baku. As far

as I was able to observe there were six complete battalions of British infantry along this line, one battalion of British cavalry, and nearly two battalions of Ghurkas in addition to the special detachments and Indian troops nearer the Mesopotamian end of the line. Some detachments of Australian and Indian troops were observed and there were a number of Canadian and New Zealand officers on duty at headquarters in Hamadan. The officers accompanying the Dunster force, in addition to those belonging to the regular battalions of troops, were mostly picked men and considered to be especially capable. I understand that the British now completely control the Caspian and its shipping and I know that bodies of marines, naval men, and inland water transportation men (the latter belonging to the Royal Engineers of the British army) are going at this time to the Caspian to take charge of the shipping. I have also been informed by military officers that these units probably number in all more than five hundred men and are taking with them guns of 4.7 size for mounting on ships in the Caspian, and parts for the building of mine sweepers. I was also told that some six inch naval guns were going up, but I do not believe that it would be possible to haul such heavy guns over the Bagdad-Caspian road in its present condition and with the present transportation facilities.

The third invasion of Persia by British troops has been by way of Baluchistan and thence north through eastern Persia to Meshed. From Meshed as base operations have recently been undertaken to secure the control of Krasnovodsk-Merv rail line. Latest reports indicate that these operations will be successful. This invasion of Persia has also been explained as a military necessity to meet, among other possibilities, a possible advance of the enemy across the Caspian into Turkestan and thence possibly into Afghanistan. Although nominally pro-British, the Amir of Afghanistan would, it is thought, welcome the enemy should they progress as far as his frontier.

The Persian government was not consulted by the British with reference to the sending of troops into Persia under General Dunsterville, although it was notified that this would be done. Earlier in the year the Persians in Ghilan [Gilan] province north of Resht had been organized under Kuchik Khan, a Persian political leader. These Persians, known as Jangalees [Jangalis], or Jungle tribes from the nature of their country, were induced by German and other enemy agents to attack the British. This they did. The plan was apparently that they should take Resht and thus cut the line of communication to the Caspian, by which time the Turks in Azerbaijan would come across to join them and thus cut the British off from the Caspian. Kuchik Khan was supplied with considerable money and equipment by the Germans and Turks and attacked the British several times. He was apparently acting independently of the Persian government and was actuated by the money paid him as much as by any other cause. He attacked the British at Resht on July 20, 1918, and was badly defeated. He was aided in this attack by several German and Austrian officers and soldiers who had escaped from Russia. His defeat at Resht and the failure of the Turks to get across to join him evidently discouraged him a great deal and, according to report, the British having offered a satisfactory price in gold for his goodwill, he made his peace with them during the second week in August, one of the peace conditions being, as I was told, that he would deliver up his German and Austrian assistants as prisoners to the British. The only other local or Persian opposition to the British occupation of the Bagdad-Caspian line was from the Sinjabis [Sanjabis], a Kurdish tribe on the Mesopotamian-Persian frontier. These people are reported to have been aroused by the German agent von Dreuffel, who is supposed later to have been drowned when attempting to cross a high river during the spring floods.

In their occupation of the Bagdad-Caspian line of communication the British appear to have treated the Persians living in that zone with reasonable consideration, feeding famine sufferers, giving employment in way of road building, etc., cleaning up the towns along the line both in the way of sanitation and of government, and in general doing the best they could to better the lot of the unfortunate Persian peasants who suffered so much from the Russians and the Turks. They have arrested some of the Persian officials who were considered dangerous or antagonistic because of the German propaganda to which they had been exposed, and have interfered in local Persian affairs in an apparently somewhat arbitrary manner which could not but cause ill-feeling among the Persian officials in Teheran. They have perhaps unnecessarily overlooked the sensitive feelings of the Persians in a few instances and have aroused considerable ill-will which might have been avoided by other methods. The giving of English names to the streets of the towns which they occupied seems to have been particularly offensive to Persian officials.

It seems reasonably certain that the British can and will hold the Bagdad-Caspian line of communication pending the outcome of the war, and it seems necessary, particularly to British interests, that they do so. While the Persians are quite unlikely to declare for the other side in the war, the presence of British forces in this part of Persia will check any probable advance of the enemy further into Persia, and will incidentally protect India, the British position in the Persian Gulf, and the important British-owned oil-fields in south-western Persia.

From all the information which I was able to obtain in Teheran it does not appear that the Persians committed any definitely hostile act against any one of three powers named, but have had to submit to several military invasions, principally on the ground of so-called military necessity, and to have parts of their country used as battlefields by the military forces of Russia, Turkey, and Great Britain. By Persians I mean the Persian government. Although not a belligerent Persia has suffered many damages and many of the disadvantages of a belligerent on the losing side in the world war. It is upon these grounds that the Persian government feels that Persia's position is a special one, and that as it occupies a position entirely distinct or different from that of any other neutral country it has a right to a place at the principal peace conference to occur at the close of the war; and many prominent Persian officials expressed to me the hope that the United States would support them in this claim for a place at the main peace conference. I was emphatically informed by members of the Persian government at Teheran that they considered all of these military invasions as violations of Persian neutrality, and that in no case had the Persian government been consulted or had it consented to the occupation or invasions. The fight which occurred in Persian territory has resulted in a considerable loss of Persian life and property, and the Persians consider that they should have a place at the Peace Conference in order to ask for and to secure reparations for these injuries resulting from the many violations of Persian neutrality.[9]

British Intention: Permanent Control of Persia

Southard also describes British occupation and control through various military and police organizations, including the South Persia Rifles, concluding by giving British long-range plans for the control of Persia. To Southard and American diplomats in Tehran and Mesopotamia, the so-called temporary British occupation and control of Persia was to be permanent:

I have the honor to state that the British control of Persian affairs is being further strengthened by other military measures. Next to the Bagdad-Caspian line, the control of South Persia with the assistance of the South Persia Rifles is the most important. The organization of native police or gendarmerie as initiated with the South Persia Rifles organization is being extended by the British to other parts of the country, and more particularly in central and north-central Persia. In the provinces of Kermanshah and Hamadan the organization of military police composed of Persian Kurds is already well advanced. The Germans, at the time of the Turkish occupation of this part of Persia in 1916, made serious attempts to organize such a force among the Kurds, but were prevented from completing their work by the return of the Russians and the retirement of the Turks into Mesopotamia. The Kurds themselves seem to have no patriotic objection to serving whatever government may offer them the most suitable financial inducement, and the British have been quite successful after having established an attractive scale of compensation which is as follows: Privates receive fifty krans per month; corporals receive seventy-five krans; and sergeants receive one hundred krans. In addition each man receives six krans per day in lieu of food. The Persian kran at present has an exchange value of about 19 cents in U.S. currency, although the normal value is about $0.0875. The term of enlistment is for one year, and the Persian authorities along the line have apparently been willing to assist the British in rounding up deserters from this native force.

The police have been enlisted in the number of several thousands—the exact number is not obtainable—and are drilled by British drill-sergeants. Those [enlisted men] which I saw did not impress me as having much physical or mental vigor, but they will probably serve well for the constabulary or police duty along the line of communication, which I understand is to be their work. It is presumed that when the British retire from Persia these police will be handed over to the Persian government as an organized and equipped body to be used in place of the gendarmerie organization formerly possessed by that government, but which has become almost completely disorganized since the beginning of the war.

Detachments, mostly of Indian troops, as Consular guards at various other places complete in general the organization for the military safe-guarding of British interests in Persia. In Arabistan and Luristan I understand that detachments of troops have come over from Mesopotamia for station at Maidan-i-Naphta [Meydan-e Naftun], Dizful [Dezful], Shuster [Shushtar], Ahwaz [Ahvaz], and other points of strategic importance in watching for and controlling possible disorder among somewhat troublesome tribes in that part of Persia. I understand that the placing of troops in this district is largely upon the necessity of guarding the oil-fields and pipelines of the Anglo-Persian Oil Company from possible attack by Persian tribes presumably in German pay. At Mohammerah, Bushire, and at other points along the Persian Gulf there are understood to be military detachments as well as bases for the gunboats patrolling the coast. At Yezd, Shiraz, and Kerman, the South Persia Rifles are understood to be in control, although British Consulates and Political Offices at these places have detachments of Indian troops, principally cavalry, as Consular guards. At Meshed in northeastern Persia there were, according to last reports, about five hundred British Indian troops with arrangements made for bringing in considerably greater numbers via the Quetta-Nushki railroad should it seem necessary to move into Russian Turkestan. I understand that this is now actually being done.

From the foregoing it may be understood that plans have been carefully and systematically worked out so that all parts of Persia, excepting Azerbaijan province, either are actually occupied by British military forces, or are more or less readily accessible to occupation should circumstances make it necessary. There appear to be three areas: South Persia, which is based upon the Gulf; eastern and northeastern Persia based on Baluchistan; and central and north-central Persia based upon Bagdad or other points in Mesopotamia. There is no definite information, so far as I could learn, as to British plans in Persia excepting that the British government is understood to have assured the Persian government that no part of the country will be permanently occupied; but it is evident that with their present organization it would be very easy and perhaps tempting to the British to retain permanent control of parts of southern and southeastern Persia which are so vitally important to their oil interests and to the safe-guarding of India from invasion. Although the British government seems to have been particularly anxious to disclaim any idea of permanently occupying any part of Persia, there seems to be a general feeling and attitude on the part of subordinate military and political officers in Persia that a permanent British control of Persian affairs is necessary to British interests and to Persian economic development in favor of British commercial interests particularly.[10]

Long after the conquest and occupation of Persia, British military and political capabilities were being augmented, thereby confirming suspicions about British intentions in Persia. The American consul in Baghdad sent the following telegram to Washington in August 1918: "Additional political officers from Bagdad continue to come to Persia for stay at various

points and British occupation and control seems to be receiving study and
definite strengthening. Additional batteries, aeroplanes, and armored cars
are coming in, complete hospital units accompany the forces, and large
hospital is about to be opened in Hamadan."[11] By the end of 1918,
prospects for Persia escaping from the British grip were bleak. The country
had been completely encircled and conquered. To the American chargé
d'affaires, Francis White, its very existence was now threatened:

> Great Britain would appear to favor a strong, independent, friendly Persia.
> There is no means of knowing what her intentions towards Persia will be, how-
> ever. Persia's geographical position vis-à-vis Great Britain has enormously
> changed since the war. With Mesopotamia in her possession and her activities
> in the Caucasus, which are already causing speculation and even uneasiness in
> some quarters, she has in a great measure encircled Persia. Furthermore from
> Bassra [Basra] as a base she will surely extend her interests up the Karun river
> at the same time as she expands up the Tigris. Now the history of European
> expansion in Asia has shown that it has proceeded along two general lines, by
> encirclement as in the case of Kirghiz steppes by Russia, and by expansion up
> the great river systems from a base at their mouth as in the case of Calcutta,
> Kurachee [Karachi], Rangoon, etc. These two conditions are now fulfilled as
> regards Great Britain's geographical position in relation to Persia and if Persia
> does not seize her present opportunity to put her house in order and establish
> a strong government circumstances which cannot now be foreseen may very
> easily arise in the future to impel Great Britain to absorb a part at least of Per-
> sian territory.[12]

The Appointment of Vossough-ed-Dowleh as Prime Minister

By early July 1918, with military conquest and occupation complete, the
British moved to take complete political control of Persia. Southard describes
the political situation and British policy as well as the British campaign to get
Hasan Vossough, Vossough-ed-Dowleh, appointed prime minister:

> There is considerable political unrest in Persia but owing to the impotence
> of Persian Government and the control exercised by the British in all parts of
> Persia excepting the Northwest, it is improbable that this unrest could result in
> more than local disturbances. Unrest due to enemy propaganda and Persian
> resentment [of] British military occupation and supervision of Persian affairs.
> Enemy propaganda much less by arrest or driving from the country many
> German agents and Persian agitators by the British during the last year. In the
> provinces, political conditions are closely watched by British officials and sev-
> eral Persians have been arrested and removed from office. Ten days ago British
> military arrested Governor of Hamadan and several supporters. Governor
> reported taken to Bagdad.

British are bringing about appointment of Persian officials friendly to Allied interests, a notable example being the retention of Prince Farman Farma as governor of Fars, second most important Persian province. He resides in Shiraz and is considered to be entirely in sympathy with British interests, and is influential in all parts of Persia. His son, Nosrat-ed-Douleh [Nosrat-ed-Dowleh] is reputed to be active British propagandist in Teheran. The leading Persian political party is named Democratic Party and is anti-foreigner and particularly anti-British and Russian. Most prominent Persians are Democrats. Chief Democratic activity is protesting against British occupation and in fighting growing British political influence. Principal result has been cabinet changes. . . . The cabinet is radically Democratic. There is constant agitation headed by former Prime Minister Vossough-ed-Dowleh who wishes again to be Prime Minister. He is reputed to be British agent and if appointed is expected to form new Ministry entirely friendly to Allies. Adherents of this man are waging active campaign in Teheran against the present cabinet by organizing protesting demonstrations of gendarmes and bazaar people. Quantity of money and food has been distributed by them in this connection alleged supplied by British. Some bombs have been thrown and one was exploded three nights ago in the garden [of] Minister without portfolio. Strong belief prevails that Vossough will succeed soon in causing the resignation of the Ministry and be appointed Prime Minister. In this event political as well as military situation in Persia will be well controlled by the British.[13]

Additional light on the manner in which the anti-British cabinet of Samsam-es-Saltaneh was undermined by the expenditure of funds by the British legation is provided by Caldwell: "On account of riots and scourges occasioned by food shortage and political disturbers Teheran has been placed under military government. Nothing serious is expected to happen."[14] In a subsequent dispatch Caldwell gives more information on the protests and the establishment of martial law in Tehran:

About a fortnight ago large crowds of beggars and idlers gathered at the mosques and other public places in the city and were harangued by native priests and other speakers. The object of these gatherings was said to be public protest against and a general disapproval of the do nothing policy and methods of the present Cabinet. The Cabinet and their sympathizers and followers, on the other hand, claimed that these gatherings were brought about, encouraged and financed by rival candidates for the Premiership and other Cabinet positions, and further claimed that financial assistance was being furnished by interested foreign powers. Of the truth or falsity of this latter statement this Legation has been unable to obtain any evidence or facts, but such charges are promiscuously and repeatedly made. However, there can be no doubt that much money is being spent to encourage rioting, for rice, costing about sixty cents per pound, other foodstuffs and money have been daily distributed among the crowds of agitators, the number of which vary from three hundred to five hundred. It is believed, from best reports, that an average of about a dollar per day has been given to the active agitators. Although a number of arrests were made by the local police, they seemed unable to cope with the situation, hence the order establishing martial law. The city is now quiet and no further trouble is looked for. It is my opinion that these gatherings and protests are largely, if not entirely, instigated against the present Cabinet by rival candidates for public favor, though these rival candidates may have received some encouragement and financial backing from interested foreign governments.[15]

The term "interested foreign governments" was a euphemism for Great Britain. Caldwell discusses the appointment of Vossough-ed-Dowleh. Despite several challenges, the position of the cabinet was secure by November 1918, thanks to the British:

> During 1917 and in the late spring and early summer of this year there was a considerable amount of terrorism culminating in political assassinations and bomb throwing and accompanied by demonstrations against the Samsam-es-Saltaneh cabinet, which was then in power. A great many persons took "bast" [sanctuary] in the Shah's Mosque at the instigation of the mollahs who, it is said, were paid by opponents of the then existing cabinet and the pro-British party. In order more effectively to deal with these manifestations martial law was proclaimed in Teheran on July 6th. Matters remained in very much the same state, however, for some time and nothing active or effective was done against the demonstrators except to arrest some of those taking bast in the Mosque. Matters remained in about this condition until August when the British Minister succeeded in having the Shah request the resignation of the Samsam-es-Saltaneh cabinet and appoint Vossough-ed-Dowleh in his place. Vossough-ed-Dowleh is pro-British and one of the most intelligent and competent of the present Persian statesmen and his coming to power greatly strengthened the position of the Allies in Persia. The old cabinet was very popular with the people, however, and just before leaving office it took all possible steps to discredit the new cabinet. For several days after the new cabinet assumed office there was no bread in the city. The old cabinet's action in abrogating all Russian treaties, conventions and concessions won the populace to its side. The position of the new cabinet for several days was rather difficult but things soon settled down into their normal course and no trouble arose. The democrats and other opponents of the Vossough-ed-Dowleh cabinet, who were openly questioning his motives, were only waiting for a chance to cause him embarrassment and if possible turn him out of office. The evacuation of Baku by the British and the Turkish advance in Azerbaijan, from Mianeh to a point near Zinjan [Zanjan], seemed to be the opportune moment and they, the German Legation and the Turkish Embassy used this Allied set back to the utmost. The opportunity was short lived, however, as a few days thereafter the news of the Turkish debacle in Palestine and of Bulgaria's collapse strengthened the pro-Allied party and the movement against the present cabinet ceased almost as quickly as it had begun. Now that Germany is vanquished in the West

it is not likely the Vossough-ed-Dowleh cabinet will experience any great opposition for some time to come.[16]

Southard also provides a great deal of information on the political situation after the conquest of Persia by the British. To bring about the appointment of Vossough, for instance, the British legation spent £100,000.

> The British, who are the most recent comers into northern Persia, have been very successful in their intrigues for influence at Teheran, and undoubtedly have complete control at present over the Persian government both at Teheran and in the provinces, and over Persian political affairs in general. This has been accomplished largely through the excellent work of the British Legation at Teheran with its Consuls and Political Agents stationed at all important points in the country, and by the military control of South Persia through the organization of the South Persia Rifles, and the military control of central and northern Persia by establishing the Bagdad-Caspian line of communication.
>
> The final step in British control of Persian political affairs is considered to have occurred on August 3, 1918, when the Shah was influenced to dismiss the Samsam-es-Sultaneh [Saltaneh] cabinet which was very much anti-British, and to appoint as Premier Vossough-ed-Dowleh, a very strong Persian politician with pro-British sympathies. Although Persian cabinets since the granting of the Constitution in 1906 have changed frequently, allegedly through Russian influence for the purpose of thus shaking popular confidence in representative government, the feeling in Teheran the latter part of August was that the Vossough-ed-Dowleh cabinet would probably be able to remain in power and prevent Persian governmental interference with the British plans for keeping Persia and the Caspian Sea from the enemy and damaging enemy influence. Should this cabinet fall and be succeeded by one of the more radical sort it may be taken as an indication that enemy influence is still able to interfere with the generally accepted thorough British control of Persian affairs. The methods used by the various powers in attempting to gain influence with the Teheran government are generally conceded to have been a liberal use of gold and suggestions of what might happen to Persia. It is generally stated in Teheran, both by the interested and the disinterested, that the British Legation disbursed approximately a hundred thousand pounds sterling in May, June, and July, to bring about the appointment of a Prime Minister suitable to British policy.
>
> The Minister of Interior, subject usually to the Shah's approval, appoints provincial governors. This portfolio has in the last two cabinets been held by the Prime Minister and as the present Prime Minister, Vossough-ed-Dowleh, is a reputed Anglophile it gives the British the power of securing through him a corps of provincial governors who will work in the interest of their policy as regards Persia. However, more than twenty of the twenty-eight provincial governors holding office prior to the Vossough-ed-Dowleh cabinet were considered purchasable with British influence or money, or with the money or influence of any power which might have control of affairs in Teheran.

Although the British evidently found it necessary, under the circumstances, to act in many instances with a great deal of severity and abruptness in their dealings with the Persian government, it seems not improbable that if their political representatives in Persia display the same efficiency in conciliating the Persians which they used in accomplishing the control of political affairs in the country, the next few months will see the Persians accepting with entire good-will the so-called temporary British military and political control of their country.[17]

The Consolidation of Power by Vossough

Beginning in the fall of 1918, the American legation in Tehran began submitting lengthy quarterly reports. The first eleven cover the period after the appointment of Vossough as prime minister; the eleventh specifically covers the first quarter of 1921, and provides a detailed account of the coup d'état of February 21, 1921. Deeply resentful of the fact that Vossough was a British imposition, Ahmad Shah's relationship with "his" prime minister and government was one of outright hostility. By the end of 1918, relations between Ahmad Shah and the government had practically broken down. Matters came to a head over the shah's dismissal of Qavam-es-Saltaneh, Vossough's brother, as governor-general of Khorasan. With the solid backing of Vossough by the British minister, Sir Percy Cox, Ahmad Shah was forced to concede and, in practice, the shah was publicly humiliated by the British and Vossough. Ahmad Shah's dismissal of Qavam and his subsequent humiliation are discussed by Francis White:

> The Shah felt that his dignity would not permit him to back down after having already recalled Ghavam [Qavam] and announced his intention of appointing Prince Nosra-es-Sultaneh in his place. Also he did not wish Vossough-ed-Dowleh, whom he was coming more and more to fear, to gain the added prestige which a reversal of his decision under such circumstances would give him. He finally told Cox that he did not want to do anything which was contrary to the interests of Great Britain and that he would leave Ghavam as governor but he himself would have to leave and that then the British could make Vossough dictator. Sir Percy told him that his government did not want Vossough or any one else to become dictator nor did they want the Shah to leave but that they must insist on having a friendly governor in Meshed. The Shah insisted that he would leave and go to Europe leaving Vossough in charge and that then the order could be recalled. Sir Percy pointed out that it would be very difficult traveling at this time and also it would be very inconvenient for him to go to Europe. The Shah said that he would go to Kum [Qom] but the British Minister objected on the ground that would be a protest against the pressure brought to bear by the British which was not what they wanted; they wanted the Shah to co-operate and work with them and not against them.[18]

The hostility of Ahmad Shah to the Vossough government encouraged other politicians to become active against the cabinet. But with British support, the Vossough government was "unshakable":

> The intrigues against the cabinet, carried on principally by Ain-ed-Dowleh, Saad-ed-Dowleh, and Samsam-es-Sultaneh, lost a great deal of intensity after the reconciliation between the Shah and Vossough-ed-Dowleh late in January. The British Legation was determined to support Vossough-ed-Dowleh and to keep him in power as long as possible and with this support the cabinet's position was practically unshakable. The situation is so secure that Vossough-ed-Dowleh, who has not been in the best of health recently, is considering going to Europe for a much needed change. The Shah also, I am confidentially informed, is contemplating going to Europe for the same reason but the British Government, which controls all means of transport from here, has not yet decided whether it would be convenient to have him travel at this time and consequently whether or not it will give him traveling facilities.[19]

During its first year in office, the government of Vossough-ed-Dowleh set about establishing law and order, which in practice meant consolidating its power. With its secure base, and faced with disorders in Gilan, Astarabad, and Kurdistan, the Vossough government, with British help, energetically set about establishing its control through the Persian gendarmerie and the Cossacks.[20] By the fall of 1919, the government had accomplished its goal throughout the country, including Gilan. It is very clear that the establishment of law and order, which was to be pursued much more vigorously by Reza Khan after 1921, was part of consolidation of British control of Persia.[21]

The Anglo-Persian Convention of August 9, 1919, and Vossough's Civilian Dictatorship

With complete military and seeming political control of Persia, the British intended to formalize and perpetuate their political and commercial domination through the Anglo-Persian Convention of August 9, 1919. The following account of that convention is based on a memorandum written by Augustin W. Ferrin, the American vice consul in Tehran in the second half of the 1920s. By this agreement, Britain promised to respect absolutely the independence and integrity of Persia and to supply expert advisers, at Persian expense, for the reform of the administration, to provide munitions and equipment for the creation of a modern Persian army, to arrange a loan for the Persian government to carry out these reforms, and, in the meantime, to advance some funds while withholding oil revenues.

Britain expressed its readiness to cooperate with the Persian government to encourage Anglo-Persian enterprise in railways and other forms of

FIGURE 2.1 *Hassan Vossough, Vossough-ed-Dowleh, ca. 1930.*

transport. The two governments agreed to the appointment of a joint commission for the revision of the existing customs tariff. On the same day, the British signed a supplemental agreement to loan Persia £2 million at 7 percent interest secured upon the southern customs, subject to service of a previous loan of £1.25 million made in May 1911. The loan was to be paid in installments after the arrival of a British financial adviser in Tehran. The agreement was signed by Sir Percy Cox for the British. The Persian signatories were the prime minister, Hassan Vossough-ed-Dowleh; the foreign minister, Prince Firouz Mirza Nosrat-ed-Dowleh; and the minister of finance, Prince Akbar Mirza Massoud Sarem-ed-Dowleh.

The agreement was deeply distrusted by the public, who suspected secret clauses. The suspicions were strengthened when it became known that the three Persian signatories had received £131,000 immediately after signing. In the words of Ferrin, "later the British claimed that this was an advance to the Persian government under the loan agreement of August 9, 1919, but no evidence appears ever to have been adduced to show that the money ever reached the treasury, or indeed to explain what did become of it."[22] Deeply suspicious of the affair, Caldwell describes in vivid terms the attempt to force the agreement on the Persian people through bribery, coercion, and intimidation:

> The outstanding and unique feature of the whole affair is not the treaty itself but the dexterity and celerity with which it was put over the public who were made to accept it and not allowed to even privately voice a dissenting opinion, under fear of imprisonment or deportation, though an adroit and systematic attempt was made to prepare the fallow ground of public opinion in advance, during the several months this treaty was being formulated. The reason that the particular members of the Persian Peace Commission to Paris were chosen was that it was thought best to have them out of the country at this critical time, knowing that their hands would be tied in Paris. Others of like integrity, ability and patriotism have been sent away on pretext of pilgrimage or appointment to consular posts. More remarkable, even, than this allaying and silencing of criticism was the method of openly buying and corrupting the venal priesthood, all too many of whom are known to have been given and to have accepted presents, money, pensions and other tokens. It is but fair to say, however, that a great number of the priesthood, as well as the public, could not be so reached, and the only method to silence these was through threats, fear of imprisonment, etc. Then again, a great amount of fawning and entertaining was done, of which even some of our Americans were the recipients. Favors and flattery were expended on many of these people who were of too little importance to ever have been hitherto noticed, though this procedure and unusual attention were too apparent to escape the notice of any observant person. While the war was pending it was usually sufficient, in order to stifle criticism, to loudly proclaim that any critic or objector was pro-German, but such a false weapon cannot now be employed and resort to subtler means becomes necessary.[23]

The Vossough government silenced the opposition with imprisonment and exile and imposed strict press censorship. It appears that what transpired under Vossough's government was a minor and mild version of events under Reza Khan. Caldwell writes:

> The Persian public are awaiting, Micawber like, for "something to turn up," and the wiser ones still profess to believe that the treaty can never be carried into effect. Nevertheless, the arrest and deportation of a few of the leaders, the rigid enforcement of the prevailing martial law, coupled with the natural

cowardice and timidity of the Oriental, makes it extremely unlikely that any effective measure can be taken to stop its enforcement. This is especially true in view of the presence of several thousand British soldiers in Persia, the absence of the Shah in Europe and the all too willingness of the present Cabinet to faithfully serve the power that made and maintains it.[24]

In the following account of the exile, arrest, and silencing of the opponents of the agreement, the army referred to is the British occupation army:

The four ex-Cabinet members who were banished in September and sent to Kashan are still held as prisoners and not allowed to return to Teheran. This banishment has in great measure stopped any attempt at public censure of the treaty, for the Cabinet has announced that it is prepared to take strong measures against all objectors. The Persian is by nature a moral and physical coward and much more so in the presence of an army which is located at strategic points throughout the country, ready at a moment's notice to take drastic action against either individuals or communities. Since the last report it has been discovered that a number of Members elect of the Medjliss [Majlis], who have been sojourning abroad as officials, Ministers to foreign countries, members of the Persian Peace Commission, etc., will not be permitted to return to Teheran, and have been advised accordingly. Prince Suleiman Mirza, who was arrested in Persia two years ago while returning to Teheran after having been in Turkey, although duly elected to the Medjliss, is still held by the British military authorities in Bagdad or India. He is one of the most patriotic and able Persian statesmen, even though he was apparently misled during the war. Nawab, who was Persian Minister to Germany during the war, but who is everywhere spoken of as a man of the highest type and character, will not, it is understood, be allowed to return to Persia to take his seat if and when the Medjliss is convened. The members of the Paris Peace Commission have likewise been informed that they will not be permitted to return. The Chief, Moshaver-ol-Mamalek, was offered the post of the Ambassadorship to Constantinople, which he has, I understand, declined, but he will not be permitted to return for a time, at least. Zoka-ol-Molk is also barred, while Mirza Hussein Khan, whose brother has just been removed from the Persian Ministership at London to be replaced by a more favorably inclined and pliable tool, has been told that he would not be allowed to remain in England and also that he cannot, for the present, return to Persia, but he was offered and has accepted the post of Minister to Spain, though Persia has not a single subject in Spain, nor Spain in Persia. Spain recently abolished her Legation here. The manner in which the Anglo-Persian treaty was consummated, against the wishes of the entire Persian public, and forced on the nation by the most unpopular Cabinet (which, as has been before explained was placed in power by the British authorities, and is held there by the presence of a British army, divisions of which are scattered in practically all the principal cities of Persia, including Resht, Enzeli, Tabriz, Kazvin [Qazvin], Hamadan, Kermanshah, Shiraz, Bushire, Bunder [Bandar] Abbas, Kerman, Meshed, and Nosratabad) is constantly in the thoughts of the people even though, other than the dangerous method of secretly published articles, there is no manner in which the treaty can be opposed. Silence is enforced but so far as is known, not a single Persian who is honest and uninstigated by a hope of reward is found in favor of this treaty. It is understood that in case the Medjliss is convened and in case the majority of the members should have been so well chosen as to vote in favor of the ratification of the treaty, about one third of the Democratic element would immediately resign. But even then the question of despair is asked, "What can Persia do?" for it must have money. It is the general opinion that the Treaty, if actually consummated, marks the end and downfall of Persian independence as a nation. In fact, many of the more thoughtful seem to think that Persia will not even be on a footing with Egypt under this Treaty.

At present, due mainly to the prevailing martial law, the identity of the Persian political parties has practically been lost, because there can be no public meetings and everything that is done or written publicly must be in favor of the present Government. Soon after the Anglo-Persian Treaty was made public a communiqué was issued in the local papers by what purported to be the Democratic Party (but was in effect the announcement of a small part of that party, with one of the former Democratic leaders, who found it worth their while to make such a statement) to the effect that the Democratic Party approved the treaty. Of course this announcement could not be publicly denied as that would be a form of opposition to the treaty and Government, and also no newspaper could or would accept such an announcement; but that does not mean that the statement was true, in fact the few who made the statement were immediately considered as traitors and no longer Democrats, and are not now recognized by the party. But as mentioned above, political parties are now not in evidence and to all intents and purposes might just as well not exist.

Anonymous publications in the form of blue prints are sent out from time to time, but since the police make every effort to apprehend the guilty parties, this is done with the utmost secrecy, and entails much personal danger. There are a number of secret organizations in Persia and ordinarily their efforts are felt during a crisis, but evidently the existing martial law and the proximity of the British troops to the capital have had the desired effect upon such organizations.

At present Persia is ruled with an iron hand by the Prime Minister, Vossough-ed-Dowleh. Even the slightest initiative cannot be taken by other members of the cabinet or Government without first referring the matter to him. The Valiahd [Crown Prince] is Prince Regent during the absence of his brother, the Shah, but the Valiahd has no real authority. In fact, even the Shah was forced, by foreign influence, to bend to the will of the Prime Minister. This latter has come up from the ranks and now seems not only powerful but also very prosperous, and has a new beautiful country estate in the course of construction. He has, for the last ten or fifteen years, been known as one of the most forceful characters in Persia, and now that he has the full power of the Government in his hands (under the control of the British) he is not allowing anything to stand in his way. The Persian people greatly admire a strong ruler and although they are much opposed to the actions of the present Premier, they cannot help but admire him. It has been confidentially stated that a high-up Persian advised Vossough-ed-Dowleh to get rid of all of the Princes now in Government service, as they are well known to be an intriguing and pliable set. But the Premier is said to have replied: "Everyone knows the choosing and dismissing of these men is not really in my hands, even though it is in my name." It is reliably reported that the present British Minister here, Sir Percy Cox, who recently had the honor of K.C.M.G. conferred upon him, as a result of the consummation of the treaty, is soon to be allowed to consummate his ambition to become the Governor-General of Mesopotamia, and is to be replaced by Mr. [H.] Norman. The Persian Prime Minister has also recently been knighted by the British Government, having received the Order of the Bath. This, of course, is but a red flag to the Persian nationalists.[25]

The British Propaganda Campaign: Maude Radford Warren's Visit

To help sell the agreement to Persians and to the world, the British undertook a massive propaganda campaign both in Persia and in America:

The amount of money spent in Persia on propaganda and various causes must be something enormous, and when Lord Curzon informed the Department that the British Government had expended great sums in Persia during the war he told the truth. No political campaign in Persia is comparable to the thoroughness with which this is being and has been done. In connection with the consummation of the treaty, too, should be remembered the statement of the British Minister [Charles Marling] to the undersigned in 1916, when he said, "We'll tend to Persia AFTER the war."[26]

Caldwell also describes the imposition of tight press censorship:

At present, the only public propaganda here is in favor of the British and this is continuous. Among the better class here American prestige remains high and great admiration exists for American ideals and institutions. This feeling, however, the present Cabinet endeavors to discourage by every means, and disparaging articles as to our political attitude appear frequently in the local papers. The newspapers published here continue to be practically edited by the Cabinet but "shab namehs" [anonymous publications] are scattered throughout Teheran, which latter contain some very strong statements. Recently the Prime Minister issued a manifesto announcing that the authors of these scurrilous articles were known and that they would receive condign punishment, but the articles continue to appear and the real authors are still free. The local British publication, Reuters News, which reaches here daily by telegraph, is filled by assurances by British statesmen and Persians residing in Europe that a close rapprochement and political understanding and unseverable ties of friendship exist between the two countries.[27]

In addition, Britain undertook an international campaign of deception and misinformation about British policy in Persia. Caldwell describes the fact-finding visit to Persia of Maude Radford Warren of the *Saturday Evening Post*. Formerly a British subject, Mrs. Warren had become a naturalized American citizen.

A matter of some importance was the recent arrival in Teheran, from Bagdad, of Mrs. Maude Radford Warren, from Chicago and Ithaca. She represents the Saturday Evening Post and has visited Egypt, Mesopotamia and Persia with a view of preparing some articles on these countries for publication. Upon her arrival in Bagdad the American Consul there wired this Legation as follows: "Mrs. Warren, correspondent of the Saturday Evening Post desires to proceed to Teheran, but British Political Officer offers objections unless you consent." To which I replied: "If Mrs. Warren has an honest desire to study or write of Persian affairs in good faith, I can see no objection to her coming to Teheran." Mrs. Warren arrived one week later in a British automobile and stayed in Teheran for a week, then departed by way of the Caspian Sea and the Caucasus for Constantinople. She was, I understand, given an automobile and transportation from Bagdad to Teheran, 635 miles, and from Teheran to Enzeli, 234 miles, by the British authorities gratis. Upon arrival in Teheran she came to this Legation and asked to see certain documents of a confidential nature, including the report on Persia handed to the Department by Dr. Judson, but was advised that it was not within my power to lend her such assistance. Thereupon inquiry was made from her if she desired to ascertain the full facts about Persia and the Persian situation and if she expected to write the same for publication in the Saturday Evening Post. To which she very candidly replied that she did not expect to write the facts; that she represented a magazine whose policy, as well as her own, was to bring about a closer understanding and better feeling between the Governments and people of America and Great Britain.

She was advised to see some of the leading and best informed Persians, as well as the foreign diplomats, but she replied that she did not care to do this. During the week she was here, however, she was in daily communication with the British Legation, who took great pains to be in close touch with her and gave her very detailed reports of the situation, a small part of which Mrs. Warren repeated to the undersigned, whom she advised that the British Minister said that the recent secret revision of the Persian Customs Tariff, though done by British advisers, greatly favored American trade at the expense of Great Britain. Mrs. Warren was formerly a British subject and lost no opportunity of airing her strong pro-British tendencies, sympathies and her admiration for British men and institutions. She interviewed Arbab Kaikhosrow Shahrokh, who recently returned from America, and who is the Zoroastrian member of the Persian Parliament as well as one of Persia's most honorable and best statesmen, but his interview and attitude were decidedly distasteful to Mrs. Warren.

She did not care to see the French or Belgian Ministers or the Russian Chargé d'Affaires.[28]

Majlis "Elections" and the Implementation of the Anglo-Persian Convention

Under the Persian constitution, the Anglo-Persian Convention was valid only if it was ratified by the Majlis. Shortly after it was signed, in late 1919 elections were held in certain regions for the purpose of convening the Fourth Majlis and submitting the agreement for its consideration. Caldwell describes the government's attempts to ensure that the "right" candidates would be elected, a prelude to the farcical elections that would be held during the next sixty years under the Pahlavis:

> It is quite generally understood that neither the present cabinet, who were and are as previously reported, dictated, held and placed in office by the British Legation and who have maintained their incumbency by reason of the support given by that Legation and the presence of a large number of British troops in and about Persia, nor the British Government and Legation expect or desire to await the convening of the Persian Medjliss to ratify this agreement, even though the Constitution provides that such ratification is necessary before the agreement becomes effective or of force and validity. This in spite of the fact that the present cabinet absolutely controls the appointment of Governors throughout the different provinces and that these Governors will, and in some instances have, practically chosen the members of the Medjliss from their respective provinces.[29]

By early 1920, it was becoming clear, despite the election of many "suitable" candidates, that given the popular antagonism to the agreement, there was no possibility of its approval by the Majlis. Consequently, the government decided not to convene the Majlis.

Almost immediately after the signature of the Anglo-Persian Convention, and despite lack of Majlis ratification, its main provisions had been implemented, including the appointment of British advisers:

> It is understood that the British advisers provided for in the agreement are en route here, expecting to begin work at once, though it will be months before a Persian Medjliss can be convened. Many British officers in the Indian Service are reported to be looking forward and aspiring to a better career in the Persian service and while numerous assurances and repetitions in the form of published "communiqués," "covering letters," etc., are given the public assuring that Persia's independence and integrity are to be respected, numerous well-known Persians of strong pro-British tendencies and reputation, certain news-

papers, officials and such are openly saying that "Persia is now a British dependency; we are under a British protectorate and may as well acquiesce; the best we could do was to come under this British mandate," etc. Nevertheless there is nothing in the treaty itself that necessarily implies a limitation of Persia's sovereignty; but throughout Persia the thoughtful inhabitants are inclined to regard the res gestae. These Persians point out that the really good part of the convention is not the treaty itself, but is conveyed in a "covering letter" from the British Minister. The same convention, if made with America, would probably have excited no opposition from the Persians, who desire to place such power as is therein given in the hands of a non-neighboring power who has no political interests here and who has, to quote numerous Persians: "a good reputation in dealing with small and weak nations."[30]

The Anglo-Persian Convention provided for the appointment of a British Military Mission to Persia:

A number of British military investigators have arrived in Teheran. They are headed by Major General [W. E. R.] Dickson, and most of them are connected with the Indian army. According to the Anglo-Persian agreement the present Persian forces are to be made into a uniform force. It will no doubt be of great value to have Persia's forces unified and enlarged, which heretofore has been prohibited by her neighbors, but which it is believed Great Britain now considers as necessary, and it is to be hoped that she may be allowed to have a sufficiently large force to keep her interior in a state of peace, as well as to properly safeguard and protect her territory. In order to do this she will also need to have her finances properly organized, so that she may have the wherewithal to maintain such a force. If Persia is allowed to have a proper taxation and financial administration, which it not only desires but has often tried to secure, it is believed that she will not only be able to pay all her current expenses, but she will soon also be able to pay off her debts, which in reality are not large.[31]

In his description of the rapid de facto implementation of the agreement and tariff revision Caldwell reported the appointment of newly arrived British Financial Adviser S. A. Armitage-Smith:

The recently promulgated but unratified Anglo-Persian treaty is being and has been practically put into full force and effect. The tariff has been revised by the British Commission of experts and their revision has the force of law. The Tariff Revision Commission has departed and has been replaced by a financial expert, Mr. A. Armitage-Smith as "Financial Adviser," although in effect he has the same powers or even more than Mr. Shuster had while in Persia. He has brought out a number of assistants from England, and his, as well as the Military Commission and other Departments of the Persian Government, is constantly being augmented by the arrival of newly arrived Englishmen.[32]

The Famine of 1917–1918 and the British Attempt to Stifle Persian Foreign Trade

In the winter of 1917–18, severe famine swept Persia, primarily caused by the invading Russian and Turkish armies that occupied western Iran.

> The Russians, of all the invading forces, seem to have done the Persians most harm. Along the Bagdad-Caspian line may still be seen many abandoned villages and demolished houses resulting from the Russian occupation. There is very little firewood in the country and the Russian troops are said to have taken for firewood the roofing, window and door frames, and other wooden parts of the huts of the Persian peasants. In doing this the house was, of course, made uninhabitable and as some of the destruction occurred in winter the peasants thus deprived of shelter had a very hard time of it and many died. The Russians are also said to have taken all the food to be found, to have killed domestic animals kept for breeding purposes, and to have eaten up the small stocks of seed grain in the winter of 1916–17, and in general to have been largely responsible in this way for the serious famine that occurred in that part of Persia last winter. The Russians in general seem to have behaved very badly in Persia.[33]

Southard further reports that grain was so scarce that the price of wheat exceeded 100 tomans ($200) per kharvar ($600 per ton), a substantial sum by the standards of the time. He relates that the benevolent British armies provided food to the famine victims in the spring of 1918 and gave them employment as day laborers engaged in road construction.

British benevolence was imaginary. The withholding of oil royalty payments by the British at this critical juncture will be discussed at length in chapter 9. At this point it should be pointed out that the most important source of revenue to the Persian government was tariff revenue derived from foreign commerce. With the outbreak of war in 1914, tariff revenue from the southern tariffs was greatly reduced due to the fall in commerce. Moreover, after the 1917 revolution in Russia, revenue from the northern tariffs completely dried up. With its revenues curtailed, the government was placed in great financial difficulty. To assist the Persian government, the British government gave it monthly advances of 350,000 tomans (about £70,000 at the usual exchange rate). However, while providing such assistance and food and employment for the famine victims, the British government, in addition to stopping oil payments, set about further curtailing Persia's foreign trade by imposing a tariff on Persian exports to Mesopotamia. In addition, to Caldwell's intense anger, the British did all they could to restrict Persian trade with the United States. The American consul in Baghdad reported on the imposition of duty on goods imported from Persia.[34] It is clear that the regulation was intended not only to impose a 10 percent duty, but to completely discourage trade with Persia.

Most remarkable in Caldwell's reports of British attempts to sabotage American trade with Persia was that at a time when Persia was about to plunge into a famine that claimed many victims, the British had prevented the importation of food from the United States:

It is still necessary for practically all commercial shipments to enter Persia from the South, for the routes from Trans-Caucasia are not yet open for general freight, and of course practically nothing (except oil from Baku) is now being obtained here from Russia. Having no competition from the North gives Great Britain a great advantage in securing Persian trade. Two examples of British interference with American trade in South Persia may be cited. One case occurred during the war, in August 1917. It had to do with shipments of three thousand sacks of American sugar, the first shipment of this kind ever brought into this country. A representative of the American company accompanied the shipment and upon arrival at Bunder Abbas found that all transport animals coming into that port were commandeered by the British and were controlled by them, generally being used in connection with the then newly formed South Persia Rifles. The American in charge went to the British Vice Consul in the city (who practically is in control of the place) and after much discussion it was arranged that if the former could secure transport animals outside of Bunder Abbas they would be allowed to come into the city, load and depart without any molestation from the British military or Vice Consul. The man in charge of the shipment went out of the city about twenty-five miles and was finally able to secure a caravan of three hundred and fifty camels; but the owner, who wished to avoid the commandeering of his animals would not go to the city until he had the fullest assurances that they would not be seized. He received an initial payment for the use of his animals and went to Bunder Abbas, where his caravan was commandeered and used by the British military. When the Vice Consul was appealed to he stated that even though he had given his word he could not give any assistance to the American or the owner of the caravan. Therefore the shipment of the sugar was forcibly held in Bunder Abbas five or six months and the American declares that meanwhile shipments of sugar by Hindus and British protégés were allowed to be sent inland. The British Vice Consul offered to pay him five hundred tomans (about one thousand dollars) if the shipper would give him a receipt stating that complete compensation had been received, but the Vice Consul was informed that ten thousand dollars would not fully compensate the loss suffered by this company, and the five hundred tomans was refused. In 1919 this same company again brought a shipment to Persia, this time to Mohammerah, and the representative states that the best freight rate he was able to secure from Bombay to Mohammerah was sixty five rupees per ton of forty cubic feet, whereas he knows that some British firms were at the same time able to secure a rate of forty-five rupees per ton.[35]

Having sabotaged imports from the United States, the British also prevented Persian exports to the United States. By withholding oil royalty payments and killing off Persian exports to the United States, the British intended to have Persia completely at their economic mercy.

The other instance was in Kerman, where the representative of an American rug company was stationed. This man was an Armenian, a Turkish subject, who had been in America two years, long enough to know something of it and to grow to love it better than any other that he knew. He received American papers and magazines and often quoted passages from them in favor of America, and even went so far as to state that if America had not entered the war the Allies would not have won, and America therefore was the decisive factor and had won the war. The British consul in Kerman received reports of such matters and put a spy on the trail of the offender. The Kargozar, who has local authority over cases where foreign interests are involved with Persian interests, was informed that the British Consul was not in favor of this representative of the American company, and every case that came up involving this man or his company was decided in favor of the Persians. It was made so uncomfortable for the Armenian in Kerman that he wished to leave, but he dared not to go without getting permission from the British Consul (for fear of being arrested as soon as he got out of the city) so he went to the Consul and asked for permission, whereupon he was asked: "What assurance can you give that you will never come back here again?" The man felt so persecuted that after getting the permission he had requested he actually fled from Kerman, leaving no one in charge of the interests of the firm, and the company has, in consequence, suffered great loss in that district.[36]

Through the Anglo-Persian Convention of August 1919, the British intended to turn Persia into a captive market to the exclusion of American products, as Caldwell's account of the plan to purchase American automotive products illustrates. Evidently, the British had dreams of capturing the automotive market.

Since the publishing of the Anglo-Persian Treaty, many hope for the promised establishment of motor transportation throughout the country, and as has been pointed out before, this is believed to be the temporary means of transportation best suited to Persia under present conditions. But much road construction is necessary before such transport can be put into general use. For instance, one cannot go by motor from Teheran to the important city of Meshed, nor from Teheran to Tabriz, and only with much difficulty to Shiraz and other cities of South Persia. It is therefore likely that the planned motor transport services, when put into operation, will be on long runs only and on such routes as Resht to Teheran and Bagdad to Teheran. As one example of the scores that might be cited showing the far-reaching intentions and effects of this [Anglo-Persian] convention, there is herewith submitted an extract from a letter just received at this Legation from Mr. H. Malcolm of Shiraz: "Regarding the proposed Motor Car Company, referred to in my previous communications, I beg to state for your information that several meetings have been held here since my last report, two of these being presided over by H.R.H. the Governor, Prince Farman Farma himself, and it was decided that the shareholders should select a competent person to go to the [United] States for the purchase of some forty cars and trucks as a start. The subscribers were notified that the first call would be made for the purpose shortly, but since then the matter has remained quite dormant, and it seems to me that the recent Anglo-Persian Treaty has altogether upset the arrangements and in such case, of course, I am sure the project will die a natural death."[37]

The Fall of the Vossough-ed-Dowleh Cabinet, June 1920

By early 1920, it was clear that despite all the coercion and intimidation by the British and the Vossough government, even with the "election" of the right persons, there was no possibility of the agreement being ratified by the Majlis or accepted by the population. It was clear that the civilian dictatorship of Vossough had failed. This left in limbo the many British advisers who had arrived in Persia. Meanwhile, according to Caldwell, the British were becoming "disgusted and angry" at the resistance to the advisers:

> However, it may be well to point out that the Persian Government is already saddled with a large number of British advisers and employees who have contracts for at least three years, and these men will probably be kept here for the time being, although it is doubtful if they will be allowed to accomplish much until the matter of the treaty is definitely settled, even though as one of these men, who was being retired from the regular British Government service and was assuming an important position under the Persian Government, expressed to me: "I am glad to be able to take up this work because I feel it is a good opportunity of serving my King". . . . The various British commissions have assembled in Teheran and their reports and recommendations have been made to the Persian Government, but owing to the opposition of the public it has not been possible for even Vassough-ed-Dowleh [Vossough] to proceed with the work of reorganization in accordance with these recommendations as desired. The work has, in every possible manner, been delayed and hindered, and the British are becoming impatient and disgusted. Of course the British have gone full-steam ahead under the terms of the Anglo-Persian Convention of August 9, 1919, apparently regarding it as in full force, whilst they were continually making public statements to the effect that of course the treaty could not be regarded as in effect until it was ratified by the Persian Medjliss. The Persian populace have, of course, refused to recognize its validity since it has not passed through even the sham Medjliss that the treaty's adherents were said to be about to convene.[38]

Shortly after the signature of the Anglo-Persian Convention, Ahmad Shah wisely departed on an extended European trip. He did not wish to be associated in any way with Vossough-ed-Dowleh and the agreement.[39] Caldwell describes the gradual disintegration of the Vossough government:

His Imperial Majesty, the Shah, is continuing his visit to Europe, having been officially received by the King of Italy. He is expected to return to Persia in May or June. For some time past it has been rumored that the Minister of Finance has not been on the best of terms with the Prime Minister and that the former was intriguing against the latter, but it is understood that since the Minister of Finance is very pro-British, the British Minister until recently insisted that he remain in the Cabinet. However, a short time ago the Prime Minister threatened to resign if Prince Sarem-ed-Dowleh, the Minister of Finance, did not do so, and finally the latter handed in his resignation. This was no doubt also brought about by the fact that the Minister of Finance found it burdensome to have to work under British advisers, especially since it is well known that some of them have been greatly opposed to him, and at the same time the Persian populace was bringing as much pressure as possible to bear on him not to accept the British proposals. He was replaced by the former Acting Minister of Foreign Affairs, Etela-ol-Molk, and the Chief of the Division of Neighboring Countries in the Foreign Office, Mansourol-Molk, has been appointed Acting Minister for Foreign Affairs. When the Minister of Finance resigned, the Minister of War, Sipahdar Aazam, also left the Cabinet. This man has, like the former Finance Minister, long cherished the ambition of being Prime Minister. However, it is believed that his resignation was due entirely to the undercurrent of public pressure opposed to the [British] Military Commission, and the difficulty of working with these foreign advisers. This resignation took place when the preliminary work of the Military Commission was finished, and at the same time the next most prominent Persian member of this Commission, Colonel Fazlollah Khan, committed suicide, leaving a note advising all patriotic Persians to follow his example. A new Minister of War was appointed, but never attended even one meeting of the Cabinet, and a couple of weeks later he also resigned, since when Prince Salar Lashgar (a brother of Prince Nosrat-ed-Dowleh, the present Minister of Foreign Affairs) has with great difficulty been persuaded to take charge of the Ministry of War. It is not pure accident that the Persian Ministers of War and Finance, the two main Departments of the Persian Government which the British have invaded, have had to resign. Recently it has been rumored continuously that Vossough-ed-Dowleh is about to resign and that Prince Farman Farma, the present Governor-General of the important province of Fars on the Persian Gulf, will return here to again take up the position of Prime Minister. In this case, although it is now thought by many that Vossough-ed-Dowleh would then go on a foreign tour, it is more generally believed that if the Medjliss should be opened, he, as member of that body, will be a leader in trying to secure the ratification of the Anglo-Persian treaty.[40]

Caldwell later reports the return of Ahmad Shah in 1920:

On June 2nd His Imperial Majesty, the Shah, arrived in Teheran, after having spent about ten months in Europe. He was due to arrive here several weeks earlier than he did, but he apparently much enjoyed the fetes and publicity so lavishly bestowed by interested European governments, and so prolonged his visit. But at last, on account of the heat in Mesopotamia and His Majesty's illness there and the rumblings of disorders, both in Mesopotamia and in several of the Persian provinces, he cut short his visit to the Mohammedan Holy places and hurried to his capital. The courtiers, grandees, officials and notables received His Majesty at one of his palatial garden-parks just outside the city. After that reception, which occupied about two hours, the Shah drove through the streets, which were handsomely decorated with rich oriental rugs and lined with tremendous crowds along the whole distance to Gulestan, the royal palace in Teheran. He was received with great éclat and it is believed that in Teheran, at least, his theretofore low and ebbing prestige has somewhat increased. However, in this respect, much depends on the stand taken by His Majesty and the newly formed Cabinet. His Majesty has been greatly improved by his sojourn abroad, both physically and mentally. He has lost seventy pounds in weight during his absence (which loss he could well afford) and not only does he seem to have grown much more au courant with world happenings and politics in general, but his ideas, ideals and general view of life and the world seem to have changed greatly for the better.[41]

Judging the moment to be right, Ahmad Shah quickly brought about the resignation of the Vossough-ed-Dowleh government.

As soon as His Majesty returned political intrigues commenced on every hand and numerous malcontents, of whom the Vossough-ed-Dowleh regime has produced a tremendous number, rushed to the Shah to inform him of their real and fancied wrongs and woes, and the country's plight. Vossough-ed-Dowleh, the Prime Minister, immediately informed the Shah that he was over-worked and desired to be relieved of the fatigue and burden of Government. It is true that Vossough [Vossough] has been most diligent, and whereas most Persian Prime Ministers do very little actual work, he has kept in constant and closest touch with every department of the Government, and the Ministers of his Cabinet have been allowed practically no freedom of action, for all government business has to pass through his own hands. As heretofore reported, the Shah and Vossough-ed-Dowleh have had several tilts regarding the usurpation of power by the latter and a few days after His Majesty's return the Prime Minister demanded, if he were to remain in office, plenary powers to deal with the present and portent uprisings such as those in the Northern and Western parts of Persia. But the Shah felt that upon his return from Europe a policy of appeasing the populace might work to better advantage than one of force, and therefore the requested powers were not granted to Vossough-ed-Dowleh, who thereupon stated that his resignation was final and, after days of hesitation and indecision, it was accepted.[42]

Vossough then left Teheran in greatest haste and is reported to be on his way to India and England. It is reliably reported that the British government, in making its regular monthly payments of three hundred and fifty thousand tomans to Persia, actually paid over the money to Vossough-ed-Dowleh, and that the last three of these monthly payments were retained entire by him personally, no part of the same having been turned over to the Persian Government. Immediately after the resignation of Vossough-ed-Dowleh the Shah himself sent a telegram recalling the exiles who were banished from Teheran to Kashan: Musteshar-ed-Dowleh, Mohtashem-es-Saltaneh, and Momtaz-ol-Molk, and it is generally supposed that these men will be given positions of trust under the new government. The new Prime Minister [Moshir-ed-Dowleh] also published a statement saying: "With regard to the so-called Anglo-Persian Treaty of August 9, 1919, as it is evident that this treaty must be passed by the Medjliss before being enforced, its executive operations will be discontinued for the present." When it was certain that Vossough-ed-Dowleh had resigned, several mass meetings were held in Teheran, entirely disregarding the rule of the existing martial law that no political assemblies shall take place, and the police, although aware of the meetings and even present thereat, made no attempt to disperse the crowds, feeling that the new policy of the government would be much more liberal than hitherto. At these meetings petitions were addressed to the Shah demanding: Withdrawal of existing martial law. Annulment of the Anglo-Persian Convention of August 1919. Re-election of members of the Medjliss throughout the provinces, to replace those fraudulently chosen. Immediate assembly of the national Medjliss. A separation of the powers of church and state. The latter, especially, is a remarkable demand to be made by the inhabitants of a Moslem country.[43]

The Appointment of Moshir-ed-Dowleh

After Moshir-ed-Dowleh succeeded Vossough, Caldwell expressed surprise that the British had permitted the appointment of such a person.[44] The reality appears to be that Britain's position—due to the British retreat from Enzeli and Rasht (see below), popular opposition, and the resignation of Vossough—had been greatly weakened. The fall of Vossough was a heavy blow to British prestige:

> The British have not been idle in this Prime Minister game, for they have realized that they were, in large measure, responsible for the discontent of the Persians and much of the ill will that is now and has been evinced and directed against the British. It must not be forgotten that Vossough is, body and soul, their man. So the British were most interested in keeping Vossough in power, but since that failed, they naturally tried for the one who would be most acceptable for themselves and at the same time apparently pander to the desires of the people. But most of the people want a Premier whose patriotism and integrity are unquestionable and the announcement in the local paper that the British Minister called upon the new Premier, Moshir-ed-Dowleh, and spent four hours in conference with him, immediately turned a number of Moshir's former adherents against him.[45]

By the summer of 1920, it was clear to all that the Anglo-Persian agreement was dead, with no hope of resuscitation. Caldwell observes:

> During a recent excursion from north to south, through Persia, upon discrete inquiry scarcely a Persian was found to be in favor of the recent Anglo-Persian agreement. The Cabinet seems to have definitely put off the treaty and all considerations connected therewith until the matter can be taken up by the Medjliss. Meanwhile the whole matter is being held in abeyance and practically all the British advisers employed by the Persian Government under the recent agreement have been dismissed or ostensibly sent on three months leave of absence. It is true that a few are remaining here, but these, although paid regularly, are not allowed to work on governmental business. Vossough-ed-Dowleh, the former Prime Minister, is still in India, apparently at Simla, the Summer Capital; and for the present he is keeping out of the limelight here, hardly being in communication even with his family. A telegram was received by the undersigned in a mixed commercial code from a mutual friend, stating that Vossough-ed-Dowleh was well and requesting information as to the welfare of his family here. Vossough-ed-Dowleh, the late Prime Minister, could not possibly return to Persia at this time, with the prevailing situation. The British cannot be very pleased at the turn affairs have taken since the departure from Teheran of Sir Percy Cox (who has, by the way, just arrived in Mesopotamia to take charge there, after having been for several months in England). The British have steadily lost ground, although naturally every effort has been made to keep affairs in the condition in which they wish them to be. This has happened in spite of the indefatigable efforts of the present British Minister, Mr. H. Norman. When the very popular new Prime Minister assumed his post it was agreed between the British and the Persian Government that the monthly subsidies of three hundred and fifty thousand tomans per month should be continued until the end of October, so the present Persian Government has had some money to run on, but it has certainly been very limited, and what is to happen at the end of October remains to be seen. The Foreign Minister recently told me that it was hoped to have the Medjliss opened by the early part of November, but it is certainly to be doubted if a sufficient number of members can be here and ready by that time, even if the Prime Minister seriously desires it.[46]

Caldwell then included a seemingly innocuous piece of information that would prove to be very ominous. Immediately after the return of Ahmad Shah and the impending fall of Vossough-ed-Dowleh, and even before the appointment of Moshir-ed-Dowleh, the British had begun preparations for a coup d'état: "About a month ago it was rumored that the British had reversed their policy and were about to withdraw their troops from Persia, but this is not believed to have been well founded, and doubtless the wish was further to the thought. However, General Champagne, who has for more than a year been in charge of the British forces in Persia, is recalled, and General Ironside has been sent to take over the command."[47]

Mirza Kuchik Khan and the Jangalis

It turned out that the British would not get rid of Moshir-ed-Dowleh until they were ready. The circumstances that brought about his fall in October 1920 were related to the Jangali uprising in Gilan. The Jangalis of Gilan under Mirza Kuchik Khan, like the Democrats of Azerbaijan, had been a source of great actual or potential trouble for the government of Vossough-ed-Dowleh from the beginning. After their numerous defeats by the British, the Jangalis had reached an understanding with the British, which the British later abrogated.[48]

With British assistance (including warplanes and other equipment), the Persian Cossacks defeated and dispersed the forces of Mirza Kuchik Khan in the spring of 1919. "Most of them were captured and sent to the fortress of Kelat-i-Nadiri for imprisonment and their supplies, munitions and transport were confiscated. Only the leader Kuchik Khan and one or two of his followers escaped. His whereabouts at present are unknown and he is variously reported as having gone to Kermanshah and Tabriz. In any case the Jungalee movement is at an end."[49]

It soon became apparent that the news of the demise of the Jangalis was greatly exaggerated. In January 1920 Caldwell recounts that peace negotiations between the Jangalis and the Vossough Government had been underway for several months: "In the province of Guilan [Gilan] the Government has for a long time been negotiating with the leader of the Jangalees, Kuchik Khan, and it is expected that this army of troublemakers for the Government will soon be disbanded, and the leader and men allowed to resume their positions as ordinary subjects of the Persian Government. Kuchik Khan has displayed marked ability and patriotism, and it would probably be much to the advantage of the Persian Government if it could secure his loyal services."[50]

Peace between the Jangalis and the Persian government proved elusive. By early 1920, the Vossough government was facing mounting difficulties in Gilan and Mazandaran. From an account by Caldwell dated April 10 it is clear that the Jangali movement was a nationalistic uprising against the British. The alliance of the Jangalis with the Bolsheviks was a tactical one aimed at the British aggressor:

> Bolshevistic tendencies are constantly increasing in Persia and whereas a few months ago it seemed that the Persians were firmly and unalterably opposed to the Bolsheviki, many adherents are now found for the cause here and one often hears that the Persians will welcome them with open arms if they do succeed in

pressing through the Caucasus into Persia, as is now threatened. It is believed that this growth in Bolshevism in Persia is like the former alleged pro-German sympathies of the Persians, not love for the Bolsheviki or their principles, but rather the fact that the Bolsheviki are vehemently opposed to the British— whom a great number of patriotic Persians firmly believe to be their greatest enemy, and these Persians, having faith in the ultimate independence of their country, which has existed independently throughout so many centuries, feel that the Bolsheviki will push the British out of Persia if they come here. So, although it is hardly possible that Bolshevism could ever secure a firm hold in Persia, there is, nevertheless, great danger of its spread to Persia on account of the occupation of this country by the most steadfast enemies of the Bolsheviki. Constant progress is being made by the Bolshevik agents and propagandists among the Persian people, but this is entirely in the undercurrent and never appears openly. The Persian Government has had some difficulty in keeping Governors in the northern provinces, specially along the Caspian Sea, and this trouble has been mainly due to the presence and fear of Bolshevists, for their propagandists are busy along the whole northern frontier of Persia. Our Consul in Tabriz has reported the presence of a number of their agents in the province of Azerbaijan, and it is well known that the British are forced to use every means possible against them in the province of Khorassan, for that province borders Afghanistan and is a direct approach to India, and the Bolsheviki have long been in control of Turkestan or Trans-Caspian up to the Persian frontiers. In the province of Guilan the Jangalees seem to be again on the point of causing trouble, although it was considered that they had been finally put down. Doubtless the only thing that keeps them within bounds is the presence of British troops in Resht and Enzeli, for fear of a Bolshevist invasion has caused the British military to send a force of some fifteen hundred soldiers to Enzeli on the Caspian Sea, where they have entrenched themselves and fortified the place. If the Bolsheviki should attack that quarter from the Caspian Sea, it is likely that they would find ready and able assistants on land in the person of the Jangalees.[51]

The British Driven from Enzeli and Rasht, May 1920

This is exactly what happened. The Jangalis and Bolsheviks attacked the British at Enzeli in May 1920 and drove them out. As noted, the British defeats had emboldened Ahmad Shah to dismiss Vossough in June 1920.

The British suffered great loss of prestige by their precipitous retreat from Enzeli, and a few days later they also evacuated Resht, coming to Kazvin [Qazvin]. Reinforcements were hurriedly sent up from Bagdad to Kazvin and if the Bolsheviki had advanced they would likely have been opposed near this latter place. However, they have so far occupied only Resht and the Caspian ports. At the time of the capture of Enzeli by the Bolsheviki, most foreigners fled from Resht and Enzeli, and among these refugees are the two American missionaries who are located in Resht. They have come to Teheran. All Americans are safe and it is believed that they would not have actually suffered even if they had remained in Resht.[52]

With the expulsion of the British from Gilan, the Provisional Republican Government of Gilan was formed, with Mirza Kuchik Khan as its nominal head. The provisional government proclaimed the abolition of monarchy and all treaties and agreements with Britain were declared unlawful. The remnants of the Persian Cossacks in Gilan were captured, and the officials of the Persian government were escorted out of Gilan. Caldwell concludes the following report with the observation that as long as the British remained, no peace was possible. The British, on the other hand, were determined to hold on whatever the cost:

> The revolutionary provinces have viewed the fall of Vossough-ed-Dowleh with the greatest satisfaction, but it is by no means certain that the new Cabinet can cope with or control the situation. The greatest animosity of the Persians who are not satisfied is exhibited against the British and if the latter continue to hold the upper hand in Persia, peace and content cannot be expected here for a long time to come. But, on the other hand, the British have announced that they are ready to supply whatever may be necessary of men and means to control the situation, and have announced definitely that they will continue the military occupation of Persia.[53]

The Cossacks' Triumph and Debacle, September–October 1920

In the summer of 1920, the Gilan rebels attacked Mazandaran, thereby causing a general panic in Tehran. This time, however, the Cossacks, under the command of their Russian commander, Colonel Starosselki, saved the day. The Cossack victory was a great moral boost to Ahmad Shah and the Persian government. It proved that the British were not indispensable.

> In May the British forces evacuated Enzeli and Resht and retired to Menjil [Manjil] and Kazvin, and the Bolshevists, both foreign and native, made no really serious attempt to come on to Kazvin and Teheran. However, in June and July they began spreading along the southern shore of the Caspian, in the province of Mazanderan, and there was great excitement for fear they intended invading Teheran by way of the extremely difficult route to the northeast. . . . Colonel Starosselski, the Russian Chief of the Persian Cossacks, was made a General and given full charge of the situation, evidently to the great disgust of the British, who have General Dickson here desiring and apparently still hoping to be put at the head of the Persian consolidated or uniform force. But the present Premier is endeavoring to put him off with the excuse that nothing can be done until the Medjliss is convened. . . . He [Starosselski] is a man of considerable affability and tact, and also of considerable ability. He has been at the head of the Cossacks here for about three years, and has several times been accused of intriguing with the Shah against the British. It will be remembered

that during the Spring the British demanded that the Cossack Brigade be turned over to them, but Starosselski refused to give up his command and has so far effectively resisted all efforts made against him in this connection. So it happened that the Cossacks were sent into Mazanderan, where there were so few Bolshevists that the Cossacks had a complete and easy victory—the invaders being forced to put out to sea and return to Enzeli. Starosselski himself went to Mazanderan for a few days, and upon returning after the victory was presented by the Shah with a jeweled sword and had the honorary title of Field Marshall conferred upon him.[54]

Shortly after their victory against the rebels in Mazandaran, the Cossacks attacked Enzeli, but the attackers were devastated by the heavy naval guns there.[55] Having earlier retreated from Enzeli, the British were fully aware of those guns and their allowing the ill-advised attack to take place indicates that it was a deliberate measure to destroy the Cossacks and discredit their Russian officers. Having failed earlier to get rid of the Russian officers, the British brought it about the hard way. The complicity of the British is made clear by Ironside, as reported by Sabahi: "From a political point of view it would be very advantageous to us to leave Col. Starosselski to make a mess of things as it would then be more easy for me to get rid of him." Sabahi adds that Ironside "first ordered the British advance column at Manjil not to render any help to Starosselski." And then, inexplicably and "without being seriously attacked," the British withdrew from Manjil. British headquarters in Baghdad was baffled at the British withdrawal on the eve of the Cossack offensive.[56]

As for the Bolshevik threat so often proposed in books based on the British records (e.g., Sabahi), Caldwell comments: "'The Revolutionary Red Committee of Persia,' which formed a 'Provisional Republican Government' for the province of Guilan, seems to have disappeared, together with its government. Kuchik Khan, the leader of the Jangalees in that province, at first joined the foreign invaders, but later decided that it would be best to withdraw from their association. This he did, but found himself left only with some two hundred followers, and with these he has retired to the jungle."[57] Thus by the fall of 1920, despite the Cossack disaster at Enzeli, the Jangali movement and the "Bolshevik threat" had effectively dissipated.

The Dismissal of Russian Officers and the Fall of the Moshir-ed-Dowleh Government, October 27, 1920

In the fall of 1920, the British began forcing the dismissal of the Russian officers and the downfall of the Moshir-ed-Dowleh government. The British were already deep into plotting a coup d'état in which the dismissal of the Russian officers and the assumption of control of the Cossacks by

British officers was a vital link. The British first ensured the destruction of the Cossacks as a fighting force and then set about decapitating it by depriving it of its Russian officers and taking direct control of the force.

About the end of October there was a Cabinet crisis over the British demand for the immediate dismissal of General Starosselski and his Russian Cossack officers, and the popular premier, Moshir-ed-Dowleh, fell from power. Moshir-ed-Dowleh is popular not because he has done anything to help the people, but because they have the fullest confidence in his ability and honesty and they feel that he administers the government for the best interests of Persia and not for himself or a foreign power. In fact it was quite a surprise when the British allowed him to be made Prime Minister, but quite to be expected that he should lose the Premiership within a few months, for the guiding hand over Persia's destinies found him not so pliable as were his immediate predecessors. The Russian officers in charge of the Persian Cossack Division had long been one of the greatest annoyances the British had to endure in Persia, and as frequently mentioned in previous reports, nothing was left undone to have the Russians expelled, but with the clever and astute General Starosselski at their head, the Russians were able to remain a much longer time than anyone anticipated. When Major-General Ironside assumed control of the British Norper [northern Persia] force early in October, he knew that Starosselski and the Russians had to be gotten rid of as soon as possible, and with the assistance of his compatriots in the necessary positions, especially of Major-General W. E. R. Dickson in Teheran, the task was accomplished before the end of the month. The immediate dismissal of the Russian officers on a charge of dishonesty was demanded of the Persian Government, the Prime Minister, Moshir-ed-Dowleh, refused, and politically speaking "off came his head." The Shah, who had promised Starosselski that his position was secure while he was away from Teheran directing the Persian forces against the Bolshevists and "insurgents" in the northern province of Guilan, gave in to the demands of the British and a Premier was put in power who was willing to do as the British desired.[58]

The man willing to carry out British desires was Fatollah Sipahdar Rashti (not to be confused with Mohammad Vali Khan Tonekaboni, Sipahdar Azam). The appointment of the Sipahdar cabinet resulted in demonstrations in Tehran. A telegram from C. Van Engert of the American legation describes the events:

Slight disturbances took place last night and this morning when the police and gendarmes broke up meetings held in protest against the authority of a pro-British cabinet. Bazaar and most shops closed. Excited group of about 40 students and minor government officers came to the Legation this morning to seek asylum bringing several of their number who had been injured in encounters with the police. They were of course refused admittance except two as spokesmen who desired to have the American Government informed of their treatment at the hands of what they consider the pro-British party. After talking to them for a few minutes they seemed satisfied and went away quietly.[59]

Engert concludes by confirming the dismissal of Starosselski and 140 other Russian officers and closes by reporting that "Resht appears to have been again evacuated by the Bolsheviki."[60] Caldwell relates that, immediately upon his appointment, the new premier accused Starosselski and the Russians of misappropriation of funds, although no documents were ever tendered to support the charge, and the Russians were dismissed and forced to leave Persia.[61]

The Announcement of British Withdrawal and Ahmad Shah's Urgent Appeals for American Help

Having completely neutralized Persia's defense capability—first through the defeat of the Cossacks in Enzeli, and then the dismissal of its Russian officers—the British in December 1920 announced their intention to withdraw from Persia the following spring. Even Caldwell was deceived by the ploy:

> Towards the end of November, when the British had seen that the Russians were put out and that Persia had no foreign assistance except from Britain (the Belgian customs officials and several Swedish Gendarmery officers being entirely controlled by the British) a bold stroke was decided upon. It was announced that the British would no longer consider aiding Persia and she would be left to her fate. It was evident that Persia was not anxious for the Anglo-Persian Agreement to go through and therefore the British advisers and assistants would be withdrawn from Persia, Meshed [Mashhad] would be evacuated and the British troops in East Persia withdrawn to Sistan, while the whole of the North Persia force (with headquarters at Kazvin) would be entirely withdrawn from Persia—thus leaving North Persia and Teheran entirely open to Bolshevistic attacks. (No mention was made of evacuating that part of the country bordering on India and the Persian Gulf). Prognostications of the most terrible things which would surely happen were assiduously spread broadcast. The British Foreign Office announced that all British women and children should be evacuated soon in order that the men could get away more easily later; and also British assistance was offered to all foreigners who would leave soon enough. Prominence was given to the report that not only would all British business concerns such as the telegraph, banking and transportation monopolies leave but that the British Legation itself would be evacuated before the Bolshevists arrived in Teheran.
>
> It is very evident that the British are using every means within their power to impress upon the Persians just how necessary they are to the welfare of this country. The Persians, naturally an excitable people, feel that a great attempt is being made by the British to dupe and frighten them, and they are therefore sitting calmly by, waiting for "something to turn up." The general sentiment is rather pleased at the idea of the withdrawal of the British and the concluding agreement with Russia. Persia seems always to be between the devil and the deep sea, but somehow lives in spite thereof.[62]

In several conversations with Caldwell, Ahmad Shah made urgent appeals for America to help Persia at this critical juncture. With the announced "withdrawal" of the British from Persia, and the high moral prestige of America, Caldwell concluded that an unparalleled historical opportunity had been created for the United States to assist Persia and participate in its development. On January 6, 1921, Caldwell sent a long telegram in which he urged immediate American military and economic assistance to Persia. The message concluded: "The decisions of the next few weeks will determine the fate of this part of the world for a generation and if we intend to participate in its economic development no more favorable moment will ever present itself to lay the foundation."[63] The British withdrawal was a ploy to deceive the Persians and such interested parties as the American legation. Before the United States could respond, the British struck with the coup on February 21, 1921. "The decisions of the next few weeks" were to determine the fate of Persia for generations to come.

Economic Conditions on the Eve of the Coup

The quarterly reports from the American legation contain revealing information on economic and trade matters. From these reports one may conclude that despite the attempted strangulation of its foreign trade, the loss of its customs revenues, and the withholding of oil royalties by the British, by the end of 1918 the famine had disappeared, food was plentiful, and the Persian currency, the kran, had appreciated to an all-time high of only 18 krans per pound sterling and 4.25 krans per dollar. Moreover, these reports convey the impression of a prosperous economy where poverty was uncommon. All this despite the nonpayment of oil royalties and the British attempt to curtail Persia's foreign trade.

By early 1919, the devastating famine of 1917–18 was over, and food was plentiful. "Economic conditions in the capital have been much improved during the last quarter due, in a great measure, to the appointment of a Belgian as food controller. The price of bread [sangak], which is now plentiful, has been fixed at three krans a maun [3–6 kgs.] which is low enough to allow the poor to buy sufficient for their needs. The Shah sold his grain to the food controller at a very moderate price and his example was of great assistance in making the food control a success."[64]

In the fall economic conditions continued to be favorable:

> Economic conditions in Persia have not changed much since the last quarter. The crops in most districts have been good and prices of native foodstuffs are in some instances lower. . . . Outside the province of Azerbaijan, where the Armenians and Assyrians, especially those who are refugees, suffered greatly and where the land in great measure has remained uncultivated during the last few

years, there is, so far as is known, no general destitution in Persia, and it is believed that the people will be able to get through the winter as well as usual. With the recent capture and execution of the many notorious brigands throughout the country has come a feeling of safety along the trade routes and commerce is now being carried on with much greater security than in the years past.[65]

In April 1920, Caldwell describes a relatively prosperous economy full of promise:

There have been plentiful rains throughout Persia this season and it is generally believed that this will be one of the best agricultural years Persia has had for a decade. Prices of foodstuffs, however, remain very high and it is greatly to be hoped that there will be such plentiful crops that food can be had at appreciably lower prices. This is almost a virgin field and although Persia has probably not more than ten million inhabitants, most of whom are still content with what they themselves can produce, the inhabitants need to be awakened and the country developed, and it is believed that numerous good opportunities are now dormant here. Therefore it is urgently recommended that an American commercial specialist be sent to this country for at least a short time. The value of the kran is the highest it has ever been. At present one dollar sells for only 4 1/4 krans, whereas the normal rate is 11 3/7 krans to the dollar. At the same time the pound sterling, which is normally worth 55 krans, is now worth only 18 krans. American exchange is now kept down to the level of the pound sterling by the Imperial Bank of Persia, a British institution, but if large quantities of American goods could be brought into Persia, dollar exchange would immediately rise on account of the demand for our currency to pay bills due in America. And American goods are greatly in demand here.[66]

These conditions are in sharp contrast to the picture painted in some of the recent literature.[67] They are also in stark contrast to the poverty and misery, including a severe shortage of bread, reported by American diplomats in Iran in 1940–41 (see chapter 15).

CHAPTER THREE

British Coups d'État

From Reza to Reza Shah Pahlavi, 1921–1925

WITH THE FAILURE OF THE VOSSOUGH-ED-DOWLEH experiment in civilian dictatorship, the forceful control of Persia was achieved by the British through the imposition of a military dictatorship. This was brought about by the coup d'état of February 21, 1921. The British insisted that they had no knowledge of or any part in the coup and Sabahi has declared that the British minister, Norman, "and the Legation, as well as the Foreign Office and the War Office, were completely in the dark about the planned coup."[1] Some other writers have described the coup as inspired or encouraged by the British.[2] At least from the middle of 1920, the British had made preparations for the coup. Moreover, as American diplomatic reports show, it was a completely British undertaking. In a telegram dated February 22, 1921, the American minister in Tehran, John Lawrence Caldwell, reports the first news of the coup:

> About 1,000 Persian cossacks surreptitiously marched on Teheran yesterday from Kazvin [Qazvin] and captured the capital without resistance. They immediately arrested the cabinet except the Prime Minister as well as scores of prominent officials, wealthy Persians, reactionaries and nationalists. Nonpayment of cossacks assigned as the cause. Prime Minister took refuge in the British Legation. British disclaim all knowledge of or participation in the revolution but they are visibly pleased with the situation and evidence is not lacking of their military encouraging step. Director of the movement is Seyid Ziaedin [Seyed Zia-ed-Din], editor of newspaper RAAD, who is considered British protégé and who was the confidential adviser of the ex-Prime Minister Vossough-ed-Dowleh. Persian opinion almost certain that the whole affair is a scheme of the British. Order prevails.[3]

Immediately after the coup and the arrest of the notables, the same Norman who had been supposedly in the dark about the coup describes the
coup and the arrests: "Power could not have been wrested otherwise than
by force from a small gang of men either corrupt or incapable, or both,
who have hitherto monopolized it and well neigh [sic] ruined the country,
and imprisonment and exile provide the only means of preventing them
regaining their former position and completing their evil work."[4]

Immediately after the coup, Ahmad Shah was forced to appoint Seyed
Zia-ed-Din prime minister, and an obscure officer, Reza Khan, the coup
leader, was appointed commander of the Cossacks. The next recorded
communication from Caldwell was a telegram dated February 27, 1921:

> Shah has made Seyid Ziaedin Prime Minister with dictatorial powers and he
> is forming cabinet. Rigid martial law enforced, all newspapers suppressed. Tele-
> graphic communication throughout Persia forbidden, public gatherings, and
> even discussion in homes prohibited. Many requests denied for refuge in this
> Legation; wholesale arrests amount to about 100 including four ex-Prime Min-
> isters, many other officials and rich personages. Population hostile and claim
> whole affair British coup d'état. British Legation deny all previous knowledge
> but British military at Kazvin are known to have supported the movement.
> Leaders and followers are largely British protégés and unless the movement
> strongly backed by the British military it is certain to fall. However, British
> Legation has doubtless reported fait accompli to London and is believed to have
> asked strong support for the present regime although the British military
> still contemplate evacuation of Persia in April. Shah's life in some danger
> and I believe that he contemplates abdication if and when permitted. The
> Prime Minister states that he has in mind the execution of a number of those
> arrested.[5]

On February 26, 1921, Seyed Zia-ed-Din issued his proclamation, and
the occasion was described in a dispatch from Caldwell:

> I have the honor to attach hereto and enclose herewith a translation of a
> proclamation issued February 26, 1921, by the new Prime Minister, Sayyid Zia-
> ed-Din, who assumed charge of the Persian affairs some days ago with plenary
> and dictatorial powers and is now by direction of the Shah conducting govern-
> mental business with hourly advice from the British Legation. As reported in
> cablegram No. 9 of February 26, the Premier is a British protégé whose pur-
> pose, character and antecedents are not above suspicion; in fact, he is known to
> have received, while editor of the official newspaper RAAD, a regular stipend
> from the British, and it was he who, in 1919, so violently led the editorial
> assaults and attacks on America, her people and institutions. He is a man with-
> out experience in political affairs, but was a faithful understudy of the recent
> Premier Vossough-ed-Dowleh, and is a man of some force. Many of the pas-
> sages in the proclamation are merely for home consumption. Among these may
> be noted the phrase "We are free and will remain free," and the bombastic brag-
> gadocio anent the so-called Persian army, which consists of a small motley

horde of semi-brigands. The same may be said of the announcement of the "abrogation" of the Anglo-Persian agreement of August 1919. The present Premier was one of its principal protagonists since its very inception and up to his taking office. He is known to be simply a tool for British politics and his announcement of the abrogation of a treaty not yet ratified by the Persian Parliament, as provided by the Persian Constitution, is at least a misnomer, even though an attempt was made to put the agreement into effect without such ratification. Moreover, up to the time of the present coup d'état, which permitted the present Prime Minister to assume control, it had been considered for several months past that the Anglo-Persian agreement was dead and nearly all of the British advisers had quietly left Persia, while the London Foreign Office had announced that hope of further execution of the agreement had been abandoned. However, as soon as Sayyid Zia-ed-Din came to power the remaining British advisers commenced work and assumed hopeful countenance and privately expressed the confident belief that they would now remain permanently in Persia.

Caldwell concluded his dispatch with the following:

It is perfectly apparent that the whole movement is of British origin and support, in furtherance of the scheme of forceful control of the country, its people and resources, and is looked upon with horror and deep indignation by the better class of Persians, who see in it but another and perhaps final attempt to compel them by coercion and corruption to accept a policy of undesired advisers operating through native tools.[6]

Caldwell's Account of the Coup

A detailed account of the coup is provided by the American legation. That this important document, which was declassified in 1972, more than 50 years after it was written, should have been overlooked all these years is remarkable. Selected parts of this report were recently given by Ghani. However, Ghani's version appears to differ in minor ways from the actual report existing in the U.S. archives. Moreover, Ghani had selected not to include the revealing parts about the people's hostility and distrust of the coup and its participants. One of the interesting pieces of information that emerges from Caldwell's report is that the coup leaders Reza Khan and Seyed Zia even met before the night of the coup. They had first met when Seyed Zia and Colonel Haig went out to meet the invading Cossacks supposedly for the purpose of "ascertaining their intentions." It was subsequently claimed that Colonel Haig and the representatives of the British Legation had gone out to "dissuade" Reza Khan and the Cossacks from entering Tehran.[7] Caldwell first describes events leading to the coup:

As stated in Report No. 10, for the quarter immediately proceeding that now under consideration, the Persian Government was in a most disturbed state, and that condition continues—with some developments. When the British first announced their intention of "withdrawing from Persia and leaving it to its fate," they displayed for the benefit of the Persians a glaring and horrible picture of the political and economic chaos in which this country would then find itself, when the Bolshevists had arrived and gained control. But following this scarce announcement, when nothing happened, the Persians suspected a big political game of bluff and calmly settled down to await developments—especially to see what the British actually intended doing. The London Foreign Office announced through REUTERS'S NEWS that every effort had been made to help Persia and that ungrateful Persia didn't appreciate the great efforts which had been made to help her and consequently British assistance would be withdrawn and Persia "would be left to shift for herself." After the slight excitement which was naturally experienced, the populace felt and expressed satisfaction and happiness at the prospect of being uninterfered with, but never quite got over the feeling that the British didn't mean exactly what they said.

It being announced and generally conceded that the proposed Anglo-Persian convention of August 1919 was dead with no hope of resurrection, several prominent Persians, including the Shah, suggested the possibility of securing financial and military officers from the United States in order that the latter might take charge of the Persian "army," and in case of need to repulse any possible attacks which might be made by the Russian Bolshevists after the withdrawal of the British troops. This matter was taken up with the Department (see telegram No. 3 of January 6th last) with the suggestion that it be discussed with the London Foreign Office, but from the attitude displayed by the local British authorities any such suggestion was frowned upon and received no encouragement from the London office. It was frankly the attitude of the British here that if they did leave Persia they desired that the worst happen and that "she be taught a good lesson," even though the British Minister did state, probably out of politeness, that "there might be no objection to America helping Persia."

On the evening of Sunday, February 20th, the people were surprised to learn that a force of about fifteen hundred Cossacks had marched from Kazvin and were at that moment only a few miles outside of Teheran. It was stated that they intended to take possession of the capital, but the full scope of their position was unknown. That afternoon the British Minister had gone out of the city for a walk and did not return until about five o'clock, but a couple of hours before that time the Counselor of the British Legation, Lieut. Colonel Haig, together with Sayyid Zia-ed-Din, now Premier, had gone out of the city to meet the Cossacks. The purpose of these two men was stated to be to ascertain the intentions of the invading Cossacks, but the Cossacks themselves made no secret of the fact that each one of them had been given five tomans (about five dollars) by the British just before entering the city.

It should be remarked in this connection with the invasion that these Cossacks were under the control of Colonel Smyth, an Englishman in the employment of the Persian Government who was, some months ago, in charge of the intelligence office in Kazvin, and who has for some time in the past been actually at the head of the Cossacks at that place. He made frequent trips to Teheran and it is known that he spent a good part of his time during these trips in the presence of Sayyid Zia-ed-Din. It is also known that just before the Cossack's [*sic*] departure from Kazvin, Colonel Smyth received the money to pay this force, but it seemed that he preferred that they wait for their money until their arrival in Teheran, and soon after their arrival here they were paid, and the money was drawn from the bank under Colonel Smyth's signature. But the strange point is that although this force was kept in Kazvin (the headquarters of the British forces in North Persia) under British control, they left the city with British supplies, marched a distance approximately one hundred miles in four days (there being both telephone and telegraph wires along the whole route, as well as wireless stations in the hands of the British at both Kazvin and Teheran) and that neither the Persian Government nor the British Legation here seem to have known that the Cossacks were marching on the capital with the intention of capturing it until the afternoon of the fourth day after the troops had left Kazvin, and when they were only a few miles outside Teheran. The whole thing was so well ordered and prearranged that it would have been impossible for it to have been carried out as it was, without collusion. A little after midnight on the night of February 20th, the Cossacks entered Teheran. They were joined by the Gendarmes, who are supposed to protect the capital and the interior of Persia, and when the Shah sent a Swedish officer to take charge of the Sarbaz [soldiers] of the Central Brigade, in an efforts to keep the Cossacks out of Teheran, that officer found that the Sarbaz also had joined the Cossacks. Three cannon shots were fired into the air, as were also numerous rifle shots. The only resistance encountered was that of the Police, and at their central office two men were killed before the rest surrendered. Otherwise the coup seems to have been accomplished without bloodshed.

It was soon learned that practically all of the principal figures in the movement were men who had been intimately connected with the British. Major Masoud Khan, who has since been made Minister of War, has for several months past been the personal assistant to Colonel Smyth at Kazvin. Colonel Reza Khan, who has assumed the commandership of the Cossacks, served on the Anglo-Persian Military Mission, being practically a spy for the chief of the mission [General Dickson], and for some months past has been working in close co-operation with the British in Kazvin. Sayyid Zia-ed-Din, the Prime Minister, is the owner of the semi-official, British subsidized newspaper RAAD, and as the Department has been heretofore informed, it was the RAAD which in the Autumn of 1919 vigorously attacked America, its people and institutions. Sayyid Zia-ed-Din is a man of thirty-four years of age. "Sayyid" denotes a descendent of the Prophet Mohammed, and until the coup Zia-ed-Din wore the blue turban which is the mark of a Sayyid, but now he wears a black "kola," the usual Persian headdress. He is a Persian of exceptional energy and ability and although he was a faithful understudy of Vossough-ed-Dowleh while the latter (who is known to have accepted large sums of foreign money for pursuing certain policies) was Prime Minister, and although the Sayyid himself is known by everyone to have accepted a subsidy for his newspaper, and is supposed to have received other British money, he is, nevertheless, believed by some people to be more or less honest in his present effort to establish a better government than has lately existed in this country.

The great excitement that prevailed during the first few days after the "capture" of Teheran was mainly due to the uncertainty of what might follow. It was immediately known that Sayyid Zia-ed-Din was in control of affairs and directing the movement of events here. The first matter to be attended to was the arrest of all those concerned in politics, especially those who had hitherto accumulated large amounts of money through their official positions, as well as those in poorer circumstances who might, if left at liberty, be detrimental or hostile to the present administration. In this latter category came those who were merely personal enemies of the new premier. The alleged purpose of most of these arrests was the securing of funds to meet public expenditures. However, it is difficult to see how any amount approaching the needs of the government can be secured from this source. Even the wealthiest Persians are notorious for their lack of ready cash; securities as known in America and Europe are practically unheard of here, and real estate forms by far the greater part of the wealth of these men who have been arrested. Whether this property, which is of course nearly all within this empire, is actually given outright to the Government, is confiscated by it, or promises of future payment based on the holding of the same are accepted by those in power, the amount of actual money which can be secured to meet the immediate needs of the Government, or even secured within a year, seems negligible in comparison with the amount the government must procure at once from some source if it is to continue to exist. However, the squeezing is in process and will continue until all the funds possible have been extracted.

A number of ex-cabinet officials and other prominent personages have been arrested, accused of intriguing and conspiring against the life of the Shah, but in reality to insure the official safety and political life of the present Prime Minister. Among these latter are Momtaz-ol-Molk, ex-Minister to Washington; Mosteshar-ed-Dowleh and Momtaz-ed-Dowleh, ex-cabinet officials; Mirziantz, prominent Armenian member of the Medjliss; and Mirza Sayyid Hassan Modaress [Modarres], an influential and prominent Nationalist member of the Medjliss. Moin-ot-Tojar [Tojjar], the President of the Chamber of Commerce and leader of the merchants (who was among those banished to Kashan in 1919), has already given one million dollars to secure his freedom. His contribution is partly in property and partly in the form of a receipt given to the Government for money owed to him by it.

It should be noted that such men as Moshir-ed-Dowleh, Mostefi-ol-Mamalek (both counted as honest ex-Premiers), Motamen-ol-Molk, Hakim-ol-Molk, and others of that ilk were not arrested, nor were any of the Bakhtiaris although some of the latter are notoriously crooked. Doubtless the power of the Bakhtiari tribe was feared if any of their chiefs were molested.

Within a day or two after the coup the Shah formally appointed Sayyid Zia-ed-Din Prime Minister with plenary and dictatorial powers. Martial law was declared anew and is rigidly enforced. The police have not been trusted alone, but a Cossack is stationed with each policeman. For several days all internal communication by post or wire was suspended, and no newspapers were allowed to be published. However, after about a week these bans were lifted, communications were reopened and publication of *Iran* as an official paper permitted. Gatherings are prohibited, even in private houses, and no criticism of the Government is allowed. On February 26th the Premier issued a long proclamation. It will be noticed that there is no mention of the Medjliss in the proclamation, which would indicate that the dictator does not feel any need of this constitutional requisite. Neither does he state that although the Anglo-Persian Agreement of 1919 is abrogated, it is actually being put into effect without Persia receiving any of the benefits therein stipulated, which would seem to indicate that Persia is thus a greater loser than it would have been had the agreement been put into effect as it originally stood. It is perfectly evident that some sort of secret agreement has been made for British advisers. It is unbelievable that the present regime can last unless supported with British force and funds. Feeling against the Shah runs high and it is the best opinion that he will soon abdicate and secretly leave Persia, as this is known to have long been his desire. Daily reports are coming in of large numbers of tribesmen from the Lur, Kashgai and Bakhtiari districts in the South, marching on Teheran, and such a movement is not at all unlikely for scarcely a prominent Persian is in sympathy with the present regime.[8]

Betrayal by Swedish Officers

In his report on the coup, Caldwell mentions that when on the night of the coup d'état Ahmad Shah sent for the gendarmes and the sarbaz (militia) forces to protect Tehran from the invaders, it was discovered that they too had joined the Cossacks. The British had left nothing to chance. Additional information was to be provided four years later in a dispatch from Wallace S. Murray, American chargé d'affaires ad interim. From Murray we learn that the Swedish officers were rewarded by the British for their treachery:

> The present Persian Army had its origin, as the Department is aware, in the Seyid Zia-ed-Din coup of February 21, 1921 when Colonel Reza Khan was selected by the leader of that coup to march on Teheran with a column of some eight hundred cossacks (The Honorable J.M. Balfour in his work entitled "Recent Happenings in Persia" states the number to have been twenty-five hundred), and overthrew the tottering Government of Sepahdar Azam. The fact that the old Cossack Brigade, after the dismissal of its Russian officers, was stationed in Kazvin in charge of British officers has always made it somewhat difficult to place full credence in the solemn assurances of the British Legation that the coup was executed without their knowledge or consent. The fact furthermore that both Colonel Gleerup, the Swedish commander of the Gendarmerie in Teheran, and General Westdahl, Swedish Chief of Police, had both issued summary instructions to their units to keep to their quarters during that eventful night of February 20–21, and that they were both subsequently awarded G.C.M.G. decorations by the British Government for their "loyalty to British

interests in Persia," has not tended to relieve the British of the reasonable suspicions of the Persians that the coup was not spontaneous. Even ignoring the
above facts, the action of Seyid Zia-ed-Din, once he had assumed the reins of
power, in putting into execution the spirit of the Anglo-Persian Agreement
with respect to the British and financial missions in Persia, despite the fact that
for political reasons, he had to "denounce" the agreement, has branded him as
a British agent. . . . Sardar Sepah [Reza Khan] unquestionably owed his success
to British support.[9]

General Dickson's Letters to Engert and Lord Curzon

On August 25, 1921, in a confidential dispatch, the American chargé
d'affaires in Tehran, C. Van H. Engert, informed the State Department
about his personal correspondence with Major General W. E. R. Dickson,
former president of the Anglo-Persian military commission, mentioned in
Caldwell's report. Engert enclosed Dickson's letter to himself and a copy of
Dickson's letter to Lord Curzon concerning the recent coup d'état in Persia. One of the provisions of the 1919 Anglo-Persian Treaty was the establishment of a joint Anglo-Persian military commission for the purpose of
reorganizing the Persian military forces. The person selected to head this
commission was General Dickson, Indian Army. Dickson was born in
Iran, had considerable knowledge of the country and its history, and spoke
Persian. He had a sense of loyalty and affection for Iran and its people that
was not shared by some of the members of the British legation in Tehran
and the policymakers in London. Consequently, he had been kept in the
dark about the coup of February 21, 1921. Dickson became so outraged by
the coup that he began openly criticizing British policy. In a subsequent
letter to Curzon, Dickson referred to the coup as "nothing short of black
treachery."

At the insistence of the British legation in Tehran, Dickson was removed
and subsequently was demoted to colonel for supposedly divulging state
secrets about British participation in the coup. Engert's dispatch:

> I have the honor to transmit herewith, for the Department's confidential
> information, a copy of a private letter addressed to me by Major General (now
> Colonel) W. E. R. Dickson, Indian Army, together with its two enclosures con-
> sisting of a letter from General Dickson to Lord Curzon, dated May 14, 1921,
> and a letter to General Dickson from Mr. John L. Caldwell, the late American
> Minister in Teheran, dated March 1, 1921. The Department's special attention
> is invited to the statement (on page 2 of his letter to me) that Colonel Smyth, a
> British officer in Kazvin, admitted having organized the Cossack march on
> Teheran in February last that led to the overthrow of the [Sipahdar] Govern-
> ment. "Smart" mentioned in this connection is Mr. W. A. Smart, the Oriental
> Secretary of the British Legation in Teheran, and "Haig & Company" refers to
> Lieut. Colonel T. W. Haig, then Acting Counselor of the British Legation, Lieut.
> Colonel Wickam, then acting Military Attaché, Mr. Havard, British Consul in

Teheran, and a few other Englishmen who favored drastic action. Mr. Norman, the British Minister who—it is rumored—is about to be recalled, gave me his word of honor the day after the coup d'état that he knew nothing about it. This seems to be borne out by the statements under consideration. The letter to Lord Curzon is an admirable exposé of the situation in Persia, with particular reference to British activities, and its commendable frankness is in refreshing contrast with the air of mystery many British officials in Persia give themselves. As General Dickson was almost equally outspoken in conversation while still here this doubtless led to the belief in British circles (referred to on page 5 of his letter to Lord Curzon) that he was divulging official secrets to the American Legation, and ultimately brought about his removal.[10]

Dickson's letter to Engert contained the following:

My dear Engert: I have been intending to write to you for some time but have been so busy since I got home that I have had hardly a minute to call my own. I hope that you got the letter I wrote to you from Bombay and the censorship of Said [Seyid] Zia & Co. was not in too active operation! I told you of my journey down to Baghdad, the appalling snow, though as a matter of fact, with the waiting I had to do while the roads were being cleared, I could have got a car through. I called, while at Kermanshah, on Sarem-ed-Dowleh, the Governor of the Western Province, and had quite a long conversation with him. I do not know whether you have met him, but he is rather a man who has always fascinated me. Though he is a scoundrel (he was the man who shot his mother with his own hands) I have always thought of him as an honest scoundrel, if it is not an Irishism to say so. When, for example, he was Finance Minister and wanted to rob the public till, he simply put his hands in and took the money out, made no bones about it, and did not try to cover the transaction with a facade of honest intention. He is a long way the most clever of the Persian Royal Family and at the time the present Shah was in a moral funk and wanted to abdicate I seriously suggested, at a meeting we had at Sipahdar's, (then Prime Minister) that the Shah should be allowed to abdicate and that Sarem-ed-Dowleh should be invited to seat himself on the throne. In Persia's present pitiable condition, it would be better to have at her head a strong, capable man, who, though he might rob himself, would take good care to see that no one else did so, than being as at the present, at the mercy of a whole swarm of bloodsuckers, draining her life blood. My suggestion was received with laughter! Sarem-ed-Dowleh was very interested in my news from Teheran, from where he had no reliable news. He told me what, of course, I knew, that Sayid Zia having kept the Shah and using the latter's name was a clever move, as provincial governors like himself could take no action which could be interpreted into revolt against the Shah whereas had Sayid Zia deposed the Shah, he and other governors would have led a revolt against the usurper. Sarem-ed-Dowleh told me that he was aware of Sayid Zia's intention to "grab" him and had taken due precautions. I am afraid that these precautions were not very effective as, on arrival in London, I heard that Sarem-ed-Dowleh, as well as the Qavam-es-Saltaneh at Meshed, had been seized by agents of Sayid Zia.

I saw Colonel Smyth at Kazvin when I passed through and he admitted what we all suspected, that it was he that had organized the Cossack coup on Teheran. He also told me that he had done it with the knowledge of the British Legation in Teheran. He did not say that Mr. Norman had a hand in it but admitted that Smart had. I am rather inclined to think that Smart, Haig and Co. ran the business without letting Norman into the secret. It seems a funny thing to do, run a deep political intrigue and keep the Chief of the Mission in the dark, but everything so far as I know points to this having been the case. Smyth is a man who lets his tongue run and I got a lot of interest out of him. He told me, for example, that Sayid was in a funk of Reza Khan and that he (Smyth) had been sent for to Teheran to sit on him. Smyth was confident that he had done so but I naturally laughed at him and said it was far more likely that Reza Khan would prepare a "cup of coffee" for Smyth! I have seen a paragraph in the French papers that Sayid Zia has had to flee from Persia escorted by Cossacks and that the power is in the hands of Reza Khan! I very much wonder what has really happened.

On arrival in England I went to the Foreign Office and had a very stormy interview with Oliphant, the head of the Eastern Section. I have never, to my recollection, been treated with such rudeness as on this occasion. I was treated as if I were a sort of cross between an unwholesome dog and a naughty child that needed thrashing! I kept my temper, however, and said nothing. I went to the War Office and found, from a friend there, that the Foreign Office had asked the War Office to "strafe" me, but could get no details beyond the fact that the War Office has said to the F.O. what amounted to "He is your child, if he wants smacking, do it yourself." I then wrote direct myself to Lord Curzon, and I enclose a copy of the letter. I did not get an answer for ten days, but having had occasion to go to the Foreign Office, I was treated, instead of as if I were a dog, with deference and politeness that amused me by its intensity. I finally got a letter in which I was thanked by the Secretary of State for Foreign Affairs for my services in Persia! Such a change to the strafing that they wished for me in the first instance![11]

Dickson's long letter of May 14, 1921, to Lord Curzon is an interesting document. In the final part of his letter, Dickson discusses the February coup:

With regard to the recent coup d'état I desire to deny the allegations which appear to have been made, that it was I who am responsible for the widely accepted view in Persia that the coup was a British move in disguise. So far from its being so, I was myself, for a time, among the Persians, under suspicion of having been implicated in the movement and my denials of all knowledge of the matter were, at first, obviously not credited. Sayid Zia-ud-Din, in his anxiety to stifle all possible opposition, had arrested not only rich notables from whom money could be extracted but also Nationalists and popular leaders from whom opposition to his unconstitutional action might be feared. In these circumstances Sayid Zia-ud-Din's desire for my immediate withdrawal from Teheran, not withstanding the impassability of the roads at that time, could not but be welcome to me, as it dissipated suspicions among the Persians, very distressing to myself, of having been guilty of what would have been black treachery towards those who had honored me with their confidence and friendship and on whose support in the Medjliss I could have relied for the reorganization of the army had events followed, as we had hoped they would, a constitutional course. When endeavoring to refute my denials of any knowledge of the coup d'état, Persians stated the general belief that the coup was, in reality, a British one, was based on two grounds. Firstly the fact that a large Cossack force was allowed to leave Kazvin, a place garrisoned by British troops, by stealth and to pounce on Teheran by surprise. It was strange, they pointed out, how on this occasion a large Cossack force succeeded in eluding the vigilance of the British when three months previously, on the occasion of the dismissal of the Russians, an attempt by the Russian officers to lead a much smaller body of Cossacks to Teheran was at once detected and frustrated by the British. The second point of which considerable capital was made was the fact that the Cossacks had been equipped for the march to Teheran with boots from the British Ordnance stores at Kazvin. Other reasons for the belief were also given but not resting on such tangible grounds. I was myself unaware of Colonel Smyth's share in the coup until after I had left Teheran and learned of it from Colonel Smyth himself.

Dickson then devotes a paragraph to Reza Khan, a person with whom he was well acquainted. In rebuking Curzon, Dickson does not mince words:

> With future events in Persia I am not, of course, concerned, but Your Lordship may, perhaps, forgive me for expressing doubts as to whether any beneficial results can, even assuming the best intentions on the part of those in power, be attained by a regime resting on that most insecure of all foundations, a military force which has been misused for a political purpose, which feels that it holds the reins of political power in its hands and on whose loyalty no reliance can be placed. The last remark I make advisedly, as Reza Khan, Sayid Zia's military chief, is a man with whom I am well acquainted. He was disloyal to one of his chiefs, Colonel Clergé, at the time of the 1918 emeute; last spring when the problem of bringing the Cossacks into the proposed uniform force was engaging a serious attention, he made an offer to me to betray his Russian officers, and only recently as I passed through Kazvin, Colonel Smyth told me that Sayid Zia feared his [Reza's] growing power and had desired Colonel Smyth to endeavour to control him.[12]

British Records Pertaining to Iran: A Case Study in Falsification and Mendacity

Even in their official parliamentary papers, the British continued to deny any connection to or knowledge of the coup. Shortly after the coup, the American embassy in London provided the State Department with "the official report of Questions and Answers in the House of Commons on Monday February 28, in regard to the recent revolution in Persia." The official report consisted of the following:

Lieut.-Commander Kenworthy asked the Prime Minister whether the action of the Persian Cossacks in overthrowing the Government at Teheran has been assisted or supported in any way by His Majesty's Government; whether these Persian Cossacks have been paid and provisioned by His Majesty's Government; and what is the attitude of His Majesty's Government towards their present action:

Mr. Cecil Harmsworth: As the reply is rather long, I will, with the hon. Member's permission, circulate it with the *Official Report*.[13]

The subsequently produced *Official Report* follows:

Detachments of the Persian Cossack Division, composed entirely of Persian troops under a Persian officer, marched from Kazvin on Teheran and entered the town on 21st February shortly after midnight. The Persian officer in command of this force stated that the Persian Cossacks, who had had experience of the Bolsheviks, were tired of seeing one inefficient Government succeed another in Teheran, where, apparently, no one was making any preparations to oppose a Bolshevik advance, which would follow the withdrawal of the British forces from Persia. The Cossacks professed loyalty and devotion to the Shah, but were determined to set aside the evil counselors by whom he had been surrounded. They also professed goodwill towards foreigners who, they declared, had nothing to fear from them.

As no force was available to oppose their entry into Teheran they encountered practically no resistance, and took charge of all Government establishments and picketed the streets. The local gendarmerie and police joined them, and discipline was maintained. The Government of Sipahdar naturally collapsed, and the Prime Minister sought refuge in His Majesty's Legation, but was subsequently induced to leave with an assurance that he would not be molested. The revolutionaries have not yet set up a Government, but have arrested various prominent personages. The bazaars were closed and the town was quiet on the 22nd February.

His Majesty's Government have taken no part in, and have no responsibility whatever for the action of the Persian Cossacks. The British subsidies for the maintenance of this force ceased in May, 1920. The attitude of His Majesty's Government towards the Cossacks is one of neutrality.[14]

The preceding document establishes a fundamental fact: British records on Persia contain distortions and outright lies. As a great deal of the existing written history of Persia is based on the British records, a reappraisal of all these works is clearly indicated. That the British records cannot be trusted became clear to me when I compared the contrasting accounts of the abolition of the Qajar dynasty in 1925 with the "selection" of Reza Khan as shah found in the American and British records. The British version, provided by Cyrus Ghani, gives the impression that Reza Khan was a popular national leader who was acclaimed shah by the people. However, unlike the American account, the British version fails to mention the decapitated bodies of Reza Khan's opponents appearing outside the walls of the Majlis, and the possible effect on the hapless deputies who are portrayed by Ghani as solid supporters of Reza Khan. Nor does one read in the British version about the appearance of troop detachments outside the Majlis during its critical deliberations and the effect the firing of a few random volleys had on the deputies' determination to support Reza Khan.

From the American records it is learned that in its last session prior to voting to abolish the Qajars and appoint Reza Khan as the head of the provisional government, the Majlis was about to appoint a committee to study and report on the holding of a popular referendum on the question of any changes in the Constitution. At this critical juncture, detachments of troops appeared outside the Majlis, and as noted by the American chargé d'affaires, the firing of a "few random shots" had been sufficient to "curtail unnecessary debate" by the deputies, who adjourned and fled from the Parliament building in a "state of great trepidation." In the next sitting of the Majlis, a majority voted to pass Reza Khan's agenda. In reading the American records one begins to understand the role of the British in this sorry chapter of Iran's history, and the profound sense of humiliation and resentment of the people of Iran at the unconstitutional manner in which a nearly illiterate peasant was thrust on the throne by a foreign power.

Reza Khan as Minister of War and Prime Minister, 1921–1925

With British financial assistance and the support of the British occupation forces, and having been given control of the domestic military and police forces by the British, Reza Khan quickly became the de facto dictator of Persia. The open financial assistance took the form of giving him loans from the Imperial Bank of Persia, a British-owned institution, and payments by the Anglo-Persian Oil Company, which had conveniently decided to resume royalty payments. According to Sabahi, "By allowing the Imperial Bank to supply funds to Reza Khan's army, the British government wished to curry favour with the 'winning horse.'"[15] In addition, £931,000 was paid in 1921 by the Anglo-Persian Oil Company (which was controlled by the British government) as part of the Armitage-Smith Agreement of December 1920 (described in detail in chapter 9). These payments (£125,000 in April 1921 and £808,000 in December 1921) were made after the coup d'état.[16] With such sums at his disposal, Reza Khan's rise to become military dictator of Persia was assured and viewed with great "satisfaction" by the British, who could barely conceal their joy. According to Sabahi, "Reza Khan 'frequently' assured the British officials that 'he would do with Persian hands that which the British wished to do with British hands.'"[17]

In December 1921 the British military attaché in Tehran observed with much satisfaction that Reza Khan "is now more a military dictator than ever, controls the Cabinet, has the greatest contempt for the Majlis, and is feared by the Shah."[18] In London meanwhile, Sabahi reports, "Curzon was 'amused' by the rapidity with which the officer 'without political aspiration' had turned into an almost fully fledged military dictator."[19] After a confrontation with the Majlis in 1922, Reza Khan threatened to abolish the Majlis. The British cheered him on. George Churchill, in charge of the Persian desk at the Foreign Office, wrote: "If Reza Khan's coup d'état comes off and he abolishes the Majlis and institutes a military dictatorship, the local press will close down automatically and Sir P[ercy]. Lorraine's troubles will cease. For this reason I hope that Reza Khan will succeed."[20]

In April 1921, Reza Khan became minister of war as well as commander of the armed forces. In May 1921, following a cabinet crisis engineered by Reza Khan, Seyid Zia was removed and forced to leave Iran:

> As a result of a quarrel between the Minister of War and the Prime Minister the latter was obliged to resign and fled from Teheran early this morning. The cabinet which has fallen came into power last February through a coup d'état. The immediate cause of its overthrow was the refusal of Reza Khan also known as Sardar Sipah to retain British officers or employ additional ones in return for guns and ammunition. It will be recalled that he [Reza Khan] was at the head of the Cossacks who took Teheran in February and therefore considered himself creator of the late government whose orders he refused to take. In April he ousted the Minister of War and took that portfolio himself in addition to remaining commander in chief. Since then friction between himself and the premier increased daily and the latter resigned several times but the British Legation had prevailed upon the Shah to refuse acceptance.[21]

Much was to be made later by such writers as Cyrus Ghani about Reza Khan's patriotism and his dismissal of the British officers. The whole episode was a charade by the British intended to bring Reza Khan into greater prominence and gain him political capital. Of the three British officers in the service of the Persian government, General Dickson had already returned to London and, as reported by Caldwell, the other two had already received their orders to return to their units in India before the coup. Murray also briefly alludes to the dismissal of the British officers: "One of the first acts of Sardar Sepah when he assumed charge of the army was to dismiss the British military mission, whose status was, in any case, irregular after the failure of the agreement." Despite "his gratitude to his British supporters," Murray notes, "public sentiment was so violently Anglophobe that any anti-British act on his [Reza Khan's] part could but increase his popularity with the people."[22]

Qavam-es-Saltaneh (brother of Vossough-ed-Dowleh) was put in place of Seyid Zia. But real power was in the hands of Reza Khan and the British-

FIGURE 3.1 *Ahmad Shah (right-hand figure with sash), Crown Prince Mohammad Hassan Mirza (to the left and slightly behind of Ahmad Shah), Qavam-es-Saltaneh (front row, in light-colored coat, wearing glasses), and Reza Khan (in Cossack uniform, behind and between Ahmad Shah and the prince), ca. May 1921. Courtesy of the Institute for Iranian Contemporary Historical Studies (IICHS).*

supported military. In October 1923, the American minister, Joseph S. Kornfeld, reports, "Minister of War [Reza Khan] supported by the British is using every possible pressure on the Shah to make him prime minister."[23] Ahmad Shah, shortly after, was forced to make the appointment. By then Ahmad Shah was almost a prisoner who was being openly mistreated and threatened by Reza Khan. Ahmad Shah told Lorraine that Reza Khan had "started abusing him and [Crown Prince] Valiahd quite openly and saying he could chain both brothers when it suited him."[24] Similarly, the Crown Prince informed Kornfeld "of the humiliations to which the royal family is being constantly subjected by the Minister of War. . . . The Minister of War is in complete control of the army, [and] the Shah feels that this is not the time for the measuring of strength."[25] Ahmad Shah informed Loraine of his desire to leave for Europe to be "out of the way and secure from any attempt against his life and liberty."[26] He left Iran shortly after and was never permitted to return. He died in Paris in 1930 at the age of thirty-four. The role of the British in Reza Khan's advancement was not hidden to the American diplomats. Commenting on the relentless rise of Reza Khan with British help, Kornfeld hit upon the essence of the matter:

Reza Khan's influence in Persian affairs is most sinister. He must be either curbed or crushed. Unfortunately he is receiving the secret support of the

British who feel that they can accomplish their own ends far more easily through him than through the constitutional Government. I have positive assurance from the Prime Minister [Qavam-es-Saltaneh] that at the time Persia decided to engage American advisers and to encourage America's economic cooperation, Lord Curzon protested vigorously. My own observations have forced on me the conclusion that, notwithstanding their protestations to the contrary, at heart the British are opposed to the Open Door in Persia. Finding it impossible to close the Door, they seek to bring into the house such chaos and confusion as will deter others from entering. Reza Khan is an admirable tool in their hands.[27]

Bernard Gotlieb, American consul in Tehran, reported: "The reins of government are virtually in the hands of one man, the Minister of War, the cabinet changes are kaleidoscopic, and it would need very little pressure from circumstances to result in its transformation into a military dictatorship in name as well as in reality."[28]

The move during February and March 1924 to change the country into a republic with Reza Khan as its president was, as suggested by Gotlieb and Millspaugh (see below), a thinly disguised attempt to transform the country into a military dictatorship. The manner in which this was defeated in the Majlis by Modarres and others has been described in the literature. Murray believed that Reza Khan had failed in his "republican" attempt mainly because the British were not willing to support him in that endeavor. Although weakened, Reza Khan survived the debacle and continued to remain in office thanks to the support of the military, which in practice meant the British. The episode greatly emboldened Reza Khan's opponents, including Sheikh Khaz-al of Khuzestan. The manner in which, with British assistance, Reza Khan overcame Sheikh Khaz-al's challenge is described by Sabahi. By August 1925, however, Reza Khan was again in trouble and his opponents were planning to finish him off for good. An account of what transpired during the crucial period between August and December 1925 can be constructed from the American records.

The Political Situation in August 1925: Reza Khan's Growing Weakness

A version of the manner in which Ahmad Shah was deposed and Reza Khan made Shah is given by Sabahi and Ghani. Using British records, the authors conclude, not surprisingly, that the British simply "stood aside," and observed from a distance as the events unfolded because "they were not able to influence the course of events there."[29] A vastly different version of the events appears in the detailed reports of the American chargé d'affaires, Copley Amory Jr. It emerges that the abolition of the Qajar dynasty, and the choice of Reza Khan as the new shah, was yet another British coup d'état that was rapidly and skillfully executed. After the failure of the republican movement, and despite British assistance and protection, the position of Reza Khan had been greatly weakened, and his opponents emboldened. The appointment of Nosrat-ed-Dowleh Firouz as minister of justice in December 1924 and of Shokrollah Khan Sadri (Qavam-ed-Dowleh) as interior minister was viewed as an indication of the rising influence of Modarres (whom Loraine calls "a conceited and narrow-minded bigot") and a deterioration in the political fortunes of Reza Khan.

By August 1925, Reza Khan was clearly in trouble, and it was being predicted that his conservative and clerical opponents were about to move to finish him off for good. In a dispatch dated August 29, 1925, Amory describes the situation. The rising power of Modarres, "the influential and veteran leader both in and out of the Medjliss of the clerical forces and who is allied to the group which surrounds and supports the Valiahd [Heir Apparent]," and the recent cabinet appointments of Firouz and Sadri were widely interpreted "as a sign of an increasing weakness [by Reza Khan] which, it is widely admitted, began after the failure of the attempted republican coup d'état sixteen months ago. At that time his general officers, at least, gave him loyalty and support. It is said that were a similar emergency to arise to-day the response from these subordinates would not be as complete as it was then."

In addition to pointing out Reza Khan's weakening position in the army, Amory also describes his growing unpopularity with the people: "With the common people it is apparent that Reza Khan has lost in popularity and prestige. The enclosure to this despatch recites certain recent incidents, probably not important in themselves, but which show the way the wind is blowing and which have given a decided impetus to the growing popular coolness towards the Prime Minister. The reason for these drastic and almost puerile acts on his part is attributed by some to nervousness for the safety of his person. An increasingly arbitrary attitude, especially when it takes such flagrant forms, on the part of one who comes from the people and who was originally considered a champion of their interests is regarded with particular resentment." In summing up the situation, Amory concludes that "the clerical and the conservative forces entertain suspicions and grievances against Reza Khan and are merely biding their time until they gain sufficient control to eliminate him entirely." The enclosure to the dispatch is especially revealing in its description of the political situation, the actual popularity of Ahmad Shah and Valiahd with the people, the widespread unpopularity of Reza Khan, and his brutal tendency to violence. The enclosure is given in full:

Local gossip has been busy recently with an incident attributed to the increased activity of the group surrounding the Valiahd. The alleged incident was not of course mentioned in the censored press but it is said to be significant and its reaction on Reza Khan's humor has given Teheran a new subject for talk. On August 13 [1925] a funeral service was held in the Shah Mosque for the senior Mollah of Teheran, which the Heir Apparent [Valiahd], the Prime Minister [Reza Khan], officials and many prominent persons besides a large public crowd attended. In contrast to the silence which prevailed when the Prime Minister arrived, escorted by armed guards, the Heir Apparent was welcomed with a loud and enthusiastic acclamation. At the close of the services a Seyid addressed the people on the character of the deceased and concluded his remarks by crying: "Long live the Shah and the Heir Apparent." The entire crowd responded with enthusiasm. The Seyid then cried: "Long live the Prime Minister." There was a silence except for the few persons in the immediate vicinity of the Prime Minister who immediately left the Mosque. On his way through the crowds to the bazaar he passed a merchant who was playing with his rosary. Reza Khan according to gossip demanded of the merchant whether he knew who it was who was speaking to him. The merchant muttered, "Yes, His Highness the Prime Minister." "Why then did you fail to render respect?" asked the Prime Minister, and slapped the man several times on the face.

Reza Khan went to his country place and for the next few days refused to receive visitors. On Saturday morning on his way to town he got out of his automobile and beat and kicked a policeman who fainted and was taken to the hospital, who had failed to arrange in file a group of donkeys that had blocked the road. In the village of Gulhek, Shahidi, an official of the Post office, Haik, a typist at the Internal Revenue Administration, Kooros, an alumnus of the American High School and a well known merchant in Teheran, with a number of other Persians of the better class were standing at the side of the street chatting and laughing without noticing the passing of the Premier's car. Reza Khan stopped his car, went up to the group, and took hold of Shahidi and asked who he was. When Shahidi explained that he was a government official he was slapped, thrown to the ground and kicked. Reza Khan stands six feet two and must weigh 230 pounds. Everyone in the group was treated the same way, except Kooros who protested he "had bowed and His Highness had not noticed."[30]

With such displays of popular support for himself and the obvious weakening of Reza Khan, Ahmad Shah announced that he intended to return to Persia. On September 21, 1925, Tehran newspapers published Ahmad Shah's telegram dated September 16, 1925, to "his" prime minister about his intention to return. The newspapers had also published Reza Khan's reply and his "jubilation and delight" about the return of His Majesty. Amory observes: "For months rumors have been current in regard to the return of the Shah to Persia and have increased with the growing influence and activity of the reactionary elements during the last weeks, so that this

FIGURE 3.2 *Reza Khan (front row center), prime minister, minister of war, and generalissimo of the Persian army and navy, with senior military officers, ca. 1925. Courtesy of the IICHS.*

announcement created no public excitement and very little interest. There has been no newspaper comment probably due to the press censorship."[31]

For reasons not clearly understood, bread was scarce and declining in quality in Tehran in September 1925. Despite the existence of martial law, the government permitted a demonstration on September 23, 1925, just two days after the announcement of the return of the shah. The demonstration turned violent and a mob attacked the Majlis building, beating up deputies, and demolishing some of the furniture. Amory commented, "They went as a hungry and angry mob, assaulted deputies and destroyed furnishings!" He added, "Practically no reference was made to the disorders in the strictly censored press nor indeed have the newspapers reflected to any degree the acuteness and importance which the alimentation situation has assumed."[32] The only indirect reference to the attack on Parliament was a brief announcement in the newspaper *Iran:* "Yesterday a group of people went to Parliament to complain about the lack of bread."[33] The government finally restored order and the crowd had been dispersed by the army only after some groups among them had shouted the slogan, "We Want the Shah!" That the entire episode of bread shortage had been contrived by Reza Khan to further his political ends was demonstrated by the fact that the "shortage" was quickly alleviated when the army stores of wheat were opened, and grain was transported from the provinces. The chanting of pro–Ahmad Shah slogans by demonstrators showed that Reza Khan could no longer even stage-manage a demonstration. With the weakening of Reza Khan and the impending return of Ahmad Shah, it was time again for the British to come to the former's rescue and thereafter events moved rapidly. There followed one of the most humiliating episodes in Iran's history.

The "National Movement"

The first step was to prevent the return of Ahmad Shah. The British government had "objected" to the return of Ahmad Shah to Iran because he "would certainly intrigue against Reza Khan." And in retrospect, the Foreign Office had paid Ahmad Shah the highest compliment by stating that he had done "nothing to earn him the gratitude or support of His Majesty's Government."[34] Then, beginning on October 7, 1925, the Majlis received numerous telegrams from the provinces protesting against the shah's return and expressing dissatisfaction with the Qajar dynasty. Amory comments: "These protestations would be of interest if they were spontaneous but offer an increased interest because it has become apparent that they are staged maneuvers on the part of the Prime Minister and his agents to discredit the ruling dynasty in the public mind." He went on to describe some of these protestations. Persons calling themselves a Group of Azerbaijanis Residing in Tehran had published a statement in the Tehran newspapers appealing to the Majlis deputies to oppose the return of Ahmad Shah, who was accused of occupying himself "with self-indulgence instead of the service of the country." Ahmad Shah was denounced "as being responsible for the failure of Persia to progress since the promulgation of the constitution" and was called a foreign lackey.[35] The newspapers declared, "In Azerbaijan the markets have been closed as a protest against the return of the Shah and telegrams of protest are being received by the deputies and by the Prime Minister from the inhabitants of that province."[36]

The "inhabitants" of Azerbaijan had formed the Mixed National Committee of Azerbaijan and were sending large numbers of telegrams to the Majlis and to the prime minister. Claiming to represent the people of Azerbaijan, the committee called Ahmad Shah a traitor and threatened "that relations with Teheran will be severed if the Shah is allowed to return." Similar national committees had been formed in all the provinces and cities and were flooding the Majlis with their telegrams of protest. Newspapers gave prominent exposure to the telegrams and carried reports on "bazaar closings to protest the return of the Shah."[37]

The protests against the return of the shah had been changed during the second week of the so-called National Movement to demand the abolition of the Qajar dynasty. Describing these protests, Amory writes: "The 'demonstrations' in the form of telegrams from the provinces, the 'threat' of Azerbaijan to secede and kindred gestures of the so-called national movement continued up to Friday, October 30. They were without question engineered by Pahlavi and his group. No spontaneous enthusiasm has been apparent at any stage. The 'popular' gestures of the last few weeks have been chiefly directed to the Medjliss. There has existed in many quarters a frank contempt for the Shah and some of his family and a realization of their total unfitness. But one of the chief aims of the Constitution was to make of the monarch an innocuous figurehead."[38]

Amory describes the so-called National Movement in Azerbaijan, which had been sending telegrams to the Majlis and to Reza Khan threatening to "secede" if the Qajars were not deposed.[39] The dispatch included a report from the clerk of the American consulate in Tabriz. The clerk, a native of Tabriz, states:

> The other day about 60 persons marched through the bazaars crying "long live Pahlavi" and "destruction to Kajar dynasty." I hear they were all hired for this purpose. There is still a commission at the Telegraph office sending all sorts of telegrams to Teheran in the name of the people. The commission is composed of the most notorious elements. In the evenings about 100 people are gathering at the Telegraph office and there are some speeches all for the destruction of the Kajar dynasty. The Prime Minister from Teheran has sent a telegram to the effect that "he cannot say anything against the lawful demands of the people." The bazaars are open and the movement is very weak. For such a big city as Tabriz in Persia only less than 100 people are going to the Telegraph office. The above statements are the real and actual conditions of Tabriz.[40]

The activities of the Tabriz National Committee continued. On October 26, 1925, it sent a telegram to the Majlis, demanding the deposition of the Shah and abolition of the Kajar dynasty, and threatened that "Azerbaijan will sever its relations with Teheran if the Medjliss does not arrive at a decision by Tuesday [October 27]." Another telegram asked the Azerbaijan deputies not to appear in the Majlis, and threatened them with "horrible consequences" if they did so. As reported by Amory, it announced, "Necessary action will be taken to dethrone the Shah and the Kajar dynasty." It asked "that all the provinces provide the National Committee of Tabriz with full powers" to dethrone the Shah and the Qajar dynasty.[41] Another telegram warned that the people of Azerbaijan would boycott the Majlis elections unless Parliament was given power to abolish the Qajars. In a telegram dated October 28 the Tabriz National Committee announced that "Tabriz has severed its relations with Teheran and the 'national forces' have seized the government departments." In a telegram on October 29 it declared that "a volunteer national army is being organized in Tabriz." Not to be outdone, the National Committee of Kerman sent a telegram to Reza Khan begging him "to leave the capital temporarily, so that the Kermanis may march to the capital to compel compliance with their demands." Groups allegedly representing the merchants of Tehran and the trades

union of Tehran had taken sanctuary (bast) at the Military Academy, "urging that action be taken to terminate the Kajar rule." The Tehran newspapers reported that on October 31, "Mr. Pahlavi went to the Military
Academy and visited the various groups of people who had taken 'bast.'"[42]

Proceedings of the Fifth Majlis, October 1925

The terms of the parliamentary officers were set to expire in early October
1925, just as the "national movements" and their telegrams were getting
under way. The president of the Majlis (the Majlis speaker), Mirza Hossein
Khan Pirnia (Motamen-ol-Molk), had intimated that he was not willing to
stand for reelection. On October 8 deputies met in private to discuss the
election of a new Majlis president. Mirza Hassan Khan Mostowfi (Mostefi-
ol-Mamalek) was asked to become a candidate, but he refused. Seyid
Mohammad Tadayun was considered but sufficient agreement could not
be reached on his candidacy. Despite Pirnia's refusal, he was reelected
president on October 11, and Tadayun was elected first vice president. On
October 13, Pirnia tendered his resignation. Amory writes, "A delegation of
deputies called on him at his house and tried to persuade him to withdraw
his resignation. The deputies pointed out that if the President insisted on
retiring a crisis would ensue in the conduct of Parliament and that only a
short period remained, anyway, before the expiration of the present Medjliss. Mr. Pirnia, however, refused to reconsider his decision, pleading illness and stating that he did not approve of any individual holding an office
too long in a constitutional country."[43] From October 15 to October 17
attempts were made to get Pirnia to reconsider his resignation, but to no
avail. Pirnia's resignation was officially read in Parliament.[44] That the resignation of Pirnia and the refusal of Mostowfi to run for president of the
Majlis were parliamentary maneuvers to derail the plans of the British and
Reza Khan can be seen from the following report from Amory:

> Yesterday (October 19) in the Medjliss Tadayun reported a conference with
> the Prime Minister (Reza Khan), who had asked him what action the Medjliss
> intended to take with regard to the telegrams that had recently been received
> from Tabriz with regard to the return of the Shah. Tadayun stated that he had
> not seen these telegrams. The Prime Minister asked him to express to the
> deputies his anxiety about the situation in Tabriz. The Prime Minister believed
> that the Medjliss should take a decision as soon as possible. Tadayun informed
> the deputies that a telegram had been received from Tabriz addressed to the
> President of the Medjliss, who had been asked to come to the telegraph office
> with ten deputies to communicate with Tabriz. When those who had sent the
> telegram had been informed that the President had tendered his resignation the
> two Vice Presidents were asked to come to the telegraph office with ten deputies.
> Tadayun then asked the opinion of the deputies. It was pointed out that the

telegram was addressed to the Vice Presidents, who had been asked to select the ten deputies and therefore the opinion of the Medjliss was not necessary. Thereupon, Mostowfi, Alai, Taghi Zadeh (Taqizadeh), Afshar, Arbab-Keikhosrow, Nedamani, Hekmat, Teherani and Adli were invited to go with the Vice Presidents to the Telegraph Office. After hearing the presentations that were made by telegraph from Tabriz the deputies concluded that the matter should wait until a President is elected and the Medjliss can express its opinion.[45]

Despite his refusal to be a candidate, Mirza Hassan Khan Mostowfi (Mostefi-ol-Mamalek) was elected president of the Majlis on October 20. During the next two days, Mostowfi informed all the deputies who had gone to see him that he would not accept the presidency. But he had "not yet written anything to the Medjliss to that effect."[46] On October 28 it was announced, "A special meeting will be held this morning of the officers of the Medjliss who will discuss important matters that are now before the Medjliss including the telegrams that are being received from the provinces [against the Qajar dynasty]." When Mostowfi was invited to attend this meeting, he replied that he did "not consider himself responsible for the Presidency of the Medjliss." *Iran* reported, "A private meeting of the Medjliss will be held this morning to discuss whether the above reply should be interpreted as the President's resignation."[47]

On Thursday, October 29, the following deputies "requested that the telegrams received from the provinces [against the Qajar dynasty] be read in open session": Yassa'ee, Kei-Ostovan, Dast-i-Gheyb, Engineer Emir, Prince Heshmati, Akhgar and Kumi. Amory writes, "The Petitions Committee of the Medjliss therefore reported that since the middle of Mehr [October 7] numerous telegrams, bearing the signatures of notable men, have been received from Azerbaijan, Khorassan, Kerman, Kurdistan, Birjand, Barforoush, Sari, Kermanshah, Nahavand, Malayer, etc., all of which express dissatisfaction with the Kajar dynasty and contain demands to the effect that sovereignty be taken away from the Kajars. The Committee had carefully studied the telegrams and had decided to bring them to the attention of the Medjliss, so that the latter may act in any manner appropriate."[48] After some discussion, it had been suggested by Deputy Yassa'ee that the best course of action was to hold a referendum. Based on *Setareh Iran* of October 30, Amory gives the following account: "in view of the fact that Article 35 of the Constitutional Law provides 'Sovereignty is a divine gift that is entrusted to the Kajar family by the people of Persia,' he [Yassa'ee] believed that in case the people found that the Kajar dynasty was not able to perform the duties inherent in holding this 'gift' they could take it away. The best method of doing this was in his opinion by having a referendum. It was finally suggested that a committee consisting of 12 deputies be formed to study and report on the matter."[49]

The suggestion of holding a referendum after a committee had studied and reported on the matter brought matters to a head. The appearance of Reza Khan's troops outside the walls of the Majlis at this time and the firing of shots were sufficient to frighten the deputies, who, according to Amory, "'adjourned' in a sudden panic, certain random shots having been fired in the vicinity, probably designedly, to put them into a state of trepidation and to prevent unnecessary debate." On the afternoon of the following day, Friday, October 30, "members of the Medjliss received messages to go to the Prime Minister's house. They were there asked to give a pledge to vote in favor of this law [abolition of Qajars], which was [to be] presented to the Medjliss on the following day. There appears to have been a precipitate 'climbing on the band wagon' and various forms of inducement and pressure were undoubtedly used."[50]

Abolition of the Qajar Monarchy and the Appointment of Reza Khan as Provisional Head of State

On October 31, 1925, the day after Reza Khan's "tea party" for the deputies, Amory sent a telegram marked strictly confidential and urgent: "Declaration of Prime Minister as Shah or at least convocation of constituent assembly for this purpose appears imminent. Indifference underlies artificial public demonstration in his favor. Absence of any effective coordination or leadership among elements opposed gives movement reasonable prospect of success. British Minister has delivered message from Chamberlain to Foreign Minister emphasizing strict neutrality in the crisis. European missions do not emphasize legal irregularities as serious obstacles to recognition of such a new regime."[51] That afternoon, in a vote of 80 to 5 (with 30 absent), the following law was passed by the Majlis: "In the name of the welfare of the people the national Consultative Assembly declares the abolition of the Kajar Sovereignty and within the limits of the constitution and other laws entrust Provisional Government to the person of Mr. Reza Khan Pahlavi the determining of the form of the permanent government shall be made by a constituent assembly which shall for this purpose amend Articles 36, 37, 38, and 40 of the supplement to the constitutional law."[52]

In announcing the passage of the "law" in his telegram Amory adds, "Minority contend that procedure illegal. Only deliberate genuine popular referendum can authorize constitutional change. Majority contend that recent telegrams from provinces to the Medjliss demanding abolition of Kajar dynasty constitute mandate. . . . Millspaugh is continuing his functions as heretofore but is concerned at probability of complications from existence and exercise of unconstitutional authority. Certain patriotic Persians who disapprove of the methods now recognize definitive nature of the event. No elements exist at present to contest the fait accompli especially as British neutrality appears to be more of the letter than the spirit."[53] On October 31, Crown Prince Mohammad Hassan Mirza was forced to leave Tehran for Baghdad, and his residence was seized by General Morteza Khan, commander of the Tehran army. Amory reports, "In reality the Valiahd was sent out of the country to Bagdad in very humiliating circumstances. It is said his person was searched and he was provided with practically no funds nor simple conveniences for his journey."[54]

The official justification for the Majlis action was given in a circular note dated November 1, 1925, from Foreign Minister Hassan Moshar (Moshar-ol-Molk) to the foreign legations in Tehran: "National Movement demands abolition of Kajar dynasty, which was becoming every day more violent, would have resulted in great revolution and disastrous consequences if urgent action had not been taken. National Consultative Assembly found it necessary in order to end the crisis to respond to public opinion. On October 31 it declared the abolition of Kajar sovereignty and entrusted to His Great Highness, Pahlavi, generalissimo of all the forces, the provisional Government of the country until a constituent assembly is formed to make a permanent arrangement."[55]

The "Fairy Wand"

The manner and speed with which the considerable opposition to Reza Khan had been neutralized and his plans approved by the Majlis was remarkable. It was as though he waved a fairy wand and everything fell into place. Amory writes that due "to considerable but uncoordinated opposition to the Prime Minister's plans, it appeared up to the last moment that the Prime Minister's tactics of throwing the responsibility for a decision in regard to the 'national movement' on the Medjliss would not be successful." But, miraculously, continues Amory, "on Friday, October 30, a sufficient number of deputies allowed their minds to be made up for them to enable the revolutionary program to be steam-rollered through the Medjliss on the following day. The Prime Minister supplied the necessary leadership and wafted away the opposition with a fairy wand."[56]

The magic wand was especially effective because the entire movement was "short and quick"—three weeks in all. In the words of Amory, "The first signs of it occurred less than a month ago. No time was given after it was launched for either friends or foes really to draw breath and philosophize on what was happening." Unquestionably, Reza Khan had benefited from the cowardice and moral failure of such individuals and Hassan Pirnia (Motamen-ol-Molk), and Hossein Mostowfi (Mostowfi-ol-Mamalek).

While admitting "the unquestioned integrity and patriotism" of both men, Amory declares that, "like so many of their compatriots they show a total lack of the power of decision or affirmative courage in a time of emergency, and in this instance they persisted in adopting a completely negative attitude in the face of an important issue." When faced with a grave crisis, the two men had simply walked away. Amory also observes, "Perhaps Pahlavi's fairy wand worked with special success in view of the fact that the life of the present Medjliss is nearly up and thoughts are turning to hopes of reelection," not to mention troop detachments and volleys of random shots fired outside the Majlis. The writer also notes that in addition to the judicious appointments of many governors and other provincial functionaries, "the ground containing potential opposition had been carefully watered for some time past, as, for instance, by the appointment of Prince Firouz and his friends to the Cabinet."[57]

The miracles brought forth by Reza Khan's fairy wand had been made possible with British assistance. Actually, the wand belonged to the British. After the failure of the "republican movement" in March 1924, it was apparent that, by late 1924, Reza Khan was once again considering the deposition of the Qajar dynasty. Murray, the American chargé d'affaires, writes, "A state of nervousness and uncertainty prevails today in Persian political circles that is not reassuring. The Prime Minister [Reza Khan] is believed to be desirous of a change of regime by which he may become Regent or Shah. To realize his plans he may be obliged to solicit the support of the British. I am constrained to remark that in the eventuality of the success of such a coup carried out with British support, the chances of American competition for the North Persian oil concession will, in my opinion, be greatly reduced."[58]

In a subsequent struggle with his opponents, Reza Khan was greatly weakened, thereby prompting Amory to conclude that Reza Khan was a spent force and that his opponents were preparing to finish him off for good. Encouraged by this turn of events, toward the end of September 1925, Ahmad Shah announced his intention to return home. Shortly thereafter, the National Movement was launched (October 7), the Qajar dynasty was deposed (October 31), and Reza Khan was declared head of the provisional government.[59] Amory discusses the reason for the alacrity of the events. In September 1925, when Ahmad Shah announced his intention to return, there were three ostensible political groupings: the supporters of Ahmad Shah (the Court Party), the supporters of the Valiahd (the Moderates), and Reza Khan and his supporters. Since the first two groups were obviously allied against Reza Khan, there were in practice two political groups: Reza Khan and his opponents. Amory believed that the British would have liked to see a continuation of the current status quo with Reza

Khan in actual power, or a variation by which Ahmad Shah was deposed in favor of a minor prince of the Qajar line, but with Reza Khan as regent. By October 1925, the British realized that the continuation of the status quo or its variation was no longer possible because of the growing antagonism between Pahlavi and his opponents. The status quo had broken down first due to "the intrigue by the partisans of the Shah having as its object the complete elimination of Pahlavi by the time of the Shah's expected return in November," and second due to "the growing personal antipathy of Pahlavi towards anything bearing the tag Kajar."[60]

Amory leaves no doubt as to what transpired subsequently, and the origin of the fairy wand: "The British perhaps realized the personality of Pahlavi would not permit the indefinite continuation of the status quo and that with the elimination of the irritant, the Court Party [and Ahmad Shah], a strong one man government offered the best, perhaps the only alternative. When it became obvious that this [continuation of status quo] was impossible they naturally swung into line behind Pahlavi." Amory's obvious conclusion: "This situation explains in great part the quickness with which recent events crystallized and the facility with which Pahlavi's program has been carried out."

Amory also describes the decision of the proposed Constituent Assembly: "It is widely predicted it will decide on some form of monarchy for this would appear to be Pahlavi's personal ambition and in line with British desire. It is possible, however, that the Russians and those internal elements which are resentful at the result of recent events may attempt to frustrate this program." Amory includes an observation that must have been obvious to all: "As to the future one doubts whether Pahlavi's affirmative personality will ever permit him to play the role of the usual constitutional executive. One wonders whether he realizes, with his lack of education and limited perspective, the difficulties which will confront him as intrigue and conflicting ambitions to a greater and greater extent concentrate their focus on him and on him alone."[61]

The Constituent Assembly and the "Selection" of Reza Shah

On November 4, 1925, Mohammad Ali Foroughi (Zoka-ol-Molk) was appointed acting prime minister. The next day, a large reception was held at the Majlis celebrating the abolition of the Qajars. Amory reports that newly elected Majlis President "Tadayun addressed Mr. Pahlavi and expressed to him the satisfaction felt by the deputies for having entrusted to him the prosperity and welfare of the nation." The elections to the Constituent Assembly were held from November 10 to 14. However, even before the election of the assembly, in a situation that gave rise to a feeling of déjà vu, newspapers reported that "new telegrams have been received from the provinces expressing impatience for the coronation of Mr. Pahlavi as sovereign. A telegram from Tabriz states it is not necessary to await action by the Constituent Assembly." On November 14, "at an army parade reviewed by Mr. Pahlavi the commander of the Teheran troops, General Morteza, speaking for his command, requested Mr. Pahlavi to accept the crown as Persian sovereign. Pahlavi declined, stating that he would later summon the officers and consult with them on this subject."[62]

The elections to the Constituent Assembly prompted some very undiplomatic comments by Amory:

> The press has devoted much space to the elections for the Constituent Assembly, but the news published has been altogether of a mechanical nature, merely recording the progress and the results. Indications of the significances, the spirit and attitude of public opinion have been entirely lacking. It is obvious that the policy of those in power is to have the elections carried out with as little delay as possible, just as it is predicted that action by the Constituent Assembly when once it meets will be pushed in order that opportunities for those who may desire to upset Pahlavi's program will be minimized. As the "national movement" aroused no popular enthusiasm, so the elections for the Constituent assembly have awakened no real interest. A substantial portion of those entitled to vote have not come to the polls. One might assume from the tone of these [press] reports that the flower of the country was being sent to Teheran by waves of national enthusiasm! Where ignorance and poverty are prevalent such a condition is always true to a certain extent, but in the present instance there is added a widespread feeling that the results are a foregone conclusion. Returns from the Teheran district are just coming in. Among those who appear to be leading are men who are closely identified in and out of the Medjliss with the recent "national movement." It is predicted that many members of the present Medjliss will be elected to the Constituent assembly.

Amory then makes an observation that was to prove fundamentally valid for the next fifty-three years, and was a salient characteristic of the Pahlavi system: "In general it is becoming apparent that those elected represent a new class in politics and that Pahlavi and his movement are using elements in the community which heretofore have not wielded substantial influence, elements who may be said to represent perhaps more energy, but less character and far less the established tradition than those whom the public has been accustomed to regard as the ruling class."[63]

In reading Amory's comments one begins to understand the deep humiliation and anger felt by many at this shameful charade of constitutionalism that was being staged by the British.

> Certain currents of which one has for some time been conscious are taking more definite shape as the opening of the Constituent Assembly draws near.

First of all one comes in contact more and more with indications of resentment or disgust at Pahlavi's recent course of action. The manner in which the "national movement" as well as the elections to the Constituent Assembly have been engineered might have been regarded with more charity if his motives had been accepted as more genuine. Discontent in the provinces at the arbitrary, tactless and dishonest administration of many army officers and a growing feeling that Pahlavi and his army—which represents both his political and military power—are using their position to an ever increasing extent for their own personal interests contributes largely to this attitude. The extent to which this feeling can become a determining factor will depend largely on how far Pahlavi will keep the loyalty and support of his subordinates. The fact that the army and, incidentally, its intelligence service are admirably organized discourages any insubordinate act or rival movement at the present time.[64]

With 248 of 272 elected members present in Tehran, and the remaining twenty-four en route, the Constituent Assembly was officially opened by Reza Khan on December 6 and it adjourned on December 13. On December 10 it amended Articles 36, 37, and 38 of the supplement to the Constitution. Of these, Article 36 was the most important. It was "amended" to read as follows: "The Constitutional Monarchy of Persia is vested by the people through the Constituent Assembly in the Person of His Imperial Majesty Reza Shah Pahlavi and his male heirs generation after generation."[65] On Tuesday, December 15, Reza Khan took the oath of office as shah in the Majlis and the date of his accession was officially proclaimed as December 16, 1925. The entire process, writes Amory, "was accomplished quickly and in an orderly manner; in fact, so well ordered has been the management and sequence of events that one is inclined to place credence in prevailing rumors that encouragement and friendly counsel have not been lacking from the British diplomatic representative."[66] On December 16 a grateful Reza Shah responded to a message from King George of England: "I offer to Your Majesty my deep thanks for the friendly sentiments and congratulations that Your Majesty has expressed on the occasion of my accession to the Throne. I am absolutely confident that during my reign the good relations between the two countries will more than ever be furthered and strengthened. I take this occasion to express my and my people's good wishes for the prosperity of Your Majesty and the Royal Family, and for the splendor and greatness of the noble people of England. [Signed] Reza Shah."[67]

Commenting on the role of the British in this entire process, and the implication for American interests in Persia, a clearly angered Amory had some frank comments about the British success in "launching" the new dynasty:

The British are beginning to feel that the moment is ripening for them to make more active efforts to secure, over Dr. Millspaugh's head, openings for

British capital and contracts here. Their solicitude for the successful launching of the new government has become more and more evident. The impression is current that they have left no stone unturned during the last few weeks to make the new sovereign feel they are his friends and they alone can act the part of guide and counselor. The British Minister has been ever at hand to answer questions or give friendly counsel in regard to questions of technique and ceremonial which have recently arisen. He may be said to have driven a Pahlavi bandwagon vis-à-vis the diplomatic corps and his efforts in this respect have not been unsuccessful.[68]

Amory notes that the Russians were extremely unhappy at the success of the British in getting their man on the throne and that "Soviet attempts at subversive action are based on actions that appear crude and childish in comparison with the experienced dexterity of their British rivals."[69] The British role in bringing Reza Khan to the throne and the Soviet resentment of the British coup were also of concern to officials in Washington. Commenting on the accession of Reza Khan to the throne, Wallace S. Murray, former chargé d'affaires in Tehran and future chief of the Division of Near Eastern Affairs, writes: "While the British have shown themselves unwilling to support the Shah in his previous ambition to become President it is obvious that they were more than ready to support him in overthrowing the Kajar dynasty and ascending the throne himself. It cannot be overlooked that such a procedure was extremely distasteful to the Russians."[70]

The role of the British in helping Reza Khan to the throne and his British connection was repeatedly referred to by future American ministers in Tehran. The American minister from 1930 to 1933, Charles Calmer Hart, whose dispatches we shall cite repeatedly in this study, discusses British policy in Persia during 1921–1931: "The year 1921 had seen the Seiyed Zia-ed-Din coup d'état and the beginning of the dramatic rise of Reza Shah. On him the British counted on the success of their policy. They were not mistaken in his ability to rule."[71] William H. Hornibrook, the minister from 1934 to 1936, comments on the supposed "decline" of British influence in Iran:

The fact that the present Shah owes his throne to the British and the cabinet members owe their respective posts to the Shah is enough in itself to cause any prudent observer to stop, look and listen, before believing the myth that our British cousins have lost their influence in the Persian capital. I have taken the occasion to make a rather careful check on the British connections of the present members of the Cabinet. I am convinced that fully three-fourths of them may be definitely classified as pro-British, not from choice, but from fear. I have carefully, and I hope rather adroitly, sounded out a very considerable number of Persian officials on the subject of the British influence. My reaction is that they dislike the British, possibly more than the nationals of any other country, but they do fear them, and have a very wholesome respect for any recommendation which emanates from the British Legation. The intelligence department of the Anglo-Persian Oil Company is not as effective or as well manned as it was in the days of frank British domination of the Persian foreign policy, but it still functions and functions very effectively.[72]

CHAPTER FOUR

Millspaugh and the American Financial Mission to Persia, 1922–1927

*E*VER SINCE PERSIA'S BRIEF EXPERIENCE with Morgan Shuster, who was in charge of Persia's finances in 1911, the appointment of an American financial adviser was considered key to Persia's financial and political salvation. During the brief time he was in Persia, Shuster gained the trust and affection of its people. Moreover, America was seen as a possible counter to Britain and Russia. With the appointment of Qavam-es-Saltaneh as prime minister in May 1921 and the convening of the Fourth Majlis, the appointment of an American financial adviser was pursued in earnest. To his credit, and despite his pro-British past and the fact that he was a brother of Vossough-ed-Dowleh, Qavam attempted to free Iran from the British grip and the looming nightmare of the dictatorship of Reza Khan.

Qavam tried to bring Iran closer to the United States through the establishment of an American financial mission, which, it was believed, would lead to both the political and financial involvement of the United States in Iran at the expense of the British. This policy was naturally greatly resented by the British, who regarded Iran as their exclusive domain. They never forgave Qavam. By bringing about the establishment of an American mission, Qavam and the Majlis were clearly attempting to undo the fruits of the British coup. Little wonder that Qavam was to receive, as reported by the American consul Bernard Gotlieb, a physical thrashing from Reza Khan in the presence of Ahmad Shah (see chapter 5). Qavam had instructed Hossein Alai (subsequently Hossein Ala), Iran's minister in Washington, to pursue the matter of an American financial team and possible loans to Persia, and had described the hostility of the British minister in Tehran to the proposed American initiative. Qavam concluded his message with the following statement: "You must continue your activities with complete confidence. At this critical moment, the government and the Medjliss expect a speedy result from your efforts and anxiously await a material proof of America's goodwill toward Persia."[1]

As the desperate tone of Qavam's telegram clearly shows, obtaining an American loan, the appointment of American advisers, and the vain hope of "material proof of America's goodwill" were a futile attempt by Qavam and the Majlis to save Iran from the looming abyss of Reza Khan's dictatorship, which was being rapidly cemented with British help. Sadly for Persia, the proof of America's goodwill never came. Instead, it appears that the United States agreed with the British proposal "not to allow the Persians to play us off one against the other." British displeasure at possible American assistance to Persia was directly communicated by the British minister, Sir Percy Loraine, to the American chargé d'affaires in Tehran, C. Van H. Engert. The following telegram from Engert illustrates the point: "I have just received a private letter from the British Minister expressing surprise at resolution in Medjliss re loan because the Prime Minister 'has been discussing with me since my arrival the conditions on which my Government would be willing to facilitate an advance from British sources and also because of the understanding Sir Auckland Geddes has reached with the State Department not to allow the Persians to play us off one against the other.' I am reliably informed the Premier and the British Minister had virtually agreed on terms of a loan from Anglo-Persian."[2]

The Appointment of Millspaugh, 1922

Despite British opposition, Qavam proceeded with the appointment of a financial adviser from America. In another cable to Alai, Qavam instructed him to sign Millspaugh's contract immediately: "The Madjless approved in its sitting of to-day the 23rd of Assad [August 15th] the addition of the word 'appointment' to Art. 6 of the contract and powers of the Administrator General of Finances. You are to inform Dr. Millspaugh of this and to sign his contract without loss of time.—Ghavam-os-Saltaneh."[3] The person appointed Persia's administrator general of finances was Dr. Arthur Chester Millspaugh, a thirty-eight-year-old economist with a Ph.D. from Johns Hopkins University. In addition to being an academic, Millspaugh was also an economics consultant to the State Department, which had recommended his appointment. Millspaugh arrived in Persia in November

FIGURE 4.1 *Arthur Chester Millspaugh, administrator general of the finances of Persia, ca. 1925. Courtesy of the IICHS.*

1922 and departed in August 1927. Those responsible for his departure were called traitors to Persia.

From the beginning, Millspaugh was faced with the hostility of the British and that of their chosen instrument, Reza Khan. It is usual to acknowledge the role of Qavam in the Azerbaijan Crisis of 1946–47. His brave efforts to spare Iran from the impending brutal military dictatorship also deserve recognition. The British set about sabotaging the work of the mission from the beginning, and thus the failure of the mission was a forgone conclusion. With the support and encouragement of his British protectors, Reza Khan also set about wrecking the American financial mission.

In his 1946 book, Millspaugh berates himself for having been an unwitting instrument in solidifying Reza Khan's dictatorship: "Our financial reforms helped Reza to consolidate his dictatorship."[4] The Millspaugh mission, however, had the effect of incurring the intense interest of the State Department and that of the American legation. A rich source of archival documentation was thus generated by the correspondence involving Millspaugh, the American legation in Tehran, and the State Department. In addition, Millspaugh's quarterly reports on economic and financial conditions in Persia during 1923–27 contain much general, social, economic, and political information.

British Hostility to Millspaugh and the American Mission

From the outset, American officials were keenly aware of British hostility to the American mission and to Millspaugh. The records clearly indicate that American patience was tested over British intrigue against the American team. Thomas R. Owens, American consul in Baghdad, refers to the British attitude to Millspaugh: "Many of the British in Bagdad have expressed the hope that the efforts of the American Advisers will be crowned with success, but most of these expressions are obviously insincere and ironical. All indications point to the fact that the British really hope that the mission will fail and are insidiously working to bring about the desired end."[5] By July 1923, barely six months after the arrival of the American mission, Minister Joseph Kornfeld was expressing his extreme pessimism: "Unfortunately, every recommendation for the thorough-going reformation of the Persian finances meets with decided opposition."[6] A few days later, Kornfeld again expressed his unhappiness with the British: "Relations between Millspaugh and foreign representatives cordial. British particularly affectionate, decidedly to the detriment of mission. Intention of British sinister. Having been unable to prevent mission from coming they deliberately set to work to use them and at the same time to destroy them. Unfortunately they are succeeding. The Persian Government not disposed to follow Millspaugh's advice unquestionably. Recently when in the presence of Council of Ministers he urged collection of taxes on opium in Ispahan [Esfahan], Prime Minister Moshir-ed-Dowleh declared it was a political matter and therefore outside the former's province."[7] The British were also openly threatening the American advisers that they would behave toward Millspaugh as they had toward Shuster. Kornfeld lost no time in informing the State Department: "British will support advisers only so long as it serves their purpose. Legation's despatch 205 en route reports conversation wherein secretary of British Legation said to American municipal expert who would not exempt British or any foreign subjects from road tax that if the mission persisted in its attitude towards the British they would be forced to take the position they assumed toward Shuster. Belgian charge' d'Affaires told secretary of our Legation that assistant manager of Imperial Bank of Persia stated to him in confidence that if the Persian delegation comes to London for a loan the first demand would be dismissal of American advisers."[8]

The manner in which the British sabotaged the American team is outlined in a dispatch from Bernard Gotlieb, American consul in Tehran. He states that on June 21, 1923, the Majlis passed a bill authorizing Dr. Millspaugh to borrow $5 million for the Persian government from banks in the United States. Of 73 deputies, 50 voted in favor. However, the next day, the following amendment was passed by the Majlis: "The $5,000,000 mentioned in Article 1 will be repaid (including interest) out of the revenues of the country with the exception of the revenues from the Anglo-Persian Oil Co." Thus, the British had effectively vetoed an American loan. Gotlieb reports that no American financial institution was likely to make a loan of this magnitude unless it was secured by oil revenues.

The sabotaging of the loan occasioned angry comments on British policy in Persia: "Thus Persia's one gilt-edged security cannot be utilized in this connection. There seems to be little doubt that the oil royalties are being reserved for the $10,000,000 loan which is to be made in connection with the North Persian oil concession when granted." The $10 million loan was to be a British loan in exchange for granting Britain the oil concession to the remaining five northern provinces. Commenting on the advisability of giving a loan of $5 million without using oil revenues as security, Gotlieb adds, "I do not believe that Persia's political stability is such as to justify any such investment. Four years elapsed between convocation of the last Medjliss and its predecessor and there is no certainty that a similar period may not elapse before a new Medjliss comes into being. The reins of government are virtually in the hands of one man, the Minister of War, the cabinet changes are kaleidoscopic, and it would need very little pressure from circumstances to result in its transformation into a military dictatorship in name as well as in reality."[9] Already in July 1923, several months before the appointment of Reza Khan as prime minister, in October 1923, it was clear to Gotlieb as well as to others where Persia was heading.

British intrigue against the American mission included attacks by newspapers financed by the British, as well as hostility from and sabotage by such cabinet ministers as Modir-ol-Molk, a known British agent. The press assaults continued unabated. In June 1924 a series of articles in the handful of the newspapers permitted to function by Reza Khan violently attacked Millspaugh and the American mission. Given that the newspapers functioned at the pleasure of the British, through Reza Khan, no one could doubt the source of the attacks. Kornfeld reports:

Arbab Khaikosrow and Zoka-ol-Molk were not so optimistic. While both felt that these attacks were inspired by the British, they regretted that Dr. Millspaugh's conduct was not beyond criticism. In the two conferences that I had with Dr. Millspaugh, he spoke very freely regarding the difficulties of his task, the chief of which was the opposition of Modir-ol-Molk, the Minister of Finance. In view of the fact that Modir-ol-Molk is known to be very friendly to the British, his antagonism to the American financial mission is construed by Dr. Millspaugh as reflecting British attitude. As an example of how the British work with and through Modir-ol-Molk, Colonel MacCormack, a member of the financial mission, told Mr. Murray, Secretary of the Legation, that several days ago while visiting Modir-ol-Molk, he saw a note addressed to him by Mr. Havard, the British Oriental Secretary, requesting that certain Government land that the advisers had taken from a prominent Persian because of the ridiculously low rent he had paid in the past, be returned to him at the same low rent. Dr. Millspaugh feels that there is a decided connection between this attack on the advisers and the present British protests against every American project in Persia.[10]

In his search for possible reasons, Kornfeld displayed the extent of his unhappiness at British policy in Persia, and of their opposition to the American advisers:

I have the honor to state that the views expressed by me regarding the attitude of the British towards the American advisers are amply supported by facts. The opposition of the British to the engagement of the American advisers is clearly shown in the enclosed copy of a telegram which the Persian Minister in Washington received from the Persian Prime Minister on January 15, 1922. The fact that, subsequently, the British expressed their approval of the engagement of the advisers does not in any means prove that they were favorable to it. They simply made a virtue of necessity. The reservation with which the British gave their consent is indicated in the very carefully prepared statement made by Sir Percy Loraine [sic], the British Minister in Teheran, to Mr. John Clayton of the Chicago Tribune. In that formula, it is nothing less than that, the Minister made British support of the advisers conditional on their observance of the "strictest impartiality towards foreign interests in Persia." By "foreign interests" was of course meant British interests. Though it would appear that the British Empire, being Persia's largest creditor and one of her neighbors, has a real interest in the reorganization of the finances of Persia, I regret to state that such is not the case. Persia's interests and Great Britain's interests in Persia are by no means identical. A Persia regenerated and strong would be in a position to assert herself and thereby set an example for India, which could hardly be viewed with favor by the British. Again, Persia regenerated would of necessity weaken British control in the southern part of Persia, the region of the Anglo-Persian oil fields, at present practically a British province. Again, if through the success of the American advisers, American capital felt justified in entering largely into Persia's economic life, the Imperial Bank of Persia could not manipulate the rise and fall of the kran absolutely regardless of the market price of silver. To my mind, to the extent that the American financial mission may try to make Persia more prosperous and independent, they will run counter to British interests, and consequently incur their opposition. While this opposition may not necessarily cause the defeat of the mission, it will have to be reckoned with and should be taken into account before America decides to make large commitments in Persia.[11]

The matter of British hostility to the American financial mission is also repeatedly referred to by Wallace S. Murray, chargé d'affaires ad interim, who was in charge of the American legation after Kornfeld.

> The combination of the outward espousal of the American Financial Mission by the British, together with the latter's covert obstruction to all it has attempted to accomplish, has gone far to bring their work to a standstill. This latter activity, Dr. Millspaugh now feels, has been carried out in large part by the former Minister of Finance, Modir-ol-Molk, a British appointee in the last cabinet, and who has now, fortunately, been dismissed. So convinced did Dr. Millspaugh become of the fact that the principal opposition to his work emanated from the British that he prepared at the beginning of last June a memorandum to the effect for the State Department which he showed to the American Minister, to Mr. Soper, the Sinclair representative, and to the late Vice Consul Imbrie, but which he never had the courage to despatch to its destination.[12]

Reza Khan's Hostility to Millspaugh

A main reason for Reza Khan's hostility to the recently appointed American financial mission was that from the very beginning Reza Khan wanted total control over public funds and with no accountability on how the funds were spent. Millspaugh and the financial mission were a serious obstacle to Reza Khan's designs. Millspaugh's relations with Reza Khan had been uneasy from the very beginning. In addition, Reza Khan had been emboldened in his dealings with the Americans because of the British hostility to the American mission. Millspaugh's attempts to curtail the amount of money allocated to the army, the police, and the gendarmerie (*amnieh*), instruments of coercion that sustained Reza Khan's power, created tension between Millspaugh and Reza Khan. That the maintenance of such a large army was a serious waste of resources was well recognized by observers. In his report on the military, Murray observes:

> One cannot but ask, after some observations of the present-day situation in Persia, why an army at all! And above all why one that consumes one half of the country's annual revenues? It is perfectly obvious that Persia is neither in a financial nor economic position to afford such a luxury. While draining her Treasury and depriving the farms of much needed agricultural workers, she has created neither an army that could meet alone any of her neighbors, nor one in fact that has proved its ability entirely to put down tribal rebellions in the country such as those of the Kurds and Lurs. Well-wishers of Persia cannot but regret that she has not seen the wisdom of disbanding her "army" and organizing a capable Gendarmerie of from ten to fifteen thousand men well equipped, specially trained for tribal warfare, and supplied with first rate

motor transportation to effect their rapid displacement. Such hopes are of
course in vain as long as Sardar Sepah [Reza Khan] lives; he has created the
present army, imperfect as it is, and will never consent to its reduction. However bad the Shah's [Ahmed Shah's] regime has been, but few Persians are persuaded that Sardar Sepah's would, in the long run, be an improvement.[13]

Murray also comments that the Persian army was useless because of the
six highest army commanders (*emir lashgars*), only one had any real military training and education. The remaining five emir lashgars, like Reza
Khan, lacked education and consisted of "former N.C.O.'s or petty officers
of the Cossack Brigade who were personal friends of Reza Khan before his
rise to power."[14] The outright incompetence and cowardice of these emir
lashgars was to be fully demonstrated in August 1941 at the Allied invasion of Iran, when this "national" army proved totally useless. Despite
Millspaugh's attempts to curtail military and quasi-military allocations (as
noted by Murray), 50 to 60 percent of total government funds were allocated to the army, police, and gendarmerie.

It was inevitable that, with Reza Khan's "educational and cultural shortcomings," education was not going to receive priority (see table 4.1). The
figures are only out of the regular budget and do not include expenditures
out of the oil revenues that were supposedly spent on armaments. The
budgetary allocation to the army, police, and gendarmerie in that year was
over 125 million krans, or 45 percent of the total budget. But in addition,
60 million krans (£1.2 million) was also "voted" from the oil revenues
banked in London to be spent for arms purchases. When this sum is also
added to the regular budgetary appropriations, total army, police and gendarmerie appropriations came to 67 percent of the budget. In contrast,
expenditure on education was one-fourteenth of the sums squandered on
the armed forces, whose sole purpose was to maintain the Pahlavi regime
in power. A consequence of this educational neglect, Millspaugh observes,
was that after twenty years of Reza Khan, "The masses of the Persian people are still largely illiterate and densely ignorant. . . . Yet the process of
educating the masses has hardly started and has not yet made any percep-
tible impression."[15]

Not only was the bulk of the budget allocated for the instruments of
coercion, Reza Khan insisted on no budgetary control or oversight by
Millspaugh and the Ministry of Finance, because army matters were supposedly secret. Millspaugh's insistence on instituting some degree of financial control and accountability, including an accounting for the gold and
valuables plundered from the tribes by Reza Khan and his army, resulted in
some acrimonious exchanges between Reza Khan and Millspaugh, and at
least one incident of murder of a Persian government employee who had
supplied Majlis deputy Seyed Hassan Modarres and Millspaugh with
information on financial irregularities in the Ministry of War. In order to

TABLE 4.1. Appropriations for army, police, and gendarmerie, 1925–1928 (in krans)

	1925/26	1926/27	1927/28	1928/29[a]
Ministry of War	94,000,000	94,000,000	98,000,000	98,000,000
Police	11,460,386	11,615,577	12,048,224	15,194,636
Gendarmerie (Amnieh)	5,580,000	5,580,000	5,580,000	2,211,600
Education	7,731,380	9,935,138	11,719,725	13,722,730
Total budget	246,159,072	241,215,026	243,130,815	276,828,377

[a] Projected.

Sources: Twentieth Quarterly Report of the Administrator General of Finance, June 23–September 23, 1927 (891.51/416); Twenty-first Quarterly Report of the Administrator General of Finance, September 24–December 22, 1927 (891.51/417).

discourage other government employees who contemplated providing financial information to the likes of Modarres and Millspaugh, the decapitated body of the offending accountant was placed outside the gates of the Majlis. Few could afford to ignore the message. Fortunately for historians of Iran, all this is recorded by Millspaugh's meticulous reporting and memoranda to the State Department.

Violence and Intimidation against Members of the Financial Team

Millspaugh's relations with Reza Khan, however, had a brief initial cordial phase because at first Millspaugh had caved in to Reza's financial demands. However, as Reza Khan's demands increased, the relationship quickly deteriorated. Kornfeld states: "Just now he [Millspaugh] has the support of the Minister of War whom he has guaranteed 750,000 tomans monthly. To meet expenses the government received two million tomans from the Imperial Bank of Persia against the Anglo-Persian royalties."[16] The cordial relations between Reza Khan and Millspaugh were short-lived. True to his character, to obtain more funds, Reza Khan, minister of war, resorted to physical intimidation and violence against the Americans. The beating of a Belgian employee of the Ministry of Finance by two of Reza Khan's Cossacks and the extortion of money out of the employee are described by Kornfeld, who goes on to report that Reza Khan's normal practice of extracting money through violence and intimidation had also been tried on Millspaugh, but with less success:

I have the honor to advise the Department that on the evening of August 14 a report came to me that on the morning of that day two Cossacks appeared in the office of Dr. Millspaugh, in the Ministry of Finance, and demanded in the name of the Minister of War [Reza Khan] the immediate payment of a substantial sum of money which the Ministry of Finance owed the Ministry of War.

Failing to receive a favorable response, the officers became violently abusive and threatened to close the Ministry of Finance. Finding Dr. Millspaugh, and his associates, quite calm under this show of force, the officers left without carrying out their threat. Thereupon, Dr. Millspaugh sent his chief interpreter to the Minister of War with a strong note of protest against this indignity. The Minister of War, outraged by the high-handed actions of the officers, ordered that they be severely punished, and sent Dr. Millspaugh an apology as well as his assurances of his whole-hearted cooperation. In order to have this report verified, I requested Mr. Wallace S. Murray, the Secretary of the Legation, to arrange a conference with Mr. Thomas Pearson, Secretary of Dr. Millspaugh, who was present at the incident, and therefore would be in a position to give an accurate account of what actually occurred.

Having verified the incident by Pearson and others, Kornfeld continues:

> Despite the protestation of the Minister of War of his innocence as well as ignorance of the whole affair, I am fully convinced that he had authorized the officers to do just exactly what they did. He had done exactly the same thing on several occasions with the Belgian functionaries and unquestionably, had he succeeded, he would not have been so very anxious to disavow his connection with the affair. But having found himself foiled, he naturally must seek to reinstate himself in the favor of the advisers by repudiating the action of his subordinates.[17]

After Ahmad Shah was forced to appoint Reza Khan to the post of prime minister in October 1923, and leave Iran never to return, the position of the American financial team was further weakened:

> I have the honor to advise the Department that, since becoming Prime Minister, Reza Khan has shown a contemptuous disregard of Dr. Millspaugh, the American Administrator General of Finances. The following incidents indicative of his attitude have been brought to my attention. First. After the death of Dr. Ryan, the finances of the Municipality of Teheran were so recklessly handled that, at the insistence of the Imperial Bank of Persia, in order to protect its loan, they were entrusted to Dr. Millspaugh. On becoming Prime Minister, Reza Khan issued an order that all beggars should be removed from the streets of Teheran and maintained at the expense of the Municipality. Dr. Millspaugh took exception to the Prime Minister's utter disregard of the financial advisers in failing to consult him regarding this additional burden on the Municipality. He pointed out that, with the existing obligations, the Municipality could not undertake this additional expense. That Dr. Millspaugh correctly presented the situation is clearly proved by the fact that the Prime Minister has made a private appeal for funds to support this reform. This however does not prove that the Prime Minister accepted Dr. Millspaugh's advice in a kindly spirit. On the contrary. I am reliably informed that he spoke very harshly of this attempt on the part of Dr. Millspaugh to "meddle in the affairs of the municipality" of which the Prime Minister is, by virtue of his office, the President.
>
> Second. According to the Civil Service Law, no foreigner may be in the service of the Government unless he is in possession of a contract approved by

Parliament. In the execution of this law, Dr. Millspaugh dismissed Shapurgu Bomangu Morris, a Parsee Indian, and therefore a British subject. Though only a minor official in charge of the provisions in a Government warehouse, he [Morris] succeeded in securing an audience with the Prime Minister. Without consulting Dr. Millspaugh, the latter gave instructions to the immediate superior of the discharged employee to reinstate him at once. In this instance, the Prime Minister clearly violated not only Dr. Millspaugh's contract but also the law forbidding the employment of foreigners.[18]

The American Consulate in Tehran also took a grim view of the situation and the prospects for the American financial mission. A report by Consul Gotlieb examines the relationship between the American advisers and Reza Khan since the latter's appointment as prime minister in October 1923. Having described Reza's brutish instincts, Gotlieb feared for the physical safety of the Americans:

> The Advisers themselves are in an extremely pessimistic frame of mind and prepared for any contingency. I firmly believe that if things keep on as they are, there is a very fair prospect of the Mission abandoning its work within the next six months. Their departure will be a sad blow to American prestige locally, but to speak in all frankness, their failure after the first few months was a foregone conclusion. They were attempting a superhuman piece of work with every card stacked against them. In the first place, they were not really wanted in their capacity as advisers by those few Persians who were in control of affairs and whose attitude and cooperation counted more than that of the ignorant masses, or of the few dilettante reformers who had returned from European universities to seek posts in their own country. Those directing Persia's affairs were well aware that she could not go much longer without a loan—and that no loan was obtainable from any but British sources, unless something like stable guarantees were offered. What could be better calculated to elicit ready response from American financiers than the assurance that their loans would be employed productively, under the supervision of American financiers. But the loans have not been forthcoming, and this disappointment, coupled with the unfortunate failure of the Advisers to institute striking reforms which might have served to reinforce their position, has not improved matters any. As the exactions of Reza Khan on behalf of his army and the consolidation of his own influence increase, the general desire for loans diminishes, however, because of the conviction that the bulk of any sum obtained will merely go into the Premier's pockets.
>
> The Advisers found a personnel already stocked with interpreters, counselors, confidential secretaries in the employ of the British Legation. British prestige was not especially enhanced by the collapse of the Anglo-Persian Agreement or the unceremonious dismissal of the Armitage-Smith financial mission. It is readily comprehensible that failure on the part of the Americans who came to replace them would serve by contrast to restore British prestige. Their policy of obstruction during the last half year has not been especially pronounced, however. They are lying back, waiting with folded hands for the

Advisers to accomplish their own downfall. An impartial observer of the situation is forced to the conclusion that no foreigner can control Persia's financial destinies unless he has armed force, or the threat of it, behind him. True, up to the present time, the Advisers have had the support of Reza's army, without which they would be powerless. But to what avail, if the instrument of revenue collection consumes a disproportionate share of its own gleanings (nine million tomans was the last army budget). Dr. Millspaugh has not, and cannot have, the support of his own government in the same fashion that a British financial adviser would have backing of his program by London.[19]

The Plunder of Azerbaijani Tribes by Reza Khan, 1923–1924

By late summer of 1924, relations between Millspaugh and Reza Khan had deteriorated badly. An endemic problem was the matter of the budget of the Ministry of War. Another problem was Millspaugh's insistence that Reza Khan provide an accounting of the gold and valuables that had been seized by the army from the tribes of Azerbaijan, in particular what had become of the jewelry and valuables taken from Eqbal-ol-Saltaneh, a tribal chief in Maku.

In 1923, Reza Khan's army conquered the tribes of Azerbaijan, confiscating their lands and looting their valuables. An inquiry on the part of Dr. Millspaugh as to what had become of the valuables seized brought a sharp response from Reza Khan. The subject is discussed in several diplomatic dispatches and it is possible to construct a body of evidence. Moreover, long after their "pacification," Reza Khan's exactions from these unfortunate tribal people continued. In November 1924, representatives of the Shahsavan tribes of Azerbaijan arrived in Tehran, as noted by Murray: "A picturesque episode of this struggle of the 'robber barons' was the arrival in Teheran on November 25 of a delegation of Shahsavan and other tribes of Azarbaijan which Sardar Sepah more than a year ago succeeded in disarming and subjecting to his will. These hardy mountaineer warriors had come to Teheran for the purpose of presenting to Sardar Sepah a magnificent jeweled dagger as a sign of their recognition of him as their suzerain overlord."[20]

On August 17, Millspaugh wrote to the Ministry of War asking what had become of the exactions collected by the army from the Azerbaijan tribes:

Ministry of War:
    Several months ago, the Ministry of War delivered to the Mint a certain number of foreign coins apparently received by the Army in Azarbaijan. After reminting, the Mint delivered to the Army an amount of Krs. 61231.65 and I am informed that the Ministry of War sold to a money-changer an amount of Krs. 120,000. The amount of Krs. 181,231.65 has not yet been accounted for by your Ministry. If the above amount was received by the Army from any other source than the Treasury-General, it should, of course, have been delivered to

the Treasury-General as revenue, according to the law. Therefore, unless your Ministry can show that the above-mentioned amount was received in accordance with a legal authorization, it will be my duty to deduct this amount from the Saratan [June-July] budget of your Ministry. I hope you will give me full information at the earliest possible date.

—A. C. Millspaugh, Administrator General of Finances[21]

Millspaugh's inquiry brought a sharp response from Reza Khan:

The Administrator General of Finances

In reply to your letter No. 3829 concerning foreign coins and their minting into Persian coins, I have to say that as the said affair relates to the internal matters of the Ministry of War the Ministry of Finance shall not have any interference in that.

—REZA, Minister of War and Commander-in-Chief of the Army.[22]

The above correspondence will be particularly illuminating when it is reflected that we have not yet received any accounts whatever from the Ministry of War, that it is common knowledge that economies could be made in the Ministry of War to the amount of probably 200,000 tomans a month and that the Army has collected property and funds, which it has not turned over to the Treasury, vastly in excess of the amount which I mention in my letter No. 3829. I desire also to call to your attention that, after agreeing upon a budget of 9,400,000 for the present year, the Ministry of War sent to the Medjliss, without consultation with me, a proposal for an additional credit of 500,000 tomans. It is also desirable for you to know that, having failed after efforts extending over the whole period of our stay in Persia, to compel the Ministry of Posts and Telegraphs to subject itself to our control as regards its revenues and expenditures, I gave that Ministry an order to pay the Ministry of War an amount of tomans 125,000 on account of the War budget for Saratan [June-July].

Instead of using the authority which he presumably possesses over the Ministries, the Minister of War, who is also the President of the Council, refuses to compel the Ministry of Posts and Telegraphs to pay this sum to the Ministry of War. In other words, he expects us to pay the budget of the Ministry of War even though he does not assist us in controlling the revenues and expenditures of the Ministry of Posts and Telegraphs; he expects us to pay the full budget of the Ministry of War, which amounts to 45 per cent of the total budget of the Government, even though we are already behind a full month in our payments of the expenses of the Government and face a deficit of at least one million tomans; he expects us to pay also the full amount of any additional credits he may obtain from the Medjliss; and, finally, he expects us to do all of these things without any examination of the accounts of the Ministry of War and without asking the Ministry of War to deliver to the Treasury the money which it has illegally received. It is obvious that such unreasonable demands on the Treasury, without any corresponding assistance in the collection and control of the revenue, will render impossible any effective work by us toward putting the finances on a sound basis.[23]

Murray subsequently discussed with Millspaugh the looting of the tribes by the army. He then spoke of the subject with Zoka-ol-Molk Foroughi, Reza Khan's finance minister, and the contents of both conversations are included in his dispatch of September 24, 1924:

Again on September 5, in a conference with Dr. Millspaugh, he expatiated on the impossibility of continuing further his activity as Administrator General of Finances unless a radical change in the mind and attitude of the Prime Minister [Reza Khan] meanwhile intervened. He complained bitterly of the latter's selfishness in insisting, despite all difficulties facing the advisers, that no diminution be made in the War Ministry's budget and showed me a communication from Sardar Sepah [Reza Khan] rebuking him for even suggesting that, owing to the impending deficit of a million dollars in the present fiscal year, it would be necessary to reduce the budgets of all Ministries including that of War. Dr. Millspaugh at the same time showed me a second communication from Sardar Sepah administering a further rebuke as a result of an inquiry on the part of the Administrator General into the disposition of large sums of gold and silver bullion which the Persian military is alleged to have captured and appropriated for its own needs during last year's campaign in Azarbaidjan when the rich tribal chief, Eghbal-os-Saltaneh, the Turco-Kurdish chief of Maku, and the Shahsevan Turkish chiefs were conquered and forced to disgorge their ill-gotten wealth. The sharpness of Sardar Sepah's rebuke with regard to these spoils is no doubt to be explained from the fact that this very question of confiscated spoils was to have been the subject of the Minority's interpolation of the Government which failed to take place on August 19. It is reasonable to suppose that the Prime Minister immediately suspected the Administrator General of having connived with the Minority to embarrass him. He further pointed out that he considered the unwarranted action of the Prime Minister in submitting to the Medjliss, some months ago, a bill for an additional credit of 500,000 tomans to the Ministry of War for expenses incurred in crushing the rebellion in Luristan.

As Dr. Millspaugh sees it, the Prime Minister wants the Government to foot the bills over and above his already large budget, for all military campaigns and allow him to pocket, for his own personal use, all the spoils. In the opinion of the Administrator General, if Persia is to be rescued from her present desperate financial straits, it will be necessary to reduce the budget of the Ministry of War one million tomans each year until it has reached the sum of six million tomans which he considers a reasonable sum for the maintenance of an army of 30,000 to 40,000 men.[24]

The next day, September 25, Murray held a conversation with Foroughi. Murray's dispatch records the contents of that discussion, including Foroughi's response to the looting of the tribes by Reza Khan:

With regards to the appropriation of Sardar Sepah of the gold and silver captured from Eghbal-ol-Saltaneh, he expressed little concern and even ignorance of the actual amount, adding that the conquest of Azarbaijan was of such infinitely greater importance inasmuch as this province was, for the first time in the last years, paying taxes to the central Government instead of absorbing funds from that source for its maintenance. He called my attention to the fact further that although the Prime Minister might have kept for his personal use the gold and silver captured, he had nevertheless confiscated and turned over to the Government all the properties of this rich tribal chief.[25]

Millspaugh's Confidential Letter to Dulles about Reza Khan

On September 20 Millspaugh wrote two letters to Allen W. Dulles, chief of the Division of Near Eastern Affairs, one of which was a fifteen-page confidential exposé of the situation in Persia and the difficulties of the American financial mission. The first three pages of this document (written entirely on the official stationary of the Ministry of Finance) deal with relations between the American legation and the financial mission. The remainder of the letter describes the actions of Reza Khan and conditions in Iran. Some excerpts from this lengthy document are given. By 1924, Reza Khan was already transferring large sums to foreign banks. Millspaugh also describes the gruesome murder of an accountant in the Ministry of War who had been supplying information to Modarres and the American financial mission. The prime minister, minister of war, and Sardar Sepah referred to in the letter are all Reza Khan:

> Practically all of the present difficulties of the American Mission pertain to the relations of the Mission with the present Prime Minister. It should be clearly kept in mind, of course, that the present Prime Minister, Sardar Sepah, has been Minister of War since the arrival of the American Mission and in fact for some time previously. From the start, we adopted the policy of conciliating the Minister of War in order to obtain military assistance in the collection of taxes. It was also naturally our purpose to provide for the adequate financing of the Army in order to maintain security and order in the country. We realized that the budget of the Army was too large, amounting as it did and still does to almost 50 per cent of the budget of the country. We felt that certain waste of money by the Ministry of War could be overlooked in order to establish the American Mission and get its work started. It is evident, however, that a mission which has undertaken the task of putting the country's finances on a sound foundation and establishing its credit abroad cannot indefinitely overlook waste of funds, particularly when the assistance which is expected is not forthcoming and when certain economies become vital to the work of the Mission.
>
> If the disproportionate budget of the Ministry of War is not sufficient evidence, the unnecessary expenditure will be made clear when it is known that the present Prime Minister, who a few years ago was a Cossack private standing guard at the gate of the British Legation, now owns two houses in Teheran, several villages in Mazandaran, and a fleet of automobiles; that, according to reliable information, he sent several months ago a sum of money, possibly as much

FIGURE 4.2 *Reza Khan on sentry duty at a European legation before the coup d'état. Courtesy of the IICHS.*

FIGURE 4.3 *Reza Khan with a newly acquired Rolls-Royce, 1921. Before the coup the car belonged to Nosrat-ed-Dowleh Firouz. Courtesy of the IICHS.*

as $200,000, to Europe; that he made a "gift" of 40,000 tomans to the Ministry of Public Instruction; that it was his habit, according to reliable information, to go to the treasury of the Ministry of War and take out rolls of bills without counting them; that it is notorious that the principal officers of the Army have become wealthy in the last few years; that purchases have been made of aeroplanes, tanks, armored cars and wireless equipment which, while conceivably useful, are not indispensable; and that, finally, the Ministry of War has never rendered any accounts to the Ministry of Finance although such accounts were promised by Sardar Sepah in his first interview with me. When the budget of 1303 (the present fiscal year, 1924) was under preparation, I talked with the Minister of War and induced him to consent to a budget of tomans 9,400,000 for the Ministry of War, the same as the budget of the previous year. The budget of 1303, however, included provisions for new taxes estimated to produce 1,000,000 tomans and I made clear to Sardar Sepah that if we did not get the revenue we could not pay the proposed expenses. He accepted the budget and promised to get the tax projects through the Madjless. Then the Madjless met, and instead of showing any interest whatever in the budget or the tax projects he wasted valuable weeks in attempting to coerce the Madjless into establishing a Republic (i.e., a Dictatorship).

He had in the meantime, as Prime Minister, loaded us down with a Minister of Finance named Modir-ol-Molk whose one aim was to create difficulties and embarrassment for the Americans. He not only kept this man in office after his actions had been repeatedly called to the Prime Minister's attention but the Prime Minister, in striking contrast with other Prime Ministers, studiously avoided calling me into consultation on financial questions but proceeded on the assumption that I was subject to his orders even with regard to matters which had been clearly placed within my jurisdiction in my contract. After the Republican movement had been disposed of by the Madjless, the Deputies took up the consideration of the budget and at the same time, instigated I am sure by Modir-ol-Molk, launched a series of stupid criticisms and attacks against the American Mission. A month or two of this sort of thing, after the Budget Commission had rejected the proposals for new revenue and had started to reduce the budget of the Ministry of Finance, I went to the Prime Minister and told him plainly that we could not succeed under such conditions. As a result of my interview with him, he ordered his Ministers to give us support, silenced the newspapers and published in the newspapers a signed statement to the effect that the Government was thoroughly satisfied with the work of the American Mission. After this, the open criticisms and attacks on the part of the deputies ceased to a large extent, but the Budget Commission still showed no inclination to reduce the expenditures of the Government or even to pass the budget in any form.

At about this time, Modares, the leader of the Minority, feeling the strength which he had gained as a result of his part in defeating the Republican movement, began to intimate privately that the budget of the Ministry of War should be reduced and a gelatin statement appeared setting forth the actual necessary expenditures of the Ministry of War totaling about 6,000,000 tomans a year. A few days after this statement appeared, a decapitated body was found outside one of the gates which was identified as the body of one of the accountants of the Ministry of War who, it is generally understood, prepared the statement referred to. Persians are terrorized. I have reason to believe that the stand we are taking is generally approved by the people and by the Deputies, but no one will publicly approve of it and only the most reckless boys will state to us that they approve of it. It is not to be expected that any Persian will go to the American Legation and express approval of the reduction of the War budget. I wish the Department to realize, therefore, that any yielding by us on this point now will not only create serious fiscal difficulties for us but will also be interpreted as weakness on our part and will actually result in the weakening of the position of the American Mission more than it is now weakened.[26]

When decapitated bodies begin to appear, as they did outside the gates of the Majlis, what parliament and people would not be terrorized? With such tactics, there was no possibility that the vastly inflated budget of the Ministry of War would not be approved, as Murray describes: "I have the honor to inform the Department that in an emergency session of the Medjliss on December 2, the budget of the Ministry of War for (the rest of) the present fiscal year ending March 21, 1925 and amounting to Tomans 9,200,000 was approved separately by a substantial majority." Despite the appearance of the accountant's body, some deputies courageously opposed the vote:

In an emergency session, held in the afternoon of December 2, parliament passed by 77 votes the budget of the Ministry of War. The Minority deputies, such as Saeem, Haeri Zadeh, and Modarres, were violently opposed to the passage of the budget, arguing that the appropriations of Tomans 9,200,000 was much in excess of the needs of the Ministry of War. Haeri Zadeh proposed that it be cut down to Tomans 6,000,000, stating that the actual number of troops in the Persian army was 20,000. Modarres believed that the Army did not contain more than 18,000 men and that there were too many "Marshals" in the army. Sardar Moazam, Minister of Public Works, declared that there actually were 42,000 men in the army and that there was not one officer who was not needed. In its bill asking for the passage of the budget, the Government stated to Parliament that the payment of the expenses of the Ministry of War and the salaries of the soldiers was of urgent importance.[27]

The Army's Extortion and Looting of Civilians: Fars and Khorassan

The day after the approval of the Ministry of War budget, Murray discovered other facets of Reza Khan's behavior:

On December 3, 1924, I was informed by Dr. Millspaugh that Sardar Sepah on his triumphal "march to the sea" had requisitioned funds from the financial agents and customs authorities at Isfahan and Bushire amounting to Tomans

27,000 which had been promptly charged to his account. Monsieur de Kerckheer, the Belgian Acting Director of Customs, a functionary of long experience in Persia, wisely ordered that all customs collection at Bushire be transmitted to the capital without delay when he learned that Sardar Sepah contemplated visiting the city. The instructions arrived too late however to save about Tomans 2,000 seized by the army.[28]

After Reza Khan's "triumphal march to the sea," and visit to Bushire, a detachment of the army had been stationed there. George Gregg Fuller, American vice consul in Bushire, reveals that after the pacification and looting of the unfortunate tribal population, it was then the turn of the civilians in urban areas. Fuller's dispatch is reproduced in full:

I have the honor to report several recent events which show that the Persian army is not yet the unmixed blessing a person in Teheran is led to believe. It has made transportation safer and enabled the collection of greater revenues, but the arbitrary action of men and officers is creating great dissatisfaction in the remoter provinces. Bushire offers a good opportunity to understand military conduct in the provinces. The main difficulty is that the troops' pay is six months in arrears, although some units have been paid up to four months. They are always penniless or in debt, so their undisputed power is their chief source of income. The vacant house of a wealthy merchant was commandeered for the temporary use of officers, and no compensation was offered—or expected. Goods are taken from the bazaars as fancy indicates, and the transfer of the units will relieve them of the necessity of payment. The taxi drivers were forced to carry so many free army passengers that, whereas taxis could formerly be obtained anywhere, they have completely disappeared and no one would think of restarting such a business.

Transportation from Bushire to Shiraz and the interior has always been more or less insecure because of brigandage by the tribes. The Persian army now controls this route, but shippers are little better off than before. The merchandise is not stolen but the donkeys and mules are commandeered by the army and only released on the payment of a large ransom. The result is that charvedars [muleteers] are refusing to transport merchandise. A large number of bales and boxes are lying here because caravans will not start. One European firm alone has 500 packages coming from Shiraz for which three different waybills have been received—each time the shipment has been started the animals were taken by the army and the goods dumped beside the trail.

A recent order increased annoyance to anger. Some imported French aeroplanes would not fly, so they were entrusted to the humbler but dependable porters and mules for delivery at Shiraz. The mules could not object, but the more experienced porters refused the untempting government offers. In desperation orders were issued to empress enough men, so troops scoured the city, seizing everybody with democratic justice,—tribal visitors, domestic servants, and respectable merchants. Although a good profit was realized from the seizure of wealthier merchants, others were forced to labor under the hot sun

for a bit of bread and water daily. Foreign business houses sent searchers to rescue their employees, and officials demanded the release of their servants. All
who could do so escaped from the town, or found concealment in harems. The
nomads whose tents are pitched outside the city took refuge inside this consulate. Thus the first time the Persian Government has stationed troops in
Bushire has not increased its popularity. All the censure is directed against the
Prime Minister [Reza Khan] personally for these actions.[29]

With the elevation of Reza Khan to the throne of Persia in December
1925, and his subsequent coronation in April 1926, the matter of extortion
and misconduct by his army reached new heights. What the so-called
national army did to the people of Mashhad is described by Hoffman
Philip, the American minister in Tehran:

Reports from the provinces during many months past have rendered it more
and more evident that the overbearing and oppressive attitude of the chief military commanders there has redounded to the discredit and unpopularity of
the Shah and his military establishment, among the people. These commanders
are known in several instances to have extorted large sums of money from the
civilian population and to have prevented the legal collection of taxes by the
agents of the Ministry of Finance. No definite information is available respecting the gross sums collected from the people by the army officials but they are
said to be very large. It has been reliably reported to me, for instance, that the
General in command of the Meshed [Mashhad] region gathered in the sum of
three hundred and fifty thousand tomans from the inhabitants of the city, prior
to his departure for Teheran April last for the purpose of attending the coronation of the Shah. In spite of the large sums at the disposition of the Ministry of
War, derived from the Treasury appropriations and many other sources it has
become known that the pay of the military is now greatly in arrears. It is
reported that the pay of the majority of the soldiers outside the capital has not
been forthcoming for periods ranging from eight to four months. At the same
time there has been great extravagance in all branches of the army. There is reason to suppose that the Shah cannot be unaware of the irregularities committed by his commanders for some time past. Indeed, there are those who believe
that he has benefited pecuniarily as a result of some of them.

Some months ago my attention was called by Doctor Millspaugh to the
unsatisfactory condition of affairs which existed in the financial administration
of the country owing to the independence of the Ministry of War from that
administration, and its refusal to accept any budgetary control. In short, the
Ministry of Finance continues to allot annually to the Ministry of War a global
credit amounting to nearly one half the revenues of the state but of which no
accounting is rendered. The Ministry of Finance also is aware that large sums
have been received by the army from other domestic sources of which the Ministry is unable to take official cognizance. From occasional talks with the retiring British Minister, who has never displayed any great frankness in regard to
current affairs of moment, I understand that his Government has been per-

turbed on account of the unfortunate state of the military establishment. This concern, I am told, is due to the desire of Great Britain to see the continuance of a moderately strong and efficient Persian Army on the Russian frontier.[30]

Writing about the same subject a few days later, Philip included the following: "There is little doubt that the same military misrule as is reported from Khorasan exists throughout the army quartered in other provinces. I have recently heard that much of the same state of discontent exists also in Shiraz, owing to the non payment of the soldiers on the one hand and the exactions of the military commander from civilians on the other. This condition of affairs is greatly impairing the prestige of the Shah in the country."[31]

Bank Pahlavi

All the above reports indicated that the soldiers had not been paid for months even though half the budget was appropriated to the Ministry of War. It is also intimated that the army was actually about half the size reported. What became of the money? The answer is given in a sixty-three-page memorandum by Millspaugh concerning the affairs of the army and the finances of the Ministry of War in which he documents widespread theft by army officers and leaves no doubt that the stealing took place with the knowledge, approval, and participation of Reza Khan and subsequently Reza Shah.[32]

In the same document, Millspaugh reveals another reason why the soldiers' pay was greatly in arrears. It centered around the newly established Bank Pahlavi, which had established a system of embezzlement. Not having received their pay, the soldiers could go to Bank Pahlavi, which would pay them at a discount but would in turn receive the full amount from the Ministry of War. Moreover, the bank had been established with army funds and those of the army retirement fund for the personal benefit of Reza Khan.

According to its constitution, there was established as of 1st Farvardin 1304 [March 22, 1925], a bank to be known as "Bank Pahlevi" for serving the requirements of the officers and privates of the army. The capital is fixed at a minimum of Ts. 1,000,000 and a maximum of Ts. 5,000,000, 60% of which is to be paid for from the retirement pension cash of the army. It is not clear from the constitution of the bank whether it is intended to be a private institution, a branch of the Ministry of War, or an independent governmental establishment. If it is a private institution, the use of the retirement pension funds for purchase of bank shares is illegal. According to Law, all public funds must be deposited in the Treasury General. It is understood that the funds of the municipality of Teheran have been deposited in the Pahlevi bank. Such deposit is likewise illegal for the above stated reason. If the bank is a branch of the Government, the army treasury cannot legally loan public funds to individuals without the authorization of the Ministry of Finance, and the Ministry of Finance cannot give legally such authorization without the approval of the Medjliss. Furthermore, a bank is a financial institution. My contract provides that I shall have charge of the finances of Persia. The operation of the Pahlevi Bank without my knowledge, approval, or supervision is evidently contrary to my contract.

The Bank Pahlevi has obtained a mail contract for carrying mail on the Khanikin-Teheran [Khanegein] road. I know of no legal means by which public funds paid to the Ministry of War for military purposes can be used for the purchase of automobiles and equipment for civil purposes; and I am not informed as to what disposition is made of the revenues received from the mail contract. Apart from the illegality of the Pahlevi Bank, the operations of the institution are irregular. The bank is essentially identical with the army treasury. A soldier with a month's salary in arrears presents himself to the bank. The latter pays the arrears at a discount, which goes to the profit of the bank. The same procedure takes place in the case of persons who have sold supplies to the army. They are told at the army treasury that there is no money in the treasury to pay them. They then go to the Pahlevi Bank, which is practically the same as the army treasury, and are told that they can be paid at a discount. Obviously, if the army has funds with which to run a bank and transport service and to discount arreared salaries and arreared bills, it has funds to pay arreared salaries and arreared bills.

When the American Mission came to Persia, pensions were in arrears. Pensioners sold their havalehs [drafts] at a discount to the bazaar merchants. The latter brought the havalehs to the Ministry of Finance and in many cases got them paid in full. This dishonest practice, which was profitable to those engaged in it, was immediately stopped by us. The operations of the Pahlevi Bank are, so far as I am informed, essentially the same. If the Pahlevi Bank wishes to conduct such operations, it should first place itself under the administration of the Ministry of Finance and should then ask for the approval of the Medjliss. If it does not wish to state this, it should divorce itself completely from the treasury of the army, should dispense with the use of any public funds whatever, and should be established and operated as a purely private institution with private capital, and it should refuse to deal with any arreared payments.[33]

By 1932, Bank Pahlavi had expanded considerably, and operated Tehran's autobus service, as described in a dispatch from Charles Calmer Hart:

> This is a somewhat extraordinary institution. Organized during the early years of the rising ascendancy of Persia's present Shah, it was originally designed solely as a depository for annual army appropriations which the Shah (then Minister of War) insisted should be paid six months in advance. And today, while it has invested certain surplus profits in the Teheran autobus service and makes loans to non-military persons within the country, it retains still its original military character. And the Shah is generally known to be its chief and controlling stockholder. It is still the sole Persian depository for army funds. Its President, Amir Lashgar Khodayar, and its Vice Presidential Director General,

Colonel Amir Khosrovi, are army officers. Its depositors and its creditors are almost all army officers and other ranks. Compared with the Imperial Bank of Persia the Banque Pahlevi is, of course, as a banking institution, of relatively little importance; but it serves its purpose in satisfactory fashion and is apparently so managed as to provide a regular source of modest profit to its imperial chief stockholder.[34]

In a subsequent dispatch Hart reveals that the profits of the bank were not so modest after all. The balance sheet of "Banque Pahlevi" for the period ending March 21, 1933, showed that the bank's net profit increased by 51 percent during the year, to 3.8 million rials ($230,000). Deposits had increased by 166 percent, to 38 million rials ($2.3 million), and assets had increased to 42 million rials ($2.5 million). The bank's reserve had been increased to 10 million rials ($600,000), and its capital to more than 10 million rials. Hart adds that "the new funds [are] being subscribed, I am told on good authority, by the Shah himself." He concludes that "the pleasantly liquid position reported as existing in the preceding year has become even more liquid."[35]

Hart describes the close relationship between Reza Shah and his personal banker and exclusive import agent for Pierce-Arrow automobiles, Colonel Amir Khosrovi: "The Pierce-Arrow bears somewhat the stamp of royalty here because the Shah has three or four of this make in addition to several Lincolns and a Rolls-Royce. The Shah's private banker, Colonel Reza Qoli Khan Amir Khosrovi, head of the Pahlavi Bank, is the agent of the Pierce-Arrow for all of Persia, and the Shah is his chief customer. This banker is supposed to have paid for the de luxe white and gold–trimmed Pierce-Arrow specially built for the Shah last year and received here only a few months ago."[36]

Subsequently, Amir Khosrovi, whose beating and dismissal by Reza Shah in May 1941 is described in chapter 5, was appointed head of the National Bank of Persia, and the occasion of his promotion to the rank of general was noted by William Hornibrook, the American minister: "Colonel Amir Khosrovi, Managing Director of the National Bank of Persia and the man who once visualized an exclusive automotive monopoly under his own personal direction and control, was elevated by the Shah during the New Year's festivities to the rank of General."[37]

The Sinclair Oil Concession and Bribery

In 1922 the Persian government was authorized by the Majlis to grant an oil concession to an American company for the five northern provinces that were not part of the D'Arcy Concession. Eventually, in December 1923, some two months after the premiership of Reza Khan, a concession was granted to the Sinclair Exploration Company of New York. From his early days, bribes—like the large bribes described below in connection with the Caspian fisheries—for the purpose of gaining economic and mineral concessions were routinely paid to Reza Khan and his ministers (such as Teymourtache and Foroughi). American consul Bernard Gotlieb reports: "From confidential statements made to me by the local representative of the Sinclair Company, there is a very good chance of the Premier signing the Sinclair project within the next few days. This once effected, the sanction of the Medjliss which should convene within a month would appear to be assured inasmuch as it will undoubtedly be completely subservient to Reza Khan."[38]

Two weeks later, a telegram from Gotlieb states: "This afternoon I officially witnessed signing of north Persian Oil concession by Reza Khan Prime Minister and R. Soper representing Sinclair Exploration Company."[39] In a subsequent report Gotlieb states: "A rather strange, if significant, phase of the matter is the fact that according to declarations made personally to the Sinclair representative by the Ministers of Foreign Affairs and Finance, Dr. Millspaugh, the Director-General of Finances, was kept in entire ignorance of the concession negotiations until Reza had signed it."[40] The reason Millspaugh had been kept in the dark emerged from the early days of the negotiations. Allen Dulles reported on a visit by a member of the British embassy in Washington: "Mr. Craigie of the British Embassy called and told me of reports which had reached the Embassy regarding bribes said to have been given by Sinclair Oil Company to certain prominent Persians to obtain their support of the Sinclair proposal. I said that rumors of this nature had reached the Department and presumably through the same channels as that of the British report but that we have no information whatever to substantiate these rumors."[41]

Soon after the grant of the concession, reports of large payments to Reza Khan and his foreign minister, Foroughi, began to circulate in the American press. A telegram from Secretary of State Hughes to the Tehran legation contained the following: "The Washington Herald of February 7th states: 'An American is credited with handing a bribe of one hundred thousand dollars to the Persian Foreign Minister in a bitter fight between two oil groups for control of the rich Persian oil fields.' Article further states: 'Publicity to the one hundred thousand dollar bribe has been given by the Persian Foreign Minister, proud of his own cleverness in getting the money. All the papers in the Levant are printing stories about it.'"[42] A Tehran newspaper, *Nasroll Mellah*, had printed an article claiming that a payment of 300,000 tomans ($300,000) had been made by Sinclair Oil to Reza Khan and Foroughi, of which Foroughi's share had been 100,000 tomans.[43] Embarrassed and upset at the allegations, Minister Kornfeld sent the following telegram: "Minister of Foreign Affairs man of unimpeachable integrity. *Nasroll Mellah* a paper appearing irregularly and with no standing whatever stated on January 15 that the Prime Minister received 300,000 tomans from Sinclair. Article not taken seriously by anyone. On January 24 same paper categorically retracted statement."[44]

Meanwhile, the Persian minister in Washington, Hosein Alai, had been instructed to make an appropriate response. Alai called on Dulles, the chief of Near Eastern Affairs, and the contents of the conversation are given in memorandum of conversation between Dulles and Alai:

> The Persian Minister expressed his concern at the article in Washington Herald of February 7th with regard to the alleged bribery of Persian officials in connection with the granting of the North Persian oil concession to Sinclair. The article he said was libelous, totally unsubstantiated and most distressing. It would undoubtedly injure the credit of Persia in this country and entirely unjustly since there was not the least basis of truth to the report. He had denied it in a statement to the Associated Press but his statement had not been published so far as he could find. He said that while he appreciated that it was not a matter within the competence of the Department of State, he would greatly appreciate any suggestion I could give him with regard to the action he could take to counteract the unfortunate impression which the article might create. Should he write to the editor? The story was really a libel on his country. What should he do? I told the Minister that I had noted the statement and could fully appreciate his feelings in the matter. I did not feel, however, that I was in a position to advise him. Often it is desirable to disregard sensational press statements, but he would be the best judge as to the action he should take.[45]

Pressure was also placed on Kornfeld, the American minister in Tehran, who states: "I have the honor to transmit herewith translation of a communication from Zoka-ol-Molk, Minister of Foreign Affairs, expressing his keen chagrin over the statement that appeared in the American Press alleging that he accepted a bribe of $100,000 from the Sinclair Exploration Company for the granting of the northern oil concession. As I have already advised the Department, Zoka-ol-Molk is one of the most honorable men in Persian public life. I do not know how the Department can redress this wrong, but I should respectfully suggest that it issue a statement denying unqualifiedly this absolutely unfounded charge."[46] Three days later Kornfeld sent the following telegram: "Under date of February 14th Minister of Foreign Affairs writes me: 'I regret to bring to your notice that according to a telegraphic report received yesterday from Mr. Alai the American press have not accepted contradiction of news published by them some time ago. I, therefore, request you take necessary and immediate steps toward making the press accept and publish the official denial given them by him.'"[47] The response from Hughes, dated February 16, contained a lesson in

American government and practices: "You should call to the attention of the Minister for Foreign Affairs that the executive branch of the Government cannot control expression by the press of this country. As the Minister undoubtedly knows, the courts of the country may be availed of for such legal remedies as the law allows in case of false or libelous statements."[48]

Reza Khan and Foroughi declined to avail themselves of the legal remedies open to them. That they had received substantial bribes over the Sinclair concession is clear. In a confidential letter of September 21, 1924, Millspaugh had informed Dulles that based on reliable information, Reza Khan had a few months before transferred $200,000, apparently from the Sinclair payment, to Europe. The remaining $100,000, as reported by the newspapers, had gone to Foroughi. As to Foroughi's reputed integrity, when confronted with solid evidence of his bribe taking and corruption, Minister Hart remarked that in the world of crooks and scoundrels, Foroughi was a "veritable collector's piece" (see chapter 9).

The expenditure of the large bribes by Sinclair was for naught. After the murder of Robert W. Imbrie, the American vice consul in Tehran, Sinclair abandoned its concession. This prompted Murray to express regret on the absence of American oil interests in Persia:

> It is greatly to be regretted that no American oil interest is at the present time represented in Tehran. A state of nervousness and uncertainty prevails today in Persian political circles that is not reassuring. The Prime Minister is believed to be desirous of a change of regime by which he may become Regent or Shah. To realize his plans he may be obliged to solicit the support of the British. I am constrained to remark that in the eventuality of the success of such a coup carried out with British support, the chances of American competition for the North Persian oil concession will, in my opinion, be greatly reduced.[49]

Murray's prediction turned out to be accurate. The Americans were to be shut out of Persia's oil for the next thirty years. It was not until the oil consortium agreement of 1954 that the American oil companies gained access to Persian oil.

The Caspian Fisheries

On October 1, 1927, only weeks after Millspaugh's departure from Persia, the fisheries concession to the Soviet Union, to which Millspaugh had so strenuously objected, was signed by the Iranian government. By this agreement, Persia's fisheries on the Caspian Sea were given to the Soviets for twenty-five years.[50] Three years prior to the granting of the concession, events had taken a violent turn. In May 1924, Millspaugh had ordered the seizure of the fisheries from the Soviets, who had apparently been operating them. Information is found in a press clipping: "Caspian Fisheries

Seized from Russia's Control: According to reports of the correspondent of the Russian Telegraph Agency from Teheran, the American Financial adviser in Persia, Mr. Millspaugh, ordered armed occupation of south Caspian fisheries, which have been exploited by Soviet Russia on the basis of the Russo-Persian treaty of 1921. Mr. Millspaugh employed for that purpose the military detachments at the disposal of the Persian Ministry of Finance."[51] Soviet response was rapid and decisive. American vice consul Robert W. Imbrie, in a dispatch entitled "Seizure of Persian Fisheries by Bolsheviks," states:

> I have the honor to report that recently a Bolshevik warship landed sailors with machine guns near Enzeli [Bandar-e Anzali, or Bandar-e Pahlavi] on the south shore of the Caspian Sea and there took possession of the fisheries. The seizure of these fisheries was not based on any legitimate claim that they belong to Russian subjects and, in fact, was in contravention of the rights of the Lianosoffs, Russian subjects. An emphatic protest against the seizure of these fisheries has been made by the Persian Government to the Bolshevik Minister in Teheran and through its representative in Moscow but no satisfaction has been forthcoming. Though the warship has left, the sailors and the machine guns remain and the Persian Government does not seem inclined to reduce the matter to a definite issue by sending troops against those holding the fisheries.[52]

Millspaugh's Memorandum on the Fisheries

Soon after the seizure of the fisheries by the Soviets, the fishing concession was reportedly granted to the Soviet government.[53] Imbrie did not live to follow the story. After his murder in July 1924, the matter was taken up by Murray. After the terms of the agreement were made known to Millspaugh, he strenuously objected to its provisions in a memorandum to the Persian government. A dispatch from Murray provides an interesting account of the episode and contains a copy of Millspaugh's memorandum, which was also supplied to the American legation. Murray's account follows:

> I was informed by Dr. Millspaugh on October 3 that, on the previous day, he was urgently called to the Council of Ministers where he found the Prime Minister, together with all his Cabinet Ministers, and the Soviet Minister in conference over a proposed concession granting to the Soviet Government a 50% interest with the Persian Government in the Caspian Fisheries. The details of this project are ably exposed in the accompanying enclosure of Dr. Millspaugh. The above meeting of the Council of Ministers must, as related by Dr. Millspaugh, have been exceedingly dramatic. It appears that, upon his arrival, the Soviet Minister was requested to withdraw to the next room while the Persians discussed the question confidentially. The Prime Minister, I am informed, under the influence of the Minister of Public Works, Sardar Moaz-zam Khorassani, who was sponsor of the plan, and who was, unquestionably,

appointed to this portfolio in order to put through concessions and agreements favorable to the Soviet Government, was on the point of signing the concession in question when Dr. Millspaugh arrived. At the order of Sardar Sepah, the concession was laid before the Administrator General and his opinion was requested. Although he had no previous information that such a concession was even under consideration, he observed at a glance its disastrous character and expressed his opinion in no uncertain terms. This opinion is fully outlined in his memorandum. As a result of his presentations, the decision of the Prime Minister to sign forthwith the concession was shaken, and Dr. Millspaugh informed me that since the presentation of the enclosed memorandum to the Prime Minister nothing more has been heard of the concession.[54]

Millspaugh's memorandum of October 7, 1924, delineates how the fisheries agreement completely betrayed Persia's economic and political rights. The people of Iran and those studying the history of this period owe him a great debt. In this excerpt Millspaugh discusses the economic provisions of the agreement:

These articles mean, apparently, that the Persian Government shall receive each year tomans 80,000 plus 15 per cent of the net revenue and also 50 per cent of any net revenues which remain. If there is any idea of accepting this arrangement, these articles should be made perfectly clear. According to the decision of the Arbitration Commission which decided that the Lianosoff concession was legal, the Lianosoffs were to pay the Government 50 per cent of the net profits and the Government was not required to contribute any amount whatever to the capital. According to Article 5 of this agreement, any sums due to the Persian Government on account of payment of tomans 80,000 plus 15 per cent of the net revenues shall be paid back to the Russian Government by the Persian Government on account of its loan to the Persian Government. For several years, therefore, the Persian Government will have no right to any revenue from the fisheries except, possibly, 50 per cent of the net profits. Since the revenue of the Persian Government under the agreement will be for the most part a certain percentage of the net profits, it is necessary that the Persian Government should fix the method by which the net profits are to be determined. It will be recalled that there has been much difficulty with the Anglo-Persian Oil Company with regards to this point and in the Sinclair Oil concession there are explicit provisions safeguarding the interests of the Persian Government with regard to the calculation of net profits. There are no such safeguards in the proposed fisheries agreement. The mixed company under Russian control will sell the fish and caviar either directly to the Food Department of the Soviet Government or to a Russian company organized for this purpose. The price can be fixed arbitrarily in such a way that the profits from the commercial sales will be made by the Food Department or by the Russian company and not by the mixed company established under this agreement. In this way, the Russian Government could arrange that the net profits of the mixed company would be very small while the profits from the purchase and sale of fish and caviar in Russia (and the rest of the world) would be very large. The provisions of this agreement relating to revenues and the price of the produce are full of opportunity for tricks and disputes and consequent losses to the Persian Government.

According to Article 10 of the agreement, the Russian government was to pay the Persian government 100,000 tomans for the use of the fisheries during the past two years. Millspaugh's detailed calculations on the cost of Russian actions showed that they actually owed 950,000 tomans for the forced use of the fisheries. Other damages inflicted on northern Persia on account of Russian military activity since 1918 came to nearly 3 million tomans. Millspaugh comments: "It will be seen, therefore, that in offering the Persian Government a sum of 100,000 tomans, the Soviet Legation does not show much generosity." Millspaugh then addresses the political aspects of the agreement:

The political consequences of this agreement would seriously affect the economic and financial interests of the country. It would lead to financial obligations and would be the cause of constant disputes between the two Governments. It would give the Russian Government a foothold in northern Persia. Whenever any disorder occurred, the Russians would land troops for the sake of keeping order. Sooner or later the ports along the southern coast of the Caspian would be under the control of the Russian Government. The Russian specialists engaged in the management of the fisheries could not be expected to be politically neutral. The Soviet authorities in Enzeli have already taken legal possession of a public domain property. Since the Persian Government claims ownership of rivers and coastal lands, there would be constant disputes with the Russian Government on this point. Eventually the Russian Government would interfere with other industries in the north, and it would not be long before the Russian Government would claim a definite sphere of influence in the north, as it did in 1907. It is better not to settle the fishery question at all than to settle it as proposed in this agreement. It is better to let the Russians seize the fisheries by force over the protests of the Persian Government than to surrender rights and interests which are not only valuable but absolutely vital.

Millspaugh concludes with a recommendation:

In my opinion, the proposed agreement should not be seriously considered for a moment by the Persian Government. The proper, legal, and practicable way to settle the fishery question, in conformity with the Russo-Persian treaty, is to lease or buy the Lianosoff rights or properties; second, to make an agreement with the Soviet Food Department to sell all fish (not caviar) to the Soviet Food Department at cost plus 30 per cent, and in order to give the Russian Government the right of appointing a commissioner to inspect the exploitation and shipment of fish. If the Persian Government really desires to retain its economic independence, there is another way to retain its rights. A public demand on the Russians to submit all points at issue to arbitration would, I am certain, deter them from any further arbitrary actions. If the Persian Government does not care to take this action, it should leave the matter in its present situation, continuing to protest against the Russian occupation and refusing to enter into any agreement by which the fisheries would be handed to them.[55]

The Fisheries Concession and Payments to the Shah

Less than a month after Millspaugh's memorandum on the fisheries, and despite all the points he raised, it is clear that Reza Khan had begun to accept presents from the Soviets, and was bringing pressure on Millspaugh to desist from opposing the fisheries agreement. Millspaugh's refusal to cooperate must have been very unwelcome. In a strictly confidential dispatch Murray provides real insight on the corrupt practices of Reza Khan and his close associates, such as Zoka-ol-Molk Foroughi:

> I have the honor to inform the Department that, on November 4, I was confidentially informed by Dr. A. C. Millspaugh, the Administrator of General Finances, that, on the previous day, the Soviet manager of the Caspian fisheries which are practically confiscated by the Soviet Government, handed the Prime Minister [Reza Khan] a check for 100,000 tomans on account of the fish that had been caught under Soviet exploitation of these fisheries and which is desired to export from Enzeli to Russia. The check was delivered to Dr. Millspaugh by the Minister of Finance, Zoka-ol-Molk, with the request of the Prime Minister that it be deposited in the Treasury General, and that he, the Prime Minister, be given a receipt therefor. Upon Dr. Millspaugh's inquiry as to the conditions under which the money had been paid, the Finance Minister assured him solemnly that there were no conditions whatsoever attached to it, and that the Persian Government had in no way obligated itself in the matter. It is to be noted that this remark was made despite the statement of the Prime Minister in his covering letter enclosing the check, to the effect that the advance had been made in expectation of the early signing of the fishery concession. Dr. Millspaugh thereupon committed himself in writing to the Minister of Finance protesting vigorously against what he termed a dangerous precedent to set in the case of these bitterly disputed properties. He said that it was inconceivable to him that the Soviet authorities would voluntarily deliver a check to the Prime Minister for 100,000 tomans without attaching any strings thereto, and that the acceptance of any such sum in the expectation of the final passage of the fishery concession would tie the hands of the Persian Government and render further independent negotiations impossible. Upon receipt of the written communication, the Minister of Finance again explained to Dr. Millspaugh that he had "totally misunderstood the situation," and that the Prime Minister had assumed no obligation whatsoever in accepting the money and that inasmuch as the Government was "hard up" he had better cash it at once. Dr. Millspaugh then pointed out to him, that in the first place, the check had never been endorsed by the Prime Minister, and in the second place, it was drawn on the Russo-Persian Bank of Teheran

which was notoriously without funds, so that the acceptance of such a check would not only not provide the funds in question but would render impossible an eventual protest of the Persian Government against occupation of the fisheries by the Soviet Russians. In illustrating to the Minister of Finance the unwisdom of accepting the money, he gave the following example. Any day the Russians might appear in the Caspian provinces, start to dig a well despite protests of the Persian Government, and obtain a quantity of oil which they desire to export to Russia. In case they then offered the Government a sum in payment upon this oil, which they had illegally exploited and had no right to possess, the case would be exactly identical with that of the present instance when the Soviet authorities were offering to pay 100,000 tomans for fish caught in Persian waters under illegal occupation and exploitation thereof. Although the Minister of Finance was not convinced, the check was nevertheless not presented to the bank, and it will in all probability not be accepted.[56]

Subsequent events show that despite Millspaugh's protests and opposition, Soviet inducements to Reza Khan were irresistible. Soon after Millspaugh's dismissal and departure on August 4, 1927, the fishery agreement had been concluded with the Soviets. American consul Orsen N. Neilsen relates the "rumor that the Russo-Persian dispute concerning the fisheries was to be settled by equal participation in fishing operations by both countries. Mr. Flessner reports that he is informed by Mr. Mehdi Gholi Hedayat, the Prime Minister, that an agreement to this effect shortly is to be signed."[57] The rumor was well founded. Minister Philip reports that the Caspian Fisheries Convention, which was signed on October 1 and consisted of twenty-one articles, five protocols, and five notes, had been submitted to the Majlis to be studied by the deputies. The convention was practically identical to the previous ones to which Millspaugh had objected strenuously. Philip adds: "It is the general opinion that the Caspian Fisheries Pact will be approved by the Medjliss. The department will kindly note that the treaty precludes the employment by Persia of foreigners, other than Russians, for the port and fisheries business."[58]

According to Philip, the fisheries convention and several other agreements with the Soviets "were hastily approved (by the Medjliss) on the 23rd of that month [October]." The only parliamentary opposition was from Dr. Mossadeq and Taghi Zadeh, who had pointed out several inconsistencies in the pact and had suggested that the measure be carefully examined and debated before approval. Philip continues:

> It is common knowledge that this precipitate legislation was chiefly due to the Shah's dominating tactics with the Deputies. It is reported that on the 22nd ultimo the Shah harangued a meeting of the Deputies at the Palace, again making use of the expression to the effect that "he could not sleep" until the Agreements were ratified. It was also reported to me by one of my colleagues that Teymourtache is known to have interviewed a number of Deputies for the

purpose of strongly impressing upon them the Shah's wishes in this respect. As an example of parliamentary procedure, the "railroading" of these pacts through the Medjliss is not conducive to respect for the dignity and independence of the parliamentary body. The general impression seems to be that the Soviet has derived much more tangible benefits from the Agreements than Persia.[59]

Soon after the granting of the concession, reports circulated of large presents being paid to Reza Shah. Philip relates: "The British Minister told me confidentially that he has heard the Soviet Government had paid quite heavily in presents for the purpose of obtaining the consummation of the Perso-Soviet Agreements."[60] That huge sums had been paid to Reza Shah and Teymourtache for the approval of the fishery concession was to be learned from the Agabekoff revelations (see below), and by the astute reporting of the American minister in Tehran, Charles C. Hart. In 1931, with renewed American interest in the Caspian fisheries, commercial concerns in New York made offers to market the Persian government's share of caviar and fish. After much negotiation, however, the Persian government suddenly lost interest in the American offers. Hart explained why.

The $850,000 "Present"

In June 1932, Hart met with Teymourtache, who expressed a willingness to grant a fishing concession to American interests for the Persian Gulf fisheries in place of the Caspian. Teymourtache had also revealed that although the Persian government had abandoned its talks with the Satin and Pope group of New York, "they had been of immense help to him in negotiating later with the Soviets." Hart quotes Teymourtache verbatim: "I said to the Soviets here is a serious [American] offer, exhibiting the Satin and Pope proposal, and they lost no time in coming to terms. They paid me $850,000 cash for the concession we were about to grant to Satin and Pope." Unable to contain his astonishment at Teymourtache's frank confession of the massive bribe and evidently other revelations, Hart writes, "I suspect that some of my colleagues would be startled at this information, which I shall not pass on."[61]

One regrets that Hart does not include more of what he learned from Teymourtache. In a December dispatch, written after the dismissal of Teymourtache, Hart returns to the $850,000 bribe: "It will be recalled, as reported in one of my earlier despatches, that he [Teymourtache] said he obtained $850,000 from the Soviet Government for a mere reconfirmation of its contract to purchase and market the Persian half of the caviar and other products of the Caspian Sea fisheries for which a concession was granted in October, 1927. I recall that he did not say whether this payment reached the Treasury General."[62] Earlier, Hart had noted that "a liberal portion [of the bribes]" went into the pockets of His Majesty.[63] There can be no doubt where the bulk of the above present ended up. What came to be known as the Agabekoff revelations verify the huge Soviet bribes given to Reza Shah in connection with the fisheries concession.

The Agabekoff Revelations and Williamson's Letter to Hart

In 1930 a Soviet defector, Agabekoff, wrote a book in Paris in which he describes large payments to Iranian officials for approving the Caspian fisheries concession to the Soviets in October 1927.[64] He also describes Teymourtache, Reza Shah's minister of court, as a highly effective Soviet agent who, in exchange for providing intelligence to the Soviet embassy, was being handsomely rewarded. In a confidential report Hart wonders why some of the high Persian officials named by Agabekoff had not been touched. He then provides the obvious reason.

> The Government, as reported in previous despatches, made approximately 400 arrests, but no move has been made to punish the alleged Persian agents named in Agabekoff revelations. Several aliens mentioned have been ordered out of the country. As to the Persian agents the majority of them remain in jail but one of the outstanding figures implicated, Abbas Mirza Eskandari, formerly Chief of Cabinet of the Ministry of Public Works, was released on bond after being arrested. The Persian enemies of Teymourtache, and they are without number, are ready to believe all that was said about him by Agabekoff, classifying him as the most efficient aid to Soviet ambitions in Persia and as a carrier of political secrets from other Legations to Soviet headquarters. The foreign colony also believes that Teymourtache has been guilty of everything charged against him and much more. The Persian foes of Teymourtache, in the main I would say loyal to the Shah, are disappointed that the latter ordered no drastic action against his Minister of the Court and others mentioned in the Agabekoff tale. It is not believed for one moment that the Shah is ignorant of the Agabekoff story of the use of money to buy Persian subjects for the service of Moscow, hence the disappointment. The calm that has followed the Agabekoff upheaval is so unlike what has happened on other occasions when national scandal came to the attention of the reigning Pahlevi. The one conclusion on which most observers, Persian and foreign, converge is that the Shah himself must share in the sums collected outside the law from the Soviets and concession hunters; that if the Soviet Government paid several million rubles, as Agabekoff asserts, for the oil and timber concessions in the northern provinces, some of it, a liberal portion, went into the pockets of His Majesty. There are many who do not want to believe that, but in looking for the explanation of the stuffed club treatment meted out to the alleged Persian spies for Soviet Russia

operating on Persian soil, some selling fishing rights on the Caspian Sea and others oil and timber, and some of them bartering in confidential information of the Foreign Ministry, only one solution seems plausible.

The Shah is carried away in his personal cupidity. Chatty Persians are fond of regaling the foreigners with the story that their Shah is the second richest man in the world and emphasize the ponderous achievement in the rise of an illiterate peasant's equally illiterate son to a position of power and fabulous wealth. (Encyclopedia Britannica lists the Shah as the son of an army officer, but this I think was arranged to give him distinguished background. The truth seems to be that he is the son of a very poor peasant.) Most of these riches have been acquired by confiscations or partial confiscations and by going through the motion of buying large real estate holdings for which little or no consideration has been paid.

Though knowing his worship of money and property I was long reluctant about believing that the highways and byways of graft led up to the throne. Now I am convinced of it and this despatch is written for the purposes of the archives. I believe that such facts and surmises should be made available to my successor. Had there been anything in the files to tell me that Teymourtache was an unprincipled politician, engaged in building up his personal finances at the expense of intriguing Governments and foreign concession hunters, I feel that such information would have been of vast help to me. As it was, several days were required to find him out.[65]

In a subsequent dispatch Hart reproduces part of a letter, dated February 17, 1931, that David Williamson, the American chargé d'affaires in Tehran in 1927 and now at the American embassy in Turkey, had written him upon learning of the Agabekoff revelations:

The Agabekoff revelations confirm what have always been suspected. As everyone knew in 1927, when the Fisheries agreement was being negotiated, certain highly placed officials received large—very large—presents. The date of November 1, 1927, on which day the Fisheries agreement was signed over Dr. Millspaugh's protest, sticks in my mind. That was payday; the ghost walked at the palace. Herein lies the reason why the Highest Person has not punished his second in command; *both* received their share. It seems incorrect to call either of them "agents." But I feel that Agabekoff was particularly useful in that he showed up obscure Russian agents, so difficult to detect.[66]

Hart's dispatch concludes:

I place high value on Mr. Williamson's comment as serving to confirm suspicions generally expressed by members of the foreign colony ever since Agabekoff's tale became known. It is also interesting to know that Dr. Millspaugh, American financial advisor to Persia at the time, pointed out the objectionable features of the convention. This indicates that Dr. Millspaugh did not understand the Persian mind; that he assumed that his duty lay in the direction of giving good advice, not always welcome.[67]

Millspaugh's Dismissal

As reported above, despite his own vast fortune, Reza Shah's household expenses were paid by the Ministry of War, over which Millspaugh had no control. Reza Shah also expected the Ministry of Finance to pay for the construction and improvement of his palaces. Hoffman Philip tells of Reza Shah's construction expenses, which he requested Millspaugh to pay. When Millspaugh refused, it is not surprising that he incurred royal displeasure:

> Dr. Millspaugh remarked that the Shah strikes him as a man without the sense of financial responsibility. In this connection he mentioned that the Shah has recently spent the sum of eighty thousand Tomans on improvements to the buildings and garden of his private summer residence. A request was made of the Ministry of Finance to meet this expense, but only six thousand Tomans of it were considered legitimately chargeable to that department. The Shah receives an income of forty thousand Tomans from the State, and he is commonly reported to have amassed a large private fortune in recent years.[68]

With the ascent of Reza Khan to the throne with the help of the British, the fate of the American financial mission and the future of American economic enterprise in Persia, including the granting of oil concessions to American companies, was sealed. Events leading up to and the reasons for Millspaugh's dismissal are described in various dispatches. It was clear to all that the dismissal of the American team was a signal victory for the British, and an important step in Reza Shah's control of financial affairs. The complete domination of Persia by the British and the absolute military dictatorship by Reza Khan (the two were the same) could not be achieved as long as Millspaugh and his American team were present in Persia. The American chargé d'affaires ad interim, Copley Amory Jr., writes:

> Pahlavi's animosity against the American Financial Mission in general and Dr. Millspaugh in particular has developed primarily because of a growing feeling on the part of Pahlavi that the role of the American Financial Mission of carrying out an objective economic development of Persia does not in many essential respects coincide with his personal needs and ambitions. Dr. Millspaugh attributes the chief difficulties facing his Mission to this jealousy on the part of the military elements and their desire to control sources of revenue which legally accrues to the state. He outlined this situation to me as follows: The army has received an annual blanket credit of about 9 million Tomans during the last three years. A large portion of this amount has been regularly stolen by army chiefs. During this period the army has increased in size. Wireless apparatus, tanks, aeroplanes, and other

equipment has been bought in increasing quantity. The need for greater funds has been met thus far by various forms of extortion. The common people especially in the provinces have been hit in a multitude of ways; tributes have been collected from tribes and their chiefs. It is estimated that the funds thus illegally obtained represent from 2 to 4 million Tomans, or from 25 to 50 per cent of the 9 million Tomans legally supplied by the Ministry of Finance. "Everyone steals in the army except privates." Thieving by Persian officers, like all bad habits, has increased with practice, and with the accompanying increase in legitimate expenses the need for more funds during the past year by the Ministry of War has become urgent. There are indications that many of the illegal sources of revenue are becoming dry; that extortion in its various forms is becoming more hazardous as the sources become less fruitful. There were a few isolated and abortive gestures [by the army] to grab government taxes last summer. As the autumn has progressed it has become evident that these were not spasmodic phenomena which could and would be promptly and severely stopped by the central authorities. In some cases this action appears to have originated with the local military authorities and to have been arrested by orders from Teheran. In other instances it appears that Pahlavi himself has been responsible or to have winked at such actions by his subordinates. The conflict between the military authorities, who constitute the basis of Pahlavi's political as well as military power, and the financial authorities, as represented by the American Financial Mission, is the backbone of the present trouble.

A review of the present position of the Financial Mission would not be complete without allusion to the increasing appreciation by such public opinion as exists here of the disinterested and arduous services and the very considerable results attained by Dr. Millspaugh and his assistants.

Dr. Millspaugh feels that an attempt may possibly be made, when the Constituent Assembly convenes, to pass an amendment to the Constitution which would directly or indirectly affect his status and powers as defined in his contract with the Persian Government (signed on August 14, 1922). The object of the action would be to curtail the power vested [in Millspaugh] by Article 5 of the contract: 5. That, the Imperial Persian Government agrees that no financial obligation shall be incurred by or in the name of the Persian Government without the written approval of both the Minister of Finance and the said Arthur Chester Millspaugh, and agrees further that no expenditure or transfer of Public moneys shall be made without the signature of the Minister of Finance and the counter signature of the said Arthur Chester Millspaugh.

In whatever manner this might be done Dr. Millspaugh feels it would be but to cloak Pahlavi's desire to secure direct and arbitrary control of government funds.[69]

In December 1925, a Constituent Assembly voted to replace the Qajars with Reza Khan as shah. The American chargé d'affaires made no attempt to hide his anger at the British:

Dr. Millspaugh does not show a very optimistic frame of mind as to his future relations with Pahlavi. He is inclined to emphasize the new sovereign's limited perspective arising from his lack of ordinary educational training and to his temperamental disinclination to recognize shackles of any description as warranting the belief that Pahlavi's attitude towards the constitution and constitutional rights may before long become important issues. I think it is timely to refer to the British attitude towards the financial Mission. . . . His [Reza's] relations with leading members of Persian officialdom who are known to have British sympathies have been reported of late to have been particularly close. It is pointed out by friends of the Financial Mission that one of the objects at which present British policy here is now aiming is to accentuate in high quarters the timidity, the distance, even the hopelessness of attracting American capital to Persia. It is hard to believe, with the British desire for stability in this country, that they would encourage even covertly the departure of the American Financial Mission at the present time. One concludes that they realize the impossibility of receiving Persian consent to a British administration of Persian finances. Equally well must they realize the results of Persian management of Persian finances. Perhaps they divide the functions of the American Financial Mission into two categories (1) the actual financial administration of the Ministry of Finance and (2) the general custodianship of the broader aspects of Persian economic development; and will direct their efforts against the second category of Dr. Millspaugh's activities. The comment might be made that control of the second phase is, in many ways, dependent upon the control of the first. . . . I indicated in my confidential despatch of December 4, 1925, that the effect of the unselfish, objective and efficient work of Dr. Millspaugh and his mission is having an increasingly wide and favorable effect. As in line with this condition there is transmitted with this despatch the issue of December 1, 1925 of *Hayat Vatan,* a Teheran newspaper, which contains in both Persian and English a friendly account of Dr. Millspaugh and his work.[70]

The gratitude of the people of Persia was insufficient to save the American financial mission. Millspaugh's departure from Tehran and the attitude toward it is described by Hoffman Philip, the new American minister:

I have the honor to report that Dr. A. C. Millspaugh, Administrator General of Persian Finances, left Teheran on the 4th instant for the United States. Dr. Millspaugh's departure from Teheran, after four and a half years of intense and successful devotion to the interests of the Persian people, was entirely ignored by the Shah and his Government. Largely, I think, on account of the attitude created by the Shah, whose position is that of a dictator at present, and to the confused idea of the actual facts given out by the slavish press of Teheran, there was no parliamentary or popular gesture of regret or appreciation on the occasion. The departure marked the end of a fine and courageous effort to rehabilitate and to stabilize the finances of this country and to bring about the establishment of reforms which would have been both a lasting benefit to the Persian people and the inspiration of world confidence in Persia through the medium of real financial independence. If I may be permitted apparent contradiction, I will say that the very success of this effort was one of the causes of its failure—the

rapid transition from a seemingly hopeless deficit and financial chaos to financial independence and a robust and tempting bank account, in the space of four
and a half years, has been, it appears, too much for the patience and moral equi-
librium of Persia's new Shah and his advisers. In my opinion, and in that of others, one of the chief weaknesses of Millspaugh's administration lay in the
creation and the augmentation of idle balances to the credit of the Government.
The fact that these important credits were drawing a fair rate of interest from the
Imperial Bank of Persia has no bearing on this question. The funds were there
for all to realize and covet. So long as Dr. Millspaugh was also present, they could
not be dissipated through impracticable and devious practices.

The sudden acquisition of the throne by a man of dominating character and
redolent of martial authority of camps, but otherwise devoid of education and
culture of any kind, had the effect of precipitating immediate administrative
difficulties for the American Financial Mission. Large sums were lying idle. The
Shah, the Army, called for urgent appropriation. They were told that they could
not have it without the approval of the Parliament, the appropriations for the
War Department being already overdrawn. That the demands in question were
in all probability both illegal and unreasonable did not affect the situation thus
created. The man who thus opposed the wishes of the highest power in the land
was Dr. Millspaugh. It is no exaggeration to make the broad statement that the
best classes of Persians look upon the practical dismissal of Millspaugh by the
Shah as a bold move to get possession of the funds of the State. A strange characteristic of the Persian who achieves power apparently is his belief that he is
entitled to take any liberty with the funds of the nation, though he decries such
a tendency on the part of others. My opinion is that the Millspaugh incident
will contribute very extensively to the growing unpopularity of the Shah and
his strongest advisers. For the moment, however, they constitute by far the
most powerful element in the land.[71]

In a subsequent dispatch Philip adds:

The reaction of the Millspaugh incident on the political situation has been
considerable. Although it has served as a demonstration of the Shah's dominating position in all branches of the Government, yet it has at the same time had
the effect of greatly enhancing the uneasiness and lack of confidence which is
growing in the more conservative lay and ecclesiastical Persian circles anent the
actual motives of the Shah and his chief advisers. I am convinced that the Government's methods in this matter have been quite opposed to the great consensus of opinion in this country. Fundamentally, the people trusted Millspaugh
and his colleagues and had faith in their honesty and good intentions—and,
fundamentally, they suspect the motives of the Shah and his advisers in the
means they have adopted to wrest the financial administrative power from the
hands of the Americans. As things are, the impression one receives from this
incident is that the Shah and his Government have wearied of the restrictions
imposed upon their desire for personal self determination in matters financial
by the somewhat rigid and impersonal rulings of a group of Americans, and

they desire to employ the funds of the nation as an adjunct to their political policies, as well as personal gain. Some two weeks ago a rumor was widely circulated here to the effect that a soldier had attempted the life of the Shah at his country residence. The man was said to have fired several ineffectual shots at the Shah and to have been himself immediately executed. Although there has been no further confirmation of this report, I find that it has received general credence.[72]

Conclusions

Millspaugh describes how Reza Shah "milked" Iran:

> While the Shah was working these expensive and dubious miracles, he amassed for himself a substantial fortune. . . . How did the Shah find the money? In his regime, national, municipal, and private finances were intermingled; no reliable statistics were published. . . . His private accumulations came from the produce of the agricultural lands that he appropriated, from the shares that he had in certain private enterprises, from gifts and bribes, from tributes paid by tribal chiefs, and from rakeoff that he had from others' grafting. Altogether he thoroughly milked the country, grinding down the peasants, tribesmen, and laborers, and taking heavy toll from the landlords. While his activities enriched a new class of "capitalists"—merchants, monopolists, contractors, and politician-favorites—inflation, heavy taxation, and other measures lowered the standard of living of the masses.[73]

Apart from Reza Shah's desire to gain complete control of Persia's financial resources, he had in 1927 two immediate reasons to be rid of Millspaugh and the Americans. First was the impending signing of the fisheries agreement with the Soviets and his receipt of large presents. Second, and far more important, the removal of Millspaugh was a necessary step in the plundering of Persia's oil revenues by Reza Shah. As described in detail in chapter 10, oil revenues after Millspaugh were no longer regarded as government revenue and were no longer to be part of the regular budget. Henceforth, these revenues were to be part of a reserve fund banked in London, out of which special appropriations were made each year. As I will show, during the next fourteen years nearly all of Iran's oil revenues were diverted to Reza Shah's bank accounts in Europe and the United States. In addition, as outlined in chapter 9, with impending important negotiations concerning oil matters and the British desire to revise the D'Arcy Concession, the British were especially anxious to be rid of Millspaugh.

CHAPTER FIVE

Reza Shah Pahlavi

A Study in Brutality and Greed

THROUGHOUT HIS RULE, FOREIGN NEWSPAPER references to Reza Shah's humble background became cause for diplomatic rupture. In 1936 and 1937, *Time* and the *New York Mirror* referred to Reza Khan's earlier duties as stable boy and later as sentry in front of foreign legations in Tehran.[1] The Iranian foreign minister requested of the American minister in Tehran that the offending newspapers be punished and future indiscretions prevented. When the Iranian minister, Baqer Kazemi, was informed that newspapers in America were protected by the U.S. constitution, he coolly suggested, to the disbelief of the American official, that to accommodate His Pahlevi Majesty the American constitution itself should be changed. Persian ambassadors and ministers in foreign countries were abruptly dismissed because they were perceived as not having responded in a timely or effective manner to the alleged press disrespect to the shahinshah of Iran. The same Kazemi who had suggested the changing of the American constitution was summarily dismissed as ambassador to Turkey in 1940 because of a magazine article that referred to Reza Shah's humble origins. As the accounts show, Iran had become an international laughingstock.[2] To the Iranian people, who had been brutalized for twenty years, however, it was no laughing matter.

In 1938, after a break of three years during which Iran had maintained no diplomatic representative in the United States, the State Department requested an official biography of Reza Shah from the newly reopened Iranian legation. The intention was to make the biography available to reporters so that, it was hoped, past indiscretions about His Majesty's origins would not be repeated. A biography was supplied by the Iranian minister, A. Daftary. After it was edited and polished by the State Department and approved by Daftary, it became the official biographical source on Reza Shah. The text is given in a memorandum, which gives the following introduction: "Attached is the translation of the Shah's biography furnished by Dr. Daftary, Iranian Chargé d'Affaires ad interim, together with a summary thereof prepared in the Division of Near Eastern Affairs in consultation with Dr. Daftary and approved by him in its final form." In reading Reza Shah's official biography, one cannot avoid the conclusion that everything it says about the man is a lie:

> His Imperial Majesty Reza Shah Pahlavi is descended from an old prominent family of Iranian gentry long established in the region of Sawad Kuh in the province of Mazanderan in northeastern Iran. In that region, in the town of Alacht, Reza Shah was born on March 16, 1878. Reza Shah's father was Abbas Ali Khan, Major of the First Regiment of Sawad Kuh, a regiment composed entirely of inhabitants of that region. His grandfather was a captain in the same regiment who died in battle during the Iranian siege of Herat in 1856. Reza Shah's father died on November 26, 1878, only a few months after his son's birth, and guardianship of the youth was assumed by his uncle, Nasrollah Khan, General of the Brigade of which the Sawad Kuh regiment formed a part and Commander of the garrison at Teheran. There Reza Shah was given a military education in accordance with the family tradition. In 1900 at the age of twenty-two Reza Shah entered the Iranian Cossack Brigade where he made a distinguished record and eventually rose to the rank of General. Dissatisfied with the then weak government at Teheran under which the country was fast drifting into a state of anarchy, Reza Shah (then Reza Khan) played a leading role in the coup d'état of February 21, 1921, at which time he was made Commander in Chief of the Army. Several months thereafter, on April 25, 1921, he was named Minister of War and on October 28, 1923, he was made Prime Minister. Following the abolition of the Kajar [Qajar] Dynasty, Reza Shah was named regent and Chief of the Provisional Government on October 31, 1925, and on December 12 of the same year he was chosen sovereign of Iran by a Constituent Assembly. On December 17, 1925, he took the oath to defend the Constitution, and on April 25, 1926, he was formally crowned at Teheran. According to the Constitution of Iran succession to the throne passes to the eldest son of the reigning sovereign. The present Crown Prince is His Imperial Highness Shahpur Mohammad Reza, who was born on October 26, 1919. Other children of His Majesty are Their Highnesses Prince (Shahpur) Ali Reza Pahlavi, Prince Gholam Reza Pahlavi, Prince Abdor Reza Pahlavi, Prince Ahmad Reza Pahlavi, Prince Mahmoud Reza Pahlavi, Prince Hamid Reza Pahlavi, and Their Highnesses, Princess (Shahdokht) Hamdam Khanum Atabay, Princess Schamsolmolouk Pahlavi, Princess Aschrafolmolouk Pahlavi and Princess Fatmeh Khanum Pahlavi.[3]

Reza Khan's Background and Character

Even the date of birth given in the so-called official account was false. In a 1936 report on Reza Shah's state of health, Gordon P. Merriam, American chargé d'affaires ad interim, observes: "The Shah's age is believed to be about sixty-nine, although there seems to be an effort to create the impression that he is ten years younger."[4] Few journalists and writers paid attention to Reza Shah's official biography. In a *Washington Post* article on the British General Sir Edmund Ironside, journalist Jack Culmer refers to Reza Khan: "Four years later, Reza Khan, peasant, half-Cossack and half-bandit, occupied the Peacock Throne of Persia vacated by the deposed Ahmad Shah."[5] After desperate representation by the State Department, the *Post* quickly published a retraction and apology.

In his 1939 book *Inside Asia*, John Gunther devotes a chapter to Reza Shah. On political prisoners, Gunther writes, "There is no trial, no sentence. Enemies are supposed to be removed, if removal for good is deemed necessary, not by the headman's ax or firing squad but by the more melodramatic method of poisoning. The disgruntled call it cheerlessly the inoculation Pahlevi. A pellet in the breakfast coffee one fine day—and then there aren't any more fine days. It may be announced that the victim died of a stroke." Gunther reveals that not even dogs had been spared the brutality of His Majesty: "When the Shah travels (and he travels incessantly) the dogs are killed in any village that he spends the night. This is because he is a light sleeper, easily disturbed by noise." Gunther also notes, "The Shah is believed to be the largest individual landowner in Asia, except possibly the Emperor of Japan. He owns vast properties throughout Iran, largely confiscated from rebellious former owners. . . . His Imperial Majesty is, oddly enough, the only monarch in the world in the hotel business. Travel in Persia is a state monopoly; the Shah personally owns most of the hotels, especially those along the Caspian."[6]

The descriptions given by other contemporaries, such as Millspaugh, and in the confidential American diplomatic reports were also vastly different from the "official" biography. According to Millspaugh, Reza was the "son of Mazanderan peasants," and "a creature of primitive instincts, undisciplined by education and experience, surrounded by servile flatterers, advised by the timid and the selfish. . . . Brutality and greed, already well marked among his traits of character, grew to dominate his behavior. . . . In any event, as time passed he put aside his more or less decent counselors and surrounded himself with the worst elements of the Empire. These he made his accomplices. To these he gave privileges and favors. With amazing thoroughness, he rewarded vice and punished virtue. At the same time, he presented to his impressionable people a personal example of colossal corruption."[7]

In a highly confidential report obtained with difficulty by the American embassy in London, the description of Reza Shah's background is very different from the official version given by the Iranian government and polished by the Division of Near Eastern Affairs of the State Department. A strictly confidential letter, dated May 29, 1936, from Ray Atherton, counselor at the American embassy in London, to Wallace S. Murray, chief of Near Eastern affairs at the State Department, contains part of the confidential State Department report. (Atherton mentions Hugh Millard, second secretary of the American legation in Tehran in 1930.)

Dear Wallace: With reference to your letter of April 7th regarding the early life of the Shah of Persia, the following is the pertinent portion of a strictly confidential biographical sketch of his life which the Embassy was permitted to copy as a personal favor.

"Pahlavi, Reza Shah. Born about 1873. Comes of a small family of Sawad Kuh in Mazandaran. His father was a Persian and his mother of Caucasian stock, whose parents sought refuge in Persia when certain Caucasian districts were ceded to Russia under the treaty of Turkomanchai. He entered the Persian Cossack Brigade at the age of 15 and was employed as a stable boy. He rose from the ranks and gained the approval of the Russian instructors of the brigade for his courage and fearlessness, and whenever an expedition was sent to any part of the country to round up brigands or quell a disturbance he seems to have taken part in it. At the beginning of the War he had been promoted to Colonel, and in 1921 when the Cossack Brigade, previously transformed into a division, was deprived of its Russian officers in Northern Persia and was in need of a resolute leader, the choice fell on Reza Khan." The above mentioned report makes no reference to the Shah as "formerly a stable boy in the British legation at Teheran." Millard tells me that when he was in Teheran he asked someone, whom he thinks was the head of the Imperial Bank of Persia, Wilkinson, whether it was true that there had existed a photograph of the Shah, then a Cossack soldier, standing guard at the Bank, and he was informed that it was true. Millard also tells me that there was a similar picture of the Shah standing guard in front of the British Legation. Millard did not see either of these alleged pictures. He also tells me that his Persian cook told him that he had been (presumably before the War) second cook at the German Legation and more than once on cold nights, when parties were being given, he had sent coffee out to his old friend, Reza Khan, on guard duty in front of the Legation.[8]

On June 16 Murray sent the following confidential reply to Atherton: "Dear Ray: Many thanks for your letter of May 29, 1936, quoting a pertinent portion of a strictly confidential biographic sketch of the Shah. This sketch was exactly what we wanted and confirms our own information.

You may be assured that the sketch itself as well as the source from which it was obtained will be regarded as strictly confidential."[9] In 1939, Murray would polish up Reza Khan's "official" biography, intended for distribution to journalists.

The American diplomatic dispatches from Tehran are rife with observations of this nature about Reza Shah's peasant background and his total lack of formal education and culture. For instance, in a confidential report the American minister, Charles C. Hart, refers to Reza Shah as "an illiterate peasant's equally illiterate son."[10] In another dispatch Hart comments: "Five years of wielding the Imperial Power from the Peacock Throne of the Shahinshahs of Persia has changed but little the rough and direct drill-sergeant characteristics of the founder of the Pahlavi dynasty. I need not, I believe, elaborate this point. Incidents reported in my despatches and in those of my predecessors and the general opinion of competent local observers point to this statement as being almost axiomatic."[11]

Reporting on his first meeting with Reza Shah in February 1930, Hart observes: "I may yet change my opinion, but I departed with the conviction that I had met a man who was only a few jumps from savagery."[12] Extensive excerpts from this first encounter with Reza Shah are given below. At this point, suffice it to say that when he left Iran four years later, not only had Hart not changed his opinion, he had become convinced that his first impression had been overly charitable.

Reports of Reza Shah's personal cruelty and violence to servants, gardeners, elderly newspaper editors, senior army officers, and cabinet ministers are scattered throughout the American diplomatic reports. It is reported that laborers building the railroads were whipped on orders of Reza Shah because His Majesty did not consider them sufficiently energetic; that construction workers and masons working on His Majesty's palaces were beaten up by the shah because their work was deemed unsatisfactory; that newspaper editors were harshly dealt with.

In his report "Character of Reza Khan," the American military attaché, Captain Frank C. Jedlicka, states:

> Reza Khan the new Prime Minister of Persia even though he has risen to the highest political post in the country, has not been able to refrain from carrying with him at least one acquisition of his early days, when he was a Cossack soldier and officer. . . . Reza Khan has not lost this tendency to personally deal out punishment to those who cross his will. As War Minister, in moments of passion, he slapped the faces of and otherwise physically assaulted a Prime Minister, a chief of police, newspaper editors, officers and others. Within the last two weeks he has again been the subject of several outbursts of wrath, where the causes thereof received immediate physical punishment administered personally by the Premier. His latest victims are reported to be a police officer and a

pseudo-mullah. This lack of restraint of the primitive instinct on the part of
Reza Khan is undoubtedly deplorable. It arouses adverse comment, particularly
among foreigners. A Teheran journal which had the audacity to criticize Reza
Khan on this score was promptly suppressed. To properly understand these acts
of the Premier, it is necessary to take into consideration his early environment
and the physical and mental make up of the man.[13]

The Suppression of Newspapers

While reporting on the physical violence toward newspaper editors, the
military attaché also describes the rapid disappearance of Tehran's newspapers: "Since the accession of Reza Khan to the Premiership [October
1923] several of the leading newspapers of Teheran have been suppressed,
while others have gone out of existence. It is expected that under the present regime, of the thirty or more Persian papers, which have been appearing during the last two years, at most, ten of the leading ones will survive.
It can be assumed that those journals which survive will do so by virtue of
their pro-Reza Khan activity, or because they will abstain from attacking or
criticizing the Government."[14] The suppression of newspapers by Reza
Khan had begun long before he became prime minister, but the atmosphere of terror created by the British through Reza Khan and the silencing
of the newspapers was far more than that created under Vossough-ed-
Dowleh just two or three years earlier. A dispatch of March 1, 1922, from
C. Van H. Engert, American chargé d'affaires ad interim, includes "a rather
pathetic farewell address to its readers by the newspaper *Nejat-i-Iran* [Sal-
vation of Iran] which, together with numerous other newspapers in
Teheran, was suppressed by the order of the Minister of War because they
had expressed themselves somewhat freely as to the share Reza Khan had in
the coup d'état of last year. One or two of the editors were flogged." The
text of the letter follows:

Compatriots:
   Farewell! The newspapers *Setareeh-i-Iran* [Star of Iran] and *Setareeh-i-
Shargh* [Star of the East] have vanished. We too drop our pen and voluntarily
discontinue the newspaper *Nejat-i-Iran*. We leave this task to our colleagues. The
anniversary of the 21st of February 1921, and we also are expecting imprisonment and suppression. We go today and you tomorrow! If you venture to search
for the real author of the coup d'état, you will be arrested, put in jail and punished. You, the deputies of the Medjliss, who laugh now and then at the editors
of the newspapers being flogged at Isfahan and Teheran! If this condition continues, you yourself will be bastinadoed right in front of the Medjliss! Then the
people will laugh at you! It is during your Premiership, Moshir-ed-Dowleh, that
we are forced to undergo pressure and restriction. This ignominy will always be
a stain on you. History will preserve it. Censorship of the very air we breathe does

not allow us to further disclose our opinions. Compatriots! Farewell!
 —February 24, 1922[15]

A month later, Engert relayed a press clipping from the newspaper *Haghi-gat* (Truth) of April 3:

Today and the Past. Is there a law authorizing the Military Government to threaten the speakers and journalists with "cutting their tongues" and "break- ing their pens"? Does the law authorize the Military Government to imprison and banish editors of the newspapers? Does the law prescribe to the printing offices to refuse printing articles attacking the Military Government? Does the law provide that a member of the Cabinet [Reza Khan] can at the same time hold the portfolio of the Minister of War and be the Commander-in-Chief of the Army, the Director-General of Indirect Taxes, and also in the name of mar- tial law to interfere in judicial and other Government affairs? Is this monopoly permitted by the Constitution? Is it not despotism? Did the law forbid the peo- ple of Tabriz from complaining when their houses and stores were plundered by the Cossacks after the defeat of Lahouti? Does the law forgive Mokhber-os- Saltaneh, the assassin of Sheikh Mohammad Khiabani, the late leader of the democratic party of Azerbaijan, and grant him a seat in Parliament? It is reac- tion which forces Farrokhi, the editor of *Toufan*, and Falsafi, the editor of *Hayat*, to take asylum in the Soviet Legation and at the Shah Abdul Azim Shrine, respectively. We say the Constitution, which is the cost of the blood of our patriotic martyrs of liberty, must not be trampled upon. We say a member of the Cabinet must not have arbitrary powers.[16]

Finally, the complete silencing of Iran's newspapers was achieved with the brutal murder of the poet and anti-British newspaper editor Mirza Zadeh Eshghi in July 1924 as he emerged from his house (see chapter 6). Although the three masked murderers were not caught, few had any doubt as to who the real assassin was.[17] With the silencing of the newspapers, a significant obstacle to the complete dictatorship of Reza Khan had been erased. The British were well on their way to achieving their objectives in Persia: complete political control, the unhampered exploitation and plun- der of Iran's oil resources, and the development of Iran's economy along lines conducive to British interests.

Incidents of Personal Brutality

In a confidential report from 1923 the American consul Bernard Gotlieb provides evidence of Reza Khan's brutality:

The present Premier is an ignorant peasant of brutish instincts who has risen to the present position through a certain native shrewdness, resolution and firmness of character rarely found in a Persian. He is a man of uncontrolled pas- sions—he personally assaulted the former Prime Minister, Ghavam[Qavam]-

es-Saltaneh (in the presence of the Shah it is reported); administered a terrible beating with his own hands to an offending journalist, an old white-bearded Persian—this in the presence of a member of the American colony who states that it was the most pitiful and degraded exhibition of brutality that he had ever witnessed, and since his accession as Premier, he has on several occasions publicly assaulted members of his suite or offending officials including a severe beating administered to an old Sheikh who because of defective eyesight failed to rise as Reza Khan entered the room where he was sitting. I repeat that it is not absolutely outside the bounds of probability that upon the first real hint of opposition by a finance official, the Premier's animal instincts may get the better of him, and an incident created which will have far-reaching results.[18]

Even before becoming prime minister, Reza Khan had developed a habit of savagely beating newspaper editors, as attested by the American minister Joseph S. Kornfeld:

As an indication of Reza Khan's brutality, I would cite two very recent occurrences. Two days ago one of the newspapers had the courage to demand that the Minister of War present his budget to Parliament like any other Minister. Forthwith he had the editor brought to his office, personally beat him most brutally, knocking out several of his teeth, and had him imprisoned. This savage assault was reported to me by an American who was an eye-witness. The other incident which throws light on Reza Khan's character was related to me by the Belgian Minister. One of his Cossack officers came to the office of a Belgian functionary in the Ministry of Finance and demanded 3000 tomans on the order of the Minister of War. The functionary remonstrated, pleading that he could not honor the voucher unless endorsed by the Minister of Finance. Thereupon, the Cossack proceeded to beat him, locked him up in his office, and detained him there until he extorted the money.[19]

Nearly a dozen years later, there had been no abatement of Reza Khan's brutality to those who could not defend themselves. In March 1935 the American minister William H. Hornibrook reported in passing Reza Shah's beating of the editor of a scholarly publication: "Only a month or two ago Seif-i-Azad, publisher of *Iran-i-Bastan,* was summoned to appear before His Majesty and roundly scorned. Rumor has it that at the conclusion of the interview the publisher was personally given a thrashing by the Shah."[20] Violence against subordinates had not abated even on happier occasions. In May 1936, Reza Shah traveled to Bandar-e Pahlavi (Enzeli) to meet his son and designated successor, Mohammad Reza, who was returning after five years of study in Switzerland. On the way to Pahlavi, Reza Shah stopped at Chalus:

The Shah stopped at Chalus for luncheon en route to Pahlevi. All that morning gardeners had been rushing to and fro watering the plants to have everything fresh and green. The following scene is related by Major Pybus, the British Military Attaché, who witnessed it from the window of the hotel there. Upon descending from his automobile, almost the first thing the Shah did was to strike one of the gardeners in the face with the full sweep of his arm. He similarly struck two other gardeners before he left, and had two trees uprooted that had been planted in a manner or position not to his liking. When the Shah left, the general relief was both great and apparent.[21]

The Shah's violence to high government officials was a common occurrence. As described by Hart, a most shocking incidence of personal savagery was the Shah's 1933 prison beating of Teymourtache, which left him unconscious (see chapter 6). In 1938, Engert reported other beatings, such as that of General Amanullah Jehanbani. In July 1937 there was a rumor that the French military mission in Tehran would be replaced with a German mission. The French minister, Monsieur Bodard, sought the assistance of General Jehanbani, a Francophile who had studied in France. Jehanbani conveyed the French minister's concern to the shah:

> The Shah was so infuriated by what he considered as unwarranted interference on the part of the French Minister that he struck Jehanbani in the face, ordered him to take off his uniform, and told him never to show his face again. The entire incident, although fantastic from our point of view, is very typical of the present regime. The Shah is so utterly unfamiliar with Western notions of liberty and justice, and lives in such Oriental isolation that he never developed the slightest regard for human susceptibilities. His truculent manners, his intolerance of the slightest opposition or criticism, and his directness of action have made him undisputed master of his subjects. He has no use whatever for politicians and diplomats, and apparently enjoys treating them with the strong-arm methods of the "man-on-horseback." That this has already had deplorable effects on the diplomatic relations of Iran with certain other countries is notorious, and in this particular case all efforts to improve relations with France have been practically nullified.[22]

The beating of General Reza Qoli Amir Khosrovi, Minister of Finance, is also recorded in detail by Moose. Prior to becoming minister of finance in 1940, Amir Khosrovi had served as head of the National Bank for nearly a decade, and prior to that he had served as head of Bank Pahlevi, Reza Shah's personal bank. "Colonel Amir Khosrovi, Managing Director of the National Bank of Persia and the man who once visualized an exclusive automotive monopoly under his own personal direction and control, was elevated by the Shah during the New Year's festivities to the rank of General."[23]

Few other individuals had helped Reza Shah in transferring his fortune to foreign banks as much as Amir Khosrovi. Such was Reza Shah's affection for Amir Khosrovi that he was sometimes jokingly referred to in the diplomatic reports as Madame Pahlevi. On May 18, 1941, it was announced that

Amir Khosrovi had been excused from his duties as minister of finance, and had been replaced by Abbas Qoli Golshayan. James S. Moose, chargé d'affaires ad interim, reports:

> The underlying reason which prompted the Shah to remove General Khosrovi is not yet apparent. The Shah was absent from Tehran during the first half of May, traveling in the Caspian provinces; and he is reported to have returned to Tehran in a bad humor. At a meeting of the Iranian cabinet, the Shah is said to have called for certain papers; and when General Khosrovi failed to produce them, the Shah expressed his disapproval by beating General Khosrovi with his riding crop in the presence of the other cabinet members, and by telling him to go to his house and stay there—the Pahlavi phraseology of dismissal. . . . The same report comes from many sources, and it fits well with the Shah's treatment of his officials, so that there is slight reason to doubt that it is essentially accurate. General Khosrovi was outstanding because of the favor which the Shah had formerly shown him."[24]

Hart's First Impressions of Reza Shah

Late in 1929 the State Department announced the appointment of Charles Calmer Hart, the American minister in Albania, as the new minister in Tehran. Hart and his family arrived in Tehran in early January 1930, and for the next four years Hart was to provide much useful reporting on political and financial matters. Hart describes his first meeting with the shah, on the occasion of the presentation of his papers as Minister Plenipotentiary and Envoy Extraordinary of the United States:

> Notwithstanding these cares notice came on February 6 that the Shah would receive me at the Gholestan Palace three days later, Sunday the 9th. The only unusual feature of the occasion was that both of the Imperial cars sent to convey me and my staff to the palace were of American make. Otherwise I sensed nothing to sweeten an atmosphere perceptibly befogged by the overhanging mood of a medieval mentality, disappointed and disgruntled. The ceremony was carried through with precision, but to me the Shah gave the appearance of uneasiness. He read his speech in reply stammeringly and greeted me with an artificial smile as he extended his hand. It is plausible that he feared I might take advantage of the occasion to bring up the question of the railroad. On the other hand it had been suggested to me beforehand that I should be prepared should he project the question into our first exchange. But nothing of the kind. Manifestly he was at a loss for anything to say and leaned heavily during the brief chat on the cerebrum of his Minister of Court, who, in the presence of his chief, is not the cocksure chanticleer that he is on other occasions and in other company.
> I relieved the situation by asking permission to present my staff, which consisted of Mr. Millard, whose assignment to this post was a most happy selection. After a few words by the Shah, as laid down by the protocols, he took leave and hastened to the door, which he opened himself, leading out of the large room

FIGURE 5.1 *Charles Calmer Hart, American minister to Persia, 1930–1933. Courtesy of the National Archives.*

where the reception took place. For that provision of the protocols I thanked somebody. How much simpler than to have to back out of a large room bowing. When the Shah hurried away, Teymourtache, his Minister of Court, rushed after him, first trying to open the door and then making a move to accompany his chief into the next room but was waved back. What happened looked like a sharp rebuff but was explained later to me by the Turkish Ambassador as nothing more than the Shah's customary rudeness to everyone about him. It is the custom after meeting a new monarch, or a national executive, to give a rather pleasing account of one's impressions. I may change my opinion, but I departed with a conviction that I had met a man who was only a few jumps from savagery; that he has achieved his imperial position by a form of brute sagacity which gave him control of the army and the tribal genius to use it to his own ends, which I should say is not so much for the good of Persia or its people but for self-glorification and personal aggrandizement. His imperial strutting proves one proposition, and the almost limitless estates he has bought or confiscated in districts he expects the railroad to develop establishes the other.

The crudity of his mind is brought into relief by a bit of information dropped at the Legation a few days ago by my German colleague who has been here for seven years. Describing the Monarch's idiosyncrasies he said that when out motoring it is not unusual, if a puncture occurs, for the Shah to draw his pistol and threaten to shoot the chauffeur. A. W. Dubois, Manager for Ulen & Company, said that, when on a recent tragic inspection trip of the railroad in the South, the Shah suddenly decided that some of the laborers were not showing enough energy. He pointed to them and ordered some soldiers to give them a lashing. He was satisfied when the whip had been severely applied to a considerable number of the men on the work. My impressions are so far unfavorable because, coming from Albania which was once termed "little bit of Asia set down in Europe," and which was regarded by some as more oriental than Turkey, I had expected something better in Persia. I am forced to the conclusion that [King] Zog of Albania is not less than one century ahead of the Shah and that the Albanian peasant is an aristocrat as compared with the poor peasants of

FIGURE 5.2 *Reza Shah Pahlavi. This framed needlework portrait hung in the bedroom of Mohammad Reza Shah in Niavaran Palace. Courtesy of the Organization of National Cultural Heritage, Ministry of Education and Islamic Guidance, Tehran.*

Persia. In Albania peasants live in real houses, while in Persia many of the peasants are virtually unclad, and have nothing but mud or thatched huts devoid of furnishings. However, I find my surroundings just as interesting as I anticipated, and am more than grateful for the opportunity to come to this post.[25]

Reza Khan's Early Avarice

Based on State Department records, we know that as soon as he had been placed in power by the British, Reza Khan began amassing wealth. The process included the blackmail and other forms of extortion from wealthy individuals. From Engert we also learn that Reza Khan had attempted extortion from Ahmad Shah: "The Shah has officially announced his intention to leave for Europe on the 25th instant expecting to be absent six months ostensibly for reasons of health. The Legation is reliably informed that the real reason for the Shah's determination to leave is the insistent demand for money made upon him by the Minister of War which he refused."[26]

Reza Khan transferred vast sums to foreign banks (his transfer of $200,000 to Europe was noted in chapter 4). By 1926, Reza Shah's transfers to foreign banks had evidently reached such a level that it was felt necessary to deny them. American minister Hoffman Philip describes an army announcement dated April 29, 1926, just days after the coronation of Reza Shah, that contains "a categorical denial that the Shah or any member of the Royal family had any savings deposited in a foreign or domestic bank. Officers, therefore, are strictly prohibited from such practices as inimical to the country's interests. This statement on behalf of the Shah has given rise to considerable speculation as to the source of his own reputedly large fortune."[27]

By 1924, few, including Wallace S. Murray, chargé d'affaires ad interim, had any illusions about the unlimited greed of Reza Khan: "While it is generally admitted that he has robbed less than many would have done in his place with about $10,000,000 a year at his absolute disposal, it is nevertheless a fact that he has in the last two years acquired great wealth at the expense of a bankrupt country, and so hypnotized has everyone been that no one dared to question his right to plunder, and even the American financial mission has been unable to force him to account." The $10 million Murray refers to is the annual budget of the Ministry of War, which constituted nearly half the entire government budget. Moreover, no accounting as to how this money was spent was ever given. Murray had also included the following: "I am sure that the Department will be interested to know of a conversation I had on September 25 with the adjutant to the Prime Minister, Major Ruhollah Khan, to whom reference has frequently been made in the Legation's despatches since the Imbrie incident.

Much to my astonishment, Major Ruhollah Khan discussed his plans for the future, stating that nothing more was to be hoped from Sardar Sepah [Reza Khan] who was a hopeless opium addict and whose only desire now was to pile up an immense fortune, invest it in Europe, and get out when things got too hot."[28] And this is exactly what happened in 1941, but it is getting ahead of our story.

As noted in chapter 1, Major Ruhollah Khan was among those executed for his part in the Pouladian attempt to assassinate Reza Shah. Following the passage of the universal military service law on June 6, 1925, Murray expressed his cynicism as to its real purpose: "On June 6th Parliament approved bill imposing universal military service in Persia. The obvious advantages that Reza Khan will personally realize from the new legislation are that: 1. His power and prestige as 'Generalissimo of all the Land and Sea forces of the Persian Empire' will be greatly enhanced. 2. By the pressure of the present law he will be able to exact substantial bribes from rich Persian grandees who may desire to have their relatives exempted from military service."[29]

Acquisition of Land by Reza Shah

During the twenty years that Reza Khan was dictator of Iran, vast areas of the country, including some 7,000 villages, hamlets, and pastures, were transformed into his private estate. According to a map prepared by the American Embassy in 1954 to show the proposed sale and distribution of the "Pahlavi estates" from 1952, vast areas in northern and western Iran (practically all of Luristan and much of northern Khuzistan) were acquired by Reza Shah and subsequently became the property of his son. The relocation of the Lur and Arab tribes, the very people whose land in Luristan and northern Khuzistan had been confiscated by Reza Shah, is described in detail by Hart and his report is given below.

Hart comments that in 1932 Reza Shah was by far the largest landowner in the world. He speculates that Reza Shah's dream was to travel hundreds of miles of Iranian territory and be able to call everything in sight his own.[30] As the map shows, this dream was fully realized. Reza Shah had become the largest private landowner not only in the history of Iran, but in all likelihood in the recorded history of mankind. The manner in which this land was forcibly acquired from its owners and the brutality and mayhem that was visited on them—including execution, death in prison, and exile—would require many volumes to describe. I have described elsewhere what transpired from 1932 to 1935 in a small corner of Mazandaran when Reza Shah set about acquiring the land there.[31]

From the American diplomatic reports it is learned that the process of land acquisition on a large scale began soon after Reza Khan became shah.

In a March 1927 report Philip describes Reza Shah's "pilgrimage" to Qom: "The Shah left Teheran by automobile on the 16th instant, his birthday, ostensibly on a visit to the shrine at Kum. The most recent report of his movements is to the effect that he went to Isfahan and from there proceeded to Khoramabad in Luristan on the 20th instant. It is variously stated that the latter journey has been due to the Shah's desire to visit property which he is said to have acquired in that region."[32] The property consisted of land confiscated from the unfortunate tribes of Luristan by Reza Khan.

Shortly after this report, we learn (not surprisingly) that Reza Shah's land acquisition also involved his relatives and associates, and was not confined to rural properties, as Philip indicates:

> It is generally believed that the Shah, since his accession, is continuing to enrich himself by irregular means both at the expense of the State and of private individuals. This is said to involve questionable annexation by the Shah and his relatives of villages and lands in various parts of the country as well as acceptance of "presents" from various sources. In this connection, it may be mentioned that the private town Palace of the Shah—an extensive property which he has improved and embellished and where he resides when he is in Teheran—was formerly owned by the Kadjar Prince Firouz, now Minister of Finance. Gossip has it that this residence was "presented" to Reza Pahlavi.[33] Also, it has been suggested to me that the entire expenses of the Shah's household are supplied from funds placed at his disposal by the Ministry of War and that, consequently, the money supplied by the Ministry of Finance for the budget expenses of the household goes to swell the Shah's private fortune. I am told that the Shah probably would oppose the renewal of Millspaugh's contractual right to pass upon foreign concessions granted by the Government, for the reason that he contemplates granting to the Soviet the right to exploit certain of the northern oil fields covered by what is known as the Semnan Oil Company (also known as Khorian Company), a Persian corporation under the nominal direction of Amir Monazzam, a wealthy friend of the Shah, in which the Shah and Teymourtache are believed to be very large share holders. I mention the above reports, all of which have reached me through trustworthy sources, as a means of conveying to the Department the "background" of the situation as it actually exists here.[34]

Reports on Reza Shah's predatory acquisition of wealth continued. In October 1927, Philip reports: "The domestic political situation of the moment impresses me as unsound and as fundamentally unsatisfactory to all concerned with it. I have heard the opinion expressed here that the Shah, having amassed a great private fortune, is now doing his utmost to promote the interests of his Government and the people. I am prepared to believe that this might be the case, though I fail to perceive why he does not call into his councils the Persians of best repute rather than of the worst."[35] In his next dispatch, Philip explains that since the new railway was being built through the land "acquired" by Reza Shah, its value would be greatly enhanced. "The Shah is still away in Mazandaran with the Minister of the Court and other personages. It is reported that he visited Astara, Bander-Gaz, etc. He is supposed to have acquired extensive properties in the Mazandaran region contiguous to the projected line of railway. The British Minister told me confidentially that he has heard the Soviet Government had paid quite heavily in presents for the purpose of obtaining the consummation of the Perso-Soviet Agreements."[36]

Hart's Observations on Reza Shah's Extortion and Land Acquisition

Reporting shortly after his arrival on the disruption of commerce due to the imposition of foreign exchange controls (see chapter 14), Hart describes the difficulties that one of the wealthiest merchants, Haj Moin-ot-Tojjar Bushehri, was experiencing with His Majesty:

> Aside from the upsetting effect in trade caused by measures aimed at the control of foreign exchange, there is a story circulating in Teheran, and supported by the British Acting Commercial Attaché, concerning difficulties confronting Hadji Moin-ot-Tujjar Bushiri, one of the richest merchant princes of Persia. Bushiri, who is said to be worth 3,000,000 to 4,000,000 tomans, owns a fleet of steamers on the Karun River, vast holdings in Khuzistan, the Government concession for the iron oxide on the Hormuz Island in the Persian Gulf, and until recently a large lumbering concession in the Caspian province of Mazandaran. It is this last property which, according to reports, has brought him to grief. Bushiri, like the Shah, sold railway ties to the Syndicate from forests in Mazandaran but, though both are said to have profiteered largely but equally, the Shah concluded that Bushiri was the only profiteer of the two and seized his interests in mills and forests in that province. The report alleges that now Bushiri has been called upon to pay 600,000 tomans to His Majesty or be subjected to the indignity of having a street run through his handsome residence property in Teheran, destroying two houses.[37]

Hart refers to Bushehri's other troubles in subsequent reports. In his dispatch on the Agabekoff revelations Hart details a case of land "purchase" by Reza Shah:

> He likes money, but evidently only for the love of counting it, because he is a man of no luxuries and no vices except his opium pipe. Within the year 1930 it is safe to estimate that he increased his property holdings not less than $2,000,000. The largest part of this came in the purchase of a valuable piece of land in northern Persia from Hadji Moin Bushehri who never received the 350,000 tomans stated as the consideration although compelled to pay 50,000 tomans to the Minister of Court as a commission on the sale. The story of this transaction leaked out, so soon after the Minister of the Court demanded and

received his commission that officials of the Imperial Bank of Persia were able to recognize the 50,000 toman check when it came for collection.

The same man who sold the land and received nothing, though a very rich man, suffered other heavy losses in about the same way. Bushehri, 90 years old and a man of patriarchal appearance, is just the kind of individual the Shah would be expected to want in his scheme for modernization and industrialization, but no. Bushehri, old as he is, put transports on the Karoun River and the Gulf which proved a great help and convenience to Ulen and Company in moving their railroad construction materials. He also established lumber mills in the north which produced ties for the railroad building project in that section. Word came to the Shah that Bushehri was making a profit on selling in this way indirectly to the Government and confiscated his river and gulf transports, his mills and timber in Mazandaran. All confiscations are made in the name of the Shah and the property so taken passes to him, not the Government. The present Shah, taken all in all, is from what I know the best man from almost every standpoint that has ruled Persia in several centuries. He is constructive. Only but for his lust of riches, an attribute generally known and recognized, he might be the equal of some of the lesser monarchs in Europe. And at that I would say he is superior to King Carroll of Roumania. Though knowing his worship of money and property I was long reluctant about believing that the highways and byways of graft led up to the throne. Now I am convinced of it and this despatch is written for the purposes of the archives.[38]

Bushehri's case is particularly interesting because it confirms that Reza Shah confiscated not only agricultural properties, but also industrial mills and even river and sea transportation. In reading this case, one begins to understand why Iran, despite its oil income, never developed an industrial economy. Security of and respect for private property and laws was destroyed by Reza Shah, and then by his son and successor. In discussing the role of Teymourtache, minister of the court, Hart recounts the arrest of Bushehri's son:

While the Minister of Court may have no illusion about his popularity, I doubt that the Shah really knows how he stands in the estimation of his subjects. This is not to be wondered at since he is surrounded by people who are afraid to tell His Majesty any unpleasant truth. His temper is notoriously short, and his punishments swift and severe, so no one wishes to risk incurring His Majesty's displeasure. How frank the Minister of Court has been is not clear, but judging by the enormous amount of property that the Shah is said ruthlessly to have taken and continues to take from the owners, it would appear that Teymourtache has done little to check his Sovereign's avarice. This greed for wealth has done more than anything else to make the Shah unpopular, and though no one dares to say a word against him, I am told that he is as much hated as he is feared. With reference to a young man named Bushiri, the wife of one of the high officials of the Foreign Office was asked if he was the son of the wealthy merchant Bushiri who was having some difficulties with the Shah. She said he was, adding with a smile, "all wealthy men have difficulties with His Majesty." With reference to the Shah and his propensity for acquiring property, another of my colleagues remarked bluntly: "I wonder why someone doesn't kill him."[39]

It was later learned that the British took substantial care to safeguard the life of Reza Shah. The noted presence of the British military attaché during Reza Shah's trips underscored the point. Hart nevertheless concludes, "The Shah is nevertheless a man of unquestionable courage and I believe despite his shortcomings he is no doubt the best man in Persia for Sovereign. The thought of what will happen when he dies gives one pause."[40] One year later, Hart was finally to undergo a drastic change of opinion.

Reza Shah's Trips to the Caspian Region

On April 29, 1931, Reza Shah traveled to Gilan, where he opened a bridge over the Sefid Rud River and then, according to Hart,

proceeded to Barfarush to visit his extensive estates in that district. He returned to Tehran on May 12, and the Minister of the Court, who had accompanied the Shah, reached Tehran several days earlier. The brother-in-law of one the Shah's suite recounted to an American in Tehran the following incidents that took place during the trip.

Due to an unfortunate misunderstanding, the Governor and Chief of Police at Barfarush were not accurately advised of the Shah's plans and failed to meet him at his arrival. This started things off badly and when he inspected a new building being erected on his property he called the lieutenant in charge of the work and the following conversation took place.

H.M. Don't you think this is a rotten Job?
Lieut. Yes, Your Majesty.
H.M. How much money did I send you for the construction?
Lieut. Six thousand tomans, Your Majesty.
H.M. You must have wiped your boots with it.
Lieut. Yes, Your Majesty.
H.M. Aren't you a damned fool?
Lieut. Yes, Your Majesty.

Taking exception to the manner in which two masons were conducting their work the Shah beat them. Later, royal clemency was appealed to on behalf of an officer who had been imprisoned and fined 400 tomans for failure to complete a building quickly enough. The officer had served his time but the Governor suggested that it was not the man's fault and that the 400 tomans might be returned to him. The Shah said, "No. He will work better in the future." At Sari, the Shah was greeted by the Governor, who is a very stout man with rolls of fat over his collar. Turning to the crowd he asked if they didn't think this was a funny man to have for governor. This started off His Excellency badly and he had the greatest difficulty in making convincing the various requests and explanations which he subsequently submitted to the Shah. At the same town when the Shah was inspecting the station and other buildings erected by the German consortium he had the following conversation with the Persian in charge:

H.M. What is that building over there across the tracks?
Eng[ineer]. Those are the living quarters for the railway personnel, Your Majesty.
H.M. They don't need such fine quarters and anyway isn't it built on my property?
Eng. Yes, Your Majesty, but it wasn't Your Majesty's property when the building was erected.
H.M. Well it is now and so is the building. Go and seal it up.
Eng. Yes, Your Majesty.[41]

What became of the hapless workers who had inhabited His Majesty's property is not described by Hart. Hart's conclusion to his dispatch is revealing: "Though the foregoing incidents seem to indicate a harshness of character, I am not at all convinced that Persia is not just as well off for such displays of temper on the part of its Sovereign and the results tend to indicate that the Shah knows best how to govern his people."[42]

Reza Shah's frequent trips to the Caspian region are described by Hart in his numerous reports. A dispatch from November 1931 contains the following:

Again, I have the honor to report, the Shah is traveling in the northern provinces of his realm. But just over a month after his return from the tour of inspection, His Majesty again left the capital for what, probably because it is his birthplace, is his favorite as well as the most favored region of the Empire. The rich Caspian coastal province of Mazanderan has been the greater part of His Majesty's travels. His itinerary was via the ancient road, now modern and as well built a motor highway as the country boasts, one hundred miles from Tehran eastward along the mountainous northern edge of the central Persian plateau to Firuzkuh, altitude 7,500 feet, and thence northward down the fifty mile valley leading to Aliabad and Barfurush on the Caspian plain, 86 feet below sea level.

Near the latter town there is a royal palace and extensive land belonging to the Crown. The former, now renamed Shahi, is the westernmost station of the eighty mile northern trial section of the projected trans-Persian railway. The distance between the two towns is almost twenty miles. At a somewhat shorter distance to the north lies the fishing port of Meshed-i-Sar [Mashhad], famous for its caviar, wild boar, and salmon. From Meshed-i-Sar it is some two hundred miles by coastal road to Resht [Rasht] and Pahlevi on the opposite, southwestern, corner of the Caspian. Halfway between the two is the new port of Habibabad which is to be the northern extremity of the so-called Chalus road that will bring the capital within some three to four hours driving (by automobile) distance of the Caspian.

At Habibabad the Shah owns extensive properties, largely acquired since his accession to the Throne, near the scene of his birthplace. These properties, too, he is visiting during the course of his present trip. Then, weather permitting, for the Caspian rains have begun and much of the coastal plain resembles one great field of rice, its most notable agricultural product, His Majesty will continue on to Pahlevi and return to Tehran via the old Russian-built Resht-Kazvin post road.

A story. There are three ways by which His Majesty is said to have acquired his extensive land holdings near Habibabad. Certain lands were purchased, or, as some say, acquired by the time honored Persian practice of forcing the landlords to transfer title for a fraction of the property's real value. These originally acquired lands were scattered. They had, under Persia's new laws, to be registered. This step was taken. But, at the same time, all small alien bits of land lying within the boundaries of such property were also registered in His Majesty's name. And, if the Shah's holdings were small, why then any lands lying between them and his larger holdings were also included. The net result, I am told, is that practically the whole of that part of Mazanderan is now registered in His Majesty's name. The largest single tract was acquired by purchase, but the purchase price was never delivered although the former owner was compelled to pay a commission of 50,000 tomans on the sale.[43]

Reza Shah's Maniacal Avarice

In discussing Reza Shah's fear of communism, Hart includes the following observation:

> His natural avarice alone is sufficient to cause him to shudder when he thinks of the confiscation and nationalization of private property. On this question the Shah is a man of deep convictions.
>
> If there is anything Reza Shah loves more than another it is private property; that is, private property that he can call his own. In a way he favors nationalization but not nationalization in the name of the state. In the name of the head of state, that would be different. I have not the least doubt that he stands ready to take title to every foot of earth in Persia if this can be accomplished without inciting a revolution. He is reported to be today, perhaps, the largest single landowner in the old world. If one travels along almost any highway in Persia with an individual familiar with the lay of the land it is constantly being pointed out that "this village belongs to the Shah," or some limitless stretch of land "belongs to His Majesty." It can be safely said, also, that hundreds of more villages and thousands upon thousands more hectares of land are already earmarked for registry in the name of Shahinshah, may his reign endure forever,

just as soon as the transfers can be arranged in a manner not to cause too strong
a revulsion of public or private feeling.[44]

On December 28, 1932, at the height of the "dispute" with Britain over oil,
the minister of the court, Abdol Hosein Teymourtache, was dismissed and
arrested. In "Teymourtache To Be Tried: Strictly Confidential Musings on
His Pahlevi Majesty" Hart accurately predicts, "As for my own views, I do
not give the one-time Minister of the Court a beggar's chance to escape from
the worst that could happen." He continues about Reza Shah and his rule:

> The world has been regaled for ten years with stories of the advanced con-
> ceptions of Reza Shah Pahlevi. Sometimes I have been guilty of paying too
> much tribute to his construction of boulevards, highways and schools; to the
> success of his drill-sergeant-like re-establishment of a considerable measure of
> public security throughout the scattered provinces of this realm; and to the
> notable progress made in breaking feudalist powers of provincial landlords and
> tribal chieftains. Just now I am not sure that I have not been a dupe.
>
> Reza Shah is just as Oriental in his mentality as any of his predecessors and
> perhaps is the least educated of all the rulers of Persia in several centuries. Much
> has been made by me and others of his policies of centralization, public
> improvements, et cetera; but I fear that all of us, in so reporting, have failed to
> take into consideration the ultimate ends which he had ambition to achieve.
>
> To many of those predecessors, even the truly great Shah Abbas is not
> entirely guiltless, the mark of progress may be epitomized as the building of
> luxurious palaces, not that gorgeous palaces were best for the country or that
> the attendant development of the arts would advance the economic betterment
> of the masses of their subjects, but that such achievements would stand out in
> future history as monuments to their procreators. I have arrived at the conclu-
> sion that, just as former Shahs constructed palaces for their own personal glory,
> so Reza Shah has been constructing railroads, highways and boulevards for his
> own personal glory and with the added aim of private aggrandizement. What I
> mean by private aggrandizement will be explained by what is to follow.
>
> It is my opinion that the present Shah has never had in mind the real
> advancement of his subjects or the establishment of safeguards for those who
> have honestly come into possession of money or property—that his conception
> of kingly duty has not included the lifting of the impoverished masses, four-
> fifths of the country's 13,000,000 population, from their filth and squalor.
>
> On account of his maniacal personal avarice, which today is unsurpassed in
> the history of kings—for it has grown fat on the feedings of the past ten years—
> I would say that, rather than making Persia a good place for Persians, his inten-
> tions have been to make Persia a good place for Reza Shah. I have heard it said
> there is not a day when he does not quietly gather in a new estate in some part
> of the country. In transferring the private property of others to his own name
> he is reputed to have become the largest single landowner in the world. This is
> perhaps true.
>
> It appears entirely probable today that his single aim has become the
> building of a personal empire, or a new spectacular Garden of Allah, where

the chief title role would be played by himself and where as nearly as possible, every piece of arable land on his horizon can be called his own; that he may be able to travel for hundreds, yes, thousands, of miles and point to every-thing within his vision as "mine." The roads and the railroads which he is building would therefore become nothing more than communications between all of his vast estates. Besides the rapid acquisition of land in his name which has been going on from the day of his accession to the throne, measures have obviously been underway to squeeze the last bit of property and money out of the hands of the heretofore prosperous class. For instance, the prominent Kazeruni family has virtually been reduced to the pauper level, and the Bushehri family is on the way out. Since taking over the largest of the Bushehri estates in Mazanderan three years ago and refusing later to pay the purchase price of 350,000 tomans although the now suppressed Minister of Court compelled Bushehri to pay a commission of 50,000 tomans on the sale the Shah has been relentless in the pursuit of the family. Sometime after that profitable transaction was carried out the Government confiscated the Bushehri sawmills and adjacent lands in Mazandaran and Bushehri boats on the Karun River on the pretext that Bushehri interests were making too large profits in selling ties to the northern railway and in transporting supplies to the Ulen and Company work in the south.

From Persian authority I had it a few days ago that a recent assessment of 2,000,000 tomans had been levied on the Bushehri family and payment com-pelled although receipts were produced to prove that the family taxes had at no time been delinquent. It has been reported, and is probably true, that Aqa Reza Dehdashti Bushehri, one of the younger members of the family, Deputy in the last Majlis and a man of culture and polish educated in England, has been thrown in jail within the last two weeks on some charge linking him with the Teymourtache operations. In Shiraz a few weeks ago I heard the declaration that Solat-ed-Doleh, Kashqai chieftain, was not seized and taken to prison in Teheran because of actual evidence of plotting against the Government. His arrest, the confident belief was expressed, was ordered that the Shah might be free to gobble up all of his lands and houses, among the richest estates remain-ing in southern Persia.

Human instincts, I would say, will never intervene to save Teymourtache from punishment as barbarous or diabolical as that earlier Shahs visited upon officials who had fallen into disfavor. In my despatch No. 16 of February 11, 1930, reporting my presentations of my papers to the Shah three years ago I wrote: I may change my opinion, but I departed with the conviction that I had met a man who was only a few jumps from savagery. Later I revised that opinion somewhat but in recent months the bulk of evidence, not all of it hearsay by any means, has tended to support that first impression. There is no end to the stories one hears of Reza Shah's personal cruelties. Chauffeurs, butlers, cooks, personal servants, all tell the same poignant tales of how they have been brutalized by him, and not even Ministers have escaped his corpo-ral wrath.[45]

Reza Shah's Tribal Policy

It is claimed in the literature that Reza Khan's greatest achievement was the establishment of a "national" army which was used for the unification of Iran. In a 1930 report Hart describes prevailing views of the army's achievements:

> In the opinion of many competent observers, the principal accomplishment of the present regime is the building of a comparatively well-organized and well-disciplined army of some 40,000 men and the effective use of that force in bringing order out of internal chaos. Without it the tribes would never have been subdued. Subjection was a necessary preliminary to the government's present policy of establishing schools among the almost one hundred per cent illiterate tribesmen and of moving certain of them to available agricultural lands in the settled portions of the plateau. Reza Shah may be said to have created this new army. With its support he became Shah. With Teymourtache, his able Minister of the Court, he has since utilized it as the sole means of establishing control over, controlling, and of taking the initial steps towards modernizing the country. He is sometimes criticized for having appropriated so much— over fifty per cent—of the national budget to its use.[46]

In his description of British justification of their policies in Persia and their support of Reza Shah, Hart quotes Tehran's "leading foreign banker," E. Wilkinson, head of the British-owned Imperial Bank of Persia: "The army pays for itself; it and only it has made possible the regular collection of taxes—reasonable and modest ones—throughout the country; the increased tax returns more than pay the army's expenses of upkeep."[47]

Additional insight on some of the contemporary views on tribal policy and unification can be gleaned from a 1932 commencement speech by Dr. Samuel M. Jordan, as reported by Hart: "Thirty years ago when I came to Persia, feudalism was in full swing. Each clan and tribe was ruled by its own chief who was disobedient to the Central Government. Now we have come into a new era and a youthful fortune. Under the able leadership of His Imperial Majesty Pahlevi, the Shahinshah of Persia (applause and clapping of hands), the country has a powerful and successful Central Government. Now Persia has a unified people, one Government, one State, and one Sovereign. As a result of this political unity, brought about with sacrifice by the Shahinshah, old differences no longer exist."[48]

Hart points out that Jordan's views were not shared by all foreign observers. By way of contrast, he offers the views of Professor Ernst Herzfeld, a prominent Iranologist. The "consequences" that Herzfeld refers to did not become fully apparent until 1979: "It is a system of ruining established authorities of old, without replacing them with anything at all. Everywhere we see methodic destruction of religious customs and feelings. The result is a vacuum. One day the consequences will appear. For, unfortunately, consequences of acts are unavoidable."[49]

The Relocation of Lur and Arab Tribes

Reza Shah's tribal policy and his unification of Iran consisted of massive doses of brutality as well as plunder of one-quarter of the country's population. As outlined above, the tribes of Azerbaijan had been conquered by Reza Khan's army in 1923–24, their lands seized, and their valuables plundered. The tribal policy was not confined to their subjugation and the looting of their valuables. Some information on the forcible transfer of tribal people from Luristan to other parts of Persia is reported by American chargé d'affaires David Williamson in December 1929: "It is not known accurately what numbers are involved in this enforced migration. The press gave out that 110 families, or approximately 600 persons, had been transferred to villages near Kazvin. It is learned from other sources, however, that the number of deportations is far larger than reported. . . . The condition of the deportees is said to be lamentable."[50] In a February 1931 dispatch Hart tells of thousands of people, including old men, women, and children, being made to walk hundreds of miles from Luristan and Khuzistan to remote points in Khorrasan, in forced marches reminiscent of the Soviet Union under Stalin.

> Some light on the forced migration of the Lurs was shed in the Medjliss on the night of February 1, 1931, when Taghi-Zadeh [Taqizadeh], as Minister of Finance, presented a "doubly urgent" bill providing for an additional appropriation of 50,000 tomans for the rehabilitation of Luristan. This money, it is explained, is not only for the rehabilitation of the province but also to give assistance to the thousands of tribesmen, actual number not known, who have been transferred to remote districts, mainly to Khorassan. The introduction of the bill brought forth some information on the circumstances attending the forced migration of the Lurs about which there has long been so much mystery. "The Lurs who have been shifted," said Deputy Yassaii, "have been imposed on the peasants. Numerous complaints," he continued, "are reported to have been received by the authorities concerning the forced migration of the Lurs, the non-payment of their rations, the cost of transport and other incidental expenses. It might be well for the Minister of Finance to explain who is responsible for this situation and for the attendant expenses. Which Ministry, I should like to know, handles such complaints, and who is the competent authority to administer justice to these people? What disposition, tell me please, has been made for the appropriations that have been voted for this purpose? It is reported that these appropriations are not properly spent," Yassaii is further quoted as saying, by the *Ettela'at,* Teheran newspaper. "For example," he proceeded, according to that newspaper, "the camel-drivers who transported the Lurs' effects have not been paid. The camel-drivers have, therefore, complained to all the authorities and have received no answer. I want to know to whom

these camel-drivers should be referred, to the Ministry of War or the Ministry of Finance?" "This matter is handled under the strict control of the Ministry of Finance," Taghi-Zadeh replied to Yassaii's interpolations, "and under the supervision of honest and energetic officials who report to me every week. I may present a full report on the subject. Great care is taken in the payment of medical and living expenses of the shifted tribesmen. I have taken the deepest personal interest in the medical treatment of their sick and have done everything within my powers to help them. The above measures also were taken in connection with the Arab tribes. The question of the Lurs is much more difficult. They must be made to accustom themselves to home life. As to the complaints you have heard let me know what the complaints are and I will do everything possible to remove their causes."

"Expenses," Taghi-Zadeh said in further development of the subject, "are met from the auspices of both the civil and military officials. A number of the Lurs were sent to Khorassan, a number to Zarand, Saveh and Khar. They were not until recently settled in those places. Missions have been sent to investigate and report on the expenses involved in the colonizing operations and statements of accounts are now being received. In the beginning the landowners in places to which the Lurs were shifted were required to ration the tribesmen. Subsequently it was decided that the Government should assume this responsibility. Lands, seed and oxen have been supplied to the transplanted tribesmen in Khorassan that they may be productively engaged and enabled to live comfortably. Physicians have been sent to attend both the Arabs and Lurs now lodged in Zarand, Saveh and Khar. The Red Lion and Sun [similar to the Red Cross] also has lent much assistance, and has supplied them with clothing and pusteens (heavy sheepskin garments). Lands and dwellings have been purchased for them. They receive the most painstaking sanitary attention. The Health Department detailed the physicians required. The problem in Luristan itself is a much more difficult problem. There the Lurs have no idea of home life and the Government is making every effort to acquaint them with advanced methods of living. I have received no complaints from camel-drivers. Such complaints I shall be glad to remove when received." Mohit Larijani, deputy from Khar and Veramin [Varamin], asserted that the Lurs who have been removed to those two districts have deprived the native residents of all their ease and comfort. "It might be well," Deputy Larijani said, "to take this point into consideration and to take such measures as will relieve the people of their consternation," which brought from Davar, Minister of Justice, the tart reply that "It does not matter if two men in Veramin should suffer when it is a question of public interest and the establishment of peace and security in the country."

The vote was taken and the bill was approved by 85 of the 98 deputies on the floor. No votes were cast in opposition. The conclusion of the dispatch is classic Hart:

Since the transfer of the Lurs began months ago no information has been available on the subject from Government sources. The estimates of the number moved were based on the information of travelers who saw large contingents of marching tribesmen either on the road from Luristan to Teheran or scattered for three hundred miles along the road to Meshed [Mashhad]. Some estimates I have heard have been as high as 15,000, others still higher. Just what is meant by the rehabilitation of Luristan is not quite clear. It is assumed, however, that the expectation is to settle much of the country formerly occupied by Lur tribesmen by more domesticated Persians of peasant experience. I have also been told that in shifting these tribesmen the Government tried to differentiate between those tribesmen of brigand inclinations and those disposed to more settled lives. Just how this could be done I do not know, because no Lur in his present unintelligent state could hardly see a future for himself in other than predatory pursuits.[51]

The Relocation of Kurdish Tribes

In a subsequent report, Hart provides the following translation of a newspaper account, still chilling in its detailing of Reza Khan's brutal tribal policy. The special correspondent describes the relocation of the Kurdish Djalali clan to northeast Azerbaijan and their tragic attempts to break out of their predicament:

> Last year General Zafar-ed-Dowleh, ex-Commander of the Division in Azerbaijan, disarmed a part of the famous Djalali clan of the Kurdish tribes, who are renowned for their indomitable courage, and transplanted them in the region of Ahar. (Translator's note: A not infertile region lying to the northeast of Tabriz rather less than half way to the Caspian Sea.) For reasons still remaining mysterious and unelucidated, some number of families of this clan (some 200 in number) took flight, taking with them their cattle and livestock. They passed the Eve-Oghli mountains within 28 kilometers of Khoy by midnight. There they separated into three groups. One proceeded towards Markhane, the second towards Tchelleh-Khaneh about six kilometers from Khoy, and the third towards the villages of Al-Gouyrouk and Revand. The military commander of Khoy, Captain Hossein Khan Moghaddam, upon hearing the news, proceeded at once with 200 men towards Markane, situated within the circumscription of Maku, and sent detachments towards the direction of Tchelleh-Khaneh and Eve-Oghli. The inhabitants of Markane had already barred the road to the fugitives before the arrival of the Government troops, and were valiantly fighting them. A pitched conflict ensued after the arrival of the Government forces, resulting in numerous deaths and casualties on the part of the Kurds who left 30 women and children as captives. The remainder managed to escape. Also at Tchelleh-Khaneh the army with the help of the population of Khoy killed a few the fugitives and captured 20. Again, the rest managed to escape. At this juncture, a corporal and a soldier, who had gone to the village of Heydar-Abad on an entirely different mission, encountered on the road nine Kurds and a Kurdish woman and were suddenly attacked by the fugitives. The corporal took refuge back of a rock and fought the assailants for two hours, killing seven of the men and the woman. The two surviving Kurds fled. The third group, which had taken the direction of Al-Gouyrouk and Revand,

invaded the latter village where they pillaged the cattle and livestock. The inhabitants of the village called the inhabitants of a neighboring village to their help. Amongst the latter was a young man, Ibrahim Aqa Taheri, 30 years of age, who assumed the leadership of a group of peasants, determined to give chase to the brigands. But, upon overtaking the latter, the villagers, unaccustomed to finding themselves under musketry fire, were terrified and dispersed. Their youthful leader was left alone under fire. He fought the Kurds courageously, killing four of them, but was finally shot from the rear in a most dastardly fashion. Meanwhile military reinforcements arrived. The fugitives lost a number of lives and left a number of captives. . . .

The captured women and children have been sent back under military escort to the place to which they had been originally shifted for definitive residence. The men will be turned over to the military courts. The bravery of the military forces is worthy of full praise and admiration.[52]

Hart concludes his dispatch with the following observation:

This tale, exaggerated and inaccurate though it is in parts, and other recent references in the local press to the Government's policy of settling the tribes has led me to make an informal inquiry at the Foreign Office regarding the extent to which an effort has been made to carry out the policy. In reply I am told that full statistics will be requested of the Ministry of the Interior and in due course communicated to the Legation. I know of no other source whence such statistics could be obtained. They should prove of real interest and assistance in estimating the success of what is most often referred to here as "the Shah's tribal policy."[53]

A reply to Hart's inquiry was given by Mohammed Schayesteh, director of the Bureau of European and American Affairs at the Foreign Ministry, who included no actual numbers of relocated tribesmen and their families.

The Views of Dr. Samuel M. Jordan

By 1936 some foreign observers had become accustomed to Reza Shah's avarice and other shortcomings. The American legation reported the view of Dr. Samuel M. Jordan, president of the American College in Tehran, that the shah's "predatory activities of this kind had slackened of late." Jordan's claim that Iranians tacitly approved Reza Shah's acquisition of wealth is recorded in a strictly confidential memorandum of a conversation between Jordan and the American chargé d'affaires, Gordon P. Merriam:

Dr. Jordan considers that intelligent Iranians of means and position are fully aware of the Shah's cultural shortcomings as evidenced by his present attitude towards the United States and the reasons therefor. But the impression is widespread that broadly speaking His Majesty is doing very good work for the country and for the present, at least, there is a general willingness to overlook his failings in the direction mentioned, and to blink at the large amount of property and wealth he has gathered unto himself, in large part by coercive measures. Parenthetically, it appears that the means used by the Shah to acquire real property has been to offer the owner about ten per cent of the value with the advice that ten per cent was better than nothing and that if the owner did not choose to accept that amount, the property would be taken over without any compensation whatever. Dr. Jordan understood, however, that predatory activities of this kind had slackened of late. He thinks that the retention by the Shah of the form of a constitutional monarchy has done much to make bearable the present regime, which is absolute in fact. Influential people have said to themselves: "True, Parliament is now nothing but a rubber stamp. But it sits, it acts, and we are learning how to conduct Parliamentary business. If within a few years the Shah dies, we will say to his son: 'Either you rule as a true constitutional monarch, or we shall have to get rid of you.'" The implication here is, apparently, that Iran has paid a high price for the services of the present Shah, and there is a general feeling that he is worth it. As to American affairs, Dr. Jordan felt that the Shah was doing immeasurable damage to his own country by his attitude toward a people which had repeatedly, over a long series of years, shown its disinterested friendship for Iran. Dr. Jordan was full of admiration for the material progress that Iran has achieved under His Majesty and pointed out, as one example, that there is not a single street in Teheran at the present time which is not superior to the best street in the city two years ago.[54]

Unfortunately, the views of Dr. Samuel Jordan had no link to reality. One cannot help but suspect that like Mrs. Maude Radford Warren, correspondent for the Chicago *Herald*, Jordan also possessed a hidden and sinister agenda: Not only were Reza Shah's predatory acts not "blinked at," there was no indication that they had slackened. The opposite appears to have been true: they had become more venerable with age. The case of the silk weavers of Yazd and their deportation to Mazandaran will establish the point.

The Shah's Silk Mill in Mazandaran

In addition to acquiring vast areas of northern Iran and building roads and railroads to connect these lands with domestic and foreign markets, Reza Shah also established numerous textile mills in Mazandaran. The primary impetus appears to have been the trade monopoly laws that severely restricted imports of textiles, and as with silk imports, banned them altogether (see chapter 14). Clearly, large profits could be realized. Hart describes the opening of a spinning mill in Shahi (formerly Aliabad), near Sari in Mazandaran, on February 14, 1932: "The Shah did not, as he did in the case of the Kahrizak [sugar] refinery, attend the inauguration ceremonies of the Shahi mill. But he is in a more personal sense interested in its success. For, from British Commercial Attaché Lingeman, I have confirmation of a report that, of the 500,000 tomans [about $220,000] capital subscribed for the building and opening of the mill, His Majesty furnished two-fifths. A like amount was subscribed by the National Bank of Persia and the remaining fifth by the German firm of Siemens Schukert which supplied and installed the machinery." Hart concludes with a quote from the speech of Dr. Kurt Lindenblatt, director of the National Bank of Persia, at the opening ceremonies: "I conclude as did Dr. Lindenblatt's address: 'May Allah lengthen the years of His Beloved Imperial Majesty, may our souls be sacrificed for Him, may His reign long endure and His shadow never grow less.'"[55]

By 1938, His Majesty's shadow had grown to encompass a silk mill in Chalus, Mazandaran, of which he was sole owner. A strictly confidential report from 1939 (given in its entirety) by the American consul James S. Moose Jr. reveals, contrary to Jordan's assertion, a heightened level of brutality and predatory tactics by Reza Shah:

> I have the honor to report that numbers of Yazd silk weavers are being deported to Mazandaran. As the Department is no doubt aware, silk weaving is one of the important industries in Yazd. Prior to the rise of the present Shah, all Persian dignitaries and notables wore brocade robes, and much of the brocade was woven in Yazd. With the adoption of European style clothing, the use of brocade robes was discontinued, but the weaving of Yazd silk survived. No mulberry trees grow there, nor is there sufficient water to permit their cultivation. Consequently, cocoons produced in Mazandaran and Guilan are shipped to Yazd where the silk is spun and woven; and the textiles are sold in Teheran and elsewhere in Iran.
>
> Several years ago, under authority of the Foreign Trade Monopoly Law, the importation of silk into Iran was forbidden, and about a year ago a silk mill belonging to the Shah personally was opened at Chalus in Mazandaran. Apparently there has been difficulty in securing satisfactory mill hands to tend the Shah's looms; and recently weavers have been deported from Yazd to Mazandaran for that purpose. Yazd is high (some three thousand feet above sea level) and extremely dry. If it rains three days a year in Yazd, the season is considered to be very wet. The local inhabitants do not emigrate to Mazandaran voluntarily because they usually suffer from malaria, tuberculosis and other diseases when transplanted to the steamy below-sea-level Caspian Provinces. The problem of inducing Yazdis to emigrate to Mazandaran has been solved by the Iranian police. All persons known to be silk weavers have been arrested; and as soon as a truck load had been assembled in the police station, they were shipped off to Mazandaran to tend the Shah's looms almost without pay. The figure of one rial a day (3 cents at the commercial rate of exchange) has been mentioned; but the undersigned officer is inclined to think that one rial is too low.
>
> Much of the silk weaving in Yazd is home industry, and the police have made house to house searches to locate looms and ferret out the weavers. Persons who were taken into police custody and who denied they could operate a loom were beaten unmercifully by the police until either they confessed or the police were convinced that they were not weavers. No less than 350 men have been deported, and the search merrily continues. No women and children are

known to have been impressed into the Shah's service. The forgoing information was vouched for by a responsible European business man who has lived in
Yazd for the past two years. In describing the procedure in recruiting His Imperial Majesty's mill hands, he characterizes it as "nothing short of slavery."[56]

The banning of silk imports created opportunities to earn serious money.
Responding to those opportunities, Reza Shah not only "recruited" workers for his silk mill in Chalus, he obviously set about destroying the silk
industry in Yazd because it would compete with His Majesty's mill.

Urban "Modernization"

The reign of terror inflicted on the rural and tribal population had a coun-
terpart in the urban areas: forced modernization of the towns and widening of the streets. The annual real estate tax in urban areas had been 5
percent of the value of the house. In February 1931 the Council of Ministers approved a bill submitted by the Tehran municipal council proposing
that property taxes be raised 60 percent. Article One stated: "In addition to
the 5 percent real estate taxes voted by the National Consultative Assembly
3 per-cent municipal taxes shall be collected." Article Three declared that
the additional levy would become effective on March 22, 1931—that is,
almost immediately.

The approval of the new tax prompted Hart to comment on Reza Shah's
urban policy: "The story of taxes and more taxes in all of Persia, and in
Teheran particularly, would be an almost endless tale. The municipality,
urged on by the Shah, is trying to modernize the capital of Persia so rapidly
that property owners find it almost impossible to keep up with the
progress which is wiping out liberal areas of their real estate, for most of
which they receive limited or no compensation. Property owners, besides
having to give up much real estate, have been compelled to see the demolition of their houses and to replace them at their own expense by better
structures constructed on designs prescribed by municipal planning commission. The old mud walls they have been required to replace by brick
walls, the design of which must harmonize with the architecture of the
house." Hart then informs us of the widespread system of extortion from
households and of the extralegal taxes required from property owners:
"Now and then a policeman, accompanied by a soldier, calls upon every
householder on a street and informs him that for the rebuilding or upkeep
of the thoroughfare he is required to pay at once the sum of one toman or
two tomans for every person residing in the house. Similar policy appears
to prevail in many of the outlying communities as judged by requests for
advice which reach the Legation from American missionaries in several
parts of Persia."[57]

The large-scale forced demolition of old houses in Tehran and other cities on the orders of Reza Shah and their replacement by modern buildings was a destruction of Iran's architectural and cultural heritage. This modernization also included the cutting of the ancient trees that had lined the streets of Tehran when they were widened and made to resemble boulevards. Engert, the American chargé d'affaires who earlier had incredulously reported on the proposed sale of Iran's historic crown jewels on the orders of Reza Shah (chapter 13), was now forced to relate the wanton destruction of Tehran's old buildings and ancient trees. To explain such a cultural calamity, Hart offered that when an "illiterate son of an equally illiterate peasant" was made the absolute dictator of Persia by the British, what else could be expected?[58]

On March 6, 1939, the cabinet approved a decree that prohibited the felling of trees that were more than 100 years old without authorization from the Ministry of Interior. Engert notes that "this should help to preserve what is left of the pleasant landmarks in the form of centuries old plane trees which, usually in the vicinity of mosques and shrines, have been providing grateful shade to the wayfarer." But it was too little and too late to save the ancient trees that had been cut down when the streets in Tehran were widened on the orders of Reza Shah. With obvious sadness, Engert adds: "One cannot help but wish that such a step had been taken many years ago. In fact, nothing is more depressing to those who have recently returned to Iran after an absence to ten or fifteen years than the ruthless manner in which whole avenues of majestic trees have been sacrificed on the altar of 'progress.'"[59]

In another report Engert had provided an account of the destruction of the old houses. Engert had included the following:

> I have the honor to inform the Department that during the past six months there has been an intensification of the campaign to modernize Tehran. To beautify his capital has long been close to the present Shah's heart and the appearance of Tehran has undergone remarkable changes since His Majesty came to the throne. Streets have been widened and paved; trees have been planted to take the place of the old ones destroyed by the alterations; modern government buildings have been erected in various parts of the city, and a number of small parks in local squares are being landscaped. Previous efforts, however, are not to be compared with the present activity under the direction of the Acting Chief of the Tehran Municipality, Mr. Gholam Hossein Ebtehaj. Avenue Shah Reza, which is the continuation of the road from Kazvin and runs from west to east in the northern part of Tehran, not far from this Legation, seems destined by the Shah to be the most imposing thoroughfare of the city. It is being paved, widened and landscaped with concrete islands at regular intervals down the center where small trees are planted. Old buildings as well as a good many new ones are being demolished along its whole length from Avenue

Pahlevi to the Shimran road, and their places are being taken by impressive apartment houses of two and three stories.

The demolition of old buildings is being carried out in various other sections of Tehran, notably along Avenue Lalezar, the shopping district, and in Sangalaj, a densely populated slum district in the central part of Tehran. Tehranis say that an army of scorpions marched out when the wreckers began their work on the last named part of town. A stock exchange is to be erected in this district. Avenue Shah, the present main street, Avenue Pahlavi, and other principal streets are also undergoing alterations. Buildings on all main streets must be at least two stories high to add more dignity to the city. Estimates of the number of houses recently torn down range from 15,000 to 30,000 and Tehran looks as if it had been destroyed by an earthquake.

The Municipality is, of course, simply carrying out the orders of the Shah. The ruthlessness of its methods is bewildering to anyone not used to the ways of modern Iran. Each landholder receives orders that another story must be erected on his single story building, or that his building must be torn down and a new one erected. If he pleads lack of funds the Municipality suggests that a loan be obtained. If the man is unable to obtain a loan the Municipality finds a purchaser for the property who has sufficient funds to make the required improvements and forces the original owner to sell, usually at a considerable loss. The Shah is determined to have a modern, dignified and beautiful city. The cost to the taxpayer or property holder is not, of course, a consideration provided the change which has been decreed is effected immediately.

At the same time that houses are being torn down streets are being torn up. In the course of times these streets will be well-paved boulevards, but the interim period is trying both to pedestrian and motorist. O'Donovan in his work "The Merv Oasis" published in 1882 refers several times when describing Tehran to the deplorable condition of its streets and to the holes a pedestrian could fall into if he did not take every precaution.[60] The danger can be no less today. A street for instance which was untouched in the morning may be completely torn up by evening and as no effort is made to warn the public by barriers or red lanterns there is the constant risk of falling into a ditch or hole. The underground water courses or *qanats* by which water is brought to the city further complicate the situation. Unused *qanats* the existence of which has been forgotten may give way under the weight of a passing motor car. Only two years ago a saddle horse belonging to the British Legation fell through the middle of a perfectly safe appearing Tehran street and dropped thirty feet to the bottom of the *qanat*. He was extricated after five days of digging little the worse off for his experience having been supplied with food and water each day. Local residents refer facetiously to the two-mile length of Avenue Shah Reza as the "Maginot Line," and walking or motoring in Tehran has become both difficult and dangerous.[61]

CHAPTER SIX

A Reign of Terror and Murder

THE ESTABLISHMENT AND MAINTENANCE OF a military dictatorship and the plundering of Iran by the British and Reza Khan necessitated the elimination of actual and potential opponents through a reign of terror. The list of those destined for elimination by Reza Shah's "poison squad" was to be a long one. Teymourtache, Sardar Assad, Firouz, and Modarres were to be the most prominent victims who met a grisly end in Reza Shah's prison. The fortunate ones like Taqizadeh, Dadgar, and Rahnema were sent into exile. Others like Ali Dashti were allowed to languish in a prison hospital. The reign of terror culminated in the slaughter of July 12–14, 1935, when machine guns were fired against demonstrators in Mashhad.

The reign of terror that had prevailed since 1921 became completely institutionalized by 1928, when the plunder of oil royalties by Reza Shah began in earnest. Hoffman Philip, the American minister, declares that an oppressive dictatorship had been established by 1928:

> The marked unpopularity of the existing Government and the wide spread discontent that is observable among all classes, save those under the immediate aegis of the Shah, create an oppressive atmosphere of unrest and suspense which is far from prepossessing. The Minister of the Court, Abdul Hussein Teymourtache, has assumed the executive reins of the government in all matters of state and now occupies the position of virtual Premier, without the portfolio. The other Ministers of the cabinet seem entirely subservient to the leadership and policies of Teymourtache in his capacity as chief representative of the Shah. The actual Premier, Mr. Hedayat, appears content with a very minor role in governmental affairs which, at least, affords him opportunity to obtain official

positions for his many relatives. The Medjliss displays practically no constructive independence in legislative matters, and an overwhelming majority is always available to those who present bills in the passage of which the Shah is known to be interested. In short, the Government as now conducted savors most strongly of despotic oriental monarchy. Its chief element of strength, of course, lies in the Army. In this department the Shah maintains his active and dominating interest—Sardar Assad Bakhtiari, the Minister of War, occupying little more than a nominal position in military affairs.[1]

The Eshghi and Imbrie Murders, July 1924

The complete silencing of Iran's newspapers was achieved by the brutal murders of the poet and anti-British newspaper editor Eshghi and of the American vice consul, Robert W. Imbrie. Kornfeld reports: "I have the honor to advise the Department that on Thursday, July 3, [1924], Mirza Zadeh Eshghi, editor of the Opposition paper GHARN-I-BISTOM was assassinated. The funeral which took place on July 4 was attended by 30,000 people. The opponents do not conceal their suspicion of the Government's complicity in the crime. The editors of twelve Opposition papers have taken bast [sanctuary] in Parliamant."[2] It was pointed out that just prior to his murder, Eshghi had written several anti-government and anti-British pieces in his newspaper. The subject was discussed by Vice Consul Robert W. Imbrie in his report of July 14, 1924, titled "Political and Religious Demonstrations in Teheran," which is particularly important. This dispatch, which was to be Imbrie's last report, not only provides insight on the Eshghi murder but also throws considerable light on Imbrie's own brutal murder on July 18, 1924. Immediately after the murder of Eshghi, massive anti-government demonstrations had broken out. Out of a population of 150,000, Imbrie reports that no less than 30,000 had taken part in the anti-government demonstrations:

> The unrest originally grew out of the assassination, on the morning of July 3rd, of one Mirza Zadeh Eshghi, a journalist, poet, and anti-republican writer who was shot down in his home, in Teheran, by three armed men. Though Eshghi was a notorious character, a man of evil repute, whose death might very well have been the result of his own wrongful acts, political significance was at once attached, by the minority in Parliament, to the assassination. It was pointed out in the press that the murdered man had just published several articles and poems against Government leaders, and significance was also attached to the fact that the last cartoon published by him, just prior to his assassination, was aimed against the British. In this connection the Ghanoon, organ of the minority party in Parliament, said under date of July 6: "The world will not forget that Eshghi was killed as being responsible for the cartoon of John Bull and

his attack on the colonial policy of Great Britain." . . . Whether this assassination was politically inspired cannot be determined, but it is a significant fact that immediately following the murder twelve editors and writers of the opposition press sought bast (asylum) in the Medjliss.

On July 4th Mir Zadeh Eshghi was buried. His funeral was the occasion of a tremendous demonstration, excited by the Mullahs, in which thirty thousand shouting, frenzied people took part. Reza Khan was denounced as a murderer and assassin and oppressor of the people. The demonstration and the disorder continued into the night. Throughout the fifth and sixth of July demonstrations against the Government continued.[3]

On Monday, July 6, demonstrations of another sort had been organized by the government. The purpose of these demonstrations was to divert the attention of the people from the murder of Eshghi. These demonstrations, Imbrie continues,

> subsidized by the Government, took the form of anti-Bahaist manifestations. At every teahouse a Mullah harranged the crowd. Mobs, fired by oratory and hashish, swarmed through the streets, unhindered by the Police, crying against the Bahaists. In the bazaar all shops belonging to Bahaists closed. A big demonstration against the two American Bahaist Missionaries, here in Teheran, was staged and their quarters, though not attacked, was booed and hissed. My request for Police protection for these ladies was, however, promptly acceded to and a guard has since been maintained about their house.

Imbrie informs us that this government-instigated lawlessness "continued throughout the week ending July 12th, when, having served their purpose in diverting the attention of the people from the murder of Eshghi, they were allowed to die out and now, at the time of this writing, Teheran has assumed almost its state of normalcy."[4]

On July 18, 1924, Imbrie was allegedly attacked by the mob that he described, and he was murdered. Certain key facts about the murder of Imbrie are established. The assault on Imbrie by the "government-subsidized" mob took place right outside the main barracks of the Pahlavi regiment, Reza Khan's household regiment, and Reza Khan's Cossacks actually participated in the beating of Imbrie and his companion. Severely injured, Imbrie was murdered shortly after as he lay helpless in the hospital inside the police headquarters in Tehran.[5] There can be no doubt that this brutal murder, similar to that of Eshghi, was at the instigation of Reza Khan. The murder of Imbrie, declared Colonel W.A.K. Fraser, the British military attaché in Tehran, gave Reza Khan "the excuse for declaring martial law and a censorship of the Press. . . . Numerous arrests have been made, chiefly of political opponents of the Prime Minister."[6] Major Sherman Miles of the American

Army, who was sent to investigate, had no doubt that the murder of Imbrie was deliberate so that Reza Khan "could declare martial law and check the power of the Mullahs."[7] Although no evidence has been found linking the British directly to these murders, the fact remains that they were beneficiaries of these crimes. Moreover, the government-instigated and -financed "anti-Bahaist" incidents were similar to the "anti-Jewish incidents" that had been staged by Reza Khan in September 1922.

The "Anti-Jewish" Incidents of September 1922

On December 14, 1931, Samuel Haim, former Jewish deputy to the Fifth Majlis, who had been arrested and imprisoned since 1926 on charges of plotting against the person and rule of Reza Shah, was suddenly executed after a "trial" by a military tribunal. According to Charles C. Hart, he had been arrested for conspiring with Colonel Mahmoud Poulladin, commanding officer of the crack Pahlavi Regiment, Reza Shah's household regiment, and Major Ruhollah Khan, "against the person and reign of Reza Shah whose coronation ceremony had been held with much high pomp on April 25 of the same year."[8] Colonel Poulladin, Major Ruhollah Khan, and several others were executed in 1928, but Haim languished in jail for three more years. One of the charges against Haim was that he had been the real instigator of the 1922 disturbances in the Jewish neighborhoods of Tehran, disturbances that American minister Joseph S. Kornfeld had claimed Reza Khan had engineered in order to provoke a cabinet crisis. In addition, Haim was condemned for plotting against Reza Shah. His execution was the beginning of a campaign that was to claim many victims.

From September 19 to September 22, 1922, parts of Tehran had been shaken by what appeared to be anti-Jewish incidents. Kornfeld, himself a rabbi, had obtained firsthand evidence that not only had the Cossacks and police not done anything to enforce law and order, but they had been the instigators of the incidents. Kornfeld had no doubt that Reza Khan (and by implication the British) were the real authors of the disturbances. Kornfeld's report includes the following:

> The immediate cause of the disturbances which lasted from September 19 to September 22, was a quarrel between a domestic of the Alliance Israelite Universelle with a servant of a mulla. They were taken to the Commissariat who, after a careful inquiry into the nature of the controversy, decided against the servant of the mulla. As soon as this became known among the Moslems, a mob formed and at once rushed to the Alliance school, which is located in the Jewish quarter. After having forced the school to close, the mob made a general

attack on the Jews. For a time it looked as if it might turn into a general massacre, but happily it never reached that stage.[9]

One of the employees of the legation was injured, prompting the intervention of Kornfeld, who had protested to the Foreign Ministry that in a city where the government maintained 8,000 troops, such lawlessness was uncalled for. The next morning, Kornfeld instructed the legation's interpreter, Ali Pasha Saleh, "a Moslem of distinguished family," to go to the Jewish quarter and investigate. Kornfeld continues:

As I surmised, the situation had not improved. The shops in the Jewish quarter were still closed, and the mob as aggressive as the day before. On approaching the mob, our interpreter inquired regarding the cause of the commotion. Immediately, a commissioned Cossack officer proceeded to insult and attack him and, had not two mounted gendarmes come to his assistance, he might have been seriously injured. Upon informing them of who he was, they had led him to a place of safety, but when he requested that they arrest the Cossack, or at least they ascertain his identity, they refused to do so. However, he did succeed in inducing them to take him to the Commissariat to have the incident recorded, though even then they avoided making reference to the criminal action of the Cossack. After reaching his home, the interpreter advised me by phone of what had happened. I immediately communicated with the Minister of Foreign Affairs and asked him to come to the Legation at once. He promptly complied with my request. We had a very serious conference. I made clear to him that the situation had become intolerable, and that I was forced to cable my Government, and that unless order was speedily restored, I apprehended serious international complications. That same evening the mob made another attack. This time however the Gendarmes fired on the rioters who immediately dispersed. Since then there has been no disorder. The city has resumed its normal life.

Now as to the real significance of the riot. It was not a spontaneous outburst of indignation on the part of the Moslems against the Jews, but a well-planned plot of Reza Khan, Minister of War, to overthrow the Government. This is not his first attempt at a coup d'état. He prides himself on the fact that it was he who brought about the coup d'état of February 1921. He was also responsible for the resignation of Moshir-ed-Dowleh, the recent Prime Minister, but before he brought about his fall, he succeeded in having him turn over to him the department of Indirect Taxation so that he might have financial resources entirely free from the control of the Ministry of Finance for the maintenance of HIS army. Since Ghavam-os-Saltaneh has become Prime Minister, the Minister of War has been using every conceivable pressure to secure the control of the Teheran Gendarmerie which is still under the Ministry of Interior so that he might be in absolute command of all the military forces, and thereby ensure for himself their undivided support. Thus far he has failed. Hence his exasperation. He has another grievance against the present Cabinet and Parliament, and that is the engagement of American financial advisers because of the authority delegated to them to supervise the public funds. For these reasons he is making desperate efforts to overthrow the Government. He is unquestionably directly responsible for this riot, which he had hoped would become sufficiently serious to bring about the fall of the Cabinet and give him the opportunity to carry out his designs. That is why his Cossacks, instead of protecting life and property, were either indifferent or actually acquiesced in this outrage. Fortunately his plot miscarried.[10]

The newspaper *Shafaq-i-Sorkh* describes another charge on which Haim was executed. Before World War I, Haim had been an employee of the Persian customs administration.

> Soon after the outbreak of the World War Haim quitted the service of the Persian Government and joined the British Intelligence Service. [After the 1921 coup] he organized a Zionist Society, published a newspaper in Persian and in Hebrew, conducted energetic propaganda and was on the verge of deluding his Jewish compatriots with the absurd plan of leaving their country for the torrid desert of Palestine. But as the Persian Jews still hesitated to abandon their home, Haim, to provoke them against their Moslem compatriots, engineered that most deplorable incident of the Jewish Quarter of Teheran [1922]. In one week's time the entire quarter was ruled by panic and commotion, and to a certain extent his plan was successful, for certain families left for Palestine. In the meantime he had gained a certain degree of reputation and popularity with the Jews and was elected to the Fifth Medjliss [1924–26]. However, as the Deputies were aware of his past career, they long retarded recognizing his credentials, and he was not re-elected to the Sixth Medjliss [1926–28]. Furious at this, Haim had then embarked upon his dangerous revolutionary conspiracy.[11]

According to *Shafaq-i-Sorkh,* Haim made a full confession of his part in the plot. Hart learned from Professor Herrick B. Young of the American College that Haim had been tortured into making his confession. Young's personal servant was a nephew of Haim, and he had confirmed the allegation of torture. Hart adds:

> And from other generally well-informed Persian sources there is direct confirmation of the truth of the allegation. As to what has transpired since Haim's arrest, there is again general agreement as to the facts. He has, for the past five years, been continuously in custody, frequently brought before the Military Tribunal for retrial or further questioning. And I find none who question seriously the obvious probability that, between trials, he was submitted to the Persian equivalent of an almost continuous "Third Degree." That Haim was able so long to defy his questioners is all that seems to call for astonished comment.

Hart concludes:

> And, if there is any conclusion which I may draw from the present incident, it is that, after six years on the throne of the ShahinShahs, the seat of Reza Pahlavi is firmer than it has ever been before. There are, of course, ups and

downs of Imperial popularity, and some of the measures of reform sponsored by His Majesty have been more truly acclaimed than others. But Persia has, I venture to state without fear of successful contradiction, made real progress under his aegis, both during the decade following the 1921 coup d'état and that which has followed his accession.[12]

Hart needed one more year and the brutal treatment and murder of his friend Teymourtache to realize that the so-called progress under Reza Shah was a myth, a mirage.

Abdol Hossein Teymourtache

On December 22, 1932, in the midst of the dispute with the Anglo-Persian Oil Company following the annulment of the D'Arcy Concession, His Highness, Abdol Hossein Khan Teymourtache, the former Sardar Moaz-zam Khorassani, minister of the imperial court since 1925, was suddenly dismissed. The once omnipotent Teymourtache, often described as the shah's alter ego and right-hand man, had been shunted aside, and the oil negotiations, once his exclusive domain, had been taken out of his hands. But his sudden dismissal was unexpected. Shortly after his dismissal, he was arrested, tried on numerous charges, and sentenced to ten years' solitary confinement. In early October 1933, it was announced that he had died of heart failure while in prison.

Teymourtache was born in Khorasan around 1880 and was educated at the Czarist Cavalry School in Russia. It appears that in 1920 he was elected as a deputy from Neishabur to the Third Majlis. Hart describes the circumstances surrounding his election: "It is perhaps of interest to mention that some years ago when he was of no importance in Persian politics Teymourtache came to Mr. Havard [the long-time oriental secretary at the British legation in Tehran] and requested that the British Consul in Sistan be asked to lend his influence toward the election of Teymourtache to the Medjliss. The request was granted."[13] With this background, it was not surprising that Teymourtache had thrown in his lot with Reza Khan, the principal British tool. When Reza Khan became prime minister in October 1923, Sardar Moazzam (as Teymourtache was then known) became minister of justice in Reza Khan's first cabinet. In 1924, he was made minister of public works. With the advent of the Pahlavi monarchy in 1925, Teymourtache was appointed minister of the imperial court, the post he held until his dismissal, on December 22, 1932. For seven years Teymourtache completely dominated the affairs of Persia.

The arrest and subsequent death of Teymourtache were reported in a series of brilliant dispatches by Hart. In his years in Tehran as the American minister, Hart had become friends with Teymourtache. While freely admitting his utter corruption, Hart greatly respected his friend's towering intellect and was grieved and angered at his treatment.

"Teymourtache Dismissed and Great Was the Fall Thereof"

In his report Hart looks for reasons for the unexpected dismissal, about which no facts were as yet known:

> The exact moment when the ax fell is not known. Stories differ. Eugene Lyons, Moscow correspondent of the United Press of America, was the first to discover the summary action of the Shah, understood that the removal order was communicated to the Minister of the Court late in the night of December 22. Others say the action was taken early the next morning. But to show that the move was predicated on no shifting sands, the Teymourtache motor cars appeared on the streets of Teheran, hours before the big news was out, with white plaques supplanting the gold tags accorded to Palace officials. Also soon after the plaques were changed armed emissaries of the Shah entered the Teymourtache premises and, without requesting the key, broke open the garage in which a large Pierce-Arrow car considered the property of the Government and not belonging to the Minister of the Court. The car was taken to the Shah's residential palace. Stories and rumors as to the Shah's precipitate action are numerous and varying.[14]

One rumor was that Teymourtache, Dr. Kurt Lindenblatt of the National Bank of Persia, and Herr Vogel, Lindenblatt's assistant, had embezzled 3 million tomans ($1 million). Another was that Teymourtache had been planning to overthrow the Pahlavi monarchy. It was also said that he had become too powerful and that in the event of Reza Khan's passing he would have been a threat to the succession of Mohammad Reza, Reza Shah's heir apparent. Another rumor was that Teymourtache had given bad advice in the matter of the cancellation of the D'Arcy Concession. Although Hart could tender no convincing reason, he summed up the position by declaring that, "while any one of these reasons for the Shah's action advanced by rumor could be sufficient, in the opinion of anyone familiar with Reza's peasant mentality, the truth probably is more nearly that a vast combination of circumstances and developments led to the precipitate action which cast into private life the foremost, if not the only, intellectual giant Persia has known in a century."

> In the passing of Abdol Hossein Khan Teymourtache, Minister of the Imperial Pahlevi Court since December, 1925, oblivion has swallowed a mouthful. Few men in history, I would say, have stamped their personalities so indelibly on the politics of any country. Had this man been scrupulous while in power, with a larger and more important field in which to employ his talents, he might easily have gone down to posterity as one of the wizards of the age. Now the senior member of the diplomatic corps, I can say that I perhaps know him more intimately than any of my present colleagues. I confess I approached him

FIGURE 6.1 *Abdol Hossein Teymourtache, ca. 1930. Courtesy of the IICHS.*

three years ago with certain prejudices. However, it was not long until I began to feel myself in the presence of a mighty genius every time I called on him.

My profession, it is to be recalled, for several years before coming abroad had placed me in the way of the so-called great men. It was in my line to make their acquaintance and to interview them. I have met the most diverse types, some great only by reputation and other actually deserving of the high positions accredited to them in the intellectual, social or political life of the world.

Only one man out of every one hundred credited with greatness actually attains that stature when one comes into contact with him. Teymourtache impressed me at once as an original character and the most strikingly alert human being within the memory of my acquaintance. The only man I have ever met who was at all comparable on one side of his mental makeup was Leonard Wood. General Wood had the faculty of carrying a vast mass of detail in his mind and, months after some matter of business had passed over his desk, he was not required to send for the file to discuss it intelligently. The American general, however, it will be appreciated was engaged in only one realm. The subjects that came to his attention were myriad but not especially diverse in character. Teymourtache was the active head of the Persian Government. He took business out of the hands of all the cabinet ministers and discussed every problem in minutest detail, as if he might have had it solely in charge.

After my first few meetings with him I began to suspect that his brilliancy had the elements of madness. He impressed me as just too bright. I intimated some such conviction in a personal letter to Mr. Murray under date of July 9, 1930. That was because the man's gifts were so extraordinary as to appear unnatural. Whether it was foreign affairs, the construction of railways or highways, reforms in posts and telegraphs, educational administration or finance, he, as a rule, could discuss those subjects more intelligently than the so-called competent ministers. Besides, he devised formulas for the country's economic rehabilitation, made treaties, supervised the complicated questions regarding what to do with the tribes and told the War Minister much he did not know about organizing a system of national defense. The Soviet commercial treaty and the trade monopoly laws are unmistakable monuments to his versatility. At my last conference with him I had occasion to refer to some not too important statement that I had made to him more than two years before. He said he recalled it and proved the truth of it by taking the words out of my mouth. Wherever he sits today, though shorn of the honors of office, whether he be in prison or under guard in his house, I can say one thing about him: The shadows are stretching themselves across the figure of a strong man.

I know him to a certainty to be a strong man. The chief weapon of diplomacy in the East for the last century has been to picture the bad impression that some ill-advised act on the part of the particular government in question would make on the world at large. To say to Teymourtache that if the Persian Government followed a certain course would make an unfortunate impression only made one ridiculous. Hammer and tongs diplomacy was sure to get one nowhere and to achieve that end with lightning rapidity. He was quick to recognize attempted coercion and to repulse it without regard to the feelings of the instrument of its application. As the Department is aware there were times when I found myself under strong compulsion to make strong representations. At first on such occasions Teymourtache would cut in with sharp interruptions which often diverted the conversation so far off the charted course as to confuse the issues. I finally adopted the method of requesting him to permit me to complete my statement after which he would discuss the points of my representations. This proved the solution. If he wished to interrupt he would courteously inquire, "May I answer that point right now?" When at the close of one of these conferences I sensed that my representation had left a raw edge I applied the healing lotion of a story. Invariably he was ready any time to exchange savage emotions for a laugh. It was in this way I discovered the identity of the very limited number of persons with whom he fraternized.

Tell him a story that amused him and at the first meeting with Ghaffary, Undersecretary for Foreign Affairs, I was informed that the Minister of the Court had suggested that he have me repeat the story to him. Aside from Ghaffary I never could detect any close friendships between him and anyone else. Abdol Hossein Khan Diba, Chief accountant of the Court, by public associations, gave the appearance of being a friend, but this connection I think was misunderstood. Teymourtache could not have admired Diba because the latter is possessed of a mentality that comprehends only the grosser things of life. He possesses none of Teymourtache's sparkling humor and is as stodgy as Satan without any of the latter's cunning. In him Teymourtache unquestionably found a poker companion to whom he could lose and not be compelled to pay. But Diba's functions in the Court were more far flung than that. Salaries of Court officials are relatively trivial and through the activities of Diba and Mohammad Mirza Khosrovani, Chief of Cabinet of the Ministry, the Court was made to pay its way with good sums for beautiful summer houses in Shimran, a splendid variety of the most luxurious American motor cars and abundant left over for poker and baccarat, both here and, last winter, in Paris.

I have no doubt that most of my colleagues are gloating over the dismissal of Teymourtache. I am certainly sure that all my former colleagues who departed since my arrival are pleased. I cannot say that I feel that way about it. Persia still remains an integral part of the Orient and I am not so optimistic as to anticipate any sweeping resurgence of political and intellectual honesty in this part of the world. Persia has lost, at least for the time being, its one true statesman. Another dishonest man is sure to succeed him, if a successor is named. Teymourtache had this advantage, the advantage of being intelligent. I would rather deal at any time with a dishonest man who is intelligent and industrious than with an honest man who is both lazy and heavy in the head. I like Foroughi, for example. Foroughi is honest, but Foroughi is lazy and he does not just quite get around to doing the things he promises with the best of intentions to do. . . . In all my rovings Teymourtache has impressed me more as a vibrant, captivating personality than any other human being that I have known. Born pragmatist, his piquancy is of a quality usually described in books and seldom found in the flesh. At a dinner party, although he had been working laboriously all day at his office and was the last to arrive, he soon became the life of the assemblage. It was worth a good period of one's time to observe him as he entered the reception room and went forth to shake hands with, maybe, thirty to fifty other guests. When he had completed this social nicety one looked back on it as a worth-while exhibition in itself.

At the table he instilled life into the dullest personalities it ever was my misfortune to meet. Why, I cannot conceive, but for some reason foreign governments when it comes to filling the post at Teheran, cast about for the most egregious bores within their realms. They come and stay but they never get beyond that conversational stage which dwells on the theme of what a terrible place Teheran is as a residence. The same individuals any place in the world would find life somber because they themselves radiate dullness. There have been very notable exceptions, of course.

Teymourtache always gave the impression of being honestly happy when reflecting his own magnetism to every part of a long table or ballroom, and, I judge, usually was. Never but once did he give the least inkling that he was not so happy as he seemed. One evening when he had all the speechless men and women within sound of his voice in an uproar he turned to me and congratulated me on not having languages. He remarked: "It must be a great help."

In my official conversations with him he seldom, if ever, raised the question of nationalism. It would not have mattered had he done so because I would have perceived he was not sincere. Not sincere, because most of the notables of large responsibilities in high public life of the East are not honest in their nationalistic rantings. Nationalism is just one devious way of making the ignorant masses feel that their interests are being zealously, even jealously, guarded by those in power. The American politician, to achieve the same end, prates lachrymosely and loudly of the need of social justice. Ever since coming to Persia stories have been related to me, usually by persons who have never lived, of Teymourtache's dissipation and general pursuit of vices. I heard many times of his "getting too much to drink," but I confess that I never saw any true evidence of it. His favorite drink is champagne of which nothing was known in the Prophet's time.

As to vice, does the term mean anything in this part of the world? Let it be remembered that Teymourtache was born into the world as a follower of Mohammed. If Teymourtache has recognized any of the teachings of Islam it was to seek, as best as he could, to observe within reasonable limitations that part of the law relating to marriages and consort with concubines. The Islamic law places its faithful followers on a quota basis as to wives. The Prophet allows the faithful one to take four wives. Teymourtache has only three, but he is now barely past fifty years old. Islam also allows the faithful follower to have as many concubines as he can afford. I doubt if Teymourtache exceeded the limits of this inhibition, though he is said to have patronized many. I have, however, no way of knowing what Bradstreet or Dun would say about his ability to afford them.

I could go on indefinitely depicting the life and characteristics of this most picturesque of human figures but regulations, I find, require me to confine my reports to despatches, with no allowance for a book on any subject no matter how romantic.[15]

The Arrest and Suspected Fate of Teymourtache: "Not a Beggar's Chance"

On January 18, 1933, a Tehran newspaper announced that Teymourtache had been arrested and was to be tried. Hart reports and discusses the news, and the remainder, which deals with Reza Shah's avarice and acquisition of wealth, is given in another chapter.

No question, I have the honor to report, looms quite so large in Persia just now as that of what will happen to Abdol Hossein Khan Teymourtache whose summary dismissal as Minister of the Court was reported in my despatch No. 1310 of December 29, 1932. While the newspapers, evidently enjoined from exploiting the news of the Teymourtache debacle, continue to concentrate on the controversy of the Anglo-Persian Oil Company concession cancellation, the public is far more deeply engrossed in the possible fate of this deposed states-man and bon vivant extraordinary. An atmosphere of suspense hangs over Teheran. A public hungry for some information received its first appetizing morsel in three weeks when a Teheran newspaper announced on January 18 that Teymourtache had been placed under guard at his home. This report had the effect of upsetting stories going the rounds, circulated by friends of the for-mer Minister of the Court, that his suspension was only of a temporary variety applied by juvenile courts as a form of probationary discipline. The announce-ment was brief and appeared in but one newspaper, indicating that the press remained in doubt as to how far to go in covering the news of this particular event. Meanwhile the subject continued to be threshed over with an intensity of interest whenever men came together, in clubs, drawing rooms or bazaar.

No further information reached the public until today when the *Kouresh* under the caption, "The Trial of Teymourtache," published the following laconic item: "We have obtained information that Teymourtache will shortly be brought before a tribunal for trial." Not the least inkling has been given of the charges lodged against the one-time exalted head of the Imperial Court. The surmise most generally heard, however, is that he is to be tried on an indict-ment growing out of the alleged manipulation of funds of the National Bank of Persia. While newspapers have been keeping a closed mouth up to this time, it is possible that more of the actual character of Teymourtache's difficulties may be revealed in immediately succeeding days. The reason for such anticipation is that British newspapers appear to have commented in complimentary terms on the ability and statesmanlike genius of the deposed official. Several of Teheran's newspapers today referred caustically to this attitude of the British press. "Such expressions of sympathy and partiality by the *Times* and other London news-papers," declared editor Safavi of *Kushesh*, "create suspicion in the mind of the reader. A bad odor is scented and certain facts may in the future be disclosed." The favor shown to Teymourtache by the British press, it is to be expected, may cause the Shah to give local newspapers the same carte blanche on the subject that they have enjoyed with reference to the Anglo-Persian oil controversy.

That the former Minister of the Court is not beleaguered on a mere misde-meanor indictment is evident from the strength of the guard thrown about his house. It is known that his Armenian wife, hostess of his residential home, and their two children are not permitted to see him. Neither have his mother, now approaching eighty years, and his favorite daughter, Madame Gharagozlou, here from London, been permitted to see him since the guard was posted, I am informed. While in foreign circles I still note some skepticism as to the acute nature of the charges against him and the prospects of condign punishment, Persians, I am informed, agree almost unanimously that he is more than likely to go the way of viziers, ministers and princes who offended Shahs of other days. A Persian of high intelligence who circulates widely among the upper class of his countrymen, chiefly those who are in the political life, informs me that nine out of every ten Persians are confident that the former Court Minister is to be put out of the way. Interesting is the parallel drawn between this dismissal and that of Finance Minister Prince Firouz two years ago. Firouz had risen too high, was too independent, had to be broken. First placed under guard, as I reported at the time, in a manner not unsimilar to that used in the present instance, Firouz was eventually put on trial, convicted of having taken a paltry bribe of less than $5,000 and has since been confined to the Farmaniyeh estate near Teheran. In the present case, too, a vast mass of rumor must be panned to obtain a few nuggets of facts. Among the rumors that have been circulated within the last several days were stories: first, that the distinguished prisoner had disappeared; second, that he had been taken to Kasr-Kadjar [Qasr-Qajar] prison; third, that he had been removed to the prison at police headquarters a couple of days ago; fourth, that he was to have been taken to prison but for illness which caused the Shah to relent; fifth, a report from his two brothers-in-law that his mother was permitted to see him at his house only night before last.

As for my own views, I do not give the one-time Minister of the Court a beggar's chance to escape from the worst that can happen.[16]

As the dispatch continues, Hart reveals his realization that the so-called progress under Reza Shah was all a facade, a clever myth skillfully engineered by the British. He also speculates on the fate of Teymourtache:

Human instincts, I would say, will never intervene to save Teymourtache from punishment as barbarous and diabolical as that which earlier Shahs visited upon officials who had fallen into disfavor. . . . Certainly he will not blind his deposed Minister of the Court or bury his body in quicklime to his neck to be eaten alive, as other Shahs have done when their Ministers came into disfavor, because Persia is no longer shut away from the world as in those earlier days. Reza Shah sneers at the frown of Allah but stands in horror of the judgment of civilization on his acts. Therefore he is content to have an offending official shot, "poisoned by mistake," or drilled through while "trying to escape."

Reza Shah's experience as head of the Imperial Government admittedly has expanded his outlook but it has removed none of the suspicion from his Oriental mentality. To be suspected by this monarch is the equivalent of conviction and later condemnation is merely a sequential detail.

Nadir Shah, it will be recalled, suspecting his son, Riza Kula Mirza, of disloyalty ordered the prince's eyes removed. Later he regretted his act, and some historians say that all the spectators of the blinding were put to death on the pretext that they should have offered their lives to save the eyes of a Prince who was the glory of Persia. The Prince, a most enlightened young man of his time, is credited with remarking, "it is not my eyes you have put out but the eyes of Persia."

Because he was believed to have assumed too much power, a charge similar to that thought to lie against Teymourtache, Kaim Makam, ablest of Mohammed Shah's ministers, was ordered strangled to death. Amir-i-Nazam

[Amir-i-Kabir], unquestionably one of the notable Persian patriots of history, was put to death in the Royal Garden of Fin at Kashan by having his veins opened, because he appeared to have gained overmuch popularity with the army. The excesses recounted above were the acts of monarchs much more brilliant than Reza Shah, monarchs who were educated, even cultured, monarchs some of whom had even been to Europe and India.

If reports are true, Government authorities have set out to round up every person who is suspected of being in league with Teymourtache. I have heretofore mentioned the reported imprisonment of deputy Bushehri. Rumors have it that several other persons are now prisoners in one jail or another. Abdol Hossein Diba, deposed Chief Accountant of the Court, over whose person the wrath of the Shah first broke, is the subject of numerous reports as to his whereabouts. For some time after his dismissal he was held a prisoner in the office of the Chief Prosecutor but stories going the rounds now have it that he has been banished to one of the provinces, presumably Azerbaijan from whence he originally came. The next two weeks, I apprehend, will bring forth interesting developments.[17]

The Trial and Conviction of Teymourtache

Among those who pleaded for mercy for the fallen minister of the court, Hart reveals, was the crown prince, Mohammad Reza Pahlavi, who had sent a telegram from Switzerland to his father. Teymourtache's son was a schoolmate of Mohammad Reza. Hart also says that Ali Akbar Davar, the minister of justice, who was in Europe at the time, had gone to see the crown prince, and it was widely believed that the telegram was sent at the instigation of Davar. Consequently, it had no impact on Reza Shah. The indictment against Teymourtache accused him of accepting bribes and embezzling public funds. Hart informs us that Teymourtache had been moved to the police prison the previous week. Earlier Hart had noted that all of Teymourtache's property had been seized, his servants and his cook had also been arrested, and his wife, Tatiana, had undergone several grueling questioning sessions by the police. In prison, Teymourtache was stricken with a heart ailment and was transported to the prison hospital. Hart discusses the charges against him:

Published charges indicate that he has been indicted for manipulations of National Bank funds, particularly with reference to the foreign exchange transactions. His alleged crime is that of a variety common to Persia, the illicit taking of money. This indictment is used to cover the more serious suspicion or belief, no doubt, that he was intriguing to overthrow the imperial regime.

Two or three days, it is learned, were devoted by the Public Prosecutor to an examination of the former Minister of the Court before his removal to prison. From responsible authority not to be quoted I have it that the deposed minister had lost none of his old punch when approached by his inquisitors. When asked if it was true that he had taken money his reply was reported to have been: "Of course I have stolen money but I am not the big thief." This retort is said to have been directly responsible for the decision to remove him to prison. On a previous occasion he is said to have informed one of his former trustworthy friends that he was not acting for himself in all of his known irregularities. He was said to have added that it would be dangerous to put him on trial, he "might talk too much." The former protege, being Persian, was, Persian-like, ready to desert a sinking ship and carried the tale direct to the Shah, with the harsh result that followed. Since then not only has he been incarcerated but personal property has been seized to cover debts and alleged peculations of large sums.[18]

According to newspaper announcements, "The one-time distinguished official is charged with fraud, embezzlement and receiving bribes. The money alleged to have been involved is divided into 1,800 British pounds and 100,000 tomans ($35,000 at last quoted rate of exchange)." Hart also reports, "In the meantime the Teymourtache family have become virtually destitute, a fact supported by Madame Teymourtache's offering most, if not all, of her better clothing, including evening and dinner gowns purchased in Paris, for sale at a well known clothing exchange in Teheran."[19]

By this time, the British had openly turned against Teymourtache. At first, the British newspapers had praised his "intelligence and statesmanship qualities." The praise, according to Hart, infuriated Reza Shah further. Suddenly, it seemed, the British had begun to play a different tune, showing their anxiety about the succession issue in Persia. The entire episode makes one suspect that the British may have had a hand in Teymourtache's downfall, and may have been the ones to tip off Reza Shah. In a London *Times* article the paper's purported former correspondent in Persia writes, "The prospect of a regency occupies his [the shah's] mind today. What chance would his 13-year-old son have should this Regency fall to a man still young, ambitious, and entirely unscrupulous?"[20]

The trial took place on March 17, 1933, in front of the high court of the state. After only a few hours, the accused was found guilty of all the charges and was sentenced to five years of solitary confinement. In June he was tried on another bribery charge, convicted, and received an additional five-year term. His appeals for clemency to the shah and the Court of Cassation, Iran's highest court, were summarily dismissed. Hart also reports that Teymourtache had been taken from prison to the courthouse on foot, under guard, paraded through the streets of Tehran like a common criminal.

Rising Repression

As these remarkable dispatches were being received from Hart, Wallace S. Murray, former chargé d'affaires in Tehran (1924–25) and now chief of the State Department's Near Eastern Division, provided an assessment of the political situation in Persia. Having served in Tehran from 1922 to 1925, Murray had no illusions about Reza Khan:

Politically speaking, Persia is a constitutional monarchy which, however, amounts in fact to a complete dictatorship. Reza Shah Pahlavi, founder of the present dynasty, has ruled the country for the last seven years, during which time he has built up a strong centralized government, controlled by himself, and based on the support of the army. His Prime Minister [Foroughi] is little more than a figurehead, his Cabinet Ministers are the equivalent of a secretariat, and the Mejliss, or Parliament, acts only as a rubber stamp. Elections to the latter are controlled from the Palace and the deputies vote in accordance with Palace dictates. Up to a short time ago, the Persian scene was dominated by a figure almost as striking as that of the Shah. His Highness Teymourtache, Minister of Court, was the Shah's chief counselor and executor of the royal will. Shrewd, intelligent, unscrupulous, his power had grown to a point which led to his dismissal, and today the Shah alone presides at all Cabinet meetings and decides all questions. In contrast to his former right hand man, the Shah is untutored, irascible, ruthless, and totally lacking in cosmopolitanism or knowledge of the world.[21]

Shortly before his death, Teymourtache received a savage beating in his prison cell at the hands of Reza Shah. While Hart was writing the following dispatch, predicting the impending death of Teymourtache, the prisoner was already dead or about to expire:

The story of Teymourtache's relegation to darkness and solitude has reached me from two Persian sources which I regard as reliable. The two versions are in practical agreement that while the Shah was driving down Shimran road several weeks ago he sighted head carriers turning into the driveway leading to Kasr-Kajar prison. Each carrier held poised on top of his head a large tray which appeared to contain food. The imperial car was stopped and the carriers were asked where they were going and to whom they were delivering food. They answered that they were ordered to take food to Teymourtache. The Shah, instantly in a rage, knocked trays from the heads of the two men and proceeded to the prison. He went direct to the cell of Teymourtache and demanded to know if he thought he was so much better than other prisoners that he could enjoy special privileges such as food from outside and additional prison comforts not provided by regulations. A violent assault is said to have followed which, according to one of my informants, left the distinguished prisoner on the concrete floor of his cell in an insensible condition.

At the same time the Shah gave orders that the prisoner was to be deprived of his special bed, that his carpet and all movable furniture in the cell were to be taken away, with all books and paper and other means with which to read or write or otherwise occupy his time; and that the one-time Minister of the Court should be placed on an equality with the lowest criminal of Kasr-Kajar.

The report of the Shah's violence was not long, as usual, in reaching the ears of Persians, although foreigners in Teheran generally appear to have obtained few details. By Persians the story is accepted as a fact, probably because they have information to confirm it from someone among the wardens of the jail. The result has been to cause apprehension among friends of the prisoner, and there are whisperings that one may expect the announcement at some not distant day that the man who once made cabinet ministers step at the snap of his finger has suddenly expired from apoplexy or some affection of the heart. But those who anticipate such announcement do not mean that they will accept any such diagnosis of death cause. What they mean is that the government will find a method of doing away with the quondam Minister of the Court and that, of course, no autopsy will be permitted to determine the truth.

Such apprehensions appear to be justified by what seems to have happened only recently to Solat-ed-Doleh, Kashgai chief, whose body was viewed in the hands of body washers at the morgue a few weeks ago but whose death was never announced. Some even express the fear that Teymourtache already has passed on and that his death is being kept secret. So strong is this fear or suspicion, whichever it may be termed, that Teheran is filled with sporadic rumors of his death.

Of course, no one believes that Solat-ed-Doleh died a natural death, and his end, it is felt, justified Teymourtache on insisting that his food be brought in from the outside so long as allowable.[22]

The Little White Pill

Hart's dispatch of October 3 proved prophetic. On October 6, Hart sent the following telegram: "Teymourtache body removed from prison, buried yesterday. Understood to have died October 3 or 4 but death not announced to date either officially or by press."[23] The next day he submitted his report:

I am now required by the course of events to supplement my prophetic despatch No. 1542 of October 3, 1933, by reporting the death in prison on the following day, October 4, of Abdol Hossein Khan Teymourtache, who was placed under arrest by orders of the Shah on December 22, 1932. The public is hazy as to the date of the Teymourtache demise, some holding he passed away on October 3 while others declare he died the following day. News of the death first spread through Teheran on October 5, coming not from the officials of the jail or from the Government but from servants of the Teymourtache household. The body was buried at Shah Abdul Azim on the afternoon of October 5 with wives No. 1 and 2 as chief mourners.

Two days have passed since the burial, but the Government has made no announcement and the newspapers of Teheran obviously have been forbidden to make mention. The Teheran public evidently was prepared for the news to an extent to absorb much of the shock because it had so long been predicted in private conversations that Teymourtache would never be permitted to leave the jail alive.

The word has been passed around that death was due to heart failure, but so are all deaths. I doubt if there is a Persian in Teheran, and certainly there is no foreigner here, who does not believe that another surreptitious lynching, such as have characterized the history of the Shahs for centuries, has taken place. All accept the statement that Teymourtache died of heart failure, but if allowed to pursue an inquiry I am sure every one would go back to ascertain the nature of the astringent that caused the heart to fail. One of the servants in reporting the death remarked, "he died from a little white pill."

If the deposed Minister was put to death according to the formula suspected generally in Teheran, the way was prepared several weeks ago when the Shah gave orders that Teymourtache's personal physician was no longer to be admitted to the jail. Any required medical service was to be ministered by the prison physician who is a political appointee of the Chief of Imperial Police. This order was given by Reza Shah at the time of his assault on Teymourtache in Kasr-Kajar prison described in my despatch No. 1542.

The shocking news of Teymourtache's passing has revived conjectures as to the causes of his downfall. There is quite general agreement that the Shah moved so harshly against his brilliant and forceful Court Minister partly because of fear of his growing influence and power. But some say this was not all. Some well-informed Persians, I learn, have declared that the Shah was displeased with the enthusiastic reception of Teymourtache in Moscow on the occasion of his return from a visit to Europe in the early part of 1932. Responding to the cordial greetings of high Soviet authorities at the time Teymourtache is said to have delivered a powerful speech dwelling upon the imperative need for sympathetic cooperation between the Soviets and Persia. In this speech he invited Litvinoff, Commissar for Foreign affairs, to visit Teheran as a guest of the Shah. Litvinoff never came, but on the day of Teymourtache's death Karakhan, assistant Commissar for Foreign Affairs, was winding up a long series of honors at official receptions and dinners in Teheran. Karakhan was regarded as Teymourtache's ardent friend, his real liaison with the Government in Moscow. It was with Karakhan that he carried on supplemental negotiations with regard to the Perso-Soviet commercial treaty. . . . One is even told that a visit made by Karakhan to Kasr-Kajar prison on the last day of his sojourn was designed on his part as a gesture of friendship toward his old friend the one-time Minister of the Imperial Court then shut up in a bleak and barren little cell of this Persian Bastille. . . .

Albeit he had enemies and ardent ones, I doubt that anyone could be found in Persia having any familiarity with the deeds and accomplishments of Teymourtache who would gainsay his right to a place in history as perhaps the most commanding intellect that has risen in the country in two centuries. Whatever evil there was in him having been interred with his bones, it is my opinion that his name will be idealized when that of the tyrant, Reza Shah, has become nothing more than a haunting memory.[24]

It was subsequently revealed that Karakhan had intended to visit Teymourtache in his prison cell, which may have hastened the latter's end. William H. Hornibrook, Hart's successor as minister, compares Teymourtache's prison death with that of Sardar Assad Bakhtiari (see below), on whose behalf, he says, the ulema had planned to plead with Reza Shah:

> There is, of course, a certain verisimilitude attaching to this version from the parallel which it has, in certain particulars, with the circumstances attending the end of Teymourtache. It will be recalled in that instance that it was on the occasion of the visit to Teheran of Vice Commissar Karakhan of the Soviet Commissariat of Foreign Affairs of the U.S.S.R. that Teymourtache met his end and it was then reported that Teymourtache was liquidated in anticipation of the intercession in his behalf of Karakhan or for fear that Karakhan might seek to visit his old acquaintance and obtain from him disclosures embarrassing to the Persian Government.[25]

Pahlavi's Poison Squad

Hart describes the official announcement of Teymourtache's death:

> I have the honor to report that after suppressing news of the death in prison of Abdol Hossein Khan Teymourtache for three days, the *Ettela'at* of Teheran carried this brief announcement on the evening of October 7: "Teymourtache who was in Qasr-i-Qajar prison died two nights ago from angine de poitrine (angine [sic] pectoris) and cardiopathy from which he was suffering and due to which physicians expected an apoplectic fit." The *Shafaq-i-Sorkh* of October 8 reported that Teymourtache died on Wednesday, October 4, adding that "his body, after being examined by the legal physician [of the Ministry of Justice], was buried at Imamzadeh Abdullah." The date of death appears to have been October 4, which was the day after I wrote my sadly divinatory despatch No. 1542, which reads today as if I had received advance information from the Shah's poison squad.
>
> Imperial malevolence toward the distinguished prisoner persisted even to the grave. The body, as that of a common criminal, was carried to its last resting place by four common policemen of the 14-toman the month variety, and no word of honorable mention of the man's life or distinguished services was permitted to be made. The scene at the cemetery enacted by his oldest daughter, Iran Khanum, who was educated at the American school, is too harrowing for description.
>
> One surprising feature of the depressing incident was that Persians of all walks of life were permitted for days to call at the Teymourtache home, the house occupied by the first wife, who is Persian, to express their sympathy. Cars and carriages began gathering in front of the house early every morning for several days and by the end of the afternoons the street was blocked.
>
> Persian women who enjoy the widest latitude in their gossip, I am informed by an American woman who speaks full-fluted Persian and sees many of them,

talk freely of how Teymourtache was poisoned. The statement has been made to me by a Persian that there is not a subject of Reza Shah in Teheran and elsewhere in Persia who does not take it for granted that the sensationally abrupt death was due to foul play under orders from the Palace.

As expressed in my despatch No. 1550, I am convinced that the name of Teymourtache will live through the ages and that the cause of death will be accurately catalogued by future histories of Persia just as today one reads in the record of the past that the veins of the great one-time Prime Minister Emir-i-Kebir were opened by orders of Naser-ed-Din Shah in the garden of the Shah [Bagh-i-Shah] at Fin, near Kashan.

While it is true that shahs from the inception of Persian dynasties have been past masters at wrecking souls and destroying bodies, not even the indomitable Reza Shah has yet contrived to extinguish the human soul. Among Teymourtache's enemies, I am told, were many who had such stolid faith in the superhuman powers of the man who once all but dominated Persia that they thought it wise to watch their step. No word was uttered by them even after his arrest, which might reach the ears of the noted prisoner because they could not convince themselves that his phenomenal genius would not in the end solve the riddle of his incarceration and permit a return to official activity with a reassertion of his old influence. And there are those today, perhaps, who are not willing to believe that the real Teymourtache has been put secretly away. And these cannot assure themselves, if so, that the Persian wizard of the age will not some day, in his own mysterious way, dig himself out.

And such cautious souls doubtless will whistle any time they chance to be passing the old Mohammedan burying ground at Shah Abdol Azim whether it be day or night.[26]

Solat-ed-Dowleh Qashqai, Sardar Ashayer

When a detailed history of the brave resistance of the southern tribes to British conquest of south Persia is finally written, the name of Mirza Esmail Khan Qashqai, Solat-ed-Dowleh, will assuredly be honored. Hart mentions him in his dispatch of October 3, 1933 (quoted above), but earlier, after a trip to Shiraz, he had reported the arrest of Solat-ed-Dowleh: "In Shiraz a few weeks ago I heard the declaration that Solat-ed-Dowleh, Kashqai chieftain, was not seized and taken to prison in Teheran because of actual evidence of plotting against the Government. His arrest, the confident belief was expressed, was ordered that the Shah might be free to gobble up all of his lands and houses, among the richest estates remaining in southern Persia."[27] Additional information on the arrest and dispossession of Solat-ed-Dowleh and Qavam-ol-Molk Shirazi is provided in a March 1933 dispatch.[28]

On October 20, 1932, the Majlis enacted the following law: "Preamble: There are times when the exigencies of the country warrant the exchange of the land and water interests of certain persons, including tribal chiefs and others, for parcels of public domain. Voted: For two years from the date of this law the Government is authorized to transfer to such persons lands forming part of the public domains, when the political exigencies of the country warrant the transfer of their interests from one zone to another."[29]

The purpose of the measure was twofold. First, it enabled Reza Shah to "exchange" barren lands belonging to the government for valuable agricultural land belonging to private individuals. The valuable exchanged land was then "purchased" by Reza Shah from the government. Its second purpose was to deprive the tribal leaders of their property and influence. The above law had been passed after an earlier pilot project had been tried in Fars. Hart reported that on June 7, 1932, the Majlis had approved "a Government bill dispossessing one of the last great feudal landowners of the Shiraz region, Qavam-ol-Molk, hereditary chief of the Khamsa Arab tribes." Hart had included the following quotation from the bill: "The Ministry of Finance is authorized to exchange, through official title deed, all the water and land interests of Mirza Ibrahim Qavam situated in the province of Fars against public domains, including lands, water rights, qanats, et cetera in Ashraf, Semnan, Damghan, Neishapur, Kashan and Torqozabad, on the basis of equality of revenues."[30]

Having noted the exchange (read *confiscation*) of the lands of Qavam for lands in distant Khorasan and Damghan, where Qavam exercised no political influence, Hart reports on "the effective suppression of the influence of the second leading Shiraz feudal family, i.e., that headed by Solat-ed-Doleh, paramount chief and leading deputy of the warlike Qashqai tribes." He also describes the process to be used against the unfortunate Bakhtiari tribal leaders.

On the proposition of the Minister of the Interior, the Majlis on August 30, 1932, voted to deprive "Ismail Khan Qashqai (Solat-ed-Doleh) and Nasser Khan (one of his sons)" of their parliamentary immunity, "authorizing the Government to subject them to criminal prosecution." My scrap on this development is the following extract from the Minister's remarks when introducing the motion: "The Government has conclusive evidence of the implication of the two deputies in an intrigue and conspiracy to neutralize the efforts towards stabilization and tranquillity in South Persia. The current drought in Fars has created a delicate situation affording those who entertain mischievous ideas an opportunity for subversive action. Others being implicated, it is obvious that the details of this intrigue must be kept secret." Persistent rumor at the time had it that the motive behind this charge, allegedly a trumped-up one, was that Solat had not shown the same compliance as had the Qavam in submitting to the royal will by agreeing to an exchange of his Shiraz properties. Since this Majlis vote there has been absolute official silence as to the fate of the two deputies, but it is generally believed that they are still held in Kasr Kajar Prison at Teheran.[31]

FIGURE 6.2 *Solat-ed-Dowleh Qashqai (left), Nosrat-ed-Dowleh Firouz (center), and three sons of Solat-ed-Dowleh (Mohammad Nasser, Khosrow, and Mohammad Hossein), 1923. Courtesy of the IICHS.*

The next news about Solat-ed-Dowleh, Sardar Ashayer, was when his body had been seen in the hands of the body washers in the morgue in Tehran in 1933. Though the news of his passing had not been announced, it was confirmed by Hart: "Mirza Esmail Khan Qashqai (best known by his former titles Sardar Ashayer and Solat-ed-Doleh), wealthy anti-British chief of the Qashqai tribe who was last year imprisoned by the authority of the Majlis (despatch No. 1393 of March 25, 1933), is said to have died in prison a week ago. His death was not reported in any local newspaper."

In the same dispatch (1393), Hart also provides some observations on Reza Shah's policy of centralization, which necessitated the brutal suppression of tribal life. Hart calls centralization

the outstanding feature of the Pahlavi regime distinguishing it from that of Reza Shah's Kajar predecessors. That feature may be summed up in the word centralization—centralization of power in His Majesty's own hands, centralized finances and a much Europeanized Capital which is the seat not only of centralized administration but also of a disciplined modernized army and a radial system of motor roads rendering mobile the mainstay of the new regime. Here we touch the particular subject of the present despatch: the breaking of feudalism and the settlement of the nomadic tribes which form at least a quarter of the country's population. This constitutes another of the essential elements of the Shah's centralization policy. Its progressive application throughout the country has, of course, been evident ever since Pahlavi, even before he was chosen Shah, became the virtual ruler of Persia. Never has there been any abating. The feudal power of the tribal chiefs, be they submissive or not to the central authority, the Shah has consistently held, must be broken.[32]

The Shah's Invitation: The Fate of Ali Khan Qashqai

In reporting the death of Solat-ed-Dowleh, Hart also includes a piece from the newspaper *Shafaq-i-Sorkh* of July 31, 1933, about the recent arrest of his younger brother, Ali Khan Qashqai:

The most important news of this region is the surrender of Ali Khan Qashqai to the Government forces. This event was made the occasion for public jubilation, for it means the extermination of sedition and outlawry in the south. Frequently, during the last few years, Ali Khan Qashqai has disturbed peace and security in the province of Fars. His followers have plundered villages and travelers, at times descending even to massacre and other outrages. Troops were ordered early in the summer to pursue and suppress the band. The operations have been successful, and the band defeated and dispersed, and Ali Khan forced to surrender. Other minor outlaws, encouraged by his acts of brigandage, have also been suppressed.[33]

On the gruesome fate of Ali Khan's older brother, Solat-ed-Dowleh, Hart comments: "One wonders how long the younger brother will live in captivity." The actual circumstances surrounding the "surrender" and "capture" of Ali Khan Qashqai is described by Hart in a report dated October 4:

Ali Khan Qashqai, respected—I use the adjective advisedly—brigand chieftain of the great southern province of Fars, last July "surrendered" to the military forces of Reza Shah. That, at least, was the term used in the report quoted in my above-mentioned despatch [no. 1508]. Now from Herr Friedrich Krefter, Acting Director of the American archeological mission at Persepolis, who traveled from Shiraz to Teheran in Ali Khan's company, I learn a different tale. The latter is that, as in the cases of Mashallah and Simko, Ali Khan was not captured by the Persian military but accepted the invitation of the Shah to visit Teheran as an honored guest. He was conducted to the capital by a guard of honor. Frequent stops were made en route at estates of friendly Persian notables. Courtesies from civil and military authorities were the order of the day. Krefter was proceeding to Teheran in connection with affairs of the Persepolis archeological expedition. Rule had it that he might not proceed by night. But rules were broken by Ali Khan. Krefter accepted readily an invitation to join the tribal leader's suite. He found of vivid human interest both the pageantry of the journey and the naiveté of his honored host going, all unwittingly it seemed, to an almost certain doom. It is now reported in usually well informed Persian circles that Ali Khan was not received by the Shah but, instead, has been held in the same house in which a year ago his deputy brother, Solat-ed-Doleh, was led, never to leave alive, to Kasr Kajar, Persia's Sing Sing. I know of none in Teheran who doubt that Ali Khan will follow in the footsteps of his onetime distinguished elder brother.[34]

The Arrest of Bakhtiari Tribal Leaders, 1933

Among those who had pleaded with Reza Shah to show mercy to Teymourtache was Jafar Qoli Khan, Sardar Assad Bakhtiari, nominally the minister of war:

As evidence that no letdown is likely in the prosecution of Teymourtache, I am informed that Sardar Assad, Minister of War, has virtually abandoned his intercessions. Of all the men surrounding the Shah only one appears to have been informed at any time as to his mind with regard to his deposed Minister of the Court or to have known anything of the various steps in the prosecution. This man was Sardar Assad who was once the Shah's commander. Reza Khan, as he was known in those days following the promulgation of the constitution, served for five years as a private under his present Minister of War and always has been grateful for the kindness shown him by the Sardar (Sardar is the

Bakhtiari title which means general commander). Sardar Assad was the most ardent friend of Teymourtache in high office. It is known that following the arrest he interceded many times with the Shah to be lenient with the disgraced official. On at least two occasions he had reason, it is known, to believe that his supplications were about to be successful, then came startling revelations of more huge peculations in National Bank funds, which were shared with no one else, stories of political intrigue, then praise in the British newspapers for the ability of the distinguished prisoner, and all hopes were dashed.[35]

Soon after the burial of Teymourtache, it was the turn of the same Sardar Assad Bakhtiari to be arrested and die in prison. George Wadsworth, chargé d'affaires ad interim, describes the arrest of Sardar Assad and many of his close relatives on November 28, 1933:

> Sardar Assad, Minister of War, longtime friend and supporter of the Shah was placed under arrest, sent under guard to the capital and incarcerated in Qasr Qajar prison. And on the following day a dozen or so members of the family of Bakhtiari Khans—of whom Sardar Assad is, of course, one—resident in Teheran were similarly arrested by the police or held "in quarters" in their regiments. Among them is Sardar Assad's brother, Sardar Bahadur, a colonel in one of the cavalry regiments stationed in Teheran. "Why?" has been the question which all of Teheran has asked itself since the news of the arrests became generally known yesterday. From such generally well informed sources as colleagues and American missionaries I could learn nothing.[36]

Wadsworth conversed with Edward Wilkinson, manager of the Imperial Bank of Persia, and George McGill, a representative of a British manufacturing concern. McGill felt that the arrest of Sardar Assad was related to an article in the London *Times* by its correspondent in Tehran, DeBathe. According to McGill, the article "derides the Shah, his ministers, his officials, his accomplishments and his program; exaggerates reports of unrest—which is only natural—among the tribes; predicts revolution." Wadsworth then adds: "But Mr. Wilkinson felt there must be something more to the situation than the DeBathe article. He couldn't for a moment believe that Sardar Assad was disloyal to the Shah. Twenty years experience militated against such a supposition. Nor did he know of any serious reasons for discontent among the Bakhtiari. There was, of course, on the other side of the question the incontrovertible proposition that one of the Shah's basic policies is to 'liquidate' any and all Persians whose influence might be such, upon his death, as to threaten the continuation of the Pahlavi dynasty. And Sardar Assad, a leading Chief of the as yet not disarmed powerful Bakhtiari tribe, could readily be conceived as at least a potential menace to the realization of that aim."[37]

The detainees included three Majlis deputies whose parliamentary immunity had been removed by the Majlis on December 10, 1933: Mohammad Taqi Khan Assad Bakhtiari (Amir Jang), Amir Hossein Khan Ilkhan Bakhtiari, and Mirza Ebrahim Khan Qavam (Qavam-ol-Molk), leader of the Khamseh tribes in Fars. Wadsworth reports on the Majlis proceedings concerning the revocation of the parliamentary immunity of these members. On December 10, 1933, the minister of the interior had made the following speech:

The honorable gentlemen are aware of the sacrifices made toward the security of the country since the progressive movement started under His Imperial Majesty's rulership. Unfortunately in certain cases and localities certain individuals finding this condition detrimental to their personal interests have resorted to certain futile measures which could best be likened to the contortions of a dying man (Cheers). It is to be regretted that in certain recent developments three deputies are accused of complicity; namely, Amir Hussein Khan Ilkhan, Mohammad Taqi Khan Assad (formerly Amir Jang) and Mirza Ebrahim Khan Ghavam-i-Shirazi (formerly Ghavam-ol-Molk). As they must be legally prosecuted, the National Consultative Assembly is hereby requested to divest them of their parliamentary immunity so that the Government may be able to subject them to prosecution according to the requirements of the law.[38]

As expected, the Majlis had voted (no doubt unanimously) to divest the three of their immunity. Wadsworth then provides a reason for the wholesale arrests:

The facts on which this conspiracy charge was lodged have not been made known. From Professor H. B. Young of the American College in Teheran, who has several Bakhtiari boys in his classes, I have the following tale: Their fathers had met, as was their common practice, to discuss the affairs of the tribe, then about to leave its summer quarters to the west of Isfahan for winter grazing in Khuzistan. Following the meeting they had written a long letter to their "brother," the Khan Baba Khan, leading chief with the tribesmen. This letter, sent by special messenger, was intercepted in Isfahan. In it were at least two unfortunate references: One to certain stores of ammunition held by the tribesmen; the other to the internal political situation, in connection with which it was added that in the event of any untoward development—presumably the death of the Shah—their position was, to translate the Persian phrase: "One for all and all for one." The story of this letter, with varying versions as to its contents, is confirmed by other sources, as are later stories of the discovery and seizure of large supplies of ammunition hidden in two or more of the tribe's summer villages. Late reports have it that a board of inquiry into the matter has been sitting in the Ministry of War, that all prisoners have been closely questioned by a military prosecutor and that sentences of death have been recommended in the cases of five of the Bakhtiaris, including Sardar Assad, his brother Amir Jang and their nephew Amir Hussein.

The arrests have acutely revived local discussion of the question of dynastic succession. The days of Sardar Assad's father are recalled; of how in 1909 he had seriously considered the idea of overthrowing the Qajars and establishing a Bakhtiari dynasty; of the ensuing Bakhtiari march on the capital as the force most responsible for the restoration of constitutionalism and the abdication of Mohammad Ali Shah. As one critic put it: "With the Shah the question of dynastic succession has become an obsession." There is, of course, nothing new in the question per se. During my three years at this post the query I have heard perhaps most often put to persons with long experience in this country has been: "What may we anticipate will transpire when the Shah dies?" A complete answer might be: "Almost anything. Certainly we may expect intrigue on every side. There will be partisan cliques within and without the Army. One of the dozen generals might conceivably gain the throne. The Crown Prince will have his supporters but in their case also self interest will be a guiding motive." To this composite answer comment of the last year [may] be added with growing conviction: "Teymourtache, formerly all-powerful Minister of the Court, was crushed because the Shah felt with reason that he could not count on his Minister's loyalty. All others that His Majesty may distrust will be similarly crushed. We are dealing with an oriental despot who will show no pity, shrewd in a knowledge of his own people, violent by nature but brutal in an occidental rather than in oriental sense and, above all, almost unique among Persians in a calculating and dominating perseverance to attain his ends."[39]

The Prison Death of Sardar Assad

Shortly after the above dispatch was completed, a new American minister arrived in Tehran, William H. Hornibrook, a Roosevelt appointee. Before he left he visited the White House, accompanied by Wallace S. Murray. As an indication of Roosevelt's special interest in Persia and the Middle East, the president requested Hornibrook to periodically submit a report on conditions in Persia directly to him. In his first report, Hornibrook had spoken favorably about Reza Shah and the progress and modernization being carried out under his leadership. He referred to the freeing of Persia from British domination and control. Soon, however, and like Hart, he was disabused of such illusions.

The reality of the reign of terror that prevailed in Persia had become clear to him when Sardar Assad was murdered in prison in the manner of Teymourtache. Soon after Sardar Assad's "heart failure" in prison, Hornibrook had to report on the executions of the Bakhtiari tribal leaders and the long jail sentences handed to others. And before long it was his duty to narrate the bloody massacre by machine gun and bayonet of the protesters and pilgrims in the holy shrine of Imam Reza in Mashhad between July 12 and 14, 1935. He submitted no other report on progress under Reza Shah.

FIGURE 6.3 *Jaffar Qoli Bakhtiari, Sardar Assad, ca. 1930. Courtesy of the IICHS.*

In a telegram dated April 2, 1934, Hornibrook reported: "Former Minister of War died quote of apoplexy unquote in prison on Friday according to a brief press item without comment."[40] He went on to describe Sardar Assad's death in an April 7 dispatch:

> While the most generally accepted version of the events leading to the arrest of Sardar Assad and other prominent Bakhtiari is that given in the last-mentioned despatch [1656, February 10, 1934; see note 38], few are disposed to

credit the Bakhtiari either individually or collectively as a tribe with having had specific treasonable designs; the most that is attributed to them is that of taking precautions to be prepared for any eventuality following the Shah's death. That Sardar Assad himself possessed the following or strength of character to warrant the supposition that he had dynastic ambitions is doubted by those familiar with him who describe him rather as an inoffensive and somewhat colorless character lifted to a position of responsibility as Minister of War by the personal favor of the Shah. For some weeks previous to his actual death rumors were rife that he had passed the way of the Qashqai chief, Solat-ed-Dowleh and of Teymourtache. Nothing was heard until the brief announcement published in the *Ettela'at* on the evening of March 31, 1934, in an obscure corner of that newspaper, as follows, in translation: "Ja'far Qoli Khan Assad Bakhtiari died during the night of Friday in the hospital of the prison of Kasr Kajar from an attack of the apoplexy." That is all, not a word or a line more in the *Ettela'at* or any other of the newspapers which republished the news but, of course, columns may be and have been read between the lines.

Hornibrook then describes the British attempt to portray the death of Sardar Assad as natural:

> According to the Oriental Secretary of the British Legation, Sardar Assad actually suffered a stroke of apoplexy something more than a year ago and there is a remote possibility that his death occurred from this natural cause. But there are few who hold to this view. Rather the opinion is generally heard that Sardar Assad has been another victim incident to the ruthless application by the Shah of two policies: the one, the extinction of the feudal elements in Persia as exemplified by the tribes and tribal leaders, and the second, the liquidation of any and every individual whom the Shah conceives may stand directly or indirectly in the way of the maintenance of the Pahlavi dynasty. Of course, the first policy naturally forms part of the second and broader one.

> The question uppermost today in men's minds in Persia was raised with Mr. Herrick Young of the American college in Teheran by one of the leaders of the Bakhtiari—and therefore all the more entitled to credence as confirming the tragic end of Sardar Assad—how much longer is such a state of affairs to continue? A second question, implicit therein, is who will be the next victim? While it is common agreement of those with whom I have discussed the situation set forth above that there is probably not a single person in all of Persia who does not bear the most sullen resentment, fear and hatred of the Shah, the circumstances surrounding the death of Sardar Assad would not appear to have aroused, even amongst the Bakhtiari, emotions of an explosive character. Perhaps the apparently silent undemonstrative acceptance of the situation is to be found in the fatalistic character of the Persian religion which animates and conditions the Persian's attitude towards life. However that may be, there has been no appreciable reaction to an occurrence which is assuming the character of a fixed tradition with the Shah. It is doubtful, nevertheless, in the light of the past history of the Persians, if their patience will prove inexhaustible and it is

believed by me, on the basis of my own brief observations and on the information I have gathered from my colleagues and others that the seed which is now
being sown may bear its expected fruit of bitterness against the Pahlavi dynasty
with the passing from the scene of the dominating figure of the Shah.

Hornibrook goes on to recount the release of Ebrahim Qavam from
Qasr-Qajar:

> Some few days before the Now-Ruz, however, or about the middle of March,
> to the general surprise of Teheran, there was released from the Kasr Kajar prison
> the Qavam-ol-Molk, otherwise known as Mirza Ebrahim Khan Qavam, who
> had been imprisoned coincident with Sardar Assad. Those who have seen the
> latter since his release report that, although a man in his early forties, he has suf-
> fered a complete whitening of the hair. At the same time he states that he was
> well treated in prison and permitted to have such comforts as he desired but that
> not the slightest hint was ever given him of the reasons for his incarceration.[41]

In a later report Hornibrook further recounts the death and burial of Sardar Assad:

> From other sources I have heard that the body of Sardar Assad was sent
> immediately from Teheran, under a military escort, to Isfahan; that the body
> was kept outside of the city until the relatives could be notified and that they
> were then informed that the funeral services must be limited to the attendance
> of only a few chosen close relatives and that no examination of the body would
> be permitted. As the Dutch Chargé d'Affaires pertinently remarked, with the
> thought of van der Lubbe obviously in his mind, "it is not only in Germany that
> bodies of dead men are thus dealt with."
>
> A version of the circumstances leading to his death, of which I have been
> able to obtain from one of my colleagues some corroboration—so far as such
> is possible in this country of extensive rumors and limited sources of exact
> information—is that the death of Sardar Assad was a sequel to appeals which
> the mullahs had intended to present in his behalf to the Shah. The story is that
> the mullahs resolved, on the occasion of the Now-Ruz reception at the Golestan
> Palace on March 21, 1934, to request the Shah to exercise clemency on behalf of
> Sardar Assad. It is recounted that the Shah, before entering the audience cham-
> ber where the mullahs, in accordance with traditional practice, were permitted
> to remain seated until his entrance, had apparently been advised of the inten-
> tions in this respect of the mullahs. In any event, upon entering the audience
> chamber the Shah launched into a violent and bitter upbraiding of a mullah
> who had not, in the Shah's opinion, shown sufficient alacrity in rising in the
> August presence of His Majesty. So furious was the Shah, and so caustic was he
> in his comments on the alleged disrespect shown him that, so the story goes,
> the mullahs were so intimidated that they failed completely to muster the nec-
> essary courage to advance the plea for clemency on behalf of Sardar Assad as
> they had intended. A few days later, in the night of March 29th, the end came to
> Sardar Assad.[42]

The Fate of Other Tribal Detainees

Hornibrook also describes the sentences of those who had been arrested along with Sardar Assad. Thirty-five individuals had been tried in military courts, and the sentences had "been published in two successive days in the vernacular Persian press":

> The first announcement of the sentences was published in the evening issue of *Ettela'at* on November 27th, in translation as follows: "The following Bakhtiari, Kashgai, Boir Ahmadi, and Mamasani traitors and insurgents, who have been convicted by the military tribunal of high treason and armed insurrection, were executed:
>
> 1. Mohammad Reza Khan Bakhtiari (Sardar Fateh)
> 2. Mohammad Jevad Khan Esfandiari (Sardar Eqbal)
> 3. Ali Mardan Khan Chahar Lang
> 4. Aqa Gudarz Ahmad Khosrovi Bakhtiari
> 5. Sartip Khan Boir Ahmadi
> 6. Shokrollah Khan Boir Ahmadi
> 7. Hossein Khan Darreshiri Kashgai
> 8. Imam Qoli Khan Mamasani.

To this the *Setareh ye Djehane* on November 29th added the information, after listing those executed, that "the verdict of the War Council has been put into execution and the traitors mentioned above have been shot." In the evening of November 28, 1934, the *Ettela'at*, followed by other newspapers thereafter, published a list of the others affected by the sentences of the court-martial, as follows:

1. Mohammad Taqi Khan Assad (Amir Jang), life imprisonment
2. Esmail Khan Zarasvand Bakhtiari, life imprisonment
3. Musa Khan Bakhtiari (Bahador-os-Saltaneh), life imprisonment
4. Mollah Kheirollah Janaki Bakhtiari, life imprisonment
5. Manucher Khan Assad, ten years imprisonment with hard labor
6. Ahmad Khan Ilkhan, ten years imprisonment with hard labor
7. Yusef Khan Amir Mojahed, ten years imprisonment in solitary confinement
8. Nosratollah Khan Ilkhan, eight years imprisonment with hard labor
9. Aqa Eskandar Baba Ahmadi Bakhtiari, eight years imprisonment with hard labor
10. Mostafa Khan Ajami Behdarvand Bakhtiari, seven years imprisonment in solitary confinement.
11. Khan Baba Khan Assad, six years imprisonment with hard labor

12. Ali Mohammad Khan Il-Beig Bakhtiari, six years imprisonment with hard labor

13. Mohammad Khan Assad (Salar A'zam), five years imprisonment with hard labor

14. Abdol Karim Khan Esfandiari Bakhtiari, five years imprisonment with hard labor

15. Mirza Aqa Il-Beig Bakhtiari, five years imprisonment with hard labor

16. Aqa Lotfeh Ahmad Khosrovi Bakhtiari, five years imprisonment in solitary confinement

17. Amir Hosein Khan Ilkhan, three years imprisonment with hard labor

18. Aqa Nasrollah Khan Sulmuli Bakhtiari, three years correctional imprisonment

19. Teimur Khan Bakhtiari, one year correctional imprisonment.

The following were acquitted:

1. Haji Soltan Ali Khan (Shehab-os-Saltaneh)

2. Mohammad Qoli Khan Assad (Sardar Bahador)

3. Rahim Khan Amir Bakhtiari

4. Esmail Khan Esfandiari

5. Parviz Khan Esfandiari

6. Habibollah Khan Esfandiari

7. Ali Mohammad Khan Ilkhan

8. Elias Khan Ilkhan.

The press, of course, confined itself to publishing the names without adding anything whatsoever in the way of comment on the sentences.

Hornibrook, however, adds his own commentary on the sentences and on some of the unfortunate individuals:

It will be recalled from the Legation's previous despatches which have been cited, that the arrest of Sardar Assad and his Bakhtiari and other colleagues would appear to have been occasioned by the interception of a letter from Khan Baba Khan, who has now been sentenced to seven years imprisonment, which, though admittedly indiscreet, is not generally considered to have been implicit of more than the ordinary foresight which the tribe might have been expected to take in the event of the Shah's death, namely, that of concerting measures to deal with such an event by the united counsel of the tribe. It now appears, from such information as it has been possible to obtain, that the Government, finding it impossible to convict the Bakhtiaris and their immediate tribal neighbors who were imprisoned on the charges of treason in connection with the incident of 1933, proceeded against them on the basis of the rebellion of 1929 which was reported in the Legation's despatches of July 13 and July 19, 1929. At that time, consequent upon the disaffection of certain of the tribal leaders residing in the Bakhtiari country and vicinity against their leaders who spent most of their time in Teheran, a rebellion against the authority of the latter was initiated and the Government sent both Sardar Assad and his brother, Mohammed Taqi Khan Assad Bakhtiari (Amir Jang), to put down the disaffection. Due to the inability of these to put the rebellion down the Government was subsequently forced to despatch other government troops. Of the eight now executed, all were leaders of that rebellion, including Sardar Eqbal, Sardar Fateh (born in 1886, the cultivated son of the former Ilkhani and brother of the present Ilkhani), Ali Mardan Khan, Sartip Khan and Shokrollah Khan, the two last named being young men.

Of those sentenced to imprisonment, Salar Az'am, the brother of Amir Jang, is described as an entirely harmless individual, who is addicted to needle work and it is related of him that he is now engaged in making a large pillow case bearing the Shah's portrait in the confident expectation that when it is completed and it is seen by the Shah he will be released. The comparative mildness of the sentence of seven years upon Khan Baba Khan, the recipient of the alleged intercepted letter of 1934, is generally ascribed to his consummate cleverness. Some years ago when his home was visited by the authorities and the complaint was made that his house contained no portrait of the Shah, Khan Baba is reported to have placed his hand upon his breast and to have remarked with great simulated feeling: "true enough, but then I am one of those who bears always the portrait of the Shah in my heart."

Of all the measures taken against the tribes by the Shah, beginning with those directed to the undermining of the authority of the Sheikh of Mohammerah and including the measures taken against the Kurds, the Turcomans, the Kashgais, the Lurs and the Ghavams, those which have now been taken against the Bakhtiaris and their neighbors are considered as the most severe. Besides court-martialling of these prominent members of the southern tribes, it is understood that for the past two months government assessors have been at work in the Bakhtiari country appraising the lands of the principal Bakhtiari chieftains with a view of enforcing an exchange of their properties for land in other parts of Persia. No immediate disturbances are anticipated as a reaction to the Government's present action as it is felt that the Shah has the army too well in hand to permit of the successful outcome of any open disaffection. Moreover, there may be quoted the conclusion of the cultured son of one of the Bakhtiari leaders that "there is nothing to be done," which may be accepted, it is believed, as characteristic of the reception of the news of those directly or indirectly affected. "It is God's will," such is the defense mechanism offered by the Bakhtiari and by Persians to cover their present inability to react actively; but, when the banked fires of resentment find an outlet with the Shah's death, "God's will" may possibly express itself in something more than a passive manner. In the Legation's despatch No. 22 of April 7, 1934, it was stated that the execution of Sardar Assad exemplified the application of two policies on the part of the Shah: the one, the extinction of the feudal elements in Persia as exemplified by the tribes and tribal leaders, and the second, the liquidation of any and every individual whom the Shah conceives may stand directly or indirectly in the way of the maintenance of the Pahlevi dynasty, the first policy, obviously, forming part of the second and broader one. Only the future can tell whether he has sown the seeds of dissolution of his own dynasty or whether the action taken by him may cement the Pahlevi strength. Between these prospects it would seem that the former is more probable.[43]

The British reaction to all this is also recorded:

> In a conversation with the Oriental Secretary of the British Legation, Mr. Trott, who has served for some years in Persia, the most profound regret was expressed at the action of the Government which was characterized as excessively severe. In the opinion of the British Oriental Secretary, who has perhaps a more profound knowledge of Persian conditions than any member of the staff of the British Legation, the action of the Persian Government in this instance, instead of cementing the dynastic succession—its presumed purpose—is more likely than not to lead to profound disaffection among the tribes concerned which will smolder on until the Shah's death and will then assert itself in perhaps active rebellion.[44]

The Persian Bastille

Following the 1931–34 murders and arrests, there are many reports that Reza Shah embarked on an orgy of terror against prominent people as well as ordinary citizens. Some of the political prisoners from this grim period were held in Qasr-Qajar prison, which Hart had called the Persian Bastille or the Persian Sing Sing. Built in 1929, Qasr-Qajar (Qajar palace) was designed by Teymourtache, after prisons he had inspected in Europe, "to provide suitable accommodation for political prisoners." It was here that Teymourtache was himself incarcerated and met his end. Described as "one of the most prominent landmarks of the northeastern suburbs of Teheran, [this] extensive one-storied structure" was clearly designed to strike terror into the hearts of would-be "political offenders."[45]

In 1938, the prison was renamed on orders of the shah, as reported by James S. Moose Jr., chargé d'affaires ad interim: "I have the honor to inform the Department that, on orders of the Shah, the prison for Iranian political offenders known as Qasr-e-Qajar will henceforth be designated Bissim (pronounced Bee-Seem), the Persian word for wireless. A military radio station is located directly north of the prison. This name was not referred to the Iranian Academy, but its disapproval is unlikely."[46]

In April 1935 the American chargé d'affaires J. Rives Childs toured the prison with a sociology class from the American College:

> The prison is capable of accommodating some 1,200 to 1,500 prisoners and this number is generally filled. I was greatly impressed by the order and system maintained in the Kasr-Kajar prison and by the apparently humane provisions

made for the prisoners, as well as by the intelligence of its governor. I saw a number of rooms reserved for political prisoners and a number of the political prisoners themselves, including many of the Bakhtiari tribesmen recently sentenced to varying degrees of imprisonment, and the accommodations provided them seemed to leave nothing to be desired short of private baths and radio sets. Unless the prisoners had been given special fare for some days before our visit in order to give them the appearance of being well-fed it was otherwise impossible to avoid drawing the conclusion that they were well provided for. At the end of our visit we were received by the governor who replied to all questions put to him. When the governor was asked as to the hours allowed political prisoners for reception of friends his answer was given in the interrogation, "Did you ever know any political prisoners to have friends?"[47]

New Arrivals at Qasr-Qajar: Dashti, Rahnema, and Others

Just four days after describing his visit, Childs reported that to the guest list at Qasr-Qajar had been added numerous notable names. Two of the new arrivals were Ali Dashti and Zein-ol-Abedine Rahnema, prominent Majlis deputies and newspaper editors. Rahnema's brother, A. R. Tajaddod (Sheikh-ol-Araqeinzadeh), had also been brought in for good measure. Just as surprising were the arrests of Farajollah Bahrami, "the former Minister of Posts and Telegraphs, who was more recently Governor General of Khorassan, and his coadjutor, Mirza Musa Khan Maham." Childs's report continues:

> The only public announcement in any way indicative of the Government's action was the brief notice in the vernacular press on April 16th of the suppression by the Ministry of Education of the *Shafaq-i-Sorkh* and the withdrawal of the license of Rahnema as the publisher of the *Iran*, it being added that the *Iran*, however, would continue to be published but by a different editor. It will be recalled that both Dashti and Rahnema failed of election to the Tenth Majlis, their parliamentary immunity as deputies to the Ninth Majlis expiring, consequently, only a few days ago. Rahnema's career has been largely devoted to journalism. Of his colleague, Dashti, it suffices to state that his career likewise has been largely confined to journalism, although it cannot be said that the *Shafaq-i-Sorkh* has ever enjoyed the reputation as that of the semi-official government mouthpiece, the *Iran*, of which Rahnema was the editor. Some warning of the disfavor into which Rahnema and Dashti had fallen with the Shah was given on the occasion of the No-Ruz reception at the Palace when His Majesty spoke in very uncomplimentary terms publicly of the vernacular press of the capital generally. There are now some who see in a series of satirical articles regarding taxation published in the *Shafaq-i-Sorkh* signed "Droshky Driver" the occasion of the disfavor into which Dashti, the editor of that journal, has fallen. For although a rigorous censorship is maintained by the police over the press, as the Department is aware, I understand that in recent months the newspapers have been accorded greater latitude in the exercise of their own discretion over material to be published.

Tajaddod's principal offense may have been that he was the brother of Rahnema, although he was at one time also a deputy, as well as the editor of the now defunct *Tajaddod*. In September, 1926, he was arrested with several military officers charged with a plot against the life of the Shah. After his release he was compelled to leave the country, settling in Iraq. Upon being accorded permission to reenter the country he was appointed a judge.

The possible reasons for the sudden arrest of Bahrami and his associate, Maham, are also discussed:

Mirza Farajollah Khan Bahrami served from March, 1932, to September, 1933, as Minister of Posts and Telegraphs, after having previously served as confidential secretary to the Shah, and as Governor of Isfahan and Governor General of Fars. From 1933 to the latter part of 1934 he was Governor General of Khorassan, having been recalled from that post immediately prior to the visit of the foreign orientalists to the tomb of Ferdosi, a recall which excited no little comment at that time. It was rumored at the time that his recall at that time was due to his report to the Shah, when he was instructed to make preparations for the lodging of the visiting orientalists, that it was not possible to provide adequate accommodation for the visitors in Meshed on such short notice. There are others, however, who place greater importance, as a factor in his recall, upon lack of judgment which he is said to have displayed in reporting directly to the Shah, prior to His Majesty's anticipated visit to Meshed, an anonymous letter which had been received threatening an attempt against the Shah's life. The Shah is said to have expressed particular indignation at Bahrami's referring the matter to him without having apparently taken such measures for the security of the Shah as the latter deemed the circumstances to warrant. The arrest, with Bahrami, of Mirza Musa Khan Maham would appear to be due to the close association long maintained between the two, the latter having served with Bahrami in Isfahan, having been appointed by him as his Under Secretary in the Ministry of Posts and Telegraphs and having been named Chief of the Municipality in Meshed when Bahrami took up the post of Governor General of Khorassan.

Childs points out that all these supposed reasons were mere speculation. No one knew, not even the senior ministers:

Conjecture, of course, is general regarding the reasons prompting the disfavor into which the arrested men have fallen with the Shah. The Shah himself is alone able to provide the explicit reasons contributing to the disgrace of these prominent men and he is known to keep his own counsel. The difficulty of learning the truth under such circumstances has been well given voice to by a prominent official who, when the subject was brought up, aptly countered with the interrogation of "does anyone really know all the causes contributing to the downfall of Teymourtache?" In the case of the present arrests the causes of their disgrace were more than likely due to a variety of reasons, including, it has been suggested, not least to the fact that they were known as friends of Teymourtache.

Some light on the difficulties of determining the precise causes of the downfall of the arrested men is afforded by a reported authentic story of a conversation between the Shah and an Iranian official who received him in Khorassan when the former visited Meshed to participate in the Ferdosi celebration, a story which throws considerable light also on the Shah's character. According to this story, the Iranian official, in an endeavor to flatter His Majesty, remarked that there was only one previous ruler of Iran who deserved to be compared in any way with His Majesty, namely, Nadir Shah. "What, that brigand?" the Shah remarked, adding that he could perceive no similarities either in their careers or character. "The great defect in the character of Nadir Shah," the Shah continued, "was that he could not keep his own counsel, while I know well the advantages of keeping mine."[48]

The above five were lucky in that their sojourn in Qasr-Qajar was brief and they had escaped the fate of Teymourtache and Sardar Assad. Their punishment is reported by Hornibrook: "The Legation has been informed from a credible Iranian source that the former Minister of Posts and Telegraphs Bahrami had been exiled to Malayer; that Dashti, former editor of the *Shafaq-i-Sorkh,* who is now ill in the police hospital, will, upon his recovery be exiled to the district of Bushire from which he had been elected to the Ninth Majlis; while Rahnema, editor of the *Iran,* and his brother, A. R. Tajaddod, have been permitted to leave Iran and are now in the Lebanon."[49]

The Next Victim: His Highness Dadgar

According to Childs, on or about the day that he reported the imprisonment of Dashti and Rahnema (April 19, 1935), "summary measures were taken by the authorities against the President of the Majlis, His Highness Dadgar." However, this time it appeared that the British had intervened to save one of their own:

> A day or two after the imprisonment of Messrs. Dashti, Rahnema, and Bahrami, it appears that a police guard was thrown about the home of Dadgar. Upon perceiving the situation of police surveillance in which he was thus suddenly placed, it is reported that Dadgar communicated with the Shah and asked to be permitted to leave the country, promising never to return. It is generally agreed that, in any case, permission was suddenly accorded to him and a passport issued him, and that he took his departure, with his son, for the frontier about April 21st. Since that time there have been rumors that he was detained at the frontier and had been brought back to Teheran for imprisonment but these rumors are not generally accredited, the British Minister informing me that he had been assured by the Iranian Under Secretary for Foreign Affairs that Dadgar had left the country.

Childs then searches for reasons for the sudden fall of Dadgar, whose association with Reza Shah extended to the 1921 coup:

> The summary action taken against Dadgar is generally believed to have been prompted by the same causes which were responsible for the imprisonment of editors Dashti and Rahnema. In my previous despatch I have touched upon the difficulty of ascertaining the actual reasons prompting the action of the Shah against these prominent personalities. More cynical observers cite the large property interests of Dadgar in Teheran and elsewhere in Iran as having contributed to the Shah's desire to be rid of him, while others contend that it is quite characteristic of the Shah that he should seize any opportunity presented to rid himself of men such as Rahnema and Dadgar who assisted him in his rise to power, the one, it is recalled, having proposed the conferring of the Shahdom upon the former Prime Minister in the Constitutional Assembly of 1925 and the other having seconded the proposal.

Childs describes the prevailing view of the reasons for the shah's action against Dashti, Rahnema, and Dadgar:

> The interpretation of the Shah's action which is now gaining favor is that it was occasioned by a movement led by Rahnema and Dashti in the Majlis for the reassertion of the integrity of that institution. It is stated that dissatisfaction had been mounting in the Majlis for the reassertion of the integrity of that institution. It is said that dissatisfaction was mounting in the Majlis against the use of that body more and more as a mere rubber stamp by the Shah, particularly so far as it concerned taxation projects. The articles mentioned in my previous despatch as published in *Shafaq-i-Sorkh* mildly critical of the taxation measures of the Government were, it is said, intended by this group to break the ground for an organized movement in the Majlis looking for the reassertion of the authority of that body. While it is alleged that Dadgar was not privy to the movement in question, it is said that the Shah's resentment against him was occasioned by his failure to report the existence of such a movement in the Majlis as that represented to have been conceived by Dashti and Rahnema.

Childs concludes with the reality of "constitutional" rule under Reza Shah:

> There are not lacking deputies who are of the opinion that the Shah, in his concern over the independent action contemplated by the deputies Dashti and Rahnema, may decide upon the indefinite postponement of the convening of the Tenth Majlis which should be assembled within a few weeks. Others are rather of the opinion that the Shah finds the facade of constitutionalism implicit in the continued existence of a Majlis useful for his purposes and that he may be slow in doing away with a body which is altogether innocuous, which is entirely within his control, and offers the convenient illusion of constitutionalism to those naive ones amongst his subjects who continue to confuse the shadow of a thing with its substance.[50]

The Exile of Mossadegh and Taqizadeh

One of those exiled in 1927, Dr. Mohammad Mossadeq, a Majlis deputy, made a speech criticizing the financial practices of the imperial court. Seyed Hassan Taqizadeh, another Majlis deputy, criticized the practice of approving financial legislation on the basis of double urgency—that is, no debate or analysis was allowed prior to the vote. Both men incurred royal displeasure. Hart describes what followed: "In this connection this Department will recall the fate of Mossadegh, a rich, well educated and able man and a former deputy who served as a Cabinet Minister several times. Mossadegh in discussing the budget about three years ago referred among other things to the abuses of Court officials. He was brought before the Shah, to whom he explained that he made the statements only in the interest of His Majesty. This was to no avail and, after being subjected to months of persecution, he was allowed to retire to his villages, where he has since spent his time."[51]

Hoffman Philip gives the text of a Majlis speech given by Taqizadeh on February 29, 1928:

> In other countries the Government first publish their bills in the press for the information of the public. Here even the deputies know nothing about the bills. Bills are presented in an urgent and sudden form. The fundamental laws of the constitution provide that the budget should be submitted to the Medjliss six months before the end of the year. We wait until the end of the very last month of the year when the budget is finally presented in an urgent form and we are then expected to approve it without even knowing what it is. One of the most important functions of the Medjliss is to supervise the budget. The Medjliss should express its views in every detail of the budget. Three months ago the general budget of the Empire was taken up and then excluded from the agenda. It was probably deferred intentionally in order that they should come to us at the close of the year and urge immediate approval. The budget comprises the principles of the policy of the Empire and it should be discussed. I was opposed to probably 99% of the bills that have been voted. I was hoping that all items would appear separately in the budget so that we could discuss them all at once.
>
> Fortunately the country has been freed from many bonds. Now is the time to formulate a practical plan for the progress and prosperity of the country. The country is now at a historical juncture. We have an extraordinary and historical and miraculous opportunity of which we should avail ourselves. A hundred years ago this country was entangled by certain bonds which found their origin in Turkomanchai. The entire budget should be laid before the chamber in order that it may be determined which items are important and which are more important. It is my conscientious duty to point out this matter to the gentlemen. Education and public instruction should be developed and once the mass steps into the path of educational growth all anxieties will cease. Education is the sine qua non of all reforms. In so far as the budget is concerned I believe

that it should be discussed at length. I did not know that this bill would all of a sudden fall into the chamber from the sky at this time of the night and it would be railroaded through the Medjliss in one hour. I believe that the Medjliss should be allowed to consider it for ten days, for the bill constitutes the basis of all the reforms of the Empire.[52]

Hart relates Taqizadeh's "difficulties" after his speech:

> It will be recalled that Tagi-Zadeh [Taqizadeh], a close friend of Mossadegh, suffered from the same persecution due to bold statements he made at about the same time. Mr. Saleh, the Legation's interpreter, tells me that Tagi-Zadeh made several visits to his house during that period and even expressed the fear that he might be starved to death. Though Tagi-Zadeh's troubles appear to have blown over no one appears to have dared to speak very frankly to the Shah since the incidents referred to above, which to be sure is not to be wondered at under the circumstances. Memdouh Chevket Bey, the Turkish Ambassador, regards this as a serious matter and believes that fear, amounting to nearly terror, which His Majesty instills in his subjects makes it impossible for him to hear anything but flattering acquiescence. The Ambassador said that General Kerim Agha, the former Minister of Public Works, and at present the Mayor of Tehran, has a particularly pernicious influence on the Shah by praising his every word.[53]

By 1935, however, Seyed Hasan Taqizadeh, minister of finance at the time of the 1933 oil concession agreement, was again in trouble. Certain French newspapers had made unfavorable comments about Iran and Taqizadeh, Iran's minister in Paris, had not shown sufficient energy to "suppress" the offending papers. Fortunately for him, he was outside Iran when ordered back; he declined and proceeded to Germany, his wife being German. It is difficult to believe that Reza Shah thought the French press could be managed as he did the Iranian press. In the opinion of Hornibrook, "his [Taqizadeh's] ability and statesmanship were too well known to the majority of his people and his popularity was too universally conceded to permit his continuing serving in a high official position under the present dynasty. The incident was seized by the Shah to relieve him of his post and thus disgrace a possible contender for the throne or the Presidency of an Iranian Republic." The Taqizadeh incident provided Hornibrook with an opportunity to describe the reign of terror and mention a system of espionage that would do credit to that "maintained by any government in time of war":

> Since the accession of Reza Shah to the throne the political history of Iran is clogged with similar incidents. It will not be necessary to mention the long list of sudden deaths, imprisonments or of those who have been exiled from the country. The archives of the State Department contain reports covering these cases, but it might be worth while to mention similar events which have happened during the past two or three months. Dadgar, former President of the

Majlis, was exiled to Europe. Dashti, former Deputy and Editor of the suppressed *Shafaq-i-Sorkh*, is now ill in the police hospital. Rahnema, former
Deputy and Editor of the *Iran*, has been exiled to Iraq and with him in exile is
also his brother Tajadod. Bahrami, former Governor-General of Khorasan, is
still in jail.

It will be observed from the above record, which can be supplemented by a
long list of unpleasant events, including, of course, the downfall of Teymour-
tash, General Sheibani and Sardar Assad, that it is part of the plan and program
of the present dynasty to eliminate from the scene of political activity those
whose abilities, patriotism or ambition might prove a menace to the orderly
succession of the son of the present ruler to the throne. A system of espionage
has been perfected in Iran which would do credit to that maintained by any government in time of war. The various cabinet ministers and members of parliament have become pliable and willing tools of Reza Shah, functioning only as
part of the governmental scenic effects. The army and the police have been completely reorganized, the older and more experienced officers having been for the
most part replaced by younger and more dependable men and no one dares to
utter a word of criticism or complaint. The Shah is in complete and absolute
control and his slightest whim immediately becomes the law of the land.

Hornibrook then refers to the people's rising discontent and level of hostility to the Pahlavi regime:

But, underneath the surface there is running a feeling of hostility to the present regime. It is not vocal, but it is none the less potent in shaping the views of
the people. What many believe to be unnecessary improvements resulting in
heavy taxation, the wholesale imprisonments, legal murders and exile of
prominent citizens, to say nothing of the introduction of European reforms in
the headgear of men and the proposed unveiling of Moslem women, have left
their impress upon the minds of the inhabitants and at some future time may
be expected to result in an incident which may prove to be the end of the present dynasty. Many people believe that the Shah is so firmly entrenched, his
army so loyal and his people so thoroughly afraid, that nothing can happen to
the present regime. For the moment this is perhaps true, but the recent rioting
in Meshed, the opposition of the Mullahs to the introduction of European customs and the fact that it was only a little more than a year ago that Teheran witnessed sadistic religious rites that spelled nothing other than fanaticism of the
worst form, does not hold out that hope for the future stability that is the fond
desire of both better class of Iranians and Europeans domiciled in this country.

Hornibrook also describes his conversation with the British minister:

It was only a few days ago that I discussed confidentially with the British Minister the possibility of the death of Reza Shah and what might be expected as an
aftermath of such an event. Both the Minister and myself attempted to put our
finger upon a single Iranian now in public life who is qualified by training, temperament and ability to assume the leadership in such an emergency. No name

could be suggested which appeared to measure up to such a Herculean task. We both agreed that out of the difficulties resulting from the possible death of Reza Shah some comparatively unknown man, probably an army officer, would arise and perhaps be able to successfully take command of the ship of state.

Hornibrook's last sentence turned out to be prophetic: "My own impression is that the Shah's wholesale introduction of European customs, his hostility to the clergy, [and] his ruthless methods may possibly result in a bitter anti-foreign feeling in the event of his demise."[54]

CHAPTER SEVEN

The Massacre in Mashhad

THE MASSACRE THAT TOOK PLACE IN AND NEAR the holy shrine of Imam Reza in Mashhad from July 12 to 14, 1935, was one of the bloodiest and most brutal in Iran's history. The only other remotely comparable incident was the suppression of the protests of June 5–8, 1963, when troops killed many protesters. The Mashhad massacre was especially significant because the outrage took place at a sacred shrine of the Shia faith. As Hornibrook reported, machine gun fire had been directed at the protesters and pilgrims, resulting in "a frightful loss of life." Thereafter, the people said, "Our holy shrine has been desecrated and bathed in blood," and they predicted the end of Reza Khan.

The end came six years later, but what the people did not predict was that Reza Khan would be rescued by his British masters and shielded from justice. The events of July 12–14, 1935, in the city of Mashhad in the province of Khorassan were considered at the time the gravest crisis in Iran's recent history. The response was an accentuation of the reign of terror, including the search for and the punishment of those allegedly responsible.

European Headgear, the Banning of Ashura, and the Unveiling of Women, 1935

Reza Shah's campaign to force Muslim women to discard the veil began in earnest in the summer of 1934 with the campaign to force Persian men to discard the *kolah,* the traditional Persian head covering, in favor of the "European" hat. In a June 1934 announcement, Prime Minister Foroughi gave the implausible reason: "By order of His Imperial Majesty the Shah, the President of the Council of Ministers enjoins all Ministries and

Administrations to inform their subordinate services that workers having to work in the open air under the sun, should wear in the future a hat with a brim capable of offering protection against sunstroke."[1]

At the opening of the Tenth Majlis in June 1935, it was officially announced that the Pahlavi hat was to be discarded in favor of the European hat. Hornibrook comments: "I am informed that, following the Shah's decision to abandon the official use of the Pahlavi hat, he is stated to have remarked that the use of western headgear by Iranian men made the continued use of the chador by Iranian women altogether incongruous. I understand that, as a result of these observations made by the Shah to his counselors, which carry, of course the weight of command, there has already been initiated on the part of the women of the younger generation, a movement looking to the giving over the use of the veil."[2]

Hornibrook reports that the campaign "to give practical application to the expression of the wishes of His Majesty" to ban the Islamic veil was officially launched by Foroughi, who as prime minister was to give a tea party at the Iran Club on June 28, 1935. All members of the cabinet and the undersecretaries were invited with their wives, who were to attend unveiled. Hornibrook adds, "It is understood that this tea by the Prime Minister will be followed by similar teas offered by members of the cabinet and their wives to their colleagues."[3] And then the colleagues would give tea parties for their subordinates and their wives, and so the process was to continue.

The adoption of the European hat and the proposed unveiling of women was part of a continuous Westernization campaign whose primary aim was to weaken Islam and the ulema. In early April 1935 the government imposed severe restrictions on the observance of Ashura, the most somber day of mourning, which commemorates the martyrdom of Imam Hossein. Mourning processions were prohibited. The prohibitions and the subsequent "disturbances" in several cities are reported by J. Rives Childs, chargé d'affaires ad interim:

> This year the police order is understood to have gone forth that no mourning processions were to be allowed to parade in the streets as in previous years. A few days before the advent of Ashura, which fell this year on April 14th, certain mullahs are known to have addressed telegrams directly to the Shah appealing for the removal of the restrictions imposed on observance of the day. The mullahs who took action in Kermanshah and in Teheran are known to have been placed promptly under detention until after the day had passed. Likewise in Babol, where the most serious disturbances are understood to have occurred, it appears that an application was made by the mullahs to the authorities for the holding of public processions. Subsequent to the failure of these efforts to obtain the desired permission an earthquake occurred in Babol on the night of the 13th. In consequence the excited population, unexpectedly

moved to mourning for causes even much more immediate than those concerned with the death of Hussein more than a thousand years ago, proceeded
into the streets and, in defiance of the ban, undertook to assemble in mourning
processions. Policemen who sought to disperse the mourners were roughly
handled and in the ensuing melee it is reported that at least two of the police
were killed. Disturbances of lesser gravity are said also to have occurred in
other parts of the country, the localities mentioned as affected being Meshed
[Mashhad], Kum [Qom], Kerman, and Yezd [Yazd].

In Teheran such mourning as took place was rigidly confined to the
mosques and to the privacy of the homes of the mourners, but even then
the mourners were careful to avoid extending their exhibitions of grief to
anything more than the mild beating of their breasts with their hands.[4] A
simmering tension between the civilian population and the Pahlavi instruments of repression appears to have been endemic. The imposition of
reforms and modernization often provoked opposition and outbreaks of
violence. The resistance of the people of Tabriz to the introduction of con-
scription and the response of the regime was described in 1928 by Augustin
W. Ferrin, American consul:

> According to a report just received from Hassan Ali Khan Asaf, clerk in
> charge of the Tabriz Consulate, the conscription [compulsory military service]
> proclamation was posted on the afternoon of October 12. The next morning
> bazaars were closed, the people began to gather at a mosque and some assem-
> bled at the houses of the mujtahids, Mirza Sadigh Agha and Haji Mirza Abdul
> Hassan Agha, the religious leaders of Tabriz. Telegrams were sent to Teheran
> protesting against conscription, also against the Pahlevi hat and the proposed
> unveiling of women. On October 14 a crowd going to the conscription head-
> quarters was scattered by shots fired in the air by the military. On October 17
> another crowd marched toward the Russian Consulate, with what object it is
> not apparent, possibly to put itself under Russian protection. A few shots by the
> military sufficed to disperse this crowd also. That night the mujtahids and a
> number of prominent merchants, including Kerbasi, were placed under arrest.
> On October 18 the bazaars were reopened and it was believed that the move-
> ment was at an end. The population of Tabriz is unarmed and the military force
> there is large and efficient.[5]

What was different with the unveiling of women was the magnitude of
the opposition which appears to have caught the British and Reza Shah by
surprise. The popular resistance to this measure is recorded in a dispatch
from Hornibrook vastly different in tone from the one on the proposed tea
parties he had written just five days before. In less than a week, the situation had deteriorated badly.

> The construction of a modern system of public highways at the expense of
> the taxpayers, the widening of the streets at the cost of abutting property

owners, and the project for building a railway from the Caspian to the Gulf in order to provide quick means of transportation for the produce raised on the Shah's large private holdings in northern Iran, were all accepted by the people of this country as an expensive luxury. But, when the suggestion is made that veils should be removed from Moslem women, His Majesty steps upon something which is far more important to the Islamic mind than a material increase in the burden of taxation. He steps upon a tradition of long standing, a custom which has been observed for centuries, and does violence to the feelings of his own people. Behind the forced nods of approval and public expressions of agreement with the Shah in his determination to bring about this reform, there is a hidden hostility to the entire program on the part of a very considerable number of Moslems. Cabinet officers who desire to retain their posts will unquestionably force their wives to permanently remove their veils and their example will be followed by lesser officials and other residents who are not particularly wedded to the old regime. However, many official faces which give the smile of sanction in public, frown at the proposal in private. The members of the clergy who have already been driven to the point of distraction by what they term, "the irreligion of the Shah" have a new weapon with which to wage their clandestine warfare. Intimate friends and close relatives of prisoners who have died a mysterious death in jail, or who have been summarily exiled, have been given new ammunition to use against the present dynasty.[6]

Hornibrook's comments on the opposition to the unveiling of women continue in a follow-up dispatch:

No innovation inaugurated during the reign of Reza Shah has caused the same feeling of unrest and uncertainty, or the same feeling of open resentment to the present regime as the proposal for the unveiling of Moslem women. It may be stated with certainty that members of the clergy are bitterly opposed to the removal of the Chador and that the great majority of Moslems are enraged as a result of the reform. The substitution of the so-called "international" [hats] for Pahlevi hats which, incidentally no longer retain their "Pahlevi" designation, was accepted with good natured tolerance by most Iranians of the upper and middle classes, while it is being imposed on people of the lower walks of life by intimidation and violence. The more progressive and enlightened even welcomed the change, but many of those who could see virtue in European headgear for men could only see evil in the proposed innovation in the attire for women. As a protest to the unveiling of women, and to a lesser degree, to the change in the headgear of men, Haji Aqa Hossein Qomi of Meshed, one of the three ranking Mullahs in Khorassan, first wired his views to the Shah and then proceeded to Teheran to make such a protest in person. He arrived at Shah Abdul Azim in the vicinity of the capital and his presence promptly created an incident of no minor importance. Rumors as to his arrival soon reached the ears of devout Moslems and on July 4 most of the bazaars closed. Hundreds of people then proceeded to the mosque to obtain his advice and counsel on the

recent innovations. Uniformed police and plain-clothes detectives were immediately despatched to the mosque and contact with the Mullah thus prevented.
Since that date a strong police guard has been maintained and I presume will
remain on duty until the Mullah concludes to take his departure. On July 6 the
bazaars closed again, but were promptly reopened by the police under threats
that the penalty would be the immediate sale of their merchandise by government officials. Rumors as to serious rioting in Tabriz have, thus far, lacked
confirmation.

Haji Sheikh Abdol Karim, Mullah of Kum, is reported to have sent a polite
telegram to the Shah, soliciting prevention of acts forbidden by Islam. The
Shah is said to have sent an immediate reply to the effect that the elimination of
the Pahlevi hat has no direct or indirect connection with religion and that as yet
he has issued no orders requiring the women of Iran to unveil. The Shah is also
said to have issued orders providing that no officer in the army must hereafter
be seen upon the streets in company with a veiled woman. If this is correct, and
it has been confirmed by an army officer of high standing, the Shah has taken
the tremendous risk of breeding discord among his own troops. That there is a
deep seated and growing feeling of hostility to the Shah's program there can be
no possible doubt. Reports obtained by the Consulate confirm those obtained
by the Legation and only a modification of the present program can, in my
opinion, remove the present feeling of open hostility toward the Shah on the
part of the clergy and a very considerable number of the population. Whether
he is prepared to abandon the plan or not is a mere matter of conjecture, but to
do so would unquestionably result in a loss of prestige. As long as the troops
and police remain loyal, and as yet there is no indication of difficulty from this
source, any reform which pleases Reza Shah must be accepted by the Iranians.[7]

News of the Uprising in Mashhad: Strict Censorship

On July 12, 1935, the public and the American legation sensed that a
serious incident had taken place, although they did not know where.
Hornibrook reports that rumors of serious rioting in Tabriz were dis-
proved by the Tabriz consulates of Turkey and Britain.[8] Nor had reports of
rioting in Shiraz been confirmed by Dr. Schmidt of the American archeological team. Hornibrook's "coded telegraphic message" to Dr. Donaldson,
an American missionary in Mashhad, was intercepted by the police and
was not delivered. It is indicative of the degree of censorship that the
American legation had not been able to communicate with Mashhad and
learn about the uprising there for about a week.

Finally, news of the protests reached the legation in a telegram dated July
18, although the legation remained ignorant of the incident's true date or
any details: "Rioting in Meshed on July 8th as a protest against European
headgear and proposed unveiling of women resulted in death of several

policemen and troops were finally called out to restore order. Rigid censorship prevented confirmation of rumor until today when it was officially confirmed by Ministry of Interior. Edict requiring European headgear being rigidly enforced. No formal order issued requiring women to unveil. No rioting in Teheran and Government in complete control of the situation in Meshed."[9]

The government communiqué about the Mashhad incident, which continued to mislead as to the date of the event, was issued also on July 18 and is described in a dispatch from Hornibrook:

> That the rioting currently reported to have taken place in Tabriz and vociferously denied by officials of the Iranian government, in fact took place on July 8 in Meshed, was officially confirmed today by the Minister of Interior. The communiqué fails to disclose the number of civilians who were killed or wounded and the censorship which was immediately established upon all news emanating from Meshed following the rioting makes it difficult to obtain further details than that included in the formal statement issued by the Minister of the Interior. It is interesting to note that during the past ten days there have been rumors of rioting in Tabriz, Shiraz and Kum, but none to the effect that there has been any disorder in Meshed. The rumors emanating from the first three mentioned cities were easily disproved, but the atmosphere has been tense and there appeared to be a general feeling of uncertainty among the people.

Hornibrook includes a translation of a statement by the Minister of Interior about the events in Mashhad:

> According to a report received from the Governor general of Khorasan in the evening of July 8 one Sheikh Bohlul, who has a notorious record of sedition and intrigue and who had on a previous occasion been subject to prosecution, called a gathering of the simple-minded and illiterate riffraff to hear his sermons which continued for two or three days. Rogues and scoundrels assembled and Bohlul proceeded with absurd talks on the subject of the new headgear and dress. When he resorted to scurrilous language the police authorities endeavored in vain to dissuade him from making irregular statements which were apt to stir up unrest and cause disorder and insecurity. The people expressed their concern and police officials decided to disperse the mob which showed resistance, assailing, wounding and killing some of them. The police were obliged to call upon the military forces for help. The insurgents engaged in a fight with the regulars using mortal weapons which they had in their hands. The regulars found themselves forced to reestablish order by resort to firearms. The rascals and ruffians were either captured or scattered, but unfortunately the author of this sedition, namely Sheikh Bohlul, succeeded in escaping. Order and security has been thoroughly re-established. The police are now following up the incident with a view to discovering the facts.

Not to be outdone, the daily newspaper *Le Journal de Teheran,* while reporting the minister's communiqué, added:

Why did this intriguer with his deplorable past choose the day of July 11 to try to create this sad incident? Because for nearly twenty-five years following the bombardment of the dome of the shrine of Imam Reza by Tzarist troops on the day of July 11, every year the local population gathers at the sanctuary on that day in token of respect and regret. The Sheikh and his blackguards assembled at the sanctuary of the said mosque, a place of asylum, but were forced to escape in order to save their lives. He was no idealist but a mean dastard who will be arrested and punished as an assassin or malefactor. This was no popular movement, for all the people of Meshed were opposed to the rioters. It is an intrigue, the ignominy of a reactionary of no faith or honor who unfortunately caused the death of some policemen and soldiers, victims of duty, before whom we bow in respect.

Not a single mention of the heavy civilian casualties had been made so far. The tyranny and absurdity of forcing the male population to wear the European instead of the Pahlavi hat is seen from the following:

For the present, at least, the Shah has determined to confine his activities to enforcing his decree that the Pahlavi hat must go. Police have been vigilantly enforcing the command of the Shah and there can no longer be any question or doubt that the male Iranians will hereafter appear in European hats, thus at least adopting the veneer of European civilization. Police officers have removed these hats from the heads of the peasantry and destroyed them in public. There has been no compromise or suggestion of compromise on this issue, and the net result has been that hundreds of the indigent have found it necessary to proceed to and from their places of employment without any headgear. Only a few days ago I noted a horseman riding at rapid pace down the Lalezar, tearing the Pahlavi hat into small pieces and casting them at the crowd.

Still unaware of the extent of the bloodshed in Mashhad, Hornibrook concludes his dispatch with the following lighthearted observation: "The Pahlavi hat must first be definitely and finally abolished from all Iran and then it may be reasonably expected that the removal of the veils will be made an issue of major importance. The promulgation of such a decree will, in my opinion, make Teheran one of the most interesting posts in the Foreign Service."[10]

Hornibrook first learned the details of the shocking incident in Mashhad from the Afghan ambassador:

A conference with the Afghan Ambassador on the subject of advices which he received from the Afghan Consul General in Meshed resulted as follows: The Ambassador advised me that he had received a detailed account of the situation in a coded message from the Consul General; that eight Afghans had been killed during the rioting, five hundred people had been killed, eight hundred

wounded and that approximately two thousand people had either been confined to jail or disappeared. The information received from the Afghan Consul
General is to the effect that the rioting did not take place on July 8 as indicated
in the formal statement issued by the Minister of the Interior, but that it started
on July 12 and lasted long into the night of July 13. According to the Ambassador's report vast throngs of people assembled in the mosque, as a protest to
the new innovations proposed by the Shah, were ordered to disperse by the
police and refused. The Shah was then appealed to by the Governor General for
definite telegraphic instructions. These instructions were to give them another
opportunity to leave peaceably and in the event of their failure to do so to call
out the troops and disperse them by force. Rifle fire was first used by soldiers in
an effort to dislodge the inhabitants from their sanctuary and then machine
guns were brought into play, resulting in a frightful loss of life.

The military is in complete and absolute control of the situation, but the
atmosphere is tense. No Americans or Europeans were killed or injured. The
Ambassador has wired his Consul General in Meshed for the names and pass-
port numbers of the eight Afghan pilgrims whom he alleges were killed in the
rioting and proposes to make formal representations to the Iranian Government as soon as this data is published.

Hornibrook then records a conversation with Dr. Donaldson, an American missionary who had arrived in Tehran on July 20:

Dr. Donaldson, whom I tried unsuccessfully to reach by wire prior to his
arrival gave the following facts to me. The rioting started in the morning of July
12, and was precipitated by an Iranian Mullah who mounted the rostrum in the
Shrine and opened a bitter tirade against the new innovations proposed by the
Shah. Guards pulled him down from the rostrum and placed him in temporary
confinement. Rioting started, the Mullah was rescued from the guards and
again harangued the crowds which by this time were becoming larger. Police
reserves were rushed to the scene and their unsuccessful efforts to disperse the
mob resulted in several casualties before nightfall. The Governor general
appealed by wire to the Shah early the following morning and received in reply
a telegram to the effect that all available troops should be called out, and the
mob dispersed by force, even though it became necessary to level the Shrine in
so doing. This telegram was read to the fast-growing number of rioters as soon
as the same was received. Late during the afternoon of July 14 the mob in the
Shrine and the grounds numbered more than ten thousand people. The
Meshed troops lacked discipline and some of them declined to obey the com-
mands of their officers and fire on the rioters. Two of those who declined to
obey such command were shot down by their officers. One committed suicide
and several officers were later arrested because of their inability to obtain obedience from the enlisted men.

Because of this situation five hundred regulars were rushed from a nearby
town and it was this body of troops that later turned the machine guns on the

Shrine and finally dispersed the mob. More than two thousand troops in all participated in the fighting. Rifle fire and the machine guns were first turned on the Mosque causing serious but not irreparable damage. The firing was first directed far above the heads of the occupants and gradually the aim was lowered until it resulted in a frightful loss of life. Local missionaries estimate that between four and five hundred were either killed or wounded and there were easily between five and six hundred arrests. Police and soldiers were numbered among the killed and wounded, but for the most part they were civilians.[11]

Casualty Estimates by the British

At first the British tried to play down this tragedy. Just as the British had attributed the prison death of Sardar Assad and others to natural causes, they now tried to minimize the number of casualties. Hornibrook narrates his dealings with the British legation:

> The British Minister had left Chimeran on a camping trip when the news of the rioting first reached Teheran and his subordinates were unwilling to give me any information until he could be reached and had authorized them to communicate the substance of the report from the British Consul. When this consent was obtained the entire record was disclosed by the Secretary. It confirmed in the main the statements made by the Afghan Ambassador and Dr. Donaldson, with the exception of the number killed, wounded and arrested. British Legation estimates are as follows: Killed, sixty; wounded, one hundred and fifty; arrested eight hundred. Official figures obtained from the Meshed police by the British Consul are as follows: Killed, twenty-eight and wounded, sixty.[12]

In the meantime, the British revised their estimates of those killed and injured. Hornibrook reports:

> I conferred with the Afghan Ambassador this morning and he asserted that his Consul General at Meshed had not revised the figures killed, wounded and incarcerated and that he was personally convinced that the estimate was approximately correct. I also obtained from the British Minister the contents of the latest official despatches received from Meshed. Written and telegraphic reports were opened freely for my inspection and in the main, coincided quite well with the information which already has been submitted to the Department. The Minister now roughly estimates the number of killed and wounded at between four and five hundred. I quote below certain statements which were made by the British Consul at Meshed and turned over to me confidentially by the Minister.

Hornibrook then provides an excerpt from the British report:

> One hundred and twenty-eight dead have been buried in trenches by the military authorities. The number of wounded is not less than two or three hundred.

Five hundred and four persons are now confined in military barracks, of whom two hundred are wounded. In the civil jail three hundred and eleven are confined and of this number twenty-eight are wounded. Prisoners in the barracks are flogged daily in groups of thirty. Two officers and eighteen soldiers were killed and fourteen men were wounded. Thirteen Afghan pilgrims were slain (the Afghan Ambassador placed the number at eight). The number of arrests now number more than eight hundred. The first bloodshed took place on the night of the 11th and resulted from the fact that the Commanding Officer was thrown into the "jube" [drainage channel] by the rioters. The officer then ordered his troops to fire at the mob. Casualties resulting therefrom were eighteen killed and fifty wounded. The crowd swelled on the 12th and 13th and rioting became more general, culminating in the slaughter on the night of the 14th.

Disaffection among the Meshed contingent of the troops caused the Commanding Officer to disarm many of them and place the men under military guard during the second two days of the rioting. The Mullahs in the Shrine openly assailed the Shah and called upon Allah to protect them against European innovations and high taxes. The same sentiments were echoed by the rioters, both in the Shrine and in the public streets. . . .

He [the British Minister] also showed me a telegram received yesterday from the British Consul at Tabriz. It stated that refugees from Meshed have arrived in Tabriz with reports of the recent massacre and that there is a strong feeling of indignation against the Shah. . . . Our sacred Shrine has been bathed in blood. This is one of the stock expressions whispered by devout Moslems in Teheran, and it has unquestionably left its impress upon the minds of the people. I think I am quite safe in asserting that among the civilian population, and to a lesser extent among the official classes, the Shah has definitely lost his popularity. Many of those who only a month ago hailed him as "Reza Shah the Great," now secretly condemn him for the Meshed massacre. I am also advised that even among the more cultured and progressive Iranians holding high positions, it is freely admitted that a grave blunder was perpetrated and that the Shah's prestige has suffered very materially in consequence thereof.[13]

The Execution of the Acting Custodian of the Shrine

Immediately after the tragedy, the search for scapegoats was on. According to press reports, at an audience of Majlis deputies at Sadabad Palace held on July 24, 1935, Reza Shah "made certain declarations of the highest importance," as relayed by Hornibrook:

I am advised confidentially from a source which I regard as reliable, that on the above occasion the Shah made the following statement: A shrine should be reserved for a place of worship, and not for the purpose of sedition. It was intimated very clearly by His Majesty that in view of the seditious conduct of many of those who took refuge in the Shrine, any action, including that of demolishing the edifice, would have been quite justified under the circumstance. He paid his respects in no uncertain terms to the young Mullah who led the rioting and charged that in Syria he had been engaged in pernicious propaganda against the Iranian Government. He then launched into a vehement attack upon the tactless Government officials at Meshed for what he termed their inefficiency and cowardice. His position was that bloodshed could have been averted and the rioters easily dispersed had the civil authorities shown that initiative and courage which might be expected of men stationed in such responsible posts. He concluded by singling out Deputy Asadi, the son of the Acting Custodian of the Shrine, and humiliated him in the presence of the assembled deputies.[14]

It was clear that Asadi had already been singled out to serve as a scapegoat and that his end was near. In a dispatch entitled "Wholesale Arrests of Public Officials—Execution of Mohammad Vali Asadi," Hornibrook describes the fate of the hapless Custodian of the Shrine, and the continuing reign of terror:

It has been officially announced that Mohammad Vali Asadi, until recently the Shah's agent in personal charge of the treasure and other affairs pertaining to the sacred Shrine at Meshed, was executed on December 21st. A court martial convicted Asadi of being the real author of the Meshed riots and therefore guilty of high treason. Authorities assert that he made a full and complete confession before sentence was pronounced. It is interesting to note in connection with the execution of Asadi that it was on his behalf that the former Prime Minister is alleged to have interceded with the Shah. It has since been learned from a personal friend of the former Prime Minister that he vigorously denies that he attempted to obtain the release of Asadi. The past two weeks have also been notable because of a series of arrests of public officials and dismissals from the public service. Salman Asadi, son of Mohammad Vali Asadi, was dismissed as Managing Director of the Agricultural Bank of Iran. Ali Akbar Asadi, son of the executed Treasurer of the Shrine, has found it prudent to refrain from attending sessions of the Majlis and will doubtless later be impeached by his colleagues. Mohammad Razavi, Under Secretary of Posts, Telegraphs and Telephones, was arrested and later released. S. M. Hejazi, Chef de Cabinet of the Minister of Finance, was also arrested and released. Both of the last two mentioned were arrested on the charge of embezzlement of the public funds but allowed to resume their offices when released. Abdol Ali Lotfi, Chief Justice of Khorasan, is now under trial by court martial and a number of lesser officials have been arrested, most of whom are held on the charge of embezzlement. Haji Qaem-Maqam-ot-Tolieh, Aqa Zadeh and other Meshed Mullahs were arrested and banished from Khorasan.[15]

Reza Shah's Personal Security: The British Role

At the end of his July 25 dispatch, Hornibrook alludes to some of the measures the British had taken to safeguard the person of Reza Shah and to shield him from assassination. It is no wonder that they quickly whisked him away to security and comfort in 1941. The presence of the British military attaché, Major Pybus, during Reza Shah's 1936 trip to Chalus and Pahlavi was noted in chapter 6. Now we can begin to understand the proximity of the British attaché to the person of the shah during his trips: it was to ensure Reza Shah's security. Moreover, by protecting him, the British guaranteed that the killings would continue. Nosrat-ed-Dowleh and Modarres, not to mention Asadi and Davar, were to follow shortly:

> All members of the diplomatic corps with whom I have discussed the matter agree that the Meshed riot was the most serious incident that has happened during the reign of the present monarch, and that his victory for law and order was more than offset by his loss of popularity and prestige. The British Minister regards the present situation as one of the most critical in the history of the country. His fears are predicated not upon the ability of the Shah to maintain law and order, but upon the possibility of his assassination. He confirmed prior reports that I had received to the effect that a double guard had been placed around the Shah's palace in Chimeron and added that the public has been excluded from the hills in the vicinity of the royal residence.
>
> That the military authorities took no chances on the Meshed situation spreading to other cities and towns in the Kingdom is indicated by a statement made to me by a member of the American Archaeological Expedition at Ray. On the day following the Meshed riots he observed forty truckloads of soldiers passing the compound en route to Kum, second only to Meshed as a hot bed of fanaticism.[16]

CHAPTER EIGHT

The Reign of Terror and Murder Continues

O<small>N</small> FEBRUARY 10, 1937, THE MINISTER OF
finance, Ali Akbar Davar, died. He had served many years as minister of
finance and minister of justice and was considered one of Iran's most capable administrators. Although the official announced cause of death was
apoplexy, Davar had committed suicide in order to escape a fate similar to
that of his friends Teymourtache and Sardar Assad.

That Davar was doomed was clear from 1934. In a report on the death
of Sardar Assad, Minister Hornibrook had also tentatively predicted the
end of Davar. He reported that at the Now-Ruz audience,

> [t]he Shah manifested in the presence of his Ministers extreme displeasure
> with Minister of Finance Davar, the manifestation of his displeasure taking the
> form of an inquiry regarding the number of executive assistants attached to the
> Ministry of Finance. Upon being informed that there were in the Ministry of
> Finance an Under-Secretary and two Directors General, the Shah is reported to
> have remarked that, since this was out of all proportion to the executive assistants
> attached to the other Ministries, he failed to understand, in those circumstances,
> the reason for the inability of the Minister of Finance to perform his work satis-
> factorily. Such a comment can only be interpreted as evidence of the extreme
> capriciousness of the Shah, as well as the developing disfavor in which able lieu-
> tenants would seem to be held by him, in view of the well known competence of
> Davar who is considered the ablest member of the Cabinet. Perhaps, his ability,
> as in the case of Teymourtache, may be in the end the means of his undoing.[1]

By July 1934, Hornibrook had no doubt that Davar was destined to meet
his end à la Teymourtache and that he had "been marked out for eventual
elimination by reason of his very strength." Hornibrook's report continues:

The latest in a series of developments involving the relations of Davar and the Shah is reliably reported to have occurred only a few days before the Shah's departure for Turkey when he expostulated with Davar by reason of the diminishing returns from customs dues and asked Davar to account for the decrease. In answer the Shah's Minister of Finance explained that the decline in customs dues was attributable to the world economic crisis which was affecting Persia no less than other countries. To this the Shah, whose ears have been filled with the sycophantic assurances of his entourage that Persia had been spared from the effects of the world crisis owing to the genius of His Majesty, replied with the exclamation that in Persia no economic crisis existed. As expressed to me, for a Persian it is not sufficient to vent one's displeasure by casting an opponent out of the second-story window of a house; the victim must needs be conducted to the highest point possible and cast from there to the depths.

Hornibrook examined Davar's options. The first two, remaining as minister of finance or being appointed ambassador to Moscow, were deemed unrealistic.

The third alternative which may determine Davar's fate is, of course, his imprisonment in the Qasr Qajar prison, following the precedent established in respect of his distinguished official predecessors, Teymourtache, Minister of the Court, and Sardar Assad, Minister of War. Such a policy would be strictly in line with that followed by the Shah with a view of eliminating from public office all men of ability or of strength who, in the opinion of His Majesty, offer any promise of attracting support to themselves which might stand in the way of the accession to the Throne of the Shah's son.

The concluding paragraph of the report proved to be prophetic:

Moreover, in view of Davar's intimate association with Teymourtache and Firouz, the three, as the Department is aware, at one time forming the so-called Triumvirate in Persian political life, the Shah's attitude towards the last of these, Davar, remaining alive or possessing any influence, is all the more easily understood. Davar's outstanding ability and his self-effacement in respect of the Shah, extending even to his concurrence as Minister of Justice in the punishment meted out to his old associates have been the factors which have contributed so far to the maintenance of his position; it remains to be seen for how long.

That Davar lived for another two and a half years was a tribute to his ability. Moreover, shortly after Davar, it was to be the turn of Firouz.[2]

Davar's Suicide

Davar's suicide, on February 10, 1937, is described by Gordon P. Merriam, chargé d'affaires ad interim. It is clear that Davar had been contemplating suicide for some weeks:

Some weeks ago, Davar retained a quantity of morphine which his administration had confiscated from smugglers. A few days before his death, he obtained a quantity of opium which had been prepared by his administration for sale, and closely questioned the official in charge regarding its purity, receiving satisfactory replies. He took both packets to his office in his home, where they were noticed by his wife. She inquiring what they were and whether they would not be dangerous for the children to play with, he replied: "It is nothing" and swept them into a drawer. On the days just prior to the 10th, his colleagues and associates noticed nothing wrong; in fact, it is generally agreed that Davar's decisions had never been more sound or clear. He came home on the evening of the ninth and asked to have a bed made up in his office as he intended to work late, and gave orders that he be called at seven the following morning. The place was strewn with dossiers, for the man literally never stopped working. He was heard walking about in the office until two or three A.M., when it is conjectured that, having taken the opium and the morphine, he went to lie down, not in his office, but in the adjoining salon where a bed had also been prepared, in the knowledge that as soon as he should be discovered a great crowd would immediately gather and that the salon would be more dignified and appropriate to these circumstances.

His servant knocked to awaken him at the desired hour; after pounding hard on the door without obtaining a response, he notified Mme. Davar. She immediately rushed from bed, and entering the room was unable to awaken her husband. Without dressing, she ran as she was next door to summon Dr. Sami'i, brother of the Foreign Minister, and within a short time a large number of doctors and other persons assembled. One of the Directors-General of the Ministry of Finance, Mr. Allah Yar Saleh, a former interpreter of this Legation, lived around the corner. Upon hearing the news he immediately fetched his brother, Dr. Jehan Shah Saleh, a graduate of Syracuse University, and upon entering the room where Davar lay, his face black and surrounded by doctors and friends, found that it had been concluded that he was suffering from some kind of poisoning, but no one knew what, or how to proceed. It appears that Dr. Saleh at once gave a diagnosis of opium poisoning, which caused a general shaking of heads, for this way of taking one's life is not highly regarded among the Iranians. (It was perhaps taken by Davar to spare his family the terror and nastiness of a shot wound.) His mouth was opened and the odor of opium which issued was recognized at once. The proper measures were taken, but it was much too late. Davar, lying unconscious in the arms of Mr. Allah Yar Saleh, who was rubbing the temples in an effort to keep circulation going in accordance with instructions from his brother, suddenly opened his eyes upon him, gave a shudder, and expired at about nine A.M. In accordance with the wishes of the Shah, the cause of death was given out as heart failure [not apoplexy as first reported]. Moreover, there is not a member of the diplomatic corps or person of any standing in Teheran who does not know the truth, so much so that in discussing the matter the real fact is not even mentioned as rumor, for this would be an insult to one's information and intelligence, but the discussion immediately passes to the reasons why Davar took his life.

Those reasons are not known to anyone save the Shah, whose lips will doubtless remain sealed. The hypothesis and rumors that have been advanced are as follows: 1. Not long ago there was a scene between His Majesty and Davar during which the latter was seized by the lapel and shaken vigorously.

FIGURE 8.1 *Ali Akbar Davar, ca. 1930.*

The Shah's complaint was that petitions and information had come in from the merchants that Davar's economic program had taken away all their business and put it in the hands of the Government; the merchants had not been recompensed and had no way to make a living. Davar realized that the economic framework he had run up was tottering and put an end to himself before it should fall, bringing disgrace and probably death. Some color to this story is lent by the fact that Davar recently canceled a few, though unimportant monopolies. 2. Another version also pictures the scene abovementioned, but gives the reason for the Shah's wrath the lack of wheat in Khorasan. Famine in that area was in fact narrowly averted by extraordinary and efficient measures taken by Davar, who sent out his best officials to all parts of the country to make transport available by unlocking the passes, thereby releasing hundreds of trucks which had long been snowbound. He also borrowed transport from the Anglo-Iranian Oil Company, and compelled the sorely-harassed automobile dealers to carry wheat at less than market transport rates. Now, although the crisis had been met, the Shah might well have asked: "What sort of a policy is this which ships wheat out of Khorasan for Russia (and which incidentally lies rotting at Bandar-i-Shah) thereby creating a shortage in Khorasan?" 3. The story runs that Davar received $50,000 from the American interests concerned for granting the oil and pipe-line concessions. So far as I am aware, this is being repeated as a rumor but it is not gaining credence, because Davar's integrity has never been questioned. 4. The Shah feared Davar, not so much perhaps for himself as to the succession to the throne. The army had been showing a tendency to look to the Minister of Finance as the future source of power and authority. Should this man, who held the economic life of the country in the hollow of his hand, also be in a position to acquire the army at the Shah's death, the accession of the Crown Prince would be in grave danger. Consequently, the argument runs, the Shah had determined to put an end to Davar's authority; Davar saw the writing on the wall and preferred to end his life at the height of his power, rather than await disgrace and almost certain death later on. Support to this view is lent by the arrest and imprisonment of Forouhar, the recently recalled Iranian Minister in Paris, and a close friend of Davar. Forouhar was arrested the very morning of Davar's death, and although Davar could hardly have known of it, he may nevertheless have perceived the lay of the land or had it intimated to him.

As the days pass, it becomes more and more clearly indicated that the fourth and last account of the motives which led Davar to take his life is the true one. It is thought that the Shah did indeed make a scene with his Minister of Finance, but that the precise subject of the conversation at the time is of little moment. It was enough for Davar that the Shah's attitude plainly showed he had finished with him. What did Davar himself say on the subject? The night before his death he wrote three letters: one to the Shah, one to his wife, and one to his mother.

The last two letters were actually personal in nature. The letter to His Majesty has been read to the council of Ministers. In it Davar merely said that he was doing this because he was tired.

The whole thing is perhaps well summarized by the cynical remark of several members of the Diplomatic Corps: "Well, anyway, he lasted longer than the others." Here it is of interest to note that while every preparation had been made to honor his memory to the utmost, when the Shah perceived the extent of the popular emotion, these preparations were suddenly canceled. I am reliably informed in strict confidence that the newspapers had prepared material on Davar to cover their entire front pages, but that by order of the Imperial Police it was all suppressed. The matter that has appeared since the day following the death has been perfunctory and brief. Even the title "Excellency" has now disappeared; he is referred to as "the late Davar." The fact and manner of the death of the Minister of Finance have brought consternation to all the higher officials of the Government. There is not one who pretends to Davar's competence and courage. They have seen a remarkable and unselfish man give his ability and energy unstintingly to carry out the Shah's wishes. He was no Teymourtache who swaggered about displaying the evidences of his power to the Iranian and foreign community. Davar worked quietly, unceasingly, forcefully, without sparing himself. He shunned society of all kinds, and particularly foreign society; moreover, he had no time for it. Davar's reward was to be placed in a position where he felt self-destruction to be expedient and to his interest. Such a reward on the part of the Shah does not appear well calculated to bring the best qualities out of his servants. There is no doubt that the manner of Davar's death has caused loss of respect for his memory. The general view cannot account for Davar's breakdown except on the ground that he was completely worn out from overwork and had no fight left in him. The general feeling is that he should have fought it out. Supposing that, like Teymourtache and others, he had been sent to prison. It is not beyond the bounds of possibility that a popular movement would have arisen and driven the Shah from the Throne. In this connection, it is said that the Iranians would have revolted long ago were they capable of concerted action and of trusting one another sufficiently for the purpose of delivering the Iranians from the prison in which they now live.[3]

History is likely to judge Davar harshly. Having served as a principal instrument of Reza Shah's brutality and corruption, Davar in the end took the easy way out.

The Murder of Nosrat-ed-Dowleh Firouz

Less than a year after the death of Davar, it was the turn of Nosrat-ed-Dowleh Firouz, the eldest son of Prince Farman Farma, to meet his death at the hands of the Pahlavi poison squad. Firouz's death was announced in a telegram dated January 15, 1938 from C. Van H. Engert, chargé d'affaires ad interim: "I learn from an absolutely reliable source that Prince Firouz eldest son of Farman Farma was mysteriously killed a few days ago while he was under Government surveillance. This removes a man whose ability the Shah has always envied and whose potential influence he feared."[4] Wallace S. Murray, chief of the Division of Near Eastern Affairs, sent the following memorandum to the secretary of state:

The mysterious killing of Prince Firouz while under Government surveillance, merits a few comments that may throw some light on the present situation in Iran and particularly on the mentality of the Shah. Prince Firouz was a direct descendant of the Kajar kings of Persia whose dynasty was overthrown in 1925 by the present Reza Shah Pahlavi. The Prince had the unenviable reputation of having been chiefly instrumental in pushing through the notorious and ill-fated Anglo-Persian Agreement of 1919 sponsored by Lord Curzon and which would, if successful, have made Iran a British protectorate. The Prince, who was at that time Minister for Foreign Affairs, shared with the then Prime Minister and Minister of Finance in the bribe of £131,000 given by the British in recognition of the unpatriotic services of these three Iranian grandees. During the period when the American Financial Mission under Dr. Millspaugh was functioning in Iran [1922–27] Prince Firouz was the most implacable opponent of the Mission and succeeded in preventing the renewal of Dr. Millspaugh's contract in 1927. Following up his victory, the Prince became Minister of Finance in that year, only to be arrested two years later for alleged conspiracy and embezzlement. Being convicted of the charges in 1930 he was deprived of his civil rights and sentenced to prison. He was later released, but has been compelled since that time to remain on his country estate outside Teheran under close surveillance. As a condition for his release, the Prince was obliged to hand over to the Shah his share of the bribe accepted from the British in 1919.

Since his disgrace and confinement in 1930 the Prince has seen one after the other of his corrupt associates broken or destroyed. That the Shah has been so long in wreaking vengeance upon the Prince has always been difficult to understand. The probable explanation is that by sparing the Prince's life this long the Shah has been able to squeeze considerable sums out of the Prince's wealthy old father. Prince Firouz was generally recognized as one of the most intelligent and gifted Iranians of his generation, but he was as corrupt as he was talented. The fate of Prince Firouz typifies the problem which the Shah has faced in his efforts to modernize his country. The problem lies not in the lack of talent but in the widespread absence of simple honesty and integrity. That is the tragedy of Iran, and, unfortunately, the example set by the Shah himself cannot bear too close a scrutiny.[5]

FIGURE 8.2 *Nosrat-ed-Dowleh Firouz, ca. 1915. Courtesy of the IICHS.*

Sharing Wealth with Reza Shah

The example set by the shah and the blackmail of Farman Farma to spare his son, Prince Firouz, is reported by David Williamson, chargé d'affaires ad interim. He also comments on a trip the shah made in October 1929 to the western provinces of Azerbaijan, Kermanshah, and Kurdistan:

> Private advices relate that His Majesty has been in a very bad humor during a part, at least, of his trip. Instead of showing himself the gracious Monarch and the indulgent father of his people, he is said to have descended upon his cities in the guise of a usurping despot, a whip in one hand and a contribution plate in the other, suspicious of everyone and critical of everything. A persistent rumor is abroad linking the Shah's visit to Kurdistan with Prince Firouz's incarceration. It is said that Farman Farma, Firouz's father, has transferred to the Shah the title to several villages north of Kermanshah as a ransom for his son; that the Shah desired to appraise the value of the property before releasing Firouz; and that, if the villages are satisfactory, Firouz will be released upon the Shah's return to Teheran. The royal bribe is claimed to be equivalent to a million tomans.[6]

In March 1930, Ali Akbar Davar, the minister of justice, introduced a bill in the Majlis authorizing the trial by the Supreme Court of Nosrat-ed-Dowleh, who was charged with taking a bribe of 5,000 tomans when he was minister of finance. Hugh Millard, second secretary of the legation, reiterates the belief that the arrest of Nosrat-ed-Dowleh and his subsequent "trial" and "conviction" were means of forcing the prince and his father to share his wealth with Reza Shah:

> Since Davar and Firouz are close friends and both are intimate with Teymourtache, who is credited with having frequently shielded Firouz, it is generally accepted that the Shah himself is responsible for the presentation of the bill to the Medjliss. This is also the opinion of G. T. Havard, Oriental Secretary of the British Legation. It is too soon to comment on this affair, but perhaps it will take a clearer aspect later. I cannot help but feel that it is simply a means of making Firouz share some of his wealth. Though there is no indication thus far that Teymourtache is involved in this affair, he is said to have shielded his friend frequently, and should Firouz be convicted this will certainly not strengthen his position.[7]

On May 1, 1930, Nosrat-ed-Dowleh was found guilty of having accepted a bribe of 5,808 tomans. He was sentenced to four months "correctional imprisonment," fined, and deprived of his public rights (office) for life.[8]

The murder of Nosrat-ed-Dowleh in 1938 was a heavy blow to his aged father, whose death on November 22, 1939 is reported by Engert:

> I have the honor to report the death, which took place early this morning, of His Highness Prince Farman Farma at the age of about 93. He was a member of the Kajar family and a direct descendant (great-grandson) of Fateh Ali Shah who ruled in Persia from 1797 to 1834. With him disappears a picturesque personage of a bygone age, and although he took no active part in politics after the advent of Reza Shah, he was occasionally seen at official functions and always acted with much dignity and self-respect. I had known him when I was here in 1920–22 and saw him last about a year and a half ago. He remained, despite his deafness, an interesting character to the last. I am told, however, that he never quite recovered after the tragic death of his eldest son, Prince Firouz.[9]

The passing of Farman Farma was also reported by the British envoy. A comparison of the American and British dispatches illustrates the mendacity in the British records. Since the British knew they were ultimately responsible for Pahlavi's savagery, they tried to conceal or trivialize its brutal impact. In this instance, by suggesting that the prison murder of Nosrat-ed-Dowleh had no impact on his aged father, the British were attempting to dehumanize both victims. According to the British, despite the murder of his son, Farman Farma had allegedly "spent his latter years in free and quiet residence in Tehran, in undisturbed enjoyment of his astonishing powers of procreation. . . . Until almost the end of his days he was mating and breeding."[10] In the British scheme of things, the dignity and human rights of the people of Iran counted for naught.

Ayatollah Seyed Hassan Modarres

Following the murder of Firouz, the 1938 prison murder of Ayatollah Seyed Hassan Modarres, an old man of nearly eighty-five years who had spent the last ten years in prison, was shocking even by the standards of Reza Khan. Of all those who opposed the rise of Reza Khan as military dictator of Persia, none did so more effectively and courageously than Modarres, whose biography is sketched in a dispatch from Copley Amory Jr., American chargé d'affaires.

Modarres was born at Esfahan (in the village of Asfeh) in about 1855. He studied Islamic law in Esfahan and Najaf, reaching the rank of ijtehad (the highest degree of learning) in Najaf. For many years he was a professor in the religious colleges in Esfahan. In 1906 and 1907, when the Constitution had been recently ratified, Modarres was elected to the provincial administrative council of Esfahan. He was a member of the Second Majlis (1909–11), having been elected by the mujtahids of Najaf to the High Body of Clerical Superintendents.

Modarres began his active political career in 1911, when he organized a campaign against Nasser-ol-Molk, then regent, whom he denounced for having deliberately postponed elections to the Third Majlis. He subsequently served in the Third, Fourth, and Fifth Majlis. Amory's biography continues:

> After the Third Medjliss [1914–15] he joined the nationalists who emigrated abroad as a protest against the Russian invasion of Persia. Upon returning to Teheran [1918] he helped Vossough-ed-Dowleh in becoming Prime Minister. Their political friendship ended soon, and in 1919, when Vossough signed the Anglo-Persian Agreement, Modarres organized a campaign against it in Teheran. He obtained most of his prestige by this successful campaign. After the Coup d'état [February 21, 1921] he was imprisoned by the then Prime Minister Seyid Zia-ed-Din on the grounds of his alleged anti-British activities. In the Fourth Medjliss [1921–23] he was leader of the reactionary majority and supported the Cabinet of Ghavam-os-Saltaneh. In the Fifth Medjliss [1924–26] he was for long the leader of the minority group opposed to Reza Khan. In the beginning of the Medjliss [March 1924] he defeated the movement for a republic led by Reza Khan. Later, in 1925, after the latter had failed to establish the republic, he became increasingly friendly with Reza Khan and has recently succeeded in obtaining portfolios for his friends: Prince Firouz [minister of jus-

FIGURE 8.3 *Ayatollah Seyed Hassan Modarres and his son Baqer, 1922. Courtesy of
the IICHS.*

tice], Mirza Shokrollah Khan Sadri [Ghavam-ed-Dowleh, minister of the inte-
rior], and Fatemi [minister of education]. Modarres is extremely bold and
obstinate; is temperamentally conservative, as would be natural in a Persian
clerical leader. Has an unusual gift for speaking and successfully plays the dem-
agogue and enjoys great influence among the masses. Is nationalistic and anti-
foreign at heart. Especially professes to be anti-British. Has on occasion
expressed himself as being friendly to America. Poses as being extremely poor,
but is said to own considerable property.[11]

From a confidential report by Millspaugh, we learn that Modarres subsequently headed the Majlis movement to reduce the army's budget.[12] A
few days later, the decapitated body of an accountant in the Ministry of

War who had been supplying Modarres with information on army finances was found outside the gates of the Majlis. The message to Reza Khan's opponents was clear.

Though not mentioned in Amory's sketch, Modarres narrowly escaped an assassination attempt. On October 30, 1926, at 6 A.M., Modarres was attacked by three masked gunmen and was severely wounded. Although two of the assailants were caught by police, the results of the subsequent "investigation" were kept secret. No one doubted that Reza Shah had been the instigator of the attack, despite his visits to Modarres's hospital bed. In 1928, Modarres was defeated in the elections to the Seventh Majlis and was arrested and exiled shortly after, as reported by Augustin W. Ferrin, American consul in Tehran. In the conclusion of his dispatch on the unrest in Tabriz, Ferrin observes: "Teheran is tranquil. About 10,000 troops are in Teheran and any open opposition to the government can be quickly quelled. About 10 days ago, Seyed Hassan Modarres, a mullah and ex-deputy, was arrested and deported for alleged sedition."[13]

In late 1931, rumors that Modarres had been strangled in prison became widespread, prompting an official denial in *Shafaq-i-Sorkh*, which Charles C. Hart describes:

> "Modarres." Of late this name, I have the honor to report, has appeared again in headlines in the local press and has been again a subject of discussion in diplomatic circles in Teheran. It was an editorial in the local newspaper *Shafaq-i-Sorkh* of November 3, last, which occasioned this revival of interest in a personage once known to every bazaarchi and official, native and foreign, of this Capital. I shall refer to the substance of this editorial below. To me the chief interest in the incident there recounted is not the fact that a Persian-language communist sheet published in Germany has been suppressed, nor that the consensus of local opinion supports the thesis that Modarres is still alive. Rather it is that in this discussion I sense again the important changes which have been brought to this country by what one observer has called the "drill-sergeant dictatorship" of its present Shah.
>
> In the career of Seyid Hassan Modarres one may trace, in its broader outline, the history of modern Persia. A member of every Medjliss, from the Second which convened in 1908, to the Sixth which closed in 1927, Modarres, early principal spokesman for the clerical faction, played a leading role in the political life of his country during that formative period when an absolute monarchy gave way to parliamentary constitutionalism. And during the decade which followed the Zia-ed-Din coup d'état of 1921, those years which saw the star of Reza Khan rise from over the Kazvin [Qazvin] camp of the revolutionaries to the Ministry of War, Premiership and finally Throne of the Shahinshahs, Modarres maintained his position of conservative clerical leader.

Then came his fall. He had, perhaps, more than any other, blocked Reza Khan's 1924 republican movement. In 1925 the Legation reported an apparent reconciliation. But in 1928 the unforgiving Shah, whose predominant influence had been consolidated during the first two years of his reign, saw to it that Modarres was defeated in the elections to the Seventh Medjliss—to quote from a despatch of that year, "on account of his loud and outspoken opposition to the Government."

One year later, Modarres was "banished" to an insignificant town in Khorassan, some miles south of Meshed near the Afghan border. The circumstances were at the time reported by the Legation as follows (despatch 821, 891.00/1472, dated May 2, 1929, from David Williamson, Chargé d'Affaires ad interim): "The Shah is continuing his quiet but effective war against the clerical party. His methods are simplicity itself. An influential mullah or dervish is secretly seized and conducted to a prison far from his native city. It is remarked that very often those so abducted never return. Among the prominent men that have disappeared this way is Modarres—but it is rumored that he is no longer alive. Others said to be in Helat, also near Meshed, are Agha Seyed Mohammad Sadegh Tabatabai, once Ambassador to Turkey, and Nasr-i-Islam, both important clerical politicians, and leaders of anti-Governmental opinion. With what specific offense they are charged is not known."

Since that report was written Modarres has become hardly more than a memory of a passing phase of the kaleidoscopic political changes which have been witnessed in post-War Persia. To the older foreign resident his name still carries memories of actual events. To the newcomer he has less substance than the Nitti to the student of comparative politics in fascist Italy of today. The achievements of both are largely submerged in the rapid march of subsequent events. Both are wholly overshadowed by the positive personalities which have made subsequent history in their respective countries.

The chief interest, then, in the editorial in question was in the memories to which it gave rise. It warrants, however, I believe, for its other and current interest, brief quotation. I have chosen the following extracts: "The communist paper *Peykar*, which was formerly published in Berlin in the Persian language and which was recently suppressed by the German Government, reported in one of its last issues that the erstwhile famous opposition leader, Seyid Hassan Modarres, had been strangled in his Khorassan prison. We deny this false report; and we affirm that Modarres is still alive in the village of Khaf, to which he was banished by the order of the Government, and that his family receives letters from him every week. We ridicule also the Persian paper *Chehreh-Nema* of Cairo which published recently a letter from a correspondent denying what it spoke of as 'the rumored stifling of Modarres' but averring that he had died of natural death. As for the communist *Peykar* and the country of which it is a partisan, we ask: How about all the murders, executions, banishments and imprisonments of which we hear in communist Russia? By what authorities are such punishments meted out to the adversaries of the Bolsheviks? Why does the

Cheka or the G.P.U. keep its prisons full of political prisoners in each town in Russia? Is not their excuse that the Soviet Government's adversaries should be annihilated? We confess that we regretted the necessity for Modarres' banishment. It was the interest of the Empire which warranted his being forced to leave the Capital. But more important is it that we realize that there are those who, being envious of the progress achieved by Persia, invent all manner of false news to delude the public."

Two further comments are perhaps of interest in connection with the subject matter of the foregoing extracts. The first was that of the Secretary of the German Legation to the effect that the German Government had been long hoping that an incident might occur which would furnish it with the desired opportunity to suppress this communist sheet, *Peykar.* The second comment is that of Count Monteforte, Oriental Attaché of the Italian Legation. After concurring with what I have described above as a general consensus of opinion that Modarres is not dead, he observed what he sensed in a very positive way was an undercurrent of opposition and carefully concealed intrigue in high Persian circles, both military and civil, against the present dictatorship regime of Reza Shah. All open opposition had, he said, been quashed for the time being. Since the so-called banishments of 1929, of which Modarres was one of the victims, there had been few persons of influence left in Teheran who were not outwardly at least strong partisans of the Shah. Firouz had been left, but he was now in disgrace, living in strictest retirement; and the one-time favorite General Shaybani, well known for his military operations against the Kashgai in 1929, had been broken because he had become too popular with a certain faction in the Army.

Count Monteforte's conclusion was that the progress of modern Persia under Reza Shah is not built on the solid foundation of a willing cooperation between sovereign, officialdom and people. But he added, that progress may last. The Shah still controls the Army. He is certainly driving a new spirit into some at least of his higher officials. And he has strong personal supporters, not only among old associates in the Army but also such really able men as Teymourtache, Minister of the Court, and Davar, Minister of Justice. "Things are like that in Persia," he said, "the Persians have to be ruled, have to be taught how to fit into the Shah's policy of West-inspired modernization. We may some day see trouble, but we are certainly seeing great changes and progress— of a sort."

There is nothing, I venture to believe, in this interesting and worthwhile informal comment which seems contrary to the many references in my own despatches to the changes and progress which have been made in the life and institutions of this country during the ten years following the 1921 coup d'état, particularly during the second period of that decade, the period which followed Reza Shah's coronation. Persia may, according to the point of view taken, be suffering under or profiting from its "drill-sergeant dictatorship."

Personally, I believe there is in the present situation far more profit than suffering.[14]

Not long after writing the preceding report, Hart underwent a drastic change of opinion concerning the balance between profit and suffering. In his next dispatch he castigated himself for being duped by the outward manifestations of progress:

I have the honor to refer to my current despatch no. 947 of November 27, 1931, reporting regarding the recent local interest in the fate of Seyid Hassan Modarres, former parliamentary clerical leader and political power in this country, and to quote below, as of interest in that connection, a memorandum prepared by the Legation's able interpreter, Mr. Ali Pasha Saleh, on certain of the legal phases of Modarres' "imprisonment": Strictly speaking Modarres is not within the walls of a "prison," as is generally believed. A prison, in the true sense of the word, is a public building for confining persons, either to insure their production in court or to punish them as criminals (see Bouvier's Law Dictionary). Otherwise phrased, "prison" includes every place of custody under legal process or lawful arrest. Modarres has not been convicted of any crime or sentenced by any court. So much for the technical meaning of the word "prison" in so far as it applies to the person of Modarres. In a broader sense of the word, however, a small town, such as Kaien [Kain] or Khaf in Khorassan, his reported place of incarceration, or even one of the larger provincial towns would, to an ambitious man of this type, be decidedly nothing but a prison, were he, as in the case, to be kept under constant police or military surveillance, deprived of liberty and forbidden to leave its narrow provincial limits.

Banishment, if I understand it correctly, is a punishment inflicted on criminals by compelling them to quit a city, place or country for a specified period of time or for life. To be lawful such a form of punishment must be based on a public edict or sentence. Exile differs from banishment in that the former applies only to removal under constraint from one's own country. Hence, both words, banishment and prison, may, I believe, if viewed in their broader meanings, appropriately be applied to the case under discussion. Technically, I suppose, Modarres is neither in prison nor in banishment; because he has not been convicted by court sentence. Actually he is in both. Apart from the foregoing technical considerations, the following extracts, quoted from the Supplementary Fundamental Laws of the Persian Constitution of October 7, 1907, will, I believe, throw further interesting light on the status of the Modarres affair: "*Article 9*. All individuals are protected and safeguarded in respect to their lives, property, home and honor from every kind of interference, and none shall molest them save in such case and in such way as the laws of the land shall determine." "*Article 10*. No one can be summarily arrested save flagrante delicto in the commission of some crime or misdemeanor or grave offense except on the written authority of the President of the Tribunal of Justice, given in conformity with law. Even in such case the accused must immediately or at least in the course of the next twenty-four hours be informed and notified of the nature of his guilt." "*Article 12.* No punishment can be decreed or executed save in conformity with the law." "*Article 14.* No Persian can be exiled from the country, or prevented from residing in any part thereof or compelled to reside in any specified part thereof save in such cases as the law may explicitly determine."

Obviously, then, the whole procedure in the case of Modarres is, to put it mildly, extra-legal, as is the similar procedure taken in other similar cases. With the conclusion drawn in this helpful memorandum I believe the Department will agree.[15]

Conclusion

Shortly after Reza Shah's downfall in September 1941, the American minister, Louis G. Dreyfus, Jr., commented on the long reign of terror and murder: "Hundreds of persons were thrown into prisons by Shah Reza, without cause and without trial, because of personal whim or because they became too powerful. Many were so adequately disposed of that they will never return."[16] On torture in Reza Shah's prisons, he adds, "The newspaper Kushesh on October 30 referred to the torturing of prisoners by the Chief of Police and demanded that torturing be stopped at once and apparatus used therefore done away with."[17]

Dreyfus also records in the same dispatch the general demand for the punishment of those involved in torture and murder of prisoners: "The opposition in the Majlis has been demanding with some violence the apprehension and punishment of officials who had any part in this unsavory procedure and of physicians who are said to have disposed effectively of many prisoners. As a result, General Mokhtar, former Chief of the Imperial Police, has been arrested. It is also announced that Colonel Mostapha Rasekh, former warden of the prison, Arabshahi, former Chief of the Detective force, and Javanshir and A'yan, high police officials, have been arrested and are being held for prosecution. . . . The opposition is now demanding the arrest of a Dr. Ahmadi, a pseudo-physician who is said to have been the Shah's agent in giving 'injections' to many prisoners now numbered among the missing."[18] The execution of "Dr." Ahmadi in October 1944 was witnessed by the American chargé d'affaires, Richard Ford, and his report and comments on the event are given in chapter 15.

In January 1943, Millspaugh had returned to Iran: "I was informed on my return to Persia that he [Reza Shah] had imprisoned thousands and killed hundreds, some of the latter by his own hand."[19] From Dreyfus's report it is learned that while a police official had been arrested for the murder of Modarres, Modarres may have been among those murdered by Reza Shah himself: "The Chief of Police of Qum, Jehansuzi, has been arrested and held for the murder of Modarres, a parliamentary leader whose death, allegedly at the hands of the Shah, created a sensation."[20]

CHAPTER NINE

Britain and Persian Oil, 1911–1951

Forty Years of Plunder

MUCH HAS BEEN WRITTEN ON THE HISTORY of Persian oil, including several volumes on the history of the British Petroleum Company, put out by the company itself.[1] A general shortcoming of these histories is the paucity of data. In addition, some have relied extensively on British records, thereby reducing their value. However, the confidential report "Nationalization of the Iranian Oil Industry," apparently prepared by the World Bank and found in a U.S. Treasury Department file, is a rich source of data on Iranian oil from 1911 to 1951.[2] Its date, February 1952, suggests that it served as a background paper during the oil crisis of 1951–53, and its attention to detail intimates the American government's keen interest in Iran's oil.

Much has also been written about the alleged economic development and modernization brought about by Reza Shah from 1921 to 1941. The World Bank report discusses the impact of Iran's oil industry on the country's economy: "Over the past 40 years, Iran's 13–18 million people have been engaged principally in agriculture and to a limited extent in commerce and the manufacture of textiles. No heavy industry or raw material production or processing other than oil exists, despite the availability of raw materials, labor, and access to the sea. There is probably no country in the world with comparable resources so retarded in its economic development as Iran. Yet it contains undoubtedly the largest single integrated oil operation with the lowest production cost in the world. What contribution has this oil industry made to the Iranian economy?" The report compares a lack of progress in Iran with the rapid economic progress made "in the last thirty years by Turkey—less bountifully endowed with resources."[3] Sadly, Iran had derived not a single benefit from its oil.

Oil production in Iran began in 1911. From 1911 to 1920, Iran received £325,000 (about $1.6 million) in oil royalties. From 1921 to 1931, Iran received about $60 million; from 1931 to 1941, $125 million; from 1941 to 1951, $250 million. For the Reza Shah years (1921–41), oil royalty payments amounted to $185 million. For the entire forty years (1911–51) Iran received £113 million, or about $435 million. The total published profits of the Anglo-Iranian Oil Company during this period were $5 billion, not counting the profits of the subsidiary companies. In other words, Iran received a little over 8 percent of the profits calculated by the oil company.

The World Bank report reveals: "On the basis of these estimates, the [Anglo-Iranian Oil] Company deprived Iran of some $1,200 million [$1.2 billion] by failing to perform its obligations in good faith under the D'Arcy Concession and by engineering its replacement with the unfavorable agreement in 1933."[4] By the standards of 1911–51, and for a poor country, $1.2 billion was an unimaginable amount of money. In 1925, for example, the Iranian government spent only $20 million. The report adds that the actual plunder of Iran's oil by the British was considerably greater than $1.2 billion, a figure based on the company's own published accounts.

In this chapter I will first discuss the D'Arcy Concession and its replacement by the 1933 Agreement, and the manner in which the British stole Iran's oil. The following chapters will document how, from 1921 to 1941, Reza Shah stole much of the $185 million the British paid Iran and diverted it to his bank accounts in London, Switzerland, and New York. The history of Persian oil from 1911 to 1941 can aptly be called the thirty-year plunder.

The D'Arcy Concession

In May 1901 a British subject, William Knox D'Arcy, obtained a sixty-year concession for the exclusive right to explore, extract, and refine petroleum products, as well as exclusive right to lay pipelines in all of Persia, except the five northern provinces that bordered on Russia. The concession area covered about 400,000 square miles. "In return, the concessionaire [D'Arcy] agreed to make a cash payment of £20,000 [about $100,000] and issue to Iran paid-up shares representing a 10% ownership in the 'First Exploitation Company.' In addition, the concessionaire agreed to pay Iran a royalty of 16% of the profits. At the end of the concession, all the assets of the company, *both in Iran and abroad*, were to be vested in the Iranian Govern-

ment."[5] The concession terms did not exempt the concessionaire from payment of Iranian income taxes.

For sixty years under the Pahlavis and continuing to this day, it has been
the practice to denounce the D'Arcy Concession. For example, in 1931 Ali
Dashti writes in the newspaper *Shafaq-i-Sorkh:* "Thirty years ago the ignorant and corrupt gloomy court [of Mozzafar-ed-Din Shah Qajar] granted
the D'Arcy concession. The people rose against that court, one of whose
misdeeds was the granting of this oil concession. The regime was overthrown. A flood of Persian gold poured out of the country in the shape of
oil. It is by no means fair that the owner of this resource should starve to
death, and her riches in the name of the D'Arcy concession be used for the
luxury of others. We do not say that the Persian Government should abolish the concession, but we do say that it should be revised. We have been
very badly cheated in this bargain."[6] Sixty years later, the criticism continued in Mostafa Elm's 1992 book *Oil, Power and Principle*. Yet the truth
appears to have been the exact opposite.

The D'Arcy Concession was extremely favorable to Iran—a tribute to
the sagacity and negotiating skills of Mozzafar-ed-Din Shah and his ministers. The World Bank report states:

> The terms of the agreement—if carried out in good faith by the concession-
> aire—were very favorable, and in fact no better terms have since been offered
> to Iran. The concession provided an arrangement by which D'Arcy could build
> up an oil industry in return for giving Iran a 10% ownership and 16% of the
> profits, or a claim approximating one-quarter of total earnings. Over a sixty-
> year period, the concessionaire would have enjoyed about 75% of the profits. In
> 1961 Iran would have obtained ownership and control of the Company's prop-
> erties, *both in Iran and elsewhere*. . . . In 1950 these properties amounted to over
> one billion dollars on the basis of original cost.[7]

The implication was that the market value of these properties were many
times more than the $1 billion they originally cost.

From the beginning, the British considered the terms of the D'Arcy
Concession to be "far too liberal for Iran."[8] The *Economist* of London was
to describe the D'Arcy Concession as "a naive document in light of the
place Iranian oil was to take in the world market."[9] In 1909 the concessionaire, with the participation of Burma Oil Company, set up the Anglo-
Persian Oil Company (APOC; later renamed the Anglo-Iranian Oil
Company, AIOC). The new company had a capital of £1 million. Moreover, the exploration, production, refining, and marketing rights were
transferred from the First Exploitation Company to the new company in
consideration of a token royalty. In the words of the World Bank report,
"Iran suddenly found that she no longer had a 10% interest in the operating concern, but only a 10% interest in the royalties received by the First

Exploitation Company from the Anglo-Persian Oil Company. This dual company device was the first step in watering down what was considered an overly generous agreement. Furthermore, royalties paid by APOC to the First Exploitation Company were charged off as costs and thereby reduced profits on which royalties of 16% were due."[10]

British Political Mischief and the Systematic Violation of the D'Arcy Concession

In 1914, the British government acquired a majority ownership in APOC; thereafter the Company and the British government became indistinguishable. The World Bank report declares, "Throughout its history the Company directed, if not dictated, the policy of the British Government in its relations with Iran. Few Iranian officials or individuals would risk the displeasure of the Company, and those who dared to do so were liable to disgrace or dismissal, and the Company fostered the belief in its omnipotence in order to strengthen its influence and domination." Quoting from Vincent Sheean's 1927 book *The New Persia*, the report notes: "Persia was filled with British agents, and bribery was the accepted means of persuasion. The expenses of the British establishment in Teheran were enormous, and British agents quite openly worked in elections, in Parliament, and in every political activity. The British Legation in Teheran is very large (larger than some embassies in Europe), and the British business men and traders throughout the country may be considered, in a sense, 'agents.'"[11]

The British set about undermining the authority of the Iranian government. The report declares that, "with the help of British Government officials stationed in Iran, [the Company] established itself as an independent power in the territories surrounding its concession." This was especially true where the Company's drilling and extraction activities were located, the Khuzistan and Bakhtiari regions. In the case of Khuzistan, "the feudal Sheikh of Mohammerah was encouraged to disregard the Iranian Government and to establish an autonomous Sheikhdom in Khuzestan and to bring the oil bearing territories under British suzerainty and control. The Iranian Government has also published the text of a letter from the British Resident and Consul General to Sheikh Khazal of Mohammerah guaranteeing him protection against the central Iranian Government."[12]

As for the Bakhtiari tribal chiefs, the report states: "To win support of these local chiefs, the Company engaged in a systematic program of encouraging their insubordination and supporting them against the central government under a policy of divide and rule." APOC even established a subsidiary, the Bakhtiari Oil Company, "for the purpose of issuing free stock to the chiefs of the Bakhtiari tribes."[13]

As soon as oil production began and the size of the reserves was known, the Company stopped payment of royalties to Iran.

The British Government had barely got into the picture before the Company began exerting pressure to amend the D'Arcy Concession. Its first move was to stop payments of royalties to Iran. This was done on the grounds that a neighboring government [Ottoman Turkey] had incited the sabotage of the pipelines. Although the actual damage did not exceed $100,000 [about £20,000], the Company used this as a pretext to withhold royalty payments for 5 years and even claimed some $2 million in compensation. Article 14 of the Concession provided that Iran was *only* obligated to protect the property of the Company and the lives of its employees, but was not liable for any loss or damage caused by acts beyond its control. Another reason given for withholding payments was that the Company had to pay a 3% royalty to the owners of the land on which the wells had been drilled. Article 3 of the Concession provided that the concessionaire was to recompense landowners for private lands taken for this purpose.[14]

Through its serious violations of the D'Arcy Concession, the Anglo-Persian Oil Company reduced the royalties due Iran. APOC established numerous subsidiary companies into which "profits were siphoned." In addition, "the Company was diverting an abnormally large share of profits into various reserves used to finance its phenomenal expansion abroad. Fed by an increasing stream of profits, these reserve accounts continued to grow rapidly. The extent to which the Company was built up out of profits from Iranian oil was bluntly stated in the annual report of the Chairman of the Board for 1924: 'Since we first became a revenue producing concession in 1914, we have provided out of earnings no less than £19,000,000 for expenditures of a capital nature.'"[15] In 1914, APOC entered into a contractual agreement with the British Admiralty to supply it with fuel "at cost," which reduced profits at the expense of the Iranian government, whose royalty was supposed to be 16 percent of the profits. The savings to the British Admiralty during 1914–51 alone exceeded $500 million, considerably greater than the total of $435 million paid to Iran between 1911 and 1951.[16]

In direct violation of the D'Arcy Concession, APOC frustrated Iran's attempts to inspect its books by issuing misleading figures. Commenting on the published accounting practices of APOC which "lumped together the investments and advances to subsidiaries," the *Economist* noted:

The public which is interested through the Government's holding has the right to protest against the cloaking of these important financial operations by one single unintelligible item in the parent company's balance sheet. . . . The combined effects of these practices, Iran concluded, was to evade or minimize royalty payments and use the funds so withheld for the expansion of the Company. Refusal of the Company to make full disclosure of its earnings, and the fact that its published accounts obviously showed only a small fraction of the real profits, created an intense distrust of the Company and its accounting methods.[17]

The World Bank report notes:

> Despite cut-rate fuel oil supplied to the Admiralty and profits siphoned off into subsidiaries, the Company accounts disclose sizable profits, as the following statements of its Board Chairman, Sir Charles Greenway, show: "(1) We have surplus assets at the end of March 31, 1919, of nearly £6,000,000 [$30 million]. (2) During the fiscal years 1921–1923, APOC spent for capital installations £32,000,000 [$160 million]. (3) Between fiscal years 1914–1923, the Company made capital expenditures of £19,000,000 [$95 million] out of earnings and paid £9,500,000 in dividends and interest."[18]

Despite these vast *reported* profits (which did not include those siphoned into the subsidiaries), during the 1932–33 oil dispute with the Anglo-Persian Oil Company the British foreign secretary, Sir John Simon, declared in Geneva that the oil royalties paid to Persia from 1913 to 1919 amounted to £325,000 ($1.6 million).[19] In addition, a lump sum of £1 million was paid in 1921, bringing the total to £1,325,000. (Similarly, Millspaugh's royalty figures for 1913 through 1920 total £1,333,285.)[20] This compared to £19 million in capital expenditures "out of earnings" and £9.5 million in dividends and interest for the same period. However, it should be stressed that of the £1.3 million in royalties, £1 million consisted of the payment made in 1921 as part of the Armitage-Smith Agreement. By contrast, royalty payments for 1921–1925 amounted to £2,833,755, or an average of £566,751 ($2.8 million) per year.

The Armitage-Smith Agreement

Affairs between the Persian government and the Anglo-Persian Oil Company were regulated by the so-called Armitage-Smith Agreement of December 1920. S. A. Armitage-Smith, who had been appointed the British financial adviser to Persia under the provisions of the August 1919 Anglo-Persian Treaty, negotiated with the Company on behalf of the Persian government. The best-known provision of the 1920 agreement was a payment of £1 million to settle all back royalties and other disputes related to the war years. The actual payment amounted to £933,000 of which £125,000 was paid by APOC in April 1921 as an advance on Iran's 1921 royalties,[21] and £808,000 was paid in December 1921. C. Van H. Engert, the American chargé d'affaires ad interim in Tehran, reports:

> I have the honor to transmit herewith translation of a statement published by the Ministry of Finance, which appeared in the newspaper *Setareh Iran* on January 1, 1922, giving certain details as to remittances received from the

Anglo-Persian Oil Company (usually referred to as the "Southern Oil Company") totaling £808,000. This represents the sum allotted to Persia as her share of profits of the subsidiary companies of the Anglo-Persian Oil Company. Up to 1920 this claim of the Persian Government had always been refused by the Anglo-Persian Oil Company, and it was only after Mr. Armitage-Smith, the then British financial advisor to the Persian Government, had in person pressed the matter in London that the reclamation was allowed. It is generally believed that the British Government, in order to facilitate the work of the financial mission in Persia, intimated to the company that it desired the claim to be settled in Persia's favor if there was any reasonable doubt as to the correctness of the company's attitude.[22]

The £933,000 paid by APOC was nearly 5 million tomans, or a quarter of the entire budget of the Persian government. With this money at his disposal, and having been given control of the armed forces by the British, Reza Khan's continued rapid rise to the dictatorship of Persia was assured.

Commenting on this settlement, the World Bank report does not mince words: "This sum in comparison with the savings of the Admiralty, taxes paid to the United Kingdom and profits distributed or reinvested, does not constitute more than 3% of the Company's profits. Iran, under its concession, was entitled to 16% of profits and thus the 'settlement' was grossly inadequate and consequently was never ratified by Iran."[23] In addition, under the D'Arcy Concession, Iran owned 10 percent of the Company. Thus, instead of £1 million, Iran should have received at least £8 million.

Armitage-Smith also reached an agreement with APOC on the manner in which net profits were to be determined. Profits were to be calculated before the payment of British income tax and were to include the profits of all the Company's operations, inside and outside Iran. The single exception was profits arising from the transportation of oil by ship. The World Bank report continues: "This exception was a particularly sore point with Iranians who argued that the tanker fleet was built out of oil profits on which the Iranian Government had not received its share of royalty and would now be deprived of its share of the tanker profits. In addition, this exception provided a ready means of skimming off profits through excessive transportation charges. It is of interest to note that the British Tanker Company—the wholly owned fleet-arm of APOC—had earned so much profit during World War I that in 1918 it purchased $8.6 million of APOC's debentures. At the same time, the Company's investments and advances to its subsidiaries increased by $24 million."[24]

It was later learned that the Armitage-Smith Agreement had altered a key provision of the original D'Arcy Concession, namely, the 16 percent of profits accruing to the Persian government. Under the new agreement, and until the annulment of the D'Arcy Concession on November 27, 1932,

Persia's share was to be 10 percent of the profits, as determined by APOC. For instance, 1923 royalties were £565,250 (about $2,825,000). In a June 1924 report on the operation of APOC in south Persia the American consul in Bushire writes: "There is no doubt as to the high profits made by the Anglo-Persian Company . . . At this rate the profits for the year just past would be about $28,000,000. The British seem to have no anxiety of any kind as to trouble in the oil fields, but they are unanimous in stating that if any disturbances occur they will promptly protect the fields with troops. At all costs the oil must flow without interruption."[25] Out of a profit of $28 million, as computed by the British themselves, $2.8 million was paid to the Persian government on the basis of the Armitage-Smith Agreement.

Four Shillings per Ton

From 1926 through 1930, oil royalties had averaged £1.1 million per year, with an average of 5.6 million tons of oil extracted per year, according to T. L. Jacks, resident director of APOC (in a report by Hart). The 1930 royalties were £1,323,679 and 2 shillings, or slightly less than those of 1929 (£1.4 million). Based on figures provided by Jacks and R. E. Lingeman, British commercial attaché, total royalties payment for the four years and nine months was £5.2 million on a production of 26.5 million tons. Yearly average figures were £1,100,000 and 5,600,000 tons. Hart notes that the de facto average royalty payment on Persian oil was 4 shillings per ton, the same as on Iraqi oil.[26] Henry S. Villard, former consul at Tehran, and now at the Division of Near Eastern Affairs, notes that, based on Hart's figures, APOC had apparently been paying only 10 percent in royalties (not 16 percent) since the Armitage-Smith Agreement; Murray concurs.[27]

After the settlement of the oil dispute in 1933, the "new" basis of royalty payment was to be 4 shillings per ton. It turned out that under the 10 percent rule, this was already being paid by the British. In return for the new payment basis, the concession period was extended for another thirty-two years. Thus the British had disengaged themselves from their obligations under the D'Arcy Concession and obtained an extension of the concession practically free. The only apparent cost to them was a "large present" to Reza Shah (reputedly between £5 million and £8 million).

APOC's Early Attempts to Revise the D'Arcy Concession

From 1920, APOC had earnestly attempted to revise the D'Arcy Concession. In particular, it wanted to get rid of the clause concerning the transfer of all assets to the Iranian government, both inside and outside the country, at the termination of the concession in 1961. Second, APOC wanted to be free of the obligation of giving Iran access to its books and records and thus maintain the secrecy of its real profits. It also wanted an extension of its concession period. In addition, from the beginning, APOC had displayed a preference for a royalty based on a flat rate per ton exported in lieu of a share of profits, as stipulated by the D'Arcy Concession. The World Bank report states: "While the negotiations regarding overdue royalties and the method of arriving at profits were going on in 1920, the Company approached Mr. Armitage-Smith with a proposal to change the basis of the royalty payment from 16% of the profits to a flat rate on tonnage exported. After consulting experts, Mr. Armitage-Smith advised the Iranian Government against such a change. The Company nevertheless continued to make similar proposals from time to time."[28]

The new chairman of the board of directors of the Anglo-Persian was Sir John Cadman, a person who had taken great pains to cultivate amicable relations with Reza Khan. His visit to Tehran in April 1926 to attend the coronation ceremony of Reza Khan prompted the American minister, Hoffman Philip, to remark: "Sir John Cadman's arrival in Teheran coincided with the Coronation, on which occasion he attended the ceremonies in the suite of the British Minister. I am told that Sir John Cadman is expected to become Chairman of the Board of Directors of the Anglo-Persian Oil Company, in the near future. He is the first director of that Company, I believe, to have visited Persia or, at least, Teheran."[29]

By early 1929, negotiations were well on their way between the two sides, and Cadman had come to Tehran. R. A. Wallace Treat, chargé d'affaires ad interim, writes, "Both the Persian Government and Sir John are being exceedingly discreet regarding the progress of their negotiations. From the Persian side I have learned that much progress is being brought to bear for a revision of the terms of the D'Arcy Concession as to the territory over which the Company may work, and for increased royalties. . . . Also, I have gathered that the Anglo-Persian is already endeavoring to arrange at this early date for a prolongation of its concession."[30]

Rumors of negotiations between the Anglo-Persian Oil Company and the Persian government to revise the D'Arcy Concession persisted after 1929. Consul Henry S. Villard, American consul at Tehran, reported that ever since the forfeiture of the banknote monopoly of the Imperial Bank of Persia on May 13, 1930, there had been persistent rumors that the APOC was negotiating for an extension of its concession for a period of 50 years in return for which the Persian share of profits would be raised from 16 percent to 20–24 percent. In addition, the government was to receive a "loan for £10,000,000 towards the cost of railways." Villard reported that the rumors emanated from authoritative sources and concludes his report with the following:

The effect of this news on the Persian public, should it prove to be true, would no doubt be most unfavorable, particularly in the South of Persia, where considerable anti-British sentiment exists. When the bank-note monopoly of the Imperial Bank of Persia was forfeited in May, the talk in the street turned eagerly toward a possible cancellation of the Anglo-Persian Oil Company's contract as being the next step in Persia's march to freedom from foreign exploitation. An extension of the concession, instead of its abrogation, would doubtless prove exceedingly disappointing to a large section of the populace.[31]

The proposal referred to in Villard's dispatch was known as the Three Star Agreement, submitted by APOC in 1929. Instead of a fixed percentage of profits, the Company proposed to pay 4–5 shillings per ton of oil produced. "This proposed agreement included a provision that the Iranian Government would be given the opportunity to acquire up to 25% of the stock of the Company. It also provided for an extension of the concession by an additional thirty years. The Three Star proposal received no consideration from the Iranian Government because of distrust of the Company's accounting practices and because of its provision for the extension of the concession to 1989."[32] In fact, the Iranian government at this time consisted solely of Abdol Hossein Teymourtache. By turning down APOC's proposal, Teymourtache was already entering dangerous territory.

APOC persisted in its attempts to revise the D'Arcy Concession. Hart, citing a conversation with T. L. Jacks, reports on renewed rumors that APOC was trying to negotiate for an extension of its concession: "But regarding the further rumor that the Shah was prepared to grant (the Medjliss is his puppet) an extension of the Company's concession on the payment of five million pounds, Mr. Jacks observed that he had no doubt that His Majesty would be very pleased to do so for the sum in question."[33] Hart later comments on the negotiations over the extension of APOC's concession: "It is stated that during his stay in London, His Highness Teymourtache will not even discuss the renewal of the Concession on account of the fact that in high circles a certain disposition was manifested which, it is understood, was so exacting as to render impossible a resumption of the negotiations which were so much talked of at Teheran in 1930."[34] It is clear that by the end of 1931, APOC had got nowhere in its attempts to revise the D'Arcy Concession.

Max M. Dixon and the Northern Oil Concession, 1930–1931

In March 1930, Max M. Dixon, an American representing the Petroleum Bond and Share Corporation of New York, arrived in Tehran accompanied by one Hussein Moustafaeff (Hassan Moustafa Bey) seeking an oil concession in the five northern provinces that were not part of the Anglo-Persian Oil Company's concession. His endeavors were ultimately unsuccessful, but his negotiations with Teymourtache, Foroughi, and Diba, the court accountant, throw light on the system of bribes given in high places and how the proceeds were divided between Reza Shah and his subordinates, at least up to 1930–31. Augustin W. Ferrin, former American consul in Persia, observes: "Mr. Dixon's conversations with Persian officials concerning a northern oil concession constitute a new and curious story, which will be found in confidential files of the Department."[35]

Soon after his arrival in Tehran, Dixon began negotiations with Teymourtache, Reza Shah's minister of the court. Fortunately, Dixon had kept the American minister, Charles C. Hart, fully informed of the progress of his negotiations, and Hart dutifully kept the State Department informed. On his conversation with Dixon concerning the oil negotiations between Dixon and Teymourtache, Hart writes,

> Mr. Dixon said that he hoped to reach an agreement on the oil concession with the Minister of the Court in a few weeks, and that the principal question at issue was how much money was to be paid for the concession. In this relation he said that Teymourtache was only acting as an agent for the Shah. Asked if the Persian officials displayed any reticence in approaching the subject of payment to be made for the concession he said it was quite the contrary. He made no reference to the matter of payment, and when the official with whom negotiations are being conducted asked that an "advance," as he euphemistically described it, be paid, he replied that American companies were not accustomed to making "advances." The ready wit of the official [Teymourtache] was, as usual, up to the situation and he remarked that he had noted in the press that even an American cabinet officer had accepted an "advance" from an American oil company. From then on the question was discussed without reserve; in fact the Persian official said frankly that in this country one never knew when one would be out of office and he felt that he should make enough to be assured of a comfortable retirement in Europe should this become necessary. Mr. Dixon added that from his experience in Turkey he had expected a great deal of circumlocution would be necessary before getting down to the subject of "advances."

Hart then describes the actual terms of negotiation, stipulating that Persia's share of the oil was inversely related to the amount of the bribe paid:

> The concession was to provide that the Petroleum Bond and Share Corporation might explore for oil for two or three years and if unsuccessful the concession could be voided by that corporation. Mr. Dixon at first told the Legation that he thought that he could get the concession for $50,000, providing for royalties amounting to 8 per-cent of the total crude oil produced, and for $100,000 if the royalties amounted to 5 per-cent of the total production. Since the Minister of the Court had expressed his preference for royalties based on a specified amount per ton of crude oil, as in the case of the Turkish Petroleum Company in Iraq, the negotiations were being conducted with this end in

view. He added that he expected to settle for about $50,000. He is endeavoring
to have the concession good for ninety years, while the Persians are negotiating
on the basis of sixty years. Mr. Dixon said that he could get it signed at once if
he were willing to pay enough for it. He seemed to have a very low opinion of
the scruples of Persian officials. Should all go well and oil be found a further
sum of about 100,000 pounds sterling would have to be paid, apparently in the
same manner as the money referred to above. Mr. Dixon also said that he had
learned on good authority that the Anglo-Persian Oil Company had made a
standing offer of 3,000,000 tomans for an oil concession for the five northern
provinces not included in the D'Arcy concession, but that the Persian officials
handling the matter were "afraid to take it."

From Hart's dispatch we also learn about the role of Foroughi:

> Mr. Dixon hoped that Foroughi, former Ambassador to Turkey, who
> appears to be on the point of reluctantly accepting the post of Minister of Eco-
> nomics, will sign the concession for the Persian Government and that it will be
> ratified by the Medjliss before the chamber adjourns on about May 15 for the
> summer. Negotiations for the concession were commenced with Foroughi in
> Angora. As to the important question of the right of transit of the oil through
> the territory included in the Anglo-Persian Oil Company's concession, he said
> that this would have to be settled before the large payment, estimated at
> 100,000 sterling, is paid. He did not seem to think that this offered great diffi-
> culties, since the Harriman interests and the Persian Government would be
> able to persuade the Anglo-Persian Oil Company to permit this. . . . He also said
> that both Teymourtache and Mirza Abdul Hussein Khan Diba, a Court official,
> told him that the late Vice-Consul Imbrie was killed at the instigation of the
> present head of the Anglo-Persian Oil Company, presumably Mr. T. Lavington
> Jacks, and they offered Mr. Dixon police protection in Teheran which he
> refused. This, I hear, was one of the wild stories current at the time of the
> tragedy.[36]

In another conversation with Dixon, Hart learned more of the negotiations for the proposed concession and how Reza Shah, Teymourtache,
Diba, and Foroughi divided the bribe:

> He [Dixon] informs the Legation that in a recent conversation, discussing
> the desired concession, the Minister of the Court, Teymourtache, suggested
> that a royalty of 4 shillings per ton of crude oil should be paid to the Persian
> Government with a sliding scale up to 6 shillings per ton, depending on the
> world market price of oil. Mr. Dixon had offered 8 per-cent of the gross oil pro-
> duced at the price at the wells; that is to say, the world market price at a refin-
> ery, less the cost of transport. In view of Teymourtache's proposal he is now
> negotiating on the basis of 4 shillings per ton of crude oil without the sliding
> scale referred to above. . . .

Mr. Dixon said that Diba, a Court official, told him that in all transactions such as this one, the Shah and Teymourtache shared equally and that he, Diba, received his portion from the latter's half of the profits.

Dixon confirms that Foroughi received the alleged payment of $100,000 by the Sinclair Oil Company in 1924, a fact Foroughi vehemently denied:

Mr. Dixon said that Foroughi, the newly appointed Minister of Economics, was a partner with him and Hassan Moustafaeff, and that they had sent to Foroughi a letter confirming the partnership. Thus the Minister of Economics is entitled to share equally with Mr. Dixon and Moustafaeff any profits which they may realize as negotiators for the Petroleum Bond & Share Corporation. Needless to say, this was told in the utmost confidence. He does not believe that Foroughi will accept the full one-third share but would accept a present. Despite this Mr. Dixon expressed the opinion that Foroughi was the most upright man of his acquaintance in Persia. . . .

This takes my recollection back to Albania. When I was reading the despatches from Tirana in the Department in 1925, preliminary to going to that post, I came across a despatch which quoted a certain Albanian as remarking that another of his fellow countrymen, a member of the bey class, was in his opinion the only patriot, the only honest man in the country. This statement interested me at the time and, afterwards, caused the keenest inward amusement when I became acquainted with this great character who stood alone as a paladin of virtue. The acquaintance had proceeded but a brief span when I discovered that as a consummate scoundrel this lone good man was what the art connoisseur would describe as a "collection piece."[37]

Hart informs us that since the negotiations had been going very slowly, the "collection piece," Foroughi, recommended that it might be wise if Dixon left Persia for two or three months in order to give the impression that he was not overly anxious to get the concession. Accordingly, Dixon announced that he planned to leave for the summer and probably would not return until the fall. As to the possibility of granting Anglo-Persian a concession in the north, Foroughi informed Dixon that "this would cause an actual revolution."

Anglo-Persian's Offer to Reza Shah

Dixon did take a long leave, as suggested by Foroughi. Villard reports his return to Tehran in the fall of 1930 after an absence of several months. He states that this time Dixon represented the John Hays Hammond group of Washington and New York, the A. W. Harriman group having lost interest because of the stock market crash and subsequent depression. As previously, Dixon was accompanied by Hassan Moustafa Bey and a Russian prince, now a Persian subject. Villard continues: "Although Mr. Dixon's negotiations did not bear fruit on his previous visit, largely because of the fact that he could not see his way to the donation of a cash 'present' in the proper quarter, he seems confident that they will now lead to success."[38]

Fortunately for historians, upon his return to Tehran, Dixon continued to keep Hart abreast of his negotiations. In an account of his conversation with Dixon on the progress of his negotiations with Teymourtache, Hart reveals that the plan was for the Hammond group to spend a minimum of $100,000 per year for three years. If the explorations were successful, the Persian government's share of the oil would be 8 percent, or its equivalent in money, should the government prefer to sell the oil to granters. Hart includes the following vital information about the visit of Sir John Cadman, APOC's managing director, in relation to the company's desire to extend its concession for another thirty years:

> According to Mr. Dixon he received the following information from his Turkish interpreter, Hasan Moustafa Bey, who acts as an intermediary between him and the Persian Government, concerning conversations between the Persian Government and Sir John Cadman of the Anglo-Persian Oil Company on his recent flying visit to Teheran. In reference to the Anglo-Persian Oil Company's desire for a renewal of its concession, Teymourtache, the Minister of the Court, told Mr. Dixon's interpreter that in an audience with the Shah, at which Teymourtache was present, Sir John offered 5,000,000 pounds sterling cash for a renewal of the Company's concession for thirty years, and 8,000,000 pounds sterling if the five northern provinces were included. According to this report the Minister of the Court expressed the opinion that the Anglo-Persian Oil Company "had not begun to talk," adding that an American Company had offered 100,000,000 dollars for these rights after the expiration of the Anglo-Persian Oil Company's concession. This alleged American offer sounds highly improbable but, if thirty years hence the concession is allowed to expire, the property might very conceivably be worth many times that sum.[39]

In the above report, we likely have found the reason for the dismissal and arrest of Teymourtache in December 1932—in the midst of the negotiations with APOC—and his subsequent murder in prison. After spurning APOC's earlier proposals, Teymourtache still insisted that despite its offer of £5–8 million, APOC "had not begun to talk." In addition, Reza Shah was not going to share the money offered for a thirty-year extension of the oil concession.

The oil negotiations were continued by Teymourtache during his European tour of 1931–32. The purpose was to revise the Armitage-Smith Agreement, and after weeks of careful negotiations, an initial agreement was reached. According to Hart, the lawyers' fees alone came to £10,000. The agreement was brought to Tehran in February 1932 and studied by the shah and his ministers. At that time, the matter was taken out of the hands of Teymourtache, who had conducted all previous oil negotiations, and given to Seyed Hassan Taqizadeh, minister of finance, who had no previous experience in oil matters. Thereafter, negotiations continued between Jacks and Taqizadeh for nine months, until the "annulment" of the D'Arcy Concession on November 27, 1932.

The Press Campaign against the D'Arcy Concession

That the cancellation of the D'Arcy Concession had been carefully engineered by the British can be seen from a violent newspaper campaign that, by carefully measured steps, first demanded a revision of the agreement and then its cancellation. Hart comments:

> The press has carried out a campaign against this company more ruthless than those directed against other foreign concessions. The coolest foreigner in all of Persia is T. L. Jacks, resident director of the Anglo-Persian. If he ever worries about anything it is not discernible. Persian direction of the oil concession suggests something very amusing to him. He declares that under Persian management the country's oil resources would peter out in three years. What would please the Persians most is to have the Government wrest the oil concession from the Anglo-Persian Oil Company.[40]

By the spring of 1931, Hart reported some of the invective demanding a "revision" of the D'Arcy Concession. Seyed Ebrahim Zia of *Iran-i-Azad* comments:

> Where did the Anglo-Persian Oil Company collect this colossal capital? Doubtless in Persia and from the Persian oil fields. In other words this tremendous wealth has leaked from our home. But what has been the share of the landlord, Persia? The Imperial Government should give the following points full consideration: In the first place it should most carefully investigate the past accounts of the Anglo-Persian Oil Company. In the second place the Government should effect a revision in the Concession and should change the basis of its royalties, i.e. 16% revenue. This is the worst means of determining the Government's royalties because it cannot be determined which expenses should be charged to the Government in computation of net revenues. Supposing they would like to lessen the Government's share, they may very easily increase the item of expenses. Why does not the Government of His Imperial Majesty Pahlevi, which has the honor of having effected all these reforms, take action to restore its rights?

Where Zia left off, Ali Dashti of *Shafaq-i-Sorkh* took up: "Our authority in revising the concession is the Constitutional Revolution." Four days later Dashti declared, "I do not want to insist on the abolition of the concession. No, because regardless of the important work achieved by the company, we have no means of operating an oil-field ourselves. We do not believe that a Company which has made such a huge organization out of nothing should be deprived of its rights. But the following adjustments are essential." The most important of the adjustments was more royalty payments to the government and payment of various taxes by APOC, such as the road tax and import-export duties. Hart wryly observes that "this prolific publicist [Dashti] is careful to say that it is revision and not abolition of the concession that is desired." Most significantly, Hart comments, "T. L. Jacks, the Resident Director of the Anglo-Persian Oil Company, assured Teymourtache some time ago that he was quite willing at any time to discuss the revision of the D'Arcy Concession."[41]

By April 1931, however, the newspapers were demanding the cancellation of the D'Arcy Concession. Hart reports that one particular article in *Shafaq-i-Sorkh* issue of April 22, 1931, entitled "Government Is Justified If It Should Cancel the D'Arcy Concession," had been particularly violent. The semi-official newspaper *Iran-i-Azad* and its editor, Zein-ol-Abedine Rahnema, were not to be outdone by *Shafaq-i-Sorkh* and Ali Dashti. In editorials from October 27 to November 7, the paper stated:

> The Anglo-Persian Oil Company is more or less a political institution whose high grade Persian employees draw their salaries from the British Government, not from the budget of the Company. Half the shares of the Company belong to the British Government. Mr. Jacks, Chief Manager of the Company residing in Teheran, is a second British Minister. Meager salaries are paid the Persian staff as compared with the British staff. The latter draw from 300 to 3,000 tomans monthly salaries. There are some 10,000 Persian laborers at work in the various establishments of the Company, but that the clerical offices are preponderantly staffed by Indians, is a well known fact. When it comes to curtailment of staff the few Persian clerks are the first victims. Further, the British chiefs treat the Persian employees as their slaves. I do not exaggerate when I say that the British chiefs of the Anglo-Persian Oil Company treat their Persian subordinates like Negroes or the way Nebuchadnezzar, who captured Jerusalem, brutalized the Jews. Cancellation of the Company's concession, obtained some 30 years ago by fraud and artifice and bribing of the late Mozaffar-ed-Din Shah, is the only satisfactory solution to this appalling situation.

Showing that he was fully aware of the realities of the so-called press campaign, Hart remarks: "Mr. Jacks, questioned as to whether he, Second British Minister to Persia, had paid for the insertion of these articles, replied: 'Most certainly not, but, what is more to the point, we didn't pay to keep them out either.' Perhaps Mr. Jacks deserves the honorary title thus given him."[42]

Iran's Annulment of the D'Arcy Concession

Following the press attacks the stage was set for the annulment of the D'Arcy Concession and its replacement by an agreement favorable to APOC. Two matters had provoked a crisis. First was the matter of income taxes. Second, there was a drastic decline in oil royalties for 1931. In 1930 the first income tax was enacted in Iran, but APOC, claiming exemption from taxes, refused to abide by it. According to the World Bank report, "The Company's refusal was not justifiable inasmuch as Article 7 of the Concession only exempted the concessionaire from land tax, export taxes and import duties. It could not have specified exemption against income taxes because no such tax then existed. Finally, in 1931, the Company admitted liability and offered to pay 4% of its profits, but this offer was tied up with other outstanding issues which could not be readily resolved."[43]

In the spring of 1932, the Anglo-Persian Oil Company announced that due to the world economic crisis, its profits had declined by 50 percent and consequently royalties for 1931 had been drastically reduced. Hart reports that, upon being informed that the 1931 royalties came to exactly £306,872, compared to £1.4 million for 1929 and £1.3 million for 1930, Reza Shah had shown extreme displeasure. "During the intervening month the local vernacular press, encouraged if not actually inspired by intimation of this royal displeasure, entered upon an extensive campaign of vitriolic criticism of the Company and all its works. All of the old alleged grounds of complaint were dug out of the editorial morgues and joyously re-burnished for the new fray."[44] The World Bank report notes:

> The low profit figures were neither justified by the volume of production (5,750,000 tons), which declined by only 4% compared with the preceding year, nor by any considerable drop in oil prices. Furthermore, in the following three years from 1932 to 1935—the depth of the depression—the Company paid royalties averaging $10 million, and yet managed to show average annual profits after royalties of $20 million. Consequently, the Iranians believe that the 1931 financial statement was deliberately manipulated as part of a plan to precipitate a crisis. . . . At this juncture the Company adopted an attitude of sweet reasonableness and claimed that the fault lay with the terms of the D'Arcy Concession which made payments to Iran dependent on profits. It suggested that this provision as well as other terms of the concession were not suited to the times and circumstances. It went so far as to say that the Iranian Government was entitled to minimum annual royalty payments, irrespective of the Company's profits. In retrospect, it would seem that the Company itself engineered the annulment.[45]

On November 27, 1932, Reza Shah ordered that the Company be notified of the cancellation of the D'Arcy Concession. In his cancellation letter to Jacks, Taqizadeh had informed him of the government's desire to enter into new discussions for the purpose of granting a new concession. In the meantime, Hart reported that neither Jacks nor the British minister had shown any alarm at the new situation. Concerning the operations of the APOC, Hart comments: "In the meantime the Persian Government appears to have taken no action to interfere with the Company's continued exploitation of the southern oil fields. A rumor circulated widely yesterday to the effect that orders had been sent to the Persian authorities in Khouzistan to take over the wells on the grounds that, the concession being canceled, the oil therein became the sole property of Persia. Today, this rumor has been denied, apparently officially."[46] The World Bank report states: "When the Iranian Government annulled the concession it expected only a token protest from the British Government, followed by arbitration in Teheran as provided for in the concession agreement. To its surprise, however, the British reaction was most severe."[47]

Hart gives the substance of Jacks's reply of November 30 to Taqizadeh's note of November 27, 1932, in which Jacks denied the right of the Persian government to cancel the concession. Jacks also stated the Company's willingness to enter into early negotiations for the modification of the Armitage-Smith Agreement and other "collateral matters." Hart reiterated that there had been no interference with the operations of the Company and none were intended. Subsequently, a conversation occurred between the American Dr. Ossip Friedlander and Teymourtache. The latter had denied the rumor that the annulment had been agreed to previously with the Company. Taqizadeh's note to Jacks was to be seen as a warning: "Of course, the Persian Government has no intention of interfering in any way with the continued operation of the oil fields, but something had to be done. We have talked and argued and negotiated for so long without getting anywhere that it was necessary to write to them something firm and definite. Call it, if you wish, a warning."[48]

A synopsis of events from December 2 to December 28, 1932, is provided by a memorandum from Murray. On December 2, the British minister submitted a protest note that contained a demand for the withdrawal of the notice of November 27, 1932: "His Majesty's Government will not tolerate any damage to the Company's interests or interference with their premises or business activities in Persia." The note added, "His Majesty's Government would not hesitate to take all legitimate measures to protect their just and indisputable interests."[49] Following naval demonstrations in the Persian Gulf and implied threats, declared the World Bank report, "To add legal veneer, the British Government petitioned the Court of International Justice at the Hague and the League of Nations in Geneva. The stage was thus set for the negotiation of a new concession that would further water down the old D'Arcy Concession."[50]

On February 7, 1933, Sir John Simon, the British foreign secretary, announced in the House of Commons that the Company and the Persian government would resume direct negotiations, and that all actions before the Council of the League of Nations had been suspended (reported by Ray Atherton). Simon added, "It is further agreed that during the period of negotiations and until a final settlement is reached, the work and operations of the Anglo-Persian Oil Company will continue to be carried on as they were carried on before the 27th November, 1932, that is before the Persian Government claimed to cancel the concession." Atherton concludes:

> The Embassy understands that a compelling reason for the Anglo-Persian Oil Company's willingness to negotiate in private and directly with the Persian Government was the former's fear of the embarrassment which would probably ensue from a public hearing. This arose from the Company's alleged bookkeeping methods. The Persians contend, apparently with justification, that the small royalties paid to the Shah by the Company resulted from the Company's practice of deducting from the profits derived from its operations in Persia the losses which the Company incurred in its Venezuela oil adventure and the expenses connected with the granting of the Iraq concession.[51]

Hart reports that it was officially announced that Sir John Cadman, chairman of the board of directors of APOC, would travel to Tehran to conduct direct negotiations with the Persian government.[52] Cadman left London on March 2 and arrived in Tehran on April 3, 1933 with an impressive team of experts, including W. Fraser, deputy chairman of APOC, and T. L. Jacks, resident director. The Persian negotiators were Taqizadeh, Foroughi, Davar, and Alai. By this time, Persia's most capable negotiator, Teymourtache, was incarcerated in the Persian Bastille.

The 1933 Agreement: A Historic Betrayal

A new concession agreement was signed on April 30, 1933, after only three weeks of negotiations. The initial announcement of a deal was reported by Atherton in London. Although its terms were secret, its main components were as follows: "The new agreement cancels the former 16% basis of royalty and provides for the payment of 4 shillings (gold) per ton on all oil extracted with a minimum of 5,000,000 tons yearly; also that it provides for the payment of £2,000,000 (gold) against outstanding claims and last year's royalty; and that the company receives a thirty years extension of its concession."[53] The concession agreement was voted on by the Majlis on May 28, 1933 on a "doubly urgent basis"—that is, with no debate or discussion. Of the 113 votes, there were 105 yeas. Hart reports, "No explanation was given of the opposing votes or abstentions."[54]

After Majlis ratification, the sum of £4,107,660 was paid by the Company. Of this sum, however, £384,765 consisted of the first and second installments for 1933 royalties. In effect, instead of the £4 million expected, the Persian government had received £3,722,895. Hart observes: "The financial terms of the concession are perhaps more favorable to the Company than initial general foreign, principally British, comment in Teheran is prepared to admit."[55]

What came to be known as the 1933 Agreement was the wholesale adoption of the terms proposed by APOC. The World Bank report notes, "Iran received no consideration for giving up the right, under the D'Arcy Concession to have all of the assets of the Company both in Iran and abroad, turned over to her without financial obligation in 1961. The termination of the D'Arcy Agreement was only twenty-eight years away." Next, under the D'Arcy Concession Iran had a 10 percent ownership in APOC, which was settled for £1 million ($5 million). "Actually, the financial statements of the Company showed assets of book value of £46 million [$230 million] with a real value in excess of $500 million. Thus Iran received not 10% but 1% for its stock ownership."[56]

Subsequently, in reference to the oil nationalization crisis of 1950–53, it has been claimed that under the 1933 Agreement Iran had held an ownership share in the subsidiary companies of AIOC. Thus, by nationalizing AIOC, Mossadeq had "lost" Iran's alleged share in the subsidiary companies. A careful reading of the entire 26 Articles of the 1933 Agreement (a remarkably unambiguous document) does not support the claim. Nowhere is there any indication that Iran held an ownership share in AIOC and its subsidiaries. In fact a main purpose of the cancellation of the D'Arcy Concession was to deprive Iran of its ownership share in the oil company and its subsidiaries. Whatever the pros and cons of nationalization of the Oil Company in 1951, the loss of the subsidiaries was not one of them.[57]

Under the new agreement, in lieu of 16 percent of the profits under the D'Arcy Concession, royalty payment was to be a flat rate of 4 shillings per ton produced. This was supposed to represent an increase in royalty payments. The World Bank report declares, "This increase, however, was more of an illusion than reality. It did not take into consideration the profits on refining and distribution which were subject to royalty under the D'Arcy Concession."[58] Moreover, as duly observed and reported by Hart, APOC's de facto royalty payment to Iran had consisted of 4 shillings per ton for some years, the same as was being paid in Iraq, the D'Arcy Concession notwithstanding. Regardless of any increase in the price of oil, Iran's share remained at 4 shillings per ton. As an inducement, APOC "offered an arrangement under which Iran would receive an additional royalty equal to 20 percent of the amount of dividends declared by the company in excess of $3,356,250 (£671,250)."[59] Next, Iran gave up the right to levy an income tax on APOC for thirty years. In return, APOC agreed to pay 9 pence per ton for the first 6 million tons, and 6 pence for every additional ton for the first fifteen years. The amounts were to increase to 15 pence and 9 pence respectively for the following fifteen years. "These rates," the World Bank notes, "were to be frozen despite what might happen to price levels or company profits over the next thirty years." Next, the duration of the concession was raised by thirty years, to 1993, and the concession area was reduced to 100,000 square miles. "Despite this shrinkage in area, the concession area, which still yielded the Company a monopoly over all the proved reserves, was far too great to be compatible with modern conditions."[60]

In short, the 1933 Agreement was a complete sell-out. The cancellation of the D'Arcy Concession by Reza Shah and its replacement by the 1933 Agreement must be considered his biggest betrayal of Iran and its rights as well as his greatest service to his British masters and protectors. In comparing the two agreements, the World Bank report does not mince words: "Comparison of the terms of the two agreements and the obvious manipulation by the Company of its 1931 financial statement conclusively prove that the alleged 1933 agreement was economically unsound and to the disadvantage of Iran. All factors considered, the new terms appeared patently less favorable to Iran than those of the D'Arcy Concession."[61]

The plunder of Iran translated into vast profits for the Anglo-Iranian Oil Company (AIOC, the new name of the Company after 1935).

> Over 18 years of operation under the 1933 Agreement, prices for petroleum products increased from 200 to 300 percent, while costs tended to decline reflecting operations at the greater volume and improvements in the techniques of production and refining. As a result, AIOC's profits reached unprecedented heights. Thanks to the policy of ploughing its profits into expansion, the AIOC today is the largest Oil Company outside the United States. In total world-wide production, refining, transportation and marketing it is a close second to the Standard Oil Company of New Jersey. This position has been attained by the Company almost entirely from profits on its integrated operations based on Iranian Oil. . . . Despite its incredibly profitable operations the Company displayed an irresistible urge to minimize its obligations in regard to royalty payments and other benefits required by this agreement, and, at every opportunity, to enhance its profits at the expense of Iran.[62]

As an example of this systematic violation of the 1933 Agreement the report cites AIOC's dividend policy. As compensation for a flat rate of 4 shillings per ton irrespective of oil price rises, AIOC had offered Iran a payment, representing 20 percent of distributed dividends, of over £621,250. According to the Company's published accounts, profits increased from $24 million in 1933 to $422 million in 1950. Despite this vast increase in profits, dividends were increased by only $15 million, with the result that Iran's share in any one year was less than $3 million. The World Bank report draws the obvious conclusion: "The Company circumvented the explicit purpose

of this arrangement in order to reduce royalty payments to the lowest possible level." The report repeats time and again that these published profits of
$422 million "do not include all profits because they exclude 59 distributing
subsidiaries and allied companies located outside the United Kingdom." As
for the allocation of this $422 million profits in 1950:

> British income taxes—$142 million, allocation to reserves and carry for-
> ward—$215 million, royalties—$45 million and total dividends—$20 million.
> To repeat, these figures do not include the operations of the Company's sub-
> sidiaries, the profits of which are not published and are therefore unknown. To
> the reviewer not familiar with AIOC practices, AIOC's published statement
> would give an entirely erroneous impression. Profits of [about] $370 million
> after royalties shown by AIOC in 1950 exclude profits on subsidiary and allied
> companies. Moreover, this figure is understated by the amount of discounts on
> sales designed to shift profits to subsidiaries and to the British Government on
> deliveries under the Admiralty Contract, and by concealing profits through
> excessive depreciation charges.[63]

The World Bank report then tries to quantify the amounts Iran had
been deprived of by the British. From 1911 to 1951, total published Company profits had amounted to $5,000 million. Under the D'Arcy Conces-
sion, 16 percent ($800 million) was due in royalties to Iran. For Iran's
10 percent ownership, a 10 percent share of dividends on 50 percent gross
profits is conservatively assumed, or $250 million. Finally, applying the
Iranian income tax rate of 15 percent to the appropriate period and earnings results in a tax liability of $600 million. Total payments to Iran should
have been $1,650 million. Actual payments during 1911–51 came to $450
million. The report concludes that "the Company deprived Iran of some
$1,200 million by failing to perform its obligation in good faith under the
D'Arcy Concession and by engineering its replacement with the unfavorable agreement in 1933."[64] To appreciate the importance of $1,200 million,
remember that Iran's total budget in 1925 was $20 million.

The report is quick to point out that the sums lost to Iran were far
greater than the $1.2 billion noted above because the latter amount was
based on *published* accounts of earnings. In practice, "[t]here appears little
doubt that AIOC's financial statements grossly understate earnings which
are hidden by the following practices: sales to the Admiralty at about cost,
sales to subsidiaries at less than commercial prices thereby shifting profits
to accounts which are not published, and excessive depreciation
allowances charged as costs. While the amounts lost to Iran by these practices cannot be substantiated, its proportion is suggested by the estimated
$500 million discount to the Admiralty and the 1950 depreciation of $168
million deducted as costs."[65] To get a measure of these hidden profits for
1950, the report notes that despite a very liberal cost and depreciation

allowance, "The profits derived from Iranian oil alone amounted to $450 million." Add the profits on tankers and those of the fifty-nine subsidiary distributing companies, and total profits "might run as high as $650 million."[66] Total payments to Iran for 1950 were $45 million, a mere 7 percent of profits.

As described by Hart, after the breakdown of negotiations, Reza Shah had forced the Iranian negotiators to accept the terms proposed by APOC.[67] In a 1950 speech to the Majlis, Seyed Hassan Taqizadeh, the finance minister in 1933, summed up the situation at the time of the signing of the 1933 Agreement: "We were a few helpless men without authority who did not agree with it and we were exceedingly sorry that it had to happen. I must say that I had nothing to do with this matter except that my signature was appended to that Agreement but whether that signature was mine or someone else's it would not have made the slightest difference. What happened would have happened in any case. Personally I did not approve the agreement nor did the others who participated in the negotiations."[68] In fairness to Taqizadeh, his refusal to sign the agreement would have meant certain death, one similar to that of Teymourtache.

The Personal Role of Reza Shah: A Conversation with T. L. Jacks

On the afternoon of May 3, 1933, George Wadsworth, secretary of the American legation, played golf with T. L. Jacks, resident director of the Anglo-Persian Oil Company. As on previous such occasions, playing golf had put Jacks in "a pleasantly communicative frame of mind," and the ensuing conversation details Reza Shah's role in the granting of the new concession to the British. In an earlier dispatch, Hart discusses the rise of Reza Shah from 1921: "The year 1921 had seen the Seyed Zia-ed-Din coup d'état, [and] the beginning of the dramatic rise of Reza Shah. On him the British had counted for the success of their policy. They were not mistaken in his ability to rule."[69]

Perhaps no other document besides Wadsworth's record of his conversation with Jacks better illustrates the role of Reza Shah as an instrument of British policy in Persia. To gain the satisfaction of the British, and for his own personal financial gains, Reza Shah had betrayed the fundamental interests of Persia and its people. Hart's dispatch and its enclosure are given in full:

> I have the honor to enclose a memorandum of an interesting conversation between the Legation's Secretary, Mr. Wadsworth, and Mr. T. L. Jacks, Resident Director of the Anglo-Persian Oil Company, in which the latter recounted certain of the circumstances attending the recent negotiations which resulted in the signature on April 30 of the Company's new concession. I have left untouched the informal style of the memorandum in the thought that, keeping as it does closely to the language used by Mr. Jacks, it best depicts the true

course of the conversation. The dramatis personae referred to therein are, in order of their appearance: Sir John Cadman, A.P.O.C. Board Chairman, W. Fraser, Esq., A.P.O.C. Vice Chairman, Taqizadeh, Persian Finance Minister, Foroughi, Persian Foreign Minister, Dr. V. Idolson, A.P.O.C. Jurisconsult, [and] Davar, Persian Minister of Justice.

Mr. Hart: I played golf with Jacks yesterday afternoon and, as usual, discussed Teheran gossip and the affairs of nations with him afterwards at tea. He raised the question of the A.P.O.C. settlement himself by asking: "What are people saying about it?" I answered that most uninformed comment was to the effect that the Company had been done in the eye but that I differed; that I wondered somewhat if I was right. And would he, I asked, tell me a bit about it? There follows a recapitulation of his reply, my few comments and questions omitted:

Certainly! I've rather wanted to tell you about it, now it is over; but not, please, for spreading about just yet. Personally, I think you are quite right. I am satisfied, and I am sure the Persians are. I consider, too, that we have signed a concession essentially beneficial, as you say, to both sides. The Shah gets what he wanted from the start, an assurance of steady income. The new agreement should net him a royalty at least some 40 per cent better than the average of the last four years, including 1932. We, in our turn, get a thirty-odd year extension of our concession. We clear up all past difficulties and claims. We start again with a clean slate. We are paying a fair price for it. And I can't see any reason why it won't work out as we hope and expect.

One interesting thing is that I am more than ever convinced I was quite right in urging on London the need for holding the conference here. There was a time when the negotiations had broken down flatly. We just couldn't agree. If we hadn't been here; if we couldn't have gone directly to the Shah; if he hadn't taken the matter in his own hands: we should have failed and we should have had to go back to Geneva. There no one can tell what would have happened. At least, there would have been months more of discussion and delay.

It was on April 24. Our position from the start was that of a buyer. We said, in effect: "What have you to give? Let us know your terms. Then we can discuss them." They hedged, of course; tried to get us to make an offer. But we stuck to our guns. Finally, after 15 days they presented a project. Frankly, it was fantastic and impossible of fulfillment. They had included such points as a requirement that we produce an annual minimum of 6,000,000 tons, to increase progressively to 10,000,000, and grant them share participation in the Company, directors, and what not. We answered in 48 hours.

Cadman, as you know, kept out of the picture, leaving all the meetings and discussion to Fraser. He was brilliant in his presentation of our reply; answered every article point by point; showed them we couldn't possibly accept. Taqizadeh, however, was adamant; fought tooth and nail for every point, phrase and word of their draft. He was honest but so unwilling to yield an inch that finally we saw it was no go. I advised we could only succeed if we called their bluff. So Fraser made his "final" speech: "We were sorry; direct negotiations had failed; we parted good friends; we would find another way; and all that." Then the planes were ordered up for a trial flight preparatory to leaving, and we actually would have left had there been no change.

Cadman, too, on my advice, asked through Fraser and Foroughi for an audience with the Shah, to say good-bye. Foroughi was hesitant, but Cadman insisted he must at least pay his respects before leaving, and the interview was granted. It couldn't, as I thought, well be refused. Foroughi telephoned me at eight that evening, the 24th. Had he not done so, Cadman, et al. would have left the next morning. The audience was the next morning. What happened can be boiled down to this: Cadman actually said good-bye and that he was sorry the negotiations had failed. And to that the Shah replied: "But I won't have it." Then they got down to whys and wherefores. Cadman told him what we were prepared to give. It was, and I was convinced of it, essentially what the Shah wanted, if not in the form his ministers and experts recommended. The result was that the Shah met that afternoon with Taqizadeh and Foroughi, Cadman and Fraser. At that meeting they went through the whole business of the negotiations. The Shah *ordered* agreement along the lines of our counter proposals. He recognized they were essentially sound and made in a spirit of wishing to meet his views and wishes.

So the negotiations started again. But again, after several days, we met a snag; two of them in fact: area and duration of the concession. So, again, Cadman went to the Shah. He had, he said, been at first most pleased with the second phase of the negotiations. Whereas at first we had met nothing but obstructionism on every side and on every point, now we saw a clear possibility of success. Only two points remained to be settled. They were—in just about ten minutes. The Shah gave his orders. We met again on the 28th. All was settled. The Shah was told, approved and went off to Mazandaran the following morning. The next day—and evening up till two o'clock—we spent putting finishing touches on the drafting. It is really an excellent piece of work; and I have to hand it wholeheartedly to Idolson that he is the ablest attorney I have ever seen work—equally at home in four or five languages and keen as they come. Even Davar would turn to Idolson and say on a discussed point of his own: "Well then you draft it." Of the signature you know. You missed the champagne supper, but you didn't miss much, for we were fagged to a frazzle, all of us.

But remember one thing or, better, two. The first is that it was the Shah and only the Shah that made settlement possible; for, without him, we should still be talking—or back home with nothing at all accomplished. The second is— and you can tell it safely to your people at home—that we have done a really good job of work in the interest of the petroleum industry at large.

There Jacks' "speech" ended. It was made in all sincerity. He was really proud of the job and its doing. As "Political Adviser" he has, I think, a right to be. And, concluding, he again asked that we consider his remarks, at least for the time being, as strictly confidential. He didn't, he explained, want the idea to get about that the Company was overpleased; for, were it to do so, there might, perhaps, be some slip—though he couldn't see any real possibility of it—in getting the

Majlis ratification. After all, he explained, Persians are still Persians and if they get the idea the Company thinks it has the better of the deal they will want to start negotiations all over again.[70]

The Temporary Adjustment of August 1940 and the Transfer of Royalties to New York

The new concession operated seemingly to the satisfaction of both sides until 1940. In that year, when it was announced that due to the outbreak of World War II and the loss of the European markets, royalties for 1939 would be about £750,000—the minimum under the 1933 Agreement and considerably less than those of the preceding years (about £2.5 million for 1937)—reports of new difficulties between the Iranian government and the Company began to circulate. In a July 1940 dispatch, the American chargé d'affaires ad interim, C. Van H. Engert, who had also served in Iran from 1920 to 1922, reports that relations between the two sides had reached an acute stage that could easily end in an open breach.[71] Ostensibly, the Iranians were complaining that the Company was restricting production and thereby reducing the payments of royalties to Iran.

Another point the Iranian government was secretly demanding is revealed in a confidential telegram from Engert in which he had reported his conversation with the British minister. The matter concerned "the transfer of the oil royalties from England to the United States at favorable rate" of exchange.[72] In a series of confidential telegrams, Engert elaborates:

> Minister of Finance has now officially informed the Anglo-Iranian Oil Company that royalties must be paid on the basis of highest past production and be annually increased irrespective of actual production. Also Iranian funds now in London and future royalties must be converted into dollars at a more favorable rate than market or all funds be converted into gold. Unless these demands are complied with the concession will be canceled.[73]

On July 29 he offers:

> I learn in strictest confidence that the British Government has expressed willingness to permit transfer of funds from England to America at the official rate but not to exceed 3,000,000 pounds sterling per annum prorated monthly. The company has refused to consider any new basis for payment of royalties but would be prepared to make advances to help the Iranian Government during the war. Incidentally when the British Government and the company pointed out that the concession specifically provided for arbitration of all disputes the Minister of Finance replied coolly that the Iranian Government would not feel bound by any arbitral award![74]

On August 22, Engert reports:

I am reliably informed that the Anglo-Persian Oil Company has agreed to pay royalties based on highest production in recent years irrespective of output. Agreement to this effect was signed yesterday but I understand with the proviso that it was a temporary arrangement which could not serve as a precedent nor modify the terms of the concession. The actions of the Iranian Government closely resemble blackmail and the local press has contained nothing but ill informed criticism and grotesque distortions of the truth.[75]

It turned out that this blackmail of the British in their desperate hour in 1940 was one that the British never forgave Reza Shah.

More specific information on the final settlement is provided in Engert's September 2 dispatch:

The net result of the negotiations has been that the Government will receive £1,500,000 in addition to the royalties it has already received for the years 1938 and 1939, and will receive £4,000,000, in round figures, for each of the years 1940 and 1941. This sum is reached by taking the peak year 1937 as a basis and adding thereto, more or less arbitrarily, a sum estimated to represent the drop in the value of the pound. On the other hand, the Company has received a written assurance that this special arrangement does not affect the terms of the concession. How much value may be attached to the undertaking remains to be seen.[76]

Engert then provided a key piece of information, designated by the State Department "strictly confidential—not for publication":

Although the question of the conversion into dollars of sterling funds derived from royalties was constantly injected into the negotiations by the Iranian Government, the Company refused to have anything to do with it and referred the authorities to the British Government. As stated in my telegram No. 179, July 29, 8 p.m., the British Government has already consented to the conversion of not more than £3,000,000 per annum at the official rate. I understand that this is to be transferred to Ottawa and there turned into gold to be available for Iranian purchases in the United States.[77]

As documented below, immediately after the signing of the "temporary adjustment" to the concession, Iran's oil revenue was transferred to Ottawa, where it was turned into gold and subsequently transferred to the Irving Trust Company of New York. Thereafter, the gold melted away without a trace.

CHAPTER TEN

The Reserve Fund of the Nation and the Plunder of Iran's Oil Revenues by Reza Shah, 1927–1941

O N SEPTEMBER 30, 1941, JUST TWO DAYS AFTER Reza Shah had departed Iran, a one-article law was enacted by the Majlis. A report by the American minister Louis G. Dreyfus Jr. confirms that Iran's oil revenues and the supposed reserve fund to which they had been paid were not under the control of the Iranian government. Moreover, Iran's annual oil revenues were not part of the government's regular budget (see fig. 10.1).

> The revenues and royalties from the Anglo-Iranian Oil Company have been, as the Department knows, paid into a special reserve fund and have not been included in the regular budget. The fund was always operated secretly, although the public was usually informed when the annual budget was presented to the Majlis that certain sums from the reserve fund were being expended for the army, for road building, or other purposes. The purpose of this law, therefore, is to bring the revenues and the fund within the regular budget of the country, certainly a necessary action if the Iranian Government intends to establish a proper budget to replace the former misleading and meaningless figures.[1]

Dreyfus's report then indicates the amount of oil revenues paid by the Anglo-Iranian Oil Company from 1927 to 1941 and what became of that money. Basically, since the revenues were not part of the budget, no one

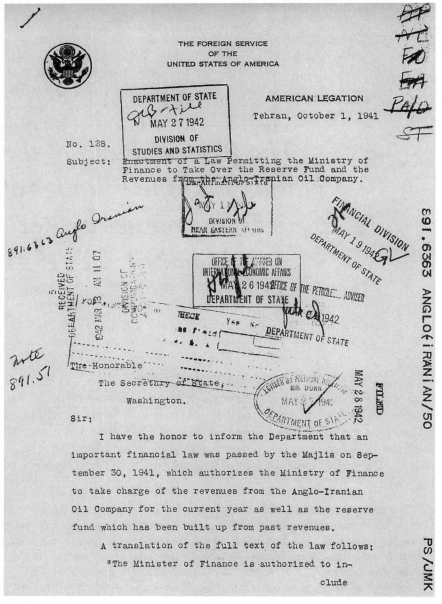

FIGURE 10.1 *Dispatch from Louis G. Dreyfus Jr., American legation, October 1, 1941, confirming that oil revenues during Reza Shah's reign were not under the control of the Iranian government.*

knew what had become of them. For fourteen years the people had been kept in ignorance about what was described as their "most valuable economic asset."

> Figures on the Iranian reserve fund were for the first time made public in the Majlis in discussing the above quoted law. It was revealed by Deputy Etebar, reporter for the budget committee, that the fund had earned in the fourteen years of its operation £31,000,000, of which £27,000,000 have been spent and £3,000,000 used for the purchase of gold. There is a present balance, he says, of £1,300,000 after deducting £600,000 of current obligation against the fund. Although Mr. Etebar's arithmetic is far from perfect, it is believed that £1,300,000 may be taken to represent the official figure of the present reserve fund balance. The reporter for the budget committee said that he did not know how the £27,000,000 were spent and he could only wish that more of it had been used to purchase gold. It would appear, if the above figures may be accepted as authentic, that the income from the Anglo-Iranian Oil Company has averaged more than £2,000,000 a year during the past fourteen years. The Government still does not reveal the amount of current revenues from this source but the Legation is reliably informed that it amounts to £4,000,000 annually for the current and past year.[2]

Commenting on this law in a subsequent dispatch, Dreyfus states, "The Majlis by a law of September 30 took possession of the annual oil royalties and of the reserve fund of the State, which had formerly been a plaything of Shah Reza outside the regular budget."[3]

This chapter will describe how £20–30 million—that is, the bulk of Iran's oil revenues during 1927–41—were diverted to Reza Shah's bank accounts in Europe and the United States on the pretext of buying armaments. We also know that this money had been inherited by Reza Shah's son and successor, Mohammad Reza Pahlavi. State Department records (given below) reveal that Mohammad Reza Pahlavi had a bank account in London in the 1950s that contained in excess of £20 million. The British had blocked this money, and the shah was unable to convert it into dollars or Swiss francs. But this is running ahead of our story.

How the bulk of the £27 million mentioned in Dreyfus's report ($135 million, a vast sum by the standards of the day) was appropriated and supposedly spent on "military purchases" will be documented below. Thanks to American military intelligence and legation reports, we have a complete inventory of Iranian military equipment purchased during 1927–41 (down to the number of light machine guns possessed by each regiment). From the American legation's reports on financial matters we are able to construct a complete list of appropriations from the Reserve Fund.

The sums indicated were certainly not used to purchase arms. As outlined below, the price of the most advanced American warplane in 1941 was $70,000 (including a weapons system and even the cost of providing mechanics for servicing the machine), and the most advanced tank in the American arsenal was $20,000. If the money had been spent on armaments, Iran could have had a large number of the most advanced warplanes and tanks. In 1941, Iran had 200 modern British-made warplanes and 100 tanks made in Czechoslovakia. Its supplies of artillery ammunition were barely sufficient for one day's fighting. As documented below, Iran's "new" navy, on which allegedly large sums had been spent, consisted of reconditioned ships and those that had been made out of scrap metal. Not even the engines on these ships were new. The spokesman for the Majlis commission charged with examining oil revenues during Reza Shah's regime frankly admitted that the commission had no idea how £27 million (out of £31 million) had been spent.

What follows is an attempt to describe the appropriation of this sum. The chapter begins by first describing the establishment of the sterling Reserve Fund of the Nation referred to in Dreyfus's dispatch. The Reserve Fund operated from 1927 to 1941, and it was through this mechanism that Iran's oil revenues (the £27 million not accounted for) were diverted to Reza Shah's personal bank accounts in Europe and America.

The Sterling Reserve Fund of the Nation

With oil production rising after 1925, oil royalties increased substantially as well. Output in 1922 was 2.3 million tons and rose to about 5.5 million tons in the late 1920s. In 1927, royalties exceeded £1.4 million ($7 million), a sizable sum at the time. The *Twentieth Quarterly Report of the Administrator General of Finance* states:

> The royalties of the Anglo-Persian Oil Company during this year amount to £1,400,000 or nearly Krs. 70,000,000, while dues from the same source have been estimated at Krs. 44,000,000 in the budget of 1306. The Government is confident that the decrease in tax revenues will be made up from the same source, and has therefore deposited the Royalties received from the Anglo-Persian Oil Company with the Imperial Bank of Persia in London at a rate of 4{fr}7/16{fr}% interest, and up to this moment when we are approaching the end of the year, the Government has not been in the necessity of spending more than £200,000 of the Sterling deposit.[4]

Table 5 of the same report shows that oil royalty payment for 1927 amounted to £1,453,567.14.0, and that this sum was deposited with the London branch of the Imperial Bank of Persia (IBP). According to table 8 of the report, the distribution in the five different accounts was:

Treasury General Ordinary Sterling No. 1 account I.B.P.,
    London £500,000.0.0

Treasury General Ordinary Sterling No. 2 account I.B.P.,
  London £400,000.0.0
Treasury General Ordinary Sterling No. 3 account I.B.P.,
  London £300,000.0.0
Treasury General Sterling Account I.B.P., London £65,734.5.7
Trust Account I.B.P., London £200,000.0.0

Depositing the oil revenues in London was a radical departure from past practice. Prior to 1927 the oil royalties had been paid in sterling by APOC into the London branch of the IBP, and the funds had been subsequently transferred to Persia. From 1927, the funds were no longer transferred to Persia but instead were kept in London as a reserve fund. The other radical departure from past practice consisted of separating the oil revenues from the regular budget. Henceforth, oil revenues were no longer regarded as regular government revenue, and did not enter into normal budgetary affairs. For the next fourteen years, for all practical purposes, Persia was a non-oil economy. Moreover, whereas up to 1927 the oil royalty payments had been regularly published and announced by the Persian government, until 1941 they were not published by the government.

No wonder Reza Shah was so anxious to be rid of Millspaugh and the American financial advisers. The *Twenty-First Quarterly Report of the Administrator General of Finance* declares:

> In spite of the fall in the revenues of certain items given in detail above, it is a source of keen satisfaction to state that the country's finances in 1306 have been managed in such a manner that at the end of the year, in addition to other economies, which will be given in detail later on, a surplus of £1,200,000 [about 6 million tomans], the amount of which has never had a precedent in the Finances of Persia, has come to existence. It is now the second period of 6 months that the above sum is deposited with the Imperial Bank of Persia in London at a per annum interest of 4 7/16%. At the end of the first six months' period a sum of nearly £30,000 was obtained by the Treasury as interest on the above deposit. In the previous report a hint was given as to the probable existence of such a surplus, but in this report we are in a position to assert definitely that the above mentioned amount can be considered as a decisive surplus of 1306, which has been economized at the end of the year after payment of the whole of the expenses of the country.[5]

The Twenty-Third Quarterly Report, covering the period from March 21 to September 22, 1928, one year after Millspaugh's departure, states:

> Notwithstanding the fact that the Ministry of Finance has not yet benefited from the Anglo-Persian Oil Company royalties due in 1306 (which sum is deposited with sure banks as Public Reserve Fund); and in spite of the fact that during the first six months, it has not received its share of this period from the same royalties due in 1307 (1928/29), yet all State expenses have been

punctually paid. Although the revenue derived from oil royalties in 1306, which comparatively is an important item in State revenues, was transferred to 1307, and although the State budget, which was voted during this Semester, compared with previous budgets has a much greater weight, yet without any need of the oil royalties, the Ministry of Finance has succeeded to secure the payment and actually pay the approved State expenses by means of the development which has taken place in sources of other State revenues and by means of increase obtained from them.[6]

The retention of the oil revenues in London and their exclusion from the budget and budgetary control had been controversial from the beginning. The American diplomats took special care to point out that the budget figures did not include the oil royalties. They also revealed that henceforth allocations from the London Reserve Fund would be through special appropriations voted on by the Majlis, usually on the double urgency basis—that is, with no discussion of the subject. In a report on the budget of 1308 (1929/30), American consul Augustin W. Ferrin points out:

> The ordinary budget does not include the large royalties from the Anglo-Persian Oil Company which will constitute a Treasury Reserve in sterling estimated at £2,826,146 (equivalent at Krans 48.00 to the pound to Krans 125,655,000). Addendum. Since the foregoing was written the Minister of Finance has asked the Parliament to authorize an advance from the Reserve Fund to the Ministry of War of Krans 60,000,000. The Minister of Finance stated that the advance of Krans 60,000,000 to the Ministry of War would be restored to the Reserve Fund by means of economies in the 1929–30 and 1930–31 budgets, but he had previously said that the expenditures already estimated for 1929–30 could not be reduced.[7]

In a subsequent report, Ferrin reveals that of a total expenditure of 349,452,601 krans, nearly half (157,550,107 krans) was spent on the army, police, and gendarmerie. An additional appropriation of 60 million krans was made by the Majlis out of the nation's sterling Reserve Fund maintained in London for the purpose of "purchasing and completing the munitions of the army." Thus the total appropriated to the military and security establishments was 217,550,107 krans, nearly two-thirds (62%) of all government expenditures. In contrast, the total allocated to the Ministry of Public Instruction was 18,483,755 krans, one-twentieth of the total budget, and one-twelfth of the military and security expenditure.[8]

In the Iran of Reza Khan education and culture had little weight, rhetoric and propaganda notwithstanding. Ferrin's report lists 1 million krans as "advances to the cultivators of crown lands." In other words, Reza Shah not only confiscated private property, but the advances to his cultivators had to come from the public purse (table 10.1)! Ferrin also informs us that total revenues amounted to 301,124,040 krans. Thus the government was faced with a deficit of nearly 50 million krans (£1 million), which could have been easily covered from the oil royalties. However, Ferrin reminds us,

> The budget as above stated does not include royalties received from the Anglo-Persian Oil Company deposited in London in sterling and regarded as a Treasury Reserve Fund. It is estimated that this fund will amount on March 21, 1930, the end of the fiscal year, to pounds sterling 2,826,146, equivalent to Krans 125,655,008. From it the Parliament, in approving the budget, authorized an advance to the military establishment of Krans 60,000,000, which will reduce the reserve as of March 21, 1930, to Krans 65,655,008. The military is pledged to return the whole advance by March 21, 1931.[9]

The retention of the oil royalties in London, compared to the previous practice of converting the sterling funds into Krans, resulted in a catastrophic decline in the foreign exchange value of the kran from 1929. Its consequences for the Iranian economy were disastrous. Except for small sums, the Persian government was unwilling to draw on the sterling balances in order to support the kran. Nevertheless, Teymourtache claimed that the maintenance of the Reserve Fund in London had a stabilizing effect on the exchange value of the kran (see chapter 14).

Military Appropriations from the Sterling Reserve Fund, 1928–1941

The American minister, Hoffman Philip, discusses the passage of a supplemental law to the budget of 1308 (1929/30): "I have the honor to report that the Budget law voted on March 17, 1929, contained authorization to withdraw 6,000,000 Tomans from the 'reserve funds of the nation' for the purchase of arms and ammunition. The reserve funds mentioned are of course the accrued royalties paid by the Anglo-Persian Oil Company and

TABLE 10.1. Selected items of expenditure, 1929/30 budget (in krans)

Ministry of War	
General budget	98,000,000
Arsenal and air	25,000,000
Purchase and repair of boats	4,000,000
Police	17,538,507
Gendarmerie	13,011,600
Ministry of Public Instruction	18,483,755
Advances to cultivators of crown lands	1,000,000

Source: A. W. Ferrin, report on the budget of 1308 (1929–30) (891.51/421), March 30, 1929.

deposited in London. 6,000,000 Tomans is equivalent to approximately £1,132,000."[10] Philip includes the text of a supplement to the budget bill for 1930, passed on March 17, 1929:

> In view of the urgent need felt for completing the Army's munitions it is respectfully requested that the following note be inserted at the end of Article 2 of the Budget Bill of the Empire for the year 1308 (1929). *Note*: Out of precautionary reserve funds of the Nation the Ministry of Finance is authorized to place the sum of six million tomans at the disposal of the Ministry of War in order to prepare and complete the munitions of the army. The Ministry of Finance will reimburse this sum to the reserve fund of the Empire through the savings to be effected in the general budget of the country in the year 1308 and 1309 [March 21, 1929, to March 21, 1930, and March 21, 1930, to March 20, 1931].[11]

The supposed savings and reimbursement never materialized. The above procedure was to become the mechanism by which at least £25 million ($125 million) in oil revenues was to be appropriated and spent on arms purchases, railways, and ports from 1929 to 1941. Moreover, thanks to the astute reporting of Hart, we can be confident that much of the £1,132,000 voted for arms purchases in 1929–30 went into Reza Shah's personal bank accounts.

In September 1931, Britain suspended the convertibility of sterling into gold, in effect devaluing the pound. Hart records Reza Shah's response to the news of the devaluation:

> First word of the suspension of the gold standard by the British Government, I have the honor to report, reached Teheran just one week ago. The result has been financial chaos. The Shah, as already reported, was on a tour of the northern provinces. When, telegraphed to him from Teheran, the news reached him at Kermanshah, he is reported to have lost entire control of himself and his temper, to have cursed the British, his advisers, his entourage and himself, to have ended by having an apoplectic stroke. The reason, it was said was obvious. Not only is it generally recognized that the Persian Government has banked abroad in sterling deposits some four to five million pounds, but the Shah is also credited with having himself banked more than a million abroad. Thirty per cent of all this gone in a flash of an eye! It was too much.[12]

That the bulk of the money had gone into Reza Shah's account was subsequently confirmed in a dispatch by George Wadsworth, secretary of the American legation. On March 10, 1932, a special bill was approved by the Majlis appropriating £1.5 million from the Reserve Fund for the purchase of munitions. Wadsworth notes that it was the second law of its kind, the first being that of March 17, 1929, in which, as stated above, about £1.2 million was appropriated: "The principal purchases under the former law were 100,000 new rifles and a small number (probably not over 300) of sub-machine guns of Czechoslovak manufacture and small quantities of ammunition of Czechoslovak and French manufacture." Wadsworth reported that on the basis of conversations with French and Czech officials, the material had been delivered to the Persian government in 1930 and 1931 and no additional orders had been received. But he also says that Persian customs statistics show imports of 80,000 krans (£1,500) from France and 21,400,000 (£350,000) from Czechoslovakia, the implication being that the remaining £800,000 had not been spent on armaments but, as suspected by Hart, had been transferred to Reza Shah's account.[13]

For the year 1309 (1930/31) Consul Henry S. Villard reports that Persian government revenues totaled $28,613,346, and expenditures were $28,582,006. Villard also points out that, "the budget does not include the Anglo-Persian Oil Company royalties which are held as a treasury reserve fund in European banks and which are thought to amount this year to between 1,250,000 and 1,500,000 pounds sterling." Villard also reports, "It is reported that approximately one million pounds sterling have been assigned for the purchase of ammunition and other war materials, chiefly Czech-Slovakia. This sum, which is rumored to have been borrowed against the oil royalties, does not appear in the budget, nor is it known how many other items of expenditure have been similarly disguised."[14] In all, the $7–$8 million in oil revenues amounted to more than a quarter of the government budget.

In a subsequent dispatch, Hart reports that by the spring of 1931 the government had about £4 million on hand in London. The following figures were supplied to Hart by R. E. Lingeman, commercial attaché to the British legation. On March 30, 1929, the government had more than £1.9 million in London, composed of royalties for 1926–27 amounting to more than £1.3 million, and for 1927–28 amounting to about £600,000, plus a small sum from the Sugar and Tea Monopoly fund. Another £500,000 was paid on account of the 1928 royalties (APOC having changed its fiscal year). Of this total, £1 million was allocated for military purchases (referred to in Villard's report), leaving a balance of £1.4 million. Adding the royalties for the twelve months ending December 31, 1929, the balance becomes £2,650,000. Assuming that the 1930 royalties remained the same as those of 1929, the government had about £4 million ($20 million), a sum equal to 70 percent of the total budget for the year 1930/31.[15]

Despite the availability of this vast sum in London, Hart reports that government salaries were months behind. To pay the salaries, the government borrowed 3 million tomans from Bank Melli and said that the rumors that the government was going to draw on the London fund to pay the salaries of its workers were inaccurate.[16]

Wadsworth reports that from the British and French military attachés it was learned that the purpose of the new £1.5 million appropriation was to

purchase airplanes, ammunition, and a supply of machine and subma-
chine guns. Wadsworth reminds us that this sterling allocation is not
included in the regular army allocation that last year amounted to 44% of
the regular budget. Wadsworth also informs us that £390,000 had been
appropriated in October 1931 for the purchase of four navy ships in Italy.
According to his estimates, the reserves in London were estimated at
£4,500,000 before these appropriations. Consequently, these new appropriation constituted 40 percent of the reserves.[17]

Hart reveals that the London funds were decimated and that the naval
appropriation was raised by another £390,000, to £780,000. As reported by
Hart, on March 21, 1931, the reserve fund contained £2,993,000, and with
£1=$4.86, it amounted to about $14,500,000. Almost two years later, it had
fallen to $6,500,000 (table 10.2).[18] The balance in the fund was £1.9 mil-
lion. However, with the devaluation of the pound sterling (the new rate
was £1 = $3.44), this came to $6.5 million. Thanks to the financial genius
of Reza Khan and his advisers, a balance of nearly $22 million had been
reduced to $6.5 million. In addition, while large sums were being spent on
the military and the police, not only were government salaries months
behind, but education was being starved of funds.

Hart later reports that for 1312 (1933/34), the Ministry of War's budgetary appropriation (not including the appropriation from the reserve
fund) was 210 million rials, or 40 percent of the entire budget. The appropriation of the Ministry of Interior was 48 million rials, of which half was
allotted to the police. In contrast, the total education allocation was 41 million rials, or 8 percent of the budget.[19]

Following the 1933 oil concession with Britain, William H. Hornibrook,
Hart's successor as American minister in Tehran, reports that a credit of £2
million was provided out of the London reserve fund "for purchases of

TABLE 10.2. Payments into and withdrawals from the
London "Reserve Fund of the Nation"

Credits	
Balance as of 3/21/1931	£2,993,000
1930 royalty, paid after 3/20/1931	£1,228,000
1931 royalty, paid in 1932	£307,000
Total	£4,528,000
Debits	
Army appropriation from 1929 (1308)	£348,000
Navy appropriations, 1931 and 1932	£780,000
Army appropriation, 1932	£1,500,000
Total	£2,628,000

Source: Charles C. Hart, dispatch 1357 (891.51/463),
February 20, 1933.

new military equipment." He also comments, "The correspondent of the London *Times* in Persia, Mr. Hicks, has informed Mr. Childs, Secretary of the Legation, that the Government has spent at least £10,000,000 on the army since the advent of the present Shah, that is to say, since 1921."[20] A report by the National Bank of Persia explains that these high military expenditures "correspond to the enormous tasks imposed by the immense extent of the territory and the frontiers of Persia." The following items were excluded from the regular budget revenues: oil royalties received from the Anglo-Persian Oil Company, receipts of the Sugar and Tea Monopoly fund, revenues of the road tax, and revenue from the Caspian fisheries concession, stated to be 9 million rials per year.[21]

APOC royalties for 1933 were reported to be £1,785,013. When added to the £3,772,895 received under the May 1933 concession, the total sterling payment for the year into the reserve fund was £5,507,905. Adding the £1,900,000 balance from 1932, the sum came to £7,407,905, or about $35 million (the dollar had since been devalued and the previous exchange rate of £1 = $5 had been restored). This exceeded the total domestic revenues of the Iranian government. It is also clear that by 1936–37, the money had vanished. As described below, in 1936, the national bank did not possess sufficient foreign exchange to meet its drafts and obligations in foreign currency. Hornibrook reports that in the 1934/35 budget, another £2 million had been set aside for the purchase of armaments abroad:

As previously, the budget of the Ministry of War makes the greatest proportional drain on the public Treasury, the amounts allotted that Ministry in the general budget comprising a total of 232,934,980 rials, as compared with 209,934,980 rials in 1933–34, an increase of 23,000,000 rials. In 1312 [1933–34] expenditures on the Ministry of War and the Road Guards constituted 41.22 per cent of the budget. While, in 1313 [1934–35] this proportion, in the general budget, is only 37.52 per cent, it should be noted that, in addition to the sums earmarked in the general budget for the military establishment, the law enacting the budget provides for the setting aside by the Ministry of Finance of no less than £2,000,000 from the Reserve Fund of the State "for the purchase and improvement of military stores for the Army." Were this sum included in the budget, the expenditure authorized for the Ministry of War and the Road Guards would represent no less than 50 per cent of the budget, or in dollars some $14,558,436 plus £2,000,000, a total of approximately $25,000,000. The large appropriation of £2,000,000 for the purchase of military supplies is believed to envisage the purchase of some eighty or more airplanes for the air force, as well as providing a sum for the continuance of the Government's policy of completely modernizing its military equipment.

Such an expenditure may be even more clearly viewed in perspective and in relation to the budget of the State as a whole when it is remarked that the sum allotted for all purposes of education in the new budget represents only 7.4 per

cent of the entire budget, as compared with 8 per cent for a like purpose in
1933–34 and this, notwithstanding that the new budget includes new items of
2,000,000 rials for the purchase of land and building of a university and
1,000,000 rials for the construction of secondary schools. The relatively large
proportion of the public revenues devoted to military expenditures and a corresponding marked paucity of revenue for the education of a population
marked by one of the largest proportions of illiteracy in the world, as well as the
continued absence of provisions for the improvement of public hygiene or the
making available of a suitable water supply in the capital, where neither a
sewage nor a water works system exists, alike reflect upon and adequately dis-
tinguish the character of the budget under review.[22]

Total receipts for the 1935/36 budget were estimated at 751,123,487 rials
and expenditures authorized were 750,872,790 rials, or about $55.2 mil-
lion. However, the revenues excluded the Anglo-Persian oil royalties
deposited in London, Sugar and Tea Monopoly tax earmarked for railway
construction, and the road tax allocated for highway construction and
maintenance. The expenditure figures, Hornibrook declares,

> are not representative of the complete budgetary accounts for the reason
> that on March 14, 1935, in the supplementary budget voted by the Majlis no
> less than £2,705,000 was appropriated from the Reserve Fund for various extra-
> ordinary expenditures, including £2,000,000 for the Ministry of War, £600,000
> for railway construction, £80,000 for the payment of installments falling due
> for the sugar refineries, and £25,000 to the Government as a credit for
> unknown purposes. If these amounts are converted at the current rate of the
> pound sterling of 65 rials the budgetary expenditures envisaged for 1935–1936
> are increased by 175,825,000 rials to 926,762,790 rials. It may be added, for
> purposes of comparison, that a similar credit of £2,000,000 was voted in
> 1934–35 from the Reserve Fund for the Ministry of War. As previously, the
> budget of the Ministry of War makes the greatest proportional drain on the
> public Treasury. As in the previous year, however, a sum of £2,000,000 is set
> aside from the Reserve Fund especially earmarked for the needs of the Ministry
> of War. If this and other sums allotted from the Reserve Fund in pounds ster-
> ling be added to the general budget, and the two million pound appropriation,
> representing 130,000,000 rials be added (to the allotment of the Ministry of
> War), the resultant sum of 379,408,380 rials will be found to represent 40.9 per
> cent of expenditures appearing in the general and supplementary budgets.
>
> The relatively important sums on which the Government may count in
> royalties from the Anglo-Iranian Oil Company annually alone make possible
> the large sums which continue to be expended on the army. Similarly, the
> heavy monopoly taxes imposed on three of the most important items entering
> into the import trade of the country, namely, sugar, tea, and cotton textiles,
> make possible the pouring of millions of rials into so unproductive an enter-
> prise as the Trans-Iranian Railway or into industrial enterprises which may be

long in yielding returns in any way commensurate with the amounts expended on them.[23]

Despite the deteriorating economic conditions, Gordon P. Merriam, chargé d'affaires ad interim, reports that in the 1936/37 (1315) budget, while the customary allocation of £2 million for the purchase of armaments had continued, the railway appropriation had been increased. A Supplementary Budget Law provided for the following sterling allocations from the Reserve Fund: Ministry of War, £2 million; Ministry of Roads and Communications, £1 million; Ministry of Industry (installments for the purchase of sugar factories), £80,000. As discussed below, there was an acute shortage of foreign exchange in 1936; consequently, in the 1937/38 budget, there was no army appropriation out of the reserve funds. But the railway appropriation had continued at the same level.[24]

In the 1937/38 (1316) budget ordinary revenues were $78,125,138 and expenditures were $78,001,984. Supplementary budget revenues are not given, but Merriam lists allocations totaling $20 million: "It will be observed that as in previous years, receipts are not given in the supplementary budget. In consequence the estimated returns in the form of royalties from the Anglo-Iranian Oil Company which are banked in the state sterling reserve fund in London, are unavailable." The Supplementary Budget Law allocated £1 million to "cover the deficit for the construction of the Trans-Iranian railways." No sterling appropriation for Ministry of War was reported.[25]

Merriam's successor, C. Van H. Engert, reports that although figures on oil royalties for the 1938/39 (1317) budget, as usual, are not given, the 1936 figure obtained from a reliable source was £2,358,000. The appropriation for the army from the Reserve Fund is the customary £2 million, as provided by Article 3 of the Supplementary Budget Law: "The Ministry of Finance is authorized to pay two million pounds sterling for the requirements of the army out of the reserve funds of the country, the use of this sum not being limited to one fiscal year." The £800,000 assigned as a loan to the Ministry of Roads and Communications for budget year 1935–36 was now declared to be a definite expenditure.[26]

For the 1939/40 (1318) budget Engert reveals that for the past two years, oil royalties had averaged £2.5 million per year. For the current budget the army appropriation out of the Reserve Fund was £2 million, and £1 million was allocated "for railways and the ports of Bandar Shah and Bandar Shahpour." This was despite the fact that the Trans-Iranian railway was completed in 1938 and was in operation.[27]

In his report on the budget for 1319 (1940/41) Engert lists the expected £2 million allotment for the army. However, due to a decline in oil royalties, the usual £1 million for railways had been omitted. Engert concludes his report with the following observation:

> The weakness of all Iranian budgets is that the public is never informed on the workings of the previous budgets, and therefore to what extent the Government has been successful in meeting its estimates is never known. It should be observed, however, that in commenting on the Iranian budget observers are handicapped by the fact that there is no such thing as free parliamentary debate—the budget being unanimously approved each year by the Majlis without question or objection or critical comment—and the local press, far from examining the law judiciously, only falls over itself in its efforts to heap praise on the budget, Iran, and His Imperial Majesty the Shah.[28]

The report on Reza Shah's last budget, that of 1320 (1941/42), was written by Dreyfus, the American minister in Tehran. The army appropriation remained the same at £2,000,000 and the usual £1,000,000 for railway construction and maintenance had been restored. Dreyfus draws the obvious conclusion from these figures in relation to the adjustment to the August 1940 oil concession, that the army and railway appropriations from the Reserve Fund was the same amount the British government had agreed to convert into dollars, transferable to banks in New York:

> It should be observed that the royalties from the Anglo-Iranian Oil Company, which are understood to amount to £4,000,000, have, as in the past, been paid into a sterling reserve fund and not included in the budget as revenue. However, two items of expenditure have been charged against this reserve account, £2,000,000 for the needs of the Army and £1,000,000 for railway construction and maintenance. In connection with this sterling reserve fund it is interesting to observe here that the British Government has granted permission to the Iranian Government to convert up to £3,000,000 a year of its oil revenues into dollars.[29]

Dreyfus's remarks came after reports that Reza Shah was transferring large sums to American banks. Moreover, as demonstrated below, by 1941, numerous agencies of the American government, including the Federal Bureau of Investigation and the State Department, were fully aware that large sums were being transferred into bank accounts in New York that belonged to "Iranians," even though American exports to Iran had all but ceased because of wartime restrictions. Dreyfus provides a sampling of the comments on the budget. The report by the budget committee of the Majlis states: "This is a situation which shows the progress and reforms realized under the high guidance and the powerful will of our Great Sovereign and we ask the all powerful God to facilitate the task of our Great Restorer in perfecting us still more in all these social branches." A Majlis deputy then remarked: "It is a great satisfaction for us to see our budget increased every year. It is testimony to the prosperity and progress of the nation." Not to be outdone, the *Journal de Teheran* editorialized in its issue of March 8, 1941, "Each year all Iranians without exception receive with joy and pride the increase in the budget of the country for all the receipts are expended for useful works, undertakings and initiatives which assure for all, calm, tranquillity, and prosperity."[30] At the time these words were written, Iran was faced with food shortages in urban areas and famine in rural areas. Tehran itself had witnessed bread riots.

Other Appropriations out of the London Reserve Fund

Military appropriations from the sterling Reserve Fund for 1928 through 1941 amounted to £18,412,000. It was noted above that in 1941 Majlis Deputy Etebar had reported to the Majlis that £3 million of the oil royalties had been spent on the purchase of gold. The veracity of this claim is confirmed by George Wadsworth, who claims that the quantity of gold purchased locally in 1933 and 1934 was reported by the local press at 52.56 kharvars (15,768 kg.), and was placed on deposit at the National Bank.[31] Hart reports that part of the 1933 oil royalties had been spent on the purchase of gold. In addition 178 kharvars (53,400 kg.) of bar silver had been imported. The value of these purchases, according to Leon Smets, the Belgian treasurer general of Persia, was £3 million.[32]

In 1932, the bank note monopoly concession held by the Imperial Bank of Persia was canceled and the right was transferred to the National Bank of Persia. Hart reports that the Imperial Bank of Persia was compensated £200,000. In addition, some £100,000 of machinery was imported for printing the new currency. The total had been appropriated from the Reserve Fund.[33]

Many other appropriations were voted by the Majlis. Hart notes that 150,000 rials (£3,000) were voted on October 4, 1932, "for the rehabilitation and settlement of the tribes."[34] Wadsworth states that for the 1933/34 budget, just as the previous year, 1 million rials were allocated to the tribes from the budget, and 300,000 rials (£6,000) were taken out of the Reserve Fund (the year before 150,000 rials had been taken out of the Reserve Fund for this purpose). The exchange rate was said to be fifteen rials to the dollar.[35]

Following the 1933 Anglo-Persian Oil Agreement, which paid Persia a lump sum of £4,107,660, Hart reports that £490,000, one-third of Persia's funded debt, was repaid from the Reserve Fund.[36] He later notes that £360,000 was voted from the Reserve Fund for the building of six sugar refineries, two of which, in Varamin and Shahi, were on His Majesty's estates.[37] A year later, on June 5, 1934, the Majlis approved the following bill on a doubly urgent basis:

Sole Article. To pay the installments, complete construction work, purchase secondary necessary equipment, make preparations for exploitation and meet all the work and expense related to sugar refineries, chintz manufacturing and silk weaving mills, etc., as well as the cost of establishment for tarring sleepers, coal tar and creosote, the Ministry of Finance is authorized to place at the disposal of the Department of Agriculture and Industry the sum of £250,000 out of the reserve funds of the country for payments that must be made in foreign exchange. Moreover, to meet the expenses incurred in the interior of the country for the aforementioned purposes, the Ministry of Finance is authorized to make a long term loan of 30,000,000 rials from the National Bank of Persia and place it at the disposal of the Department of Agriculture and Industry.[38]

On August 4, 1935, the Majlis approved a bill on a doubly urgent basis to grant a loan of £200,000 to the Ministry of Ways and Communications for railway construction and purchase of railway material. As reported by Hornibrook, the bill stipulated that "this sum must be reimbursed later by the Ministry of Ways and Communications." Hornibrook also provides a summary of the previous sterling loans for railways: November 9, 1933, £150,000; June 24, 1934, £400,000; March 14, 1935, £600,000; August 4, 1935, £200,000; total, £1,350,000.[39]

According to Engert, the government had submitted a bill before the Majlis to provide for the following sterling appropriations out of the Reserve Fund. He had no doubt as to its approval: £60,000 for an iron foundry at Amin Abad, £79,046 for the purchase of six locomotives, £79,829 for the construction of a dry dock at Bandar Pahlavi, giving a total of £218,875. The measure concluded: "These sums are to be paid out of the reserves of the country in foreign exchange, and of course certain amounts have also been provided for in Rials to complete the expenditure."[40]

By 1938, the sterling funds were also being drawn upon supposedly for the construction of seaports. James S. Moose, Jr., American consul in Tehran, reports that on October 28, 1938, the Iranian Parliament passed a bill authorizing the Ministry of Finance to spend £500,000 from the Reserve Fund "for port development at Bandar Shahpour and for railway expenses." Moose adds, "There is nothing to indicate why these two items were taken up in a special bill rather than in the regular budget."[41] Nor is it made clear why the construction of port facilities on the Persian Gulf necessitated expenditures of this magnitude in foreign exchange. Three months later, the same Majlis "approved" another large sterling appropriation for the same port. Moose reports that on January 15, 1939, the Majlis passed another law authorizing the Ministry of Finance to spend £300,000 on "railway expenses and for the harbor project at Bandar Shahpour," and "for other unspecified requirements—presumably military and for the wedding of the Crown Prince."[42] The total reported nonmilitary appropri-

TABLE 10.3. Nonmilitary appropriations from
the "Reserve Fund of the Nation," 1928–1941

Railways	£5,429,046
Purchase of gold	£3,000,000
Port construction and railway maintenance	£879,829
Sugar refineries	£520,000
Debt repayment	£490,000
Support for exchange rate of the kran, 1930	£300,000
Imperial Bank of Persia	£200,000
Printing press	£100,000
Iron foundry	£60,000
Unspecified	£25,000
Tribal resettlement	£9,000
Total	£11,012,875

Source: Records of the Department of State.

ations out of the sterling Reserve Fund from 1928 to 1941 amounted to
£11,012,875 (table 10.3).

Summary

Total appropriations out of the Reserve Fund of the Nation during 1928–41
amounted to £29,424,875 (£18,412,000 for the military, £11,012,875 for
nonmilitary). When added to the remaining balance of £1,900,000 in 1941,
the total oil royalties for 1927–41 amounted to £31,324,875, nearly identical to the sum of £31,000,000 given by Deputy Etebar (as reported by Dreyfus). The consistency of the figures and the complete accounting of the
appropriations is a tribute to the painstaking reporting on financial matters
by the American legation and consulate in Tehran. Furthermore,
£6,308,875 was allocated to cover the deficit incurred by the railways and
their maintenance and to construct port facilities.

Why such expenditures required the use of foreign exchange is not
explained. The construction of a harbor on the Persian Gulf and the
Caspian did not entail the expenditure of sterling. The railway and port
appropriations served to convert the income from properties and assets
confiscated by Reza Shah into foreign exchange at the favorable official rate
for deposit in foreign banks.

Of the £18,412,000 in military appropriations, at most £4.5 million was
spent on arms purchases. The remaining £14 million was stolen by Reza
Shah. Adding the more than £6 million in railways and ports appropriations to the £14 million, it follows that His Pahlevi Majesty stole in excess

of £20 million out of £31 million in oil revenues. Moreover, the Shah's London bank accounts that had contained £20–30 million are completely determined. By the standards of the time, this was a truly vast sum of money. Had this money been used to purchase shares in the Anglo-Persian Oil Company, Iran could have purchased many of the shares not owned by the British government and the crisis of 1951–53 might have been avoided.

CHAPTER ELEVEN

The Purchase of Armaments, 1928–1941

LIKE ITS KEEN INTEREST IN OIL AND financial matters, the American legation in Tehran also maintained a keen interest in matters related to the armed forces and the purchase of armaments overseas. These reports provide a detailed account of the equipment purchased by Iran from 1921 to 1941. In a lengthy report from July 1941, Dreyfus details the weaponry of each regiment in the Iranian army. He also encloses a document entitled "The Battle Order of the Iranian Army," which provides a complete inventory of Iran's weapons on the eve of the Allied invasion of Iran.[1] From this document and the information on specific purchases given in other reports, it is obvious that only a small fraction of the £18,412,000 supposedly spent on armaments was actually used for that purpose.

The Iranian Army

From the very beginning, Reza Khan showed interest in purchasing arms for his army. And although the American government had refused to sell arms to him, the American legation had provided detailed reports on arms delivery from other sources. The American military attaché declares: "Latest reports indicate that Persia has purchased abroad the following materials for military purposes: From France: 2 combat planes, 10 instruction planes, 10 small tractors, 4 small tanks. From Germany: 2 motor repair trucks, 30 motor trucks 1½ ton each, a quantity of machine guns, automatic rifles, rifles and small arms ammunition. From Great Britain:

2 Rolls-Royce armored cars." The attaché reveals that the Rolls-Royces were a gift to Reza Khan from the Anglo-Persian Oil Company:

> In connection with the Rolls-Royce armored cars above mentioned the War Ministry is actually receiving four. Two are a present from the Sheikh of Mohammerah and two are declared to have been purchased in England. This latter purchase is doubted. It is believed that the Anglo-Persian Oil Company presented two of these armored cars to Reza Khan, but for political reasons Reza Khan has kept the nature of the gifts secret. The cars are said to cost 5,000 English pounds each. . . . Moreover representatives of the Anglo-Persian Oil Co. at Baghdad last summer casually mentioned the shipping of Rolls-Royce armored cars for the War Minister.[2]

These same four armored cars were to take part in every annual parade from 1926 to 1941 celebrating the coup d'état of February 21, 1921.

In September 1923, American minister Joseph Kornfeld announced the delivery of some of the arms purchased from Germany: "I have the honor to advise the Department that in the latter part of the month of August a German boat arrived at the port of Enzeli [Bandar-e Anzali]. In its cargo were 17,000 rifles and a large quantity of ammunition which the Persian Government had bought from Germany before the war."[3] Shortly thereafter, Sheldon Whitehouse, American chargé d'affaires ad interim in Paris, provided more accurate information: "According to British sources, a consignment of German war material was on August 27 landed at Enzeli from a German steamer named Enseli, which made the journey via Russian waterways. The consignment which was addressed to Colonel Ismael Khan, consisted of 1150 rifles, 1000 carbines, 25 automatic rifles, detached parts of cannon and machine-guns, and 1800 cases of ammunition for small-caliber arms."[4]

In December, Kornfeld reported, "According to reliable information, the Persian Government has purchased from France three tanks which will arrive shortly."[5] He also informed the State Department of imminent arrival in Persia of arms purchased from Germany: "The Persian Government has purchased in Germany forty army lorries and trailers. The sale of this material on the part of Germany is manifestly in contravention to Article 170, Part 5, Chapter 2, of the Treaty of Versailles. The Chief of Staff of the Persian army stated unofficially that this material is brought into Persia on a Russian invoice."[6]

Throughout the 1920s and 1930s, army purchases of arms and ammunition appear to have been negligible. In 1927, American minister Hoffman Philip states that the "Majlis voted 8 million francs to be paid to Schneider-Creusot for ammunition purchased many years ago."[7] Some of the ammunition was purchased for the Schneider horse-drawn artillery guns of 1901 vintage, which were derided by American diplomats when displayed in the annual parade honoring the coup. The lack of modern weaponry, however, did not discourage extravagant comments by newspapers. On the tenth anniversary of the coup, for instance, one newspaper comments: "The splendor and worth of the new military organization is due to the energy and patriotism of the country's indomitable leader, His Imperial Majesty, Reza Shah Pahlavi. Persia whose new life began with the 1921 Coup d'état, will be able, thanks to its powerful new army, to live henceforth its own life independently, free from fear of repetition of the woes of the past century—because we know that the words peace and disarmament are today but words and nothing but words."[8]

William H. Hornibrook reveals that in early 1935 the army possessed only four armored cars (apparently the same ones that were presents from the sheikh of Mohammerah and APOC) and six tanks, all of which were obsolete. He states that in 1934 the Indianapolis-based Marmon-Herrington Company sold nineteen heavy trucks to the Persian army and in 1935 negotiated for the sale of thirty-six more trucks and twelve armored cars. The company had also been asked to enter a bid for 100 light tanks that Persia reportedly wanted to purchase abroad.[9] However, J. Rives Childs of the American legation declares: "I am confidentially informed that the twelve armored cars supplied recently by the Marmon-Herrington Company of Indianapolis, while capable of resisting fire from Iranian rifles, are not capable of withstanding fire from such modern rifles as those used by the United States Army."[10]

Hornibrook states that the War Ministry placed a firm order for fifty-six Skoda light tanks in Czechoslovakia, much to the disappointment of Marmon-Herrington.[11] The actual contract, it was later revealed, had actually been concluded a year ago, but not announced. In a conversation with Wallace S. Murray, chief of the State Department's Division of Near Eastern Affairs, Colonel Arthur Herrington, chairman of Marmon-Herrington, revealed that the initial contract with Iran was for $300,000 (£60,000), and had increased to $1 million (£200,000).[12] The company was in the process of concluding another contract for $1 million in heavy trucks and armored cars when the member of the Iranian Purchasing Commission in Bern was called back to Tehran. When he returned to Bern, he informed the company that the shah, greatly angered over articles in *Time* and the *Mirror* that referred to His Majesty's humble origins, had vetoed the purchase of American arms. The connection with the Indianapolis company turns out to be important because it demonstrates how the money appropriated for arms purchase was diverted into Reza Shah's bank accounts in New York and Switzerland.

The American minister reports that in the 1936 coup d'état parade about sixty planes took part in the flyby but no stunts were attempted, in view of a crash a few days before in which two officers were killed. Hornibrook ends his report with observations on the general state of the Iranian army:

The infantry units all possessed machine-gun batteries, and a few of the infantrymen were armed with automatic rifles. Although both horse-drawn and motorized light and medium field-artillery were in evidence, as well as eight motorized anti-aircraft guns, chief emphasis appears to be placed upon mountain guns, knocked down and carried on mules. The cavalry, splendidly mounted, was armed in part with lances, in part with carbines. The men appeared to be hardy, well-equipped and well-disciplined. The review went off without a hitch, and may be considered a good exhibition when the large numbers of animals in line is remembered. The Shah stood at attention, almost continuously at salute, during the three hours of the march-past. One was left with the impression that His Majesty has built an effective force for use, during his lifetime, in maintaining the unity of the country and its obedience to central authority. The force would, however, be of little account if faced with the power of Great Britain or Russia.[13]

In a November 1937 report, C. Van H. Engert gives the strength of the Persian army as 105,000 men (not including 8,000 gendarmes) and that of the air force, 1,000. The army had 268 artillery field guns and had purchased 156 heavy trucks and caterpillar tractors, and 78 armored cars and tanks. The air force consisted of 157 airplanes, of which only 134 were serviceable. The remaining 23 he deemed beyond repair. The total military expenditure from the regular budget was $16,740,000, or 37.5 percent of all expenditures. In addition, £2 million ($10 million) was allocated annually from the Reserve Fund. When this is included, total military appropriation was 60 percent of government expenditure.[14]

Engert reports an increase in the number of tanks and armored cars displayed in the coup parade of 1938. About 30,000 troops and officers had taken part in the parade on 3 Esfand 1299 (February 21, 1921). "The mechanized units particularly attracted great attention, and I am told that never before had so many tanks and armored cars been seen in Iran." The tank force consisted of 50 Czech-Moravska light tanks (3.5 tons), and 50 medium tanks (7.5 tons) of the same make. The armored division consisted of 4 Rolls-Royce and 12 Marmon-Herrington cars, and 28 Büssing-NAG German armored trucks. In addition, 65 army planes in formations of five flew overhead. Engert, however, could not resist the following observation about the state of the Iranian army: "The mules of the mountain batteries were exceptionally fine animals and appeared well groomed. The same was true of most of the horses. Incidentally, I learn that half of the draft horses of the field artillery had been imported at great expense from Hungary, but that many of them died shortly after arrival. I am also informed by one of the military attachés that the Schneider guns of the horse artillery are of a 1901 model and would be quite useless in modern warfare."[15]

Engert's report for the coup d'état day parade reported that the air force flyby comprised 75 British planes: 25 de Havilland Tiger Moths, 25 Hawker Audaxes, 10 Hawker Furies, and 15 Hawker Hinds. The mechanized brigade consisted of 25 medium and 25 light Czech tanks, 4 Rolls Royce and 12 Marmon-Herrington armored cars, and 48 Büssing-NAG armored trucks. Again, Engert sarcastically added, "The horsemanship seemed distinctly good, but the rear ranks were apt to crowd the front ranks too much. Most of the bays were sturdy Kurdish ponies."[16]

Engert's last report on a coup d'état parade contains disturbing, remarkably accurate information on the state of the Iranian army: "90 airplanes, in flights of five, flew past the saluting base at the unusually low altitude of between 200–500 feet." However, he reports, "No guns were observed on any of the planes." As to the armored forces, the same 49 light and 49 medium tanks, together with the same and by now habitual four Rolls-Royce armored cars took part in the parade. Although the number of the Marmon-Herrington armored cars had increased to 16, the 48 German Büssing-NAG armored trucks were the same as in previous years. In the display of the mountain artillery, the horse-drawn 1901 Schneider guns featured prominently. Engert concludes:

It was observed that although, in view of the possibility of surprises, the country is gradually being put in a state of defense, no units of the Tehran garrison were missing from the review. This would indicate that for the present the Iranian troops standing guard on the Russian frontier have been drawn chiefly from local garrisons and from provinces outside of Tehran. In this connection I have recently had interesting conversations with several foreign military attachés from which I deduct the following conclusions. The war in Finland has led the Iranian army to believe that the Soviets do no longer constitute a serious military menace. As a matter of fact there is no comparison between the Finnish army and the Iranian either with respect to size, equipment, or morale. So far the defense requirements of Iran's *international* position have been almost entirely neglected, and the army has been built up largely to meet *internal* demands, such as the suppression of the tribal revolts and to ensure the stability of the Shah's regime. The reliability of the new Iranian army has not been tested, but competent observers do not believe it would be capable of offering more than very brief resistance if a Soviet army should invade Iran.

In the first place, Iran's frontiers are not properly fortified and the northern provinces are in an exposed and vulnerable position. In the second place, it is very doubtful whether any well-planned or well-organized operations are contemplated in resisting an invasion. But by far the greatest difficulty would be that of equipping and maintaining an army in the field in accordance with the standards of modern requirements. Many weaknesses seem to exist in the Iranian military organization: (a) although what there is of the equipment is good, there is not nearly enough of it, and the scarcity of heavy ammunition is so great that (it is said) it would last only for about one day's fighting; (b) with the mechanization of a portion of the infantry and artillery the rank and file find it difficult to handle complicated modern military machinery; (c) this difficulty is increased by the great diversity of mechanical equipment (e.g. Czechoslovak, German, British, Swedish, French, etc.); (d) the army training is still very sketchy and the tactics rather primitive; (e) there is a distinct lack of capable officer personnel and the staff work is reported to be notoriously poor; (f) and as the Iranian army has as yet no fighting tradition behind it, it is probable that in an emergency it would suffer from bad leadership and inferior morale.[17]

It appears that toward the end of Reza Shah's rule, the army was no longer an entirely reliable instrument to preserve the regime. In a telegram dated December 1, 1939, Engert reports: "I now learn from a fairly reliable source that a plot to assassinate the Shah was discovered and that nearly 300 army officers are at present under arrest. According to a rumor, the five who were first arrested have already been executed."[18] A subsequent telegram states: "My 153, December 1, 10 p.m. Since then an Iranian colonel has been court-martialed and shot for alleged espionage on behalf of Russia."[19]

In his report on the twentieth anniversary of the coup parade, the American minister Dreyfus relates that the pilot of one of the airplanes that was to take part in the flyby had instead flown to Russia. To prevent a recurrence of the episode, it was reported that gasoline was being rationed to pilots in very small quantities. Dreyfus adds: "The fact that such a thing could happen and that the authorities find it necessary to take steps to prevent a repetition places the Iranian forces in none too favorable a light." Summing up the obvious, he concludes: "The army is untried as to fighting quality and morale, is insufficiently equipped with too diverse and little understood machinery, and is deficient in officer personnel. The frontiers are not well fortified and it is doubtful if Iran could put up more than a momentary and extremely weak resistance to Russia or any other modern nation."[20]

The minister, however, refrains from stating the other obvious conclusion. In a country where, for the past twenty years, at least 60 percent of the entire government expenditure had been devoted to the military, and where at least 60 percent of the oil revenues had supposedly been spent to "complete the purchase of armaments and munitions of the army," why was the Iranian army in such a state of unpreparedness and so ill-equipped? What had happened to the vast sums supposedly spent on the military?

The most complete report on the Iranian armed forces, "The Battle Order of the Iranian Army," details the active troop strength and matériel of all army, navy, and air force regiments as of June 15, 1941, two months before the Allied invasion of Iran.[21] Total army strength was listed at 126,400 men, not including 9,750 gendarmerie personnel. The army was organized into 18 divisions and possessed 448 artillery guns (including the 1901 Schneider models), and 76 anti-aircraft guns. It had one mechanized brigade consisting of three mechanized regiments—all located in Tehran. The 100 tanks, 24 armored cars, and 50 armored trucks possessed by the army (its armored corps) were also all in Tehran, not at the frontiers (table 11.1).

The real preparedness of the army can be seen from the limited strength of the divisions assigned to the northern frontier (table 11.2), a 2,000-kilo-meter border Iran shared with its northern neighbor, the Soviet Union. Given that none of the divisions possessed any armored vehicles, given that the artillery was all horse drawn, and given the near absence of anti-aircraft and aerial defenses, Iran's northern borders were for all practical purposes undefended. When the Soviets attacked on August 25, 1941, they met only brief resistance in Gilan. Azerbaijan and Khorasan were taken without any meaningful opposition.

Finally, a tally of the armor and artillery held by the army indicates that the actual sums spent for armaments had been relatively small. For instance, the cost of 20 armored cars and about 200 trucks and tractors

TABLE 11.1. Mechanized arm of the Iranian army, 1941, on the eve of the Allied invasion

One light tank battalion, Czecho-Moravska (3.5 ton)	50
One medium tank battalion, Czecho-Moravska (7.5 ton)	50
One armored car battalion	
Marmon-Herrington	20
Rolls-Royce	4
Bussing-Nag armored lorries	50
F.N.B. motorcycles	50
Harley-Davidson 2-cylinder motorcycles	16
Repair trucks	4
Mechanical transport	
Trucks	306
Ambulances	12
Other (including tractors)	150

Source: "The Battle Order of the Iranian Army," enclosure to dispatch 102 (891.415/27), July 21, 1941, from Louis G. Dreyfus, Jr.

TABLE 11.2. Strength of the Iranian army in northern Iran, July 1941

DIVISION	MEN	ARTILLERY GUNS	ANTI-AIRCRAFT GUNS
Third (eastern Azerbaijan)	8,500	28	4
Fourth (western Azerbaijan)	8,000	28	0
Fifteenth (Ardebil)	3,000	12	0
Eleventh (Gilan)	3,300	12	0
Tenth (Gorgan)	3,500	14	0
Ninth (Khorassan)	8,000	28	4
Total	34,300	122	8

Source: "The Battle Order of the Iranian Army," dispatch 102 (891.415/27), July 21, 1941, from Louis G. Dreyfus, Jr.

purchased from the Marmon-Herrington Company was, as reported by the company's chairman, $1 million (£200,000). The cost of a British-made Tiger Moth fighter plane, including weapons, was £3,750 in 1933. Even assuming that a light or medium Czechoslovak tank cost the same as an English fighter, the entire force of 100 tanks would have cost only £375,000. In all, it is clear that total purchases for the army during 1928–41 was at most £1.5 million, a small fraction of the £18,412,000 that had been appropriated for "completing the munitions of the Army."

The Iranian Navy

George Gregg Fuller, the American vice consul in Bushire, gives an informative and amusing report on the status of Iran's Persian Gulf navy:

I have the honor to report certain observations regarding the Persian Navy, in view of Persia's demands that the policing of the Gulf to stop illicit arms traffic should be assigned to Persia instead of Great Britain. The largest vessels in the Persian navy are the Persepolis and the Muzafferi, neither of which can be moved. One of these attempted a trip to Bombay some years ago, but as it was constantly on the point of sinking, the Captain refused to take it out again. In fact, both are expected to drop to the bottom soon. The crews strike for their pay at intervals, but are rounded up by the military and taken on board or to jail. The pride of the navy is the motor launch "Pehlevi" [Pahlavi], delivered this year by a German firm,—or almost delivered, as she ran out of provisions and fuel a few miles down the Gulf and the crew rowed to Bushire. A Persian crew was placed on board, under a German deck hand, promoted to Captain. The crew, unpaid, began to sell the ship's fittings in the bazaar, so a guard was detailed from the army to save the navy from itself. Then some army guns were placed on deck, and the "Pehlevi" was ordered to Mohammerah. The whole town turned out to witness the departure,—the event being only marred by the inability of the crew to find out how to get started. The ship was carried up the harbor by the tide, but her anchor was dropped in time to save her. She eventually reached Mohammerah, and will be left there for some time because of the expense of fuel. There are two armed launches now under the Customs Administration; one has been out of repair for over a year, and the other is at Mohammerah. A fine sailing craft was purchased in place of one launch, but the motor installed is too small to move the craft against strong currents. This and another sailing craft are the only vessels acting against smugglers. They [the ship's crew] frequently capture prizes and if their pay is not received, they can live by levying on the smugglers.[22]

The circumstances surrounding the purchase of the *Pahlavi* are detailed by Murray, then American chargé d'affaires in Tehran:

I have the honor to inform the Department that in the *Vatan* of November there appeared a statement that the Persian battleship *Pehlevi* would shortly arrive in Bushire. The paper further stated "this ship was built by the best manufacturers in Germany, and was recently supplied with arms and armor in the port of Naples, Italy. It is built according to the latest German system of battleships and is equipped with all the necessary wireless apparatus. Germany could not supply the Pehlevi with arms and armor on account of the restrictions upon her by the treaty of Versailles." I have verified the accuracy of this statement through the German Legation in Teheran and am informed that the "battleship" in question is an old mine-sweeper entirely unequipped which the Persian Government purchased some months ago from the German Government. The latest reports state that the boat has already arrived at Bushire and has been inspected by the Prime Minister [Reza Khan] who reached there with his army. I was informed by Ezzatollah Khan Hedayat, who has recently returned from Berlin where he was Secretary of Legation, that negotiations for the purchase of German ships for the Persian "navy" have been going on for several years. Previous to the arrival of Colonel Ismail Khan, who was sent as a special representative of the Prime Minister to finish the negotiations, a deal was practically closed for the purchase of three old torpedo boats for £3,800. Colonel Ismail Khan however saw fit to purchase the present "warship," a former mine-sweeper, for £4,000. A large part of this sum is supposed to have gone into his own pocket.

In view of the shipment of arms and ammunition from Germany, which reached Teheran in September 1923, consisting of about 2,100 Mauser rifles, 20 automatic rifles with about 200,000 rounds of rifle ammunition, and the purchase of thirty 1.5-ton motor trucks and two motor repair trucks, together with a quantity of machine guns from Germany, which arrived in Teheran about January of the present year, the present purchase of the so-called battleship from Germany is not without interest. The Department was also informed of the engagement of a former German army officer named Hartman to take charge of the arsenals at Teheran and Bushire for the repair and eventual manufacture of rifles for the Persian army.[23]

In 1928, 200,000 tomans (about $200,000) was approved by the Majlis for expanding the navy.[24] Augustin W. Ferrin, American consul in Tehran, reports: "Recently an Italian naval engineer engaged by the Persian Government has been inspecting the Persian Gulf coast and now it is announced that a Persian navy will be created under the command of Captain del Prato, an Italian line officer. The Persian Government now possesses about five small vessels and it is reported that five more will be purchased, presumably from Italy, also that dockyards will be developed. It is said that the object of a marine establishment is to chase pirates and smugglers, especially of arms."[25]

In a subsequent despatch, Ferrin states:

> In the 1929–30 budget Tomans 400,000 (about the same in dollars) is appropriated to "the purchase and repair of boats and expenses of foreign functionaries for the marine." It is said that some six small vessels will be purchased, probably in Italy, four for the Gulf and two, perhaps, for the Caspian. There has been much gun running on the Gulf coast which has interfered with the disarmament of the turbulent southern tribes, and it is believed that smuggling in the area costs the sugar and tea monopoly, whose revenues are allocated to railway construction, at least Tomans 1,000,000 a year. If the navy can suppress this smuggling it will prove a profitable investment.[26]

What became of the 600,000 tomans appropriated for the navy is not known because two years later we learn from Hart that the Persian Navy, "now chief rival of the Swiss," was to be reinforced with four gunboats ordered in Italy. Their cost, reportedly £390,000, was to be charged against the Reserve Fund. Captain del Prato, locally referred to as Admiral Sinbad, was to train Persian sailors, who then were to be taken to Italy to take command of the ships when launched. Like Ferrin, Hart supports the anti-smuggling initiative:

> There is a real need for efficient coast guard service along Persia's thousand mile southern coast. Smuggling is extensive and gun running a lucrative profession. The Government's action in purchasing these four gunboats and its plan for their use in coast guard service should go far towards improving the situation. Their cost, especially at this time of economic crisis, perhaps an inordinate charge against the undernourished Government treasury. But the expenditure, unlike that of the more advanced western nations on their naval armaments, may be classed as a productive one. For, with the suppression or limitation of smuggling, customs revenues may be expected to show a not inconsiderable increase.[27]

On February 18, 1932, the Majlis approved, on a doubly urgent basis, a single-article bill submitted by Ali Akbar Davar, the minister of finance. The new law provided an additional £75,000 (in addition to the £390,000 already approved), "to meet the remaining cost and transport expenses of Government vessels, payment to be made out of the reserve funds of the country."[28] In October, Hart reports, Davar introduced another bill allocating an additional £135,000 for naval expenditures out of the Reserve Fund. The bill was passed without debate. The total naval appropriation had come to £600,000 (390,000 + 75,000 + 135,000), or about $3 million, not counting the $600,000 appropriated in 1928 and 1929. Hart continues: "From my Italian colleague I learn that the number of gunboats is six—not nine as press reports have it, the other three 'boats' being small motor boats carried on the larger gunboats. The local press hails the completion of the new gunboats as a 'further notable achievement of the august reign of the Shahinshah who never fails to make his own interests those of his loyal subjects and who in the present instance confers inestimable advantages on honest Persian merchants by rendering possible the prevention of the increasing contraband in the Persian Gulf.'"[29]

The motor gunboats *Babr* and *Palang* each weighed 950 tons and cost $1,049,160. The four other vessels—*Shahrokh, Simorgh, Karkas,* and *Chahbahar*—each weighed 350 tons and cost $795,544 in total.[30] So satisfied were the Iranians with the supposedly new Italian boats that in August 1934 the Persian government contracted with Cantieri Navali Riuniti of Palermo for the construction of three patrol boats. The delivery date for the twenty-eight-ton boats was set for early 1935 and they were completed by the summer.[31]

Hornibrook reveals that the six ships originally purchased from Italy for nearly $3 million were reconditioned vessels, not new: "As one further item of incidental interest regarding Persian armament, I may mention that the British Military Attaché has informed the Legation that it has been learned that the gunboats purchased some time ago by the Persian Government in Italy for use in the Gulf are not new but represent reconditioned material. When the boats recently went into dry-dock at Bombay it was learned that the hull and bows were made of scrap iron and that even the engines were old."[32] In view of the revelations concerning the "new battleship *Pehlevi*" that had been purchased by the Persian government in 1924, Hornibrook's report should have come as no surprise. An internal State Department memorandum on the Persian navy had described the battleship *Pahlavi* as a reconditioned 1917 German minesweeper "whose effectiveness today can probably be questioned" and added that two other ships, the *Persepolis* (built in 1885) and the *Muzafferi* (built about 1900), were no longer seaworthy.[33]

"The Battle Order of the Iranian Army" also provides complete inventory of the Iranian navy. The main part of the Persian Gulf navy consisted of two sloops (950 tons each) and four patrol vessels (331 tons each). The

Caspian navy consisted of four vedette boats (28 tons each), and the Royal yacht *Shahsavar*.[34] Most of the southern fleet was sunk by the British in the early hours of August 25, 1941, while the Caspian fleet was seized by the Soviets and taken to Russia. In view of the reported figures, out of the £18,412,000 appropriated for the purchase of armaments, at most £1 million had been spent on the "new" navy.

The Iranian Air Force

On January 15, 1923 the Persian minister in Washington, Hossein Alai, wrote to Allen W. Dulles, chief of the Division of Near Eastern Affairs, seeking assistance and information about a small air force that his government wanted to organize.[35] In 1924, the Persian government purchased six French and two Russian planes.[36] Not long after their arrival, half the French airplanes were out of action: "three have been damaged in their flight through Persia; two are reported to be beyond repair. Ignorance on the part of the French aviator in charge of their delivery is supposed to be the cause of the mishap."[37] Kornfeld describes the aviator the government had contracted: "Captain Berault has arrived in Teheran, having been engaged by the Persian Government as instructor of Aviation in the Persian Army. At present he is preparing a landing place for the aeroplanes which the Persian Government bought in France."[38]

The attrition rate through accidents and the replacement rate were about equal. Kornfeld reports, "Regarding the purchase of wireless stations and aeroplanes from Russia, I have the honor to state that two of these aeroplanes arrived in Teheran on May 12, 1924."[39] French aviation and aviators continued to experience difficulty in Persia. Airplanes were lost almost as fast as they arrived, demonstrating the waste of precious resources by Reza Khan.

It appears that the Persians subsequently attempted to use American engines on the European aeroplanes. In July 1929 the Persian minister in Washington wrote to the secretary of state seeking assistance for the purchase of twenty-three Liberty engines.[40] Each engine cost $250, and the total, including transportation from New York, came to $5,761.95. The War Department described them as "reconditioned engines which have been overhauled once by the Air Corps. They are unserviceable for flying in their present condition and must be overhauled before being used."[41]

In October 1930 Consul Villard reported that at most twenty planes were in flying condition.[42] Despite the strictest secrecy maintained by the government, Hart was able to report that a contract for twenty de Havilland Tiger Moth training planes had been awarded to the British firm of de Havilland. Each plane cost £3,000, exclusive of armaments. When armed by Vickers the total cost of the planes was £75,000.[43] In the coup d'état parade of 1933, eighteen of the new Fox Moths were displayed. After ship-ment to Bushire and assembly there, the planes had been flown to Tehran. One had crashed on the way and one was unaccounted for.[44] Hart reports: "In the matter of the plane lost between Bushire and Teheran, I am reliably informed that the pilot was killed and the plane irreparably damaged and that the Persian military authorities are now insisting that the dead pilot's family make good the cost of the lost plane!" Subsequently two more planes collided in midair, killing one pilot and injuring the other. Thus, soon after delivery of the twenty planes, four had been lost.[45]

In all the shah purchased fifty military aircraft, twenty of which were the de Havilland trainers.[46] The other thirty, some day bombers and some fighters, were ordered from Hawker. The order, which totaled £200,000, was placed in June 1932, following a visit to London by the Persian military mission. The planes were to be fitted with the American-made Pratt and Whitney engines, each costing $7,075 (around £1,400), bringing the total cost of the planes to £242,000. Ten spares were also purchased from Pratt and Whitney for £14,000.[47] When the cost of the twenty trainer planes were added, total aviation purchases came to £331,000, out of a £1.5 million appropriation.

After the crash of the two Tiger Moth trainers, nine more were ordered from de Havilland, and ten de Havilland R5s were purchased from the Soviet Union. The tally of seventy-seven serviceable planes as of September 1933 included eleven old planes still in service and sixty-six planes pur-chased within the year (26 de Havillands, 30 Hawkers, and 10 Russian R5s). The eleven old planes still in service, Hart reveals, were part of a batch of thirty-two used machines purchased in 1931.[48]

Hart's successor as minister in Tehran, William H. Hornibrook, took a keen interest in aviation. He reports an order for six anti-aircraft batteries from Bofors in Sweden, each battery consisting of six guns, and an order for twelve armored cars from Marmon-Herrington. He also reveals that of the thirty Hawker fighters, twelve were single-seater pursuit and eighteen were double-seaters. In addition, twenty-four new Hawker two-seaters had been ordered for delivery in October 1934. Another order for twelve to twenty-four de Havillands had also been placed with the British.[49] In short, the British had effectively monopolized the Persian aviation market (see table 11.3).

British Domination of Persian Aviation

In the spring of 1934, William C. Gould, representative of the American firm Pratt and Whitney, visited Tehran in connection with the difficulties encountered by the American concern in Persia. Pratt and Whitney had sold forty R-1860 Hornet engines to Persia, thirty of which were mounted

TABLE 11.3. Composition of Iranian Air Force, 1934

Old planes	11
Planes purchased or ordered in 1933	
British de Havillands, Gypsy engines	26
(training planes)	
British Hawkers, Bristol Mercury engines	12
British Hawkers, Hornet engines	18
Planes purchased or ordered in 1934	
British Hawkers, Hornet engines	12
British Hawkers, Bristol Pegasus engines	12
British de Havillands, Gypsy engines	16
Total	107

Source: William H. Hornibrook, dispatch 53
(891.20/81), May 7, 1934.

on the Hawker planes purchased from Britain, and the rest were spares. (The cost of a regular Hornet engine was $6,640, and that of the super-charged variety, $7,075.)[50] This was to be the last aviation purchase from the United States. Thereafter, Persia purchased only British aviation equipment. The total British control of Persian affairs and especially of Persian aviation is highlighted by a lengthy report from Hornibrook, which begins:

The difficulties and obstructions placed in the way of the development of business in Persia by the American Pratt & Whitney Company would now appear to be part of a general and subtle offensive instigated under British inspiration, alarmed at the prospect of the equipment of the Persian Air Force with 200 modern airplane engines in a country contiguous as Persia is to India. This opinion is not only shared by Major Arfa, former Chief Purchasing Agent of the Persian Government in Bern, who was responsible for placing the initial order for airplane motors with Pratt & Whitney Company and who has since been superseded as the result of the intrigues instigated against him, but also by my Swedish colleague, the Swedish Chargé d'Affaires, as well as by Captain L. G. True, the American engineer loaned for one year by Pratt & Whitney to the Persian Government.

My attention was first called to this development by Captain L. G. True when reporting to me the difficulty he was having in collecting his salary from the Persian Government and the fact that, while on June 6, 1934, he had received no salary since March 5, 1934, the mechanics of the Hawker and de Havilland companies, similarly seconded by the British companies to work in Persia, were being paid and, moreover, had not been made to sign contracts as onerous as his. He likewise reported to me that rumors were being circulated that Colonel Nordquist [a Swede employed by the Persian air force] had accepted an automobile as a present from Pratt & Whitney Company before his termination of his contract by the Persian Government.

Moreover, he recounted a conversation which he had with Lady Hoare, wife of the British Minister in Teheran, who had inquired of him why American airplane engines were so unsatisfactory in their performance in Persia and when he replied that they were the best in the world and gave as satisfactory a performance in Persia as anywhere else, she observed in an unguarded moment that no more would be purchased by the Persian Government and then added: "Oh! I shouldn't have told you that." This remark may be recalled in connection with the somewhat similar statement respecting the unsuitability of American aircraft in Persia which was made by Mr. T. L. Jacks, Resident Director of Anglo-Persian Oil Company, to Mr. T. L. Washburn of the Socony-Vacuum Corporation.51

In another dispatch Hornibrook writes:

The British are in complete and absolute control of the Persian aviation corps and are therefore in a position to force the purchase of British planes and name all foreign advisers and employees maintained by such Department. . . . More notable examples of British influence in other governmental departments could be given, but the above illustration, which a personal investigation has substantiated, should suffice for the purpose of this report. . . .

Soon after the date of my arrival in Teheran, and on numerous other occasions thereafter, I was advised by both British and American residents that the influence of the former had ceased to be a potent factor in molding Persian official opinion. This viewpoint, predicated, I think, upon the inspired "mouthings" of the Persian press, and doubtless given the smile of approval of the British Legation, has disarmed many American nationals. The fact that the present Shah owes his throne to the British and the cabinet members owe their respective posts to the Shah, is enough in itself to cause any prudent observer to stop, look and listen, before believing the myth that our British cousins have lost their influence in the Persian capital. I have taken the occasion to make a rather careful check on the British connections of the present members of the Cabinet. I am convinced that fully three-fourths of them may be definitely classified as pro-British, not from choice, but from fear. I have carefully, and I hope rather adroitly, sounded out a very considerable number of Persian officials on the subject of the British influence. My reaction is that they dislike the British, possibly more than the nationals of any other country, but they do fear them, and have a very wholesome respect for any recommendation which emanates from the British Legation. The intelligence department of the Anglo-Persian Oil Company is not as effective or as well manned as it was in the days of frank British domination of the Persian foreign policy, but it still functions and functions very effectively.52

In a letter to Thomas F. Hamilton, European representative of Pratt and Whitney, Captain Leland G. True of the same firm had informed his superior that the British had obtained a monopoly on Persian aviation: "It is perfectly clear that the British rule the roost at the present time and that Swedes, Americans or any other nationality are out of the picture until these people get sick of the English. I understand that His Majesty has ordered that there will be no further mixture of equipment from different nations. In the future it is to be all English aircraft with English engines."[53] By the end of 1934, it was clear that the American aircraft industry had been excluded from Persia by the British. Hornibrook states that the Persian government had ordered twenty-four additional planes from de Havilland, of which four were to be used for the establishment of a passenger and air mail service.[54]

Hornibrook also reports that the Persian air force at the end of 1934 consisted of 145 serviceable airplanes either on hand or ordered: de Havilland Tiger Moths, 59; Hawker Audaxes, 49; Hawker Furies, 30; de Havilland Dragon Moths, 3; German Junkers, 3; American Wright Fledgling, 1. Furthermore, during 1934 thirty-eight additional planes were ordered and American aviation totally excluded. Hornibrook reports that, based on credible sources, it had been the government's intention to build a force of 200 modern planes by the end of 1935. But it was the opinion of Captain True of Pratt and Whitney that "no further orders will be placed for some time and he [True] is even doubtful whether the Government may be able to provide the proper facilities for making use of the airplanes already on hand and ordered. The problem of trained personnel alone, in his opinion, renders highly problematical the possibility of the efficient exploitation of the present strength within the next three or four years."[55] The latter prediction proved to be accurate. As shown below, the bulk of the air force purchases had been completed by 1934, and the planes that were subsequently purchased consisted mostly of trainers for use by the Teheran Aero Club.

In an April 1935 dispatch Hornibrook notes that despite severe technical problems associated with the fleet of about 160 airplanes, once again £2 million was appropriated from the London sterling Reserve Fund for armaments, of which one-third was to be spent on the purchase of airplanes.[56] What he did not know was that each year for the next five years the same amount would be allocated for arms purchases. Meanwhile a steady stream of mishaps had persisted. In early February 1935, as preparation for the coup d'état day parade, two Tiger Moths from a formation of fourteen had collided in the air; one crashed, killing the pilot, the other landed with extensive damage. Meanwhile, the accident was witnessed by the dead pilot's brother, who was also flying a plane. He was so affected that he crash landed his plane, causing extensive damage. On the same day, two Audaxes also collided in the air, but incurred only minor damage to the wing tips. Subsequently, one pilot developed such a case of nerves that he refused to take off.

In March 1935 five Hawker Audaxes, shipped from England to Ahwaz and assembled there, left Ahwaz for Tehran.

> Encountering storms on the way from Ahwaz to Teheran all of the planes were eventually compelled to land for lack of fuel. Two, which kept their approximate direction, were able to fuel and arrived in Teheran on March 24 and 26, 1935. Two turned over upon landing near Kashan, suffering twenty per cent damage to the planes and having to be brought in by truck. One of the planes, piloted by a Belgian, however, so far lost direction as to be deflected over the Lut or great salt desert between Teheran and Meshed. Forced to land for lack of fuel with some slight damage to the propeller. It was not until March 29th that Teheran received news of his fate. So upset was His Majesty over the mishaps incident to the flight of the five planes from Ahwaz to Teheran that General Nakhjevan, Chief of the Air Service, was placed under confinement to his quarters for two days from which he was subsequently released and restored to his command.[57]

Despite these difficulties, the chief of the air force, General Nakhjevan, announced to cheers and applause: "Aerial supremacy means victory in war. His Imperial Majesty has this point in mind, and I am going to give the progressive youth of my country the good news that the Imperial Iranian Air Force will in a short time be on the same footing with that of any of the foreign powers which are first and foremost in this field."[58]

In 1934 the government also decided to build an airplane factory, to be completely managed by the British. Construction started two years later, and it was expected to come into production by 1937 or 1938. The chief engineer was formerly with Imperial Airways, the assistant engineer was formerly with the Hawker plant in Kingston; other officials had worked for de Havilland, the Bristol Company, and Hawker. James Moose, the American consul, reports that in February 1938 the first planes manufactured in Iran, five Tiger Moths, rolled out of the Shahbaz factory, near Doshan Tepe. On July 21, 1938, the shah and crown prince were present for the inauguration of the next batch, a group of Hawker Audaxes. Moose adds:

> The plant was designed in England, and equipment, motors, and other material and all skilled personnel were imported from that country. In the ceremony inaugurations and press descriptions of the factory and the planes, British participation was not mentioned. British technicians employed in the factory are reluctant to estimate the capacity of the plant, because of the unpredictable policy to be pursued by the Iranian military authorities. The officially

inspired press states that five planes will be turned out every two months, and that additional types of planes will also be produced.[59]

Meanwhile accidents and the suppression of all news thereof had continued. An air force plane crashed on November 17, 1938, above Darband, killing the pilot and demolishing the plane. No mention of the crash was made in any of the media.[60] From his verandah Engert witnessed another fatal air force crash near his house in Dezashub on August 13, 1939: "As usual in Iran, not a word about the accident has been permitted to get into the newspapers."[61]

"The Battle Order of the Iranian Army" gives a complete catalogue of the stock possessed by the Iranian air force on June 15, 1941, just two months before the Allied invasion and occupation of Iran (table 11.4). In 1934 the air force had consisted of 138 relatively modern British-made planes, and by 1941, it had increased to 233.[62]

In 1933 a de Havilland Tiger Moth fighter, including weapons, cost £3,750, while a Hawker bomber was £8,000. Thus the air force had £853,250 invested in these two models alone (59 de Havilland Tiger Moths and 79 Hawkers). Between 1934 and 1939 (the year in which British deliveries of airplanes to Iran ceased because of the outbreak of war with Germany), Iran purchased 32 de Havillands, 54 Hawker Hinds, and 11 Hawker Audaxes. If prices had remained at the 1933 level, the cost of the new acquisitions would have been £640,000. Even assuming that aircraft prices dou-

TABLE 11.4. Composition of Iranian Air Force in 1934 and on June 15, 1941

TYPE OF AIRCRAFT	1934	1941
De Havilland "Tiger Moth"	59	91
Hawker "Hind"	0	54
Hawker "Audax"	49	60
Hawker "Fury"	30	28
Other	7	12
Total	145	245

Source: American Legation, report (891.796/43), September 12, 1934, and dispatch 229 (891.248/58), October 2, 1934, both from William H. Hornibrook, "The Battle Order of the Iranian Army," enclosure to dispatch 102 (891.415/27), July 21, 1941, from Louis G. Dreyfus, Jr.

Note: Old airplanes in 1941 included two Junker W33s, three Airspeed Oxfords, two de Havilland Rapides, and one each of Wacko, Praga Sports, R.W. 10, Curtiss Wright, and Hurricane (described as unserviceable).

bled between 1933 and 1939, a highly unlikely assumption because of the Great Depression, total aircraft purchases by Iran between 1934 and 1941 amounted at most to £1,280,000. (That this is a highly inflated figure can be seen from the fact that in 1941, at the height of the Second World War, the complete cost of the most advanced fighter-bomber in the American arsenal, including weapons and the services of trained mechanics for one year, was £14,400.) Yet this liberal estimate is only one-tenth of the £12 million appropriated during that period (1934–41) from the Reserve Fund of the Nation for the purchase of armaments.

Summary

A detailed analysis of arms purchases shows that at most £2 million had been spent for warplanes, £1.5 million for the army, and £1 million on the navy, bearing in mind that its supposedly new ships were not new. Of the £18,412,000 ($92,060,000) allocated from 1928 to 1941 for the purchase of arms in Europe and America, at most £4.5 million had actually been spent for that purpose. As shown below, the unused balance of this sum at the end of Reza Shah's reign was only $508,000 (about £101,000). Had $91 million actually been spent on armaments Iran would have possessed an army and air force many times greater than it actually possessed in 1941. Even using the highly inflated 1941 prices for the most advanced American weapons ($70,000 for a warplane, $25,000 for a tank, and $5,000 for a truck), Iran could have potentially purchased 1,300 advanced American fighter-bombers, or over 3,500 tanks, or 18,000 trucks, or any appropriate combination thereof. In 1941, however, Iran actually possessed 245 warplanes, 100 tanks, and at most 500 trucks and tractors. Moreover, the army had only enough ammunition to last one or two days of fighting.

The evidence indicates that at least £14 million was diverted to Reza Shah's bank accounts. Thus, the claim by Dr. Mohammad Mossadeq that the bulk of Iran's oil revenues had been diverted to Reza Shah's accounts in Europe and America is substantiated. As for about £6.3 million ($31.5 million) supposedly allocated to such projects as port construction, railways, or railway maintenance, one can be fairly confident that the money was used to convert the income from Reza Shah's domestic assets into foreign exchange for deposit in foreign banks.[63] The data and analysis indicate that at least £20 million ($100 million), or two-thirds of Iran's oil royalties during 1927–41, was stolen and diverted by Reza Shah. As shown in chapter 12, confirmation was to come from unexpected sources. To appreciate the magnitude of this sum, the entire credit guarantee limit of the United States Export-Import Bank in 1940 was $100 million.

CHAPTER TWELVE

The Diversion of Iran's Oil Revenues and Reza Shah's Foreign Bank Accounts

O N JANUARY 25, 1941, THE ÐIVISION OF Near Eastern Affairs at the State Department in Washington received an unusual letter from Robert B. Malloch, a vice president of Indiana National Bank in Indianapolis (see fig. 12.1). Enclosed was a photostatic copy of two signatures which the bank was asking the State Department to certify. The letter also provides background to the affair.

The ranking officer referred to in the letter was Colonel Sadiq Shaybani, chief of the Iranian Military Purchasing Mission in Europe. The mission's agency through which the purchase of arms was handled was known as the Imperial Iranian Army Purchasing Commission, located in Bern. In addition to its bank account with the Swiss National Bank, the commission held bank accounts in the countries from which Iran purchased arms. One such account was with Indiana National Bank in Indianapolis, location of the Marmon-Herrington Company, which had supplied the Iranian army with armored cars and trucks.

Shaybani was murdered on July 19, 1940, in his office by a fellow officer who had also reportedly shot another officer before committing suicide. The circumstances surrounding this tragic affair and its bizarre aftermath are described by the American chargé d'affaires in Tehran, C. Van H. Engert:

I have the honor to report that on July 19, 1940, Colonel Sadiq Shaybani, Chief of the Iranian Military Mission in Europe, was killed in Bern, Switzerland,

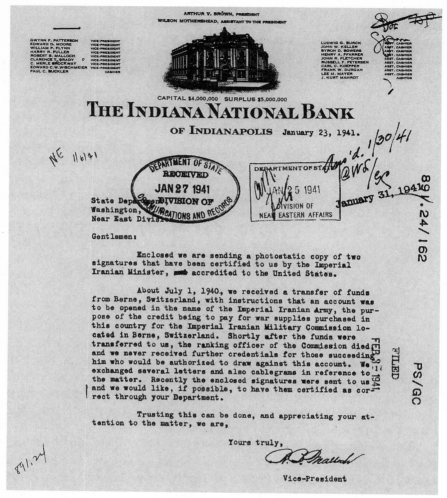

FIGURE 12.1 *Letter dated January 23, 1941, from Indiana National Bank to the State Department concerning Iranian army funds and requesting certification of the signatures of two individuals supposedly authorized to withdraw funds from the account.*

by Captain Farzin, a member of his staff. No reference to the incident has been permitted to appear in the local press, and it is only now that rumors regarding it are beginning to leak out. No government official has been allowed to mention it. As far as can be privately ascertained at this time the affray took place in Colonel Shaybani's office. Captain Farzin had been accused of appropriating some of the Mission's funds and had been dismissed. He refused to return to

Iran—where he would have been court-martialled—and asked to be reinstated. When his demand was refused he shot and killed Colonel Shaybani and wounded Major Khanlar, another member of the Mission. He then shot and killed himself. Major Khanlar is expected to recover. As both Colonel Shaybani and Captain Farzin belonged to very prominent Iranian families—Farzin was the son of Mohammad Ali Farzin, President of the National Bank of Iran—their tragic deaths have caused consternation in Tehran social circles, which was rendered all the more poignant because the friends and relatives of the two officers have not dared to speak of their grief for fear of incurring the displeasure of the authorities. Colonel Shaybani (also spelt Sheybani or Shaibani) was considered a very able man and, besides having for a number of years headed the Mission which was purchasing armaments for the Iranian army, he is also said to have been accredited as Military Attaché in London, Paris, and Bern. I am told he also spent some time in the United States to buy military equipment four or five years ago, but the index cards of the Legation do not refer to him.[1]

In the enforced silence that followed it was as though the two officers had never existed. The secrecy surrounding the incident tells us something about the reality of life in Iran under Reza Shah.

The Iranian minister in Washington mentioned in the letter from Indiana National Bank was Mohammad Schayesteh, who served as Iran's minister in Washington from 1939 to 1944, one of the longest terms of any Iranian envoy in Washington. Schayesteh's name came up again in relation to the Royal Bank of Canada (not to be confused with Canada's central bank, the Bank of Canada). On July 2, 1941, George T. Summerlin, chief of the protocol division at the State Department, received an unusual letter (dated June 5) from the Agency of the Royal Bank of Canada in New York:

My dear Mr. Summerlin:

We would be very grateful if you would please certify to us that Mr. Mohammed Schayesteh is, according to your present records, the Envoy Extraordinary and Minister Plenipotentiary of Iran. We may mention that one of our Toronto branches has some pending business with Mr. Schayesteh which will require his signature as Iran Minister and we, of course, are very anxious to satisfy ourselves that he is considered by your Department as the accredited representative of that country. It may be that his credentials as represented to your Department may also give him the power to represent his country in the Dominion of Canada, and if you can advise us on this point, it will be greatly appreciated. Thanking you in advance for your kind cooperation, we are, Yours very truly, N. C. Allingham, Assistant Agent[2]

Summerlin's reply was routine and noncommittal:

My dear Mr. Allingham:

In reply to your inquiry of June 5, 1941, the Honorable Mohammed Schayesteh, having presented letters of credence to the President on February

13, 1940, is the duly accredited Minister of Iran to the United States. Since his letters of credence presented to the President apply only to this Government, it is suggested that you communicate with the Iranian Legation, 2315 Massachusetts Avenue, Northwest, Washington, D.C., to ascertain whether the Minister is accredited also to Canada. It is not believed, however, that he is accredited also to that country.[3]

Summerlin could have added that since Iran possessed its own legation in Ottawa, the Royal Bank of Canada should have directed its inquiries there and not to Washington.

That the State Department was not overly happy about its involvement in these unusual banking affairs can be seen from its response to Indiana National Bank and the Royal Bank of Canada. A letter from Wallace Murray to R. B. Malloch of Indiana National Bank includes the following:

Although the photostat copy of the Minister's signature corresponds with his signature appearing on official documents in the Department, it is not possible for the Department to certify a Photostat copy of a signature. It is therefore suggested that you might care to have the Minister submit to the Department an original certification of the signatures of the two gentlemen in question. The Minister's signature will then be authenticated and the document returned to him for transmission to you, or will be forwarded direct to you if that should be his wish. The Department is unable to certify to the correctness of the signatures of the two persons mentioned in the Minister's certification, but possibly this will not be necessary for your purpose if the signature of the Minister is authenticated.[4]

Malloch immediately replied that his bank no longer wished to pursue the matter:

My dear Mr. Murray:
We thank you for your letter of January 31st, replying to our request that the photostatic copy of two signatures which were sent to you on January 23rd with request that they be certified, and which you were unable to do but suggested that the Iranian Minister's signature be certified by you. However, we will proceed no further, if you will kindly return the copy of the signatures to us, we will appreciate it.[5]

Murray returned the photostatic copy of the two signatures, but who were these two individuals who were now authorized to make transfers from the account of the Imperial Iranian Army at Indiana National Bank? Unfortunately, their identities are not given in State Department files. Shortly thereafter, a large transfer was made from the Iranian Army's account at Indiana National Bank to the Swiss National Bank.

The Transfer of Iranian Army Funds

On May 5, 1941, Wallace S. Murray, formerly in Tehran and now chief of Near Eastern Affairs at the State Department, received a visit from George E. Reynolds, manager of the Washington office of the Marmon-Herrington Company of Indianapolis. Reynolds had come to convey information he had received from Colonel Herrington, one of the company's partners. A State Department memorandum of the conversation includes the following:

> The Marmon-Herrington Company has been for several years manufacturing and selling to the Iranian Government large orders of military equipment. To pay for this equipment, the Iranian Government has maintained considerable dollar deposits in the Indiana National Bank at Indianapolis. The Marmon-Herrington Company has regularly drawn on these deposits to pay for the military shipments which have been going forward regularly to Iran. This morning a telegram was received by Indiana National Bank from the Iranian Purchasing Commission in Bern, Switzerland, to transfer all funds deposited in this country to Switzerland. There are, at the present time, said to be several hundred thousand dollars of such deposits. Mr. Reynolds said he felt quite sure this action of the Iranian Purchasing Commission was a direct result of the following United Press report that was broadcast over the radio on Saturday: Secretary of State Hull reveals that the Government is considering freezing the funds of all foreign countries. No decision has been reached. Hull said that such a general freezing order has been under study rather than a proposal to freeze only Axis funds. Under such procedure, the United States would not necessarily prevent the spending of frozen funds, but transactions then could only take place under licenses in which the applicants must state their reasons for wanting to spend the money. Mr. Reynolds stated that this action would undoubtedly be very detrimental to the interests of the Marmon-Herrington Company and he would be appreciative of any suggestions that the Department might have to make under the circumstances.[6]

It was in response to this approach that the State Department asked Treasury to ascertain if Iranian funds had been withdrawn from the United States. The Treasury Department responded that far from withdrawing the funds, the Iranians had been increasing their assets in the United States by shipping gold from Canada to the Irving Trust Company of New York. Thanks to the intervention of the FBI and its undercover investigation of foreign funds in the United States after 1938, we can piece together how Iran's oil revenues were diverted on the pretext of buying arms. We also know that the Iranian government funds kept at Indiana National Bank were not spent on the purchase of military supplies. Instead, the money was transferred to the Imperial Iranian Army Commission account with the Swiss National Bank at the National City Bank of New York. Thereafter, the money disappeared. We know this because the money was never transferred to the Iranian Army Commission account in Switzerland, where it was supposed to go.

The events surrounding Iranian funds at Indiana National Bank attracted the attention of the FBI, which subsequently launched an investigation. On July 5, 1941, FBI director J. Edgar Hoover sent a confidential letter, delivered by special messenger, to Adolf A. Berle Jr., assistant secretary of state, in which he describes the transfer of over $1 million from Indiana National Bank to the Imperial Iranian Army Commission account in Zurich (see fig. 12.2).

It is clear that the elaborate layers of banking (Indiana National Bank, Swiss National Bank, Bank of Canada, Royal Bank of Canada, and National City Bank of New York, not to mention the Irving Trust Company) were not consistent with the practices one expects to find in the normal handling of government funds and those of Bank Melli. The banking layers were intended to facilitate the disappearance of the money in the same manner that the gold shipments from Canada had vanished. Moreover, as described in the next chapter, the New York branches of Swiss banks (including the Swiss National Bank) played a crucial part in laundering and transferring Iranian funds to and from Switzerland.

In this particular case, we know that not only was the $1.13 million never spent on military supplies, but that the money was never returned to the account of the Imperial Iranian Army Purchasing Commission in Bern. In a State Department memorandum, J. J. Reinstein reports: "Mr. Fox telephoned me today to inform me that the Swiss National Bank recently transferred $508,000 to a New York bank for the account of Bank Mellie. The transfer was effected under the Swiss general license. The Treasury Department thought that the Department might have some interest in the information."[7] A copy of this memorandum was forwarded to the American legation in Tehran, and the American chargé d'affaires was informed that "[t]he information may be brought, in the discretion of the Officer in charge, to Dr. Millspaugh for his information or for any comment he may desire to make."[8]

Following the downfall of Reza Shah, Dr. A. C. Millspaugh had once again been made administrator general of Iranian finances in January 1943. Just as he had done from 1922 to 1927, Millspaugh again provided historians and posterity with valuable information. Millspaugh's response concerning the money transferred to New York was reported in a dispatch from Richard Ford, American chargé d'affaires ad interim in Tehran (see fig. 12.3).[9]

Sadly, of the $92 million appropriated for the purchase of armaments, only $508,000 remained. The remainder had vanished. It is also clear that the Swiss National Bank had been an accomplice in the diversion and loot-

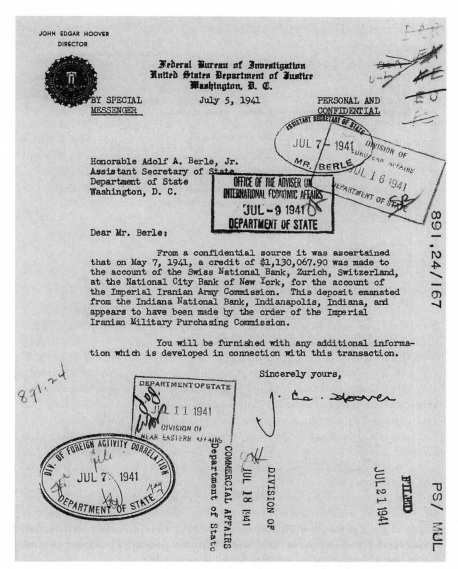

FIGURE 12.2 *Letter from J. Edgar Hoover, FBI director, to Adolf A. Berle Jr., assistant secretary of state, July 5, 1941, reporting a transfer of $1,130,067.90 from the account of the Iranian Army at Indiana National Bank to the Swiss National Bank.*

ing of Iran's oil revenues. From the analysis given in the previous chapter, it can be concluded that of the £18,412,000 appropriated for arms purchases abroad, at most £4.5 million was actually spent on the purchase of arms, and the remaining £14 million ($70 million) appears, as claimed by Mossadeq, to have been diverted to Reza Shah's bank accounts in Europe

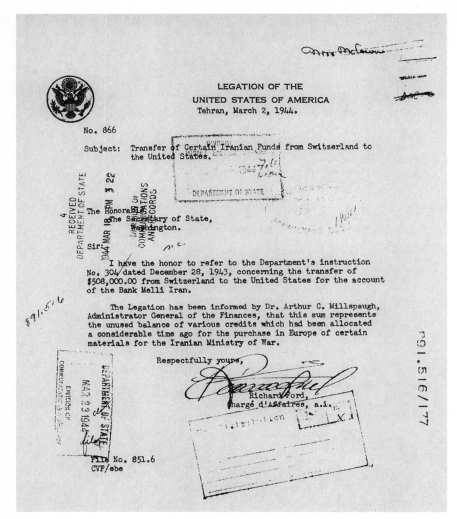

FIGURE 12.3 *Dispatch from Richard Ford, March 2, 1944, revealing the balance of unused funds remaining in the account of the Iranian Military Purchasing Commission in Switzerland at the end of Reza Shah's reign in 1941.*

and America. As described above, in 1939, 1940, and 1941, £2 million had been set aside each year to buy arms.

After the outbreak of World War II in 1939, however, no weapons could have been bought from the four main European belligerents—Britain, France, Germany, and Italy. Czechoslovakia, from whom Iran had purchased a hundred tanks, had been occupied by Germany in 1938. Moreover, as the State Department documents prove, all of Iran's requests for arms from the United States had been routinely rejected by the American government after 1939. Even the tinplate requested for Reza Shah's canning factory had been summarily rejected by the export control commission. American rejection of Iran's requests was in part due to British request that no arms be supplied to Reza Shah after 1939, as well as the urgent needs of the United States and the urgent war needs of Britain for war matériel and weapons.

The diversion of the Iranian Army funds to Swiss banks documented above was part of a pattern of the general plunder of Iran's oil revenues, especially in the last years of Reza Shah's rule. According to the adjustment agreement of August 1940 between the Anglo-Iranian Oil Company and the government of Iran, Iran's oil royalty for the year was to be £4 million, with an additional £1.5 million to be paid by the Company for 1938 and 1939. In other words, £5.5 million ($27.5 million) had been paid into the London Reserve Fund in 1940 alone. However, in September 1941, just after Reza Shah's downfall, there was a balance of £1.9 million in the Reserve Fund, against which there was a debit of £600,000, leaving a balance of £1.3 million.

Given that Iran received £5.5 million from APOC after the so-called adjustment to the concession, what had happened to the remaining £3.6 million? We know that it was not used to import goods into Iran. Furthermore, as documented below, imports from the United States to Iran were for all practical purposes prohibited. The few items Iran desired to purchase from the United States were not available, and nearly all Iranian applications for export licenses had been rejected.

Gold Shipments to New York

Documentary evidence also suggests that some of Iran's oil revenues were converted into gold and deposited in commercial banks in New York, after which the gold had simply disappeared without a trace. As outlined above, as part of the adjustment agreement in August 1940, the British government had agreed to convert up to £3 million per year into dollars or gold at the official rate of exchange. The evidence indicates that as soon as the agreement was signed, London instructed the Bank of Canada to supply the government of Iran with gold, and gold shipments from Canada to the Bank Melli account at the Irving Trust Company of New York had begun. Information on gold shipments from Canada to the Irving Trust Company of New York is given in a memorandum of conversation dated October 18, 1940, between L. W. Knoke of the Federal Reserve Bank of New York, and Governor Towers of the Bank of Canada (Canada's central bank):

> Governor Towers of the Bank of Canada called this afternoon at 4:20 p.m. We might be interested, he said, in a little background of two transactions

recently put through by them as follows: (1) a gold shipment from Ottawa to Irving Trust Company of about 115,000 ounces [$2,022,000] for account of Banque Millie Iran, and (2) a payment to Chemical National Bank of $643,000–odd for account of Central Bank of Bolivia. In both cases Bank of Canada received instructions from London, in connection with certain British payment agreements, to place gold in the name of the Banque Millie Iran and the Central Bank of Bolivia, respectively. Thereupon, under instructions from the people concerned, they made the above shipment to the Irving Trust Company and the above payment to the Chemical National Bank.[10]

Given that the instructions had come from London, and in light of Engert's report, it is clear that the gold constituted payment for Iran's oil exports. What is noteworthy is that the gold had been shipped to Irving Trust Company and not to the Federal Reserve Bank of New York, where ordinarily Iran's gold reserves should have been kept. Moreover, given the date of Governor Towers's call, gold shipments from Canada to New York had begun almost immediately after the signing of the adjustment agreement between the Iranian government and the Anglo-Iranian Oil Company. It is also clear that the gold shipments had continued. Evidence is found in a memorandum from the Treasury Department to the State Department.

In early 1941, there had been rumors of an impending freeze on all foreign funds in the United States. This had caused some concern that Iranian funds in U.S. banks might be transferred to Switzerland. The matter of Iranian funds had been discussed within the State and Treasury Departments, and the results are given in the following memo from a treasury official to Murray at the State Department:

> I discussed this matter with Mr. Livesey, EA [Economic Affairs], who states that it is not known whether or not there is to be a general freezing of funds, and that, therefore, no statement can be made concerning the question. It is his opinion that, since no reassurances can be given to Mr. Reynolds or to the Iranians, there is nothing which can be done. Mr. Livesey communicated with Mr. Cochran of the Treasury Department and ascertained that there have been no substantial withdrawals of Iranian funds from the Irving Trust Company, where it is understood that the Iranians keep most of their funds in the U.S. for distribution to meet payments for materials ordered. On the other hand, the Iranians have been bringing gold in from Canada to augment their assets.[11]

It is also clear that the gold had subsequently disappeared without a trace. In 1943, Millspaugh suggested that to counter inflation some gold should be sold to the public. This measure was intended to reduce the war-induced liquidity in the Iranian economy. By converting the public's cash into gold and not goods, inflation pressures would abate. The suggestion had met with approval from the American government and it was agreed between the U.S. Treasury Department and Bank Melli Iran that gold was to be shipped from the United States to Iran.

Numerous shipments of gold by air from New York to Iran were made between 1943 and 1945. In 1943, however, despite all the gold shipments mentioned in the State Department memo and by Governor Towers of the Bank of Canada, Bank Melli Iran did not own any gold in the United States. According to Treasury records, Iran had to buy the gold from the Treasury Department and pay for it with dollars. The department had been prepared to sell up to $8 million in gold to Bank Melli Iran.[12]

Reza Shah's Foreign Bank Accounts

State Department records provide a rich source of documentation on Reza Shah's fortune in foreign banks. Based on these records we know that his bank deposits in London exceeded £20 million ($100 million), and were most likely as high as £25 million ($125 million). The 1941 Census of Foreign-Owned Assets in the United States indicates that Reza Shah's assets in the United States at the time of his abdication were at least $18.5 million. From reports by American diplomats in Switzerland, we can conclude that Reza Shah's accounts with Swiss banks were considerable. In addition, in 1941, the shah had $50 million on deposit with Iranian banks. The shah had thus amassed at least $200 million in banks in London, New York, Switzerland, Tehran, and Toronto. In today's terms, that sum is equivalent to at least $7 billion and does not include stocks and bonds in America and Europe, his vast holdings of real estate, agricultural land, industrial and commercial establishments, and the finest pieces of Iran's ancient crown jewels. In relative as well as absolute terms, it ranks as one of the greatest robberies of all time by an individual. It also shows how easy it is to plunder a nation, keep the loot, and pass it on to the next generation.

At the time of his abdication and flight in September 1941, there was endless speculation about the existence of vast sums Reza Shah had supposedly stashed in foreign banks. Dreyfus, the American minister in Tehran, describes the confusion and deception surrounding this matter:

> There has been no end of conjecture and false reports concerning the former Shah's deposits abroad, some persons declaring that they amount to more than one hundred million dollars. Speeches and reports concerning these foreign deposits have been typical of the confusion reigning in government circles since officials have had to begin to think for themselves. Speakers or writers would report that steps were being taken to obtain possession of the deposits only to state next day that investigation had shown that there were no such deposits and to return the following day to the previous or another stand. As a matter of fact, no evidence of any deposits in foreign banks or holdings of properties or valuables in foreign countries has yet been produced. The Prime Minister

informed the Majlis on September 28 that, in order to relieve the fears of the people on this score, the Government had obtained from the former Shah a document signed before a notary public which states that he agrees that any sums he may possess in foreign banks are to be considered as included in the transfer of his property to the Shah. . . .

   Nothing has been said, it may be noted, as to the disposition of stocks and bonds which the ex-Shah may possess in foreign countries.[13]

The governments of both Britain and Iran, especially Mohammad Ali Foroughi, Reza Shah's old crony, had participated in a cover-up of the shah's foreign bank accounts. As his partner, the British had a vested interest in concealing the extent of the plunder. Similarly, Foroughi had been a partner in Reza Shah's corruption and a beneficiary of bribes and presents.

   The Iranians who had aided Reza Shah's transfer of funds to foreign banks and were knowledgeable on the subject were all in Iran and continued to hold high positions. All the former heads of Bank Melli and chiefs of the Foreign Exchange Commission of the Ministry of Finance were also all there, and most continued to hold high positions. Two of Foroughi's ministers, Abbas Qoli Golshayan and Yadollah Azodi, had served as chiefs of the Foreign Exchange Commission. Two individuals who had served for many years as heads of Bank Melli since 1933—General Reza Qoli Amir Khosrovi and Mohammad Ali Farzin—were also in Iran. As described below, Reza Shah's instructions for transfers from Midland Bank, where Iran's oil revenues were kept, to his personal accounts at the Westminster Bank had been handled by Amir Khosrovi. These people must have been knowledgeable about Reza Shah's foreign bank accounts. All these people had continued to maintain silence evidently because Reza Shah's son and successor made it worthwhile for them.[14]

Reza Shah's London Account

In 1931, Charles C. Hart, the American minister in Tehran, reported that Reza Shah had personally banked more than a million pounds in London. From a handful of banking documents that the Pahlavis had neglected to destroy prior to their mass flight from Iran in 1978, we learn that Hart's caustic remarks about Reza Shah's London bank accounts were not baseless speculation. What Hart did not know was that Reza Shah already held dollar-denominated accounts in London, Geneva, and Berlin. The surviving documents reveal the diversion of Iran's oil revenues to Reza Shah's personal bank accounts.[15]

   In a confidential letter dated August 17, 1931, Colonel Reza-Qoli Amir Khosrovi, director general of Banque Pahlevi (Pahlavi Bank) told Dr. Kurt Lindenblatt, president of the National Bank of Persia (Bank Melli): "Excel-

lency, Based on His Majesty's order, I beg you to send telegraphic instruction to the Midland Bank in London to deposit $150,000 in His Majesty's
account at the Westminster Bank, and confirm it by wire. With my highest
esteem to you, Mr. President, Director General, Colonel Amir Khosrovi."[16]
Lindenblatt replied: "Excellency, Following receipt of your instruction
number 5170 of 17 August, I have the honor to inform you that yesterday
immediately following the receipt of your letter, I gave telegraphic instruction to the Midland Bank Ltd. of London to deposit $150,000 to the
account of His Majesty at the Westminster Bank Ltd., London. The Westminster Bank has received our telegraphic instructions and will inform
you of the receipt of the money. My highest salutation and consideration to
Your Excellency. Dr. Lindenblatt, National Bank of Persia."[17]

On September 4, 1931, the Westminster Bank acknowledged a deposit of
$150,000. The transfer of money in $150,000 amounts to Reza Shah's
accounts continued. For instance, on August 25, 1932, the Westminster
Bank acknowledged another deposit of $150,000 to His Majesty's account.
In 1931, in addition to his London accounts, $150,000 was deposited in both
the Union de Banque Suisse and the Reich Kredit Gesellschaft of Berlin.

The significance of the above correspondence is not the amounts
involved. By Reza Shah's standards, $150,000 was a small sum, a fraction of
the monthly transfers from New York to Switzerland. The important fact is
that the oil revenues paid by the Anglo-Persian Oil Company were paid to
Iran's Reserve Fund in London. This fund was at first banked at the London office of the Imperial Bank of Persia. Subsequently, the funds were
deposited in the Midland Bank in London. Here is a clear indication that
Reza Shah was diverting Iran's oil revenues to his own personal accounts.

Immediately after the invasion and occupation of Iran in August 1941,
the British government had announced that "Iranians" holding sterling
deposits in London would continue to have full access to the money, subject to the exchange controls. A report in the London magazine *Economist*
includes the following: "The Anglo-Russian entry into Iran is not being
accompanied by the customary financial trappings of belligerency. Iran is
not to share the fate of enemy and enemy-occupied territories, or even
Japan, in having its sterling assets frozen. Iranian nationals are to have
complete freedom—within the framework of sterling exchange control, of
course—to operate their sterling accounts and deal with their sterling
securities."[18]

As reported above, at the time of this announcement, the net amount
remaining in the Reserve Fund was only £1.3 million. The Iranian national
holding vast sums in sterling was of course Reza Shah. The announcement
was intended to reassure him and encourage him to cooperate. He was to
quickly surrender and leave quietly on a British ship. That the shah had

nearly £30 million in London was also known in Iran at the time. Abdol Hossein Hajir, a trusted Pahlavi aide, "had gone to England in the early 1940s, it was said, to rescue Reza Shah's fortune—some £20 million to £30 million or more—which the British Government had locked up until after the war."[19]

After Reza Shah's death in July 1944, this money had been inherited by his son and successor, Mohammad Reza Shah. Confirmation of this matter was to come from a totally unexpected source. In the fall of 1957, Reza Afshar, who had held several important posts under Reza Shah, including the governorship of Gilan, visited the United States. While in the nation's capital, Afshar, then managing director of Iranian Airways, predecessor to Iran National Airlines (Iran Air), had called on the State Department. His conversation with State Department officials Murat W. Williams, Grant E. Mouser, and Howard J. Ashford is reported in a confidential memorandum (see fig. 12.4).[20]

The shah's money was blocked by the British restrictions on exchange and capital transfers that had been imposed since the beginning of World War II.[21] By purchasing planes and other equipment from Britain and paying in pounds, the shah would be repaid by the Iranian government in dollars or another fully convertible currency, such as Swiss francs. The huge sums in the Shah's London accounts explain the large-scale purchase of British equipment during the 1950s, including several thousand British-made Massey-Harris tractors bought in 1954–55 and apparently paid for from the shah's London accounts. The fleet of British Leyland double-decker buses for use in Tehran had been purchased (at a cost of £5 million) from the same account. We also learn from the State Department memorandum that for some time presumably funds from the account went for British planes, including a plane purchased by the Imperial Iranian Air Force (IIAF) under the guise of the Iranian Aero Club: "He [Afshar] referred in a critical fashion to the role of General Gilanshah, Chief of the IIAF General Staff, in his capacity as head of the Iranian Aero Club and the fact that the Club was now using three recently-purchased British pioneer aircraft to accept revenue traffic for flights within Iran."[22]

After all these purchases, £20 million still remained in the shah's London accounts. Having served as an instrument and pretext for diverting Iran's oil revenues to Reza Shah's London bank accounts in the 1930s, Iranian aviation was still being used in the 1950s as a way of converting these sterling balances into dollars and Swiss francs. Once again, Great Britain and the Pahlavis were the winners. The Iranian people were the losers. Moreover, given the timing of Afshar's conversation and given that Britain had imposed exchange restrictions since 1939, there can be no doubt that this money was part of Iran's oil revenues that had been stolen by Reza Shah.

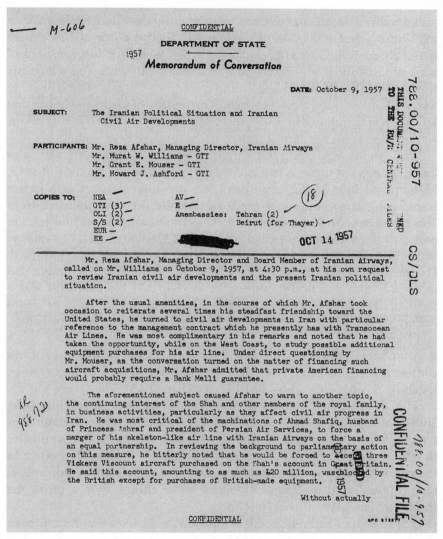

FIGURE 12.4 *Memorandum of conversation between Reza Afshar, managing director of Iranian Airways, and State Department officials, October 9, 1957. Afshar reveals that the shah's account in London was "as much as £20 million"—doubtless the part of Iran's oil reserves that had been diverted by Reza Shah.*

Reza Shah's Fortune in New York

Rumors that Reza Shah was transferring large sums to American banks had circulated widely in Tehran. In June 1941, pursuant to an executive order from President Roosevelt, the Treasury Department conducted a census of foreign-owned assets in the United States as of June 14, 1941.[23] The findings, published in 1945, allow a relatively accurate estimate of Reza Shah's assets in the United States at the time of his downfall. Total assets owned by Iranian nationals amounted to $18.5 million. Of this, $14.1 million consisted of bank deposits and gold bullion held with commercial banks. This was clearly Iran's oil revenue that had been transferred from Canada. The remaining $4.4 million consisted almost entirely of ownership of stocks and bonds that Dreyfus had mentioned in his dispatch. The assets owned by Iranian nationals doubtless consisted almost entirely of the funds of Reza Shah.[24]

While funds were being transferred to New York, large sums were also being transferred to Swiss banks. As documented below, from April 1943, Mohammad Reza Shah, Reza Shah's son and successor, had also begun transferring large sums to New York. Despite the new transfers from Tehran to New York, by October 1943 private balances held by Iranian nationals in American banks had fallen to $12,359,000 (from $14.1 million in 1941), a clear indication that the transfers to Swiss banks had continued. On the other hand, official balances held by the Iranian government had increased from practically nothing in 1939 to $21,145,000. This was a result of converting 60 percent of Iran's oil revenues for 1942 and 1943 into dollars, as provided for in the 1942 financial agreement between Britain and Iran.[25]

After Reza Shah's death, in July 1944, two issues had created discord and conflict among his heirs. First, there was the alleged theft of Iran's crown jewels by those present at his bedside (see chapter 13). Then there was the division of Reza Shah's money in American banks. Reza Shah's third wife, Touran Amir Soleimani (Queen Touran), describes these matters in a series of letters to her son, Gholam Reza Pahlavi. Written in 1945 and 1946, shortly after Reza Shah's death and when Gholam Reza was a student at Princeton University, the letters are part of a collection of documents recently published in Tehran.[26] Among other things, they confirm the shah's vast bank accounts in New York.

Queen Touran had repeatedly complained to her son that he had been cheated out of his share of Reza Shah's fortune by Queen Taj-ol-Moluk and her children (Mohammad Reza Pahlavi, Shams Pahlavi, Ashraf Pahlavi, etc.). Queen Touran had unwisely suggested to Gholam Reza that he write a formal letter of complaint to the Majlis, declaring that he had been cheated out of his inheritance by his siblings.

The letters also reveal that Iran's new ambassador to the United States in 1945, Hossein Alai, Mohammad Schayesteh's successor, had been entrusted to contact the American banks concerning the division of the shah's money among the heirs. A year after Reza Shah's death, Amir Soleimani wrote her son:

I have learned from various sources that, apart from his official task as ambassador, Ala has another mission. It concerns Reza Shah's fortune in American banks. My dearest, please keep your ears and eyes fully open. Please do not let the events after your father's death be repeated. Remember how those scoundrels stole his jewels after his death and are now living the good life in Tehran. . . . Now that Ala has arrived in America, go and see him, speak frankly with him, and explain your situation. I have already spoken to him in Tehran and have put him in the picture.[27]

Subsequently, according to secret State Department reports, Alai had considerable difficulty with fifteen-year-old Hamid-Reza, the youngest son of Reza Shah. On several occasions he ran away to Paris from his boarding school in Newport, Rhode Island, and was threatening to repeat the pattern. One report on the "elusive prince" notes that he had "considerable funds at the time of his previous departure [for Paris], the source of which is unknown."[28] The author of the report did not have to look far to discover the source.

Reza Shah's Swiss Accounts: Villard's Final Contribution

Finally, there are indications that the transfers from New York to Swiss banks were for the benefit of Reza Shah. Moreover, he had already amassed vast sums in Swiss accounts. In September 1941, a series of reports by the British Broadcasting Corporation claimed that Reza Shah had deposited huge sums in foreign banks. When informed of the broadcasts, Reza Shah smiled bitterly and said, "I have a little over three pounds in a Swiss bank which is the balance remaining from the money I sent there for the education of my son."[29]

However, a subsequent report by Henry S. Villard showed that the Swiss transfers by Reza Shah had been considerable. Villard, who had been the American consul in Tehran from 1930 to 1932 and had subsequently served in the Division of Near Eastern Affairs, was in 1959 the U.S. representative to the International Organizations in Geneva. From May 2 to May 5, 1959, Reza Shah's son and successor, Mohammad Reza Shah Pahlavi, then shah of Iran, had visited Geneva. Villard, who maintained a keen interest in Iran, described the shah's visit, and a portion of his report is reproduced here (fig. 12.5).[30]

In view of the Villard's report, Reza Shah's transfers from New York to Swiss banks and the fact that the Imperial Iranian Army Purchasing Commission had been located in Switzerland acquire added significance. It appears that just as Swiss banks had participated in the plunder of Jewish refugees fleeing the Nazis, they had also been active collaborators in the looting of the Iranian people. After he fled Iran to Italy in August 1953, and before his restoration to power by a CIA coup, press reports in Italy and Switzerland had given the final destination of the ex-shah (the term they used) as Switzerland, supposedly because it was a neutral country and the

FOREIGN SERVICE DESPATCH

(Security Classification)

FROM : U. S. Resident Delegation and
American Consulate General, GENEVA
No. 275

TO : THE DEPARTMENT OF STATE, WASHINGTON.

May 5, 1959

REF :

ACTION	DEPT.
For Dept. Use Only	
REC'D	

SUBJECT: Shah of Iran Visits Geneva

As is customary with foreign dignitaries, the Geneva press has devoted considerable attention to the visit to Geneva, from May 2 to 5, of Shah-in-Shah Mohammad Reza Pahlevi. The Shah was met on his arrival by members of the diplomatic community, including the principal consular officers of the United Kingdom and Germany, the Pakistani charge d'affaires and Consul Stanley R. Lawson of this office. On his departure the British charge d'affaires in Bern, Consul Lawson and others were present. The Shah's host during his stay in Geneva was General Fazllolah ZAHEDI, Iranian ambassador in Geneva, who is the father-in-law of the Shah's daughter.

This is the Shah's second visit to Geneva in recent months. Press reports indicate that on May 4 he inspected a villa situated at 27, Chemin du Velours, in the Chene Bougeries district, which has been bought in his behalf by General Zahedi. Other press reports indicate that the Shah consulted with Geneva bankers handling his financial interests. According to earlier, private reports, the Shah has been purchasing apartment houses in Geneva through General Zahedi, and has rented some as furnished apartments (a more highly profitable operation than unfurnished rental) while leaving others unoccupied.

The implication gained by local observers from the press reports is that the Shah may be preparing a refuge in Geneva, in the event that he is forced by political developments to leave Iran.

Henry S. Villard
United States Representative
to International Organizations in Geneva

cc:
AmEmbassy - Bern
AmEmbassy - Tehran

DHPopper/seg

Official Use Only

REPORTER

ACTION COPY — DEPARTMENT OF STATE

The action office must return this permanent record copy to DC/R files with an endorsement of action taken.

FIGURE 12.5 *Villard's dispatch of May 5, 1959, revealing that the shah had been purchasing apartment houses in Geneva and consulting with his bankers in the city. Given the timing of the report, the shah probably paid for the Swiss real estate from funds that had been allocated to arms purchases during Reza Shah's reign and subsequently diverted to his personal account.*

ex-shah had attended school there. The main reason was that part of his inheritance from his father (his three pounds) was banked there.

Reza Shah's Domestic Accounts

With the departure of Reza Shah in September 1941, the people of Iran were able to glimpse a small part of the wealth he had accumulated from 1921 to 1941. Dreyfus reports that on September 28, 1941, Prime Minister Mohammad Ali Foroughi informed the Majlis that Reza Shah's cash deposits at Bank Melli amounted to "the unbelievable sum of 680,000,000 rials [$42.5 million]." (As the most senior American diplomat in Iran, Dreyfus's annual salary was about $8,000.) Dreyfus further comments: "There was little of value in the country, in fact, in which he [Reza Shah] was not interested. His greed knew no bounds and in addition to acquiring a large part of Mazandaran he bought city properties, built hotels and operated factories. . . . It may be mentioned that the former Shah took any and all lands he wanted to his avaricious bosom under formal or implied threat of some kind of harm to the owners. He paid whatever pleased him to pay, usually a tenth or twentieth part of the value, although it is said he paid as little as a hundredth in some cases."[31]

What Dreyfus did not know was that Foroughi and Minister of Finance Golshayan were either unaware or had deliberately failed to inform the Majlis that this was Reza Shah's *savings* account at Bank Melli. Reza Shah maintained a checking account at the same bank, with a balance of "only" 85 million rials ($5.3 million). Had it not been for Reza Shah's insistence (from exile) that this sum (in his checking account) too be converted to dollars and transferred to him, its existence may never have been noticed by historians. In a letter to his son and successor, sent from Mauritius and published after the Islamic revolution, Reza Shah shows that, despite the vast sums already stashed in foreign banks, he could not bear to forgo this final $5.3 million:

> The other matter that I wanted to bring to your attention is that it has been some time that no money has been sent to me [from Iran]. When I left Iran, I had in excess of 85,000,000 rials in my current account with Bank Melli. I placed this money at the disposal of [Mahmud] Jam so that it can be sent to me when needed. After a while a letter came from Jam informing us that he was leaving on a mission, and he had entrusted the money to your care. This money has still not been converted into foreign exchange and sent to me. So as not to keep me waiting, it is necessary that you should arrange for its conversion into foreign exchange and transfer it to me.[32]

The New Shah's Money Transfers via Diplomatic Pouch, 1943–1952

Soon after succeeding his father, Mohammad Reza Shah with remarkable continuity carried on his father's practice of transferring money from Iran to banks in the United States, as documented by declassified State Department files. In March 1943, the new shah opened an account under his own name at the Guaranty Trust Company of New York with a deposit of $1 million. We have a record of this matter because the shah requested the assistance of the American legation in Tehran and the use of the diplomatic pouch to send the papers to New York. On March 10, 1943, the American Minister in Tehran, Louis G. Dreyfus, Jr., had sent a strictly confidential telegram to the Secretary of State (fig. 12.6).[33]

Acting Secretary of State Wells replied: "Strictly confidential, to be decoded by the Minister only. Your 255, March 10. Department assumes that funds involved are legitimate personal property of Shah. If this is the case, you are authorized to transmit the letter in question in diplomatic pouch. Wells."[34] Despite twenty years of American diplomatic reports from Tehran on the manner in which Reza Shah had acquired his wealth and despite the State Department's knowledge that Iran's oil revenues were being diverted to his accounts in New York and in Europe, the department assumed "that funds involved are legitimate property of Shah." Moreover, the same Dreyfus who had written that "the former Shah took any and all lands he wanted to his avaricious bosom under formal or implied threat of some kind of harm to the owners" was now accepting the proposition that the money derived by such methods constituted legitimate property.

The shah's application and the following letter from the chief manager and chief accountant of the Imperial Bank of Iran, dated March 7, were sent to Guaranty Trust in the American diplomatic pouch:

> We enclose a request addressed to you by His Imperial Majesty Mohammad Reza Shah Pahlavi, Shah of Iran, for the opening in your books of a current account in his name. We feel sure that you will be willing to accede to the request of His Imperial Majesty and we hereby authorize you to debit our account with you with Dollars 1,000,000—(One million dollars)—for the credit of his account.
>
> We shall be obliged if you will treat all correspondence relating to this account as strictly confidential, and address any communications to us, marked confidential, for transmission by us to His Imperial Majesty. On receipt of this letter please confirm to us by telegram that the account has been opened and please send us a cheque book for transmission by us to H.I.M. for use on the account.
>
> P.S. We suggest you send any written communications on this subject through our London Office who will forward them to us.[35]

TELEGRAM RECEIVED

CORRECTED COPY
~~FROM~~

Tehran

Dated March 10, 1943

Rec'd 4:51 p.m.

Secretary of State,

Washington.

891.001/72

255, March 10, 3 p.m.

FC NE FF

STRICTLY CONFIDENTIAL.

F.W. 891.001/72

I have been requested to transmit in pouch a
letter addressed by Imperial Bank of Iran to Guaranty
Trust Company enclosing application of His Majesty
the Shah for the opening of a private account in his
own name of one million dollars. Before complying I
should appreciate Department's instructions.

I understand that the rials with which the dollars
were purchased were part of the more than six hundred
millions left by Shah Reza to present Shah. It would
appear that Shah desires to have money abroad for two
reasons: (1) to take care of himself and family should
he ever have to leave Iran and (2) because he is being
mulcted out of his money through contributions under
pressure for charitable and other purposes.

This matter is being treated with utmost secrecy
here since its disclosure might have repercussions
extremely harmful to Iran's delicate political situation.

Transmission

FIGURE 12.6 *Telegram from Dreyfus, March 10, 1943, reporting the shah's request to use the American embassy's diplomatic pouch to transfer his application to open a personal account with an initial deposit of $1 million at the Guaranty Trust Company of New York.*

In the shah's application the opening balance is given as $1 million, which "would be remitted through the Imperial Bank of Iran."[36] The application and enclosures were forwarded to Guaranty Trust Company on April 19 by Paul H. Alling, who succeeded Wallace Murray as chief of the Division of Near Eastern Affairs. On the same day, the State Department sent the following strictly confidential telegram: "To the American Minister, Tehran. The Secretary of State acknowledges receipt of the Minister's despatch no. 491 of March 18, 1943, enclosing a letter addressed by the Imperial Bank of Iran to the Guaranty Trust Company of New York. The enclosure in question has been forwarded to the Guaranty Trust Company of New York."[37] Finally, on April 21, Harold F. Anderson, second vice president of Guaranty Trust Company of New York, replied to Alling (fig. 12.7).[38]

Subsequent documents reveal that the shah's $1 million deposit was made at Guaranty Trust (fig. 12.8). The shah's transfer of funds to New York through the British-owned Imperial Bank of Iran continued from 1943 until the latter bank was forced to leave Iran by Dr. Mossadeq in 1952. Thereafter, according to State Department records, the department's diplomatic pouch once again became the conveyance for His Majesty's transactions with New York banks (see figs. 12.9, 12.10).[39]

At a time when, due to war and foreign occupation, the people of Iran were faced with famine and suffering, the new shah, then twenty-four and following in the footsteps of his father, had begun transferring money to foreign banks, especially in America. We must conclude that during the next thirty-five years he transferred vast sums out of the country. The State Department's role in facilitating this transfer was assuredly a breach of American law because the department had ample evidence that the money had been acquired illegally, that it rightly belonged to the people of Iran. Why was the U.S. government so anxious to help and protect Mohammad Reza Shah and his regime that it even facilitated his money transfers? The short answer is found in the presidential finding signed by Franklin D. Roosevelt on March 10, 1942, which states that "the defense of the Government of Iran is vital to the defense of the United States."[40] For the next thirty-seven years, until the Islamic revolution, the United States was to replace Great Britain as the protector of the Pahlavi regime.

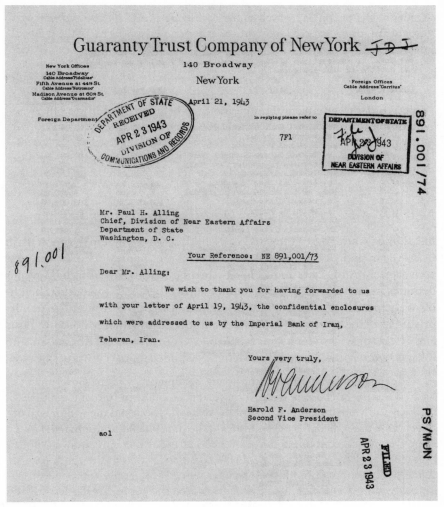

FIGURE 12.7 *Letter from the Guaranty Trust Company of New York to the State Department, April 21, 1943, acknowledging receipt of the shah's application and initial deposit ("confidential enclosures").*

During the period between January 18, 1943 and August 13, 1943, the following accounts have been opened with the Guaranty Trust Company, New York, on instructions of the Imperial Bank of Iran, whose account was debited in each instance.

Opening Date	Name	Opening Bal	Balance as of August 13, 1943
1/18/43	Mr. Sardar Sahib Singh	$30,000.00	$99,999.80
2/25	Mr. Michel Saab (Blocked France)	74,988.41	74,988.31
3/10	Dr. Mohammad Moazed	10,000.00	27,500.00
3/18	Mr. Mohamoud Pour-Reza	10,000.00	127,493.07
3/25	Mr. Rustam Rahman Shahpour Guiv	25,000.00	50,991.89
3/25	Mr. Avanees Baghdassari Garibian	15,000.00	14,999.90
4/13	Mr. Soliman Arastoonadoh	10,000.00	10,000.00
4/13	Mr. Abdollah Shoul Shashoua	19,979.98	9,971.83
4/15	Mme. Nektar Baghdassari Garibian	6,000.00	6,000.00
4/15	Mr. Sedrak Aivaz-Zadeh	100,000.00	100,000.00
4/15	Mr. Salim S. Shiry	10,000.00	80,011.46
4/15	Mrs. Gunhild Karamian	10,000.00	10,000.00
4/15	Mr. Hossein Paveh Isadi	50,000.00	1,987.78
5/11	Mr. Antoine Aysseh	95,000.00	139,993.94
4/20	His Imperial Majesty Mohammad Reza Pahlavi, Shah of Iran	1,000,000.00	1,000,000.00
5/11	General Khodayai Khodayar	15,000.00	15,000.00
6/18	Mr. Fred Abraham Tanimi	10,000.00	9,999.50
6/18	Mr. Mohammad Asseni	50,000.00	49,999.50
6/18	Mr. Kazem Behdjou	20,000.00	19,999.50
6/18	Mr. Abbass Eskandari	15,000.00	14,999.50
6/18	Mr. Heydar Gholi Hechmati	8,000.00	7,999.50
6/18	Mr. Bohaeddin Kohbod	70,000.00	75,404.18
6/18	Mr. Massoud Sabeti	20,000.00	20,000.00
6/18	Mr. Edward Minas Shismanian (Blocked France)	10,000.00	9,999.50
6/19/43	Mr. Emad Kia % Iranian Consulate New York City	55,346.00	47,991.38
5/18/43	Mr. Emir Jalil Mojdei Pasteur Avenue, St. Jalilabad No. 26, Teheran, Iran	35,000.00	34,999.90
4/25/39	Mr. Saleh Rahmin Masri % K. & E. M. Lawee Al Rashid Street Baghdad, Iraq.	10,000.00	30,380.71
4/25/39	Gourdji Rahmin Masri c/o K. & E. M. Lawee Al Rashid Street Baghdad, Iraq		76,318.21

FIGURE 12.8 *Confirmation of the shah's $1 million deposit at the Guaranty Trust Company of New York on April 20, 1943. In this report of October 19, 1943, Samuel S. Gilbert of the Treasury Department informed Francis H. Russell of the State Department: "The Federal Reserve Bank of New York has made available to this office information concerning deposits of Iranians at the Guaranty Trust Company, New York, on instructions of the Imperial Bank of Iran. Enclosed herewith is a record of these accounts which may be of interest to your department."*

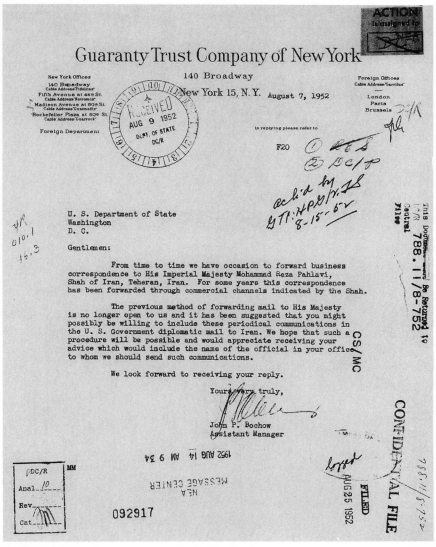

FIGURE 12.9 *Letter from the Guaranty Trust Company of New York to the State Department, August 7, 1952, requesting use of the diplomatic pouch to conduct banking business with the shah after the closure of the Imperial Bank of Iran, 1952. The letter confirms that the shah had been conducting "banking business," a euphemism for the transfer of funds to New York, through the Imperial Bank of Iran.*

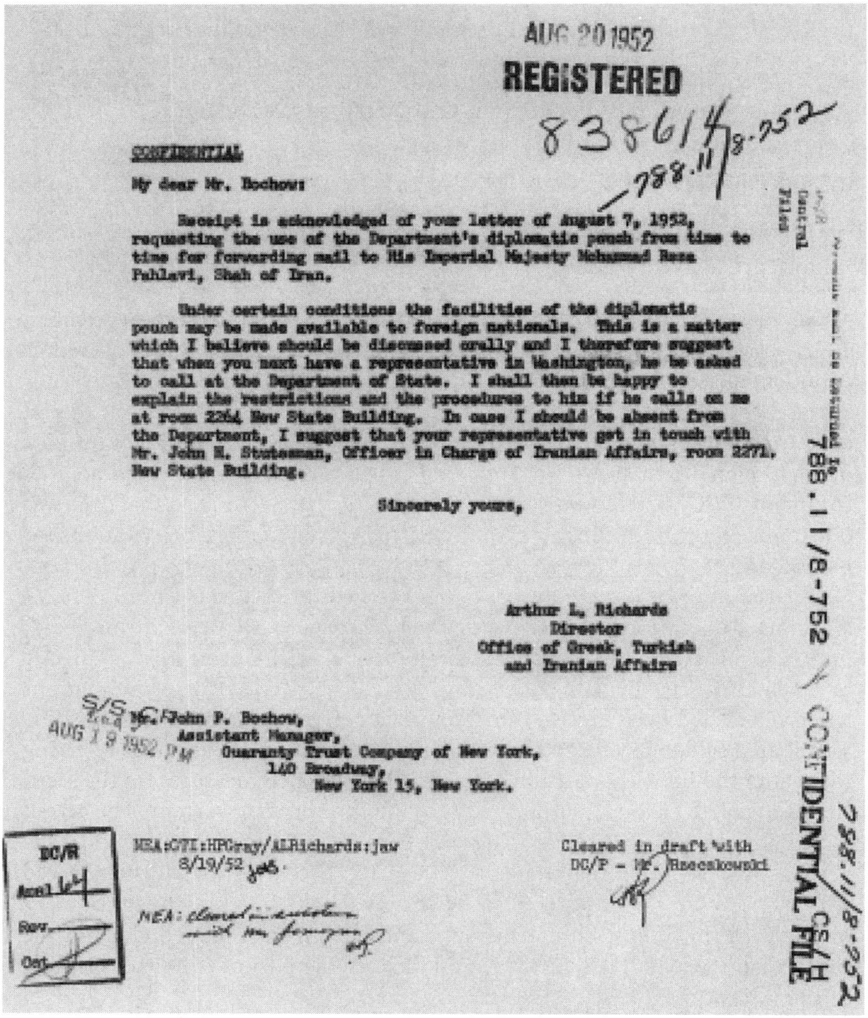

CONFIDENTIAL

My dear Mr. Bochow:

Receipt is acknowledged of your letter of August 7, 1952, requesting the use of the Department's diplomatic pouch from time to time for forwarding mail to His Imperial Majesty Mohammad Reza Pahlavi, Shah of Iran.

Under certain conditions the facilities of the diplomatic pouch may be made available to foreign nationals. This is a matter which I believe should be discussed orally and I therefore suggest that when you next have a representative in Washington, he be asked to call at the Department of State. I shall then be happy to explain the restrictions and the procedures to him if he calls on me at room 2264 New State Building. In case I should be absent from the Department, I suggest that your representative get in touch with Mr. John M. Stutesman, Officer in Charge of Iranian Affairs, room 2271, New State Building.

Sincerely yours,

Arthur L. Richards
Director
Office of Greek, Turkish
and Iranian Affairs

Mr. John P. Bochow,
Assistant Manager,
Guaranty Trust Company of New York,
140 Broadway,
New York 15, New York.

NEA:OTI:HPGray/ALRichards:jsw
8/19/52

Cleared in draft with
DC/P - Mr. Rzeczkowski

FIGURE 12.10 *Letter from Arthur L. Richards, State Department, to John P. Bochow, Guaranty Trust Company of New York, August 20, 1952, inviting a representative of the bank to come to the department for the purpose of explaining the use of the diplomatic pouch to conduct business with the shah.*

CHAPTER THIRTEEN

The Theft from Iran's Crown Jewels

AN EXCELLENT INDICATOR OF THE PEOPLE'S
hatred and distrust of Reza Shah was the general fear that he had taken some
of Iran's crown jewels with him when he went into exile in September 1941.
Dreyfus's account of the furor over the integrity of the jewels is revealing:

> The question of the crown jewels has become a *cause célèbre*. In reply to
> widespread rumors that the crown jewels had been removed from Tehran, the
> Minister of Finance [Abbas Qoli Golshayan] announced in the Majlis on Sep-
> tember 14, 1941, that all of the crown jewels, which it may be stated form part
> of the legal cover for the rial, were on deposit at the Bank Mellie, where they
> might be inspected by the deputies. The crown jewels with the exception of the
> royal regalia, he said, have been on deposit at the bank for four years, while the
> royal regalia were removed from the museum at the Gulestan Palace to the
> Bank Mellie on August 26 because of the dust caused by nearby construction.
> Little credence is given in any circle here to the Minister's statement and it is
> generally believed that the royal regalia were actually moved from Tehran and
> returned only when embarrassing questions concerning them were asked by
> the people and on the radio from London and Delhi. It is further generally
> remarked locally that the Acting Minister of Finance was promoted to the rank
> of full Minister a few hours before making the above mentioned statement to
> the Majlis as a *quid pro quo*. A commission headed by Nasrollah Akhavi, Pre-
> siding Judge of the Court of Cassation, and including Ali Hedayat, Chief of the
> Tribunal of Accounts, Hossein Ala, Ebrahim Hakimi and 12 Deputies have
> been appointed to examine the crown jewels and to report on their presence in
> the Bank Mellie and their authenticity.[1]

In a subsequent dispatch on the commission's report, Dreyfus reveals that on August 26, 1941 (4 Shahrivar 1320), "five cases and two packages of articles set gems" were transferred from "the Museum of the Golestan Palace to the treasury of the Banque Mellie. The five cases and two packages were examined, and the contents were compared with 'a list that was in the hands of Mr. Qané Basiri, the Director of the Royal Buildings Administration.'" The comparison with Mr. Basiri's list indicated that nothing was missing.[2]

Subsequently, however, it was learned that of the jewels that had been loaned on the occasion of Queen Fawzieh's wedding to the present shah, "Eight rings, 54 pearls, and one pair of diamond ear pendants were missing." Of the missing items, "one pair of brilliant pendants" and "one ring with two brilliant stones" had been taken "in the Name of Her Highness Ashraf Pahlavi." Furthermore, the report states, "Eight rings on which large brilliants are mounted. . . . were missing." They had been taken out "in the name of Her Majesty Queen Fawzieh." The inconsistency and inaccuracy in the ring count was indicative of the nature of the investigation. According to Dreyfus, however,

> The report seems, on the whole, to be satisfactory. It appears evident that almost all of the crown jewels are now in the Banque Melli and that few, if any, have been taken away. The Minister of Finance reported in a speech to the Majlis on November 4 that the only missing pieces were 5 rings, a pair of earrings and 54 pearls. The rings, he stated, had been sent to Egypt just before the wedding of the present Shah to be offered as presents. The earrings, which had been reported as missing, have now been found, he added. The pearls, he reported, had been used in making other ornaments. The Minister of Finance called attention to the fact, not commonly known, that the ex-Shah had purchased at the time of the marriage 240 carats of diamonds, which had been added to the Crown Jewels, as were numerous gifts which were made to him by foreigners or heads of States. The two following incidents will serve to show the opposition's distrust of the Government in this matter of Crown Jewels. When the Minister of Finance announced that the former Shah had purchased 240 carats of diamonds, he hastened to add, "The sellers and commission agents are present to testify." When the same Minister erroneously stated that 6 rings were missing, several deputies shouted, "No, eight." It would appear that the commission carried out its task carefully and faithfully, and that it has been reasonably established that the Iranian Crown Jewels are safe.[3]

Dreyfus's confidence was misplaced because the commission itself had admitted that its investigation was at best cursory.

The commission's report concludes: "Inasmuch as there was not much time left for investigating other jewels constituting the cover of bank notes and since because of the termination the Twelfth legislative term of the

Majlis the report had to be submitted to the Majlis and to the Government, such investigations that were possible were conducted." The commission had expressed its hope that "it is certain that the said bank note cover has remained intact and immune, and that the records and lists of Royal Buildings Administration are in perfect order."[4]

Moreover, what Dreyfus did not know was that what had remained of the crown jewels was safe. The best parts had already been taken by Reza Shah in years past.

In 1926 a law was passed by the Majlis authorizing the government to sell most of the remaining crown jewels. In 1937 another law was enacted, at the instigation of the shah, to sell parts of the crown jewels because, in the words of the minister of finance, the old jewels were "dead and useless capital." In 1941 the people of Iran had ample cause to be concerned about the safety and integrity of the crown jewels, widely regarded as part of their heritage.

The Law for the Sale of Crown Jewels, 1926

In the early months of Reza Khan's premiership, Millspaugh reports on Iran's government jewels (later called the crown jewels):

> The last appraisal of the Crown Jewels was in 1289 [1910–11] and from the results of that appraisal, it is probable that the salable jewels represent at the present time a value of many millions of tomans. At the request of the Government, a project has been prepared for submission to the Madjless proposing the reappraisal and sale, under proper control, of certain jewels. It is proposed, of course, to retain jewels that have a special historical interest and to conduct the sale in such a way as to realize for the Government the full value of this valuable property. The Royal Building and Furniture Section of the Treasury General is charged with the supervision, safe custody and accounting on behalf of the Ministry of Finance, of the Crown Jewels, the relics, and antiquities in the Royal Museum, Government documents and the Royal Library. The functions of the Royal Building and Furniture Section in charge of these valuable historical objects and articles are fully and carefully performed.[5]

Thanks to Millspaugh's reports from 1924 we can tell exactly when Reza Khan first obtained access to the crown jewels: "Due to a fear expressed by the Government in connection with the dampness in the Treasury in the Royal Palace where the Crown Jewels are stored, H.H. the Prime Minister decided that another room in the same building would be better adapted to the storage and safe-keeping of the jewels. As a consequence, the new strong-room has been made ready and the transfer of the jewels to the new location is at the pleasure of His Highness, who is expected to designate the time when transfer will be made under all due formality."[6]

The looting had started in earnest. The law allowing the sale of the jewels was passed by the Majlis in October 1926, shortly after the Reza Khan's accession to the throne.[7] No information on the sale of these jewels and the identities of the buyers was provided, but we are told that the proceeds were to be used as part of the capital for the new National Bank of Iran (Bank Melli Iran). The sale of the crown jewels was mentioned in a 1930 conversation between Hart and Teymourtache in which the latter said he had suggested to the shah that "after making a selection of a small number of the finest crown jewels the others be sold for gold." Hart also reports that "the Shah seemed to be in agreement with him [Teymourtache] on this point and that His Majesty, unlike his predecessors, does not care for jewels and is not given to wearing them."[8]

The sale of the crown jewels appears to have been a continuous process, not confined to official sales. Hart reveals one episode involving the chief accountant of the imperial court: "From a high official of the Foreign Ministry I received verification a few days ago of a rumor that [Abdol Hossein] Diba was found to have removed a ponderous emerald from the Peacock Throne more than a year ago, substituting a large nugget of ordinary green glass. The abstracted emerald was taken to Paris in the latter part of 1931 where it was sold, its proceeds defraying the expenses of a junket about Europe on which no expense was spared to make pleasant the sojourns in several capitals."[9]

The Law for the Sale of the Crown Jewels, 1937

On October 28, 1937, a bill was unexpectedly introduced in the Majlis requesting the government's authorization to sell most of the crown jewels in return for gold bullion. American chargé d'affaires Engert reports:

> The Bill provides for a Commission, consisting of the Prime Minister, two Ministers, and two Deputies, which is to classify the crown jewels according to their historic value. Those selected by the Commission are to be transferred to the National Bank of Iran which, in turn, will decide how many of them are to be sold. They will then be appraised by another Commission, which will also fix the manner of the sale. The most significant provision in the Bill is the stipulation that "the sum realized from such sale must be used exclusively for the purchase of gold bullion." I seem to recall that when I served here before [1920–22], there was some talk of using the crown jewels as collateral for a loan. Nobody probably knows their exact value, and there have been persistent rumors to the effect that many have already been sold (or have disappeared) and that some imitation stones have been substituted. However that may be, I understand that when they were last appraised in 1910 their value was estimated in the neighborhood of $30,000,000. In this connection the Department's attention is also invited to an announcement which appeared in most of the newspapers of October 27th—i.e., the day before the bill was submitted to the Chamber—that His Majesty had decided "to donate all gold belonging to his august person to the National Bank of Iran."

FIGURE 13.1 *The Peacock Throne of Persia, 1937. The original caption (in French) reads: "To remedy the financial difficulties of his country, the shah of Persia has decided to sell, either in Paris or London, two of the Crown's most precious posses- sions. One of these, shown in the photo, is the new throne, which is adorned by 140,000 precious stones and was recently appraised at £6 million."* New York Times, Paris bureau; courtesy of the National Archives (306–NT-1122–175399).

The finance minister's speech in the Majlis that day included the following: "By order of His Majesty the Shah, and with his authorization, I am pre- senting to the Chamber the project of a law regarding the sale of part of the Crown Jewels. As the deputies are aware, some of these jewels must be kept and safeguarded for the benefit of the Crown, but others are in fact a dead capital which does not serve any good purpose. The latter therefore furnish a particularly suitable means of putting into effect the Government's desire of increasing the original capital of the National Bank of Iran."[10]

The first reading of the bill took place on November 11 and it was approved just five days later. The vote was 99 for and 11 against.[11] In the meantime, rumors had begun to circulate that the jewels were much less valuable than expected and that many of the old emeralds were flawed. The entire collection, it was said, would not bring more than $6 million. It was clear to the people of Iran that the entire charade was played out to enable Reza Shah to steal the most valuable pieces of a cherished legacy of Iranian history.[12] During the past twelve years it had been amply illustrated that whenever valuable government property had been "sold," there was only one buyer: Reza Shah.

Even before the introduction of this latest bill, the newspapers were full of praise for the shah's generosity in "donating all of his gold" to the nation. An excerpt from *Ettela'at* on October 27 is typical: "Inasmuch as this unparalleled donation on the part of the Shahinshah should serve as an example to all Iranians, it behooves all owners of gold to sell their gold to the National Bank of Iran with the view of strengthening the economic structure of the country, for only in this manner will the public wealth always remain within the country, and the person who sells gold will thus be rendering an important service to the national economy."[13]

Iran was similarly extravagant in its praise: "This unprecedented donation by His Imperial Majesty is a fine example for all the people of the country, and of course every individual will willingly and eagerly follow this lofty precept. It is indeed suitable that all owners of gold should sell their gold to the National Bank of Iran with the view to strengthening the economic power of the country, for as a result of such action public wealth will be preserved in the country itself."[14]

In an editorial *Setareh-ye Jehan* gives the economic reason for the proposed sale of the crown jewels:

> The Ministry of Finance has placed before Parliament a project of a law relative to the sale of a portion of the crown jewels, the sum derived from this sale to be used exclusively for the purchase of gold bullion to increase the gold reserve of the National Bank of Iran. Only those jewels that have no historical value will be sold. Two deputies will be designated to take part in the negotiations for the sale, the choice of the jewels to be sold, the estimating of the value, etc. Such is the tenor of the project of the law submitted to Parliament and passed by that body at its first reading during the course of yesterday's session. Perhaps one will ask why the Government—by formal order of His Majesty the Shah—has taken this decision which at first approach appears somewhat surprising, because no one is ignorant of the fact that the covering reserves of our bank of issue greatly exceed the legally fixed percentage of cover for the issuance

of bank notes. What reason then have we for purchasing more gold? The question deserves an answer.

After a lengthy and arcane discussion of the supposed differences between fixed and circulating capital, the editorial concludes:

> Money, which is represented today nearly everywhere by bank notes, should be securely guaranteed by a metal reserve, preferably gold. The more money there is in circulation the more business there will be. And the more gold reserves there are the more money there will be in circulation. Herein therefore lies the reason why the Imperial Government wishes to add to the number of gold ingots held in reserve in the vaults of the National Bank of Iran. And that is why it wishes to transform into gold ingots the Crown Jewels which, being "fixed capital," will never be of any use to the national economy if permitted to sleep behind show cases in the Museum of the Golistan Palace.[15]

"A Small Portion Was Set Aside"

After all this, the government suddenly lost interest in the sale of the jewels and the matter was quietly shelved. Ali Soheili, then foreign minister, states

FIGURE 13.2 *Taking Persian art treasures to London, 1930. The original caption (in French) reads: "Art Treasures by Air. One of the most amazing collections of treasures ever assembled is now on its way to London. Cases containing choice specimens of Persian art left Tehran (Persia) by air for the island of Abadan, there to be transferred to a British ship bound for London. Photo shows a squadron of planes, laden with Persian art treasures for the International Exhibition in London, about to take off at Tehran for the coast, where the treasures were put on board a steamer for London."* New York Times, *Paris bureau; courtesy of the National Archives (306–NT-1122–17).*

that "the Iranian Government no longer has the intention of disposing of any part of the Iranian Crown Jewels."[16] Why this reversal? The answer is to be found in a speech by Majlis President Hassan Esfandiary:

> I am certain that my honorable colleagues agree with me that the lofty ideas put forth by His Imperial Majesty are all of paramount importance for the progress of work and prosperity of the entire country. As you know, only recently our great sovereign had another new idea which had not occurred to anyone before. The Crown Jewels which indeed constitute a large capital were being kept in a secluded place without anybody knowing what they are and of what benefit they might be to the country. Imperial thoughtfulness has now worked out the best use for them. The Government presented a bill to the National Consultative Assembly which, being aware of its usefulness, promptly approved it. Immediately after that a Committee which was to examine and classify the jewels proceeded with the work without delay. The Committee consisted of members of the Government and of deputies and they worked for 45 days without stopping. A full list was prepared and signed. After the detailed report was submitted to His Imperial Majesty a small portion of the jewels which were special to the Crown was set aside and the rest was transferred to the Banque Mellie Iran, delivered to the Board of Supervisors of the Bank and placed in the vaults of the Bank under their seal. All of you had heard that there were certain Crown Jewels; but as to their quantity and value we were all in the dark. Now not only the honorable deputies but all Iranians ought to know that the jewels form a very important capital, creating a very excellent credit, and a source of wealth far greater than everybody believed. All this had been kept hidden in the Imperial Treasury.
>
> His Imperial Majesty, with his royal courage and the interest he continually shows in the improvement of his country, suddenly donated this enormous and possibly peerless capital to his people, ceding it to the Banque Mellie Iran which is in fact the treasury of the country, the state and the nation. Not only the deputies, who are already well aware of the gift, but all Iranians should be grateful. All should appreciate this blessing, the blessing of a great sovereign who sees things that no one else would see and who orders everything done which may help the country thrive.
>
> I must add that after the jewels were listed and the lists were sealed by the five persons on the committee, who included Cabinet Ministers and Deputies, a copy was transmitted to the Majlis; that copy will be preserved in the safe of this Chamber. This is why I am voicing the sentiments of my respected colleagues, the deputies, and of the entire nation when I express profound appreciation of this noble gesture by His Imperial Majesty. I pray God to grant him a long life, so that the Iranian Government and people may reach the zenith of their progress under the high leadership of this great Shahinshah.[17]

Esfandiary's speech provides the answers to other questions as well. The jewels were not sold in 1937–38 because a portion that were "special to the Crown" had already been set aside (by His Pahlevi Majesty). But why were these items not noted by the Majlis commission that had investigated the crown jewels in October 1941, and had supposedly examined with care the contents of the five cases and two packages that had been moved from the museum of Golestan Palace on August 26, 1941? The reason is simple: the list of jewels used by the 1941 commission was not the list Esfandiary refers to in his speech. Nowhere in the report is there a mention of this list, which had supposedly been safely placed in the Majlis safe box.[18]

Instead, the list used by the commission was one found "in the hands of Mr. Qané Basiri, the director of Royal Buildings Administration."[19] That is, it had been prepared by the Royal Buildings Administration during the reign of Reza Shah. Given Reza Shah's limitless greed, the theft of the jewels is not surprising. On September 28, 1941, Prime Minister Foroughi "announced to the Majlis that an inventory was being made by the customs authorities at Bandar Abbas of all the goods being taken out of the country by the former sovereign, which list would in due course be made public. This was in answer to widespread reports that the great quantities of valuable objects were being taken abroad by the ex-Shah and his suite."[20] Of course, such a list was never made public; it is doubtful it was ever compiled.

Shams Pahlavi and the Two Diamond Rings

State Department records describe what became of some of the stolen jewels. In late summer of 1945, Shams Pahlavi, Reza Khan's favorite daughter, and her husband traveled to New York. Shortly after she tried to sell jewelry that she said was purchased in South Africa. In his report of a conversation with the Iranian chargé d'affaires, Dr. A. A. Daftary, George V. Allen, chief of the Division of Near Eastern Affairs, says that Shams had

> brought with her to America two valuable diamond rings, said to have been purchased in South Africa. She now desires to sell one of them. Dr. Daftary wondered whether there was any possibility, in view of the fact that she had entered the United States on a diplomatic passport and is the sister of the Shah, that she might be exempted from the necessity of paying customs duty on the ring. I replied immediately that there was no slightest possibility of customs exemption in case the Princess sold the ring. I said that I felt confident that if the Shah himself came to America and sold personal jewelry while here, American customs duty would have to be paid on the articles sold. I added, furthermore, that I hope very much that Princess Shams would not allow anyone in New York or elsewhere to delude her into any foolish action on any kind of false assurance that her status would protect her.[21]

Finally, a secret report from the American Embassy in London supports the theory that Mohammad Reza Shah was also engaged in shipping jewelry and gold from Tehran to New York in the 1950s (fig. 13.3).[22]

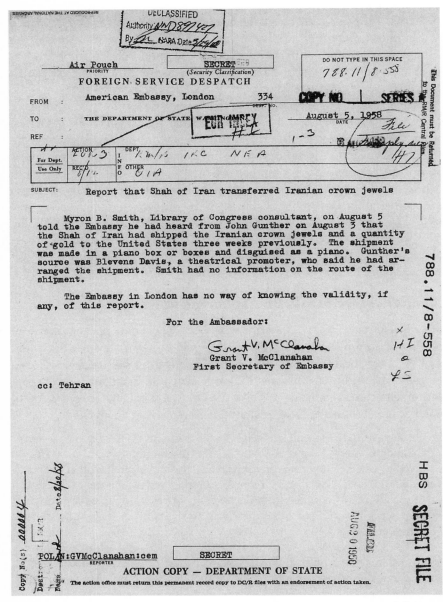

FIGURE 13.3 *Dispatch from the American embassy, London, August 5, 1958: "Report that Shah of Iran transferred Iranian crown jewels."*

CHAPTER FOURTEEN

The Foreign Exchange Crisis and the Deteriorating Economy, 1928–1941

*T*HE PLUNDER OF IRAN'S OIL BY THE BRITISH and the diversion of Iran's oil revenues to London, Switzerland, and New York as well as the de facto deprivation of oil income to Iran's economy from 1928 to 1941, resulted in the collapse of the foreign exchange value of the kran, and a prolonged foreign exchange crisis that lasted until 1941, when some of the oil revenues were at last available. During 1929–30 alone, the exchange rate of the kran fell from 48 krans per pound sterling to 67 krans, a depreciation of 40 percent. The most immediate effect was to increase the cost of imported commodities.

From the very beginning it was understood by both domestic and foreign observers that the kran's collapse was due to the diversion of Iran's oil revenues. As the documents presented in this chapter illustrate, the shortage of foreign exchange and the so-called remedies caused enormous damage to the Iranian economy. Augustin W. Ferrin, the American consul in Tehran, writes:

> The kran's decline, and still more the uncertainty as to where it will stop, has demoralized the bazaars and paralyzed the import markets. The Imperial Bank continues to attribute the exchange situation to the Anglo-Persian oil royalties, heavy importation of railway supplies and automobiles, and decreased Persian exports. It appears that formerly the Anglo-Persian oil royalties paid to the Persian Government and averaging in recent years Tomans 6,000,000 (£1,200,000) were converted on receipt into krans. In the past two years they have been kept

in sterling in London, as a Treasury reserve, amounting at present, it is under-stood, to about £3,000,000. Mr. Bushiry (former Moin-ot-Tojjar) agrees with officers of the Imperial Bank that the Persian Government could ameliorate the situation, at least temporarily, by selling this sterling reserve. It is not generally expected that the Persian Government will convert the whole sterling reserve into krans, but it is quite possible that it will allow the National Bank of Persia to draw on it in its routine commercial exchange operations.[1]

British diplomatic and banking officials in Tehran were absolutely clear on the causes of the foreign exchange crisis. Ray Atherton of the American embassy in London sent to Washington a copy of a pamphlet called *Economic Conditions in Persia,* by R. E. Lingeman, officer in charge of commercial affairs at the British legation in Tehran. On page 16 of his pamphlet, Lingeman gives the main cause of the kran's collapse:

> The oil royalty fell from £1,488,392 in the first year [1927] to £596,885 in the second year [1928], but it has since reached the £1.25 million figure once more. The Persian exchange was maintained between 45 and 48 krans to the £ until two years ago. This was due to the fact that the country's balance of trade, including the oil shipments which bring in a handsome profit to the Persian Government in the form of royalty, was a favorable one. For the last three years, however, this royalty, which is paid in sterling in London and which used to be transferred to Persia as required, has been left in London, with the result that some £3,000,000 have been withheld from the credit side of the trade balance. Under these conditions, demand for exchange far exceeded the supply.[2]

The fall of the kran was much discussed in the Tehran newspapers. Henry S. Villard, American consul, states, "Mr. E. Wilkinson, chief manager of the Imperial Bank of Persia, has addressed a letter to the Editor of *Iran* in which he lays the blame on the retention in Europe of oil royalties, the large purchases abroad of railway materials, and the stock market crash in the United States with its consequent set-back to Persian exports."[3] The newspapers made a great deal of agitation over the weakness of the kran. The controlled press and the government, in contrast, searched for other causes for the kran's decline. Hart commented on the ado in the papers:

> It has been learned from the Manager of the Imperial Bank of Persia that the Shah, on his return from the South, informed his advisers in true oriental style that the value of the kran must be jacked up at once, and he gave orders that a scheme which would bring this about be furnished him on February 8th. Since the order was issued Mr. Schniewind, the Director of General Finance, and others have been busily engaged in preparing the answer to the riddle. The German Minister told me that Schniewind and Mr. Wilkinson, Manager of the Imperial Bank of Persia, in their reports on the matter, both arrived at the conclusion that a fund should be created with which to stabilize the kran. Mr. Wilkinson had expressed the belief that one-half million sterling would be enough for this

purpose. Schniewind, on the other hand, was of the opinion that one and a half to two million might be necessary, but he thought that if this fund was created none of it would have to be spent, as its existence would have the desired effect. I understand that in these reports it was contemplated that the kran be stabilized at kran 60 to the pound sterling.[4]

The Iranian government's extreme sensitivity to criticism by foreign newspapers can be seen in its response to an article that appeared in the Baku paper *Bakinski Babotchi* criticizing Persia for keeping its oil revenues in London and blaming the fall of the kran on this policy. Teymourtache's reply in *Shafaq-i-Sorkh* amazed readers by arguing that if the oil revenues had not been kept in London, the kran's fall would have been even more drastic.[5] There were rumors that the government had briefly tried to support the kran by using its London sterling reserve. Hart reports:

> Mr. Sydney Rogers, of the London office of the Imperial Bank of Persia, has come to Teheran. He is, quite naturally, reticent concerning his negotiations with the Persian Government. In a recent conversation he told the Legation that the Minister of Court had informed him that 300,000 pounds sterling of the funds in London had recently been used to buy Persian exchange. Mr. Rogers, of course, takes the view of the Imperial Bank that arbitrarily to

FIGURE 14.1 *The Imperial Bank of Persia, Tehran, 1930. According to the original caption, the "origins of the troubles in Persia are to be found in the exploitation of the oil wells by the English." New York Times, Paris bureau; courtesy of the National Archives (306–NT-1122–18).*

maintain the kran for long at 60 to the pound sterling, which he described as "35 krans above parity," is a hopeless task in the face of the inescapable fact that the balance of the trade is unfavorable.[6]

Shortly after this report, Hart announced that the use of the London sterling Reserve Fund and the expenditure of £300,000 thereof was due to unwise currency speculation by Dr. Kurt Lindenblatt, the German president of Bank Melli Iran. The money had been used to cover the bank's foreign exchange losses: "It is revealed that Lindenblatt had been selling pounds at over 60 krans per pound [61–64], and hoping to buy them back at 60, and thus make a profit. About £250,000 were thus sold, but the appreciation of the kran did not materialize. The kran further declined to 67 krans to the pound. He was thus forced to go to Teymourtache and request the £300,000 mentioned."[7] Barely a month later, Villard, discussing the worsening economic crisis, reports that "there are many persons who believe that the large part of it [the London Reserve Fund] has been filtered away in such purchases as military supplies."[8] Clearly even by 1930 the American legation suspected that the London fund was being raided by Reza Shah.

The Foreign Exchange Control Law and Its Supplement

The government's "solution" to the crisis it had clearly created was the Foreign Exchange Control Law.[9] Enacted by the Majlis on February 25, 1930, its salient features were limitations of all foreign currency transactions to certain authorized banks; an embargo on the import and export of bullion silver; a prohibition on the export of gold in any form; the formation of a commission to fix the buying and selling of the exchange rate; and the formation of another commission from which importers were required to obtain permits before purchasing foreign drafts. The banks authorized under the law were the Imperial Bank of Persia, the National Bank of Persia, the Ottoman Bank, and the Russo-Persian Bank.[10]

Among the products whose import was entirely forbidden were vehicles of all kinds, furniture, wearing apparel, and all toiletries. Restricted goods included jewelry, precious stones, object d'art and antiques, carpets, all grains and edible cereals, fruits, milk, dairy products, livestock of all kinds, and silk and cotton cloth.[11] The new foreign trade regime is aptly described by Millspaugh:

> Faced with the foreign exchange difficulties that plagued other countries, Persia became to all intents and purposes totalitarian in trade, as it was in government, and as it strongly tended to be in industry. Parliament passed laws instituting a public monopoly of foreign exchange and of imports and exports. The government entered into barter arrangements with Germany and Soviet

Russia; unable to handle imports and exports directly, except for a few com-modities, the Shah and his favorites made extensive grants of monopoly privi-leges to private Persian companies.[12]

Villard comments on a consequence of this law on Iran's foreign trade and merchant class: "Import trade is at present completely paralyzed and demoralization reigns among merchants accustomed to stock foreign goods. Queues reminiscent of 'bread lines' during the [First World] War stand outside the commission's office to present petitions for import per-mits, but so drastic is the attitude of the commission that importers will soon no doubt become discouraged and give up attempts to bring in goods from abroad."[13]

Having stifled foreign imports, the government's next attempted fix was to effectively stifle the export trade. Supposedly to prevent capital flight from Persia, the Supplementary Foreign Exchange Control Law enacted on July 22, 1930, required exporters to sell the government 90 percent of the foreign exchange received from their exports, or 40 percent in the case of exporters who undertook to bring into the country goods for which no per-mits were required. As a consequence, Villard observes, "Persia's exports have collapsed."[14]

The large devaluation of the kran had provided the exporters of Persian products with profitable opportunities. Under the new law, however, why would anyone bother to export goods if 90 percent of the foreign exchange was to be surrendered to the government, which in practice meant Reza Shah? By such policies, the government was well on its way to decimating Iran's merchant class.

Onset of the Economic Crisis

Hart provides insights into the causes of the economic crisis of 1930:

> I have the honor to report that the financial situation in Persia is growing daily more serious. In this relation reference is made to the last paragraph of the report from the Consulate, Teheran, July 24/26, 1930: "It would almost appear that those in charge of Persia's economic destiny had begun to lose their heads and that common sense was being dumped overboard to save a foundering craft." It is doubtless true that Persia would also have suffered from the present world economic depression had the Government not launched into its patently impractical policy of fixing the rate of exchange without supporting that rate with the Government's funds abroad. This led to the exchange control laws which are ruining Persia's commerce and which have reduced the customs rev-enues, Persia's principal income, to such an extent as to make a very large bud-get deficit almost inevitable. In this connection the Turkish Ambassador remarked last winter that there was no economic crisis in Persia until the Gov-ernment by its foolish policy created one. It is generally believed in Teheran that

a serious crisis is imminent, that is to say in one or two months, unless some-thing is done to remedy the situation. On July 28 the *Iran* published an unusu-ally candid notice to the effect that the salaries in the Ministry of Economics, unpaid since March 21, 1930, "will be paid next week." The Legation hears that all Government salaries, other than those in the army and court officials, are some months in arrears.[15]

The Supplementary Exchange Law contributed to the crisis as well, as Villard reports in August:

> . . . as predicted, exporters rather than hand over their exchange to the gov-ernment or face the complications attendant upon such transactions, have shown a marked unwillingness to do business at all. Thus the new law, which has been in operation for only a month, instead of creating an improvement in conditions, has already tended to defeat the purpose for which it was intended. As an example of the check on exports exercised by the law in question, it is reported from the leading port of Bushire that no shipments whatever have been made since this measure was passed, and from Pahlavi comes the news that merchants are refusing to prepare goods for export. Businessmen every-where appear disinclined to meet the red tape necessary to sell their goods abroad which, coupled with the antagonism aroused by what is considered an arbitrary governmental decree, threatens to bring exports of Persian products to a complete standstill.[16]

One month later, Villard writes:

> Despite all the recent measures that have been passed, the economic situation in general remains unimproved and in some respects it is getting worse if any-thing. This is notably true in regard to the availability of foreign exchange at the banks, and those seeking to purchase foreign drafts, even when provided with permits from the Inspection Commission, are having an arduous task to scrape together a fraction of the amounts they need. As an example of the extraordi-nary dearth of exchange, a Persian student on the point of leaving to pursue spe-cialized courses at the American University in Beirut—a procedure encouraged by the Persian Government—was able to accumulate but $100 travel expenses out of a total of $900 approved by the Exchange Control Commission.[17]

Observers had been puzzled by the extraordinary shortage of exchange, despite exporters selling their exchange earning to the government, as required by the supplementary law. Each month the local expenditures of Anglo-Persian Oil Company alone came to between £80,000 and £100,000 ($400,000–$500,000).[18] What became of this money? Meanwhile, the price of imported products had risen sharply, by as much as 100 percent in six months. Business throughout Iran had come to a standstill. "In the case of trucks, many units sold on the installment plan have been seized owing to default in payments, only about 10 per cent in some instances having been collected on the purchase price. These vehicles are now laid up with no prospect of their taking to the road again until credit conditions become easier and the exchange situation is altered."[19]

The plight of the Persian students abroad is again noted by Villard. In 1930, 1,116 students were studying abroad, of whom 746 were studying at their parents' expense and 320 were government "boursiers" (on government scholarships). "Students in England and America are considered to need £25 a month, those in France £20, in Germany £17, in Switzerland £16, and at Beirut, Syria, £10. Owing to the inability of their parents to find enough exchange to remit to them, many of these unfortunate pupils are reported to be in dire straits." Villard reports that APOC had allocated £15,000 out of the amounts it sells in Iran each month to pay for the needs of the students.[20]

Conditions in Azerbaijan in 1930

In August 1930, U.S. consul Henry S. Villard traveled to Tabriz to close the U.S. consulate there. Ten years later another American consul, James S. Moose Jr., toured the province. Comparison of the reports of the two travelers reveals considerable deterioration in political and economic conditions over the decade. The grim circumstances described in both reports represent a side of Reza Shah's rule that has been badly neglected in the literature. Villard indicates that the population had been subdued by Reza Shah's brutal methods, and hostility and despair were its lot.

> I have the honor to report that on my recent visit to Tabriz for the purpose of closing the Consulate at that place, I had an opportunity of making a very brief survey of political and economic conditions in the province of Azerbaijan which, it is thought, may prove of interest to the Department. The results of my observations, in summary, would seem to indicate that the populace if not actually in a state of unrest is at least openly discontented and it is the opinion of many residents that should the present government's stability ever be seriously threatened the movement would receive immediate impetus from Tabriz and the vicinity. The principal cause of complaint at this time, outside of the stagnation in commercial circles, which is affecting the country as a whole, appears to be what the average person regards as over-burdensome taxation. High taxes form a leading topic of discussion, and despair seems to be mixed with the resentment that the government should, allegedly, take away practically everything which it is possible for the individual to earn. Realization of the futility of attempting to make progress under present conditions is, in my mind, partly responsible for the growing apathy noticeable in producers of Persian commodities which is everywhere hindering the development of Persia's export trade and which is particularly apparent in the Azerbaijan district. Resentment is further accentuated by comparison of the manner in which army officers are enabled to live with the general poverty of the inhabitants.

Coupled with the antagonism aroused by the current government taxation program is the oft-repeated charge that the Financial Agency of Azarbaijan is not only inefficient but corrupt. The present Director of Finance bears the brunt of these charges, which if not proclaimed from the house tops are nevertheless conspicuous in any general discussion of the situation. It is a common remark that those responsible for the departure of the Millspaugh Mission were traitors to Persia, and even those who formerly favored the dismissal of the Americans are now admitting that they were mistaken. Indicative, in fact, of an increasing sentiment for American financial administration, I repeatedly encountered the naive conviction that Dr. Millspaugh had already been invited by the government to return and that not many months would elapse before his arrival in Persia.

Although such views are more cautiously expressed, there would also seem to be an undercurrent of hostility to His Imperial Majesty Reza Shah Pahlavi. Never really popular in Azarbaijan, His Majesty is not held in respect among the inhabitants of Tabriz; one of the reasons advanced for this is that he is not of noble parentage, which forms an interesting commentary on the future of democracy in Persia. In spite of this, however, it is feared in many quarters that should the throne be vacated through death or other means, conditions would be even worse than during the Kadjar [Qajar] dynasty.[21]

Deteriorating Economic Conditions

By early 1931 the economic situation in Persia had become desperate. Hart reports a conversation with Ghaffar Khan Djalal, later Persia's minister in Washington: "I have the honor to report that Persia's economic situation steadily grows worse. I was told by Ghaffar Khan Djalal that the average foreigner in Teheran could have no comprehension of the plight of the Persian merchants. He said the number of failures has been appalling and a very large percentage of those remaining in business are now on their last legs."[22] In June 1933, Hart provided another glimpse of the grim conditions under Reza Shah:

What the year promises for the Persian people is another matter which I shall endeavor to discuss in another despatch. The internal cost of living has continued to increase. The peasant class is particularly affected, and murmurings of city dwellers, particularly the underpaid civil servants, are increasingly heard. Landlords are finding it increasingly difficult to meet tax collections. Interest rates have skied and land values have fallen. And the notable decrease in foreign trade, burdened as it is by import quotas and government "trade monopoly" restrictions favoring the large, as against small merchants, has played an important role in rendering increasingly precarious the livelihood of the commercial community.[23]

By 1935 the economy had deteriorated further. William H. Hornibrook, Hart's successor as American minister in Tehran, observes: "If the great masses of the population have not been utterly impoverished by these taxes [to support military expenditures] it may be safely said that their standard of living has been depressed to the barest subsistence level without any apparent improvement in the near future so long as they are called upon to support the building of a railway having a political rather than an economic importance."[24] By 1938, the situation had become even grimmer. In his report on the budget of 1939/40, American chargé d'affaires C. Van H. Engert remarks that, according to figures released by the National Bank of Iran, the cost of living in 1936 rose by 27 percent while the average wage of a day laborer remained at 7 rials per day.[25] In his conclusion to the budget report for 1939/40, he adds, "The cost of living of the masses is estimated by the National Bank of Iran to have increased by 31 per cent since January 1, 1937; and it continues to rise. But there is no change in the wage of the laborer which remains at 7 rials [about 42 cents] per day. The evil plight of the poor classes which was mentioned in the Legation's budget despatch for 1317 [1938/39] has become worse. If social unrest exists, it is not apparent."[26] In 1941, however, shortly after Engert's departure from Iran, social unrest and bread riots did break out (see chapter 15). Inflation, already serious by 1937, had become rampant. According to the best indexes available, the cost of living increased to 339 in 1941 (1937 = 100), an average inflation rate of 36 percent per year.[27]

Reza Shah and Teymourtache Corner the Foreign Exchange Market

In response to numerous complaints from importers of American goods, automotive parts in particular, Hart met with Foroughi in 1930 to obtain the foreign exchange to pay the American exporters for imports already delivered:

> I pointed out that the United States is relatively Persia's best customer, in that we buy at least twice as much as we sell, and let it be inferred that should we adopt retaliatory measures Persia's trade would suffer far more than ours. Persia, I said, contends that automobiles and trucks, which are obviously necessary for transport in this country, are luxuries and are therefore included in the proscribed list of imports. But are not Persian carpets, which constitute practically our entire imports from Persia, among the most luxurious articles in the world? I called Foroughi's attention to the fact that according to estimates based on consular invoices we had purchased $2,700,000 worth of Persian products during the first six months of 1930 and asked why American shippers could not have some of that exchange, less than half of which would be sufficient to pay for their shipments prior to the enforcement of the exchange

restrictions. He seemed impressed, took notes, was very courteous and sympathetic as always, but nothing came of it.[28]

An earlier dispatch shows that Hart knew why some of the dollars Persia earned from exports to the United States were not available for payment to American exporters: Reza Shah and Teymourtache had cornered the foreign exchange market, and were evidently purchasing practically all the foreign exchange.

> Despite the heavy drop in trade it is estimated that something more than $500,000 is reaching the country [per month]. But the question is asked, what becomes of it? Even the small merchant cannot obtain the paltry sums required to keep up his stocks. The banks protest always that they have no way of helping their customers who are seeking exchange or to pay for commodities shipped against documents. A statement made to me a few days ago by my British colleague seems to me to offer the most plausible answer to the puzzling situation. He said that all of the exchange was being purchased by the Shah, the Minister of the Court and Diba, accountant of the Court, with the expectation later of lifting the control and permitting exchange to run wild. Then, he said, they would purchase their krans back at a very favorable rate. This statement was made without qualification, which causes me to suspect that officials of the Imperial Bank are the source of Sir Robert's information.
>
> For more than two months a German carpet buyer has been dragging the markets for everything that had any marketable value. He has purchased $200,000 worth of carpets and has lately announced that he will purchase up to $500,000 if suitable fabrication can be found. Rumor has been that he was purchasing on account of the National Bank which it was understood had hit upon this method of obtaining foreign exchange. I learned yesterday, however, that the Government had brought him here with a commission to buy carpets to an almost unlimited amount to obtain exchange for the purchase of military equipment.[29]

The Trade Monopoly Law of March 1931

Under the trade monopoly law of March 1931, a prospective importer could not apply for an import permit under the import quotas without attaching an export certificate for the same amount. When an exporter exported goods, a certificate would be issued to the exporter. The certificate could then be sold on the market at considerable premium. An importer had to buy the certificate on the market and attach it to his import permit application. The purpose of the measure was to ensure that overall imports would be equal to exports. As a consequence of this law, imports were so restricted that the foreign exchange control laws of 1930 became redundant and were supposedly repealed. Hart notes, "Exchange obligations of the exporters, however, will remain in force as before in accordance with the 13th article of the supplement to the trade monopoly law but receipts from this source will be held by the Government in a special account for the use of holders of import permits secured on the basis of export certificates."[30]

That is, despite its "abolition," the odious regulation that mandated the surrender of 90 percent of the export earnings to the government remained in place. Hart later writes that since the repeal of the foreign exchange laws on February 15, 1932, "the exchange situations during the past fortnight has been chaos. . . . the weakness of the situation is obvious—demand for foreign exchange is greater than supply. The Government must, therefore, make available to the banks a part of its sterling reserves in London." But, he notes, "No official announcement of the Government's intention in this sense has yet been made." Not only were the oil revenues unavailable to meet the country's legitimate trade needs, but "some £200,000 sold by exporters to the National Bank of Persia under the requirements of the Trade Monopoly laws had not been sold to meet the resulting demands of authorized importers but had been utilized, supposedly as a temporary measure, by the Government to pay for imported railway construction materials." This last point was "particularly emphasized by Chief Manager Wilkinson of the Imperial Bank of Persia." That is, £200,000 of foreign exchange that should have been set aside to meet the demand of the importers, as mandated by the trade monopoly law of March 1931, had been diverted for the purchase of railway construction material.[31] A leading Tehran merchant lamented the results of the law:

> The Persian Foreign Trade Monopoly, which has since last March limited classes and quantities of permissible imports and subordinated them to the prior export of Persian products or to the purchase of export certificates at costly premiums, is generally said to have so restricted and confused foreign trading that foreign traders have felt like clearing out of the country. But, actually, the situation was almost as difficult before the Monopoly was established. For, while the Monopoly seemed to be the last straw, it was really its superposition on the uneconomic exchange laws which brought chaos.[32]

To justify their immoral policies in Persia, the British mixed hypocrisy with a heavy dose of mendacity. The British minister stated:

> After all, Persia, in the present circumstances, could do much worse than to maintain this regime in force. There were far too many Persians of the better class who were squandering their wealth on foreign luxuries. To pay the bills their peasants were made to suffer. The remedy may be drastic, but, in that field at least, it works. Such little money as the country has is being kept at home.

And, as in any event its foreign commerce plays so insignificant a part in foreign trade, it must be admitted that the temporary reduction of that commerce
is even more insignificant as a factor tending to perpetuate the financial and
economic mess which post-War Europe has got itself.[33]

Despite the desperate shortage of foreign exchange, the government did
not hesitate to pay £200,000 to the Imperial Bank of Persia for canceling its
banknote monopoly concession. In addition, the cost of importing
machinery for producing the new notes to be issued by the National Bank
was another £100,000. The required £300,000 was appropriated from the
Reserve Fund.[34] When the kran expenditures were included the cost was
£500,000 ($2.5 million). Hart comments: "In conclusion, I venture to
express the opinion, shared by many competent local observers, that this
total expenditure of some $2,500,000 will net Persia but little except the
satisfaction of seeing, first the notes of a high-credit-standing British bank
replaced by those of a Persian national bank with as yet little or no international standing and, second, the effigies of its decadent Kajar rulers
replaced on its silver coinage by that of its present royal dictator."[35]

After the granting of the new oil concession, effective on May 30, 1933,
exporters were no longer required to sell their foreign exchange to the government. A report by the National Bank of Persia (Bank Melli Iran) on Persian commerce and the exchange situation states that the deficit in the
commercial trade balance "might have been covered by the annual royalties received by the Persian Government from the Anglo-Persian Oil Company but the Government preferred to hold these in a reserve account in
London." Consequently, the report notes, the royalty paid by APOC "does
not directly affect foreign exchange on the Persian market." The resulting
plunge in the value of the kran continued despite all the various government attempts to halt the decline "because of speculation against the kran
and the hoarding of foreign exchange." The decline in the value of the kran
had finally been halted the painful way, as described in J. Rives Childs's
paraphrase of the National Bank report, "through the instrumentality of
the foreign trade monopoly law, accentuated by the deepening world economic crisis, as well as by the restrictions imposed by the Government
upon importers of certain commodities, i.e., automobiles, tires, spare parts
and so forth, to purchase their foreign exchange from the Government at
an artificial rate which lessened the demand for foreign exchange on the
open market."[36]

The era of frank discussion of economic issues in the reports of the
National Bank of Iran was brief indeed. By early 1936 the contents of Bank
Melli's annual report (Persian version) was dismissed by Hornibrook:
"[the bank report] would appear to be worthless, and the attempt will not
be made to comment upon a bank statement as general and vague as the

one contained in the report, particularly when it is considered that the accounts are not independently audited and that, in any event, no one having an intimate knowledge of the Bank's operations would dare to lift his voice in criticism."[37]

Foreign Trade and the Exchange Law of March 1, 1936

On March 1, 1936, under the by now usual double urgency procedure, the Majlis passed a law reimposing stringent controls on the foreign exchange market. The new law was in response to a continuous decline in the exchange value of the rial (the new name for the kran) during the preceding few months. Hornibrook remarks:

> Intelligent commercial opinion ascribed the fall of the rial to the working of the law of supply and demand. Despite the foreign trade monopoly law, and despite the large royalties banked abroad for the Government by the Anglo-Persian Oil Company, the demand for foreign exchange was driving the rial downward. It was predicted that the rial would go to 120 to the pound sterling. Consequently importers, foreseeing that their imports would cost more in terms of rials, tended to place orders and to make payment for several months' supply of commodities, a tendency which served to depress the rial further.[38]

This law established 80 rials to the pound and 16.02 rials to the dollar as the rate for foreign exchange. Under the old trade monopoly law the aim was to ensure that foreign trade as a whole was balanced. Under the new law the government had the discretionary power to ensure that trade with each country was balanced. In response to a question in the Majlis about exporters' foreign exchange,

> the Minister of Finance stated that exporters would not abstain from bringing in their foreign exchange and selling it to the authorized banks, because under the law they had to do so. As to the exchange held abroad prior to the enactment of the law, it would not be to the advantage of an Iranian merchant to keep it there since the National Bank would give him 12% interest, which is higher than interest rates abroad. The facts seem to be that the National Bank pays no interest on deposit accounts, and that the 12% is what it receives for money loaned by it.[39]

Article 1 of the new law established a Foreign Exchange Commission consisting of five members. Its most important duty, as outlined in Article 2, consisted of "examination of applications for permits to buy foreign exchange, and issuance of permits whenever necessary, whether such applications emanate from the Government or public institutions, companies and individuals." Article 3 required all individuals and institutions to declare all holdings of foreign exchange. Article 4 stated, "From the date of the approval of these regulations no one has the right to enter into any engagements concerning foreign exchange without the prior authorization of the Foreign Exchange Commission."[40]

Article 18 defined the obligation of exporters to sell their foreign exchange: "At the time of exporting merchandise the exporter engages to sell foreign exchange to one of the authorized banks, not later than three months thereafter, to the equivalent of the customs appraisal plus 10 per cent." Article 16 declared: "Each of the authorized banks is permitted to sell daily up to 4,000 rials [£80] worth of foreign exchange, without the permit of the Commission, for the needs of Iranian students and invalids residing abroad, for the purchase of books and magazines and for subscriptions to papers and magazines, on the condition that they never sell to any one person more than £10 per month and assure themselves that the foreign exchange sold will be expended for the purposes stated."[41]

In short, the new law imposed draconian foreign exchange controls and in practice placed the country's foreign commerce completely under the control of the government. As expected, the law made no provision for payments to foreign exporters on goods delivered before March 1, 1936. As described below, American exporters which had exported to Iran before the latter date, had still not been paid by 1941, to the intense irritation of the American legation in Tehran and, naturally, the companies affected. Moreover, as a consequence of this law, all foreign exchange accounts held by foreign and domestic exporters in Iran were blocked and they could no longer export goods already paid for without agreement to sell the proceeds to an authorized bank.

State Department files contain many complaints from American firms whose funds in Iran were blocked following this regulation. In April 1936, Vice Consul Crain noted, "Exports of every type have fallen notably since March 1st and it is believed that the Commission will have to take steps to correct the situation." The correction never materialized; things only got worse. Despite heavy penalties, as provided for in the regulations, Crain reported an active black market, with the pound selling for 103 to 106 rials, compared with the rate of 80.5 rials set by the new law.[42]

Effective Default by the National Bank of Iran, 1937

Following the new exchange and trade control measures, Gordon P. Merriam reports a serious shortage of foreign exchange, rising costs for domestic foodstuffs, and "shockingly high prices" for imported goods.[43] A few months later, Crain reports that the National Bank of Iran (Bank Melli Iran) effectively suspended payments on foreign drafts and that many foreign exchange permits were issued by the Exchange Control Commission to importers who had made the necessary rial payments. But the drafts could not be remitted because the foreign exchange was not available.

Therefore, although in theory the Melli Bank has not suspended draft payments, actually this is what it amounts to. The Melli Bank does not refuse to remit, but it involves the various importers in endless delays on the ground that documents are not in order, or on the basis of other flimsy excuses that might occur to it. This office has, for the past eight months, advocated the suspension of credit in any form to Iranian importers, regardless of their credit ratings, on the ground that there was a serious risk that payment would be delayed due to the unsatisfactory foreign exchange situation. The position is steadily growing worse and it is hoped that American firms will adopt the policy which has been recommended. There is a growing opinion of interested observers in Teheran that the Government must either make drastic reductions in official importations in order to release correspondingly greater amounts of foreign exchange to cover outstanding commercial payments, declare a moratorium, or enter into a foreign loan. It is understood that the first course suggested is being followed to a certain extent by means of reductions in importations for the Army and other Government institutions.[44]

As reported below, it turned out that in 1937 the government elected to forgo imports for the army. Thereafter army appropriations out of the Reserve Fund resumed with renewed vigor. Crain comments: "It seems almost inconceivable that a country with the resources and basic soundness of Iran could or would declare a moratorium on foreign payments, although there is always the possibility that this may be done."[45]

Contrasting American and British Views on the Economy

A comparison of reports by the American and British legations on the economic conditions in 1937 reveals the nature of the policy pursued by the British. A report by the American chargé d'affaires ad interim, C. Van H. Engert, is informative and to the point. He notes that the law of March 1, 1936, reestablished a complicated system of foreign exchange control and a strict rationing of foreign exchange for imports that had not existed since July 1933, a system that "consists of a series of measures which tend to curtail freedom of international trade, and in some cases amount to complete prohibition." Under this trade and exchange control regime, a Foreign Exchange Commission was charged with the supervision of all exchange transactions. No foreign exchange or foreign draft could be sold or bought without the commission's authorization in writing for each transaction.[46]

The commission was to examine the exchange status between Iran and the country to which remittance was desired to be made. If it found that the exchange account with that particular country was in deficit, it would not issue a permit. All merchants and private persons were required to inform the commission of their foreign exchange holdings and to hand them over to an authorized bank at the official rate of exchange. All buying and selling of authorized foreign exchange transactions was to be through one of the authorized banks, at the official rate, and the banks had to submit a daily report to the commission. With the highly overvalued rial, demand had greatly exceeded supply. Those importers who had been fortunate to obtain foreign exchange realized vast profits from the sale of the scarce imported goods.

The system was rife with corruption and bribery. On the other hand, the requirement that Iranian exporters should surrender their foreign exchange export earnings at an artificially low rate greatly discouraged exports. Finally, Engert remarked that while the foreign exchange situation had become critical, vast sums in foreign exchange earnings in the form of oil royalties were being wasted on the purchase of armaments, or railroads and port construction, activities of questionable benefit that would have a long gestation period.[47]

At about the same time Engert submitted his report, the British government put out a pamphlet by the assistant to the commercial secretary to His Britannic Majesty's legation in Tehran that paints a very different picture from that given by Engert. It does not acknowledge the existence of an economic crisis in Iran, but rather reports on the payments made by APOC:

> The royalties and taxes paid by the Anglo-Iranian Oil Company during 1936 and 1937 amounted to £4,772,127. In the supplementary laws to the budgets of 1936–37 and 1937–38 provision was made for £2,000,000 for military equipment, £2,000,000 for railway construction and £80,000 for sugar factories, a total of £4,080,000 which was presumably to be met out of reserves abroad and would leave a balance of about £690,000 out of the payments of the Anglo-Iranian Oil Company. Nothing is known of other payments into, or actual withdrawals from, the reserves abroad, the amount of which is not made known.[48]

The foreign exchange shortage, remarkably, is mentioned only in passing and is blamed on the country's rapid development. The matter of withholding the oil revenues from the trade balance and its expenditure on armaments and the construction of railroads and ports are not even mentioned. Finally, attempting to stress the positive, the pamphlet discusses Iran's gold reserves. As if to reassure the populace, it reports that the country's gold reserves of £3 million were transferred in 1935 to Bank Melli Iran. This gold and some silver, whose combined value was £5 million, formed the metallic reserve of the bank's note issue, thus providing "100 per cent coverage" for the currency. In reading this pamphlet, one begins to understand the skillful propaganda campaign by which the British have supported Reza Shah and his regime for the last eighty years.

The Nonpayment of American Exporters to Iran

An acute source of American irritation with the regime of Reza Shah after 1936 was the failure of the Iranian government to supply dollars for payment to American firms that had exported to Iran prior to March 1, 1936. Evidently, the 1936 exchange law contained no provision for compensating exporters who had exported before the law took effect. Given that the law had been approved without debate, this was not surprising. While Iranian importers of American goods had supplied the rial equivalent for the imports to Bank Melli, the Foreign Exchange Commission had not released the equivalent dollars for remittance to American firms that had exported to Iran. The American firms sought the help of the State Department and the American legation in Tehran. Numerous attempts by the legation to enable Iranian importers to purchase foreign exchange to pay American exporters had only elicited some "vague promise that the importers will be permitted to purchase export certificates of third class merchandise and present them to the Exchange Commission which, in turn, will issue the necessary permits for the purchase of the corresponding exchange."[49]

A July 1941 letter from W. F. Fischer, export manager of Tuthill Spring Company of Chicago, to Wallace S. Murray, chief of the Division of Near Eastern Affairs at the State Department, provides background:

> At this writing, we are still without funds covering commercial transactions realized in 1935. It seems to us that there is a definite lack of interest on the part of the Iranian authorities. For approximately one year we have been trying to obtain the equivalent of money owed us through the Iranian Carpet Company, which as you no doubt are aware has the monopoly for selling Iranian rugs in this country. We were prepared to accept settlement in Iranian rugs to be delivered in New York. Although we had the active cooperation of the Iranian Trade Representative in New York City, Sultan Mahmoud Amerie, no results have been obtained. As a matter of fact, our various letters to the Banks and Iranian Rug Company, Teheran, have not even been answered. It is our belief that there must be other American creditors in a similar position and the possibility this is a matter which deserves the attention of the State Department.[50]

Tuthill Spring Company was correct to assume that many other American firms were in the same situation. What it did not know was that this matter had concerned the American legation and the State Department for some time. The American consulate in Tehran had even suggested retaliatory measures against the Iranian government. In a confidential telegram to Henry F. Grady of the State Department, Engert states, "Referring to my despatch No. 1677, September 11, 1939 [see note 49], it does not appear that a single payment has been facilitated to American creditors. The Consulate therefore suggests that consideration be given to the possibility of attaching Iranian Government funds on deposit for example with Irving Trust Company and Chase National Bank of New York for the protection of the American firms."[51] In response, Grady reminds Engert: "In regard to the suggestion made at the conclusion of the Legation's telegram, it is not the Department's practice to be instrumental, in the supposed interests of American concerns, in attaching funds located in this country belonging to foreign governments. Such concerns are of course free to adopt any course which is open to them and which they may consider expedient."[52]

The American minister, Louis G. Dreyfus Jr., gives a partial list of the debtors and creditors and the amounts involved, which had been outstanding since 1936. The smallest claim was $19.44, owed by M. K. Hamneipur of Tehran to the American Newspaper Publishers Association of New York City. Nicola Sarkissian of Shahi, Mazandaran, owed $48.04 to Barnes and Noble of New York. Ovanessoff Brothers of Tehran owed $549.37 to Barcalo Manufacturing Company of Buffalo, New York; $1,221.47 to Gibson Company of Indianapolis; $9,400 to Maremont Auto Products of Chicago; $1,564.10 to E. A. Rodriguez of 55 West 42nd Street, New York City; and $430.18 to Reliable Jack Company of Dayton, Ohio. Sterling Products International of Newark, New Jersey, had a claim of $21,000 on Vakili Trading Company of Tehran. Thomas A. Edison, Inc., New York, had a claim of $1,306.45 against "an unknown Iranian customer." Princeton University had been unable to collect $313.76 from M. E. Moghadam of Tehran. Other claims of $200 to $300 remained outstanding.[53]

The total owed was below $50,000. Yet the Iranian government had not released the needed foreign exchange. With obvious irritation, Dreyfus stated,

> The present procedure for repayment has been in effect for about sixteen months—a period which would appear to be ample for a trial of its efficacy. Although it is not possible to say that no account has been paid through this procedure, the Legation knows of none; while it knows of many accounts which were owed to American exporters before the enactment of the Foreign Exchange Control Law of March 1, 1936, and which are still unpaid. . . . It scarcely seems equitable that the Legation and the Consulate should continue to sell their official drafts to the Iranian Government each month while that Government fails to make possible payment to American creditors of accounts some four years old, but has also refused to permit the purchase of trifling sums in foreign (sterling) exchange by the Legation and Consulate for the payment of official expenditures outside Iran.[54]

Failure to pay American exporters was part of a deliberate policy to discourage imports from the United States. And this policy and the encouragement of Iranian exports resulted in a substantial trade surplus for Iran, as Engert's telegram notes:

> Consul Moose and I feel the following factors should be taken into consideration in connection with Irano-American trade relations. Local dealers now claim definite discrimination against American automotive products through the operation of the clearing or barter agreements with Germany and Russia. It is said that administration of exchange control is manipulated so as to favor purchase of German automobiles. It is represented that 413 trucks have just been ordered from Ferrostahl Germany which normally would have been ordered from America. Reliable non-Iranian importer of American products states that he has seen a strictly confidential circular issued by the Ministry of Finance requiring that all bids even the lowest on supplies for the Iranian Government are to be rejected if payment is demanded in dollars unless the articles are absolutely unobtainable elsewhere. During the past year consular invoices certified for the shipment of Iranian products to the United States have doubled and local merchants report marked increase in such exports. The United States is the only important market supplying free exchange to Iranian exporters but part payment of Iranian purchases from Russia and Germany is being made in dollars.[55]

Engert refers to matters that merit additional comment. The first is Iran's balance of trade with the rest of the world. On the basis of figures found in the confidential files of the Treasury Department, from 1938 through 1940 Iran had an average annual export surplus of 116.3 million rials. The substantial surplus was not only from oil exports but from the virtual starvation of the people of Iran and severe restriction of imports through quotas and trade restrictions. In the same three years, Iran had an annual trade surplus with the United States of about $5–10 million, as a result of its deliberate restriction of U.S. imports after the outbreak of war in 1939. Late in 1939, the Iranian Military Purchasing Commission had traveled to America to buy military aircraft. After a careful consideration of Iran's request, and in view of the requirements of America's own rearmament, Wallace Murray had counseled Undersecretary of State Welles against supplying Iran with the planes, suggesting the matter be referred to President Roosevelt.[56] Welles's reply was brief: "In my judgment there is no practical way of assisting the Government of Iran in this matter. There is nothing to be gained by letting the Iranian authorities believe that there is anything this Government can do to be of assistance in this matter under present conditions."[57]

Iran's demand for civilian goods met with the same response. The reaction of W. L. Parker of the Near Eastern Affairs Division is typical:

> During a conversation yesterday Mr. Green indicated that, in view of an increasing shortage in the types of materials generally desired by the Iranian Government (such as iron steel, copper wire, tin-plate, and, of course, aluminum), most export license applications for Iran, including those sponsored by the Iranian Legation, are likely to be rejected, except in the case of a few miscellaneous commodities in which the Iranian Government does not appear to be particularly interested anyway. Mr. Green added that, by the end of July, we shall be able only to supply Britain and Canada, provide Portugal with materials for the defense of her islands, to send a certain amount of materials to China, and to squeeze out just a bit for Latin America. Mr. Green stated further that only a very mild type of recommendation could accompany the application for tin-plate for the Shah's canning-factory and that, in all probability, the application would be rejected. It was ascertained yesterday from other sources in CO [Commercial Office] that a number of applications for Iran had just been rejected by the Administrator of Export Control, and it is assumed that some of these, at least, were among those covered by the notes from the Iranian Legation. In view of the situation outlined by Mr. Green, Iran is likely to get very little in the way of supplies and practically none of the materials it appears to desire most.[58]

If there was nothing that Iran could import from the United States, what became of Iran's trade surplus with the United States? What became of Iran's oil revenues that were being converted into gold in Canada and subsequently shipped to the Irving Trust Company of New York? Why were the American exporters and firms that had claims on Iran dating back to 1935 not being paid? As documented below, in 1940 foreign employees of the Iranian government, part of whose salaries were to be paid in dollars, "had not seen a single dollar during the previous eight or nine months."[59]

The Sale of Postage Stamps for Foreign Exchange

Toward the end of Reza Shah's rule, to commemorate the shah's sixtieth birthday (March 15, 1938), a series of commemorative stamps was printed. Advance announcements of the issue stated that during the ninety days when the stamps were on sale a special cancellation would be in use.

> On March 15, 1938, the local post-office was open in the morning for the convenience of the purchasers of the new stamps. Several dealers and many collectors applied for stamps, and secured all denominations, perforated and imperforate, except those of 1 rial and 2 rials. The post-office employees apparently told conflicting tales about these two denominations. At least one prospective purchaser was told that 1–rial and 2–rial stamps had not been printed. Another was told that the supply was exhausted. After a day or two, it

became apparent that the entire supply of 1–rial and 2–rial stamps had been turned over to one Asadullah Kordestani, a former member of Parliament. Under the name of Iranphilatelic he had advertised the impending issue of stamps. Mr. Kordestani stated (and produced a paper purporting to be a contract with the Iranian postal authorities to support his contention) that he had been designated by the Ministry of Posts and Telegraphs to sell the new stamps, and that he had received all stamps of 1 and 2–rial denominations, as well as all those canceled with the special cancellation stamp.

He further stated that he is permitted to sell stamps only at face value in foreign exchange, and that the foreign exchange will be delivered to the Iranian Government. Pursuing its established policy of granting monopolies, the Iranian authorities are alleged to have conceded to Mr. Kordestani an effective monopoly on the sale of complete series of the new stamps, and to have insured at the same time the delivery to the Exchange Commission of all foreign exchange arising there from. Mr. Kordestani estimates the exports of such stamps at 30,000 pounds sterling. Possibly this is the first instance where a state has demanded payment in foreign currency for its own postage stamps. It illustrates, if any evidence were needed, the length to which the Iranian Government will go to secure relatively small amounts of foreign exchange.[60]

Why was the Iranian government going to such lengths to bring in even small quantities of dollars? What explains the extraordinary shortage of dollars? The answer is to be found in the transfer of Iranian funds to New York and Swiss banks.

Transfers of Iranian Funds to New York

While dollars had not been seen in Tehran for some time, while some postage stamps were available for foreign exchange only, considerable sums were being transferred into New York bank accounts held by Iranians. Much of these funds were then transferred from New York to Swiss banks. Unbeknown to Reza Shah and his financial managers and advisers, the U.S. Treasury Department had begun to monitor the flow of foreign funds into banks in New York and other cities. The department's main purpose was to oversee funds belonging to the governments and nationals of Germany, Italy, and Japan, and their use of the Swiss banks to transfer funds into and out of the United States. An unintended by-product of this investigation was information on the transfer of Iranian funds to the United States and Switzerland, a subject that merits an in-depth study of its own.

While researching another matter, I came across daily reports prepared by the Treasury Department on transfers into and out of foreign accounts held at certain New York banks between January 2 and June 26, 1941, the final months of Reza Shah's rule. Table 14.1 summarizes the transfers into ostensibly Iranian accounts in those banks by amount and source. The transfer of nearly $4.4 million of Iranian funds to New York at the height of World War II, in addition to the transfer of oil revenues, was clearly the main cause of the acute dollar shortage in Tehran. While misery and poverty prevailed in Iran, vast sums were being transferred to New York. The sources of the transfers are of interest.

Given that Iranian exports to Switzerland were negligible in normal times and practically nonexistent during the war in Europe, and in view of the transfer of Iranian funds from Switzerland to Indiana National Bank (see above), the transfer of funds from Switzerland to New York must be related to the Imperial Iranian Army Purchasing Commission in Bern. Evidently, it was hoped that the small transfers (spread over months, mostly in amounts of $20,000 to $200,000) would escape notice. Since the accounts were being monitored, however, even smaller transfers were recorded.

The $570,005 listed under Hong Kong and China consisted of a payment of $420,000 by Hong Kong and $150,005 from China, certainly payments for Iran's export of opium to these countries. Since Hong Kong was a British colony, it is interesting that in addition to converting most of Iran's oil royalties into dollars, the British had also been forced to pay with dollars for Iran's opium. The Italian transfer was in payment for Iranian exports, mainly rugs and agricultural products.

The payments by the Soviet Union (four transfers for $250,000 each, one for $100,000, and one for $119,997) are perhaps the most revealing. These were for exports of grain and livestock from northern Iran. As described below, in conditions of near famine in Iran in 1940–41 substantial amounts of agricultural products were being exported from Iran to the Soviet Union, including some 200,000 head of the cattle that roamed the Caspian region. As described by Consul Moose during his visit to Bojnurd, in northern Khorasan, in 1941, despite the desperate conditions, agents of the "grain monopoly" were out in force, collecting grain from the peasants for the purpose of exporting it. Since the entire Caspian region and Bojnurd had been acquired by Reza Shah, the export revenues accrued to him directly. The exports of wheat, rice, cotton, and livestock from northern Iran to the Soviet Union provided him with dollars paid into his bank accounts in New York and eventually to Swiss banks. No wonder that, until the very end of his rule, Reza Shah was aggressively acquiring land in areas adjacent to the Soviet Union. As for transfers from Iran, the largest was $600,000. If, instead of being transferred to New York, this money had been placed at the disposal of people like the above-mentioned Mr. Ham-

TABLE 14.1. Transfers into Iranian accounts
in New York banks, January 2–June 26, 1941

SOURCE OF TRANSFER	AMOUNTS
Soviet Union	$1,219,997
Switzerland	$1,193,934
Hong Kong and China	$570,005
Italy	$150,000
Iran	$1,265,881
Total	$4,399,817

Source: U.S. Department of the Treasury,
Division of Monetary Research.

TABLE 14.2. Transfers from
Iranian accounts in New York to
Switzerland, January–June 1941

MONTH OF TRANSFER	AMOUNT
January	$600,377
February	$138,675
March	$235,601
April	$565,634
May	$144,017
June 1–26	$305,808
Total	$1,990,112

Source: U.S. Department of
the Treasury, Division of Monetary
Research.

neipur and Miss Sarkissian and others who paid in rials back in 1935 but
were unable to acquire the trivial amounts of dollars to settle debts
incurred then, their lives would have been much easier.

Given that practically nothing could at that time be imported from the
United States, the transfer of Iranian funds and export earnings to New
York contributed to rumors in Iran concerning Reza Shah's deposits of his
wealth in American banks. As described in 1940 by a Belgian employee of
the American International Telephone and Telegraph Company in Tehran,
Albert C. C. Embrechts (see chapter 15), the dollar scarcity in Iran was due
to Reza Shah's transfer of his wealth from Iran to America, and rumors to
this effect circulating in Iran were accurate. Unbeknown to Embrechts and
his contemporaries, while large sums were being transferred to New York,
substantial sums were being transferred from New York to Swiss banks, as
documented by Treasury Department records. Table 14.2 shows that

between January 2 and June 16, 1941, nearly $2 million was transferred from New York banks to Swiss banks—a sum almost identical to the amount received from the Soviet Union, Hong Kong, China, and Italy ($1,940,002). Moreover, $1.13 million of Iranian army funds were transferred from Indiana National Bank to the Swiss National Bank. The data strongly suggest that the transfer of the funds to New York served as an elaborate cover and an intermediate step in the transfer of the funds to their ultimate destination, the Swiss banks. For instance, on June 11 and June 13, 1941, the Soviet Union made two payments of $250,000 each. On June 16, 1941, $305,808 was transferred from an Iranian account in New York to Switzerland.

Millspaugh noted that in the twenty years that Reza Shah ruled Iran, "he amassed for himself a substantial fortune. . . . Altogether he thoroughly milked the country."[61] The transfers to New York and Swiss banks (in addition to his London bank accounts) indicate that Reza Shah's plunder of Iran was more complete than even that suspected by Millspaugh. The main reason for the painful shortage of foreign exchange in Iran during 1928–41 was because the bulk of the foreign exchange earned by Iran's economy was seized by Reza Shah and diverted to his bank accounts in Europe and America.

CHAPTER FIFTEEN

Iran in 1941 and the Downfall of Reza Shah

FROM THE STATE DEPARTMENT FILES ON conditions in Iran at the end of Reza Shah's rule, we learn that after twenty years of plunder and brutality by the British and their partner the shah, Iran was a wasteland of poverty and famine. Social unrest and bread riots broke out in Tehran in 1940 and 1941. And by 1939 it was obvious to all foreign observers that Reza Shah's days were numbered. The shah himself sensed this, but his desperate attempts to save his tottering regime—some described in American diplomatic reports—only weakened his position further.

Reza Shah's Volte-Face

With power slipping from his hands and with conditions deteriorating rapidly, Reza Shah tightened censorship and repression. American chargé d'affaires C. Van H. Engert translates an Interior Ministry notice that appeared on October 16, 1939, and was published in all the Tehran newspapers: "Persons who disseminate false reports in order to mislead the public are notified that the dissemination of such reports is forbidden and that they will be prosecuted by the police and severely punished." Engert then comments:

> It is generally assumed that the publication of this warning is due chiefly to the large number of more or less alarming rumors which have been current regarding Soviet intentions. It is, of course, inevitable that under an authoritarian rule

such as the Shah's, which never permits the people to form an exact idea of the true situation, more fantasy than fact should from day to day be put into circulation by word of mouth. A strictly censored press—and the censorship has been considerably tightened since the outbreak of the war—has accustomed a long-suffering public to an atmosphere of mystery. Having for years had their minds confused by half-truths which only serve to conceal material facts, it is but natural that in times of alarm and agitation the people should always be ready to believe stories which in their calmer moments they would reject as unfounded rumors. It may therefore be doubted whether the present attempt to repress even whispers by punitive legislation will have much success.[1]

Realizing that repression alone was no longer sufficient to keep him in power, Reza Shah also sought to strengthen his position by introducing a small dose of liberalization. Engert had reported the following example, an announcement that appeared in all the papers: "In conformity with Article 55 of the Penal Code, and upon the recommendation of the Acting Minister of Justice, His Imperial Majesty has decided to remit the punishment of 92 prisoners in the hands of the Tehran police who have been condemned by the competent courts; consequently twenty of the said prisoners have been released, and the remainder will be released as soon as the reduction in their sentences has been calculated." Engert adds: "In the absence of information to the contrary they were all accused of being 'Communists.'"[2] Nearly forty years later, in 1978, Reza Shah's son and successor also released political prisoners in an attempt to liberalize, and thus save, a foundering regime. Both attempts, predicated on weakness, had earned the contempt of observers.

On Saturday, June 29, 1940, during an audience of a delegation of Majlis deputies at Saadabad Palace, and in the presence of newspaper reporters, Reza Shah terrified the gathered deputies and astounded Tehran political and diplomatic circles by denouncing the government for failing to take the people into its confidence and for neglecting to prepare them for the difficult days that lay ahead. He demanded that public opinion be aroused and the people informed of the state of the nation. He expressed his impatience at obsequious officials who bowed deeply in his presence, addressed him as Your Majesty, and assured him that everything was all right. According to Engert, there was little in the speech "to remind us of the Shah we know except the brusque manner in which he flung his admonitions at the heads of his terrified audience." Engert describes Reza Shah's regime as "a military dictatorship with a civilian propaganda department" and further comments:

> The Shah's revolutionary statements had been entirely unexpected and caused a great sensation. The Department is sufficiently familiar with my views regarding the Crown, the Cabinet, and Parliament to realize that only a great shock could have induced the Shah to say the things he said on Saturday. That

this totalitarian autocrat, who has held power by suppressing all enemies and eliminating all personal liberties, should suddenly declare that present conditions were a serious reproach to the Government as it stood today, or that this despot whose voiceless people and controlled press were obliged to breathe universal obsequiousness should brusquely announce that he was tired of fawning flattery and wished Parliament and the press to prepare the people to hear the truth may well portend some dramatic political changes. It is as yet too early to determine what precisely prompted the Shah to direct attention to the ominous cracks in the plaster facade of his Government. . . . By taking Parliament and the press into his confidence the Shah may be hoping to introduce a healthier atmosphere into public life and bridge the existing gap between his regime and the masses.[3]

The Scarcity of Bread in Tehran

The final years of Reza Shah, 1939–41, saw desperate economic, political, and social conditions in Iran. The extreme deprivation included a serious bread shortage in Tehran, described by American minister Louis G. Dreyfus Jr.:

> The severe shortage of wheat which has prevailed in Iran since the fall of 1940, I have the honor to inform the Department, has been partially alleviated and a serious crisis averted by the importation of wheat from India. That the situation caused by the shortage of wheat has been serious is only now beginning to be fully realized and, had the Iranian Government not been sufficiently alert to arrange for importation from India, it might have developed into a crisis of greater proportions. The mere fact of importations shows that the shortage is acute, for Iran is self-sufficient in wheat and does not import except during famines. The Government's grave view of the situation is revealed by its drastic action in requiring the delivery to it of all surplus wheat and providing penalties of confiscation and prosecution for noncompliance.[4]

An announcement in *Ettela'at* warned owners of wheat to deliver it to the grain stores of the Ministry of Finance by February 19, 1941, or be fined 100 rials per kharvar (the current price was 140 rials per kharvar).[5] Anyone caught in possession of wheat after March 1941 faced stiff jail terms and confiscation of the grain. Despite these penalties, Dreyfus concludes:

> Merchants and others with whom I have discussed the matter believe that the Government will find it difficult to obtain possession of even a small portion of the wheat now in the hands of growers and middlemen. It is said that already growers have sold large quantities of their wheat to private hoarders at as much as three times the price fixed by the government purchasing agency. This is done by bribing officials, by misdeclaring amounts held, or by obtaining a favorable ruling as to how much of quantities held may be considered surplus.

Dreyfus continues with a description of the wheat shortage:

> The dearth, although less severe, continues, particularly in the provinces where bread is being made wholly or partially from substitutes such as barley.

Tehran has suffered also, bread in recent months having been of a very inferior quality, but relief offered by imported wheat has made itself felt here to a greater extent than in the provinces. I was personally able to verify the shortage by visiting a mill several miles from Tehran. The miller informed me that for more than 40 days his mill had been closed except for grinding of a small amount of wheat carried over by individual growers. The scarcity of this invaluable item in Iran's diet may be attributed to two factors, neither of which in itself would have been sufficient to cause a severe shortage. First, wheat was exported to Germany just before the outbreak of war, reducing the normal car-ryover, and secondly, the crop in 1940 was very poor. The army has not helped the situation with its program of laying up strategic stores. It is not believed that wheat has been exported since the 1940 crop came in, although there are rumors to that effect.[6]

Dreyfus soon discovered that the rumors of continuing wheat exports were accurate. While traveling in the vicinity of Bojnurd, in northeastern Iran, in May 1941, the American consul James S. Moose Jr. came across officials of the grain monopoly who were collecting grain for export, although the country was experiencing near famine and importing wheat from India. What he did not mention was that Bojnurd was part of Reza Shah's private estate. Exports of grain and livestock from northern Iran to the Soviet Union, as documented above, translated into dollars deposited in Reza Shah's accounts in New York. Not only were the people of Iran being robbed, they were being starved. Dreyfus comments:

The matter has not been without its political repercussions. It is generally known that Gholam Hossein Ebtehaj was removed from his position as acting mayor of Tehran because of incidents caused by it. It is said that the Shah was furious because Ebtehaj permitted what in some cases almost amounted to bread riots and hence ordered his removal. . . . It is probable that the situation will be relieved sufficiently by the importation of wheat to avoid any serious consequences. However, should the 1941 crop, which comes in about July, be below average, it would be necessary to import considerable quantities or face another year of even more acute shortage.[7]

As subsequent reports were to show, the shortage was indeed to become more acute by the summer of 1941.

Reports of Worsening Conditions

By the late 1930s it was obvious to Reza Shah himself and the diplomatic community in Tehran that the days of the old dictator were numbered. Months before the Allied invasion of Iran, it was clear that, despite the shah's complete about-face, he would be unable to save himself. The American legation in Tehran was predicting the end of the Pahlavi dynasty. Foreign employees of American and European firms had begun to warn their employers that the sociopolitical situation was on the point of breakdown and serious trouble was inevitable and recommended plans to vacate Iran as soon as possible. It was no longer a question of if but when Reza Shah would be overthrown by a domestic revolution. In January 1941, a Belgian named Albert Casimir Corneille Embrechts, the Tehran representative of the International Telephone and Telegraph Corporation of New York, sent a report to Frank C. Page, the corporation's vice president. Page, who had himself recently visited Iran, realized that the report should be brought to the attention of Secretary of State Cordell Hull. Coming from the vice president of IT&T, the report promptly caught Hull's attention.

Embrechts had informed Page that, because of increasing censorship and vigilance by the Iranian police and the regime's sensitivity to any criticism, he had destroyed previous reports he had written on conditions in Iran. The enclosed report was hand delivered by a trusted source. The report paints a grim picture of repression and censorship, the desperate suffering of the people, and the exorbitant levels of taxation. It describes the acute food and bread shortages caused mainly by the government's continued policy of exporting large amounts of grain and livestock to Germany and the USSR:

> In many places in the country people have been eating barley bread or any other substitute bread which they could find, since last spring. Evidence of meat shortage is also apparent, but this is mainly due to the fact that a deal was recently made with Russia whereby Iran would supply 400,000 sheep, 200,000 pigs and 200,000 head of cattle. Personally I cannot imagine where the cattle could be found without seeing any effect on the local meat market although I was told by an official who should know that there are several hundred thousand head of cattle running wild in the hills and woods on the southern shore of the Caspian Sea (His Majesty's property).[8]

As reported above, Reza Shah had evidently found an ingenious way of turning even the cattle roaming the Caspian region into dollars in New York.

Embrechts also comments on Iran's construction program: "Apart from the railroad building programme there is a house building craze (under Government compulsion) and the construction of vast new ministerial palaces, mostly of the 1000 to 2000 room variety, calling for vast non-productive expenditures, such as is only rarely seen in peace time anywhere in the world, let alone during a war." He states that because of the government's trade monopolies, private business had come to a standstill. Inflation was rife and wages were totally inadequate to provide a bare subsistence. Most significant, Embrechts is certain that "it was no longer a question of if turmoil and revolution is on the way, it is only a question of when." The most telling sign, he says, was that Reza Shah was frantically transferring money out of Iran and into American banks. Pointing to Iran's sizable oil revenues (about $20 million per year), which were now being paid in dollars, and to Iran's substantial merchandise trade surplus, including an excess of exports over imports to the United States, the acute shortage of dollars, Embrechts reasons, was most likely due to the fact that the trade surplus dollars were being appropriated and deposited to Reza Shah's bank accounts in New York (he was unaware of the transfers to Switzerland).

Embrechts notes that dollars had not been seen in Tehran for a year. The reason, it turns out, was simple. All the dollars, including Iran's oil revenues paid by the Anglo-Iranian Oil Company, were going to New York:

> With the royalties obtained from the Anglo-Iranian, other exports to the British Empire and the United States and certain other countries able to pay in either pounds or free exchange, minus imports of sugar and tea, there remains a sizable sum in free dollars which could relatively easily pay for the required imports from the United States and there would actually be no or a very small shortage of liquid dollars. Quite the contrary is true. When the sum total is made, approximate of course due to lack of accurate information, of all revenue in free currency on the one side and all expenditure on the other, there is an unexplainable gap [surplus] of extra revenue which does not explain the very real shortage and the difficulty in obtaining dollars even by those required to pay the dollar salaries of foreign government employees who have not seen a dollar for the last eight or nine months. Rumours, trying to explain, are circulating most of which are entirely unfounded. One seems quite possible. Apparently, H.M. [His Majesty] has been transferring his private fortune to the U.S. . . . This kind of rumour or explanation should be easier to check in the U.S. than here.

Embrechts also explains the unavailability of dollars to purchase goods from the United States:

> At present time practically the only exporter and importer is the Government and business has to be done through the Department of Economics of the Ministry of Finance. The foreign trade situation as far as the Government is interested is well summarized by the regulation issued by the Ministry of Finance to all other Ministries, in which regulation instructions are given that any order issued by the Government Departments should be placed in Germany at whatever price. No dollars are available for purchases from U.S. Orders to the U.S. are only placed after decision by the Department of Economics, that is to say that goods may only be ordered from the U.S. when they cannot possibly be obtained anywhere else. I have seen this regulation with my own eyes.

Azerbaijan and Northwest Iran in 1940

Exactly ten years after Consul Henry S. Villard had visited Azerbaijan and reported on conditions in the province, a successor of Villard, James

S. Moose Jr., took two extensive trips (the second at his own expense) to Mazandaran, Gilan, Azerbaijan, Kermanshahan, Hamedan, and Zanjan, "for the purpose of familiarizing myself with the Tehran consular district and of collecting commercial and other information." Moose found conditions in Azerbaijan far worse even than those reported by Villard in 1930. Apart from the miserable economic conditions Moose describes in his "random glimpses of Iran in the Pahlavi era," Reza Shah's supposed achievements of national unification and domestic security had evaporated by 1940:

> To my mind, the outstanding feature observed on the trips was the condition of the peasants. There has been a shortage of bread, flour and sugar in Tehran for several months past, and the further I traveled from the capital, the more acute the shortage became. The situation will be remedied in a short time by the harvest now in progress, though there is reason to believe that it may recur.
>
> A plausible and commonly accepted explanation of the shortage is that the official grain monopoly has contracted for exports based on the surplus available in 1938 above domestic needs. With fixed quantities of grain set aside for export, any deficiency must be made by reducing domestic consumption. It now appears that the 1938 harvest was better than average, so that in a normal year there will be a deficiency, and in bad crop years a serious shortage.
>
> Peasants complained (as I assumed they always do) about taxation and about the price paid for grain by the government monopoly. In some villages they said that taxes amounted to half the crop, and in others the proportion was placed at two-sevenths. Probably the latter figure is more nearly accurate. After setting aside a quantity estimated to be sufficient for the peasants' needs, the remainder is taken by the monopoly at a fixed price. For example: a peasant in the Sultanabad area now receives from the monopoly 140 rials per kharvar [300 kilograms] of wheat. Twenty years ago he received the same price. In the bad old days of Kajar [Qajar] rule, he could sell freely to any purchaser; the grain was sold "as is," including dirt, stones, and such extraneous matter from the threshing floor; and he was paid in silver krans. Now, however, he must sell to the monopoly. That organization deducts an arbitrary 20% from the gross weight of the grain to allow for dirt and trash, thus reducing the price by one fifth; and it pays him in paper rials nominally of the same value as the silver krans, but which in reality have about one-seventh of the kran's purchasing power of twenty years ago. In other districts conditions are parallel. Only the poppy-growers seem to be cheerful.
>
> In Mazandaran, which is virtually the Shah's private estate, his administrators have constructed new mud houses of uniform design along the main roads, and attempt to make the peasants live in them. At any rate, they charge the peasants rent, and collect it when they can. Despite strong measures of encouragement such as burning the thatched huts which the peasants are

accustomed to occupy, many of the new houses are vacant. One or two persons are hurriedly put into each house just before the Shah passes by, and then they are permitted to return to their habitual domiciles. The Shah's silk mill at Chalus is doubtless a source of Imperial satisfaction, but the European foremen describe the conditions under which the women and children work as appalling, and the pay they receive as totally inadequate.

On the other hand, the appearance of the larger towns and villages is constantly improved. Broad avenues, two of which are inevitably named "Pahlavi" and "Shahpur," have been opened; and new buildings have been constructed along them. Sometimes a compromise is reached by the construction of a new facade to an old structure.

The Iranian Government continues work on the Tabriz railway, and much activity is visible all along the route from Tehran to Mianeh. There the railroad turns westward to Maragha [Maragheh], and thence northward along the eastern shore of Lake Rezaieh to Tabriz. Work on the way from Mianeh to Tabriz has scarcely started. The main highways are being improved by the construction of culverts and cut-offs. There is talk of the construction of an automobile road from Pahlavi to Astara, but the present road is only a track through forests and rice fields. A fairly good road has recently been completed from Shahrud to Shahpasand which could facilitate the invasion of Iran by Soviet troops through the province of Gurgan [Gorgan] at the south-eastern corner of the Caspian Sea. A road from Astara to Pahlavi could likewise facilitate the invasion of Iran at the south-western corner of the Caspian.

Many trucks were on the roads of Azerbaijan hauling to Trebizond [Trabzon] cotton and other goods destined for Germany. These shipments go by sea from Trebizond to Constanza, and hence by rail to destination. . . . Some time ago the Soviet Government was claiming cotton contracted for but not delivered by Iran; and this may have a bearing on the route chosen for exports of cotton. The price of sugar decreased as I approached the Soviet frontier, thus indicating the existence of a certain amount of illicit trade.

Throughout Azerbaijan the army was much in evidence. At Astara there was one division of troops; at Ardebil, two; at Mishkinshahr probably one; at Ahar, a regiment; at Tabriz, two divisions; and at Makou only soldiers were in evidence. Barracks and troops were noted in other places as well. Insofar as it was possible to ascertain, the people in Azarbaijan share the general Iranian feeling of admiration and sympathy for Germany and fear of the U.S.S.R. The value of real estate in Tabriz has fallen to about one-fourth of what it was five years ago, thus reflecting the apprehension of invasion by Soviet forces. Armenians and Assyrians form a minority which feels, or appears to feel, that almost any kind of change would be for the better. In Kurdistan there have been several marauding expeditions by Kurds, allegedly from Iraq. I passed over one road where a caravan had been held up and looted only two days before. Suppression of such banditry by the army is certain to be costly, and in the Afshar region the depredations have reached such proportions that the Iranian authorities are reported to have under consideration the re-arming of the villagers to permit them to defend themselves.[9]

Although he was originally a peasant himself, "Reza Shah cruelly exploited the peasants who form the mass of the population."[10]

Eastern and Southern Iran, April 1941

In April 1941, Consul Moose visited Gurgan, Khorasan, Kerman, Zahedan, Fars, and Esfahan. In a confidential report on the twenty-five-day trip, sent to Wallace S. Murray, he states that food shortages had become more severe than what he had reported a few months before:

> I think that the most striking feature of the trip was the scarcity of food throughout the country. With one unimportant exception, every place on the route was short of food, and in many, no bread whatever was obtainable. Abundant rains during the late spring, and the good harvest now in prospect, may save the situation for the moment. . . .
>
> The Iranian authorities did not restrict the exportation of foodstuffs after a severe shortage in 1940; and there is slight reason to believe that the shortage will make them more prudent in the future. In fact, grain monopoly agents were collecting grain in the region about Bojnord when I passed through, for export to Germany via the Soviet Union. As might be expected when rations are short, there was much grumbling against the government everywhere. Generally, it was anti-British because the British are popularly believed to be responsible for everything which occurs in Iran. Only in Bandar Abbass did there appear to be genuine pro-Nazi sentiment. This was attributed to the activities of the Germans who recently constructed a fish cannery there and who supplied free moving pictures and other desiderata to the local inhabitants.
>
> Naturally, it is difficult in these times to distinguish anti-British feeling from pro-Nazi feeling; but I believe that the basic desire of the people with whom I came in contact was for a change of some sort—of any sort, for that matter. There was a noticeable relaxation in the police control and supervision in the region of Gurgan (Astarabad). Last year there was much questioning of travelers by the police, and at one time the Ministry of Foreign Affairs sent out a circular to the various diplomatic missions which suggested that members of the missions should not go to Gurgan province (among other places) without first consulting the Ministry of Foreign Affairs. At one time, all the non-Iranians in the area were arrested, for no known reason, and were detained for some time at Gurgan. Beggars were as numerous and as insistent as they usually are in

Iran. There seemed to be a working agreement between the police and the beggars at various places along the way. The police would delay the car, and the beggars would make such a nuisance of themselves that I would often subsidize them to go away. I do not know of any other country where one can be a philanthropist so cheaply, and can contribute to local charity with a sum as small as ten shahis (1 cent).[11]

Minor's Report, August 1941: Reza Shah Must Go

Embrechts's report, described above, was carefully studied in Washington. Many of his views, however, had already been shared by the American legation in Tehran. A lengthy commentary on the report was prepared by Harold G. Minor, the legation's secretary, just two weeks before Allied forces entered Iran and the shah fell. In transmitting the report, Minister Dreyfus had stated that "Mr. Minor had taken great pains in the preparation of this report and in my opinion it is a piece of work which accurately presents the current situation in Iran." Minor had found the work sound and added that many persons perhaps believed that "Embrechts' views, which are those of a hard headed business man faced with practical problems, are much sounder than those of a theorizing diplomatic officer." Minor's report includes the following:

> There is no doubt that there is very real discontent on the part of the masses, whose lot has not been an easy one. . . . The exploitation of the masses has, indeed, reached a high, or rather a low, point. This is a phase in which I am particularly interested and I have discussed it with persons in all walks of life. For example, Dr. Shafter, the well known British missionary doctor at Isfahan, made the following comment to me one day in Isfahan on seeing a group of conscripts pass through the streets. These boys, he said, were bled by their officers from before they went into the army until they left, money being extracted from them for the privilege of being sent or not sent to a particular camp, for leave privileges, for special consideration, for better food, and for freedom from corporal punishment. An official of the [British Imperial] Bank of Iran told me only yesterday that one of his clerks came back from military service with his head shaved, which is required by military regulations. He explained indignantly that he had paid an officer 270 rials to keep from having his head shaved but that immunity had lasted only until the end of his service when another officer had demanded an additional 300 rials, which he refused to pay. These soldiers are paid an unbelievably low wage of 7.50 rials a *month* and this amount is often taken by the officers so that at the end of the month they have nothing, or actually have a minus account if they have resources of their own or a relative who will pay. No provision is made for their families while they are serving.

Wages are certainly insufficient for more than bare existence, amounting for a common laborer to from four to ten rials a day with an average of perhaps eight. Disregarding the foreign exchange value of the rial, it may be said that it will purchase a loaf of white bread or that a worker must pay from three to seven rials a day for his food. Thus, it will be seen that the wage is insufficient even for food for a family and most workers have a starvation diet consisting of tea, native (not white) bread, cheese and onions, with occasional greens and grapes and infrequent rice and cheap meat. It is not possible to buy adequate clothing or even dream of luxuries such as education of the children. Sometimes the workers' one or more wives and the children work to bring in additional income to make possible a slightly higher standard of living.

The cost of living in Iran has increased to the point where the toman (10 rials) has about the same purchasing power as the rial had twenty years ago. Wages have increased about five to seven fold, so that there has been indeed a severe decline in real income. . . . The result of the increased living costs and low wages has been an increase in graft. Graft and corruption are all too common here. Certain it is that the system is widespread and that many officials depend on graft for supplementing their inadequate salaries to provide a proper standard of living. The very worst phase of graft here is the practice of stealing part of the wages of soldiers and other under-paid persons.

Expropriation of property is made, usually for the Shah's benefit, for only a fraction of the value of the property. There is great dissatisfaction at the Shah's predatory tactics in gaining gradual but sure control over a large part of the land and wealth of the country. It is said that the Shah has bought the Municipal garden in Tehran for [1%] of its value. The government has a neat trick in taking [urban] lands under the right of eminent domain. They may take, for example, ten feet of land for the purpose of building or widening a street, paying the owner arbitrary compensation. They then hold that the entire property has been increased in value by the building of the street and require the owner to pay in cash within a certain specified time a sum representing the appreciation in value of his land. This procedure, which was formerly done illegally, was made legal by a law reported in the Legation's despatch No. 99 dated July 12, 1941. Forced labor, amounting almost to slavery, exists on some of the Shah's properties with wages as low as three and a half rials a day, from which the local police take a cut. Exploitation of the people, truly, has become scandalous and malodorous.

Rumors as to the Shah's private investments in the United States and Great Britain are venerable with age. They have never been confirmed but, taking into consideration his great avarice, one would guess that they are true. . . . Advantage was taken last year of Britain's bad situation to force the Anglo-Iranian Oil Company to change its agreement with the Iranian Government. Under this revised agreement, the Government received £4,000,000 a year instead of the former payment based on royalties, under which less than £1,000,000 was being received. An official of the British Legation told me in confidence that "the British will not forget this blackmail."

Most observers here view the local situation very pessimistically. There is no doubt that discontent is widespread and on the increase. This may be attributed to the increase in the cost of living, high taxation, dissatisfaction with the Shah's greedy acquisition of a large part of the wealth of the country, to the mushroom building program and its attendant ills, to the personal restrictions caused by the monopoly system, and to the general shortsighted commercial and financial policy. There is muttering for the first time in the army. In spite of this I do not believe that the means or the fortitude [exist] to translate this discontent into corrective measures or revolt. They suffer well.

I should not be surprised, although I dislike predictions, if the days of the Pahlevi regime were numbered. It would seem that Iran must, due to the war, fall at least temporarily under foreign domination. If this domination is by the Germans, the present regime would undoubtedly be found unsatisfactory. If, as at the moment seems not unlikely, the country is brought under British domination, there are indications that the Shah would not be found persona grata. A British diplomatic officer told me only recently that he considered it essential to get rid of the Shah, not only because of his shallow policies and his blackmail of the British, but also because he is too closely associated in the minds of the Iranian people with Great Britain, of which he is considered by them to be a creature and tool. The Iranians usually, in deploring their present hard lot, lay the primary responsibility at the door of the Shah but hold the British almost equally responsible. The Shah has overplayed his hand in all things and in all directions.

Iran suffers, I should like to add in closing, from what I like to term an aggravated case of "facade-itis." This great love of outward show has led to a shallowness of policy and distortion of values which have done great harm. Governmental action, always with the facade in full view and the back rooms forgotten, is too often based on the effect which will be produced on the observer, failing to take into consideration the welfare of the people or the practicability of the individual project. There seems to me to be little hope for the country without a return to common sense and, above all, human values.[12]

The Allied Invasion, August 25, 1941

This book began with the British invasion of Iran in the spring of 1918. It ends with another British invasion, this one in August 1941. Reza Shah's close association with the British and his extreme unpopularity with the people, as well as the very real possibility of turmoil and revolution, made it imperative for the British to discard their long time ally and protégé. By his miscalculations, such as forcing the British to increase the oil royalties in 1940 (the British called it blackmail) and convert the payment for oil and opium into dollars to be transferred to New York, Reza Shah had made the British task easier; they would suffer no guilty conscience. Allied objections to the presence of (at most) 2,500 German technicians and "tourists" in Iran was an excuse seized by the British and the Russians.

In the early hours of August 25, 1941, British and Soviet forces invaded Iran from the west and the north. In view of the reports on the Iranian military given above, the invading forces were not surprised when the army and the regime of Reza Shah collapsed like a house of cards. The so-called national army—on which every year for the past twenty vast sums, amounting to at least half of all government expenditures had been spent (not to mention the looting of the civilian population and the exactions by the same army), the army for whom arms and ammunition were supposedly imported by most of Iran's oil revenues from 1925 to 1941–hardly fired a shot in the defense of the country.

Only in Gilan had the Eleventh Army offered some resistance to the Soviets. It was later learned that on the first day of the Soviet invasion the Iranian army in Azerbaijan—the same army that had so "bravely" subdued the unfortunate tribes in 1923–24 and had plundered their valuables and properties (thereby precipitating the acrimonious exchange between Millspaugh and Reza Khan about the fate of the gold and silver looted by the army), the same army that had massacred the fleeing "relocated" Kurds in 1931–had melted away and had abandoned Azerbaijan to the Soviets, who had taken Tabriz and the other cities in less than a day. The army commander (Amir Lashgar), General Iraj Matbui, and the governor-general of Azerbaijan had both fled on the first day and had used army trucks to transport their household belongings, including the commander's flock of turkeys. And in Khorasan, the same army that had massacred unarmed pilgrims and protesters with machine guns in the shrine of Imam Reza in Mashhad in July 1935 had surrendered without resistance. The army commander in Khorasan, General Mohammad Mohtashemi, had donned civilian clothes and escaped.[13]

Virtually all government officials, from lowly district administrators to provincial governors, had fled their posts when they were most needed. It was not clear whom they feared most, the local people, whom they had brutalized, oppressed, and plundered, or the invading forces. Of the provincial governors it was learned later that only two did not abandon their posts during the Soviet invasion. With the dissolution of the civilian administration and law enforcement organizations, the government's authority in the provinces disappeared overnight. In light of the conditions in Iran, the deep dissatisfaction of the people, and the widespread corruption, the rapid collapse of the regime of Reza Shah was not surprising.

American diplomatic reports reveal that Reza Shah himself sought refuge in the British legation in Tehran but was turned away. In the end he wished to return whence he came. Dreyfus reports: "The Shah sent Ebrahim Ghavam, the father of his son-in-law, to the British Minister to express his anxiety at the delay and the continuance of hostilities. Ghavam also sounded out the British Minister on the possibility of the Shah taking asylum in the British Legation because of his fear of the Russians but received little encouragement on this score."[14] Reza Shah's fear was not from the Soviets but from the people of Iran, who, given the slightest chance, would have torn him to pieces.

The Abdication of Reza Shah and the Succession of Mohammad Reza Shah

The government of Ali Mansur resigned on August 26, 1941. The person selected by the British to carry out their designs was Mohammad Ali Foroughi, Zoka-ol-Molk, who became prime minister on August 28, 1941. Foroughi's cabinet had all served in prominent positions under Reza Shah and had been beneficiaries of his rule. On the face of it, for both Reza Shah and Foroughi, the circle was complete. Foroughi had served in nearly all of Reza Khan's cabinets up to 1935. He was Reza Shah's first prime minister and was to be his last. He had served as minister of war, minister of justice, minister of finance, minister of foreign affairs, and ambassador to Turkey. As noted by Murray, Foroughi's relationship with Reza Khan was intimate. That relationship, and no doubt Foroughi's close relationship with the British, had saved him from a fate similar to that of his colleagues.

The British desired to preserve their position in Iran and to ensure that the dismal record of the previous twenty years, the plunder and the brutality, would be destroyed or remain concealed for as long as possible. That could only be done if Reza Shah was removed and his son put in his place. Foroughi was the chosen instrument of this policy, just as Reza Khan had been the instrument in 1921. In saving the Pahlavi regime, the British were also determined to save their old partner from retribution and justice at the hands of his own people. The British were not about to totally abandon one who had so faithfully served them these many years. Having been assured that his London bank accounts were secure and at his disposal, Reza Khan was whisked away to Bandar Abbas, where he boarded a British ship in the safety and comfort of the vast fortune that he had stolen from the people of Iran.

FIGURE 15.1 *Mohammad Ali Foroughi, Zoka-ol-Molk, ca. 1930.*

As in 1921, when the British had pretended ignorance of the coup by Reza Khan, they tried to portray themselves as innocent bystanders in 1941. In his conversations with the American minister Dreyfus, Sir Reader Bullard, the British minister, portrayed the removal of Reza Shah and the installation of his son as a free choice. Telegrams from Dreyfus about the abdication of Reza Shah and the succession of his son show that neither the Iranian people nor Foroughi had any control over the proceedings. How could they? Iran was under a complete military occupation and the authority of its government had all but vanished. With the flight of the vast majority of government employees and the dissolution of the armed forces, gendarmerie, even the police, Foroughi's government existed only on paper.

   The British decided the changes at the top. On the night of September 11, 1941, Dreyfus spoke with Bullard. His telegram the next day reveals what the minister had told him:

> The Prime Minister informed British Minister last night that a special meeting of the Medjliss [Majlis] would be called Saturday to consider constitutional reforms. He added that while the Shah will have no alternative but to approve such reforms he will when possible take action against any who actively support them. He then in the strictest confidence made the important statement that he (and the British Minister gained the impression that the Prime Minister was speaking for the Cabinet) was of the opinion that Iranians must now get rid of the Shah. He was further of the opinion that the Crown Prince would be acceptable to Iranians if surrounded by good advisers. The British Minister believes the British Government would probably accept Crown Prince if he is free Iranian choice. It would seem to me, in view of fact that Crown Prince is generally considered weak, incompetent, and pro-German, that British could accept him if at all only as a stop-gap in order to avoid consequences of too radical a change in government or as a puppet with competent advisers.[15]

   After Foroughi's alleged suggestion that the Iranians must now get rid of the shah, British radio broadcast a series of reports in Persian declaring that Reza Shah had amassed vast sums in foreign banks and had stolen large amounts of valuable real estate. Dreyfus comments:

> The campaign against the Shah reached a climax in a broadcast last night in Iranian from London. It was stated that the Shah had stolen a large part of the valuable real estate in the country giving payment if at all only a small fraction of the value; that owners have been forced to sell under threat of death, imprisonment or insult and that poverty stricken peasants must sweat to fill the Shah's pockets with gold. The broadcast ended with a poem said to have been written by a man who was imprisoned by the Shah eight years ago. This poem likens the Shah to the legendary tyrant Zohak and asked where today are the men like Feridun and Kawa [Kaveh] who conquered the tyrant.

In contrast to 1935, when the British had attempted to downplay the numbers massacred in the shrine of Imam Reza, in 1941 they broadcast statements by former prisoners. From Dreyfus's telegram it is also learned that "[t]he Medjliss in secret session on Saturday appointed a committee to request Shah personally to refrain from exceeding his constitutional authority. The committee delivered its message as directed on Saturday night."[16]

   However, at 9 A.M. the next day, September 16, the day after Dreyfus had reported on the action of the Majlis committee, Reza Shah abdicated, which came as a surprise to the Majlis. Dreyfus sent the following urgent telegram: "The Shah has just now abdicated in favor of the Crown Prince and has fled to Ispahan [Esfahan] from whence it is thought he will go to India. Russian troops are approaching Tehran from Kazvin and British troops have moved up to Qum. No details yet available."[17] In Esfahan, Reza

Khan was safe under British army protection. News of the decision of the Majlis to accept the abdication of Reza Shah and the succession of his son was reported by Dreyfus the next day: "The Majlis yesterday accepted the abdication of the Shah. The new Shah will be known as His Imperial Majesty, Mohammad Reza Shah Pahlavi, and will take the oath before the Majlis this afternoon as required by constitution."[18]

As in 1925, in the decision process the Iranian people were conspicuous by their absence. Dreyfus paraphrases Reza Shah's abdication statement: "The former Shah in his abdication statement declared substantially as follows: 'I am ceding the reign to my son because I have become exhausted and feel that now is the time when a younger force should attend to the affairs of the country which require constant surveillance and prepare for the prosperity of the people.' . . . The Prime Minister yesterday conveyed to the Majlis an informal statement by the new Shah, the substance of which follows: 'Let it be known to the Iranian people that I am a fully law-abiding Sovereign and my definite decision is thoroughly to observe and protect the fundamental law which governs the country and people of Iran, and to insure normal course of the laws which the Majlis have enacted or will enact. If, in the past, the people have been the object of encroachments collectively or individually, and from whatever source, let them be assured from top to bottom that we will take action to remove those encroachments and to make redress as far as possible.'"[19]

Dreyfus also gives the news of the formal accession of Mohammad Reza Shah on September 17, 1941:

> The Shah took oath yesterday afternoon before Majlis. Invitation given diplomatic corps was canceled by Iranian Government an hour before ceremony because British and Russians made known that they were unwilling to attend pending absence of instructions from their Governments to do so. British Minister attributes his lack of instructions to delay in telegraph service and does not believe it signifies refusal to recognize Shah. In his speech after taking oath Shah promised constitutional Government protection of individual rights, a wide program of reform and cooperation with Governments whose interests are closely allied with Iran's. In addition to reforms indicated above the Shah it is understood will declare general amnesty and cede his father's properties to the state. Majlis yesterday promised immediate action on following: investigation as to Crown jewels, protection of rights and well-being of people, restoration of property seized by former Shah, abolition of several laws, reduction of budget and taxation, liberation of innocent prisoners and abolition of law permitting sale of pious foundation properties. British and Russian troops have stopped on outskirts of Tehran and do not intend at the moment to enter or pass through city or relieve the civil or military authorities of their duties. Tehran is calm, the people having been reassured by action of their Government by presence of British troops and by fact that Russians have not entered the city.

Iranian reaction to the Shah's abdication is almost universally one of relief and joy that the tyrant is gone and that they are at last free to do things long forbidden and express thoughts so long pent up. Their great disappointment that a member of the despised Pahlavi family is still on the throne is counterbalanced somewhat by satisfaction that the new Shah has taken active steps to correct evils and redress wrong. While future of Shah will depend on his conduct and on British and Russian policy there can be no doubt that he has made a wise and active beginning.[20]

So much for the British claim that the new Shah was "the free choice of the Iranian people." However, the "[r]emoval of Reza Shah Pahlevi was alone of incalculable value, and for that service his former subjects should be grateful."[21]

News of the detention of Reza Khan in Esfahan and the recognition of the new Shah by the British and the Soviets is given by Dreyfus: "The ex-Shah is being held in Ispahan for negotiations as to the disposition of his properties. The British Minister informs me that he and Soviet Ambassador have now received instructions from their Governments agreeing to the succession of the new Shah to throne. This approval is contingent in both cases on Shah's future good conduct. Iranian Government has been notified both of the approval and contingency on which it is placed."[22]

American recognition of the new shah took a few days, as indicated by Secretary of State Cordell Hull's telegram to Dreyfus: "Since the British and Soviet Governments have recognized the new Shah, the Department perceives no reason why this Government should not do so. You are authorized in your discretion to take appropriate steps to indicate that this Government accords him recognition."[23] Dreyfus reports that Reza Khan sailed from Bandar Abbas on September 28, 1941, on an English ship, accompanied by one wife, six sons, two daughters, a son-in-law (Djam), a secretary, and eleven servants. Only Mohammad Reza, Ashraf, and their mother remained in Iran. Dreyfus adds that "the Iranian Government is endeavoring through their Minister in Washington [Mohammad Schayesteh] to obtain visas for the Shah and his suite to enter Argentina, where it is said the Shah has elected to reside. The itinerary of the voyage is still indefinite; however, it is understood that the S.S. Bandera was cleared for Mauritius."[24] The announced desire to go to Argentina was evidently a deception on the part of Reza Shah while he was still in Iran. Upon reaching Mauritius, the ex-shah demanded to go to Canada on the grounds that the climate there was similar to some parts of Iran. Likely added attractions were his deposits with the Royal Bank of Canada and the fact that in the final years of his rule, Iran's oil revenues had been channeled through Canada on their way from London to New York.

Information on the proposed trip to Canada is provided in a series of diplomatic cables between London, Washington, Cairo, and Tehran. On

December 17 the American ambassador to London sent the following secret cable to Secretary of State Hull: "Shah of Persia is still in Mauritius and is not particularly happy at remaining there. I think he wants to go to Canada and I doubt if objection will be made provided Canada approves. The British do not want him to get into hands of the Germans who would undoubtedly use him to their political advantage. Please treat this message as strictly confidential. Winant"[25] On February 5, 1942, Dreyfus replied: "The British Minister informs me his government has given permission for ex-Shah to proceed to Canada via South Africa."[26]

En route to Canada, Reza Khan and his party stopped in South Africa. While there, he became very ill and was unable to proceed further. The American ambassador in Cairo cabled Washington: "With regard to recent reports regarding the illness of the ex-Shah of Iran I am confidently advised that, despite efforts to give him the best medical care possible, it is not expected that he will live more than six months. Kirk"[27] Reza Khan died in Johannesburg on July 26, 1944.

The Prosecution of Police Chief Mokhtari and the Execution of Prison "Doctor" Ahmadi

With Reza Shah's escape from justice with the help of the British and with the release of political prisoners and their accounts of the horror in Reza Shah's prisons, the people of Iran turned on police and prison officials who had committed murder and acts of brutality. Those who had allowed Reza Shah to escape were now attempting to save some of his henchmen. Dreyfus reports:

> The current trial of ex-police chief General Mokhtari and 16 other subordinate police officials, I have the honor to inform the Department, is deeply stirring the Iranian public and contributing to the general feeling of unrest in the country. I had occasion in despatch No. 209 of February 12, 1942, to call the Department's attention to the fact that General Mokhtari and other police officials had been arrested and held for trial and I indicated that popular feeling was running high against all persons responsible for atrocities and injustices committed during the regime of Shah Reza. Feeling against Mokhtari and the other accused is being whipped up by a vindictive and irresponsible press until the public is literally crying for blood. Particular indignation is being expressed that the trials are being conducted by a special court set up about 1928 to deal with cases of embezzlement and bribery by government officials, a court that by law cannot hand down death sentences. The press is demanding that the cases be transferred to the criminal courts, which are permitted to give death sentences, and a petition to this effect has been introduced into the Majlis by a number of deputies. To turn now to consideration of press articles on this subject, the writer counted 53 editorials in 14 different newspapers about the trials since July 20, the day the bill of indictment was handed down.[28]

FIGURE 15.2 *Reza Khan with Shams Pahlavi and Ali Reza Pahlavi, Johannesburg, 1944. Courtesy of the IICHS.*

Dreyfus then provides a few of the typical newspaper editorials. *Keyhan* attacked Majid Ahi, the minister of justice, because he had permitted the trials to be held in the special rather than the criminal court: "These criminals should receive the most violent punishment in order to serve as a lesson to history. It is hoped that with the departure of Ahy [Ahi] the laws enacted during the dictatorial regime under Ahy will be revised." In an editorial entitled "Death to Mokhtari," *Mardom* called Mokhtari a sadist who killed hundreds of people, who enjoyed torturing people and stifling the nation. The paper called upon the judges to consider their reputations before posterity when handing down judgment. *Setareh* stated, "Fifteen million Iranians are earnestly hoping that General Mokhtari will be put to death and torn to pieces. Out of respect for public sentiment, the Government should turn him over to the Criminal Courts so that he can be sentenced to death." The same paper later remarked, "I have heard that in America there is a practice or law called lynching by which a criminal who is violently hated because of his appalling and ghastly crimes is punished and put to death by the people without trial and the formalities of law. Do not God and conscience demand that Mokhtari and his accomplices be placed in the hands of mothers whose sons were killed or children whose parents were liquidated in order that they take their revenge and that the sore heart of the public be soothed."[29]

In the end, after lengthy trials all but one of those charged with heinous crimes escaped with light sentences. Richard Ford, the American chargé d'affaires reports that General Mokhtari, ex-chief of the Tehran police, was sentenced to a total of ten years in prison for complicity in the murder of well-known figures. Colonel Mostapha Rasekh, former chief warden of the Tehran police prison, received six years for complicity in the murder of Jafar Qoli Bakhtiari, Sardar Assad, former minister of war. Colonel Hosein Nirumand, another former chief warden of the prison, was sentenced to life in prison for participation in the murder of Khan Baba Bakhtiari, a brother of Sardar Assad, and of Mohammad Farrokhi, a poet and newspaper editor. Dr. Ahmad Ahmadi, former prison "physician," was sentenced to death for the murder of Sardar Asad and Farrokhi. The accused were also charged with the murder of Dr. Taqi Erani, a communist leader who had died in Reza Shah's prison, but they were acquitted on that charge.[30]

Ford concludes by stating that the trials had brought "some criticism of the [criminal] court on the part of some sections of the press. The press also takes the line that many other criminals of the former regime remain to be punished, among them men in high places. In general, however, the recently completed trial has been hailed with satisfaction, as at least a good beginning in punishing the injustices committed by Reza Shah's agents."[31] Rather than the beginning, the execution of Ahmadi was the end of the punishment of those who had committed acts of outrage under Reza Shah. Others found guilty were promptly pardoned by Reza Shah's son and successor.[32] Ahmadi's execution is described by Richard Ford:

> I have the honor to report that Pezeshk Ahmadi, prison physician under the Shah Reza regime and the convicted murderer of a number of prominent Iranians, was publicly hanged in the Maidan-e-Shah at dawn on October 14

[1944] in the presence of some 20,000 persons. Ahmadi, as the Department will recall, was the sadistic hypodermic manipulator of the old Shah and the man who saw to it that the former monarch's enemies died in prison of "heart failure." He was arrested about two years ago and sentenced to death, but delayed his execution by a series of appeals through all the courts of the country, maintaining that while he had actually killed the men in question, it was done under duress and that he could hardly refuse to obey the orders of the Shah as relayed through General Mokhtari, the Chief of Police. Under Iranian law, however, a person can only be guilty of murder if he actually killed a person and accessories before the fact escape unscathed. Consequently Mokhtari and Nirumand, the Governor of the prison, who were certainly as guilty as Ahmadi, cannot be charged with these crimes and cannot be executed. Considerable attention has been drawn to this fact in the press and the papers without exception are dissatisfied with this loophole in Iranian Law and are crying for blood.

It is interesting to note that Ahmadi was hanged in the main square of Tehran alongside of a garish equestrian statue of Shah Reza and that the Iranian Government is still in mourning over the latter's decease, the man really guilty of the crimes for which Ahmadi was hanged. However, there can be little doubt but that Ahmadi deserved his fate, Ahmadi the dreaded executioner of political prisoners whose appearance in a cell with his hypodermic was designed to terrify the stoutest heart. Amir Jang, the Bakhtiari Chieftain and Majlis deputy, has described to a member of the staff his experiences in prison and how Ahmadi gave him no less than seventeen injections, intended to terrify rather than kill. Amir Jang stated that he has led a violent life and has been involved in many battles, but that he has never experienced anything to compare with the stark terror that would overcome him as Ahmadi entered his cell.

The execution of Ahmadi should (but probably will not) serve as a grim reminder to the Iranian people of the ever-present danger of tyranny and brutality in this country and that the greatest care must be taken to prevent the country's ever falling again into the hands of a despot of Reza Shah's ilk.[33]

As Ford's dispatch shows, it was easy to lose sight of the fact that the tyranny and brutality inflicted on Iran from 1921 to 1941 was of a British variety. But the country had fallen into the hands of such a despot precisely because of the British, whose instrument and creation Reza Khan had always been.

1. Introduction

1. For instance, I could not find a detailed account of the British invasion and occupation of Persia in Olson, *Anglo-Iranian Relations.* Cronin mentions the Dunster Force once in passing. See Cronin, *Creation of the Pahlavi State.* Similarly, Ghani barely discusses the invasion and occupation of Iran in 1918. See Ghani, *Iran and the Rise of Reza Shah.* Brief references are contained in Keddie, *Roots of Revolution.*

2. Sabahi, *British Policy in Persia.* The British invasion is portrayed as relatively benign. To Sabahi, "the power of the [British] purse" exceeded the "diplomacy of violence."

3. A few of the more prominent examples of this view are: Banani, *Modernization of Iran;* Wilber, *Riza Shah Pahlavi;* Lenczowski, *Iran under the Pahlavis;* and Ghani, *Iran and the Rise of Reza Shah.* The most notable exception to the above interpretation is the account given in Millspaugh, *Americans in Persia.*

4. Alam, *Diaries of Alam,* 162, 337.

5. See Sabahi, *British Policy in Persia,* 141–54.

6. Millspaugh provides a summary of Reza Shah's terror: "The practice of terror came naturally to Reza Shah. While I was still close enough to observe, instances of his brutality came to my attention; but after the first years of his reign, the terror intensified. Apparently he did not carry out any general purge at any one time, though one sizable massacre is said to have taken place. I was informed on my return to Persia that he had imprisoned thousands and killed hundreds, some of the latter by his own hands. Several prominent men, I was told, were poisoned in prison; for example, Firouz, former Minister of Finance; Teymour Tash, once the trusted Minister of the Court; and Sardar Assad, a chief of the Bakhtiari who at one time had been Minister of War. Davar, already referred to as an exceptionally able official, committed suicide. Kheykosrow Shahrokh, Parsee deputy, respected business man, and a former friend of the American Mission, was murdered by air injection. Religious sanctity or sanctuaries did not deter the despot. He desecrated shrines and beat up and killed holy men. . . . Fear settled upon the people. No one knew whom to trust; and none dared to protest or criticize. Except at the very beginning no one seems to have attempted to assassinate the Shah. He himself, it is said, believed that he was destined to live long." Millspaugh, *Americans in Persia,* 37, 82.

7. Millspaugh describes what Reza did to Iran's parliament and its press: "He did not annul the constitution, substitute decrees for laws, close the parliament, or abolish the cabinet. Constitution, laws, parliament, and cabinet survived. But in actual practice, he acted completely contrary to the spirit of the constitution and violated many of its provisions, notably the bill of rights. Elections took place, but the Shah controlled them. The puppet parliament, cowed and corrupted, passed laws in due form, but strictly in accordance with the King's orders. The Prime Minister and ministers took their appointments and instructions from Reza and resigned at his bidding. He destroyed

the freedom of the press as had previously existed, as well as freedom of speech and of assembly. . . . The Thirteenth Majlis was in session when I returned to Persia [January 1943]. This body and its successor contrasted markedly with the parliaments that I had known twenty years before. At that time the membership consisted largely of landlords who though generally selfish and reactionary so far as their privileges were concerned, entertained a rather wholesome distrust of government, and since they then paid taxes, a real desire for economy and honesty in administration. During the intervening years, Reza Shah had put into the assembly some of the worst of his self-seeking accomplices. . . . Leaving no real law-making power to those whom he favored with appointments to the Parliament, the ex-Shah had permitted them not only to share in his economic manipulations and plunderings, but also to interfere in the administrations, to entrench their relatives and friends in government jobs, and to build up personal and corrupt 'machines' in the provinces. Moreover, since the burden of taxation had been largely shifted to the backs of the poor, the deputies had little to lose and in many cases much to gain from the government's investments and subsidies, as well as from its waste and extravagance." Millspaugh, *Americans in Persia*, 36, 85–86.

8. On the basis of such reports, one is forced to question the accuracy and veracity of Abrahamian's account of prison conditions under Reza Shah. According to Abrahamian, prison torture had been "outlawed," and prison conditions were "humane" and "enlightened." The flogging of the prisoners in Mashhad "in groups of thirty" does not quite mesh with Abrahamian's description of the supposed humane treatment of prisoners. In addition, when one reads the American consul's 1939 description of the police detention and the "merciless beatings" of the silk weavers of Yazd (see chapter 5), one is forced to conclude that Abrahamian has allowed himself to be carried away.

   When people were being murdered in prison by poisoning, or as in the case of Kheykosrow Shahrokh, by air injection, how can anyone claim that prison conditions were humane? As documented in chapter 6, the "confessions" of the former Jewish Majlis deputy just before his execution in 1931 were obtained by torture. As noted in chapter 15, after the downfall of Reza Shah, some of the released political prisoners described their terror whenever the sadistic "hypodermic doctor" Ahmadi entered their prison cells. Nor does one find any reference to the 1935 massacre in Abrahamian's book. Abrahamian, *Tortured Confessions*.

9. Millspaugh, *Americans in Persia*, 24–25, 85.

10. Wilber, *Riza Shah Pahlavi*, 120. Wilber describes the Poulladin plot: "This was the first of a series of alleged military plots against the ruler. Many people were brought to trial on these charges in later years: it was thought that the alleged plots were brought to light on such occasions as the elements in opposition to the regime were becoming too bold, and selected individuals were handled in a drastic fashion in order to discourage others who might have similar ideas."

11. Millspaugh, *Americans in Persia*, 35.

2. The British Invasion and the Strangulation of Persia

1. Marling to government of Persia, March 11, 1918; in Southard, dispatch 1 (891.00/1054), September 2, 1918.

2. Southard, telegram (891.00/974), July 6, 1918.

3. Southard, telegram (891.00/975), July 7, 1918.

4. Caldwell, dispatch 393 (891.00/1017), May 27, 1918.

5. White, report (891.00/1008), May 10, 1918.

6. Caldwell, dispatch 395 (891.00/1014), May 27, 1918.

7. Southard, telegram (891.00/994), August 4, 1918.

8. Caldwell, dispatch 436 (891.00/1060), September 2, 1918.

9. Southard, "Military Invasions of Persia by Various Belligerents Engaged in the Present European War," dispatch 1 (891.00/1054), September 2, 1918.

10. Southard, "Persian Police Organized by British Military Forces in Parts of Persia," September 4, 1918. Southard also comments on the South Persia Rifles and the Persian hostility to the British-controlled force: "While the Persians very much resent the presence of British forces on the Bagdad-Caspian line of communication they seem to feel most bitterly about the organization of the South Persia Rifles."

11. American consul, telegram (891.00/1010), August 30, 1918.

12. White, Quarterly Report 2 (891.00/1088), January 10, 1919 (hereafter QR).

13. Southard, telegram (891.00/982), July 10, 1918.

14. Caldwell, telegram (891.00/976), July 7, 1918.

15. Caldwell, dispatch 415 (891.00/1056), "Martial Law in Teheran," July 9, 1918.

16. Caldwell, QR 1 (QR1) (891.00/1072), November 1, 1918.

17. Southard, dispatch 2 (891.00/1050), September 2, 1918; dispatch 3 (891.00/1048), September 3, 1918.

18. White, QR2 (891.00/1088), January 10, 1919.

19. Ibid.

20. White, QR4 (891.00/1122), July 7, 1919.

21. Caldwell, QR5 (891.00/1147), October 1, 1919.

22. Ferrin, memorandum, "Past Ten Years in Persia" (891.1510), November 8, 1930.

23. Caldwell, QR5, October 1, 1919.

24. Ibid.

25. Caldwell, QR6 (891.00/1148), January 9, 1920.

26. Ibid.

27. Caldwell, QR7 (891.00/1157), April 10, 1920.

28. Ibid.

29. Caldwell, QR5, October 1, 1919.

30. Ibid.

31. Caldwell, QR6, January 9, 1920.

32. Caldwell, QR7, April 10, 1920.

33. Southard, dispatch 1 (891.00/1054), September 2, 1918.

34. "Notice from Collector of Customs, Bagdad, dated March 22, 1918"; in American consul, Baghdad, dispatch 92 (891.00/978), April 27, 1918. The regulation was as follows: "All tobacco and merchandise imported from Persia are subject to an ad valorem duty of 10 per cent which duty is payable to the Custom House. Persons importing goods from Persia will observe the following rules: A declaration of the goods imported should be transmitted to the custom authorities either at Bagdad, Khanakin, or Mendali. If the goods should not pass via either of the routes leading to the above mentioned places, the owners of the goods will communicate, in writing, with the first Political Officer they

come in contact with on their journey, and a declaration will be made to him. The Political Officer after having obtained a guarantee from the owner, will issue a pass permitting the passage of the merchandise to Bagdad and its delivery to the Custom House for the collection of duty. The owners of the merchandise are permitted, after having paid the customs duty, to forward the whole or part of the same to any place within the territories occupied by His Britannic Majesty's Government, on notifying the Customs authorities to the effect, and obtaining a free pass declaring that the duty has been paid in full and that there is no objection to the forwarding of the merchandise. A pass should always accompany the goods stating that it is intended to pay the duty in Bagdad, or a pass declaring that the duty has been paid in full. Without either one or the other of these passes, the merchandise will be liable to seizure and confiscation."

35. Caldwell, QR6 (891.00/1148), January 9, 1920.
36. Ibid.
37. Caldwell, QR5, October 1, 1919.
38. Caldwell, QR8 (891.00/1168), July 8, 1920.
39. Caldwell also informs us that "His Imperial Majesty, the Shah, together with his suite, is staying in Europe for the Winter. He has been officially received by the British, French and Belgian rulers, but is spending most of his time in the South of France. The Persian Foreign Minister, Prince Nosrat-ed-Dowleh, who is called 'a creature of the British' went to Europe with the Shah and is attending to many political duties while there, especially in connection with the Anglo-Persian Treaty of August 9, 1919. The Prince is at present in Paris where it is asserted he will take up the matter of the Treaty before the council of the League of Nations." QR6, January 9, 1920.
40. Caldwell, QR7, April 10, 1920.
41. Caldwell, QR8 (891.00/1168), July 8, 1920.
42. It should be noted that Caldwell's account of Vossough's dismissal is radically different from the British version given by Sabahi. According to Sabahi, it was the British who had decided to get rid of Vossough because he had become a liability: "The British officials came to see that Vusuq's policies were largely responsible for the 'unusual discontent and rebellions.'" Following such a "discovery," the British minister "Norman therefore decided to jettison Vusuq, despite Curzon's continued support for him who, according to Curzon, was 'in a better position to safeguard agreement than anyone else.'" Sabahi, *British Policy in Persia*, 91–92.
43. Caldwell, QR8 (891.00/1168), July 8, 1920.
44. In the British version, it was Norman who had chosen Moshir-ed-Dowleh as Vossough's successor. According to Sabahi, "Vusuq's successor, Norman thought, 'should be a man who while willing to follow his foreign policy should adopt a different policy at home. He must at once also summon parliament and get the agreement passed.' Norman's choice, Mushir ud-Daula, seemed well suited to the part. . . . Vusuq's willingness to resign facilitated Norman's task." Sabahi, *British Policy in Persia*, 92.
45. Caldwell, QR8 (891.00/1168), July 8, 1920.
46. Ibid.
47. Ibid.
48. White, QR3, April 14, 1919.
49. White, QR4, July 14, 1919.

50. Caldwell, QR6, January 20, 1920.
51. Caldwell, QR7, April 10, 1920.
52. Caldwell, QR8, July 8, 1920.
53. Ibid.
54. Caldwell, QR9 (891.00/1169), October 5, 1920.
55. Ibid.
56. Sabahi, *British Policy in Persia,* 51, 97.
57. Caldwell, QR9 (891.00/1169), October 5, 1920.
58. Caldwell, QR10 (891.00/1195), January 15, 1921.
59. Engert, telegram (891.00/1165), October 30, 1920.
60. Ibid.
61. Caldwell, QR10 (891.00/1195), January 15, 1921.
62. Ibid.
63. Caldwell, telegram (891.00/1171, Confidential File), January 6, 1921.
64. White, QR2 of January 10, 1919.
65. Caldwell, QR5, October 1, 1919.
66. Caldwell, QR7, April 10, 1920.
67. See, for instance, Amuzegar, *Dynamics of the Iranian Revolution,* 71.

3. British Coups d' État

1. Sabahi, *British Policy in Persia,* 123.
2. See Cronin, *Creation of the Pahlavi State,* and Ghani, *Iran and the Rise of Reza Shah.*
3. Caldwell, telegram (891.00/1181), February 22, 1921.
4. Sabahi, *British Policy in Persia,* 125.
5. Caldwell, telegram, 891.00/1183 February 27, 1921.
6. Caldwell, dispatch 646 (891.00/1197), March 11, 1921, "Proclamation of New Persian Prime Minister."
7. Sabahi, *British Policy in Persia,* 123.
8. Caldwell, Quarterly Report 11, April 5, 1921 (891.00/1196).
9. Murray, dispatch 952 (891.00/1346), March 6, 1925.
10. Engert, dispatch (891.00/1202), August 25, 1921 .
11. Dickson to Engert, June 6, 1921.
12. Dickson to Lord Curzon, May 14, 1921.
13. Dispatch 4316 (891.00/1184), March 10, 1921.
14. "Report of Questions and Answers in the House of Commons, Monday, February 28, 1921. *Persia,*" given in dispatch 4316 (891.00/1184), March 10, 1921.
15. Sabahi, *British Policy in Persia,* 164. It appears certain that in addition to the above loans Reza Khan had continued to receive money from the British in other ways. For instance, C. Van H. Engert, the American chargé d'affaires ad interim, reported that Reza Khan had sold $100,000 in American currency (small denominations) in the fall of 1921. When asked where the money came from, Reza Khan responded that it had been captured from Mirza Kuchik Khan. If Kuchik Khan had access to such sums, however, he would not have frozen in the mountains of Gilan. The British were the most likely source of this money. Specifically, Engert's telegram of January 4, 1922 (891.51/242) states that the "Minister of War and Commander in Chief has within last week sold locally one hundred thousand

dollars in American bank notes (small denominations miscellaneous issues) which he claims were taken from the rebel Kuchik Khan recently killed."

16. The payment of £808,000 in December 1921 as part of the Armitage-Smith Agreement will be discussed in detail in chapter 10. The subject is also discussed by Sabahi, *British Policy in Persia*, 27. However, and most surprisingly, Sabahi claims that this money had been paid before the coup. In actuality, the money (and an additional £125,000 "advance" paid in April 1921) had been placed at the disposal of Reza Khan after the coup. Engert's dispatch on the subject dated January 4, 1922, is given in its entirety in chapter 9.

17. Sabahi, *British Policy in Persia*, 164.

18. Ibid., 161.

19. Ibid., 160.

20. Ibid., 165.

21. Engert, telegram, May 25, 1921 (891.00/1190).

22. Murray, memorandum (891.00/1346), March 6, 1925. Shortly after ascending the throne in April 1926, Reza Shah had made some anti-British statements which had been duly reported by the newly arrived American minister, Hoffman Philip. Philip had also reported on his conversation with the British minister who had expressed his government's "disappointment" with Reza Shah. Having witnessed firsthand the rise of Reza Shah from 1921, and the British role, Murray made the following remarks about Reza Shah's alleged anti-British stance: "I can not concur with Mr. Philip in the belief that the present alleged anti-British attitude on the part of the Shah and the Persian Government. It may conceivably be that the British Chargé has spoken frankly when he repeatedly emphasized to the American Minister the great disappointment felt by his government in Reza Shah and the lack of consideration which the latter appears now to be disposed to show his British protectors. I personally, however, doubt it." Murray also discussed the relationship between Reza Shah and Foroughi: "With regard to the statement that he has made no confidants among his Ministers: Has his close relationship to Zoka-ol-Molk entirely ceased since he has become Shah? Zoka formerly enjoyed the most intimate confidence of his master."

23. Kornfeld, telegram (891.001/121), October 23, 1923.

24. Sabahi, *British Policy in Persia*, 176–77.

25. Kornfeld, dispatch 260 (891.00/1251), September 15, 1923.

26. Sabahi, *British Policy in Persia*, 177.

27. Kornfeld, dispatch 244 (891.51A/115), August 21, 1923.

28. Gotlieb, dispatch 94 (891.51/318), July 23, 1923.

29. Sabahi, *British Policy in Persia*, 176; Ghani, *Iran and the Rise of Reza Shah*, 371.

30. Amory, dispatch 1204 and enclosure (891.00/1364, Confidential File), August 29, 1925.

31. Amory, dispatch 1216 (891.9111/140), September 28, 1925.

32. Ibid.

33. *Iran*, September 24, 1925.

34. Sabahi, *British Policy in Persia*, 194.

35. Amory, dispatch 1233 (891.9111/142), October 21, 1925.

36. Cited ibid.

37. Amory, ibid.

38. Amory, dispatch 1236 (891.9111/143), November 4, 1925.
39. Amory, dispatch 1237 (891.01/35), November 6, 1925.
40. Report of the clerk of the American consulate in Tabriz, October 17, 1925. Enclosure, dispatch 1237 (891.01/35), November 6, 1925.
41. Amory, dispatch 1236 (891.9111/143), November 4, 1925.
42. Ibid.
43. Amory, dispatch 1233 (891.9111/142), October 21, 1925.
44. As reported in *Iran,* October 19, 1925.
45. Amory, dispatch 1233 (891.9111/142), October 21, 1925.
46. *Iran,* October 23, 1925.
47. *Iran,* October 29, 1925.
48. Amory, dispatch 1236 (891.9111/143), November 4, 1925.
49. Ibid.
50. Ibid.
51. Amory, telegram (891.01/22), October 31, 1925.
52. Ibid.
53. Ibid.
54. Amory, telegram (891.01/24), November 1, 1925.
55. Reported ibid.
56. Amory, dispatch 1236 (891.9111/143), November 4, 1925.
57. Ibid.
58. Murray, dispatch 854 (891.6363/582), January 20, 1925.
59. Amory, dispatch 1204 (891.00/1364 Confidential File), August 29, 1925.
60. Amory, dispatch 1237 (891.01/35 Confidential File), November 6, 1925.
61. Ibid.
62. Amory, dispatch 1247 (891.9111/144), November 21, 1925.
63. Ibid.
64. Amory, dispatch 1251 (891.9111/145), December 4, 1925.
65. Amory, dispatch 1261 (891.9111/146), December 16, 1925.
66. Ibid.
67. Amory, dispatch 1266 (891.9111/147), December 31, 1925.
68. Amory, dispatch 1260 (891.51A/313), December 16, 1925.
69. Ibid.
70. Murray, memorandum (891.00/1385), October 2, 1926.
71. Hart, dispatch 1289 (891.6363/703), November 29, 1932.
72. Hornibrook, dispatch 104 (741.91/153), June 12, 1934.

4. Millspaugh and the American Financial Mission

1. Qavam, telegram, January 15, 1922, enclosure to Kornfeld, dispatch 222 (891.51/319), July 25, 1923.
2. Engert, telegram (891.51/241) January 7, 1922.
3. Qavam, telegram (891.51/287), August 16, 1922.
4. Millspaugh, *Americans in Persia,* 253.
5. Owens, dispatch (891.51A/89), December 7, 1922.
6. Kornfeld, dispatch 203 (891.51/315), July 5, 1923.

7. Kornfeld, telegram (891.51A/97), July 9, 1923.

8. Kornfeld, telegram (891.51A/101), July 23, 1923.

9. Gotlieb, dispatch 94 (891.51/318), July 23, 1923.

10. Kornfeld, dispatch 538 (891.01A/87), June 11, 1924.

11. Kornfeld, dispatch 222 (891.51/319), July 25, 1923.

12. Murray, dispatch 638 (891.51A/199), September 8, 1924.

13. Murray, report (891.00/1346), March 6, 1925.

14. Ibid.

15. Millspaugh, *Americans in Persia,* 75.

16. Kornfeld, telegram (891.51A/93), of February 9, 1923.

17. Kornfeld, dispatch 244 (891.51A/115), August 21, 1923.

18. Kornfeld, dispatch 317 (891.51a/135), December 8, 1923.

19. Gotlieb, "The Present Political Situation in Persia as Affecting the American Advisers and Prospective American Trade" (891.51A/137), December 2, 1923.

20. Murray, dispatch 16 (891.00/1319), December 19, 1924.

21. Millspaugh to Murray, letter 3829 (891.51A/197), September 5, 1924.

22. Reza Khan to Millspaugh, August 25, 1924. Enclosure to (891.51A/197), September 5, 1924.

23. Millspaugh to Murray, letter 3829 (891.51A/197), September 5, 1924.

24. Murray, dispatch 637 (891.51A/198), September 24, 1924.

25. Ibid.

26. Millspaugh to Dulles (891.51A/202), September 20, 1924.

27. Murray, dispatch 776 (891.51/369), December 3, 1924.

28. Ibid.

29. Fuller, dispatch 59 (891.20/57), August 22, 1925.

30. Philip, dispatch 116 (891.20/59), June 30, 1926.

31. Philip, dispatch 121 (891.20/60), July 3, 1926.

32. Millspaugh, memo (891.51A/325), July 13, 1926. In *Americans in Persia,* Millspaugh gives the following account: "For months I was receiving reports from all parts of the country concerning the illegal requisitioning of men, horses, grain, and money from the villages. In fact, the looting in some places was so thorough as to leave nothing for the payment of taxes. After Reza became Shah, I sought an audience and gave him a summary of the reports that I had. He fingered his beads rapidly, a familiar sign of anger; in spite of the respect that I took pains to show him and in spite of the facts, his anger was directed at me and not at the Army. It was well known that Reza helped himself liberally to army funds and used the proceeds for personal purposes. He was already receiving 'gifts' of villages, 'gifts' proffered under duress or from fear. At the time he became Shah, his amazing greed had already made him wealthy" (25).

33. Millspaugh, memo (891.51A/325), July 13, 1926.

34. Hart, dispatch 1240 (891.516/61), October 1, 1932.

35. Hart, dispatch 1606 (891.516/81), December 26, 1933.

36. Hart, dispatch 325 (891.5151/56), January 28, 1931.

37. Hornibrook, dispatch 393 (891.001 P 15/115), March 25, 1935.

38. Gotlieb, report (891.6363/312), December 5, 1923.

39. Gotlieb, telegram (891.6363/318), December 20, 1923.

40. Gotlieb, report (891.6363/321) December 27, 1923.

41. Dulles, memorandum (891.6363/274), January 23, 1923.

42. Hughes, telegram (891.6363/335A), February 7, 1924.

43. Ibid.

44. Kornfeld, telegram (891.63636/337), February 9, 1924.

45. State Department, memorandum (891.6363/338), February 9, 1924.

46. Kornfeld, dispatch 373 (891.6363/340), February 12, 1924.

47. Kornfeld, telegram (891.6363/344), February 15, 1924.

48. Hughes, telegram (891.6363/345), February 16, 1924.

49. Murray, dispatch 854 (891.6363/582), January 20, 1925.

50. In 1922, the American government had shown some interest in the Caspian fisheries with the view of encouraging American participation therein. The State Department had requested its representative to prepare a report on the subject. In response, a history of the operations of the fisheries up to 1922 is provided in a report by Kornfeld, the American minister in Tehran. Kornfeld, dispatch 55 (891.628/1), August 4, 1922.

51. *Economic Life,* May 20, 1924; in Commerce Department to State Department (891.628/5), June 21, 1924.

52. Imbrie, dispatch 42 (891.628/6), June 14, 1924.

53. Imbrie, dispatch 44, "Reported Agreement Between Persia and Soviet Russia on the Caspian Fisheries" (891.628/7), June 20, 1924.

54. Murray, dispatch 700 (891.628/8), October 23, 1924.

55. Millspaugh, memorandum, "The Proposed Fishery Agreement with the Russians," October 7, 1924.

56. Murray, dispatch 724 (891.628/9), November 5, 1924.

57. Neilsen, report (891.628/18), August 25, 1927.

58. Philip, dispatch 466 (761.9111/4), October 21, 1927.

59. Philip, dispatch (761.9111/6), November 3, 1927.

60. Philip, dispatch 487 (891.00/1435), November 12, 1927.

61. Hart, dispatch 1158 (891.628/33), June 14, 1932.

62. Hart, dispatch 1310 (891.44 Teymourtache, Abdol H.K./1), December 29, 1932.

63. Hart, dispatch 282 (891.00B/36), January 12, 1931.

64. Ibid.

65. Ibid.

66. Hart, dispatch 485 (891.00B/44), March 24, 1931; Williamson's emphasis in original.

67. Ibid.

68. Philip, dispatch 129 (891.51A/325), July 13, 1926.

69. Amory, dispatch 1253 (891.51A/311), December 4, 1925.

70. Amory, dispatch 1260 (891.51A/313), December 16, 1925.

71. Philip, dispatch 405 (891.51A/407), August 11, 1927.

72. Philip, dispatch 409 (891.51A/405), August 13, 1927.

73. Millspaugh, *Americans in Persia,* 34. As an example of the "dubious miracles" Millspaugh offers the construction of Fariman, in eastern Khorasan: "The model town of Fariman supplies an even more astonishing example of misplaced energy. Its location seems to have had no possibilities from the standpoint of need or development, either agricultural or industrial. Trees were planted in and about the town. Unfortunately, trees require water; and, in that irrigated region, it was necessary to draw the water from the surrounding agricultural lands. Within two years after the

Shah's abdication, half the trees had died. The farmers simply took their water back. To them, bread had priority over shade or beauty. The absurdities of Ramsar and Fariman were repeated at Teheran. Here the Shah built an opera house (where there was no opera), and a government-owned department store (in a land of bazaars and small shops). He also swept clear a block or two for a stock exchange, and is said to have specified that it must be bigger than the one in New York. Fortunately it was not constructed. . . . A large part of his construction program, in the light of the country's fundamental needs, was premature and wasteful. Not much of what he did contributed to the practical enlightenment, the basic strengthening, or the long-run strengthening of the country. He did things to the people and for the people. Little was done by them. A less superficial statesmanship might have paid more respect to intangibles and given more attention to fundamentals. . . . If Pahlevi had been more of a George Washington and had played a more restricted role, it is quite likely that the government and people would have done during this time most of the good things that are attributed to the Shah and fewer of the bad things. Moreover, the country probably would have made more real progress in the long run. During these years much of the essential economic change that occurred in Persia occurred also in Iraq, Syria, and Palestine. In these countries, too, factories were founded, cities grew, and modernistic houses appeared. Each of these countries built new hotels, and unlike Persia produced the skill to manage them." Millspaugh, *Americans in Persia*, 33–36.

5. Reza Shah Pahlavi

1. Hornibrook, telegram (123 H 781/149), March 15, 1936; Hornibrook comments on an article in the *New York Mirror* that had stated that Reza Shah "was formerly employed in stables of British legation in Tehran." The *Time* article is reported in Merriam, dispatch 1010 (891.6363 Amiranian/27), March 10, 1937.

2. News of the recall of Baqer Kazemi was given by C. Van Engert, chargé d'affaires ad interim, in dispatch 1914 (701.9167/13), September 22, 1940. Engert's report includes the following: "Mr. Baqer Kazemi, the Iranian Ambassador to Turkey, has been recalled and has not been assigned to another post. Kazemi was only appointed in October, 1939 and has therefore been in Ankara less than a year. So far it has not been possible to ascertain the reason for his recall, nor has his successor been announced."

   The reason for Kazemi's dismissal is given by the American ambassador in Turkey, J. V. A. MacMurray, in dispatch 1585 (701.9167/14), November 5, 1940: "The Iranian Ambassador here has been recalled, under circumstances which have only recently come to my knowledge. It appears that, some time ago, a writer in the French-language daily newspaper *Journal d'Orient* ventured upon the somewhat hazardous task of outlining the career of the Shah-in-shah of Iran, unfortunately including the fact that he had risen from the ranks. This indiscretion of the *Journal d'Orient* seems to have escaped notice even on the part of the Iranian Embassy. In due course, however, when a clipping of the article had reached Teheran and been noted, the Ambassador received a telegram berating him for his lack of vigilance and peremptorily directing him to protest energetically to the Turkish Government and to demand of it appropriate action in amends. It so happened that one of my colleagues, calling on the Minister for Foreign Affairs just as the Iranian Ambassador went out after fulfilling this mission, found Mr. Saracoglu in a state of half-amused bewilderment, exclaiming that while

Turkey prided herself on the relative freedom of her press, he was being importuned on behalf of a sovereign of a friendly state to have condign punishment visited on an editor for publishing something which, if it had been said about Ataturk, would have been regarded by the Turkish people as a tribute to his ability and force of character."

The response of the State Department to this episode showed just how much of a laughingstock Iran had become by 1940. In a memo to the assistant secretary, under-secretary, and secretary of state, dated December 17, 1940, Murray, who had recently polished Reza Shah's "official" biography, writes: "I believe you will be entertained by the developments reported in the accompanying despatch from Ankara regarding the recall of the Iranian Ambassador to Turkey. I related the incident to the Turkish Ambassador (who was, as you will recall, in charge of Iranian interests here during the rupture of relations with Iran), and he laughed heartily."

3. Murray, memorandum (891.001 P 15/180), January 28, 1939.

4. Merriam, dispatch 758 (891.001 P 15/127), April 9, 1936.

5. *Washington Post,* July 9, 1939; in 891.001 P 15/184, July 15, 1939.

6. Gunther, *Inside Asia,* 499–516.

7. Millspaugh, *Americans in Persia,* 21–37.

8. Atherton to Murray (701.9111/569, confidential file), May 29, 1936.

9. Murray to Atherton (701.9111/569, confidential file), June 16, 1936.

10. Hart, dispatch 282 (891.00B/36), January 10, 1931.

11. Hart, dispatch 765 (891.45/1), August 7, 1931.

12. Hart, dispatch 16 (123 H 255/75), February 11, 1930.

13. Jedlicka, dispatch 334 (2657–CC-38), November 28, 1923.

14. Jedlicka, dispatch 351, "Disappearance of Teheran's Journals" (2657–CC-40), December 10, 1923.

15. Engert, dispatch 834 (891.00/1222), March 1, 1922.

16. Engert, dispatch 848 (891.00/1223), April 3, 1922.

17. Kornfeld, dispatch 586 (891.00/1292), July 9, 1924.

18. Gotlieb, "The Present Political Situation in Persia as Affecting the American Advisers and Prospective American Trade" (891.51A/137), December 2, 1923.

19. Kornfeld, dispatch 244 (891.51A/115), August 21, 1923.

20. Hornibrook, dispatch 393 (891.001 P 15/115), March 25, 1935.

21. Gordon P. Merriam, American chargé d'affaires ad interim, dispatch 797 (891.001 P 15/128), May 15, 1936.

22. Engert, dispatch 1212 (891.00/1676), January 13, 1938.

23. Hornibrook, dispatch 393 (891.001 P 15/115), 25 March 1935.

24. Moose, dispatch 78 (891.00/1814), May 28, 1941.

25. Hart, dispatch 16 (123 H 255/75), February 11, 1930.

26. Engert, telegram (891.001/44), January 15, 1922.

27. Philip, dispatch 188 (891.00/1389), October 7, 1926.

28. Murray, dispatch 663 (891.00/1306), September 28, 1924.

29. Murray, dispatch 1160 (891.22/2), June 19, 1925.

30. Hart, dispatch 1031 (661.9131/82), January 29, 1932.

31. Mohammad Gholi Majd, *Resistance to the Shah: Landowners and Ulama in Iran* (Gainesville: University Press of Florida, 2000), chap. 3.

32. Philip, dispatch 295 (891.001P15/46), March 21, 1927.

33. The house and garden so donated had actually belonged to Prince Farman Farma, the father of Nosrat-ed-Dowleh. See Farman Farmaian, *Daughter of Persia.*

34. Philip, dispatch 378 (891.51A/379), June 27, 1927.

35. Philip, dispatch 486 (891.00/1433), October 19, 1927.

36. Philip, dispatch 487 (891.00/1435), November 12, 1927.

37. Hart, dispatch 36 (891.515/12), March 22, 1930.

38. Hart, dispatch 282 (891.00B/36), January 1, 1931.

39. Hart, dispatch 132 (891.00/221), August 11, 1930.

40. Ibid.

41. Hart, dispatch 630 (891.00 P 15/72), May 19, 1931.

42. Ibid.

43. Hart, dispatch 937 (891.001 P 15/76), November 17, 1931.

44. Hart, dispatch 1031 (661.9131/82), January 29, 1932.

45. Hart, dispatch 1339 (891.44/Teymourtache, Abdol H. K./4), January 26, 1933.

46. Hart, dispatch 666 (891.00/1527), June 10, 1930.

47. Ibid.

48. In Hart, dispatch 1393 (891.00/1562), March 25, 1932.

49. Ibid.

50. Williamson, dispatch 988 (891.00/1499), December 13, 1929.

51. Hart, dispatch 338 (891.00/1515), February 4, 1931.

52. *Setareh-ye Jehan,* September 16, 1931; translation in Hart, dispatch 867 (891.00/1532), September 23, 1931.

53. Hart, dispatch 867 (891.00/1532), September 23, 1931.

54. Merriam, dispatch 842 (891.00/1643), July 8, 1936.

55. Hart, dispatch 1061 (891.655/16), February 25, 1932.

56. Moose, report 154 (891.6552/4), April 6, 1939.

57. Hart, dispatch 387 (891.5123/5), February 20, 1931.

58. Hart, dispatch 282 (891.0013/36), January 12, 1931.

59. Engert, dispatch 1631 (891.6171/6), July 13, 1939.

60. Edmond O'Donovan, *The Merv Oasis: Travels and Adventures East of the Caspian during the Years 1879–80–81, Including Five Months' Residence among the Tekkes of Merv,* 2 vols. (London: Smith Elder, 1882).

61. Engert, dispatch 1830, "Changes in the City of Tehran" (891.101/3), May 10, 1940.

6. A Reign of Terror and Murder

1. Philip, dispatch 543 (891.00/1439), February 21, 1928.

2. Kornfeld, dispatch 586 (891.00/1292), July 9, 1924.

3. Imbrie, report 57 (891.00/1297), July 14, 1924.

4. Ibid.

5. Zirinsky, "Blood, Power, and Hypocricy," 276.

6. Ibid.

7. Ibid.

8. Hart, dispatch 998 (891.00/1537), December 30, 1931.

9. Kornfeld, dispatch 75 (891.00/1229), September 29, 1922.

10. Ibid.

11. *Shafaq-i-Sorkh,* December 17, 1931.

12. Hart, dispatch 998 (891.00/1537), December 30, 1931.

13. Hart, dispatch 410 (891.20/67), March 7, 1931.

14. Hart, "Teymourtache Dismissed and Great was the Fall Thereof," dispatch 1310 (891.44 Teymourtache, Abdol H.K./1), December 29, 1932.

15. Ibid.

16. Reported in Hart, "Teymourtache to be Tried: Strictly Confidential Musings on His Pahlevi Majesty," dispatch 1339 (891.44 Teymourtache, Abdol H.K./4 Confidential File), January 26, 1933.

17. Ibid.

18. Hart, dispatch 1366 (891.44 Teymourtache, Abdol H.K./6), February 24, 1933.

19. Reported in Hart, dispatch 1380 (891.44 Teymourtache, Abdol H.K./7), March 11, 1933.

20. Ibid.

21. Murray, memorandum (891.00/1821), March 18, 1933.

22. Hart, dispatch 1542 (891.44 Teymourtache, Abdol H.K./11), October 3, 1933.

23. Hart, telegram (891.44 Teymourtache, Abdol H.K./12), October 6, 1933.

24. Hart, dispatch 1550 (891.44 Teymourtache, Abdol H.K./12), October 7, 1933.

25. Hornibrook, dispatch 29 (891.00/1592), April 14, 1934.

26. Hart, dispatch 1553 (891.44 Teymourtache, Abdol H.K./13), October 12, 1933.

27. Hart, dispatch 1339 (891.44 Teymourtache, Abdol H.K./4), January 26, 1933.

28. Hart, dispatch 1393 (891.00/1562), March 25, 1933.

29. Ibid.

30. Ibid.

31. Ibid.

32. Ibid.

33. Hart, dispatch 1508 (891.9111/335), August 11, 1933.

34. Hart, dispatch 1543 (891.00/1579), October 4, 1933.

35. Hart, dispatch 1366 (891.44 Teymourtache, Abdol H.K./5), February 24, 1933.

36. Wadsworth, dispatch 1583 (741.9114/2), December 1, 1933.

37. Ibid.

38. Wadsworth, dispatch 1656 (891.00/1587), February 10, 1934.

39. Ibid.

40. Hornibrook, telegram (891.00/1509), April 2, 1934.

41. Hornibrook, dispatch 22 (891.00/1590), April 7, 1934.

42. Hornibrook, dispatch 29 (891.00/1592), April 14, 1934.

43. Hornibrook, dispatch 275 (891.00/1598), November 28, 1934; dispatch 281 (891.00/1599), December 4, 1934.

44. Ibid.

45. J. Rives Childs, chargé d'affaires, dispatch 416 (891.131/4), April 15, 1935.

46. Moose, dispatch 1362 (891.131/8), August 4, 1938.

47. Childs, dispatch 416 (891.131/4), April 15, 1935.

48. Childs, dispatch 422 (891.00/1601), April 19, 1935.

49. Hornibrook, dispatch 482 (891.00/1608), June 22, 1935.

50. Childs, dispatch 437 (891.00/1603), May 4, 1935.

51. Hart, dispatch 132 (891.00/221), August 11, 1930.

52. Philip, dispatch 566 (891.51/414), March 24, 1928.

53. Hart, dispatch 132 (891.00/221), August 11, 1930.

54. Hornibrook, dispatch 510 (891.00/1613), July 18, 1935.

7. The Massacre in Mashhad

1. *Setareh-ye Jehan,* June 29, 1934; in Hornibrook, dispatch 143 (891.4051/15), July 12, 1934.

2. Hornibrook, dispatch 478 (891.4051/19), June 18, 1935.

3. Hornibrook, dispatch 487 (891.4051/20), June 27, 1935.

4. Childs, dispatch 429 (891.404/40), April 29, 1935.

5. Ferrin, dispatch 20 (891.00/1475), October 22, 1928.

6. Hornibrook, dispatch 491 (891.4051/22), July 2, 1935.

7. Hornibrook, dispatch 503 (891.4051/23), July 9, 1935.

8. Hornibrook, dispatch 507 (891.4051/24), July 12, 1935.

9. Hornibrook, telegram (891.00/1605), July 18, 1935.

10. Hornibrook, dispatch 509 (891.00/1610), July 18, 1935.

11. Hornibrook, dispatch 512 (891.00/1611), July 21, 1935.

12. Ibid.

13. Hornibrook, dispatch 518 (891.00/1612), July 25, 1935.

14. Ibid.

15. Hornibrook, "Wholesale Arrests of Public Officials--Execution of Mohammad Vali Asadi," dispatch number 660 (891.00/1629), December 24, 1935.

16. Hornibrook, dispatch 518 (891.00/1612), July 25, 1935.

8. The Reign of Terror and Murder Continues

1. Hornibrook, dispatch 29 (891.00/1592), April 14, 1934.

2. Hornibrook, "The Shah Prepares Another Victim in the Person of the Minister of Finance," dispatch 140 (891.00/1595), July 12, 1934.

3. Merriam, dispatch 992 (891.00/1654), February 15, 1937.

4. Engert, telegram (891.00/1668), January 15, 1938.

5. Murray, memorandum to secretary of state, January 17, 1938.

6. Williamson, dispatch 967 (891.00/1495), October 31, 1929.

7. Millard, dispatch 37 (891.002/212), March 22, 1930.

8. Hart, dispatch 77 (891.002/217), May 3, 1930.

9. Engert, dispatch 1727 (891.44/9), November 22, 1939.

10. The entire dispatch from the British legation, dated November 25, 1939, is given in Farmanfarmaian and Farmanfarmaian, *Blood and Oil,* 481–82.

11. Amory, dispatch 1213 (891.00/1365), September 14, 1925.

12. Millspaugh to Dulles (891.51A/202), September 20, 1924.

13. Ferrin, dispatch 20 (891.00/1475), October 22.

14. Hart, dispatch 947 (891.00/1534), November 27, 1931.

15. Hart, dispatch 948 (891.00/1535), November 28, 1931.

16. Dreyfus, dispatch 146 (891.00/1809), November 3, 1941.

17. Ibid.

18. Ibid.

19. Millspaugh, *Americans in Persia,* 37.

20. Dreyfus, dispatch 146 (891.00/1809), November 3, 1941.

9. Britain and Persian Oil

1. See, for example Elm, *Oil, Power, and Principle;* Farmanfarmaian and Farmanfarmaian, *Blood and Oil;* Elwell-Sutton, *Persian Oil.*

2. World Bank, "Nationalization of the Iranian Oil Industry: An Outline of Its Origins and Issues," February 19, 1952; in U.S. Department of the Treasury, file 306/7/362, doc. 541.

3. Ibid., 3.

4. Ibid., 21.

5. Ibid., 2, emphasis added.

6. Ali Dashti, *Shafaq-i-Sorkh,* March 2, 1931; in Hart, dispatch 429 (891.6363/675), March 9, 1931. Dashti's relationship with the British had soured by this time. According to Hart, Dashti had turned against the British for two reasons: "The first was a request that a personal friend be granted the local distributing privileges of Anglo-Persian oil at Bushire. The second request was that a personal friend be given a position with the Company. Both requests were denied by the company. Then, further widening the breach, was the policy of the oil company in ignoring the Dashti paper in the allotment of advertising copy. All other Persian newspapers carry regularly advertising copy for the Anglo-Persian, which is their best and only steady advertiser, but *Shafaq-i-Sorkh* had not been patronized in that way. The Soviets, my informant said, had shown more cleverness in handling Dashti. When something more than a year ago Dashti was attacking the Soviets with the same violence that he now criticizes the Anglo-Persian Oil Company and other British interests, the editor was invited to visit the Soviet Embassy. The conference appeared to have been entirely satisfactory, he said, for Dashti received a gift of a new and modern printing press which was imported from Russia and the attacks ceased to appear. Of late there has been some mild criticism of the Soviets in *Shafaq-i-Sorkh.*" Hart's informant told him that the attacks had resumed in part "because of the feeling that his long silence should by this time have become full compensation for the printing press."

7. World Bank, "Nationalization of the Iranian Oil Industry," 2, emphasis added.

8. Ibid.

9. Ibid.

10. Ibid., 3–4.

11. Ibid., 7.

12. Ibid., 6.

13. Ibid., 3.

14. Ibid., 5; emphasis added.

15. Ibid., 6–7.

16. Ibid., 4.

17. Ibid., 5.

18. Ibid., 7.

19. Atherton, dispatch 658 (891.6363/729), February 9, 1933.

20. *Fourteenth Quarterly Report of the Administrator General of the Finances of Persia* (December 22, 1925–March 21, 1926), enclosure to dispatch 145 (891.51/394), August 11, 1926, from Philip.

21. W. C. Fairley, representative of APOC, to editor of *Iran,* January 1, 1922.

22. Engert, dispatch 797 (891.51/256), January 4, 1922.

23. World Bank, "Nationalization of the Iranian Oil Industry," 7.

24. Ibid.
25. George Gregg Fuller, dispatch (891.6363/527), June 10, 1924.
26. In Hart, dispatch 855 (891.6363/680), September 16, 1931.
27. Villard, memorandum (891.6363/680), December 12, 1931.
28. World Bank, "Nationalization of the Iranian Oil Industry," 9.
29. Philip, "Presence of Sir John Cadman in Teheran," dispatch 109 (891.6363/611), June 14, 1926.
30. Treat, dispatch 789 (891.6363/640), March 16, 1929.
31. Villard, confidential report (891.6363/656), July 11, 1930.
32. World Bank, "Nationalization of the Iranian Oil Industry," 9.
33. Hart, dispatch 738 (891.6363/678), July 21, 1931.
34. Hart, dispatch 929 (891.6363/681), November 7, 1931.
35. Ferrin, memorandum (891.6363/655), May 28, 1930.
36. Hart, dispatch 51 (891.6363/653), April 5, 1930.
37. Hart, dispatch 61 (891.6363/654), April 17, 1930.
38. Villard, dispatch (891.6363/663), December 15, 1930.
39. Hart, dispatch 354 (891.6363/673), February 6, 1931.
40. Hart, dispatch 254 (891.6363/670), December 30, 1930.
41. Seyed Ebrahim Zia, *Iran-i-Azad,* February 23, 1931; Ali Dashti, *Shafaq-i-Sorkh,* March 2 and 6, 1931; in Hart, dispatch 429 (891.6363/675), March 9, 1931.
42. Hart, dispatch 581 (891.6363/6760), May 1, 1931.
43. World Bank, "Nationalization of the Iranian Oil Industry," 9.
44. Hart, dispatch 1187 (891.6363/684), July 14, 1932.
45. World Bank, "Nationalization of the Iranian Oil Industry," 9–10.
46. Hart, dispatch 1295 (891.6363/704), December 3, 1932.
47. World Bank, "Nationalization of the Iranian Oil Industry," 10.
48. Hart, dispatch 1295 (891.6363/704), December 3, 1932.
49. Murray, memorandum (891.6363/710), December 28, 1932.
50. World Bank, "Nationalization of the Iranian Oil Industry," 10.
51. Atherton, dispatch 658 (891.6363/729), February 9, 1933.
52. Hart, dispatch 1362 (891.6363/739), February 24, 1933.
53. Atherton, dispatch 850 (891.6363/747), May 1, 1933.
54. Hart, dispatch 1487 (891.6363/Anglo-Persian/8), July 15, 1933.
55. Hart, dispatch 1423 (891.6363/Anglo-Persian/1), May 2, 1933.
56. World Bank, "Nationalization of the Iranian Oil Industry," 11.
57. Whereas under the D'Arcy Concession all the worldwide assets of the Company became the property of Iran in 1961, under the 1933 Agreement only the assets *located in Persia* became the property of Iran at the end of the concession. So as to leave no ambiguity, the same point is repeated in two separate articles. Article 20 (part II) reads: "At the end of the Concession, whether by expiration of time or otherwise, all the property of the Company *in Persia* shall become the property of the Government in proper working order and free of any expenses and of any encumbrances" (emphasis added). Article 25 repeats the same point: "The Company shall have the right to surrender this Concession at the end of any Christian calendar year, on giving to the Government notice in writing two years previously. On the expiry of the

above period provided, the whole of the property of the Company *in Persia,* defined in Article 20 (III), shall become free of cost and without encumbrances the property of the Government."

Article 10 (part III) contains the following: "On the expiration of this Concession, as well as in the case of surrender by the Company under Article 25 the Company shall pay to the Government a sum equal to twenty per cent (20%) of: (a) the surplus difference between the amount of the reserves (General Reserve) of the Anglo-Persian Oil Company Limited, at the date of the expiration of the Concession or of its surrender, and the amount of the same reserves at 31st December, 1932; (b) the surplus difference between the balance carried forward by the Anglo-Persian Oil Company Limited at the date of the expiration of the Concession or of its surrender and the balance carried forward by the Company at 31st December 1932." Suffice it to say that both the reserves and the balance carried forward were completely at the discretion of the Company and could have been reduced to zero at the end of the concession. The clause was a hoax. Nor did it provide ownership rights to the Iranian government.

58. World Bank, "Nationalization of the Iranian Oil Industry," 11.
59. Ibid.
60. Ibid.
61. Ibid., 14.
62. Ibid., 15–16.
63. Ibid., 17.
64. Ibid., 21.
65. Ibid.
66. Ibid., 22.
67. Hart, dispatch 1426 (891.6363/Anglo-Persion/2), May 4, 1933.
68. World Bank, "Nationalization of the Iranian Oil Industry," 14.
69. Hart, dispatch 1289 (891.6363/703), November 29, 1932.
70. Wadsworth, memorandum; in Hart, dispatch 1426 (891.6363/Anglo-Persian/2), May 4, 1933; emphasis in original.
71. Engert, dispatch 1870 (891.6363/43), July 9, 1940.
72. Engert, telegram (891.6363/35), July 8, 1940.
73. Engert, telegram (891.6363/38), July 18, 1940.
74. Engert, telegram (891.6363/40), July 29, 1940.
75. Engert, telegram (891.6363/41), August 22, 1940.
76. Engert, dispatch 1903 (891.6363/48), September 2, 1940.
77. Ibid. Payment of oil royalties to Iran from 1942 to 1945 was established by the Anglo-Iranian Financial Agreement of May 26, 1942. It was signed by Sir Reader Bullard, British minister, and Ali Soheili, the Iranian prime minister. The main provision of the agreement concerned oil royalty payments during the war years. It fixed annual royalties at £4 million per year for the duration of the war. It also provided for the conversion of 40 percent of the royalties into dollars or gold for the purpose of importing goods from North America. In the following year, this proportion was raised to 60 percent. That is, each year £2.4 million could be converted into gold or dollars and deposited in New York. The rapid increase in Iranian "official" dollar holdings in New York from 1943 reflected this fact.

10. The Reserve Fund and the Plunder of Oil Revenues

1. Dreyfus, dispatch 128 (891.6363/Anglo-Iranian/50), October 1, 1941.

2. Ibid.

3. Dreyfus, dispatch 146 (891.00/1809), November 3, 1941.

4. *Twentieth Quarterly Report of the Administrator General of Finances of Persia,* enclo-sure to dispatch 662 (891.51/416), August 17, 1928, from Philip, 11–12. In the same dispatch, Hoffman Philip provides a stunning piece of evidence concerning British espionage and de facto control over Reza Shah: "In this connection, I had the oppor-tunity to learn on September 18th, 1928, while visiting Baghdad, Iraq, that His High-ness Teymourtache while in Europe was instructed by the Shah to purchase 200,000 rifles and ammunition. After negotiating in England, Germany and France, His High-ness reported to His Majesty that the German offer was nearly 50% cheaper than the lowest bid elsewhere. This information was given to me by the Intelligence Officers of the Royal Air Force in Baghdad, who intercepted and translated all telegrams exchanged between the Shah and Teymourtache. No more striking example of the efficiency of British espionage can be found. The officers in Baghdad knew more of Teymourtache's movements than did the Shah himself, and proved it to me by laugh-ingly informing me from what city the next wire to His Majesty would come."

5. *Twenty-First Quarterly Report of the Administrator General of Finances of Persia,* enclosure to dispatch 715 (891.51/417), December 1, 1928, from R. A. Wallace, 2.

6. *Twenty-Third Report of the Ministry of Finance,* enclosure to letter from Ferrin (891.51/427), September 18, 1929, 2. The British legation also informed Hart that a credit of £500,000 had been extended to the bank from the Reserve Fund in London. Soon after this dispatch was written, Lingeman of the British legation informed Hart that the credit had been contemplated but never made. Instead, the 3 million tomans had been taken out of the Sugar and Tea Monopoly fund that was supposed to be spent only on railway construction (891.51/439, September 6, 1930). This loan was to be repaid on the last day of the year ending March 21, 1931 (891.51/442, April 16, 1931). Hart reported that the interest on the loan was only 1 percent. Hart adds that "the loan was obtained to pay government salaries which were at the time far in arrears."

   In addition to the high oil revenues, the Iranian government had garnered large sums from the Sugar and Tea Monopoly tax and from the road tax. Information on these items is contained in Hart, dispatch 1125 (891.51/456), April 27, 1932. According to his figures, payments into the Sugar and Tea Monopoly fund totaled 400 million krans over six years, or at least $3.5 million per year. The road tax had brought in about $4 million per year. Oil royalties for 1930 were £1,325,000, or about $6.5 million, and had averaged about $7 million per year in the previous three years. These unlisted items, not included in the regular budget, were equivalent to 50 percent of the sums shown in the regular budget, which for 1311 (1932/33) amounted to $30 million. Yet, to pay the salaries of government employees, money had to be borrowed from the National Bank.

7. Ferrin, report on the budget of 1308 (891.51/419), January 29, 1929.

8. Ferrin, report on the budget of 1308 (891.51/421), March 30, 1929.

9. Ibid.

10. Supplement to Article 2 of Budget Bill for 1930; in Philip, dispatch 857 (891.243/1), June 13, 1929.

11. Ibid.

12. Hart, dispatch 876 (891.51/448), September 30, 1931.

13. Wadsworth, dispatch 1114 (891.20/73), April 9, 1932.

14. Villard, report (891.51/434), April 12, 1930.

15. Hart, dispatch 64 (891.51/435), April 18, 1930.

16. Hart, dispatch 146 (891.51/438), August 25, 1930.

17. Wadsworth, dispatch 1114 (891.20/73), April 9, 1932.

18. Hart, dispatch 1357 (891.51/463), February 20, 1933.

19. Hart, dispatch 1452 (891.51/468), June 1, 1933.

20. Hornibrook, dispatch 5 (891.20/80), March 23, 1934.

21. National Bank of Persia, bulletin no. 3, June 1934.

22. Hornibrook, dispatch 26 (891.51/479), April 11, 1934.

23. Hornibrook, dispatch 400 (891.51/486), April 1, 1935.

24. Merriam, dispatch 761 (891.51/495), April 11, 1937.

25. Merriam, dispatch 1048 (891.51/500), May 3, 1937.

26. Engert, dispatch 1272 (891.51/510), April 10, 1938.

27. Engert, dispatch 1565 (891.51/518), March 30, 1939.

28. Engert, dispatch 1799 (891.51/535), March 25, 1940.

29. Dreyfus, dispatch 53 (891.51/541), April 3, 1941.

30. Ibid.

31. Wadsworth, dispatch 1630 (891.515/48), January 20, 1934.

32. Hart, report (891.6363 Anglo-Persian/8), July 15, 1933.

33. Hart, dispatch 1213 (891.515/40), August 24, 1932.

34. Hart, dispatch 1342 (891.00/1556), February 3, 1933.

35. Wadsworth, dispatch 1664 (891.00/1588), February 23, 1934.

36. Hart, dispatch 1453 (891.51/469), June 1, 1933.

37. Hart, dispatch 1510 (891.51/472), August 12, 1933.

38. Hornibrook, report (891.51/480), June 14, 1934.

39. Hornibrook, dispatch 581 (891.51/492), August 9, 1935.

40. Engert, dispatch 1150 (891.51/504), October 29, 1937.

41. Moose, dispatch 1416 (891.51/516), October 3, 1938.

42. Moose, dispatch 1511 (891.51/517), January 23, 1939.

11. The Purchase of Armaments

1. Dreyfus, dispatch 102 (891.415/27), July 21, 1941.

2. American military attaché, report 395 (2724–CC-5), January 17, 1923.

3. Kornfeld, dispatch 257 (891.24/7), September 8, 1923.

4. Whitehouse, dispatch 3545 (891.24/6), October 1, 1923.

5. Kornfeld, dispatch 328 (891.24/8), December 21, 1923.

6. Kornfeld, dispatch 354 (891.24/9), January 15, 1924.

7. Philip, dispatch 339 (891.24/13), May 5, 1927.

8. In Charles C. Hart, dispatch 1076 (891.20/71), March 7, 1931.

9. Hornibrook, dispatch 350 (891.24/66), February 9, 1935.

10. Childs, dispatch 453 (891.24/73), May 1, 1935.

11. Hornibrook, dispatch 488 (891.24/85), June 28, 1935.

12. State Department memo (891.24/101), July 10, 1936.
13. Hornibrook, dispatch 727 (891.20/90), February 27, 1936.
14. Engert, dispatch 1152 (891.20/91), November 1, 1937.
15. Engert, dispatch 1245 (891/1679), February 26, 1938.
16. Engert, dispatch 1538 (891.415/24), February 25, 1939.
17. Engert, dispatch 1779 (891.415/25), February 26, 1940; emphasis in original.
18. Engert, telegram 153 (891.001 P15/192), December 1, 1939.
19. Engert, telegram 166 (891.001 P15/193), December 18, 1939. For a detailed account of this affair, see Cronin, "Politics of Radicalism."
20. Dreyfus, dispatch 39 (891.415/26), March 3, 1941.
21. In Dreyfus, dispatch 102 (891.415/27), July 21, 1941.
22. Fuller, dispatch 61 (891.34/2), August 22, 1925.
23. Murray, dispatch 768 (891.34/1), November 30, 1924.
24. Hoffman Philip, dispatch 570 (891.34/3), April 3, 1928.
25. Ferrin, dispatch 39 (891.30/4), February 20, 1929.
26. Ferrin, dispatch 56 (891.30/5), April 13, 1929.
27. Hart, dispatch 874 (891.30/6), September 30, 1931.
28. Hart, dispatch 1063 (891.34/11), February 26, 1932.
29. Hart, dispatch 1241 (891.34/13), October 4, 1932.
30. John W. Garrett, American Consul in Rome, dispatch 1576 (891.34/12), September 21, 1932.
31. Rossi, Italian chargé d'affaires in Washington, to Cordell Hull, Department of State (891.34/32), August 8, August 20, 1934.
32. Hornibrook, dispatch 53 (891.20/81), May 7, 1934.
33. State Department, memorandum (891.30/11), March 5, 1935.
34. "The Battle Order of the Iranian Army," Dreyfus, dispatch 102 (891.415/27), July 21, 1941.
35. Alai to Allen W. Dulles, chief of Division of Near Eastern Affairs (891.248/1), January 15, 1923.
36. Murray, dispatch 773 (891.248/9), November 30, 1924.
37. Kornfeld, dispatch 440 (891.248/6), April 1, 1924.
38. Kornfeld, dispatch 484 (891.248/7), May 8, 1924.
39. Kornfeld, dispatch 495 (891.248/8), May 14, 1924. A dispatch from Murray is informative and amusing: "Lieutenant Berault, a French aviator who, in the Spring of 1924, was employed by the Persian Government for the service of the six French aeroplanes purchased from France, and who was with the Prime Minister [Reza Khan] 'at the front' in Arabistan during the recent troubles with the Sheikh of Mohammerah, left Bebehan for Isfahan on December 17 and disappeared completely, leaving no trace for more than nineteen days. While exact details are still not obtainable, it is now nevertheless established that Berault has safely reached Isfahan after a crash of his machine. His French companion and mechanic likewise escaped without harm. On the occasion of the Prime Minister's reception to diplomatic representatives on January 5, in celebration of his victorious return from Arabistan, the French Minister informed him for the first time of Lieutenant Berault's safe escape. While the Prime Minister seemed gratified that he had escaped with his life, he nevertheless was heard to remark to his Persian companions: 'That is the third machine that Berault has demolished for me.'

The series of disasters met by all the six French aeroplanes delivered in March 1924 by the French to the Persian Government is remarkable. The entire lot are now for one reason or another out of commission, thus leaving the German Junkers and the two Russian planes supreme in the aerial field of Persia, much to the annoyance of the French. There would seem to be little question but that the French had unloaded defective war material on the Persians, on the theory that anything was good enough for them." Murray, dispatch 832 (891.248/10), January 7, 1925.

40. D. Meftah, Persian minister in Washington, to Stimson, Secretary of State (891.248/14), July 15, 1929.

41. War Department to Stimson, August 24, 1929.

42. Villard, report (891.248/22), October 22, 1930.

43. Hart's earlier dispatch 1250 (891.248/34), October 7, 1932.

44. Hart, dispatch 1367 (891.20/75), February 23, 1933.

45. Hart (891.248/38), March 8, 1933.

46. Ibid.

47. Ray Atherton, dispatch 591, London (891.248/36), January 3, 1933; Hart, dispatch 1534 (891.248/43), September 20, 1933.

48. Hart, ibid.

49. Hornibrook, dispatch 53 (891.20/81), May 7, 1934.

50. Hornibrook, dispatch 220 (891.24/55), September 21, 1934.

51. Hornibrook, dispatch 105 (891.248/48), June 12, 1934.

52. Hornibrook, dispatch 104 (741.91/153), June 12, 1934.

53. Hamilton to True, June 6, 1934; in Hornibrook, dispatch 104 (741.91/153), June 12, 1934.

54. Hornibrook, report (891.796/43), September 12, 1934.

55. Hornibrook, dispatch 229 (891.248/58), October 2, 1934.

56. Hornibrook, dispatch 418 (891.248/61), April 16, 1935.

57. Ibid.

58. *Ettela'at*, March 11, 1935; in Hornibrook, dispatch 390 (891.248/60), March 21, 1935.

59. Moose, dispatch 1356 (891.248/70), July 28, 1938.

60. Moose (891.248/72).

61. Engert (891.248/73).

62. "The Battle Order of the Iranian Army." Dreyfus, dispatch 102 (891.415/27), July 21, 1941.

63. The conversion of Reza Shah's domestic income into foreign exchange and its deposit in foreign banks is discussed in Majd, *Resistance to the Shah*, 35–36.

12. The Diversion of Oil Revenues and Reza Shah's Foreign Bank Accounts

1. Engert, "Murder of Colonel Shaybani in Bern. Suicide of Captain Farzin," dispatch 1887 (891.20/126), August 5, 1940.

2. Agency of the Royal Bank of Canada to Summerlin (701.9111/721), June 5, 1941.

3. Summerlin to Royal Bank of Canada (701.9111/721), July 2, 1941.

4. Murray to Malloch (891.24/162), January 31, 1941.

5. Malloch to Murray (891.24/164), February 4, 1941.

6. State Department, memorandum (891.24/168), May 5, 1941.

7. Reinstein, memorandum of conversation (891.51/595), December 9, 1943.

8. State Department Instruction no. 304, December 28, 1943.

9. Ford, dispatch 866 (891.516/177), March 2, 1944.

10. Knoke, memorandum, October 18, 1940.

11. "WLP" to Murray, May 7, 1941.

12. Treasury Dept. memo (891.51/556), March 3, 1943.

13. Dreyfus, dispatch 131 (891.00/1845), October 1, 1941.

14. From the declassified files of the Department of State we learn that such individuals as Amir Khosrovi and Azodi received large payments in New York following Reza Shah's abdication. In the two instances for which documentation exists, we know that a check for $102,660, to be drawn on the account of Bank Melli at the Irving Trust Company in New York, was issued to Amir Khosrovi, and the amount was paid on May 9, 1943, to "Son Excellence Monsieur le Général Reza Amirkhosrovi." Richard Ford, American chargé d'affaires ad interim, confidential dispatch 1044 (891.51/7–2744), July 27, 1944; State Department confidential cable 35 (891.51/10–2744), November 6, 1944.

The appointment of Yadollah Azodi as Iran's ambassador to Brazil in 1943 was severely criticized in the newspapers. In a confidential dispatch Ford states that "on September 7, 1943, the Bank Melli had transferred $117,780 to New York for Azodi's credit." It cannot be coincidence that the former heads of the Foreign Exchange Commission and Bank Melli during Reza Shah's rule were now receiving checks in excess of $100,000, payable in New York. Ford, dispatch 1043 (701.9132/7–2644), July 26, 1944.

15. The banking correspondence is included in Farasati, "German Managers of the National Bank."

16. Amir Khosrovi to Lindenblatt, August 17, 1931.

17. Lindenblatt to Amir Khosrovi, August 18, 1931.

18. *Economist*, August 30, 1941.

19. Farmanfarmaian and Farmanfarmaian, *Blood and Oil*, 204.

20. State Department, Memorandum of Conversation (788.00/10–957, Confidential File), October 9, 1957.

21. *Economist*, August 30, 1941.

22. State Department, Memorandum of Conversation (788.00/10–957, Confidential File), October 9, 1957.

23. U.S. Treasury Department, *Census of Foreign-Owned Assets*, 63.

24. U.S. Treasury Department, confidential report on Iran's economy, April 17, 1944.

25. Ibid.

26. Andarmanizadeh and Hadidi, *Children of Reza Shah*, 53–54.

27. Touran Amir Soleimani to Gholam Reza Pahlavi, August 20, 1945.

28. U.S. State Department report (891.0011/7–2947), August 18, 1947.

29. Wilber, *Riza Shah Pahlavi*, 216.

30. Villard, Foreign Service dispatch 275 (788.11/5–559), May 5, 1959.

31. Dreyfus, dispatch 131 (891.00/1845), October 1, 1941.

32. Rostami, *Reza Shah*, 207.

33. Dreyfus, telegram 255 (F.W. 891.001/72), March 10, 1943.

34. Wells to Dreyfus, March 12, 1943.

35. Confidential letter MF 9142, March 7, 1943; sent with dispatch 491 (891.00/73), March 18, 1943.

36. Ibid.

37. U.S. State Department, telegram 213, April 19, 1943.

38. Anderson to Alling (891.00/74), April 21, 1943.

39. Bochow to State (788.11/8–752 confidential file), August 7, 1952.

40. Roosevelt to Stettinius (891.20/133), March 10, 1942.

13. The Theft of Iran's Crown Jewels

1. Dreyfus, dispatch 131 (891.00/1845), October 1, 1941.

2. Dreyfus, dispatch 150 (891.001 P15/222), November 7, 1941.

3. Ibid.

4. Ibid.

5. Arthur C. Millspaugh, *Sixth Quarterly Report of the Administrator General of the Finances of Persia,* December 22, 1923–March 20, 1924, 45, enclosure to dispatch 646 (891.51/362), September 17, 1924, from Murray.

6. Arthur C. Millspaugh, *Eighth Quarterly Report of the Administrator General of the Finances of Persia,* June 22, 1924–September 22, 1924, 62, enclosure to dispatch 907 (891.51/375), February 17, 1925, from Murray.

7. Hoffman Philip, dispatch 202 (891.412/1), October 25, 1926.

8. Hart, dispatch 16 (891.515/9), February 22, 1930.

9. Hart, dispatch 1366 (891.44–Teymourtache, Abdol H.K./6), February 24, 1933.

10. Engert, dispatch 1155 (891.51/505), November 5, 1937.

11. Engert, dispatch 1170 (891.51/506), November 24, 1937.

12. Engert, dispatch 1224 (891.51/508), January 31, 1938.

13. *Ettela'at,* October 27, 1937; quoted in Engert, dispatch 1224 (891.51/508), January 31, 1938.

14. *Iran,* October 28, 1937; quoted in Engert, dispatch 1155 (891.51/505), November 5, 1937.

15. "The Sale of the Crown Jewels," editorial, *Setareh-ye Jehan,* November 12, 1937; in Engert dispatch 1167 (891.51/506), November 19, 1937.

16. James S. Moose, Jr., Chargé d'Affaires ad interim, dispatch 1355 (891.51/510), July 27, 1938.

17. *Ettela'at,* January 30, 1938; in Engert, dispatch 1224 (891.51/508), January 31, 1938.

18. Ibid.

19. Dreyfus, dispatch 150 (891.001 P15/222), November 7, 1941.

20. Dreyfus, dispatch 131 (891.00/1845), October 1, 1941.

21. Allen, memorandum of conversation (891.0011/9–2645), October 1, 1945.

22. McClanahan, dispatch 334 (788.11/8–558), August 5, 1958. John Gunther is the author of *Inside Asia* (see chapter 5).

14. The Foreign Exchange Crisis

1. Ferrin, "Report on Crisis in Persian Exchange" (891.5151/13), November 2, 1929.

2. In Atherton, dispatch 1113 (891.50/26), August 7, 1930.

3. Villard, report 19 (891.50/23), February 14, 1930.

4. Hart, dispatch 8 (891.00/1501), February 8, 1930.

5. *Shafaq-i-Sorkh,* March 13, 1930; in Hart, dispatch 54 (891.00/1502), April 5, 1930.

6. Hart, dispatch 53 (891.002/213), April 5, 1930.

7. Hart, dispatch 59 (891.002/214), April 14, 1930.
8. Villard, report (891.516/39), May 24, 1930.
9. State Department, memorandum (891.5151/43), November 4, 1930.
10. Villard, report (891.516/35), March 12, 1930.
11. Ibid.
12. Millspaugh, *Americans in Persia,* 30–31.
13. Villard, report (891.516/35), March 12, 1930.
14. Villard, report 64 (891.5151/49), August 23, 1930.
15. Hart, dispatch 134 (891.5151/36), August 11, 1930.
16. Villard, report 64 (891.5151/49), August 23, 1930.
17. Villard, report 71 (891.5151/39), September 27, 1930.
18. Villard, report 79 (891.5151/45), November 8, 1930.
19. Villard, report 82 (891.5151/46), December 6, 1930.
20. Ibid.
21. Villard, report 67 (891.00/1507), September 15, 1930.
22. Hart, dispatch 400 (891.515/24), February 24, 1931. As a consequence of restricting foreign exchange trading to authorized banks and requiring permits to buy foreign exchange, importers had been unable to obtain foreign exchange to pay for imports of goods already imported. In particular, Kettaneh Brothers, an importer of Dodge trucks, could not obtain $85,000 to pay for spare parts. Understandably, Dodge was pressuring its representative in Persia.
23. Hart, dispatch 1452 (891.51/468), June 1, 1933.
24. Hornibrook, dispatch 400 (891.51/486), April 1, 1935. Millspaugh offers: "The Shah's taxation policy was highly regressive, raising the cost of living and bearing heavily on the poor. He exempted the landlords from direct taxation and restored the medieval duties collected at the gates of cities." Landlords were exempted from taxation because Reza Shah was himself the biggest landlord: "various services he procured for little or nothing because suppliers learned to be afraid of presenting bills to him. He used forced labor on roads and buildings, requisitioned trucks, and doubtless had other devices for getting things done cheaply." Millspaugh, *Americans in Persia,* 34.
25. Engert, dispatch 1565 (891.51/518), March 30, 1939.
26. Ibid.
27. Millspaugh, *Americans in Persia,* 58.
28. Hart, dispatch 205 (891.5151/44), November 17, 1930.
29. Hart, dispatch 184 (891.5151/42), October 6, 1930. While His August Majesty and his minister of the court and the court accountant were participants in the foreign exchange market, the Honorable Minister of Economics Zoka-ol-Molk Foroughi, Hart had gleaned, was a participant in the silver bullion market. Hart continues, "In a conversation with Foroughi, who is Minister of Economics as well as Foreign Minister, he informed me that the Government had no immediate intention of releasing the exchange control. He said that the Government had reached the conclusion that Persia's predicament was only part of a world crisis; that when better times come in the rest of the world conditions will improve here. The one question which appeared to trouble him was whether silver will rise again."
30. Hart, telegram (891.5151/78), February 15, 1932.

31. Hart, dispatch 1080 (891.5151/84), March 9, 1932.

32. Hart, dispatch 1053 (891.5151/82), February 16, 1932.

33. Ibid.

34. Hart, dispatch 1213 (891.515/40), August 24, 1932.

35. Ibid.

36. In J. Rives Childs, dispatch 1668 (891.5151/126), February 27, 1934.

37. Hornibrook, dispatch 714 (891.516/115), February 10, 1936. Frankness had fleetingly found its way into the French version of the bank's reports. Gordon P. Merriam, chargé d'affaires ad interim, says that the French version of the National Bank Balance Sheet for 1935–36 contained the following remarkable statement: "It is known that there are no longer any publications respecting the actual receipts and expenditures of the Government." Merriam observes: "This bears out the assertion made by the Legation when transmitting the last budget to the effect that whereas an Iranian budget might look well enough, no one knew how close the Government came to carrying out its provisions. But confirmation from such a source as the National Bank of Iran was quite unexpected." Merriam, dispatch 920 (891.516/122), October 27, 1936.

38. Hornibrook, dispatch 738 (891.5151/149), March 6, 1936.

39. Ibid.

40. Vice Consul Earl T. Crain, report (891.5151/151), March 16, 1936.

41. Ibid.

42. Crain, report (891.5151/153), April 4, 1936.

43. Merriam, dispatch 956 (891.50/35), December 23, 1936.

44. Crain, report (891.516/130), April 27, 1937.

45. Ibid.

46. Engert, dispatch 1137 (891.5151/167), September 29, 1937.

47. Ibid.

48. E.A.G. Gray, "Report on Economic Conditions in Iran during 1937"; in Department of State (891.50/40).

49. Engert, dispatch 1677 (819.1515/195), September 11, 1939.

50. W. F. Fischer, export manager of Tuthill Spring Company, to Wallace S. Murray, chief of the Division of Near Eastern Affairs at the State Department (891.5151/207), July 31, 1941.

51. Engert, telegram (891.5151/201), August 28, 1940.

52. Grady, telegram (891.5151/200), October 1, 1940.

53. Dreyfus, dispatch 21(891.5151/204), January 23, 1941.

54. Ibid.

55. Engert, telegram (891.5151/201), August 28, 1940.

56. Murray to Welles (891.248/94), August 12, 1940.

57. Welles to Murray, August 14, 1940.

58. Parker, memorandum (891.24/6–1241), July 19, 1941.

59. Embrechts, "Report on Economic and Commercial Conditions in Iran" (891.00/1755), July 12, 1941.

60. James S. Moose, Jr., report (891.713/7), March 18, 1938.

61. Millspaugh, *Americans in Persia,* 34.

15. Iran in 1941 and the Downfall of Reza Shah

1. Engert, dispatch 1709 (891.00/1722), October 23, 1939.
2. Engert, dispatch 1813 (891.00/1734), April 10, 1940.
3. Engert, strictly confidential telegram, no. 145 (891.00/1740), July 2, 1940.
4. Dreyfus, dispatch 27 (891.6/311), January 30, 1941.
5. *Ettela'at,* January 14, 1940.
6. Dreyfus, dispatch 27 (891.6/311), January 30, 1941.
7. Ibid.
8. Embrechts, report (891.00/1755), January 12, 1941.
9. Moose to Wallace S. Murray, chief of the Division of Near Eastern Affairs (891.00/1758), July 20, 1940.
10. Millspaugh, *Americans in Persia,* 35.
11. Moose, confidential report (891.00/1763), May 23, 1941.
12. Minor, in dispatch 109 (891.00/1816), August 12, 1941.
13. Millspaugh gives the following account: "At first, Reza wanted to offer resistance and a few shots were fired, but his Army collapsed ignominiously. It appears that the officers quite promptly turned tail and ran; but there is at least one known exception, an officer who afterward related his experiences. Asked if he had run, he replied: 'Oh, no, I didn't run. I took off my uniform.' As a matter of fact, the officers lost more than uniforms and more than honor; they lost most of the costly armament that had delighted the Shah and helped to intimidate the populace." Millspaugh, *Americans in Persia,* 39.
14. Dreyfus, telegram (740.0011 European War 1939/14519), August 29, 1941.
15. Dreyfus, telegram (891.00/1771 Confidential file), September 12, 1941.
16. Dreyfus, telegram (891.00/1773), September 15, 1941.
17. Dreyfus, telegram (891.00/1775), September 16, 1941.
18. Dreyfus, telegram (891.00/1779 Confidential File), September 17, 1941.
19. Ibid.
20. Dreyfus, telegram (891.00/1777 Confidential File), September 18, 1941.
21. Millspaugh, *Americans in Persia,* 159.
22. Dreyfus, telegram (891.00/1778 Confidential File), September 19, 1941.
23. Hull, telegram to Dreyfus (891.00/1778), September 23, 1941.
24. Dreyfus, telegram (891.001 P15/221), September 28, 1941.
25. Winant, cable to Hull (891.001 P15/221), December 17, 1941.
26. Hull, cable to Winant (891.001 P/223), February 5, 1942.
27. Kirk, cable (891.001 P15/224), March 31, 1942.
28. Dreyfus, dispatch 322 (891.00/1914), August 11, 1942.
29. *Keyhan,* July 23, 1942; *Mardom,* July 24, 1942; *Setareh,* July 24, 1942; *Setareh,* July 31, 1942; in Dreyfus, dispatch 322 (891.00/1914), August 11, 1942.
30. Ford, dispatch 857 (891.108/3), February 28, 1944.
31. Ibid.
32. Abrahamian, *Tortured Confessions,* 72.
33. Ford, dispatch 77 (891.13/10-1744), October 17, 1944. Abrahamian's account of the execution of Ahmadi contradicts Amir Jang Bakhtiari's version: "The hanged 'doctor' was an apt symbol for the fallen regime–phony, brutal, and even deadly, but not one that tortured" (ibid.).

Abrahamian, Ervand. *Tortured Confessions: Prisons and Public Recantations in Modern Iran.* Berkeley: University of California Press, 1999.

Alam, Amir Asadollah, *Diaries of Alam, Volume One.* 2 vols. London: One World, 1992.

Amuzegar, Jahangir. *The Dynamics of the Iranian Revolution: The Pahlavis' Triumph and Tragedy.* Albany: State University of New York Press, 1991.

Andarmanizadeh, Jalal, and Mokhtar Hadidi, eds. *The Pahlavis: A Documentary Portrayal of the Pahlavi Family.* Vol. 2, *The Children of Reza Shah.* Tehran: Institute for Iranian Contemporary Historical Studies, 1999. (In Farsi.)

Banani, Amin. *The Modernization of Iran, 1921–1941.* Stanford: Stanford University Press, 1961.

Cronin, Stephanie. *The Army and the Creation of the Pahlavi State in Iran, 1910–1926.* London: I. B. Tauris, 1997.

———. "The Politics of Radicalism within the Iranian Army: The Jahansuz Group of 1939." *Iranian Studies* 32.1 (Winter 1999): 5–26.

Elm, Mostafa. *Oil, Power, and Principle: Iran's Oil Nationalization and Its Aftermath.* Syracuse: Syracuse University Press, 1992.

Elwell-Sutton, L. P. *Persian Oil: A Study in Power Politics.* London: Lawrence and Wishart, 1955.

Farasati, Reza. "Some Documents on German Managers of the National Bank of Iran during 1932–33." *Contemporary History of Iran* 7 (1995): 199–275. (In Farsi.)

Farmanfarmaian, Manucher, and Roxane Farmanfarmaian. *Blood and Oil: Memoirs of a Persian Prince.* New York: Random House, 1997.

Farman-Farmaian, Sattareh. *Daughter of Persia: A Woman's Journey from Her Father's Harem through the Islamic Revolution.* New York: Random House, 1993.

Ghani, Cyrus. *Iran and the Rise of Reza Shah: From Qajar Collapse to Pahlavi Power.* London: I. B. Tauris, 1998.

Gunther, John. *Inside Asia.* New York: Harper and Brothers, 1939.

Keddie, Nikkie R. *Roots of Revolution: An Interpretive History of Modern Iran.* New Haven: Yale University Press, 1981.

Lenczowski, George, ed. *Iran under the Pahlavis.* Stanford: Hoover Institution Press, 1978.

Majd, Mohammad Gholi. *Resistance to the Shah: Landowners and Ulama in Iran.* Gainesville: University Press of Florida, 2000.

Millspaugh, Arthur C. *Americans in Persia.* Washington, D.C.: Brookings Institution, 1946.

Olson, William J. *Anglo-Iranian Relations during World War I.* London: Frank Cass, 1984.

Rostami, Farhad, ed. *The Pahlavis: A Documentary Portrayal of the Pahlavi Family.* Vol. 1, *Reza Shah.* Tehran: Institute for Iranian Contemporary Historical Studies, 1999. (In Farsi.)

Sabahi, Houshang. *British Policy in Persia, 1918–1925.* London: Frank Cass, 1990.

United States. Department of the Treasury. *Census of Foreign-Owned Assets in the United States.* Washington, D.C.: Government Printing Office, 1945.

Wilber, Donald N. *Riza Shah Pahlavi: The Resurrection and Reconstruction of Iran.* Hicksville, N.Y.: Exposition Press, 1975.

Zirinsky, Michael P. "Blood, Power, and Hypocricy: The Murder of Robert Imbrie and American Relations with Pahlavi Iran." *International Journal of Middle East Studies* 18 (1986): 275–92

Mohammad Gholi Majd is the author of *Resistance to the Shah: Landowners and Ulama in Iran* (UPF, 2000) and of numerous articles in *Middle Eastern Studies, Middle East Journal,* and *International Journal of Middle East Studies,* among others. An independent scholar, he has taught at the Middle East Center at the University of Pennsylvania. He was born in Iran and lives in Rockville, Maryland.